CHRISTIAN PUBLISHING

·ΟΥΔΕΙΣΕω
ΝΠωΠΟΤΕ
ΓΕΝΗΣΘΣΕ
ΛΠΟΝΤΟΥΓ
)ΣΕΚΕΙΝΟΣ
ΓΛΤΟΊΚΛΙΛΥ

ΟΥΛΛΛΟΥΝΤΟΣΤΟΙ
ΧΛΟΙΣΙΛΟΥΗΜΗΤΗ|
ΛΙΟΙΛΔΕΛΦΟΙΛΥΤΟ
ΤΗΚΕΙΣΛΝΕΣωΖΗΤ
ΕΣΛΥΤωΛΛΗΣΛΙ Ο
ΠΟΚΡΙΘΕΙΣ ΕΙΠΕΝΤΟ
ΕΓΟΝΤΙΛΥΤωΤΙΣΕ
ΜΗΤΗΡΜΟΥΚΛΙΤΙΝΕ

SCRIBES AND SCRIPTURE

FROM SPOKEN WORDS
TO SACRED TEXTS

INTRODUCTION-INTERMEDIATE
NEW TESTAMENT TEXTUAL STUDIES

EDWARD D. ANDREWS

FROM SPOKEN WORDS TO SACRED TEXTS

Introduction-Intermediate New Testament Textual Studies

Edward D. Andrews

Christian Publishing House

Cambridge, Ohio

FROM SPOKEN WORDS TO SACRED TEXTS: Introduction-Intermediate New Testament Textual Studies by Edward D. Andrews

ISBN-13: **978-1-949586-98-5**

ISBN-10: **1-949586-98-7**

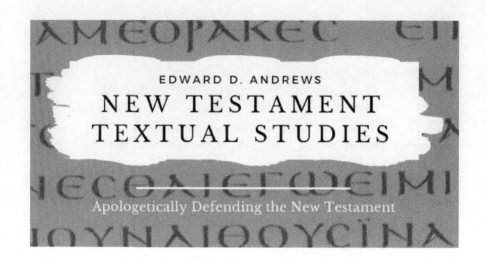

EDWARD D. ANDREWS

NEW TESTAMENT
TEXTUAL STUDIES

Apologetically Defending the New Testament

Significant English Bible Translations

Unless otherwise indicated, Scripture quotations are from the *Updated American Standard Version* (UASV) Copyright © 2022 by Christian Publishing House.

Below are some of the most significant English Bible translations of the twentieth and now twenty-first centuries. The word significant is used broadly and does not necessarily suggest a preferred or accurate translation.

It should be noted that this author prefers literal translations. Edward D. Andrews is the sole translator of the forthcoming Updated American Standard Version (UASV).

ASV American Standard Version, 1901 Public Domain

CEV Contemporary English Version, 1995 by American Bible Society

CSB Christian Standard Bible, 2017 by Holman Bible Publishers

ESV English Standard Version, 2001 by Crossway Bibles, a publishing ministry of Good News Publishers

GNT Good News Translation, 1992 by American Bible Society

KJV King James Version, 1611 Public Domain

REB Revised English Bible, 1989 by Oxford University Press and Cambridge University Press

RSV Revised Standard Version, 1946, 1952, and 1971 the Division of Christian Education of the National Council of the Churches of Christ in the United States of America

NASB New American Standard Bible, 1960, 1962, 1963, 1968, 1971, 1972, 1973, 1975, 1977, 1995 by the Lockman Foundation

NEB New English Bible, 1961 by Oxford University Press and Cambridge University Press

NIV New International Version, 2011 973, 1978, 1984, 2011 by Biblica, Inc.®

NKJV New King James Version, 1982 by Thomas Nelson

NLT New Living Translation (second edition), 2004 by Tyndale House Foundation

NRSV New Revised Standard Version, 1990 by the Division of Christian Education of the National Council of the Churches of Christ in the United States of America

TNIV Today's New International Version, 2005 by Biblica (Formerly International Bible Society)

UASV Updated American Standard Version, NT 2017 OT, 2018 by Christian Publishing House

Publication Abbreviations

AA Aland-Aland = *The Text of the New Testament, An Introduction to the Critical Editions and to the Theory and Practice of Modern Textual Criticism,* by Kurt Aland and Barbara Aland (Grand Rapids, 1987; 2nd ed., 1989).

BAA *Griechisch-Deutsches Wörterbuch zu den Schriften des Neuen Testaments und der frühchristlichen Literatur,* by W. Bauer, K. Aland, and B. Aland (6th ed.; Berlin: de Gruyter, 1988)

BAGD *A Greek-English Lexicon of the New Testament and Other Early Christian Literature,* by W. Bauer, W. F. Arndt, F. W. Gingrich, and F. W. Danker (2d ed.; Chicago: University of Chicago Press, 1979)

BDB *A Hebrew and English Lexicon of the Old Testament,* by F. Brown, S. R. Driver, and C. A. Briggs (Oxford: Clarendon, 1907)

BDF *A Greek Grammar of the New Testament and Other Early Christian Literature,* by F. Blass, A. Debrunner, and R. W. Funk (Chicago: University of Chicago Press, 1961)

BDR *Grammatik des neutestamentlichen Griechisch,* by F. Blass, A. Debrunner, and F. Rehkopf (Göttingen: Vandenhoeck & Ruprecht, 1984)

FJAH F. J. A. Hort's "Notes on Select Readings," in *The New Testament in the Original Greek,* the Text Revised by Brooke Foss Westcott and Fenton John Anthony Hort; [vol. ii] *Introduction [and] Appendix*(Cambridge and London, 1881; 2nd ed., 1896).

GMAW *Greek Manuscripts of the Ancient World* (2nd ed., E. G. Turner)

GELNTBSD Johannes P. Louw and Eugene Albert Nida, *Greek-English Lexicon of the New Testament: Based on Semantic Domains* (New York: United Bible Societies, 1996).

HIBD Brand, Chad, Charles Draper, and England Archie. *Holman Illustrated Bible Dictionary*: Revised, Updated and Expanded. Nashville, TN: Holman, 2003.

ISBE *International Standard Bible Encyclopedia* (4 vols., Bromiley) [1979–1988]

LSJ *A Greek-English Lexicon,* by H. G. Liddell, R. Scott, and H. S. Jones (Oxford: Clarendon, 1968)

LXX *Septuaginta*: With Morphology, electronic ed. (Stuttgart: Deutsche Bibelgesellschaft, 1979)

LXX Swete Henry Barclay Swete, The Old Testament in Greek: According to the Septuagint (Cambridge, UK: Cambridge University Press, 1909)

MCEDONTW Mounce, William D. *Mounce's Complete Expository Dictionary of Old & New Testament Words.* Grand Rapids, MI: Zondervan, 2006.

MM *The Vocabulary of the Greek Testament: Illustrated from the Papyri and Other Non-literary Sources,* by J. H. Moulton and G. Milligan (repr. Grand Rapids: Eerdmans, 1980)

(MT) Masoretic Text

NA[26] *Novum Testamentum Graece* (26th ed., Nestle-Aland) [1979]

NA[27] *Novum Testamentum Graece* (27th ed., Nestle-Aland) [1993]

NA[28] *Novum Testamentum Graece* (27th ed., Nestle-Aland) [2012]

NBD Wood, D R W. *New Bible Dictionary* (Third Edition). Downers Grove: InterVarsity Press, 1996.

NIDNTT *The New International Dictionary of New Testament Theology,* edited by L. Coenen, E. Beyreuther, and H. Bietenhard; English translation edited by C. Brown (4 vols.; Grand Rapids: Zondervan, 1975–86)

NU text of Nestle-Aland 26th/27th/28th [N] and the United Bible Societies 3rd/4th/5th [U]

TCGNT A TEXTUAL COMMENTARY ON THE GREEK NEW TESTAMENT by Bruce M. Metzger (German Bible Society, 1970; 2nd ed., 1994)

TDNT *Theological Dictionary of the New Testament,* edited by G. Kittel and G. Friedrich; translated and edited by G. W. Bromiley (10 vols.; Grand Rapids: Eerdmans, 1964–76)

TENTGM THE TEXT OF THE EARLIEST NEW TESTAMENT MANUSCRIPTS A Corrected, Enlarged Edition of The Complete Text of the Earliest New Testament Manuscripts by Philip W. Comfort and David P. Barrett (Tyndale House Publishers, 1999, 2nd ed., 2001)

TTNT-A *The Text of the New Testament, An Introduction to the Critical Editions and to the Theory and Practice of Modern Textual Criticism,* by Kurt Aland and Barbara Aland (Grand Rapids, 1987; 2nd ed., 1989).

TTNT-M *The Text of the New Testament, Its Transmission, Corruption, and Restoration,* by Bruce M. Metzger (Oxford, 1964; 3rd ed., 1992).

TNTCR The Text of the New Testament in Contemporary Research: Essays on the Status Quaestionis (New Testament Tools, Studies, and Documents, by Bart D. Ehrman and Michael W. Holmes (Brill, 1995; 2nd ed., 2012)

UBS³ United Bible Societies' *Greek New Testament* (3rd ed., Metzger et al) [1975]

UBS⁴ United Bible Societies' *Greek New Testament* (4th corrected ed., Metzger et al) [1993]

UBS⁵ United Bible Societies' *Greek New Testament* (4th corrected ed., Metzger et al) [2014]

VCEDONTW Vine, W E. *Vine's Expository Dictionary of Old and New Testament Words*. Nashville: Thomas Nelson, 1996.

WHI Westcott and Hort, *Introduction = The New Testament in the Original Greek*, the Text Revised by Brooke Foss Westcott and Fenton John Anthony Hort; [vol. ii] *Introduction [and] Appendix* (Cambridge and London, 1881; 2nd ed., 1896).

WPNT Robertson, A.T. *Word Pictures in the New Testament*. Oak Harbor, MI: Logos Research Systems, 1933, 1997.

WSNT Vincent, Marvin. Word Studies in the New Testament. Bellingham: Logos Research Systems, 2002.

WWSGNT Wuest, Kenneth S. *Wuest's Word Studies from the Greek New Testament*: For the English Reader. Grand Rapids: Eerdmans, 1997, c1984.

ABBREVIATIONS: Manuscripts and Ancient Versions

Textual scholars employ a symbol (called sigla; singular siglum), which indicates a manuscript and to identify the copyist or corrector of a text. Below are the sigla used in THE TEXT OF THE NEW TESTAMENT, as well as the content to the nearest book (sometimes chapter) and its date. For the complete list, please see the introduction and appendixes to UBS5 and NA[28].

- Dates are given to the nearest 25-50-year increment.

- A small cross (†) shows the content of the nearest chapter, while other times the verses are sometimes listed. For example P11 would read 1 Corinthians 1-7 † because it has many verses throughout chapters 1-7: 1:17-22, 25-27; 2:6-8, 9-12, 14; 3:1-3, 5-6, 8-10, 20, 4:3-5; 5:7-8; 6:5-9, 11-18; 7:3-6, 10-14.

- Symbol c. for "circa," or "about."

- Exact dates, like 316 C.E. for P^{10} are the result of being found with, being tied to a document with an exact date, or having an exact date on the manuscript.

- Abbreviation for text families is as follows: Alexandrian Alex.; Western West.; Caesarean Caes.; Byzantine Byz.

- Independent text is abbreviated as Ind.

PAPYRI

Papyrus, Papyri: named for the Egyptian plant from which it is made, in the proper climate this is a very durable writing material that was made by bonding vertical strips of the papyrus pith to horizontal strips. Writing could easily be done on the side with the horizontal strips, and with some difficulty on the other side (called an "opisthograph" when written on both sides). The oldest manuscripts of the NT were written on papyrus; some of them are as early as the second century.

P^1 Matt 1; c. 200 C.E. (Alex. esp. B)

P^3 Luke 7; 10; c. 6th–7th cent. C.E. (strongly Alex.)

P^4+ Luke 1–6; same as P^{64}+P^{67} Matt 3; 5; 26; c. 160-180 C.E. (Alex. esp. P^{75})

P⁵ John 1; 16; 20; c. 200-250 C.E. (Agrees with ℵ against B in John 1:34; 6:22, 27-28)

P⁶ John 10:1-2, 4-7. 9-10; 11:1-8, 45-52; c. 300-325 C.E. (More Alex. than not)

P⁷ Luke 4:1-2; c. third/fourth century C.E. (too small to determine type)

P⁸ Acts 4:1-37; 5:2-9; 6:1-6, 8-15; fourth century (Alex.)

P⁹ 1 John 4:11-12, 15-17; 275-300 C.E. (carelessly written in a common hand)

P¹⁰ Rom 1; c. 316 C.E. tied up with a contract that was dated to 316 (student trying to learn Greek)

P¹¹ 1 Cor. 1-7 †; c. sixth century C.E. (Alex.)

P¹² Heb. 1:1 c. 285 C.E. (too small)

P¹³ Hebrews 2:14-5:5; 10:8-22; 10:29-11:13; 11:28-12:17; c. 200 C.E. (Alex. Esp. B)

P¹⁴ 1 Cor. 1-3 †; c. sixth century C.E. (Alex.)

P¹⁵⁺ 1 Cor. 7:18-8:4 (proto-Alex., esp. B); **P¹⁶** Phil. 3:10-17; 4:2-8 (proto-Alex. Esp. ℵ then B; c. 250-275 C.E. (most likely the same MS)[1]

P¹⁷ Heb. 9:12-19; c. 350 C.E. (Alex.)

P¹⁸ Rev. 1:4-7; c. 275 C.E. (agreeing with C)

P¹⁹ Matt. 10:32-11:5; c. 400 C.E. (no nomina sacra, Ind. readings; Alex.)

P²⁰ Jam. 2:19-3:9; c. 175-200 C.E. (Same scribe very much likely produced **P²⁷**; proto-Alex., esp. ℵ and B)

P²¹ Matt. 12:24-26, 32-33; fourth century C.E. (mixed)

P²² John 15:25-16:2, 21-32; c. 250 C.E. (Alex)

P²³ Jam. 1:10-12, 15-18; c. 200 C.E. (proto-Alex., esp. ℵ A and C)

P²⁴ Rev 5:5-8; 6:5-8; c. 250-300 C.E. (too small to determine type)

P²⁵ Matt 18:32-34; 19:1-3, 5-7, 9-10; c. 350 C.E. (Ind.)

---

[1] Both manuscripts were discovered together and have the same formation of letters, line space, punctuation, and written in a documentary hand. While the color of ink is different, it could have been that the scribe switched to different ink after 1 Corinthians but before he started Philippians.– Comfort, Philip W.; David P. Barrett (2001). *The Text of the Earliest New Testament Greek Manuscripts*. Wheaton, Illinois: Tyndale House Publishers. p. 95.

P²⁶ Rom 1:16; c. 600 C.E.

P²⁷ Rom. 8–9 †; 175-200 C.E. (Same scribe very much likely produced **P²⁰**; Alex.)

P²⁸ John 6:8-12, 17-22; 250-300 C.E. (proto-Alex., esp. P⁷⁵)

P²⁹ Acts 26:7-8, 20; 200 C.E. (Alex. and West.)

P³⁰ 1 Thess. 4–5; 2 Thess. 1 †; c. 200-225 C.E. (Alex. esp. ℵ B)

P³¹ Rom. 12:3-8; late sixth/early seventh century C.E. (too small to determine type)

P³² Titus 1–2; c. 150-175 C.E. (Alex. esp. ℵ F and G)

P³³+P⁵⁸ Acts 7:6-10, 13-18; 15:21-24, 26-32; c. 550 C.E. (Alex.)

P³⁴ 1 Cor. 16:4-7, 10; 2 Cor. 5:18-21; 10:13-14-14; 11:2; c. 650 C. E. (Alex.)

P³⁵ Matt. 25:12-15, 20-23; c. third century C.E. (proto Alex. Handwriting resembles P⁴⁰)

P³⁶ John 3:14-18, 31-32, 34-35; c. 400-425 C.E. (Ind. text)

P³⁷ Matt. 26:19-52; late c. 260 C.E. (Ind. some similarity to P⁴⁵)

P³⁸ Acts 18:27-19:6, 12-16; c. 300 C.E. (West.)

P³⁹ John 8:14-22; c. 225-250 C.E. (proto-Alex. esp. P⁷⁵ and B)

P⁴⁰ Rom 1-4; 6; 9 †; c. 250 C.E. (proto-Alex. exemplar, mostly with ℵ followed by A and B)

P⁴¹ Acts 17-22 †; c. 750 C.E. (West.)

P⁴² Luke 1:54-55; 2:29-32; c. 700 C.E. (too small to determine type)

P⁴³ Rev. 2:12-13; 15:8-16:2; c. 600 C.E. (too small to determine type)

P⁴⁴ Matt. 17:1-3, 6-7; 18:15-17, 19; 25:8-10; c. 600 C.E. (Alex.) P¹²⁸ was formerly listed as being part of P⁴⁴.

P⁴⁵ Gospels and Acts †; c. 200 C.E. (Mark Caes.; Matt, Luke and John Alex. and West.; Acts Alex. esp. ℵ A B and C)

P⁴⁶ Rom 5-6; 8-16; 1 Cor.; 2 Cor.; Gal.; Eph.; Php; Col.; 1 Thess.; Heb.; c. 200 C.E. (Proto-Alex. esp. B in Eph., Col., and Heb.) P46 and P13 are nearly the same text. There are only seventeen disagreements out of eighty-eight variation units.

P⁴⁷ Rev. 9:10-17:2; c. 250 C.E. (Alex. esp. א and Codex 0308) The weight of P⁴⁷ and א is good but not as weighty as P¹¹⁵ A and C.

P⁴⁸ Acts 23:11-17, 23-29; c. 250 C.E. (West.)

P⁴⁹ Eph. 4:16-29; 4:31-5:13 **+P⁶⁵** 1 Thess. 1:3-10; 2:1, 6-13; c. 250 C.E. (Alex. esp. א B; the same codex; produced by same scribe)

P⁵⁰ Acts 8:26-32; 10:26-31; c. 300 C. E. (Alex. esp. א B)

P⁵¹ Gal. 1:2-10, 13, 16-20; c. 400 C.E. (Ind.)

P⁵² John 18:31-34, 37-38; c. 110-125 C.E. (Seems to be Alex.)

P⁵³ Matt. 26:29-40; Acts 9:33-10:1; c. 250-275 C.E. (proto-Alex.)

P⁵⁴ Jam. 2:16-18, 22-26; 3:2-4; c. 400-425 C.E.

P⁵⁹ John 1–2; 11–12; 17–18 †; c. 650 C.E. (Alex.)

P⁶⁰ John 16–19 †; c. 650 C.E. (Alex.)

P⁶¹ Rom 16; 1 Cor. 1; 5–6; Phil 3; Col 1; 4; 1 Thess. 1;Titus 3; Phlm †; c. 700 C.E. (Alex.)

P⁶⁶ John 1:1-6:11; 6:35-14:26, 29-30; 15:2-26; 16:2-4, 6-7; 16:10-20:20, 22-23; 20:25-21:9, 12, 17; c. 150 C.E. (Alex. esp. close to P⁷⁵, B, 016) Because P⁶⁶ is an early Papyrus near complete codex of the Gospel of John, we are adding more here. Fee studied the corrections (i.e., **P⁶⁶ᶜ**) of P⁶⁶ in John 1-9 with P⁷⁵. He found that the corrections are in more of an agreement with P⁷⁵ than the original scribe of P⁶⁶, which means that P⁶⁶ was corrected with a manuscript akin to P⁷⁵, as far as John 1-9 goes. The agreement is increased significantly when the corrections (P⁶⁶ᶜ) of John 10:1-15:8 are compared to P⁷⁵ and 15:9-21:22 with B (this section is missing from P⁷⁵).

P⁶⁶ᶜ¹ this corrector is designated as the original scribe by Comfort and Barrett.

P⁶⁶ᶜ² this corrector is designated as a second scribe in the scriptorium by Comfort and Barrett.

P⁶⁶ᶜ³ this corrector is designated as a third scribe who was also the paginator by Comfort and Barrett.[2]

P⁷⁰ Matt 2:13-16; 2:22-3:1; 11:26-27; 12:4-5; 24:3-6, 12-15; c. 250 C.E. (Alex. carelessly written but reliable)

---

[2] James Royse states that other than John 13:19, the corrections are all by the hand of the original scribe. (Royse 2008, pp. 409-21)

P⁷² 1-2 Peter, Jude †; c. 300 C.E. (Alex. esp. B and then A, and West at times (e.g. Jude)

P⁷⁴ Acts, General Epistles †; c. 650 C.E. (Alex. agrees with P¹⁰⁰) Regardless of its late date, it has an Alexandrian text, which gives a great witness for the book of Acts.

P⁷⁵ Luke 3:18-24:53 and John †; c. 175-200 C.E. (Alex.) The Christian scribe of P⁷⁵ was a professional. This was the kind of text that was used to make Codex Vaticanus. Porter shows that there is an 87% agreement between P⁷⁵ and B.

P⁷⁷ Matt 23 †; c. 175 C.E. (Alex. likely the same codex as P¹⁰³)

P⁸⁴ Mark 2; 6; John 5; 17 †; c. 550 C.E. (mixed)

P⁸⁵ Rev 9:19-10:1, 5-9; c. 350 C.E. (Alex.)

P⁸⁷ Phlm; c. 175-200 C.E. (proto-Alex.)

P⁸⁸ Mark 2:1-26; c. 350 C.E. (Alex.)

P⁹⁰ John 18:36-19:7; c. 175-200 C.E. (Alex. esp. P⁶⁶)

P⁹¹ Acts 2:30-37; 2:46-3:2; c. 250 C.E. (proto-Alex.)

P⁹² Eph. 1:11-13, 19-21; 2 Thess. 1:4-5, 11-12; c. 300 C.E. (Alex. esp. P⁴⁶ ℵ and B)

P⁹⁸ Rev. 1:13-2:21; c. 150-175 C.E. (Ind.)

P⁹⁹ Rom. 2 Cor., Gal, Eph. †; c. 400 C.E. (too fragmented)

P¹⁰⁰ Jam. 3:13-4:4; 4:9-5:1; c. 300 C.E. (Alex. agrees with P⁷⁴)

P¹⁰¹ Matt. 3:10-12; 3:16-4:3; c. 200 C.E. (Alex. more so ℵ than B

P¹⁰³ Matt. 13:55-56; 14:3-5; c. 200 C.E. (Alex. likely the same codex as P⁷⁷)

P¹⁰⁴ Matt. 21:34-37; c. 125-150 C.E. (Alex.)

P¹⁰⁶ John 1:29-35, 40-46; c. 200 C.E. (proto-Alex. esp. P⁶⁶ P⁷⁵ ℵ B)

P¹⁰⁸ John 17:23-24; 18:1-5; c. 200 C.E. (Alex. esp. ℵ)

P¹⁰⁹ John 21:18-20, 23-25; c. 200 C.E. (too small to determine type)

P¹¹⁰ Matt. 10:13-15, 25-27; c. 275-300 C.E. (Ind. Similar to P⁴⁵ and P)

P¹¹² Acts 26:31-32; 27:6-7; c. 450 C.E. (too small to determine type)

P¹¹³ Rom. 2:12-13, 29; c. 200 C.E. (too small to determine type)

P115 Rev 2-3; 5-6; 8-15 †; c. 250 C.E. (Alex. esp. A C)

P119 John 1:21, 28, 38-44; c. 250 C.E. (Alex. somewhat similar to P5)

P120 John 1:25-28, 33-38, 42-44; c. 300 C.E. (Alex. esp. P66 P75)

P121 John 19:17-18, 25-26; c. 200 C.E. (too small to determine type)

P122 John 21:11-14, 22-24; c. 350-400 C.E. (Alex. agrees with W)

P128 John 9:3-4; 12:16-18; c. 600 C. E. (Alex.) P128 was formerly listed as being part of P44.

UNCIALS

Uncial: a term commonly used to refer to majuscule (q.v.) letters (4th to 8th centuries C.E.). It is agreed, however, that the term, taken from Latin and meaning "one-twelfth," should be applied only to a particular type of Latin script or document.

א (Sinaiticus) most of NT; c. 330–360 C.E.

אa designates corrections that were done by several scribes before the manuscript left the scriptorium.

אca designates a group of correctors working at Caesarea in about the sixth or seventh century C.E., who corrected the manuscript in both the Old and New Testament.

A (Alexandrinus) most of NT; c. fifth century C.E.

B (Vaticanus) most of NT; c. 300–325

B1 designates a corrector who was contemporary with the original scribe.

B2 designates a tenth or eleventh century corrector, who also retraced the original writing, as well as adding accents and punctuation marks.[3]

C (Ephraemi Rescriptus) most of NT with many lacunae; fifth century C.E.

D (Bezae) Gospels, Acts; fifth century C.E.

D (Claromontanus) Paul's Epistles; sixth century C.E. (different MS than Bezae)

---

[3] Bruce M. Metzger, *Manuscripts of the Greek Bible: An Introduction to Greek Palaeography*, New York, Oxford: Oxford University Press, 1991, p. 74.

E (Laudianus 35) Acts; sixth century C.E.

F (Augensis) Paul's Epistles; ninth century C.E.

G (Boernerianus) Paul's Epistles; ninth century C.E.

H (Coislinianus) Paul's Epistles; sixth century C.E.

I (Freerianus or Washington) Paul's Epistles; fifth century C.E.

K (Cyprius) Gospels; ninth century C.E.

K (Mosquensis) Acts and Epistles; ninth century C.E.

L (Regius) Gospels; eighth century C.E.

M (Campianus) Gospels; ninth century C.E.

N (Petropolitanus Purpureus) Gospels; sixth century C.E.

P (Porphyrianus) Acts–Revelation; ninth century C.E.

Q (Guelferbytanus B) Luke, John; fifth century C.E.

S (Vaticanus 354) Gospels; 949 C.E.

T (Borgianus) Luke, John; fifth century C.E.

U (Nanianus) Gospels; ninth century C.E.

W (Washingtonianus or the Freer Gospels) Gospels; fifth century C.E.

X (Monacensis) Gospels; tenth century C.E.

Z (Dublinensis) Matthew; sixth century C.E.

Γ (036) Gospels; tenth century C.E.

Δ (037) Gospels; ninth century C.E.

Θ (038) Gospels; ninth century C.E.

Ξ (040) Luke; sixth century C.E.

Π (041) Gospels; ninth century C.E.

Σ (042) Matthew, Mark; sixth century C.E.

Φ (043) Matthew, Mark; sixth century C.E.

Ψ (044) Gospels, Acts, Paul's Epistles; ninth century C.E.

048 Acts, Paul's Epistles, General Epistles; fifth century C.E.

059 Mark 15; fourth-fifth century C.E.

067 Matt 14; 24-26; Mark 9; 14; sixth century C.E.

083 (with 0112) Mark 13-16; John 1; 2-4; sixth–seventh century C.E.

087 Matt 1-2; 19; 21; Mark 12; John 18; sixth century C.E.

099 Mark 16; seventh century C.E.

0102 Matt 21-24; Luke 3–4; 21; seventh century C.E.

0126 Mark 5-6; eighth century C.E.

0130 Mark 1-2; Luke 1; 2; ninth century C.E.

0131 Mark 7-9; ninth century C.E.

0132 Mark 5; ninth century C.E.

0167 Mark 4; 6; seventh century C.E.

0171 Matt 10; Luke 22; c. 300 C.E.

0187 Mark 6; sixth century C.E.

0189 Acts 5; c. 200 C.E.

0250 Gospels; eighth century C.E.

0266 Luke 20; sixth century C.E.

0274 Mark 6-10; fifth century C.E.

0278 Paul's Epistles; ninth century C.E.

0308 Rev. 11:15-18; c. 350 C.E.

MINUSCULES

Minuscule: from a Latin word meaning "somewhat smaller," a set of small, cursive Greek letters as opposed to majuscules (q.v.). In a loose sense, minuscules are often thought of as lowercase Greek letters. They seem to have been invented in the ninth century to speed and lower the cost of book production, usually on vellum or parchment

1 Gospels, Acts, Paul's Epistles; twelfth century C.E.

20 Gospels; eleventh century C.E.

22 Gospels; twelfth century C.E.

28 Gospels; eleventh century C.E.

33 All NT except Rev; ninth century C.E.

81 Acts, Paul's Epistles 1044 C.E.

137 Gospels; eleventh century C.E.

138 Gospels; eleventh century C.E.

209 All NT; fourteenth-fifteenth century C.E.

225 Gospels; 1192 C.E.

274 Gospels; tenth century C.E.

304 Gospels; twelfth century C.E.

435 Gospels; twelfth-thirteenth century C.E.

565 Gospels; ninth century C.E.

579 Gospels; thirteenth century C.E.

700 Gospels; eleventh century C.E.

892 Gospels; ninth century C.E.

954 Gospels; fifteenth century C.E.

983 Gospels; twelfth century C.E.

1216 Gospels; eleventh century C.E.

1241 Gospels, Acts, Paul's Epistles; twelfth century C.E.

1424 (or Family 1424 (a group of 29 manuscripts sharing nearly the same text) most of NT; ninth–tenth century C.E.

1582 Gospels; 949 C.E.

1739 Acts, Paul's Epistles; tenth century C.E.

2053 Rev; thirteenth century C.E.

2344 Rev; eleventh century C.E.

f[1] (a family of manuscripts including 1, 118, 131, 209) Gospels; twelfth-fourteenth century C.E.

f[13] (a family of manuscripts that include 13, 69, 124, 174, 230, 346, 543, 788, 826, 828, 983, 1689, 1709, known as the Ferrar group) Gospels; eleventh-fifteenth c.

Maj The **Majority Text**: a text of the NT in which variant readings are chosen that are found in the majority of all Greek NT manuscripts (cf. "Byzantine Family" above). One could consider this external (objective) evidence and maintain that it is the leading criterion for establishing the text.

Credit for this text is due primarily to Zane Hodges and Arthur Farstad, though the latter once humbly told me (Wilkins) that the text was mainly Hodges' work. Hodges maintained that mathematical probabilities pointed to the text with the greatest number of surviving manuscripts as the one closest to the original. Thus, the name is an accurate description, though Hodges' theory about the text's relation to the original is arguable at best. Of greater value and importance, the Majority Text has essentially purged the Byzantine text of its negative association with the Textus Receptus. Nevertheless, most textual critics maintain that those favoring the MT rely heavily on theological arguments and thin objective evidence in their defense of the text. In particular, easier readings tend to prevail over harder in the MT and BT.

Maj^a This siglum only occurs in Revelation and indicates a large group of manuscripts which contain a commentary on Revelation by Andreas of Caesarea.

Maj^k This siglum also occurs only in Revelation and indicates the large group of manuscripts which do not contain Andreas's commentary.

LECTIONARIES

Lectionaries: books of NT passages chosen by the Christian church for reading at services. For the most part, they represent the Byzantine text and are of use in reconstructing the history of that text. Below are some of the lectionaries cited in the critical editions. At present, there are 2,412 lectionaries extant.

ℓ 1 Evangelistarion (uncial); tenth century C.E.

ℓ 2 Evangelistarion (uncial); tenth century C.E.

ℓ 3 Evangelistarion (uncial); eleventh century C.E.

ℓ 4 Evangelistarion; eleventh century C.E.

ℓ 5 Evangelistarion (uncial); tenth century C.E.

ℓ 10 Evangelistarion; thirteenth century C.E.

ℓ 12 Evangelistarion; thirteenth century C.E.

ℓ 32 Evangelistarion; eleventh century C.E.

ℓ 44 Evangelistarion (uncial); ninth century C.E.

ℓ 59 Apostolos; eleventh century C.E.

ℓ 60 Evangelistarion, Apostolos; 1021 C.E.

ℓ 68 Evangelistarion; twelfth century C.E.

ℓ 69 Evangelistarion; twelfth century C.E.

ℓ 70 Evangelistarion; twelfth century C.E.

ℓ 76 Evangelistarion; twelfth century C.E.

ℓ 80 Evangelistarion; twelfth century C.E.

ℓ 127 Evangelistarion (uncial); ninth century C.E.

ℓ 147 Apostolos; twelfth century C.E.

ℓ 150 Evangelistarion (Uncial); 995 C.E.

ℓ 156 Apostolos; tenth century C.E.

ℓ 165 Apostolarion †; eleventh century C.E.

ℓ 170 Apostolarion †; fourteenth century C.E.

ℓ 184 Evangelistarion; 1319 C.E.

ℓ 185 Evangelistarion †; eleventh century C.E.

ℓ 211 Evangelistarion; twelfth century C.E.

ℓ 249 Evangelistarion, Apostolarion (uncial) ninth century C.E.

ℓ 253 Evangelistarion; 1020 C.E.

ℓ 292 Evangelistarion; ninth century C.E.

ℓ 299 Evangelistarion; eleventh century C.E.

ℓ 303 Evangelistarion; twelfth century C.E.

ANCIENT VERSIONS

Syriac (syr)

syr^c (Syriac Curetonianus) Gospels; fifth century C.E.

syr^h (Syriac Harclean) All NT; 616 C.E.

syr^h** This siglum denotes a reading in syr^h that is set off by asterisks, which questions its originality.

syr^hmg This siglum denotes a reading from the margin of syr^h.

syr^p (Peshitta) All NT except Revelation and shorter General Epistles; fourth-fifth century C.E.

syr^{pal} (Palestinian Syriac) Gospels; fifth-sixth century C.E.

syr^s (Syriac Sinaiticus) Gospels; fourth century C.E.

Old Latin (it)

it^a (Vercellensis) Gospels; fourth century C.E.

it^{aur} (Aureus) Gospels; seventh century C.E.

it^b (Veronensis) Gospels; fifth century C.E.

it^c (Colbertinus) Gospels; twelfth century C.E.

it^d (Cantabrigiensis, the Latin text of Bezae) Gospels, Acts, 3 John; fifth century C.E.

it^e (Palatinus) Gospels; fifth century C.E.

it^f (Brixianus) Gospels; sixth century C.E.

it^{ff2} (Corbeiensis II) Gospels; fifth century C.E.

it^{g1} (Sangermanensis) Matthew; eighth-ninth century C.E.

it^{gig} (Gigas) Gospels; Acts; thirteenth century C.E.

it^h (Fleury palimpsest) Matt 3–14; 18–28; Acts; Revelation; Peter's Epistles; 1 John; fifth century C.E.

it^i (Vindobonensis) Mark 2–15; Luke 10–23; fifth century C.E.

it^k (Bobbiensis) Matthew, Mark; c. 400 C.E.

it^l (Rehdigeranus) Gospels; Acts 8-11; 15; James; 1 Peter; John's Epistles; eighth century C.E.

it^q (Monacensis) Gospels; sixth-seventh century C.E.

it^r (Usserianus) Gospels, Paul's Epistles, Peter's Epistles, 1 John; seventh century C.E.

it^w (Wernigerodensis) Acts; 14th–15th c.; Peter's Epistles; 1 John; sixth century C.E.

Vulgate

The following sigla represent the major editions of the Vulgate.

vg^{cl} (Clementine) *Biblia Sacra Vulgatae Editionis Sixti Quinti Pont. Max. iussu recognita atque edita*; 1592

vgst (Stuttgart) *Biblia sacra iuxta Vulgatam versionem*; 1969 vg^{ww} (Wordsworth and White) *Novum Testamentum Domini nostri Iesu Christi latine secundum editionem Sancti Hieronymi*; 1889–1954

lat Indicates a reading supported by the Vulgate and some of the Old Latin MSS.

Coptic

The Coptic translations of the New Testament date from the 3rd century onward.

cop^{ach} (Akhmimic) John; James; fourth century C.E.

cop^{ach2} (Subakhmimic) John; fourth century C.E.

cop^{bo} (Bohairic = north Egypt) All NT; ninth century C.E.

cop^{fay} (Fayyumic = central Egypt) John; fourth-fifth century C.E.

cop^{G67} (a Middle Egyptian ms) Acts; fifth century C.E.

cop^{mae} (Middle Egyptian) Matthew; fourth-fifth century C.E.

cop^{sa} (Sahidic = southern Egypt) All NT; fourth-fifth century C.E.

Armenian

arm All NT; twelfth century C.E.

Ethiopic

eth All NT; fourteenth century C.E.

Georgian

geo All NT; eleventh century C.E.

Slavonic

slav All NT; tenth- twelfth century C.E.

Ancient Authors

The following abbreviations are used for ancient works.

1 Apol. Justin Martyr, *First Apology*

1 Clem. 1 Clement

Ann. Tacitus, *Annals*

Ant. Josephus, *Jewish Antiquities*

b. Ber. Babylonian tractate *Berakot*

Bacch. Euripides, *Bacchanals*

Cels. Origen, *Against Celsus*

Claud. Suetonius, *Claudius*

Comm. Jo. Origen, *Commentary on John*

Comm. Matt. Origen, *Commentary on Matthew*

Comm. Rom. Origen, *Commentary on Romans*

Cons. Augustine, *De consensus evangelistarum*(Harmony of the Gospels)

Dial. Justin Martyr, *Dialogue with Trypho*

Dial. Pseudo-Athanasius, *Dialogue with Zaccheus*

Did. Didache

Epist. Jerome, *Epistulae*

Fel. Augustine, *Against Felix*

Geogr. Ptolemy, *Geography*

Gos. Pet. Gospel of Peter

Haer. Irenaeus, *Against Heresies*

Hist. eccl. Eusebius, *Ecclesiastical History*

J.W. Josephus, *Jewish War*

Life Josephus, *The Life*

LXX Septuagint

Marc. Tertullian, *Against Marcion*

Onom. Eusebius, *Onomasticon*

Or.Bas. Gregory of Nazianzus, *Oratio in laudem Basilii*

Pan. Epiphanius, *Panarion (Refutation of all Heresies)*

Phaen. Aratus, *Phaenomena*

Prom. Aeschylus, *Prometheus Bound*

Pyth. Pindar, *Pythian Odes*

Quaest. Mar. Eusebius, *Quaestiones ad Marinum*

Tg. Ps.-J. Targum Pseudo-Jonathan

PREFACE

FROM SPOKEN WORDS TO SACRED TEXTS: Introduction to New Testament Textual Studies is an introduction-intermediate to New Testament textual criticism. Its objective is not to contribute to those who are already textual scholars. The objective of this book is to offer the Bible student a more detailed introductory-level look at the world of the text of New Testament textual criticism. The initial chapters are written to help the Bible student who is new to the study of textual criticism while providing in-depth benefit to the intermediate student as well.

Many good Christian biblical apologists spend a lifetime defending the trustworthiness of God's Word. Many modern-day textual scholars seem to be apologists of another sort. They seem to be apologists for **uncertainty** and **ambiguity** as Daniel Wallace in the Foreword of *MYTHS AND MISTAKES in New Testament Textual Criticism* (2019) writes, "The new generation of evangelical scholars is far **more comfortable with ambiguity and uncertainty** than previous generations." (Page xii) The book's theme should be deemed the **ambiguity and uncertainty** of the modern textual scholar.

This uncertainty and ambiguity are of their own making by presenting one hypothesis after another. A hypothesis is a supposition or proposed explanation made based on limited evidence as a starting point for further investigation. Say things like, "there was a possibility that," "it could have been," or "it might have been."

There truly has been a renewed interest in the field of textual criticism, which had lain relatively dormant for several decades. What has contributed to this renewed interest? Several factors have contributed to the rehabilitated awareness: **the internet** has provided such tools as Yahoo and Google discussion boards, where scholars and laypersons alike can discuss the science and art of textual criticism. The internet has given the layperson many websites that are free to read, which offer comprehensive information about textual criticism. **Evangelism** is another reason for the resurgence of textual criticism. Evangelism is defined as "planting the seeds of the Gospel" while Preevangelism is defined as "*tilling the soil of people's minds and hearts to help them be more willing to listen to the truth*" (Geisler and Geisler 2009, p. 22). This leads us to the third main reason for the renewed interest: The **New Atheist, Agnostic, and Skeptic**, who seek to cast doubt on the existence of God and his Word. These new critics of God and the Bible are different from those of 60 years ago or so, as they are far more evangelistic than even Christians. These modern critics pen many books, magazine articles, advertising on billboards, news, and radio shows, and publicly debate Bible scholars. They seem to be everywhere and are contributing to the spiritual shipwreck of tens of thousands of Christians.

The fourth contributing factor to this renewed interest is **scholarly books written for the layperson,** which have enabled the churchgoer to enter the conversation. We now have a plethora of books dealing with numerous biblical fields, which will allow Christians to avoid falling into the trap of doubting that what they have is, in fact, the Word of God, inspired and fully inerrant. There is absolutely no one to be blamed if we end up in repeated conversations that cast doubt on our beliefs and the Word of God, except ourselves.

If the average Christian is going to be effective in his Preevangelism (apologetics) of helping those with receptive hearts to overcome the assault on God's Word, he will need Bible study tools. One such tool is this publication, *FROM SPOKEN WORDS TO SACRED TEXTS: Introduction to New Testament Textual Studies.* There is a twofold objective within the pages of this book:

(1) We seek to educate both the churchgoer and seminary students about the field of New Testament textual studies.

(2) We offer serious Bible students an apologetic tool to use in their Preevangelism, which will enable them to overcome doubts in the Christian community and help the new believer and the unbeliever to do the same.

FROM SPOKEN WORDS TO SACRED TEXTS is written by a conservative Bible scholar, who will discuss how our text came down to us, the tools of the trade, the scribes and copyists involved, the process of textual criticism, and much more. Why is this tool even necessary? One of the most quoted textual and early Christian scholars today by atheists, Muslim apologists, and other Bible critics is Agnostic Dr. Bart D. Ehrman in his now infamous book *MISQUOTING JESUS: The Story Behind Who Changed the Bible and Why.* Ehrman has authored 20+ books with a number of them becoming New York Times Bestsellers that attack the New Testament and God Himself.

Using an apologetic approach, we will deal with such questions as, how did the New Testament authors pen their books? Were the New Testament authors even literate? Is it possible to get back to the original text of the New Testament? How do we explain all the differences in the ancient manuscripts that have come down to us? Were the early scribes trained or inexperienced? Did any of the early scribes intentionally change the text as they were copying it? How do textual scholars date the manuscripts? How are Christians to deal with the claim that there are over 400,000 variants in the manuscripts? Who are the textual scholars of the last five hundred years that have given us our modern restored text? Are our modern English translations accurate renderings of the original languages? Do they need to be? These are some of the questions that will be answered.

The primary objective of this publication is to provide knowledge and insight into how God's Word came down to us, offering encouragement based on an objective view of the evidence. Andrews will show a substantial amount of evidence that what the biblical authors penned in their New Testament books has been restored, and we can have confidence and trust in the New Testament that we have today. It is hoped that the readers of this publication will convey what they have learned herein to any who might have begun to doubt.

It should be made clear that this author is a genuine conservative Christian who believes that the originals were fully inerrant and that the Bible authors were moved along by the Holy Spirit as they authored their book(s). (2 Tim. 3:16; 2 Peter 1:21) Unlike today's modern scholars who are more comfortable with **ambiguousness**, **uncertainty**, and **pessimism**, Andrews is not. So, while they will tell their readers the glass is half empty, Andrews will tell his readers that the glass is half full. They will emphasize to their readers what we don't have as far as evidence goes and what cannot be accomplished. Andrews, on the other hand, will emphasize to his readers what we do have and what we can accomplish while being honest also about things that are ambiguous, uncertain, and where evidence is lacking.

INTRODUCTION The Making of New Testament Books

As Luke, Paul, Peter, Matthew, James, or Jude handed their authorized text off to be copied by others, i.e., published, what would it have looked like? What is the process that the New Testament writers would have followed to get their book ready to be published, copied by others? Once they were prepared for publication, how would they be copied throughout the centuries, up until the time of the printing press of 1455 C.E.?[4] As we open our Bible to the Gospel of Matthew, or the letter to the Romans, or any of the 27 books of the New Testament, how can we have confidence that what we are reading is a reflection of the original in our language? If we were to bring home from a bookstore a copy of the KJV, ASV, RSV, ESV, CSB, LEB, NASB, NLT, NIV, NRSV, UASV, or any of the other one hundred and fifty plus English translations, could we have confidence that what we are reading is, in fact, the Word of God? Some translations have footnotes throughout that say, "Other ancient MSS[5] read .... What exactly does that mean, and which is the Word of God: the words in the main text of our Bible, or the others below in the footnote?

The science and art of textual criticism have answered these questions and more. It is a science because there are rules and principles and a method

---

[4] B.C.E. means "before the Common Era," which is more accurate than B.C. ("before Christ"). C.E. denotes "Common Era," often called A.D., for *anno Domini,* meaning "in the year of our Lord."

[5] Manuscripts, MS would be singular manuscript, while MSS will refer to more than one.

or process that is to be followed if the textual scholar is to get back to the original reading.[6] It is an art because the human agent needs to be balanced with those rules and principles. It is like driving a car. The driver needs to follow all driving rules as he stays between the lines of his side of the road to reach his destination. So too, the textual scholar needs to stay within the rules to reach his destination of establishing the original words of the original texts. However, the designers of the roads were not rigid to the point of making those two lines so narrow that there was no room for the driver to miss obstructions, which might be in his path. This extra room would help the driver to avoid objects that could result in a crash. The same holds true for the textual scholar having room within the lines of his field to prevent a wreck, causing him not to reach his desired destination, i.e., the original reading.

From ancient times until 1455 C.E., anything that was authored was done literally, by hand. A "manuscript" is a handwritten text. It did not matter if it were a poem, letter, receipt, book, or marriage certificate; it would still have been produced and copied by hand. In addition, it would mostly have been done one copy at a time in the early decades of Christianity. In the second century C.E., it may have been copied in a scriptorium, i.e., a room in a monastery for storing, copying, illustrating, or reading manuscripts. In the scriptorium, there would have been a lector (reader) who would have read aloud slowly as multiple scribes or copyists took down what he was saying.

The modern-day young person is far removed from the 1920s to the 1980s where people actually used physical paper, pens, pencils, and envelopes to write letters. The same material was used for homework in school. Today, everything is digital: Microsoft Word Docx, PDFs, laptops, tablets, social media, and smartphones. A twenty-year-old today would likely find it challenging to write a letter with merely pen and paper. He would find it tedious and physically taxing. His lack of practice in writing would make it more difficult to be proficient in making the letters, and it would not be aesthetically pleasing. The hand, wrist, and forearm would get very tired to the point where he would need to take a break.

In early Christianity, manually copying a Bible text would be far more arduous than what was just described. There would be many different physical and mental tasks involved in the process of Tertius copying the book of Romans as the apostle Paul dictated to him, which would have been laborious and strenuous. The same would be even more true of the copyists

---

[6] When we use the term "original" reading or "original" text in this publication, it is a reference to the exemplar manuscript by the New Testament author (e.g. Paul) and his secretary, if he used one (e.g. Tertius), from which other copies were made for publication and distribution to the Christian communities.

who would then use Romans' original copy to make other copies. He would not have had the luxury of having the words dictated, and he would have to look at the exemplar back and forth thousands of times as he made his copy that contained 7,000+ words. Imagine if he were copying the entire Greek New Testament of 138,162 words.

Additionally, far more was involved than simply reading the exemplar and writing a word or phrase in the copy. The material that was being written on was papyrus or parchment. Papyrus was a material prepared in ancient Egypt from the pithy stem of a water plant, used in sheets throughout the ancient Mediterranean world for writing. Parchment was a stiff, flat, thin material made from the prepared skin of an animal and used as a durable writing surface in ancient and medieval times. More on this later.

When the materials used and the working environment are understood, we will fully appreciate why ancient people hired secretaries (scribes). The scribe would lay out a layer of strips that he had cut from the papyrus plant. The pithy juices of the plant would be put in the strips. Another layer would have been placed at right angles over top of the first layer. Something flat and heavy would be placed on the papyrus sheet so the two could be bonded by pressure, which would have produced what we would consider a sheet of papyrus paper. It was no easy task writing on the surface of this papyrus sheet, as the material was rough and fibrous.

The scribe could be seen sitting on the ground with his legs crossed, a board laying over his knees. He would be hunched over, holding the exemplar sheet of papyrus with the fingers of, say, his left hand and his thumb of the same hand resting on the papyrus sheet he was using to make his copy. Or, if a professional scribe, he would pin his sheets of papyrus down. To the other corner of the board would be a small container of ink that he had personally made from a mixture of soot and gum. If this scribe were not experienced at making documents, or he was using below-average level materials, his calamus, or reed pen, could very well snag and tear the papyrus, or the writing could be unreadable. To the right of this scribe, we would see a sharp knife, which would have been used to sharpen his reed pen, and a damp sponge that would be used to erase any errors he might make. Since he is copying a New Testament book, he would likely be doing his level best to write every letter with the greatest of care, meaning he would be writing slowly, all of this bringing with it some difficulty. Imagine the constant sharpening of his pen with his knife and the continuous replenishing it with ink to keep the strokes even.

Working as a scribe or copyist for long hours each day can cause back, neck, and shoulder pains, headache, eyestrain, and overuse injuries of the arms and hands. When the scribe constantly bends his head forward, the muscles in his neck, chest, and **back become almost stiffened in that position**, giving him rounded shoulders and making it more challenging for him to stand upright. Bad posture from the life of a copyist can lead to bad balance. The average human head weighs almost 12 pounds (5.44 kg). This is equal to a bowling ball! When the copyist has his neck bent to 45 degrees, his head exerts nearly 50 pounds (ca. 23 kg) of force on his neck. The weight and pressure affect his breathing and mood, aside from straining joints and muscles in his neck and shoulders.

As we can mentally picture, this scribe was carrying out many simultaneous tedious tasks as he went about copying a book of the New Testament. If he had some experience or a professional in making documents and copying literature, he would have had to consider the page before him to calculate the proper word division. He would be using stichoi notations at the end of the copying process, that is, notes on how many lines were copied to get paid, which means that he had to keep track of his lines. The scribe would always have to be conscious of an imaginary upper and lower line that he sought to keep his text between. Unlike our notebooks today, papyrus and parchment sheets did not come with ruled lines. The scribe would use an unsharpened instrument to draw 25-30 pressure lines on his page to receive the text. Before he even began the above, he would have to have the ability to estimate just how many sheets would be needed for the project. This would change if he were making a copy of an individual gospel or a codex of all four gospels, or the gospels and Acts, or a copy of Paul's epistles, or even one of Paul's epistles such as Romans. He would have to determine how he would construct the codex: was it to be one gather or multiple gathers. If it were multiple gatherings, how many sheets would he need in each gathering? To estimate these things, he would have to determine the size of the letters, how many letters to a line, how big were the margins. These are just some fundamental difficulties involved as early scribes made copies of our New Testament books.

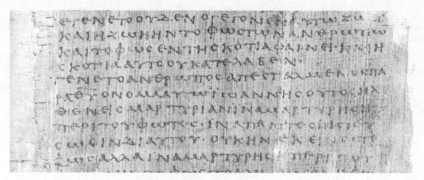

One of the Earliest New Testament Manuscripts: P⁶⁶ Papyrus

The Scroll or Roll Book

A scroll is a roll of papyrus, parchment, or other material, used for a written document. Even though it was continuous, the scroll was generally divided into pages by gluing separate sheets at the edges. Usually, the reader or lector and the writer unrolled the scroll one page at a time, leaving it rolled up on both sides of the current page that was showing. The scroll is unrolled from side to side, with the text being written or read, from top to bottom. For example, if it were Hebrew, it would be written from right to left, and one would open that scroll by rolling to the right. On the other hand, if it were Greek, it would be written from left to right, or even in an alternating direction with other languages. Boustrophedon is an ancient method of inscribing and writing in which lines are written alternately from right to left and from left to right. Usually, professional scribes would justify both sides of the pages, aligned with both left and right margins. On the papyrus scroll, Harold Greenlee writes,

> Papyrus scrolls are mentioned several times in the New Testament; references are usually translated as "book." Luke 4:17 speaks of the scroll (*biblion*) of the prophet Isaiah. John uses the same word to refer to his gospel in John 20:30. The "books" or "scrolls" mentioned in 2 Tim 4:13 may be either parchment scrolls or leather scrolls of the Old Testament. Rev 6:14 describes the sky as vanishing like "a scroll when it is rolled up."[7]

---

[7] J. Harold Greenlee, *Text of the New Testament, From the Manuscript to Modern Edition* (Grand Rapids, MI: Baker Publishing, 2008), 13-14.

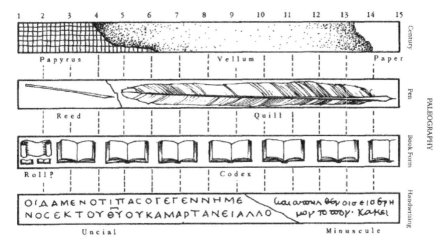

Harold Greenlee, Introduction to New Testament Textual Criticism, (p. 23)

The parchment scroll used by Moses to pen the first five books of the Old Testament; goes back to about the late sixteenth-century B.C.E. The scroll was the first form to receive writing, which was in a format that could be edited by the author or scribe and was used in the Eastern Mediterranean ancient Egyptian civilizations. The codex (bound book) got its start from Latin authors in the first-century C.E. (widely used in the second-century), some 1,500 years after the scroll. The early Christians popularized the codex in the second-century C.E. Some would even argue that the Christians invented it. However, it appears that Christians mainly began using the roll, or scroll, at least until about the end of the first century C.E. Nevertheless, from the close of the first to the third century C.E., there was a struggle between those who encouraged the use of the codex and those preferring scrolls. Traditionalists, familiar and comfortable with using the scroll, were unwilling to give up deep-rooted conventions and traditions. Nevertheless, the popularization of the codex played a significant role in the displacement of the scroll. Therefore, the scroll continued to be used for centuries.

Scrolls were used for literary works. Continuous rolls were twenty or thirty feet long and nine to ten inches high. (Psa. 40:7) The text was written in columns, which formed the pages. (Jer. 36:23) Our English word "volume" literally means *something rolled up*. Imagine being in the synagogue of Nazareth when Jesus was handed the scroll of the prophet Isaiah, where he skillfully unrolled with one hand while simultaneously rolling it up with the other hand until he reached the place he wanted to read. (Lu 4:16-17; Isa. 61:1-2) The ink used on the surface of the scrolls had to withstand being rolled and unrolled, so special ink was developed. In addition, the Jews would discard any scroll that had too many letters missing from wear and tear. It was not until about the fifth-century C.E. that the codex finally outnumbered the

35

scroll by a ten to one margin in Egypt. When we consider the surviving examples, we also see that the scroll had almost vanished by the sixth-century C.E.

The Codex Book

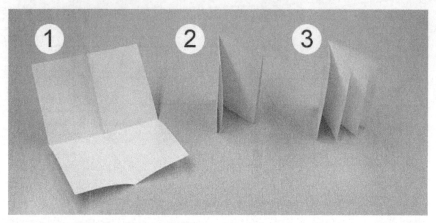

A typical four-leaf quire can be formed from a single sheet of papyrus, parchment, or paper by folding and then cutting the sheet

A codex is a collection of ancient manuscript texts, especially of the Biblical Scriptures, in book form.[8] It is made up of papyrus sheets or parchment inscribed with handwritten material, which is created by folding a single sheet of standard-sized pages, giving the scribe two leaves or four pages.

Indications of Universality

- All of the early papyrus was **in codex (book) form**. (125-400 C.E.)

- The standardization of **the nominal sacra (sacred names)** very early on: God Θεός ΘΣ; Lord Κύριος ΚΣ; Jesus Ἰησοῦς ΙΣ; Christ Χριστός ΧΣ; Spirit Πνεῦμα ΠΝΑ, being in a contracted format and with a horizontal line above the letters. Eventually, it would be 15 sacred names. The following second-century manuscripts that clearly show these nomina sacra are as follows: vP4+P64+P67 dates to (150-175 C.E.), P32 dates to (150-200 C.E.), P46 dates to 150 C.E.), P66 dates to about (150 C.E.), P75 dates to about (175 C.E.), and P90 dates to (150-200 C.E.). This means that the nomina sacra for Lord, Jesus, Christ, God, and Spirit are standard by 150 C.E.

---

[8] Late 16th century: < Latin, "block of wood, book, set of statutes"

- Initially, there were some inconsistencies in the application, but universally it was soon decided to use the nomina sacra regardless of whether the referent, meaning, or context was mundane or sacred in its use.

- By the late first century, New Testament books were being collected in codex form: the Gospels or the Gospels and Acts. The early second century saw the collection of the apostle Paul's letters, which included Hebrews.

- There was the standardization of the codex size for the Gospels, like our 8.5 x 11 inches today. The standard size in the second/third centuries was 11.5-14 cm (4.5-5.5 inches) **Width** x 14.5-17 cm (5.7-6.7) **Length**. A new standard size began to develop in the third century. Just the fact that they had a standard size for the Gospels is unusual because this is not the case for Paul's letter or any other books.

The first codices were made with waxed-coated wooden tablets. The people of Greece and Rome used waxed tablets before the Christian era. Schoolboys were sometimes given waxed tablets on which the teacher had written letters in model script with a stylus. Today, we have the blackboard (UK) or chalkboard (US), initially made of smooth, thin sheets of black or dark gray slate stone. In the early part of the 20th century, schoolchildren even had smaller slate tablets. They had a reusable writing surface on which text or drawings could be made with sticks of calcium carbonate, i.e., chalk.

Roman wax tablet and stylus

To make the waxed tablets of Jesus' day, one would slightly hollow out a flat piece of wood and fill that void with wax. These tablets were also used for temporary writing like modern chalkboards. They were also commonly used for corresponding with others. Greenlee writes, "They were also used at times for legal documents, in which case two tablets would be placed face to face with the writing inside and fastened together with leather thongs run through holes at the edges of the tablets. In one of his writings, St. Augustine mentions some tablets he owned, although his were made of ivory instead of wood."[9] An example of temporary (short-

---

[9] J. Harold Greenlee, *Introduction to New Testament Textual Criticism* (Grand Rapids, MI: Baker Academic, 1995), 8-9.

term, momentary) writing is found in the Gospel of his ability to speak, was asked what name he wanted his son to have. Luke 1:63 reports, "And he asked for a writing tablet and wrote, 'His name is John.'"

Polyptychs [**pol·yp·tych** ˈpälipˌtik] is an arrangement of three or more panels with a painting or carving on each, usually hinged together. Some were discovered at Herculaneum, an ancient Roman town near modern Naples that was destroyed along with Pompeii by the eruption of Mount Vesuvius in 79 C.E.

In time, sheets of foldable material replaced rigid tablets. The codex has been viewed as the most significant advancement in the development of the book, aside from the printing press.[10] Some of the earliest surviving codices were made of papyrus, being preserved in the dry sands of Egypt.

When we consider the thought of unrolling and using a scroll instead of the codex, we can likely think of many advantages of one over the other. The codex can contain far more written material; it is much easier to carry and more convenient. Some in the early days of the codex even mentioned these advantages. Nevertheless, some were slow to move away from the scroll's prolonged use. Again, the Christians played a significant part in the eventual death of the scroll. Their evangelism would have been far more cumbersome without the codex.

The Codex Gigas, 13th century, Bohemia.

---

[10] Colin H. Roberts; T. C. Skeat, *The Birth of the Codex*, (London, Oxford University Press, 1983), 1.

38

Compared to the scroll, the codex was also far more affordable because both sides of the pages could be written on, getting more value for one's money. Moreover, instead of having one book with each scroll, one could have the whole of the old or New Testament. The fact that one could find Bible passages far more accessible and faster, this, too, added to the codex's success. This preference for the codex was not only true for Christians but also lawyers and the like. When we think of the early Christians, we are reminded that they evangelized to the point of going from 120 disciples in the upper room on Pentecost 33 C.E. to more than one million Christians spread throughout the Roman Empire at the beginning of the second century C.E. In addition, early Christians were evangelists, who used pre-evangelism, i.e., apologetics. They could have what we now call proof texts, easily located, to make their arguments to pagans and Jews alike. Then, the fact that the codex book had a wooden cover made it more durable than the scroll, adding to its advantages. Codices were useful, sensible, and likely practical for personal reading. The Christians of the third century C.E. had parchment pocket Gospels.

Larry Hurtado, in his blog (*The Codex and Early Christians: Clarification & Corrections*), writes,

> Bagnall offered figures (pp. 72-74) comparing the number of non-Christian and Christian codices from Egypt datable to the early centuries, also giving the percentages of Christian codices of the total. His own data show, e.g., that Christian codices amount to somewhere between 22-34% of the total for the 2nd-3rd centuries CE. Yet Christian books overall amount to only ca. 2% of the total number of books (codices and rolls) of these centuries. Of course, there are more non-Christian codices, but the first point to note is that Christian codices comprise a vastly disproportionate percentage of the total number of codices in this period.

> The very data provided by Bagnall clearly show that Christians invested in the codex far more than is reflected in the larger book-culture of the time. That is, the early Christian *preference* for the codex is undeniable, and this preference is quite distinctive in that period. Bagnall actually reached the same judgment, stating, "Christian books in these centuries (2nd/3rd) are far more likely to be codices than rolls, quite the reverse of what we find with classical literature." (p. 74)

> My second point also stands and is supported by Bagnall: the early Christian preference for the codex seems to have been especially keen when it came to making copies of texts used as

scripture (i.e., read in corporate worship). For example, 95+% of Christian copies of OT writings are in codex form. As for the writings that came to form the NT, they're all in codex form except for a very few instances of NT writings copied on the back of a re-used roll (which were likely informal and personal copies made by/for readers who couldn't afford a copy on unused writing material). Here again, Bagnall grants the same conclusion, judging that, although they were ready to copy "the Christians adopted the codex as the normative format of deliberately produced public copies of scriptural texts" (p. 78), but were ready to use rolls for other texts (76).[11]

The Making of a Codex

Skin of a stillborn goat on a stretcher (modern) – The J. Paul Getty Museum

Making a codex began with a dried and treated sheepskin, goatskin, or another animal hide. "The pelts were first soaked in a lime solution to loosen the fur, which was then removed. While wet on a stretcher, the skin was scraped using a knife with a curved blade. As the skin dried, the parchment maker would adjust the tension so that the skin remained taut. This cycle of scraping and stretching was repeated over several days until the desired thinness had been achieved. Here, the skin of a stillborn goat, prized for its smoothness, is stretched on a modern frame to illustrate the parchment making process."[12] The first step for preparing the pages to receive writing was setting up the quires, i.e., a bundle of parchment sheets folded together for binding into a book, especially a four-sheet bundle folded once to make eight leaves or sixteen pages. Raymond Clemens and Timothy

---

[11] Retrieved Thursday January 17, 2019, The Codex and Early Christians: Clarification & Corrections, https://larryhurtado.wordpress.com/2014/09/16/the-codex-and-early-christians-clarification-corrections/

[12] Retrieved Monday September 15, 2014 *The Making of a Medieval Book*" The J. Paul Getty Trust. http://www.getty.edu/art/exhibitions/making/

Graham point out that "the quire was the scribe's basic writing unit throughout the Middle Ages."[13]

The Craft of the Scribe

The *recto* is the front side of a papyrus sheet or parchment sheet, while the *verso* is the back of a page. If the scribe were writing on a papyrus sheet, he would write his script on the horizontal lines of the fibers on the recto side of his sheet. If the scribe were using a parchment sheet, the manuscript had pinpricks placed in it to be ruled with lines to accommodate writing better. In some of the documents, we can still see faintly visible lines. It was similar to modern-day tablet paper, with horizontal lines running across the page to receive text, and vertical lines, which served to mark the boundaries, justify both sides. The scribal schools had different techniques for ruling manuscripts. Sometimes, a textual scholar can identify a particular manuscript's school, based on how it was ruled, giving us the place of its origin. The parchment's hair side was darker than that of the flesh side, so scribes placed the quires so that the hair side faced the hair side of the corresponding page, making it more reader-friendly.

Study of Ancient Handwriting

The study of ancient handwriting and manuscripts is an essential skill for paleographers, but also for the textual scholar as well. The style of the characters that make up an alphabet change every fifty years or so; thus, it is essential to know the eras of different styles. Moreover, scribes use abbreviations and contractions for various reasons. Therefore, the student of ancient handwriting must know how to interpret them. For example, several contractions and abbreviations are found in our earliest manuscripts of the Christian Greek New Testament.[14] We briefly mentioned this earlier.

The abbreviations that are most relevant to this discussion are what have become known as the sacred names, or nomina sacra (nomen sacrum, singular), such as Lord ($\overline{KC}$),[15] Jesus ($\overline{IH}$, $\overline{IHC}$), Christ ($\overline{XP}$, $\overline{XC}$, $\overline{XPC}$), God ($\overline{\Theta C}$), and Spirit ($\overline{\Pi NA}$). These sacred names are abbreviated or contracted

---

[13] Raymond Clemens, Timothy Graham. *Introduction to Manuscript Studies*. Ithaca: Cornell University Press, 2008, 14.

[14] It should be noted that the early manuscripts were written in what we consider all uppercase letters, known as majuscule, the large rounded letters used in ancient manuscripts. Moreover, there were no breaks between the letters, so a phrase like GODISNOWHERE could be divided as GOD IS NO WHERE or GOD IS NOW HERE.

[15] In the fourth and third centuries B.C.E., the sigma form of Σ was simplified into a C-like shape in koinē Greek.

by keeping the first letter or two and the last letter. Another essential feature is the horizontal bar placed over these letters to help readers recognize that they are encountering a contraction. The early Christian writers had three different ways that they would pen a sacred name: **(1)** suspension, **(2)** contraction, and **(3)** longer contraction. The suspension was accomplished by writing only the first two letters of "Jesus," for example (ιησους = ιη), and suspending the remaining letters (σους). The contraction was accomplished by writing only the first and last letter of Jesus (ιησους = ις) and removing the remaining letters (ησου).

The longer contraction would simply keep the first two letters and the last letter (ιης). After penning the suspension or contraction, the scribe would place a bar over the $\overline{name}$. This practice of placing a bar over the name was likely carried over from the typical way of scribes putting bars above contractions, especially numbers, which were represented by letters, e.g., $\overline{IA}$ = eleven.

When students of ancient handwriting know these individual letterforms, ligatures,[16] punctuation, and abbreviations, they can read and understand the text. Of course, textual scholars must learn the language of the manuscripts they are studying; in our case, Greek. They need to be an expert in the forms of the language, the various handwriting styles, writing customs, and able to identify different hands within the same manuscript and scribal notes and abbreviations. They also need to study the language development over the years and its history to better analyze the texts. As we have discussed, students of ancient handwriting must know the writing materials, which will enable them to better identify the period in which a document was copied.[17] One of the primary goals of paleographers is to ascertain the text's date and its place of origin. For these reasons alone, they must consider the style and formation of a manuscript and the style of handwriting used therein.

---

[16] A ligature is a character that consists of two or more letters joined together, e.g. "æ". We do not normally find ligatures in majuscule manuscripts. In the minuscule manuscripts, it can be difficult to determine a ligature due to the fact it is a manuscript with a running hand.

[17] Robert P. Gwinn, "Paleography" in the Encyclopaedia Britannica, Micropædia, Vol. IX, 1986, p. 78.

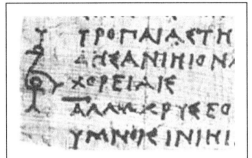

Detail of the Berlin Papyrus 9875 showing the 5th column of Timotheus' Persae, with a coronis symbol, to mark the end.

For example, with the majuscule hand, we have what is known as the **Ptolemaic Book Hand**, and how it developed is difficult to say because we have so few examples, which are not datable. It is not until we reach the third century B.C.E. that we can have confidence in the Ptolemaic bookhand era. This period's hands are stiff, awkward, and sharply defined (e.g., **E**, **Σ**, and **Ω**). Moreover, the letters evidenced no consistency in size. At times, there was a fineness, and pleasing subtlety attained. When we arrive at the second century B.C.E., we find the letters becoming more rounded and more uniform in size. However, one can detect a loss of unity in the first century. On this, Comfort writes, "Paleographers date the emergence of the Roman Uncial as coming on the heels of the Ptolemaic period, which ended in 30 BC. Thus, early Roman Uncial begins around 30 BC, and the Roman Uncial hand can be seen throughout the first two to three centuries of the Christian era. The Roman Uncial script, generally speaking, shares the characteristics of literary manuscripts in the Roman period (as distinct from the Ptolemaic period) in that these manuscripts show a greater roundness and smoothness in the forms of letters and are somewhat larger than what was penned in the Ptolemaic period. Furthermore, the Roman Uncial typically displays decorative serifs in several letters, but not all. (By contrast, the Decorated Rounded style aims at making the decorations rounded and replete.)"[18]

Majuscule Hand

During the Byzantine period (300-650 C.E.), the dominant type of book-hand became known as the biblical hand. It had its earliest beginnings toward the end of the second-century C.E., being used by all, not necessarily having any connection to Christian literature. In addition, manuscripts from Egypt, of vellum or papyrus dating to around the fourth century C.E., contained other forms of script, i.e., a sloping somewhat unpolished rough hand resulting from the literary hand, which continued until about the fifth century C.E. The three early great codices, Vaticanus and Sinaiticus of the

---

[18] Philip Comfort, *Encountering the Manuscripts: An Introduction to New Testament Paleography & Textual Criticism* (Nashville, TN: Broadman & Holman, 2005), 110.

fourth century C.E. and Alexandrinus of the fifth century C.E., were penned in majuscules of the biblical hand. The hand that produced Vaticanus is the least demonstrated. The letters are characteristic of the biblical hand but do not possess the later manuscripts' heavy look, with a greater roundness to them. Sinaiticus, which was copied shortly after that, has larger, heavier letters. In Alexandrinus, we notice a development in the form, a definite distinction between thick and thin strokes.

ΛΟΥΤΟΥΒΑCΙΛΕѠCΙΝΑ
ΜΑΓΟΙΑΠΟΑΝΑΤΟΛѠΝ
ΠΑΡΕΓΕΝΟΝΤΟΕΙCΙΕΡ
CΟΛΥΜΑΛΕΓΟΝΤΕCΠ·Υ
ΕCΤΙΝΟΤΕΧΘΕΙCΒΑCΙ
ΛΕΥCΤѠΝΙΟΥΔΑΙѠΝ
ΕΙΔΟΜΕΝΓΑΡΑΥΤΟΥΤ
ΑCΤΕΡΑΕΝΤΗΑΝΑΤΟ
ΛΗΚΑΙΗΛΘΟΜΕΝΠΡΟC
ΚΥΝΗCΑΙΑΥΤѠ ΑΚΟΥ
CΑCΔΕΟΒΑCΙΛΕΥCΗΡѠ
ΔΗCΕΤΑΡΑΧΘΗΚΑΙΠΑ

ΤΕCΤΟΥΒΑCΙΛΕѠCΕΠ·
ΡΕΥΘΗCΑΝΚΑΙΙΔΟΥΟ
ΑCΤΗΡΟΝΕΙΔΟΝΕΝΤ
ΑΝΑΤΟΛΗΠΡΟΗΓΕΝΑΥ
ΤΟΥCΕѠCΕΛΘѠΝΕCΤΑ
ΘΗΕΠΑΝѠΟΥΗΝΤΟ
ΠΑΙΔΙΟΝΙΔΟΝΤΕCΔΕ
ΤΟΝΑCΤΕΡΑΕΧΑΡΗCΑΝ
ΧΑΡΑΝΜΕΓΑΛΗΝCΦΟ
ΑΡΑΚΑΙΕΛΘΟΝΤΕCΕΙ·
ΤΗΝΟΙΚΙΑΝΕΙΔΟΝΤΟ
ΠΑΙΔΙΟΝΜΕΤΑΜΑΡΙ·

ΤΗCΤΕΛΕΥΤΗCΗΡѠΔ
ΙΝΑΠΛΗΡѠΘΗΤΟΡΗΟ
ΥΠΟΚΥΔΙΑΤΟΥΠΡΟΦ·
ΤΟΥΛΕΓΟΝΤΟCΕΞΑΙ·
ΠΤΟΥΕΚΑΛΕCΑΤΟΝΥ
ΙΟΝΜΟΥ ΤΟΤΕΗΡѠ
ΔΗCΙΔѠΝΟΤΙΕΝΕΠΑΙ
ΧΘΗΥΠΟΤѠΝΜΑΓѠΝ
ΕΘΥΜѠΘΗΛΑCΙΑΝΚΑΙΑ
ΠΟCΤΕΙΛΑCΑΝΕΙΛΕΝ
ΠΑΝΤΑCΤΟΥCΠΑΙΔΑΝ
ΤΟΥCΕΝΒΗΘΛΕΕΜΚΑΙ

Vaticanus, From Page Matthew 1:22-2:18

ΓѠΕΛΘѠΝΗΠΡΟC·
ΚΥΝΗCѠΔΥΤѠ·
ΟΙΔΕΑΚΟΥCΑΝΤΕC
ΤΟΥΚΑCΙΛΕѠCΕ
ΠΟΡΕΥΘΗCΑΝΚΑΙ
ΙΔΟΥΟΛCΤΗΡΟΝΗ
ΛΟΝΕΝΤΗΑΝΚΤΟ
ΛΗΠΡΟΗΓΕΝΑΥΤ·
ΕѠCΕΛΘѠΝΕCΤΑ
ΘΗΕΠΑΝѠΟΥΗΝ
ΤΟΠΑΙΔΙΟΝΙΔΟΝ
ΤΕCΔΕΤΟΝΑCΤΕΡ·

ΛΑΚΕΤΟΠΕΔΙΟΝ
ΚΑΙΤΗΝΜΗΤΕΡΑ
ΛΥΤΟΥΝΥΚΤΟCΚ·
ΑΝΕΧѠΡΗCΕΝΕΙ
CΑΙΓΥΠΤΟΝΚΑΙΗ·
ΕΚΙΕѠCΤΗCΤΕΛΕΥ
ΤΗCΗΡѠΔΟΥΙΝΑ
ΠΛΗΡѠΘΗΤΟΡΗΘ·
ΥΠΟΚΥΔΙΑΤΟΥΠ·
ΦΗΤΟΥΛΕΓΟΝΤΟC
ΕΞΑΙΓΥΠΤΟΥΕΚΑ
ΛΕCΑΤΟΝΥΝΜΟΥ·

ΤΕΘΝΗΚΑCΙΝΙΑΡ
ΟΙΖΗΤΟΥΝΤΕCΤΗΝ
ΨΥΧΗΝΤΟΥΠΕΔΙ·
ΟΔΕΕΓΕΡΘΟΙCΗΑΡ
ΛΑΚΕΤΟΠΑΙΔΙΟΝ·
ΚΑΙΤΗΝΜΡΑΛΥΤΟΥ
ΚΑΙΕΙCΑΘΕΝΕΙ·
ΓΗΝΙΗΛ
ΑΚΟΥCΑCΑΕΟΤΙΑΡ
ΧΕΛΛΟCΚΑCΙΛΕΥΕΙ
ΤΗCΙΟΥΔΑΙΑCΑΝΤΙ
ΤΟΥΠΡCΑΥΤΟΥΗΡ·

ΜΑΤΗΝΗΝΤΙΕΡΙ
ΤΗΝѠCΦΥΝΑΥΤΥ
ΗΔΕΤΡΟΦΗΗΝΑΥ
ΤΟΥΑΚΡΙΛCΕΟΚΑΝΜ·
ΛΙΑΠΤΙΟΝ
ΙΟΤΕΕΞΕΠΟΡΕΥΕ
ΤΟΠΡΟCΑΥΤΟΝΙ
ΕΡΟCΟΛΥΜΑΚΑΙ
ΠΑCΑΗΙΟΥΔΑΕΑ
ΚΑΙΠΕΡΙΧѠ
ΡΟCΤΟΥΙΟΡΔΑΝΟΥ
ΚΑΙΕΚΑΠΤΙΖΟΝΤ·

Sinaiticus, From Page Matthew 2:5-3:7

ΧΙΧ ΚΑΙΜΗΙΕΝΧΥCΘΘΑΙΝΥΘΟ
ΤѠΠΙΑС ΚΑΙΑCΓΕΙΒΑΥΤΟΙC
ΟΠΟΥΑΝΕΙCΕΛΘΗΤΒΕΙCΙΟΙΚΙΑΝ
ΕΚΕΙΜΕΝΕΤΑΙΕѠCΑΝΕΞΕΛΘΗ
ΤΕΟΚΕΙΘΕΝ ΚΑΙΟCΟΙΑΝ
ΜΗ ΔΕΞѠΝΤΑΙΥΜΑCΜΗΔΕ ΑΚΟΥCѠ
ѠCΙΝΥΜѠΝΕΚΠΟΡΕΥΟΜΕ
ΝΟΙΕΚΕΙΘΕΝΕΚΤΕΙΝΑΞΑΤΕΟ
ΧΟΥΝΤΟΝΥΠΟΚΑΤѠΤѠΝΠΟ
ΔѠΝΥΜѠΝΕΙCΜΑΡΤΥΡΙΟΝΑΥ
ΤΟΙC· ΑΜΗΝΛΕΓѠΥΜΙΝ
ΑΝΕΚΤΟΤΕΡΟΝΕCΤΑΙCΟΔΟΜΟΙC

ΚΑΙΡΟΥΟΤΕΠΡΟΛΗCΘΘΙΕΓΑ
ΜΕCΤΟΙCΑΥΤΟΥΑΠΗΟΝΕΘΑΜ
ΤΟΙCΜΕΡΙCΤΝCΙΝΧΥΤΟΥΚΑΙ
ΤΟΙCΧΕΙΧΑΡΧΟΙCΚΑΙΤΟΙCΠ·
ΤΟΙCΤΗCΓΑΛΙΛΑΙΟΥΤΟΙCΙCΕΙ·
ΘΟΥCΗCΤΙCΕΥΠΤΡΟΦΑΥΤΙΝ
ΤΗCΗΡΘΛΙΛΙΛΟCΚΑΙΟΡΧΗCΘ
ΜΕΝΗCΚΑΙΡΘCΑCΗCΤѠΗΡΘ·
ΔΗΚΑΙΤΟΙCΟΥΝΧΝΑΚΕΙΜΕΝ·
ΕΙΠΕΝΟΒΑCΙΛΕΥCΤѠΚΟΡΑ
CΙѠΑΙΤΗCΟΝΜΕΘΘΑΝΘΕΛ·
ΚΑΙΔѠCѠCΟΙ ΚΑΙѠΜΟCΘΝ

Codex Alexandrinus of the fifth century, The Center for the Study of New Testament Manuscripts

Once we enter the sixth century C.E., we notice in the manuscripts, vellum or papyrus, that the heavier hand became the standard but still possessed an attractive appearance. However, there was a steady decline in the centuries to come, as the writing appears to be done artificially, i.e., as a matter of duty or custom, without thought, attention. The thick strokes became heavier; the cross strokes of **T** and **Θ** and the bottom of **Δ** were equipped with sagging spurs. This era of an unpleasant hand followed in sequence, morphing from sloping to upright.

Publishing Industry of the Ancient World

Today, most people would not imagine the ancient world's having a large publishing industry, yet this was the case. The ancient writings of famous authors were great pieces of literature that were highly sought after from the moment they were penned, much as today. Thus, there was a need for the scriptorium[19] to fill orders for both pagan and civil literature and the Bible books. There was a need for hundreds of copies, and as Christianity displaced paganism, the demand would grow exponentially.

The **Autograph** ("self-written") was the text written by a New Testament author or the author and scribe as the author dictated to him. If the scribe was taking down dictation (Rom. 16:22; 1 Pet. 5:12), he might have done so in shorthand.[20] Whether by shorthand or longhand, we can assume that both the scribe and the author would check the scribe's work. The author would have authority over all corrections since the Holy Spirit did not inspire the scribe. The finished product would be the autograph if the inspired author wrote everything down as the Spirit moved him. This text is also often referred to as the **Original**. Hence, the terms *autograph* and *original* are often used interchangeably. Sometimes textual scholars prefer to distinguish, using "original" as a general reference to the text that is correctly attributed to a biblical author. This designation does not focus on the process of how a book or letter was written.

The *original* can also be referred to as the first **Authorized Text** (**Archetypal Manuscript**), i.e., the text first used to make other copies. We should also point out that some textual scholars debate whether the original or autograph of any given book was actually the first text used to make copies. And they prefer to call the latter the **Initial Text** instead, not

---

[19] A scriptorium was a room for storing, copying, illustrating, or reading manuscripts.

[20] "The usual procedure for a dictated epistle was for the amanuensis (secretary) to take down the speaker's words (often in shorthand) and then produce a transcript, which the author could then review, edit, and sign in his own handwriting. Two New Testament epistles provide the name of the amanuensis: Tertius for (Romans 16:22) and Silvanus (another name for Silas) for 1 Peter 5:12." Philip Comfort, *Encountering the Manuscripts: An Introduction to New Testament Paleography & Textual Criticism* (Nashville, TN: Broadman & Holman, 2005), 06.

Andrews qualifies what Comfort had to say about shorthand. There is the **slight possibility** of Tertius or other Bible author's scribes taking it down in shorthand and after that making out a full draft, which would have been reviewed by both Paul and Tertius. This is only the case if it is comparable to what a modern-day court reporter does. In some sense, they are taking down whoever is speaking down in shorthand. Imagine a courtroom where you have a witness talking fast, the prosecution interrupts, the defense jumps in with his rebuttal and the judge snaps his ruling, and the witness resumes his or her account of things. All of that is taken down explicitly word for word in shorthand, and if ever turned into longhand, it would be exactly what was said, down to the uh and um common in speech. So, if the shorthand of the day had that kind of capability; then, it is conceivable. We must remember these are the Bible author's dictated words to the scribe based on their inspiration, not the word choice or writing style of the scribe.

requiring that it actually be the autograph. Conservative scholars would maintain that they are the same. Neither term should be confused with what is known as an ordinary **exemplar**, which is any authorized text of the book from which other copies were made. The original text necessarily was the first exemplar used to make copies, but additional copies of high quality were used as exemplars. We will frequently use exemplar to refer to any document that serves as a standard that a scribe employed as his text for making another copy. Usually, a scribe would have a main or primary exemplar from which he makes most of his copies and one or more secondary exemplars to compare what he found in his primary exemplar. Scribes sometimes substituted text from other exemplars for what they have in their main exemplars.

We have mentioned the **Scriptorium**, a room where multiple scribes or even one scribe worked to produce the manuscript(s). A lector would read aloud from the exemplar, and the scribe(s) would write down his words. The **Corrector** was the one who checked the manuscripts for needed corrections. Corrections could be by three primary persons: **(1)** the copyist himself, **(2)** the official corrector of the scriptorium, or **(3)** a person who had purchased the copy. While those correctors were contemporaneous with the original scribe(s), others could have corrected the text centuries later. When textual scholars speak of the **Hand**, this primarily refers to a person who is making the copy, distinguishing his level of training. Paleographers have set out four basic levels of handwriting. First, there was the *common hand* of a person who was untrained in making copies. Second, there was the *documentary hand* of an individual who was trained in preparing documents. The third level was the *reformed documentary* hand of a copyist who was experienced in preparing documents and copying literature. The fourth was the *professional hand*, the scribe experienced in producing literature.[21]

We must keep in mind that we are dealing with an oral society. Therefore, the apostles, who had spent three and a half years with Jesus, first published the Good News orally. The teachers within the newly founded Christian congregations would repeat this information until it was memorized. After that, those who had heard this gospel would, in turn, share it with others (Acts 2:42, Gal 6:6). In time, they were moved by the Holy Spirit to see the need for a written record, so Matthew, Mark, Luke, and John would pen the Gospels, and other types of New Testament books would be written by Paul, James, Peter, and Jude. From the first four verses of Luke,

---

[21] Philip Comfort, *Encountering the Manuscripts: An Introduction to New Testament Paleography & Textual Criticism* (Nashville, TN: Broadman & Holman, 2005), 17-20.

we can see that Theophilus[22] was being given a written record of what he had already been taught orally. In verse 4, Luke says to Theophilus, "[My purpose is] that you may know the exact truth about the things you have been taught."

When the Son of God on Golgotha, outside of Jerusalem on Friday, Nisan 14 33 C.E. about 3:00 p.m., gave his life, Matthew, Mark, Luke, and John did not write their Gospels immediately. Matthew first wrote his Gospel in Hebrew some 12-17 years after Jesus' ascension, 45-50 C.E. Shortly after that, he translated it into Greek. Luke followed with his Gospel about 56–58 C.E. Then, Mark and his Gospel were written about 60–65 C.E. Finally, John's Gospel was written some 65 years after Jesus death in about 98 C.E. One thing few biblical scholars in the seminaries address today is how these apostles Matthew, John, and the disciples Mark and Luke were able to record the life, ministry, and death of Jesus Christ with such unerring accuracy.

The appearance of the written record did not mean the end of the oral publication. Both the oral and the written records would be used together. Many did not read the written documents themselves, as they could hear them read in the congregational meetings by the lector. This would apply to those who could read because they may not have been able to afford to have copies made for themselves. Paul and his letters came to be used in the same way as he traveled extensively but was just one man and could only be in one place at a time. It was not long before he took advantage that he could be in one place and dispatch letters to other locations through his traveling companions. These traveling companions would not only deliver the letters but also know the issues well enough to address questions that might be asked by the congregation leaders to which they had been dispatched.

In summary, the first century saw the life and ministry of Jesus Christ, the Son of God, and his death, resurrection, and ascension. After that, his disciples spread this gospel orally for at least 12-17 years before Matthew penned his gospel. The written record was used in conjunction with the oral message.

In the first-century C.E., the Bible books were being copied individually. In the late first century or the beginning of the second century, they began being copied in groups. At first, it was the four gospels and then the book of Acts with the four gospels and shortly after that a collection of the Apostle Paul's writings. Each of the individual books of the New Testament was

---

[22] Theophilus means "friend of God," was the person to whom the books of Luke and Acts were written (Lu 1:3; Ac 1:1). Theophilus was called "most excellent," which may suggest some position of high rank. On the other hand, it simply may be Luke offering an expression of respect. Theophilus had initially been orally taught about Jesus Christ and his ministry. Thereafter, it seems that the book of Acts, also by Luke, confirms that he did become a Christian. The Gospel of Luke was partially written to offer Theophilus assurances of the certainty of what he had already learned by word of mouth.

penned, edited, and published between 45 and 98 C.E. A group of the apostle Paul's letters and the gospels were copied and published between 90 to 125 C.E. The entire 27 books of the New Testament were not published as a whole until about 290 to 340 C.E.

Thus, we have the 27 books of the New Testament that were penned individually in the second half of the first century. Each of these would have been copied and recopied throughout the first century. The copies of these copies would, of course, be made as well. Some of the earliest manuscripts that we now have indicate that a professional scribe copied them. Many of the other papyri provide evidence that a semi-professional hand-copied them, while most of these early papyri give proof of being made by a copyist who was literate and experienced at making documents. Therefore, either literate or semi-professional copyists produced most of our early papyri, with some being made by professionals.

Sadly, we do not have the autographs. Even if we did, we would have no way to authenticate them. We do, however, have copies of New Testament manuscripts that go back to the second and third centuries C.E. Over the centuries, this copying of copies continued. The authors were inspired so that the originals were error-free. However, this is not the case with those who made copies; they were not under the Holy Spirit's influence while making their copies. Therefore, these copies must have contained unintentional mistakes, as well as intentional changes, differing from the originals and each other. However, this is not as problematic or alarming as it may first sound. By far, most of the copyist errors are trivial, such as differences in spelling, word order, and such.

It is true that other copyist errors, a tiny portion, are noteworthy (significant), arising from the copyist's desire to correct something in the text that he perceived as erroneous or problematic. In an even smaller number of cases, the scribe made changes to strengthen orthodox doctrine. However, these changes have little to no effect on doctrines because other passages addressing the same beliefs provide the means to analyze and correct the copyist's "corrections." Moreover, they are easily analyzed and corrected so that we know what the original contained. Furthermore, we have enough textual evidence to know what words were in the original.

In the language of textual criticism, changes to the original text introduced by copyists are called "variant readings." A variant reading is a different reading in the extant [existing] manuscripts for any given portion of the text. The process of textual criticism is examining variant readings in various ancient manuscripts to reconstruct the original wording of a written text. These variants in our copies of the New Testament manuscripts are primarily the reason for the rise of the science of textual criticism in the 16th century. After that, we have had hundreds of scholars working extremely hard over the following five centuries to restore the New Testament text to its original state. Keep in mind that textual criticism is not just performed on the Old and New Testament texts, but in all other ancient literature as well: Plato (428/427–348/347 B.C.E.), Herodotus (c. 484–c. 425 B.C.E.), Homer (Ninth or Eighth Century B.C.E.), Livy (64or 59 B.C.E.–17 C.E.), Cicero (106–43 B.C.E.), and Virgil (70–19 B.C.E.). However, as the Bible is the greatest work of all time, directly influencing countless Christians' lives (billions), it is the most crucial field.

Here, we should also expound more on the "criticism" portion of the term textual criticism. It may be helpful if, for a moment, we address biblical criticism in general, which is divided into two branches: lower criticism and higher criticism. Lower criticism, also known as textual criticism, is an investigation of manuscripts by those who are known as textual scholars, seeking to establish the original reading, which is available in the thousands of extant copies. Higher criticism, also known as literary criticism, investigates the restored text to identify any sources that may lie behind it. Therefore, we can say the following:

LOWER CRITICISM (i.e., textual criticism) has been the bedrock of scholarship over the last 500 years. It has given us a master text, i.e., a critical text, reflecting the original published Greek New Testament. It had contributed to the furtherance of Bible scholarship, removing interpolations, correcting scribal errors, and giving us a restored text, allowing us to produce better translations of the New Testament. However, of late, the dissecting higher criticism mindset of the 19th and 20th centuries has seeped into the field of New Testament Textual Studies.

HIGHER CRITICISM (i.e., literary criticism, biblical criticism) has taught that much of the Bible was composed of legend and myth. It claims that Moses did not write the first five books of the Bible, 8th century B.C.E. Isaiah did not write Isaiah, there were three authors of Isaiah, 6th century B.C.E. Daniel did not write Daniel, it was penned in the 2nd century BCE. Higher critics have taught that Jesus did not say all that the Gospels have him saying in his Sermon on the Mount and that Jesus did not condemn the Pharisees in Matthew 23, as this was Matthew because he hated the Jews. These are just the highlights, for there are thousands of tweaks that have undermined the word of God as being inspired and fully inerrant. Higher critics have dissected the Word of God until it has become the word of man and a very jumbled word at that. Higher criticism is still taught in almost all the seminaries. It is common to hear so-called Evangelical Bible scholars vehemently deny that large sections of the Bible are fully inerrant, authentic, accurate, and trustworthy. Biblical higher criticism is speculative and tentative in the extreme.

Constantine Von Tischendorf was a world-leading textual scholar and a renowned Bible scholar. Tischendorf was educated in Greek at the University of Leipzig. During his university studies, he was troubled by higher criticism of the Bible, as taught by famous German theologians, who sought to prove that the Greek New Testament was not authentic. He rejected higher criticism, which led to his noteworthy success in defending the authenticity of the Bible text. NT Textual scholar Harold Greenlee writes, "This 'higher criticism' has often been applied to the Bible in a destructive way, and it has come to be looked down on by many evangelical Christians."[23] The sad situation is that modern-day textual scholarship as a whole is unwittingly or knowingly moving the goalposts for some unknown reason. It is now the earliest knowable text in textual criticism, the sociohistorical approach to New Testament Textual Studies, and the newest trend to redate our earliest NT papyri to later dates.[24]

The New Testament in the Original Greek is a Greek-language version of the New Testament published in 1881. It is also known as the **Westcott and Hort** text, after its editors Brooke Foss Westcott (1825–1901) and Fenton John Anthony Hort (1828–1892). (Textual scholars use the abbreviation "**WH**") It is a critical text (Master Greek text of the NT seeking to ascertain the original wording of the original documents), compiled from some of the oldest New Testament fragments and texts discovered at the time. The two editors worked together for 28 years.

The Nestle Greek New Testament (first published in 1898) is a critical edition of the New Testament in its original Koine Greek, now in its 28th edition, forming the basis of most modern Bible translations and biblical criticism. It is now known as the Nestle-Aland edition after its most influential editors, Eberhard Nestle and Kurt Aland. Textual scholars use the abbreviation "**NA**." The NA is now in its 28th edition (2012), which is abbreviated NA[28]. Throughout the 130 years since 1881, there have been hundreds of manuscript discoveries, especially the early papyri that date within decades of the originals. One might expect significant changes been the WH text of 1881 and the 2012 NA[28] text. However, The NA[28] is 99.5% the same as the 1881 WH Greek New Testament.

---

[23] Greenlee, J. Harold. *The Text of the New Testament: From Manuscript to Modern Edition* (p. 2). Baker Publishing Group.

[24] For defense against this redating, see THE P52 PROJECT: Is P52 Really the Earliest Greek New Testament Manuscript? Christian Publishing House (May 26, 2020) ISBN-13: 978-1949586107

In contrast, **higher criticism** (i.e., literary criticism) has attempted to provide rational explanations for the composition of Bible books, ignoring the supernatural element and often eliminating the traditional authorship of the books. Late dating of the copy of Bible books is widespread, and the historicity of biblical accounts is called into question. It would not be an overstatement to say that the effect has often challenged and undermined the Christian's confidence in the New Testament. Fortunately, some conservative scholars[25] have rightly criticized higher critics for their illogical or unreasonable approaches in dissecting God's Word.

Importance of Textual Criticism

Christian Bible students need to be familiar with Old and New Testament textual criticism as essential foundational studies. Why? If we fail to establish what was originally authored with reasonable certainty, how can we translate or even interpret what we think is the actual Word of God? We are fortunate that there are far more existing New Testament manuscripts today than any other book from ancient history. Some ancient Greek and Latin classics are based on one existing manuscript, while with others, there are just a handful and a few exceptions that have a few hundred available. However, over 5,898[26] Greek New Testament manuscripts have been cataloged for the New Testament,[27] 10,000 Latin manuscripts, and an additional 9,300 other manuscripts in such languages as Syriac, Slavic, Gothic, and Ethiopic Coptic, and Armenian. This gives New Testament textual scholars vastly more to work within establishing the original words of the text.

---

[25] Such Bible scholars as the late R. A. Torrey, Robert L. Thomas, Norman L. Geisler, Gleason L. Archer Jr., and current scholars such as F. David Farnell, as well as many others have fought for decades to educate readers about the dangers of higher criticism.

[26] While at present here in 2020, there are 5,898 manuscripts. There are **140 listed Papyrus** manuscripts, 323 Majuscule manuscripts, 2,951 Minuscule manuscripts, and 2,484 Lectionary manuscripts, bringing the total cataloged manuscripts to 5,898 manuscripts. However, you cannot simply total the number of cataloged manuscripts because, for example, $P^{11/14}$ are the same manuscript but with different catalog numbers. The same is true of $P^{33/5}$, $P^{4/64/67}$, $P^{49/65}$ and $P^{77/103}$. Now this alone would bring our 140 listed papyrus manuscripts down to 134. Then, we turn to one example from our majuscule manuscripts where clear 0110, 0124, 0178, 0179, 0180, 0190, 0191, 0193, 0194, and 0202 are said to be part of 070. A minuscule manuscript was listed with five separate catalog numbers for 2306, which then have the letters a through e. Thus, we have the following GA numbers: 2306 for 2306a, and 2831- 2834 for 2306b-2306e.' – (Hixon 2019, 53-4) The problem is much worse when we consider that there are 323 Majuscule manuscripts and then far worse still with a listed 2,951 Minuscule and 2,484 Lectionaries. Nevertheless, those who estimate a total of 5,300 (Jacob W. Peterson, Myths and Mistakes, p. 63) 5,500 manuscripts (Dr. Ed Gravely / ehrmanproject.com/), 5,800 manuscripts (Porter 2013, 23), it is still a truckload of evidence far and above the dismal number of ancient secular author books.

[27] As of January 2016

The other difference between the New Testament manuscripts and those of the classics is that the existing copies of the New Testament date much closer to the originals. Some of the manuscripts are dated to about a thousand years after the author had penned the book in the Greek classics. Some of the Latin classics are dated from three to seven hundred years after the author wrote the book. When we look at the Greek copies of the New Testament books, some portions are within decades of the original author's book. One hundred and thirty-nine Greek NT papyri and five majuscules[28] date from 110 C.E. to 390 C.E.

Distribution of Greek New Testament Manuscripts

- The **Papyrus** is a copy of a portion of the New Testament made on papyrus. At present, we have 147 cataloged New Testament papyri, many dating between 110-350 C.E., but some as late as the 6th century C.E.

- The **Majuscule** or **Uncial** is a script of large letters commonly used in Greek and Latin manuscripts written between the 3rd and 9th centuries C.E. that resembles a modern capital letter but is more rounded. At present, we have 323 cataloged New Testament Majuscule manuscripts.

- The **Minuscule** is a small cursive style of writing used in manuscripts from the 9th to the 16th centuries, now having 2,951 Minuscule manuscripts cataloged.

- The **Lectionary** is a schedule of readings from the Bible for Christian church services during the year, in both majuscules and minuscules, dating from the 4th to the 16th centuries C.E., now having 2,484 Lectionary manuscripts cataloged.

We should clarify that of the approximate 24,000 total manuscripts of the New Testament, not all are complete books. There are fragmented manuscripts with just a few verses, but manuscripts contain an entire book, others that include numerous books, and some that have the whole New Testament, or nearly so. This is expected since the oldest manuscripts we have were copied in an era when reproducing the entire New Testament was not the norm. Instead, it was far more common to copy a single book or a

---

[28] Large lettering, often called "capital" or uncial, in which all the letters are usually the same height.

group of books (i.e., the Gospels or Paul's letters). This still does not negate the vast riches of manuscripts that we possess.

What can we conclude from this short introduction to textual criticism? There is some irony here: secular scholars have no problem accepting classic authors' wording with their minuscule amount of evidence. However, they discount the treasure trove of evidence that is available to the New Testament textual scholar. Still, this should not surprise us as the New Testament has always been under-appreciated and attacked somehow, shape, or form over the past 2,000 years.

On the contrary, in comparison to classical works, we are overwhelmed by the quantity and quality of existing New Testament manuscripts. We should also keep in mind that about seventy-five percent[29] of the New Testament does not even require the help of textual criticism because that much of the text is unanimous, and thus, we know what it says. Of the other twenty-five percent, about twenty percent make up trivial scribal mistakes that are easily corrected. Therefore, textual criticism focuses mainly on a small portion of the New Testament text. The facts are clear: the Christian, who reads the New Testament, is fortunate to have so many manuscripts, with so many dating so close to the originals, with 500 hundred years of hundreds of textual scholars who have established the text with a level of certainty unimaginable for ancient secular works.

After discussing the amount of New Testament manuscripts available, Atheist commentator Bob Seidensticker writes, "The first problem is that more manuscripts at best increase our confidence that we have the original version. That does not mean the original copy was history ...."[30] That is, Seidensticker is forced to acknowledge the reliability of the New Testament text as we have it today and can only try to deny what it says. He also tells us of the New Testament, "Compare that with 2000 copies of the Iliad, the second-best represented manuscript."[31] Of those 1,757 copies of the Iliad, how far removed are they from the alleged originals? The Iliad is dated to about 800 B.C.E. There are several fragments of the Iliad that date to the second century B.C.E. and one to the third century B.C.E., with the rest dating to the ninth century C.E. or later. That would make this handful of fragmented manuscripts 500 years removed and the rest about 1,700 years removed from their original.

---

[29] The numbers in this paragraph are rounded for simplicity purposes.

[30] 25,000 New Testament Manuscripts? Big Deal. - Patheos,

http://www.patheos.com/blogs/crossexamined/2013/11/25000-new-testament-manuscrip (accessed November 28, 2015).

[31] Ibid

The Range of Textual Criticism

The Importance and scope of New Testament textual studies can be summed up in the few words used by J. Harold Greenlee; it is "the basic biblical study, a prerequisite to all other biblical and theological work. Interpretation, systematization, and application of the teachings of the NT cannot be accomplished until textual criticism has done at least some of its work. It is, therefore, deserving of the acquaintance and attention of every serious student of the Bible."[32]

It is only reasonable to assume that the original 27 books written first-hand by the New Testament authors have not survived. Instead, we only have what we must consider being imperfect copies. **Why the Holy Spirit would miraculously inspire 27 fully inerrant texts and then allow human imperfection into the documents** is not explained for us in Scripture. (More on this later) Why didn't God inspire the copyists? We do know that imperfect humans have tended to worship relics that traditions hold to have been touched by the miraculous powers of God or to have been in direct contact with one of his special servants of old. Ultimately, though, all we know is that God had his reasons for allowing the New Testament autographs to be worn out by repeated use. From time to time, we hear of the discovery of a fragment possibly dated to the first century, but even if such a fragment is eventually verified, the dating alone can never serve as proof of an autograph; it will still be a copy in all likelihood.

If we ask why didn't God inspire copyists, then it will have to follow, why didn't God inspire translators, why didn't God inspire Bible scholars that author commentaries on the Bible, and so on? Suppose God's initial purpose was to give us a fully inerrant, authoritative, authentic, and accurate Word. Why not adequately protect the Scriptures in all facets of transmission from error: copy, translate, and interpret? If God did this, and people were moved along by the Holy Spirit, it would soon become noticeable that when people copy the texts, they would be unable to make an error or mistake or even willfully change something.

Where would it stop? Would this being moved along by the Holy Spirit apply to anyone who decided to make themselves a copy, testing to see if they too would be inspired? In time, this would prove to be actual evidence for God. This would negate the reasons why God has allowed sin, human imperfection to enter humanity in the first place, to teach them an **object lesson**, man cannot walk on his own without his Creator. God created

---

[32] J. Harold Greenlee, *Introduction to New Testament Textual Criticism* (Grand Rapids, MI: Baker Academic, 1995), 8-9.

perfect humans, giving them a perfect start, and through the abuse of free will, they rejected his sovereignty. He did not just keep creating perfect humans again and again, as though he got something wrong. God gave us his perfect Word and has again chosen to allow us to continue in our human imperfection, learning our **object lesson**. God has stepped into humanity many hundreds of times in the Bible record, maybe tens of thousands of times unbeknownst to us over the past 6,000+ years, to tweak things to get the desired outcome of his will and purposes. However, there is no aspect of life where his stepping in on any particular point was to be continuous until the return of the Son. Maybe God gave us a perfect copy of sixty-six books. Then like everything else, he placed the responsibility of copying, translating, and interpreting on us, just as he gave us the Great Commission of proclaiming that Word, explaining that Word, to make disciples. – Matthew 24:14;28-19-20; Acts 1:8.

As for errors in all the copies we have, we can say that the vast majority of the Greek text is not affected by errors. The errors occur in variant readings, i.e., portions of the text where different manuscripts disagree. Of the **small amount** of the text affected by variant readings, the vast majority of these are minor slips of the pen, misspelled words, etc., or intentional but quickly analyzed changes. We are certain what the original reading is in these places. A **far smaller number** of changes present challenges to establishing the original reading. It has always been said and remains true that no central doctrine is affected by a textual problem. Only rarely does a textual issue change the meaning of a verse.[33] Still, establishing the original text wherever there are variant readings is vitally important. Every word matters!

It is true that the Jewish copyists and the later Christian copyists were not led along by the Holy Spirit, and, therefore, their manuscripts were not inerrant, infallible. Errors (textual variants) crept into the documents unintentionally and intentionally. However, the vast majority of the Hebrew Old Testament and Greek New Testament has not been infected with textual errors. For the portions impacted with textual mistakes, we can be grateful for the tens of thousands of copies that we have to help us weed out the errors. How? Well, not every copyist made the same textual errors. Hence, by comparing the work of different copyists and manuscripts, textual scholars can identify the textual variants (errors) and remove those, leaving us with the original content.

Yes, it would be **the most significant discovery** of all time if we found the original five books penned by Moses himself, Genesis through

---

[33] Leading textual scholar Daniel Wallace tells us, after looking at all of the evidence, that the percentage of instances where the reading is uncertain and a well-attested alternative reading could change the meaning of the verse is a quarter of one percent, i.e., 0.0025%

Deuteronomy, or the original Gospels of Matthew, Mark, Luke, and John. However, first, there would be no way of establishing that they were the originals. Second, truth be told, we do not need the originals. **Yes, you heard me**. We do not need those original documents. What is so important about the documents? Nothing, it is the content on the original documents that we are after. And truly, miraculously, we have more copies than needed to do just that. **We do not need miraculous preservation** because we have miraculous restoration. We now know beyond a reasonable doubt that the Hebrew Old Testament and the Greek New Testament critical texts are about a 99.99% reflection of the content that was in those ancient original manuscripts.

CHAPTER I The New Testament Secretaries and Their Materials

One of the greatest tragedies in the modern-day history of Christianity [1880 - present] is that churchgoers have not been educated about the history of the New Testament text. They are so misinformed that many do not even realize that the Hebrew text lies behind our English Old Testament, and the Greek text lies behind our English New Testament. Sadly, many seminaries that train the pastors of today's churches have also required little or no studies in the history of the Old or New Testament texts.

Textual Criticism Defined

Again, New Testament textual criticism is the study of families of manuscripts, especially the Greek New Testament, as well as versions,[34] lectionaries,[35] and patristic quotations,[36] along with internal evidence, in order to determine which reading is the original. Comparing any two copies of a document even a few pages long will reveal variant readings. "A textual variant is simply any difference from a standard text (e.g., a printed text, a particular manuscript, etc.) that involves spelling, word order, omission, addition, substitution, or a total rewrite of the text."

---

[34] A version is a translation of the New Testament into another language, such as Latin, Syriac, Coptic, Armenian, Georgian, and so on.

[35] A Lectionary is a book containing readings from the Bible for Christian church services during the course of the year.

[36] Patristic quotations are New Testament quotations from early Christian writers, such as the Apostolic Fathers, including Clement of Rome, Ignatius of Antioch, Polycarp of Smyrna, Hermas, and Papias. There were also the Apologists: Justin Martyr, Theophilus of Antioch, Clement of Alexandria, and Tertullian, to name a few. After them came the Church Fathers, e.g. St. Augustine or St. Ambrose whose works have helped to shape the Christian Church.

Again, it needs to be repeated; when we use the term "textual *criticism*," we are not referring to something negative. In this instance, "criticism" refers to a careful, measured, or painstaking study and analysis of the internal and external evidence for producing our New Testament Greek text generally called a "critical text." Today, the goal of many New Testament textual scholars is to recover the earliest text *possible*, while the objective of the remaining few, such as the author of this book, is to get back to the *ipsissima verba* ("the very words") of the original author.[37]

> Variant readings occur only in about 5 percent of the Greek NT text, and so all the manuscripts agree about 95 percent of the time. Only about 2,100 variant readings may be considered "significant" and in no instance is any point of Christian doctrine challenged or questioned by a variant reading. Only about 1.67 percent of the entire Greek NT text still is questioned at all. We may be confident that our current eclectic, or critical, Greek NT text (an eclectic, or critical text is one based on the study of as many manuscripts as possible), is far beyond 99 percent established. In fact, there is more variation among some English translations of the Bible than there is among the manuscripts of the Greek NT. God's Word is infallible and inerrant in its original copies (autographs), all of which have perished. Textual critics of the Greek NT will continue their work until, if possible, the original of every questioned reading is firmly established.[38]

An investigation of the enormous supply of Greek manuscripts and the ancient versions in other languages shows that they have preserved for us the very Word of God.

Throughout the first five books of the Bible being penned by Moses (beginning in the late sixteenth century B.C.E.), and down to the time of the printing press (1455 C.E.)–almost 3,000 years–many forms of material have been used to receive writing. Material such as bricks, papyrus sheets, animal skin, broken pottery, metal, wooden tablets with or without wax, and much more have been used to pen or copy God's Word. The following are some of the tools and materials.

---

[37] Dr. Don Wilkins writes. "This goal, which will be mentioned in passing throughout the book, is a philosophical difference with some implications for TC practice. Both groups of critics will arrive at what they consider the earliest form of the text, but the authors take this to be the autograph as a matter of faith. One of the implications for practice is that conjectures are not considered viable options for variant readings. Another is that every word of the autograph can be found in some extant Greek NT manuscript."

[38] Charles W. Draper, "Textual Criticism, New Testament," ed. Chad Brand et al., *Holman Illustrated Bible Dictionary* (Nashville, TN: Holman Bible Publishers, 2003), 1574.

Stylus: The stylus was used to write on a waxed codex tablet. The stylus could be made of bone, metal, or ivory. It would be sharpened at one end for the purpose of writing and have a rounded knob on the other for making corrections. The stylus could also be used to write on soft metal or clay.

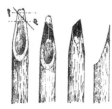
Reed Pen: The reed pen was used with ink to write on papyrus or parchment manuscripts. Καλαμος (kalamos) is the Greek word for "pen." (2 John 12; 3 John 13) There is no doubt that all the early extant papyrus manuscripts were copied with a reed pen, producing an impressive and pleasing script.

Quill Pen: The quill[39] pen came into use long after the reed pen. Quill would have been unsatisfactory for writing on papyrus, but parchment would have been an excellent surface for receiving writing from a quill pen. Of course, history shows that as parchment more fully displaced papyrus, the quill pen likewise replaced the reed pen. The quill was sharpened for use much like the reed, by having the tip sharpened and slit.

The first page of papyrus 66, showing John 1:1-13 and the opening words of v.14

Papyrus: Papyrus was the writing material used by the ancient Egyptians, Greeks, and Romans made from the pith of the stem of a water plant. It was cut into strips, with one layer laid out horizontally and the other vertically. Sometimes it was covered with a cloth and then beaten with a mallet. Scholarship has also suggested that paste may have been used between layers, and then a large stone would be placed on top until the materials were dry. Typically, a sheet of papyrus would be between 6–9 inches in width and 12–15 inches long. These sheets were then glued end to end until scribes had enough length to copy the book they were working on. The writing was done only on the horizontal side, and it was rolled so that the writing would be on the inside. If one were to attempt to write across the vertical side, it would be difficult because of the direction of the papyrus fibers. The scribe or copyist would

---

[39] The quill pen was the principal writing instrument in the Western world from the 6th to the 19th centuries C.E.

have used a reed pen to write on the papyrus sheets (cf. 3 John 13). Papyrus was the primary material used for writing until about 300 C.E. It was used with a *roll* or *scroll* (a document that is rolled up into itself), as well as the *codex* (book) form.

Writing on the papyrus sheet, even the correct side, was no easy task by any means because the surface was rough and fibrous. "Defects sometimes occurred in the making through retention of moisture between the layers or through the use of spongy strips which could cause the ink to run; such flaws necessitated the remaking of the sheet."[40] The back pain from long periods of sitting cross-legged on the ground bent over a papyrus sheet on a board made writing letters unappealing. The dealing with running ink, the reed pen possibly snagging and tearing the papyrus sheet, having to erase illegible characters were all deterrents from personally writing a letter.

Early papyrus manuscripts, such as $P^{4/64/67}$ P^{32} P^{46} P^{52} P^{66} P^{75} $P^{77/103}$ P^{101} P^{87} P^{90} P^{98} P^{104} P^{109} P^{118} P^{137}, which date 100-150/175 C.E. Then we have P^{1} P^{5} P^{13} P^{20} P^{23} P^{27} P^{29} P^{30} P^{35} P^{38} P^{39} P^{40} P^{45} P^{47} P^{48} $P^{49/65}$ P^{69} P^{71} P^{72} P^{82} P^{85} P^{95} P^{100} P^{106} P^{107} P^{108} P^{111} P^{110} P^{113} P^{115} P^{121} P^{125} P^{126} P^{133} P^{136}, which date 175-250 C.E., to mention only a few. Then, the renowned Codex Vaticanus (300-325 C.E.) and Codex Sinaiticus (325-350 C.E.) were written on parchment: creamy or yellowish material made from dried and treated sheepskin, goatskin, or other animal hides.

One may wonder why more New Testament manuscripts have not survived. It must be remembered that the Christians suffered intense persecution during intervals in the first 300 years from Pentecost 33 C.E. With this persecution from the Roman Empire came many orders to destroy Christian texts. In addition, these texts were not stored in such a way as to secure their preservation. They were actively used by the Christians in the congregation and were subject to wear and tear. Furthermore, moisture is the enemy of papyrus, and it causes them to disintegrate over time. This is why, as we will discover, the papyrus manuscripts that have survived have come from the dry sands of Egypt. Moreover, it seems not to have entered the minds of the early Christians to

Papyri copy - Greek Manuscript

---

[40] Nabia Abbot, *STUDIES IN ANCIENT ORIENTAL CIVILIZATIONS* (Chicago, IL: The University of Chicago Press, 1938), 11.

preserve their documents because their solution to the loss of manuscripts was simply to make more copies. Fortunately, making copies transitioned to the more durable animal skins, which would last much longer. Those that have survived, especially from the fourth century C.E. and earlier, are the path to restoring the original Greek New Testament.[41]

Animal Skin: About the fourth century C.E., Bible manuscripts made of papyrus began to be superseded by the use of vellum, a high-quality parchment made from calfskin, kidskin, or lambskin. Manuscripts such as the famous Codex Sinaiticus (01) and Codex Vaticanus (03, also known as B) of the fourth century C.E. are parchment, vellum, codices. This use of parchment as the leading writing material continued for almost a thousand years until it was replaced by paper. The advantages of parchment over papyrus were many, such as (1) it was much easier to write on smooth parchment, (2) one could write on both sides, (3) parchment lasted much longer, and (4) when desired, old writing could be scraped off and the parchment reused.

A 2,000-year-old Dead Sea Isaiah Scroll. It matches closely the Masoretic text and what is in the Bible today

Papyrus or Parchment?

The Hebrew Old Testament that would have been available to the early Christians was written on the processed hide of animals after the hair was removed, and the hide was smoothed out with a pumice stone.[42] Leather scrolls were sent to Alexandria, Egypt, in about 280 B.C.E., to make what we

---

[41] Cf. J. H. Greenlee, *Introduction to New Testament Textual Criticism* (Peabody: Hendrickson, 1995), 11.

[42] A very light porous rock formed from solidified lava, used in solid form as an abrasive and in powdered form as a polish.

now know as the Greek Septuagint.[43] Most of the Dead Sea scrolls discovered between 1947 and 1956 are made of leather, and it is almost certain that the scroll of Isaiah that Jesus read from in the synagogue was as well. Luke 4:17 says, "And the scroll of the prophet Isaiah was given to him. He unrolled the scroll and found the place where it was written."

The Dead Sea Scroll of Isaiah (1QIsa) dates to the end of the second century B.C.E., written on 17 sheets of parchment, one of the seven Dead Sea Scrolls that were first recovered by Bedouin shepherds in 1947. The Nash Papyrus is a collection of four papyrus fragments acquired in Egypt in 1898 by W. L. Nash, dating to about 150 B.C.E. It contains parts of the Ten Commandments from Exodus chapter 20 and some verses from Deuteronomy chapters 5 and 6. It is by far one of the oldest Hebrew manuscript fragments.

Vellum is a high-quality parchment made from calfskin, kidskin, or lambskin. After the skin was removed, it would be soaked in limewater, after which the hair would be scraped off, the skin then being scraped and dried, and rubbed afterward with chalk and pumice stone, creating an exceptionally smooth writing material. Both leather and papyrus were used before the first-century Christians. During the first three hundred years of Christianity, the secular world viewed parchment as being inferior to papyrus. It was relegated to notebooks, rough drafts, and other non-literary purposes.

A couple of myths should be dispelled before continuing. It is often remarked that papyrus is not a durable material. Both papyrus and parchment are durable under normal circumstances. This is not negating the fact that parchment is more durable than papyrus. Another often-repeated thought is that papyrus was fragile and brittle, making it an unlikely candidate to be used for a codex, which would have to be folded in half. Another issue that should be sidelined is whether it was more expensive to produce papyrus or parchment. Presently there is no data to aid in that evaluation. We know that papyrus was used for all of the Christian codex manuscripts up to the fourth century, at which time we find the two great parchment codices, the Sinaiticus and Vaticanus manuscripts. Parchment of good quality has been called "the finest writing material ever devised by man." (Roberts and Skeat, The Birth of the Codex 1987, 8) Why then did parchment take so long to replace papyrus? This may be answered by R. Reed, in *Ancient Skins, Parchments, and Leathers:*

> It is perhaps the extraordinary high durability of the product, produced by so simple a method, which has prevented most people

---

[43] A Greek translation of the Hebrew Bible started in about 280 and completed about 150 B.C.E. to meet the needs of Greek-speaking Jews outside Palestine.

from suspecting that many subtle points are involved…. The essence of the parchment process, which subjects the system of pelt to the simultaneous action of stretching and drying, is to bring about peculiar changes quite different from those applying when making leather. These are (1) reorganization of the dermal fibre network by stretching, and (2) permanently setting this new and highly stretched form of fibre network by drying the pelt fluid to a hard, glue-like consistency. In other words, the pelt fibres are fixed in a stretched condition so that they cannot revert to their original relaxed state. (Reed 1973, 119-20)

Where the medieval parchment makers were greatly superior to their modern counterparts was in the control and modification of the ground substance in the pelt, before the latter was stretched and dried …. The major point, however, which modern parchment manufacturers have not appreciated, is what might be termed the integral or collective nature of the parchment process. The bases of many different effects need to be provided for simultaneously, in one and the same operation. The properties required in the final parchment must be catered for at the wet pelt stage, for due to the peculiar nature of the parchment process, once the system has been dried, and after-treatments to modify the material produced are greatly restricted. (Reed 1973, 124)

This method, which follows those used in medieval times for making parchment of the highest quality, is preferable for it allows the grain surface of the drying pelt to be "slicked" and freed from residual fine hairs while stretching upon the frame. At the same time, any process for cleaning and smoothing the flesh side, or for controlling the thickness of the final parchment may be undertaken by working the flesh side with sharp knives which are semi-lunar in form…. To carry out such manual operations on wet stretched pelt demands great skill, speed of working, and concentrated physical effort. (Reed 1973, 138-9)

Enough has been said to suggest that behind the apparently simple instructions contained in the early medieval recipes there is a wealth of complex process detail which we are still far from understanding. Hence it remains true that parchment-making is perhaps more of an art than a science.[44]

---

[44] R. Reed, *Ancient skins, parchments and leathers* (Studies in Archaeological Science) Cambridge, MA: Seminar Press, 1973, 172.

Scroll or Roll: The scroll dominated until the beginning of the second century C.E., at which time the papyrus codex was replacing it. Papyrus enjoyed another two centuries of use until it was replaced with animal skin (vellum), which proved to be a far better writing material.

The writing on a scroll was done in 2- to 3-inch columns, which allowed the reader to have it opened, or unrolled, only partially. Although movies and television have portrayed the scroll as being opened while holding it vertically, this was not the case; scrolls were opened horizontally. It would be rolled to the left for the Greek or Latin reader as those languages were written left to right. The Jewish reader would roll it to the right as Hebrew was written right to left.

The difficulty of using a scroll should be apparent. If one had a long book (such as Isaiah) and attempted to locate a particular passage, it would not be user-friendly. An ancient saying was, "A great book, a great evil." The account in the book of Luke tells us:

Luke 4:16–21 Updated American Standard Version (UASV)

[16] And he [Jesus] came to Nazareth, where he had been brought up; and as was his custom, he went to the synagogue on the Sabbath day, and he stood up to read. [17] And the scroll[45] of the prophet Isaiah was given to him. And he unrolled the scroll[46] and found the place where it was written,

[18] "The Spirit of the Lord is upon me,
   because he has anointed me
   to proclaim good news[47] to the poor.
He has sent me to proclaim release to the captives
   and recovering of sight to the blind,
   to set free those who are oppressed,
[19] to proclaim the favorable year of the Lord."

[20] And he rolled up the scroll[48] and gave it back to the attendant and sat down; and the eyes of all in the synagogue were fixed on him. [21] And he began to say to them, "Today this Scripture has been fulfilled in your hearing."

Codex: The trunk of a tree that bears leaves only at its apex was called a *caudex* in Latin. This name was modified to *codex* and applied to a wooden tablet with raised edges, with a coat of wax placed within those raised edges.

---

[45] Or a *roll*

[46] Or *roll*

[47] Or *the gospel*

[48] Or *roll*

The dried wax would then be used to receive writing with a stylus. We might compare it to the schoolchild's slate, such as seen in some Hollywood Western movies. Around the fifth century B.C.E., some of these were being used and attached by strings that were run through the edges. It is because these bound tablets resembled a tree trunk that they were to take on the name "codex."

Codex Vaticanus ("Book from the Vatican"), Facsimile, Fourth century. It is one of the earliest manuscripts of the Bible, which includes the Greek translation of the bulk of the Hebrew Scriptures as well as most of the Christian Greek Scriptures

As we can imagine, this bulky item also was not user-friendly! Sometime later, the Romans would develop a lighter, more flexible material, the parchment notebook, which would fill the need before the development of the later book-form codex. The Latin word *membranae* (skins) is the name given to such notebooks of parchment. In fact, at 2 Timothy 4:13, the apostle Paul requested of Timothy that he "bring the cloak that I left with Carpus at Troas, also the books [scrolls], and above all the parchments [*membranas*, Greek spelling]." One might ask why Paul used a Latin word (transliterated in Greek)? Undoubtedly, it was because there was no Greek word that would serve as an equivalent to what he was requesting. It was only later that the translated "codex" was brought into the Greek language to reference what we would know as a book.

The ink of ancient manuscripts was usually one of two kinds. There was ink made of a mixture of soot and gum. These were sold in the form of a bar. It was dissolved in water in an inkwell and produced a very black ink. There was also ink made out of nutgalls, which resulted in a rusty-brown color. Aside from these materials, the scribe would have had a knife to sharpen his reed pen, as well as a sponge to erase errors. With the semi-professional and professional scribe, each character was written with care. Thus, writing was a slow, tedious, and often difficult task.

'I, Tertius, Greet You in the Lord'

Tertius is among the many greetings that we find at the end of the letter of Paul to the Romans, wherein he writes, "I am greeting you, I, Tertius, the one having written this letter, in the Lord." (Rom. 16:22) Of Paul's fourteen letters, this is the only occurrence where we find a clear reference to one of his secretaries.

Little is known of Tertius, who must have been a faithful Christian, based on the greeting "in the Lord." He may have been a member of the Corinthian congregation who likely knew many Christians in Rome, which is suggested because his name is Latin for "third." Quartus for "fourth" is one of the other two who added their greetings: "Erastus the city treasurer greets you, and Quartus the brother, i.e., a member of the Corinthian congregation. (16:23b) Some scholars have suggested that Quartus could have been the younger brother of Tertius.[49] Others have suggested that Tertius was a slave or a freedman.[50] This is also suggested by his Latin name and that slaves were commonly involved in the scribal activity. From this, we could conjecture that Tertius likely had experience as a professional scribe, who became a fellow-worker with the apostle Paul, helping compile the longest of Paul's letters. It was common for Bible authors to use a scribe, as, for example, Jeremiah similarly used Baruch, just as Peter used Silvanus (Jer. 36:4; 1 Pet. 5:12). Of Paul's fourteen letters, six certainly involved the use of a secretary: Romans (16:22), 1 Corinthians (16:21), Galatians (6:11), Colossians (4:18), 2 Thessalonians (3:17), and Philemon (19).

Penning the Book of Romans

The letter of Paul to the Romans was written while he was on his third missionary journey as a guest of Gaius in Corinth, about 55-56 C.E. (Ac 20:1-3; Rom. 16:23). We know for a certainty that Paul used Tertius as his secretary to author the book of Romans. However, we cannot say with absolute certainty how he was used. Some have argued, "from evidence outside of the

---

[49] Chad Brand et al., eds., "Tertius," *Holman Illustrated Bible Dictionary* (Nashville, TN: Holman Bible Publishers, 2003), 1573.

[50] When the Roman Empire was in power, one who was released from slavery was called a "freedman" (Gr *apeleutheros*), while a "freeman" (Gr *eleutheros*) was free from birth, having full citizenship rights, as was the case with the apostle Paul – Ac 22:28 (Balz and Schneider 1978, Vol. 1, P 121).

New Testament that it was common practice for authors to dictate their letters to an amanuensis or secretary."[51] Did the secretary take that dictation down in shorthand[52] and then compose the letter, even contributing content, with the New Testament author giving the final approval? Alternatively, was the secretary used in a more limited fashion, such as editing spelling, grammar, and syntax? Otto Roller points out that for an author to dictate a letter to a scribe verbatim would require the author to speak very slowly, i.e., syllable by syllable.[53] There will be more on this later. For now, whatever method was used, the work of a secretary was no easy job. What we do know is that the sixty-six books of the Bible were "inspired by God," and "men spoke from God as they were carried along by the Holy Spirit." – 2 Timothy 3:16; 2 Peter 1:21.

---

[51] See Gordon J. Bahr, "*Paul and Letter Writing in the First Century*," Catholic Biblical Quarterly 28 (1966): 465-77.

See also, John McRay, Paul: His Life and Teaching (Grand Rapids, MI: Baker Academics, 2003), 270.

[52] Again, there is the **slight possibility** of Tertius or other Bible author's scribes taking it down in shorthand and after that making out a full draft, which would have been reviewed by both Paul and Tertius. This is only the case if it is comparable to what a modern-day court reporter does. In some sense, they are taking down whoever is speaking down in shorthand. Imagine a courtroom where you have a witness talking fast, the prosecution interrupts, the defense jumps in with his rebuttal and the judge snaps his ruling, and the witness resumes his or her account of things. All of that is taken down explicitly word for word in shorthand, and if ever turned into longhand, it would be exactly what was said, down to the uh and um common in speech. So, if the shorthand of the day had that kind of capability; then, it is conceivable. We must remember these are the Bible author's dictated words to the scribe based on their inspiration, not the word choice or writing style of the scribe.

[53] Otto Roller, *Das Formular der Paulinischen Briefe: Ein Beitrag zur Lehre vom antiken Briefe* (Stuttgart: W. Kohlhammer, 1933), p. 333.

CHAPTER II The Book Writing Process of the New Testament: Authors and Early Christian Scribes

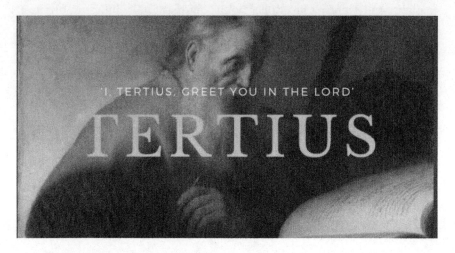

'I, TERTIUS, GREET YOU IN THE LORD'

TERTIUS

The Place of Writing

When we think of the apostle Paul penning his books that would make up most of the New Testament, some have had the anachronistic tendency to impose their modern way of thinking about him, such as presupposing where he would have written it. As I am writing this page, I am tucked away in my home office, seeking privacy from the hustle and bustle of our modern world. This was not the case in the ancient world, where Paul lived and traveled. People of that time favored a group setting, not isolation. The apostle Paul probably would have been of this mindset. Paul would not have necessarily sought a quiet place to author his letters, to escape the noise of those around him. As for myself, I struggle to get back on track if I am interrupted for more than a couple of minutes.

Most during Paul's day would have been surprised by this way of thinking, i.e., seeking quiet and solitude to focus all of one's energy on the task of writing. Those of Paul's day, including himself, would not have even noticed people talking around them, nor would they have been troubled by what we perceive as interruptions, such as others' discussions, which were neither relevant nor applicable to the subject of their letter writing.

The Scribe of the New Testament Writer

Philip W. Comfort informs us that an **amanuensis** is a "scribe or secretary. In ancient times a written document was first produced by an author who usually dictated the material to an amanuensis. The author would then read the text and make the final editorial adjustments before the document was sent or published. Paul used the writing services of Tertius to write the epistle to the Romans (Rom. 16:22), and Peter was assisted by Silvanus in writing his first Epistle (see 1 Pet. 5:12)."[54]

Dr. Don Wilkins, a Senior Translator for the NASB, also tells us that amanuensis is a "Latin term for a scribe or clerk (plural 'amanuenses'). When used in the context of textual criticism, it refers specifically to a person who served as a secretary to record first-hand the words of a New Testament book if the author chose to use a secretary rather than write down the words himself. Tertius (Rom. 16:22) is our example. The degree to which an amanuensis may have contributed to the content of any particular book of the Bible is a matter of speculation and controversy. At one end of the spectrum is the amanuensis, who merely took dictation (the position preferred here). At the other is the possibility that a New Testament author may have told his amanuensis what he wished to communicate in general terms, leaving it to the amanuensis to actually compose the book." This author would wholeheartedly disagree with the latter view, as the New Testament authors alone were inspired to give us the words of God, and the scribe was merely the vehicle for doing so.

The ancient Greco-Roman society employed secretaries or scribes for various reasons. Of course, the government employed some scribes working for chief administrators. Then, there were the scribes who were used in the private sector. These latter scribes (often slaves) usually were employed by the wealthy. However, even high-ranking slaves and freed slaves employed scribes. Many times, one would find scribes who would write letters for their friends. According to E. Randolph Richards, the skills of these unofficial secretaries "could range from a minimal competency with the language or the mechanics of writing to the highest proficiency at rapidly producing an accurate, proper, and charming letter."[55] Scribes carried out a wide range of administrative, secretarial, and literary tasks, including administrative

---

[54] Philip Comfort, *Encountering the Manuscripts: An Introduction to New Testament Paleography & Textual Criticism* (Nashville, TN: Broadman & Holman, 2005), 379.

[55] E. Randolph Richards, The Secretary in the Letters of Paul (Heidelberg, Germany: Mohr Siebeck, 1991, 11

bookkeeping (keeping records of a business or person), shorthand and taking dictation, letter-writing, and copying literary texts.

The most prominent ways that a scribe would have been used in the first century C.E. would have been as (1) a recorder, (2) an editor, and (3) a secretary for an author. At the very bottom of the writing tasks, he would be used to record information, i.e., as a record keeper. When they were needed or desired, the New Testament scribes were being used as secretaries, writing down letters by dictation. Tertius took down the book of Romans as Paul dictated to him, which was some 7,000+ words. He would have simply written out the very words that the apostle Paul spoke. Some have argued that longhand in dictation was not feasible in ancient times because the author would have to slow down to the point of speaking syllable-by-syllable. They usually cite Cicero as evidence for this argument because of his writings' numerous references to dictation. Cicero stated in a letter to his friend Varro that he had to slow down his dictation to the point of "syllable by syllable" for the sake of the scribe. However, the scribe he was using at that time was inexperienced, not his regular scribe. Of course, it would be challenging to retain one's line of thought in such a dictation process. It should be noted that Cicero had experienced scribes who could take down dictation at an average pace of speaking, even rapid speech.[56] There is evidence that scribes in those days were skilled enough to take down dictation at the average speech rate. Therefore, we should not assume that the apostles would not have had access to such scribes in the persons of Tertius, Silvanus, or even Timothy.

In fact, Marcus Fabius Quintilianus (b. 35 C.E. d. 100 C.E.) complained that a scribe who could write at the speed of everyday speech can make the speaker feel rushed, to the point of not being able to have time to ponder his thoughts.

> On the other hand, there is a fault which is precisely the opposite of this, into which those fall who insist on first making a rapid draft of their subject with the utmost speed of which their pen is capable, and write in the heat and impulse of the moment. They call this their rough copy. They then revise what they have written, and arrange their hasty outpourings. But while the words and the rhythm may be corrected, the matter is still marked by the superficiality resulting from the speed with which it was thrown together. The more correct method is, therefore, to exercise care

---

[56] E. Randolph Richards, PAUL AND FIRST-CENTURY LETTER WRITING: Secretaries, Composition and Collection (Downers Grove, IL: IVP Academic, 2004), 29-30; Murphy-O'Connor, *Paul the Letter-Writer*, 9–11; Shorthand references Plutarch, *Cato Minor*, 23.3–5; Caesar, 7.4–5; Seneca, *Epistles*, 14.208.

from the very beginning, and to form the work from the outset in such a manner that it merely requires being chiseled into shape, not fashioned anew. Sometimes, however, we must follow the stream of our emotions since their warmth will give us more than any diligence can secure. The condemnation which I have passed on such carelessness in writing will make it pretty clear what my views are on the luxury of dictation which is now so fashionable. For, when we write, however great our speed, the fact that the hand cannot follow the rapidity of our thoughts gives us time to think, whereas the presence of our amanuensis hurries us on, and at times we feel ashamed to hesitate or pause, or make some alteration, as though we were afraid to display such weakness before a witness. As a result, our language tends not merely to be haphazard and formless, but in our desire to produce a continuous flow we let slip positive improprieties of diction, which show neither the precision of the writer nor the impetuosity of the speaker. Again, if the amanuensis is a slow writer or lacking in intelligence, he becomes a stumbling-block, our speed is checked, and the thread of our ideas is interrupted by the delay or even perhaps by the loss of temper to which it gives rise.[57]

Therefore, again, we have evidence that some scribes were capable, skilled to the point of writing at the average speed of speech. While Richards says that this is by way of shorthand, saying it was more widespread than initially thought, where the secretary uses symbols in place of words, forming a rough draft that would be written out fully later,[58] this need not be the case. True, there is some evidence that shorthand existed a hundred years before Christ. However, it was still rare, with few scribes having the ability. Whether this was true of the scribes that assisted our New Testament authors is an unknown. It is improbable but not necessarily impossible.

Who in the days of the New Testament authors would use the services of scribes? Foremost would be those who did not know how to read and write. Within ancient contracts and business letters, one can find a note by the scribe (illiteracy statement), who penned it, stating he had done so because his employer could not read or write. For example, an ancient letter concludes with, "Eumelus, son of Herma, has written for him because he

---

[57] Retrieved Tuesday, February 12, 2019 (Institutio Oratoria, 10.3.17–21)

http://bit.ly/2Zazw2X

[58] E. Randolph Richards, PAUL AND FIRST-CENTURY LETTER WRITING: Secretaries, Composition and Collection (Downers Grove, IL: IVP Academic, 2004), 72.

does not know letters."[59] It may be that they were able to read but struggled with writing. Then again, it may simply be that they wrote slowly and were unwilling to spend the time improving their skills. An ancient letter from Thebes, Egypt, penned for a certain Asklepiades, concludes, "Written for him hath Eumelus the son of Herma ..., being desired so to do for that he writeth somewhat slowly."[60]

On the other hand, whether one knew how to read and write was not always the decisive issue in the use of a secretary. John L. McKenzie writes, "Even people who could read and write did not think of submitting their readers to unprofessional penmanship. It was probably not even a concern for legibility, but rather a concern for beauty, or at least for neatness," (McKenzie 1975, 14) which moved the ancients to turn to the services of a secretary. Although the educated could read and write, some likely felt that writing was tedious, trying, tiring, and frustrating, especially where lengthy and elaborate texts were concerned. It seems that if one could avoid the tremendous task of penning a lengthy letter, entrusting it to a scribe, so much the better.

The apostle Paul had over 100 traveling companions, like Aristarchus, Luke, and Timothy, who served by the apostle's side for many years. Then, there are others such as Asyncritus, Hermas, Julia, or Philologus, of whom we barely know more than their names. Many of Paul's friends traveled for the sake of the gospel, such as Achaicus, Fortunatus, Stephanas, Artemas, and Tychicus. We know that Tychicus was used by Paul to carry at least three letters now included in the Bible canon: the epistles to the Ephesians, the Colossians, and Philemon. Tychicus was not simply some mail carrier. He was a well-trusted carrier for the apostle, Paul. The final greeting from Paul to the Colossians reads,

Colossians 4:7-8 Updated American Standard Version (UASV)

[7] All my affairs Tychicus, my beloved brother and faithful minister and fellow slave in the Lord, will make known to you. [8] I have sent him to you for this very purpose, that you may know how we are and that he may encourage your hearts,

Richards offers the following about a letter carrier, saying he "was often a personal link between the author and the recipients in addition to the written link. . . . [One purpose] for needing a trustworthy carrier was, he often carried additional information. A letter may describe a situation briefly,

---

[59] See examples in Francis Exler, *The Form of the Ancient Greek Letter: A Study In Greek Epistolography* (Washington D.C.: Catholic University of America, 1922), pp. 126-7

[60] Adolf Deissmann, *LIGHT FROM THE ANCIENT EAST: The New Testament Illustrated by Recently Discovered Texts of the Graeco-Roman World* (New York and London. 1910). 166-7.

frequently with the author's assessment, but the carrier is expected to elaborate for the recipient all the details."[61] Many of Paul's letters deal with teachings and one crisis after another; the carrier was expected to be aware of these on a much deeper level so that he could orally explain and answer any questions. Therefore, he needed to be a highly trusted messenger who was literate.

As was mentioned, Tertius was the scribe Paul used to pen his letter to the Romans. We cannot assume that all of Paul's companions were proficient readers and writers. However, we can infer that Paul would task coworkers, who were able to carry and read letters and understand the condition of the people or congregation where they were being sent or stationed. Yes, at a minimum, these would have been proficient readers. In addition, the scribes whom Paul used, such as Tertius, would very likely have been semi-professional or professional. It would have been simply senseless to entrust the secretarial work of taking down the monumental words of the book of Romans, for example, to an inexperienced scribe. What skills would Tertius need to carry out the task of penning the book of Romans?

The ordinary coworker of Paul would likely have been able to read proficiently but likely possessed minimum writing skills. Paul would have chosen workers whose skills would have equipped them to carry out their assignments. Again, Tertius would have been the exception to the rule; most likely, he would have been a professional scribe. He would have been able to glue the sheets together if it was to be a roll or stitch the pages together if a codex. He would need to know the appropriate mixture of soot and gum to make ink and to be able to use his knife to make his own reed pen. Richards writes that a professional scribe would also "draw lines on the paper. Small holes were often pricked down each side, and then a straight edge and a lead disk were used to lightly draw evenly spaced lines across the sheet."[62] If Tertius had not been trained as a copyist of documents, he would have made many minor errors because his attention would have been on the sense of what he was penning, as opposed to the exact words, as is typical of the unconscious mind.

Porter writes, "Textual criticism has also recognized that even original authors may have **revised their work**, and these works have **gone through editions**." Stanley E. Porter (p. 35) *How We Got the New Testament*

---

[61] E. Randolph Richards, The Secretary in the Letters of Paul (Heidelberg, Germany: Mohr Siebeck, 1991, 7.

[62] E. Randolph Richards, PAUL AND FIRST-CENTURY LETTER WRITING: Secretaries, Composition and Collection (Downers Grove, IL: IVP Academic, 2004), 29.

Comfort writes, "When I speak of the original text, I am referring to the 'published' text— that is, the text in its **final edited form** as released for circulation in the Christian community."[63]

HOW do you edit the Holy Spirit? If the author was moved along by the Holy Spirit and all original Scripture is inspired, **why the need for editing?**

Some might say, "We believe that the NT authors themselves penned or dictated a one-time, single, and only version of their texts, unedited and uncorrected under the inspiration of the Holy Spirit."

However, I would pause to ponder Paul dictating the book of Romans to Tertius. Tertius was **not** inspired, so is he capable of going without making one single scribal error for 7,000+ words in his human imperfection? Are we removing the Holy Spirit in any way if Paul scratches out a few words that Tertius got wrong and wrote the correct word above it? Or is it the slippery slope to consider this possibility? If we hold fast to "I believe that the NT authors themselves penned or dictated a one-time, single and only version of their texts, unedited and uncorrected under the inspiration of the Holy Spirit," then we have to answer those kinds of questions. We have to raise them ourselves by writing, "some might ask, how is it ..." Peter said, "always being ready to make a defense to everyone who asks you to give an account." – 1 Peter 3:15.

We need to be willing to modify (or clarify) what we said above to include our qualification that Paul would edit the letter to the Romans as was described, as the amanuensis (i.e., Tertius) was not inspired. Paul would **not** change his original dictation in the process, and the outcome would be a single document, corrected, as necessary. We would also say that Paul might not make the actual corrections but might direct the amanuensis to do that as Paul watched. We do not go beyond this, i.e., postulating a fresh copy made from the original before publication, etc.

Did Tertius take Paul's exact dictation, word for word?

Robert H. Mounce writes,

The only legitimate question about authorship relates to the role of Tertius, who in 16:22 writes, "I Tertius, who wrote down this letter, greet you in the Lord." We know that at that time in history an amanuensis [scribe], that is, one hired to write from dictation, could serve at several levels. In some cases he would

---

[63] Philip W. Comfort (p. 19), The Quest for the Original Text of the New Testament (Grand Rapids: Baker Academic, 1992)

74

receive dictation and write it down immediately in longhand. At other times he might use a form of shorthand (tachygraphy [ancient shorthand]) to take down a letter and then later write it out in longhand. In some cases an amanuensis would simply get the gist of what a person wanted to say and then be left on his own to formulate the ideas into a letter.[64]

It might seem quite the task for Tertius to take down Paul's words in longhand. However, this is not to say that it was impossible, just difficult. Paul might have had to speak in a slow to normal speech rate, **but not** syllable-by-syllable. Tertius would indeed have been writing on a papyrus sheet with a reed pen, intending to be legible; however, he would have been very skilled in his trade. Then again, there is the **slight possibility** of Tertius taking it down in shorthand and after that making out a complete draft, which would have been reviewed by both Paul and Tertius. This is only the case if it is comparable to what a modern-day court reporter does. In some sense, they are taking down whoever is speaking down in shorthand. Imagine a courtroom where you have a witness talking fast, the prosecution interrupts, the defense jumps in with his rebuttal, and the judge snaps his ruling, and the witness resumes their account of things. All of that is taken down explicitly word for word in shorthand, and if ever turned into longhand, it would be precisely what was said, down to the uh and um common in speech. So, if the shorthand of the day had that kind of capability; then, it is conceivable. We must remember these are the Bible author's dictated words to the scribe based on their inspiration, not the scribe's word choice or writing style.

The last option by Mounce in the above is contrary to the attitudes that both the scribes and the New Testament authors would have had. Paul and Tertius knew that Paul's words were Spirit-inspired, that is, God's words. God chose to convey a message through Matthew, Mark, Luke, John, Peter, Jude, James, and Paul, not Tertius and Silvanus, Timothy, or others. We cannot say with any certainty whether Tertius or Silvanus took their authors' words down in shorthand or longhand. However, we can say that the human author was dictating the Word of God to the scribe, and in no way was it composed by the scribe. Yes, it is true that the Spirit-inspired author, who is literally moved along by the Holy Spirit, retained their style of expressing the message but not the scribe. Mark's writing style is concise, even abrupt at times. His Gospel contains rapid changes of thought. The style of writing of First and Second Timothy is the same as Titus, which adds authenticity to the letter to Titus.

---

[64] Robert H. Mounce, *Romans*, vol. 27, The New American Commentary (Nashville: Broadman & Holman Publishers, 1995), 22.

Inspiration and Inerrancy in the Writing Process

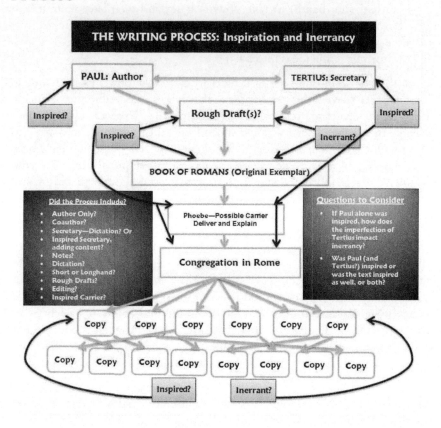

All Scripture is Inspired by God

In this context, inspiration is **the state** of a human being moved by the Holy Spirit, which results in an inspired, fully inerrant written Word of God.

Chicago Statement on Biblical Inerrancy ICBI

Article VII

We affirm that **inspiration** was the work in which God by His Spirit, through human writers, gave us His Word. The origin of Scripture is divine. The mode of divine **inspiration** remains largely a mystery to us. We deny that **inspiration** can be reduced to human insight, or to heightened states of consciousness of any kind.

Article VIII

We affirm that God in His Work of **inspiration** utilized the distinctive personalities and literary styles of the writers whom He had chosen and prepared. We deny that God, in causing these writers to use the very words that He chose, overrode their personalities. ["I would argue that if by human imperfection an author was going to choose an inappropriate word that would fail to communicate the meaning intended by God that the Holy Spirit would then override that word choice." – Edward D. Andrews]

Article IX

We affirm that **inspiration**, though not conferring omniscience, guaranteed true and trustworthy utterance on all matters of which the Biblical authors were moved to speak and write. We deny that the finitude or fallenness of these writers, by necessity or otherwise, introduced distortion or falsehood into God's Word.

Article X

We affirm that **inspiration**, strictly speaking, applies only to the autographic text of Scripture, which in the providence of God can be ascertained from available manuscripts with great accuracy. We further affirm that copies and translations of Scripture are the Word of God to the extent that they faithfully represent the original. We deny that any essential element of the Christian faith is affected by the absence of the autographs. We further deny that this absence renders the assertion of Biblical **inerrancy** invalid or irrelevant. [There is no miracle of preservation, but rather, it is preservation by restoration. Today, what we have, thanks to hundreds of textual scholars over a few hundred years, is a 99.99% restored original language text. – Edward D. Andrews]

Article XI

We affirm that Scripture, having been given by divine inspiration, is infallible, so that, far from misleading us, it is true and reliable in all the matters it addresses. We deny that it is possible for the Bible to be at the same time infallible and errant in its assertions. Infallibility and inerrancy may be distinguished, but not separated.

Inerrancy of Scripture

Inerrancy of Scripture is **the result** of the state of a human being moved by the Holy Spirit from God, which results in an inspired, fully inerrant written Word of God.

Article XII

We affirm that Scripture in its entirety is **inerrant**, being free from all falsehood, fraud, or deceit. We deny that Biblical infallibility and **inerrancy** are limited to spiritual, religious, or redemptive themes, exclusive of assertions in the fields of history and science. We further deny that scientific hypotheses about earth history may properly be used to overturn the teaching of Scripture on creation and the flood.

Article XIII

We affirm the propriety of using **inerrancy** as a theological term with reference to the complete truthfulness of Scripture. We deny that it is proper to evaluate Scripture according to standards of truth and error that are alien to its usage or purpose. We further deny that **inerrancy** is negated by Biblical phenomena such as a lack of modern technical precision, irregularities of grammar or spelling, observational descriptions of nature, the reporting of falsehoods, the use of hyperbole and round numbers, the topical arrangement of material, variant selections of material in parallel accounts, or the use of free citations.

Article XV

We affirm that the doctrine of **inerrancy** is grounded in the teaching of the Bible about **inspiration**. We deny that Jesus' teaching about Scripture may be dismissed by appeals to accommodation or to any natural limitation of His humanity.

Article XVI

We affirm that the doctrine of **inerrancy** has been integral to the Church's faith throughout its history. We deny that inerrancy is a doctrine invented by Scholastic Protestantism, or is a reactionary position postulated in response to negative higher criticism.

Authoritative Word of God

The **authoritative** aspect of Scripture is that God by way of inspiration gives the words the authors chose to use power and authority, so that the outcome (i.e., originals) is the very Word of God, as though God were speaking to us himself.

Article I

We affirm that the Holy Scriptures are to be received as the **authoritative** Word of God. We deny that the Scriptures receive their authority from the Church, tradition, or any other human source.

2 Timothy 3:16-17 Updated American Standard Version (UASV)

[16] All Scripture is inspired by God and profitable for teaching, for reproof, for correction, for training in righteousness; [17] so that the man of God may be fully competent, equipped for every good work.

What does this mean? The phrase "inspired by God" (Gr., *theopneustos*) literally means, "Breathed out by God." A related Greek word, *pneuma,* means "wind," "breath," life, "Spirit." Since *pneuma* can also mean "breath," the process of "breathing out" can rightly be said to be the work of the Holy Spirit inspiring the Scriptures. The result is that the originals were accurate, fully inerrant, and authoritative. Thus, the Holy Spirit moved human writers so that the result can truthfully be called the Word of *God,* not the word of man.

2 Peter 1:21 Updated American Standard Version (UASV)

[21] for no prophecy was ever produced by the will of man, but men carried along by the Holy Spirit spoke from God.

The Greek word here translated "men carried along by," "men moved by" (NASB)," (φέρω pherō), is used in another form at Acts 27:15, 17, which describes a ship that was driven along by the wind. So, the Holy Spirit, by analogy, 'navigated the course' of the Bible writers. While the Spirit did not give them each word by dictation,[65] it certainly kept the writers from inserting any information that did not convey the will and purpose of God.

The heart of what the International Council on Biblical Inerrancy (ICBI) stood for is apparent in "A Short Statement," produced at the Chicago conference in 1978:

A SHORT STATEMENT

1. God, who is Himself Truth and speaks truth only, has inspired Holy Scripture in order thereby to reveal Himself to lost mankind through Jesus Christ as Creator and Lord, Redeemer and Judge. Holy Scripture is God's witness to Himself.

2. Holy Scripture, being God's own Word, written by men prepared and superintended by His Spirit, is of infallible divine authority in all matters upon which it touches: it is to be believed, as God's instruction, in all that it affirms,

---

[65] Dr. Don Wilkins, Senior Translator of the NASB writes, "Exactly how the Spirit guided the writers is a mystery, and the words "thus says the Lord" in prophecy most likely do introduce a dictated message. However, those familiar with Greek can easily see stylistic differences between the NT writers which seem to reflect different personalities and rule out verbatim dictation from a single source."

obeyed, as God's command, in all that it requires; embraced, as God's pledge, in all that it promises.

3. The Holy Spirit, Scripture's divine Author, both authenticates it to us by His inward witness and opens our minds to understand its meaning.

4. Being wholly and verbally God-given, Scripture is without error or fault in all its teaching, no less in what it states about God's acts in creation, about the events of world history, and about its own literary origins under God, than in its witness to God's saving grace in individual lives.

5. The **authority of Scripture** is inescapably impaired if this total divine **inerrancy** is in any way limited or disregarded or made relative to a view of truth contrary to the Bible's own; and such lapses bring serious loss to both the individual and the Church.

Questions to Consider

We have been using the book of Romans as our example, so we will continue with it. We know that Paul was the author who gave us the inspired content of Romans, Tertius was the secretary who recorded Romans, and Phoebe was likely the one who carried the letter to Rome or else accompanied the one who did. Thus, we have at least three persons: the author, the secretary (amanuensis; scribe), and the carrier.

What is inspiration?

Inspiration is a "theological concept encompassing phenomena in which human action, skill, or utterance is immediately and extraordinarily supplied by the Spirit of God. Although various terms are employed in the Bible, the basic meaning is best served by Gk. *theopneustos* "God-breathed." (2 Tim. 3:16) This means "breathed forth by God" rather than "breathed into by God" (Warfield)." (Myers 1987, 524) **Verbal plenary inspiration** holds that "every word of Scripture was God-breathed." Human writers played a significant role. Their individual backgrounds, personal traits, and literary styles were authentically theirs but had been providentially prepared by God for use as his instrument in producing Scripture. "The Scriptures had not been dictated, but the result was as if they had been (A. A. Hodge, B. B. Warfield)."[66]

---

[66] Allen C. Myers, *The Eerdmans Bible Dictionary* (Grand Rapids, MI: Eerdmans, 1987), 525.

World-Renowned Bible Scholars Define Inspiration

Benjamin B. Warfield: "Inspiration is, therefore, usually defined as a supernatural influence exerted on the sacred writers by the Spirit of God, by virtue of which their writings are given Divine trustworthiness."[67]

Edward J. Young: "Inspiration is a superintendence of God the Holy Spirit over the writers of the Scriptures, as a result of which these Scriptures possess Divine authority and trustworthiness and, possessing such Divine authority and trustworthiness, are free from error."[68]

Charles C. Ryrie: "Inspiration is … God's superintendence of the human authors so that, using their own individual personalities, they composed and recorded without error His revelation to man in the words of the original autographs."[69]

Paul P. Enns: "There are several important elements that belong in a proper definition of inspiration: (1) the divine element–God the Holy Spirit superintended the writers, ensuring the accuracy of the writing; (2) the human element—human authors wrote according to their individual styles and personalities; (3) the result of the divine-human authorship is the recording of God's truth without error; (4) inspiration extends to the selection of words by the writers; (5) inspiration relates to the original manuscripts."[70]

Were both Paul and Tertius inspired, or just Paul?

Only Paul and other Old and New Testament authors were inspired. First, as was stated above, **Verbal plenary inspiration** holds that "every word of Scripture was God-breathed." However, God **did not**, generally speaking, dictate the books of the Bible word by word to the Bible authors as if they were dictating machines.

As the apostle Paul states, God spoke "in many ways" to his servants before the arrival of Jesus Christ. (Heb. 1:1-2) We do have one specific circumstance: The Ten Commandments, wherein the information was divinely provided in written form. Therefore, a scribe would only have to copy them into the scrolls created by Moses. (Ex. 31:18; Deut. 10:1-5) At other times, information was communicated by verbal dictation, literally word for word. When introducing the large number of laws and statutes of

---

[67] B. B. Warfield, *The Inspiration and Authority of the Bible* (Philadelphia, PA: Presbyterian and Reformed Pub. Co., 1948), p. 131.

[68] Edward J. Young, *Thy Word Is Truth* (Grand Rapids: Eerdmans, 1957), p. 27.

[69] Charles C. Ryrie, *A Survey of Bible Doctrine* (Chicago: Moody, 1972), p. 38.

[70] Paul P. Enns, *The Moody Handbook of Theology* (Chicago: Moody Press, 1989), p. 161.

the covenant with Israel, "Jehovah said to Moses: 'Write these words, for in accordance with these words I have made a covenant with you and with Israel.'" (Ex. 34:27) And on other occasions, the prophets also were frequently given precise messages that were to be delivered. These were then recorded after that, which then became part of the inspired, fully inerrant Scriptures. – 1 Kings 22:14; Jeremiah 1:7; 2:1; 11:1-5; Ezekiel 3:4; 11:5.

2 Thessalonians 3:17 Updated American Standard Version (UASV)

[17] The greeting is by my hand, Paul's,[71] which is a sign in every letter; this is the way I write.

An appended note to every letter with his signature "distinguishing mark" is like a boss signing a letter that he dictated to a secretary. It is unthinkable that Paul would sign or make a distinguishing mark on anything without reading through it and, after that, making any necessary corrections or having Tertius makes the corrections. This supposes that Paul looked over all of his letters, which would also suppose that the scribe could not have been inspired because if he were, then there would have been no mistakes in the document, which means it would not have been needed to be looked over let alone corrected. So again, there would have been no need for Paul to check the work of an inspired secretary. Again, more plainly, if Tertius had been inspired, Paul would have had no need to look the text over the moment he set the pen down. There is no need to read into silence and suggest that the secretary was inspired. While Tertius was likely a professional scribe and indeed engaged in his work, they were also coworkers and traveling companions. As was stated earlier, in a small percentage of cases, information was transmitted by verbal dictation, word for word from God by way of the Holy Spirit to the author. For example, when God delivered the large body of laws and statutes of his covenant with Israel, Jehovah instructed Moses: "Write for yourself these words." (Ex 34:27) In another example, the prophets were often given specific messages to deliver. (1 Ki 22:14; Jer. 1:7; 2:1; 11:1-5; Eze. 3:4; 11:5) Additionally, the Bible authors did dictate word for word what they received under inspiration to their secretaries, i.e., amanuenses/scribes. In other words, any word choices or writing styles belonged to the Bible author.

Jeremiah 36:4 Updated American Standard Version (UASV)

[4] Then Jeremiah called Baruch the son of Neriah, and Baruch wrote on a scroll at the **dictation of Jeremiah** all the words of Jehovah that he had spoken to him. (Bold mine)

---

[71] Lit *the greeting by my hand of Paul*

If Paul alone was inspired, how does the imperfection of Tertius affect inerrancy?

First, we should state that just because Paul used Tertius, Peter used Silvanus, or Jeremiah used Baruch to pen the Word of God, they did not thereby detract from or weaken the authority of God's Word or the inerrancy of Scripture. The dictation that Paul gave Tertius was the result of divine inspiration as he, Paul, was moved along by the Holy Spirit. Tertius merely recorded Paul's dictation, word by word. Whether Tertius was a professional scribe[72] or had the skills of a semi-professional scribe, he must have made at least a few slips of the pen, as the epistle to the Romans was some 7,000 words, and writing conditions were challenging. Afterward, however, Paul would have reviewed the document with Tertius, correcting any errors before publishing the official, authoritative text.

What about Phoebe? What role did the carrier have in the process?

Those used by New Testament authors to deliver the Word of God to people or congregations would have been some of Paul's most trusted, competent coworkers. Paul had over one hundred of these. Indeed, in the case of congregations contacting Paul with questions and concerns, Paul responded with an inspired letter, the carrier would be made aware of those questions and concerns. Paul would have spoken to the carrier at length about these matters, going over what he meant by the words he had used. This would have provided the carrier sufficient knowledge; if the person or congregation had any question(s) that the carrier could address. This process is not indicated within the Scriptures. Are we to believe God and Paul, for that matter, would send a simple carrier who was left in the dark as to what he was carrying? And that no congregational leader would have follow-up questions, which God would have foreseen? Hardly.

The Publishing, Copying, and Distributing Process

In the above, we spoke of the initial aspect of the publishing process, i.e., the moment Paul decided to pen a letter to a congregation like the Romans, the Ephesians, the Colossians, or a person such as Philemon. We discussed the process that Paul went through with his secretary (e.g., Tertius), to the carrier (e.g., Phoebe, Tychicus), and the recipients (e.g., Roman congregation). Now we turn to the circulation aspect, i.e., getting the book out to more readers. Harry Y. Gamble says the following in *The Publication and Early Dissemination of Early Christian Books*:

---

[72] In the strictest sense, a professional scribe is one who was specifically trained in that vocation and was paid for his services.

The letters of Paul to his communities, the earliest extant Christian texts, were dictated to scribal associates (presumably Christian), carried to their destinations by a traveling Christian, and read aloud to the congregations.[73] But Paul also envisioned the circulation of some of his letters beyond a single Christian group (cf. Gal. 1: 2, 'to the churches of Galatia', Rom. 1:7 'to all God's beloved in Rome'—dispersed among numerous discrete house churches, Rom. 16: 5, 10, 11, 14, 15), and the author of Colossians, if not Paul, gives instruction for the exchange of Paul's letters between different communities (Col. 4: 16), which must indeed have taken place also soon after Paul's time.[74] The gospel literature of early Christianity offers only meager hints of intentions or means of its publication and circulation. The prologue to Luke/Acts (Luke 1: 1–4) provides a dedication to 'Theophilus', who (whether or not a fictive figure) by that convention is implicitly made responsible for the dissemination of the work by encouraging and permitting copies to be made. The last chapter of the Gospel of John, an epilogue added by others after the original conclusion of the Gospel (20: 30–1), aims at least in part (21: 24–5) to insure appreciation of the book and to promote its use beyond its community of origin. To take another case, the Apocalypse, addressed to seven churches in western Asia Minor, was almost surely sent in separate copy to each. Even so, the author anticipated its wider copying and dissemination beyond those original recipients, and so warned subsequent copyists to preserve the integrity of the book, neither adding nor subtracting, for fear of religious penalty (Rev. 22:18–19). The private Christian copying and circulation that is presumed in these early writings continued to be the means for the publication and dissemination of Christian literature in the second and third centuries. It can be seen, for example, in the explicit notice in The Shepherd of Hermas (Vis. 2.4.3) that the book was to be published or released in two final copies, one for local use in Rome, the other for the transcription of further copies to be sent to Christian communities in 'cities abroad'. It can also be seen when Polycarp, bishop of Smyrna, had the letters of Ignatius copied and sent to the Christian community in Philippi, and had copies of letters from them and other churches in Asia Minor sent to Syrian Antioch (Phil. 13). It is evident

---

[73] On the dictation of Paul's letters to a scribe, see E. R. Richards, The Secretary in the Letters of Paul (WUNT 42; Tubingen: Mohr, 1991), 169–98; for couriers see Rom. 16: 1, 1 Cor. 16: 10, Eph. 6: 21, Col. 4: 7, cf. 2 Cor. 8: 16–17. Reference to their carriers is common in other early Christian letters (e.g., 1 Pet. 5: 12, 1 Clem. 65: 1, Ignatius, Phil. 11.2, Smyr. 12.1, Polycarp, Phil. 14.1). For the general practice see E. Epp, 'New Testament Papyrus Manuscripts and Letter Carrying in Greco-Roman Times', in B. A. Pearson (ed.), The Future of Early Christianity (Minneapolis: Fortress, 1991), 35–56. Reading a letter aloud to the community, which seems to be presupposed by all the letters, is stipulated only in 1 Thess. 5: 27.

[74] This is shown for an early time by the generalization of the original particular addresses of some of Paul's letters (Rom. 1: 7, 15; 1 Cor. 1: 2; cf. Eph. 1: 1).

too in the scribal colophons of the Martyrdom of Polycarp (22.2–4), and must be assumed also in connection with the letters of Dionysius, bishop of Corinth (fl. 170 ce; Eusebius, H.E. 4.23.1–12).

From another angle, the physical remains of early Christian books show that they were produced and disseminated privately within and between Christian communities. Early Christian texts, especially those of a scriptural sort, were almost always written in codices or leaf books—an informal, economical, and handy format—rather than on rolls, which were the traditional and standard vehicle of all other books. This was a sharp departure from convention, and particularly characteristic of Christians. Also distinctive to Christian books was the pervasive use of nomina sacra, divine names written in abbreviated forms, which was clearly an in-house practice of Christian scribes. Further, the preponderance in early Christian papyrus manuscripts of an informal quasi-documentary script rather than a professional bookhand also suggests that Christian writings were privately transcribed with a view to intramural circulation and use.[75]

If Christian books were disseminated in roughly the same way as other books, that is, by private seriatim copying, we might surmise that they spread slowly and gradually in ever-widening circles, first in proximity to their places of origin, then regionally, and then transregionally, and for some books this was doubtless the case. But it deserves notice that some early Christian texts appear to have enjoyed surprisingly rapid and wide circulation. Already by the early decades of the second century Papias of Hierapolis in western Asia Minor was acquainted at least with the Gospels of Mark and Matthew (Eusebius, H.E. 3.39.15–16); Clement of Rome, Ignatius of Antioch, and Polycarp of Smyrna were all acquainted with collections of Paul's letters; and papyrus copies of various early Christian texts were current in Egypt.[76] The Shepherd of Hermas, written in Rome near the mid-second century, was current and popular in Egypt not long after.[77] Equally interesting, Irenaeus' Adversus haereses, written about 180 in Gaul, is shown by papyrus fragments to have found its way to Egypt by

---

[75] On these features see H. Gamble, Books and Readers in the Early Church (New Haven: Yale University Press, 1995), 66–81, and L. Hurtado, The Earliest Christian Artifacts (Grand Rapids: Eerdmans, 2006).

[76] For Clement, Ignatius, and Polycarp, see A. F. Gregory and C. M. Tuckett, eds., The Reception of the New Testament in the Apostolic Fathers (Oxford: OUP, 2005), 142–53, 162–72, 201–18, 226–7. For early Christian papyri in Egypt see Hurtado, Earliest Christian Artifacts, appendix 1 (209–29). The most notable case is P52 (a fragment of the Gospel of John, customarily dated to the early 2nd cent.).

[77] Some papyrus fragments of Hermas are 2nd cent. (P.Oxy. 4706 and 3528, P.Mich. 130, P.Iand. 1.4).

the end of the second century, and indeed also to Carthage, where it was used by Tertullian.[78]

The brisk and broad dissemination of Christian books presumes not only a lively interest in texts among Christian communities but also efficient means for their reproduction and distribution. Such interest and means may be unexpected, given that the rate of literacy within Christianity was low, on average no greater than in the empire at large, namely in the range of 10–15 percent.[79] Yet there were some literate members in almost all Christian communities, and as long as texts could be read aloud by some, they were accessible and useful to the illiterate majority. Christian congregations were not reading communities in the same sense as elite literary or scholarly circles, but books were nevertheless important to them virtually from the beginning, for even before Christians began to compose their own texts, books of Jewish scripture played an indispensable role in their worship, teaching, and missionary preaching. Indeed, Judaism and Christianity were the only religious communities in Greco-Roman antiquity in which texts had any considerable importance, and in this, as in some other respects, Christian groups bore a greater resemblance to philosophical circles than to other religious traditions.[80]

If smaller, provincial Christian congregations were not well-equipped or well-situated for the tasks of copying and disseminating texts, larger Christian centers must have had some scriptorial capacity: already in the second century: Polycarp's handling of Ignatius' letters and letters from other churches shows its presence in Smyrna; the instruction about the publication of Hermas' The Shepherd suggests it for Rome; and it can hardly be doubted for Alexandria, since even in a provincial city like Oxyrhynchus many manuscripts of Christian texts were available.[81] The early third-century Alexandrian scriptorium devised for the production

---

[78] For the A.H. in Egypt: P.Oxy. 405; for Tertullian's use of A.H. in Carthage, see T. D. Barnes, Tertullian (Oxford: Clarendon, 1971), 127–8, 220–1.

[79] The fundamental study of literacy in antiquity is still W. V. Harris, Ancient Literacy (Cambridge, Mass.: Harvard University Press, 1989); see now also the essays in J. H. Humphrey, ed., Literacy in the Roman World (Journal of Roman Archaeology, suppl. ser. 3; Ann Arbor: University of Michigan, 1991), and in W. A. Johnson and H. N. Parker, eds., Ancient Literacies (Oxford: OUP, 2009).

[80] M. Beard, 'Writing and Religion: Ancient Religion and the Function of the Written Word in Roman Religion', in Humphrey, Literacy in the Roman World, 353–8, argues that texts played a relatively large role in Greco-Roman religions, yet characterizes that role as 'symbolic rather than utilitarian', which was clearly not the case in early Christianity. The kind of careful reading, interpretation, and exposition of texts that we see in early Christianity and in early Judaism (whether in worship or school settings) provides, mutatis mutandis, an interesting analogy to the activity of elite literary circles.

[81] On the question of early Christian scriptoria (the term may be variously construed), see Gamble, Books and Readers, 121–6. Hurtado, Earliest Christian Artifacts, 185–9, rightly calls attention to corrections by contemporary hands in early Christian papyri as pointing to at least limited activity of a scriptorial kind.

and distribution of the works of Origen (Eusebius, H.E. 6.23.2), though unique in its sponsorship by a private patron and its service to an individual writer, surely had precursors, more modest and yet efficient, in other Christian communities. It also had important successors, not the least of which was the library and scriptorium that flourished in Caesarea in the second half of the third century under the auspices of Pamphilus.[82] Absent such reliable intra-Christian means for the production of books, the range of texts known and used by Christian communities across the Mediterranean basin by the end of the second century would be without explanation.[83]

When we think of publishing a book today, there are some similarities to the ancient process, but it was not the same for Christian communities in the ancient world of the Roman Empire. Paul dispatched Tychicus as a carrier with a letter to the Ephesians, the Colossians, and Philemon and a potential fourth letter to the Laodiceans. Tychicus was competent, trusted, and a skilled coworker who delivered these letters hundreds of miles from an imprisoned Paul, with enough information to bring God's Word to the first-century Christian congregations. However, in the letter to the Colossians, Paul said, "When this letter has been read among you, have it also read in the church of the Laodiceans; and see that you also read the letter from Laodicea." (Col. 4:16) In other words, it was to be a circuit letter. Paul had also stated to the Thessalonians in a letter to them, "I put you under oath before the Lord to have this letter read to all the brothers." (1 Thess. 5:27) Paul encouraged the distribution of his letters.

Remember the process from the above; the book would be shared with friends of similar interests, and then the circles grew wider and wider to friends of friends and others. First, Paul's primary level of friends would be his more than one hundred traveling companions and fellow workers, some being the carriers who delivered the books. Second, the friends in the Christian congregation would have the letter read to them, who would then share it with other fellow congregations. In the secular (non-Christian) circle of friends, interested readers who wished to have a copy would have their

---

[82] The role of Pamphilus and the Caesarean library/scriptorium in the private production and dissemination of early Christian literature, esp. of scriptural materials, was highlighted by Eusebius in his Life of Pamphilus, as quoted by Jerome in his Apology against Rufinus (1.9).

[83] Charles E. Hill; Michael J. Kruger, *THE EARLY TEXT OF THE NEW TESTAMENT* (Oxford, United Kingdom: Oxford University Press, 2012), 32-35.

Beyond the uses of Christian texts in congregational settings, there were already in the 2nd cent. some Christian circles that pursued specialized and technical engagements with texts, usually in the service of theological arguments and exegetical agendas. The 'school-settings' of teachers such as Valentinus and Justin, and a little later of Theodotus, Clement, and Origen, were Christian approximations to the kinds of literary activity associated with 'elite' reading communities in the early empire.

slaves (i.e., scribes) make a copy or copies of a book. The same would have been valid within the Christian congregation. When the Laodiceans read the letter that Paul had sent to the Colossians, they would have had one of their wealthy members use his literate and trained scribe to make a copy for their congregation and maybe even a few copies for other members. The same would hold true when the Colossians received the letter written to the Laodiceans. Eventually, Paul's letters would have been gathered in one codex to circulate as a group, such as P[46]. Papyrus 46 is an early Greek New Testament manuscript written on papyrus. Its most probable date between 100 and 150 C.E. Michael Marlowe says that P[46] contains (in order) "the last eight chapters of Romans; all of Hebrews; virtually all of 1–2 Corinthians; all of Ephesians, Galatians, Philippians, Colossians; and two chapters of 1 Thessalonians. All of the leaves have lost some lines at the bottom through deterioration."

The scriptorium was a room for copying manuscripts, where a lector would read aloud from his exemplar, with a room full of copyists taking down his dictation. Recent scholarship has suggested that we remove the concept of the scriptorium in the time of Jesus and the apostles of the first century C.E. because this was not a practice until the fourth century C.E. Harry Y. Gamble addresses this effectively when he writes,

> It is difficult to determine just when Christian scriptoria came into existence. The problem is partly of definition, partly of evidence. If we think of the scriptorium as simply a writing center where texts were copied by more than a single scribe, then any of the larger Christian communities, such as Antioch or Rome, may have already had scriptoria in the early second century, and in view of Polycarp's activity something of the kind can be imagined for Smyrna. If we think instead of a scriptorium as being more structured, operating, for example, in a specially designed and designated location; employing particular methods of transcription; producing certain types of manuscripts; or multiplying copies on a significant scale, then it becomes more difficult to imagine that such institutions developed at an early date.[84]

Gamble goes on to inform us that Origen's scriptorium of about 230 C.E. was an exception. Just a few short years later, the scriptorium of Cyprian was a more official version of what we think of when picturing scriptoria. Then, there is the scriptorium that was attached to the Christian library in

---

[84] Henry Y. Gamble, *Books and Readers in the Early Church: A History of Early Christian Texts* (New Haven, CT, New Haven University Press, 1995), 121.

Caesarea, which we know was commissioned to produce fifty New Testament manuscripts in short order. It may even have been added in the third century when Pamphilus (latter half of the 3rd century–309 C.E.) built the library. A more official type of scriptorium could likely be found in this period at other Christian epicenters, such as Rome, Jerusalem, and Alexandria. Comfort tells us that "church history and certain manuscript discoveries from other parts in Egypt suggest that Alexandria had a Christian scriptorium or writing center."[85] Gamble adds, "It was only during the fourth and fifth centuries that the scriptoria on monastic communities came into their own, also in association with monastic libraries."[86]

While it is challenging, if not impossible, to identify a specific Alexandrian scriptorium for our early manuscripts of the second century, or even if they were produced in a scriptorium at all, we do know that professional scribes produced them. There are many possibilities: (1) the professional scribe could have produced them in a Christian scriptorium. On the other hand, (2) the professional scribe could have been a Christian who worked for a scriptorium, who then used his skills to produce copies. Then again, (3) it could have been that the scribe formerly worked in a scriptorium but now was the private scribe of a wealthy Christian who used his skills to make copies. We know that about a million Christians spread throughout the Roman Empire at the beginning of the second century (c. 130 C.E.). Therefore, the copying of manuscripts could very well have been within the Christian community, i.e., from the Christian congregation to the Christian congregation and wealthy Christians acquiring personal copies for themselves.

We have several early manuscripts that evidence that they were very likely produced in a scriptorium, even if it was simply a room attached to a Christian library, which had a handful of copyists. For example, a professional scribe undoubtedly did P46 (100-150 C.E.) because it contained stichoi marks, which are notes at the end of sections, stating how many lines were copied. This was a means of calculating how much a scribe should be paid. It is likely that an employee of the scriptorium numbered the pages, indicating the stichoi marks. Moreover, this same scribe made corrections as he went. Another example would be P[66] (also c. 100-150 C.E.) according to Comfort:

---

[85] Philip Comfort, *Encountering the Manuscripts: An Introduction to New Testament Paleography & Textual Criticism* (Nashville, TN: Broadman & Holman, 2005), 22.

[86] Henry Y. Gamble, *Books and Readers in the Early Church: A History of Early Christian Texts* (New Haven, CT, New Haven University Press, 1995), 121-2.

It is also fairly certain that P[66] was the product of a scriptorium or writing center. The first copyist of this manuscript had his work thoroughly checked by a diorthotes [corrector], according to a different exemplar—just the way it would happen in a scriptorium. Of course, it can be argued that an individual who purchased the manuscript made all the corrections, which was a common practice in ancient times. But the extent of corrections in P[66] and the fact that the paginator (a different scribe) made many of the corrections speaks against this (see description of P[66] in chap. 2). It was more the exception than the rule in ancient times that a manuscript would be fully checked by a diorthotes. P[66] has other markings of being professionally produced. The extant manuscript still shows the pinpricks in the corners of each leaf of the papyri; these served as a guide for left hand justification and right hand. The manuscript also exhibits a consistent set of marginal and interlinear correction signs. Another sign of professionally produced manuscript is the use of the diple (>) in the margin, which was used to signal a correction in the text and/or the need for a correction in the text. There are very few of these in the extant New Testament manuscripts.[87]

The production and distribution of New Testament manuscripts were carried out at the congregation and individual Christian levels in the early days of Christianity.

Moreover, this process did not negate the use of professional scribes. Just as Paul would not have used an inexperienced scribe to produce the epistle to the Romans. Congregations and wealthy Christians would have likely used professional scribes to make copies. Of course, there are exceptions to the rule, and some congregations may not have had access to a professional scribe, so they would have to have chosen to use the best person available to them. Nevertheless, if a congregation had access to a person experienced at making documents or a semi-professional or professional scribe, they would have lacked good sense or practicality not to take advantage of such a person. Think of anything we want to have done in our Christian congregation today: would we not seek a professional if we had access to one as a member, be it plumbing, wiring, teaching, or computer technology? We naturally look to the most skilled person that we can find, even if we have a clogged-up commode. Would we do any less if we were in

---

[87] Philip W. Comfort, *New Testament Text and Translation Commentary: Commentary on the Variant Readings of the Ancient New Testament Manuscripts and How They Relate to the Major English Translations* (Carol Stream, IL: Tyndale House Publishers, Inc., 2008), 26.

the first century and had just received a letter from the apostle Paul, who was imprisoned hundreds of miles away in Rome?

Why Would the Holy Spirit Miraculously Inspire 66 Fully Inerrant Texts and Then Allow Variant Errors in the Copies?

Agnostic New Testament textual and early Christianity scholar Dr. Bart D. Ehrman states, "For the only reason (I came to think) for God to inspire the Bible would be so that his people would have his actual words; but if he really wanted people to have his actual words, surely he would have miraculously preserved those words, just as he had miraculously inspired them in the first place. Given the circumstance that he didn't preserve the words, the conclusion seemed inescapable to me that he hadn't gone to the trouble of inspiring them."[88]

New Testament textual scholar Dr. Dirk Jongkind offers a brief response, "God chose not to give us exhaustive knowledge of every detail of the text, though he could have done so. Still, he has given us abundant access to his words. In other words, to say that God inspired the words of the New Testament does not mean that God is therefore under an obligation to preserve for us each and every detail."[89]

Why didn't God inspire the copyists? Some have become anxious because this question has plagued them, or some Bible critic has challenged them. Therefore, they are looking for the silver bullet to quench their personal concern or have a ready, quick response for the Bible critic. Draw comfort in that there are hundreds, if not thousands, of great responses to attacks from Bible critics that will cause them to move onto another victim in their quest to stumble God's people. However, there are good reasons, rational responses to some questions that will not be fully answered until the second coming of Jesus Christ. What lies below is the latter. Before delving into the rational, reasonable reasons why God would inspire the authors but not the copyists, let's talk a little about what we do have.

Some people have unreceptive hearts and minds. They are Pharisaical because they are not interested in an answer, and the Word of God, reason, and logic will not get through their callused hearts. Suppose I have only taught one thing in my 32 years. In that case, it is this, identify these people fast, or you will waste much of your life, giving reasonable, rational responses to then have the person reject it out of hand and move onto something else

---

[88] Misquoting Jesus: The Story Behind Who Changed the Bible and Why (San Francisco: HarperSanFrancisco, 2005), 211.

[89] An Introduction to the Greek New Testament, Produced at Tyndale House, Cambridge, Crossway.

as though they never brought it up. Mind you, an angry person, a person with doubts, is not necessarily a Pharisaical person. There are reasons for some to doubt. There are reasons for some to be angry. If the person is treating you with disdain, mocking, talking down to you, these and other things are indications of a Pharisaical attitude.

Christian Bible students need to be familiar with Old and New Testament textual studies as the two are essential foundational studies. Why? If we fail to establish what was originally authored with reasonable certainty, how are we to translate or even interpret what we think is God's actual Word? We are fortunate that there are far more existing New Testament manuscripts today than any other book from ancient history. Some ancient Greek and Latin classics are based on one existing manuscript, while with others, there are just a handful and a few exceptions that have a few hundred available. However, the New Testament has over 5,898 Greek New Testament manuscripts that have been cataloged (As of January 2021),[90] 10,000 Latin manuscripts, and an additional 9,300 other manuscripts in such languages as Syriac, Slavic, Gothic, Ethiopic, Coptic, and Armenian. This gives New Testament textual scholars vastly more to work within establishing the original words of the text.

The other difference between the New Testament manuscripts and those of the classics is that the existing copies of the New Testament date much closer to the originals. In the case of the Greek classics, some of the manuscripts are dated about a thousand years after the author had penned the book. Some of the Latin classics are dated from three to seven hundred years after the time the author wrote the book. When we look at the Greek copies of the New Testament books, some portions are within decades of the original author's book. Seventy-nine Greek papyri, along with five majuscules,[91] date from 110 C.E. to 300 C.E.

---

[90] While at present here in 2020, there are 5,898 manuscripts. There are **140 listed Papyrus** manuscripts, 323 Majuscule manuscripts, 2,951 Minuscule manuscripts, and 2,484 Lectionary manuscripts, bringing the total cataloged manuscripts to 5,898 manuscripts. However, you cannot simply total the number of cataloged manuscripts because, for example, P$^{11/14}$ are the same manuscript but with different catalog numbers. The same is true of P$^{33/5}$, P$^{4/64/67}$, P$^{49/65}$ and P$^{77/103}$. Now this alone would bring our 140 listed papyrus manuscripts down to 134. Then, we turn to one example from our majuscule manuscripts where clear 0110, 0124, 0178, 0179, 0180, 0190, 0191, 0193, 0194, and 0202 are said to be part of 070. A minuscule manuscript was listed with five separate catalog numbers for 2306, which then have the letters a through e. Thus, we have the following GA numbers: 2306 for 2306a, and 2831 - 2834 for 2306b-2306e.' – (Hixon 2019, 53-4) The problem is much worse when we consider that there are 323 Majuscule manuscripts and then far worse still with a listed 2,951 Minuscule and 2,484 Lectionaries. Nevertheless, those who estimate a total of 5,300 (Jacob W. Peterson, Myths and Mistakes, p. 63) 5,500 manuscripts (Dr. Ed Gravely / ehrmanproject.com/), 5,800 manuscripts (Porter 2013, 23), it is still a truckload of evidence far and above the dismal number of ancient secular author books.

[91] Large lettering, often called "capital" or uncial, in which all the letters are usually the same height.

Distribution of Greek New Testament Manuscripts

- The **Papyrus** is a copy of a portion of the New Testament made on papyrus. At present, we have 141 cataloged New Testament papyri, many dating between 110-350 C.E., but some as late as the 6th century C.E.

- The **Majuscule** or **Uncial** is a script of large letters commonly used in Greek and Latin manuscripts written between the 3rd and 9th centuries C.E. that resembles a modern capital letter but is more rounded. At present, we have 323 cataloged New Testament Majuscule manuscripts.

- The **Minuscule** is a small cursive style of writing used in manuscripts from the 9th to the 16th centuries, now having 2,951 Minuscule manuscripts cataloged.

- The **Lectionary** is a schedule of readings from the Bible for Christian church services during the year, in both majuscules and minuscules, dating from the 4th to the 16th centuries C.E., now having 2,484 Lectionary manuscripts cataloged.

Distribution of Papyri by Century and Type				
DATE	**ALEX**	**WEST**	**CAES**	**BYZ**
100-150/175 C.E.	7Q4? 7Q5? $P^{4/64/67}$ P^{32} P^{46} P^{52} P^{66} P^{75} $P^{77/103}$ P^{87} P^{90} P^{98} (bad shape, differences) P^{101} P^{109} (too small) P^{118} (too small) P^{137} 0189 P. Oxyrhynchus 405 P. Egerton 2	P^{104}	0	0
175-250 C.E.	P^1 P^5 P^{13} P^{20} P^{23} P^{27} P^{30} P^{35} P^{39} P^{40} P^{45} P^{47} $P^{49/65}$ P^{71} P^{72} P^{82} P^{85} P^{95} P^{100} P^{106} P^{108} P^{110} P^{111} P^{113} P^{115} P^{121} (too small) P^{125} P^{126} (too small) P^{133} P^{136} P^{141} 0220 0232	P^{29} (Metzger Western & Aland Free; too small to be certain) P^{38} P^{48} P^{69} 0171 0212 (mixed) P^{107} (Independent)	0	0

	P. Oxyrhynchus 406 P. Egerton 3			
250-300 C.E.	P8 P9 P12 P15 P16 P17 P18 P19 P24 P28 P50 P51 P53 P70 P78 P80 P86 P88 P89 (too small) P91 P92 P114 P119 P120 P129 (too small) P131 P132 too small) P134 0162 0207 0231 P. Antinoopolis 54	P37 (Free, mostly Western)	0	0
290-390 C.E.	P3 P6 P7 P10 P21 P54 P62 P81 P93 P94 P102 (too small) P117 (too small) P122 (too small) P123 P130 (too small) P139 (too small) 057 058 059 / 0215 071 0160 0163 0165 0169 0172 0173 0175 0176 0181 0182 0185 0188 0206 0214 0217 0218 0219 0221 0226 0227 0228 0230 0242 0264 0308 0312 P. Oxyrhynchus 4010 P. Oxyrhynchus 5073	P21 (mixed) P25 (independent) P112 (independent) P127 (independent; like no other)	0	0
4th / 5th Century C.E.	P11 P14 P33/P58 P56 P57 P63 P105 (too small) P124 0254			069 P. Oxyrhynchus 1077?

We should clarify that of the approximate 24,000 total manuscripts of the New Testament, not all are complete books. There are fragmented manuscripts with just a few verses, manuscripts containing an entire book, others that include numerous books, and some that have the whole New Testament, or nearly so. This is expected since the oldest manuscripts we have were copied in an era when reproducing the entire New Testament was not the norm, but rather a single book or a group of books (i.e., the Gospels or Paul's letters). This still does not negate the vast riches of manuscripts that we possess.

What can we conclude from this short introduction to New Testament textual studies? There is some irony here: secular scholars have no problem accepting classic authors' wording with their minuscule amount of evidence. However, they discount the treasure trove of evidence that is available to the New Testament textual scholar. Still, this should not surprise us, as the New Testament has always been under-appreciated and attacked in some way, shape, or form over the past 2,000 years.

On the contrary, in comparison to classical works, we are overwhelmed by the quantity and quality of existing New Testament manuscripts. We should also keep in mind that seventy-five percent[92] of the New Testament does not require textual scholars' help because that much of the text is unanimous, and thus, we know what it says. Of the other twenty-five percent, about twenty percent make up trivial scribal mistakes that are easily corrected. Therefore, textual criticism focuses mainly on a small portion of the New Testament text. The facts are clear: the Christian, who reads the New Testament, is fortunate to have so many manuscripts, with so many dating so close to the originals, with 500 hundred years of hundreds of textual scholars who have established the text with a level of certainty unimaginable for ancient secular works.

After discussing the amount of New Testament manuscripts available, Atheist commentator Bob Seidensticker, writes, "The first problem is that more manuscripts at best increase our confidence that we have the original version. That does not mean the original copy was history …."[93] That is, Seidensticker is forced to acknowledge the reliability of the New Testament text as we have it today and can only try to deny what it says. He also tells us of the New Testament, "Compare that with 2000 copies of the Iliad, the second-best represented manuscript."[94] Of those 2,000 copies of the Iliad, how far removed are they from the alleged originals? The Iliad is dated to about 1260–1180 B.C.E. The most notable Iliad manuscripts are from the 9th, 10th, and 11th centuries C.E. That would make these manuscripts over 2,000 years removed from their original.

The Range of Textual Criticism

The Importance and scope of New Testament textual criticism could be summed up in the few words used by J. Harold Greenlee; it is "the basic

---

[92] The numbers in this paragraph are rounded for simplicity purposes.

[93] 25,000 New Testament Manuscripts? Big Deal. – Patheos,

http://www.patheos.com/blogs/crossexamined/2013/11/25000-new-testament-manuscrip (Retrieved Monday, August 10, 2020).

[94] Ibid

biblical study, a prerequisite to all other biblical and theological work. Interpretation, systemization, and application of the teachings of the NT cannot be done until textual criticism has done at least some of its work. It is, therefore, deserving of the acquaintance and attention of every serious student of the Bible."[95]

It is only reasonable to assume that the Old Testament's original 39 books and the 27 books written first-hand by the New Testament authors have not survived. Instead, we only have what we must consider being imperfect copies. **Why the Holy Spirit would miraculously inspire 66 fully inerrant texts and then allow human imperfection into the copies**. This is not explained for us in Scripture. We do know that imperfect humans have tended to worship relics where traditions hold to have been touched by the miraculous powers of God or to have been in direct contact with one of his special servants of old. Ultimately, though, all we know is that God had his reasons for allowing the Old and New Testament autographs to be worn out by repeated use. From time to time, we hear of the discovery of a fragment possibly dated to the first century, but even if such a fragment is eventually verified, the dating alone can never serve as proof of an autograph; it will still be a copy in all likelihood.

Pondering: If we ask why didn't God inspire copyists, then it will have to follow, why didn't God inspire translators, why didn't God inspire Bible scholars that author commentaries on the Bible, and so on? Suppose God's initial purpose was to give us a fully inerrant, authoritative, authentic and accurate Word. Why not adequately protect the Scriptures in all facets of transmission from error: copy, translate, and interpret? If God did this, and people were moved along by the Holy Spirit, it would soon become noticeable that when people copy the texts, they would be unable to make an error or mistake or even willfully change something.

Where would it stop? Would this being moved along by the Holy Spirit apply to anyone who decided to make themselves a copy, testing to see if they too would be inspired? In time, this would prove to be actual evidence for God. This would negate the reasons why God has allowed sin, human imperfection to enter into humanity in the first place, to teach them an **object lesson**, man cannot walk on his own without his Creator. God created perfect humans, giving them a perfect start, and through the abuse of free will, they rejected his sovereignty. He did not just keep creating perfect humans again and again, as though he got something wrong. God gave us his perfect Word and has again chosen to allow us to continue in our human

---

[95] J. Harold Greenlee, Introduction to New Testament Textual Criticism (Grand Rapids, MI: Baker Academic, 1995), 8-9.

imperfection, learning our **object lesson**. God has stepped into humanity many hundreds of times in the Bible record, maybe tens of thousands of times unbeknownst to us over the past 6,000+ years, to tweak things to get the desired outcome of his will and purposes. However, there is no aspect of life where his stepping in for any particular point was to be continuous until the return of the Son. Maybe God gave us a perfect copy of sixty-six books. Then like everything else, he placed the responsibility of copying, translating, and interpreting on us, just as he gave us the Great Commission of proclaiming that Word, explaining that Word, to make disciples. – Matthew 24:14;28-19-20; Acts 1:8.

Reflecting: Some Bible critics seem, to begin with, the belief that if God inspired the originals and fully inerrant, the subsequent copies must continue to be inerrant for the inerrancy of the originals to have value. They seem to be asking, "If only the originals were inspired, and the copies were not inspired, and we do not have the originals, how are we to be certain of any passage in Scripture?" In other words, God would never allow the inspired, inerrant Word to suffer copying errors. Why would he perform the miracle of inspiring the message to be fully inerrant and not continue with the miracle of inspiring the copyists throughout the centuries to keep it inerrant? First, we must acknowledge that God has not given us the specifics of every decision he has made about humans. If we begin asking, "Why did God not do this or do that," where would it end? For example, why didn't God just produce the books himself and miraculously deliver them to people as he gave the commandments to Moses? Why not use angelic messengers to pen the message or produce the message miraculously instead of using humans? God has chosen not to tell us why he did not move the copyists along by the Holy Spirit to have perfect copies, and it remains an unknown. However, I would note that if we can restore the text to its original wording through the art and science of textual criticism, i.e., to an exact representation thereof, we have, in essence, the originals. This is the preservation of Scripture through the restoration of Scripture.

As for errors in all the copies that we have, however, we can say that the vast majority of the Greek text is not affected by errors. The errors occur in variant readings, i.e., portions of the text where different manuscripts disagree. Of the **small amount** of the text affected by variant readings, the vast majority of these are minor slips of the pen, misspelled words, etc., or intentional but quickly analyzed changes, and we are certain what the original reading is in these places. A **far smaller number** of changes present challenges to establishing the original reading. It has always been said and remains true that no central doctrine is affected by a textual problem. Only rarely does a textual issue change the meaning of a verse.[96] Still, establishing the original text wherever there are variant readings is vitally important. Every word matters!

It is true that the Jewish copyists and the later Christian copyists were not led along by the Holy Spirit, and therefore their manuscripts were not inerrant, infallible. Errors (textual variants) crept into the documents unintentionally and intentionally. However, the vast majority of the Hebrew Old Testament and Greek New Testament has not been infected with textual errors. The portions impacted by textual errors are the many tens of thousands of copies that we have to help us weed out the errors. How? Well, not every copyist made the same textual errors. Hence, by comparing the work of different copyists and manuscripts, textual scholars can identify the textual variants (errors) and remove those, leaving us with the original content.

Yes, it would be the most significant discovery of all time if we found the original five books penned by Moses himself, Genesis through Deuteronomy, or the original Gospels of Matthew, Mark, Luke, and John. However, first, there would be no way of establishing that they were the originals. Second, we do not need the originals. Third, we do not need those original documents. What is so important about the documents? It is the content on the original documents that we are after. And truly, miraculously, we have more copies than needed to do just that. We do not need miraculous preservation because we have miraculous restoration. We now know beyond a reasonable doubt that the Hebrew Old Testament and the Greek New Testament critical texts are a 99% reflection of the content in those ancient original manuscripts.

How did God inspire the Bible Authors? How Were They Moved Along by the Holy Spirit? How Did Jesus Bring Remembrance to the Apostles?

Biblical inspiration is the quality or state of being moved along or by or under the Holy Spirit's direction from God.

---

[96] Leading textual scholar Daniel Wallace tells us, after looking at all of the evidence, that the percentage of instances where the reading is uncertain and a well-attested alternative reading could change the meaning of the verse is a quarter of one percent, i.e., 0.0025%

2 Timothy 3:16 Updated American Standard Version (UASV)	2 Peter 1:21 Updated American Standard Version (UASV)	John 14:26 Updated American Standard Version (UASV)
16 All Scripture is **inspired by** God and profitable for teaching, for reproof, for correction, for training in righteousness;	21 for no prophecy was ever produced by the will of man, but men **carried along by** the Holy Spirit spoke from God.	26 But the Helper,[97] the Holy Spirit, whom the Father will send in my name, that one will teach you all things and **bring to your remembrance** all that I have said to you.

How Were the Bible Authors Inspired By God, That Is, Given Divine Direction?

Inspired By θεόπνευστος (theopneustos)

The Greek phrase "inspired by God" translates the compound Greek word θεόπνευστος (theopneustos), which literally means, literally, "God-breathed" or "breathed by God." The Greek phrase here needs to be nuanced so at not to be less than what was meant or go beyond what was meant. The Bible author was under God's influence, to the extent that he was guided or directed by God but not to the extent of dictation. To a lesser extent, Christians are guided by the inspired Word of God if they have an accurate understanding and apply it correctly in their lives. The Bible author was allowed to convey God's Word within their own writing style but would be controlled or guided to the point that he would not choose words, phrases, sentences that would miscommunicate the wrong message.

Carried Along By φερόμενοι (pheromenoi)

The Greek word φερόμενοι (pheromenoi) literally means to **cause** the Bible author to be carried along or moved along by the Holy Spirit. It means to guide, direct, lead.

Bring to Remembrance ὑπομνήσει (hupomnēsei)

The Greek word ὑπομνήσει (*hupomnēsei*) literally means to God put in the mind of the Gospel authors. God **caused** the Gospel authors (Matthew and John, Mark by way of Peter, Luke by Peter, research, and others) to recall in detail what they had formerly experienced.

The apostle Paul says that God spoke "in many ways" to his servants in Old Testament times before Christ coming. (Heb 1:1-2) The Ten Commandments were divinely provided in written form. Scribes, thereafter,

---

97 Or, *Advocate*. Or, *Comforter*. Gr., *ho … parakletos,* masc.

would have had to merely copy it into the scrolls used by Moses. (Ex. 31:18; Deut. 10:1-5) In some very special cases, the words put into Scripture by a Bible author inspired by God, moved along by the Holy Spirit, would have been transmitted by verbal dictation, literally word for word. This would have likely been the case in situations such as the Mosaic Law given to Israel. Jehovah commanded Moses: "**Write these words**, for in accordance with these words I have made a covenant with you and with Israel." (Ex 34:27) The prophets who would author Bible books were also frequently given precise messages from God that they were to deliver, and then God put these same words in the mind of the prophetic authors. God **caused** the prophet (Isaiah, Jeremiah, Ezekiel, Daniel, and others) to recall in detail what they had formerly delivered to others, now becoming Scriptures. – 1 Kings 22:14; Jeremiah 1:7; 2:1; 11:1-5; Ezekiel 3:4; 11:5.

There are other ways that the Bible authors, such as dreams and visions. We are told, "Then the mystery was revealed to Daniel in a **vision of the night**. Then Daniel blessed the God of heaven." (Dan. 2:19) "In the first year of Belshazzar king of Babylon, Daniel saw a **dream and visions** of his head as he lay in his bed. Then he wrote down the dream and told the sum of the matter." (Dan. 7:1) Readers might not know that Bible authors were more often given visions while they were awake, fully conscious, giving the author the thoughts of God directly to his mind. "In the thirtieth year, in the fourth month, on the fifth day of the month, as I was among the exiles by the Chebar canal, the heavens were opened, and **I saw visions** of God." (Eze 1:1) "In the third year of the reign of King Belshazzar **a vision appeared to me**, Daniel, after that which appeared to me at the first." (Dan. 8:1) "And this is how I saw the horses in **my vision** and those who rode them: they wore breastplates the color of fire and of sapphire and of sulfur, and the heads of the horses were like lions' heads, and fire and smoke and sulfur came out of their mouths." (Rev. 9:17) Other visions were given to the Bible author when he was in a trance. Even though the author was clearly awake and conscious, he was extremely, deeply absorbed by what he saw, blocking out all else around him. – Ac 10:9-17; 11:5-10; 22:17-21.

Another way Bible authors received the Word of God was through angelic messengers. "For if the word spoken through angels proved reliably certain, and every transgression and disobedience received a just penalty." (Heb 2:2) "You who received the law as delivered **by angels** and did not keep it." (Ac 7:53) "Why, then, the Law? It was added because of transgressions, until the seed should arrive to whom the promise had been made; and it was **transmitted through angels** by the hand of a mediator." (Gal. 3:19) The angelic representatives spoke in God's name. Therefore, the message they delivered could therefore correctly be called "the word of Jehovah." – Gen 22:11-12, 15-18; Zech. 1:7, 9.

Regardless of how the Bible author received the Word of God, be it, dictation, God directly putting words in the minds of the author, perfect recall, dreams, visions, angelic representatives, being led along by the Holy Spirit, it was all inspired by God or "God-breathed."

Authors evidenced individuality that is still compatible with the Bible's being inspired by God.

The Bible authors were not merely robots who put down dictated words, literally word for word. "The revelation of Jesus Christ, which God gave him to show to his servants the things that must soon take place. He made it known by sending his angel to his servant John, who bore witness to the word of God and to the testimony of Jesus Christ, even to all that he saw." (Rev. 1:1-2) The "God-breathed" revelation was given to him through an angel, which John then conveyed in his own words. Like many things, God allowed humans to use their God's given minds, and in the case of His Word, in choosing words and expressions (Hab. 2:2), he allowed them to use their own style, but he always maintained adequate control and guided them so that the Bible book would be accurate and true. In addition, it would also be according to God's will and purposes. (Prov. 30:5-6) This concept is even conveyed in Scripture itself. "Besides being wise, the Preacher also taught the people knowledge, weighing and studying and arranging many proverbs with great care. The Preacher sought to find words of delight, and uprightly he wrote words of truth." – See also Lu 1:1-4.

This is why every Bible commentary volume explains to its reader the style of that particular author and the background of the individual author. The ones chosen to be Bible authors were not only qualified to do so but had qualities and characteristics that moved God to choose them. In some cases, God likely got them ready before having to serve this particular purpose of being a Bible author. Matthew was a tax collector before being chosen as a disciple, so we note that he makes many particular references to numbers and money amounts. (Matt. 17:27; 26:15; 27:3) On the other hand, Luke was a "physician" (Col 4:14), so we find him using unique expressions that show that he had a medical background. – Lu 4:38; 5:12; 16:20.

In many cases where the Bible speaks about the Bible author receiving "the word of Jehovah" (UASV) or things that were said, it is likely that this was given, not word for word, but rather the author was given an image in his mind of God's purpose. After that, the author would put it in his own words. This can be inferred by the author's sating he 'saw' things rather than his 'hearing' what God said or "the word of Jehovah." – Isaiah 13:1; Micah 1:1; Habakkuk 1:1; 2:1-2.

The authors of God's Word express it that "God has given me the tongue of those who are taught, that I may know how to sustain with a word him who is weary. Morning by morning he awakens; he awakens my ear to hear as those who are taught. Jehovah God has opened my ear, and I was not rebellious; I turned not backward." (Isa 50:4-5) These authors were ready and submissive to being guided by God. Isaiah was eager to do God's will and sought to be led. "My soul yearns for you in the night; my spirit within me earnestly seeks you. For when your judgments are in the earth, the inhabitants of the world learn righteousness." (Isa 26:9) In the case of Luke, he had specific objectives that he sought to carry out. (Lu 1:1-4) In many cases, Paul was writing to fill a need. (1 Cor. 1:10-11; 5:1; 7:1) God guided these authors so that their words in their style went along with his purpose. (Prov. 16:9) These men were chosen because their hearts and minds were already in harmony with God's will and purposes. In fact, they already 'had the mind of Christ.' They were not interested in human wisdom nor in "speak[ing] visions of their own minds," as was the case with the false prophets, "who follow their own spirit." – 1 Corinthians 2:13-16; Jeremiah 23:16; Eze 13:2-3, 17.

As to the being led along by the Holy Spirit, "there are varieties of activities" that would come upon these Bible authors. (1 Cor 12:6) Much information was already at the fingertips of the authors. In other words, it already existed in manuscript evidence, such as genealogies and specific historical accounts. (Lu 1:3; 3:23-38; Num. 21:14, 15; 1 Kings 14:19, 29; 2 Kings 15:31; 24:5) In the case of using historical records, the Holy Spirit would serve as a protection against inaccurate information being part of the Bible author's book. Not everything said by other persons that would end up in the Word of God was inspired by God, but the Holy Spirit guided the author to make it part of the Scriptures and record it accurately. (Gen. 3:4-5; Job 42:3; Matt. 16:21-23) We end up with clear evidence of why it is good to heed God's Word and apply it correctly in our lives. Doing or saying what we think, feel, or believe, ignoring God's Word, or being ignorant of God and his message leads to much heartache.

Then, again, there is information in the Bible that is far beyond human abilities to acquire. We can consider what happened before the creation of the heavens and the earth, as well as man. (Gen. 1:1-26) Humans are also oblivious to what happens in the spiritual heavens as well. (Job 1:6-12, etc.) Then, we have prophecies that foretell events that are to take place decades, centuries, or millenniums after the prophets penned them. We also have revelations as to what God's will and purposes are for humanity. When we think of Solomon's wise sayings, he certainly had much life experience to share. Others had vast knowledge of the Scriptures themselves, not to mention their experience at living by God's Word. They still needed to be moved along by the Holy Spirit, so that the information that they conveyed would be "living and active and sharper than any two-edged sword and piercing as far as the division of soul and spirit, of both joints and marrow, and able to judge the thoughts and intentions of the heart." – Hebrews 4:12.

There are times that Paul said things that were not taken from anything that Jesus had taught. "To the rest, I say (**I, not the Lord**) that if any brother has a wife who is an unbeliever, and she consents to live with him, he should not divorce her." (1 Corinthians 7:12-15) The first thing to notice is Paul saying, God inspires me, so I can say this and the Lord (Jesus), did not touch on this, but I am. Let us take a look at the context and historical setting. Paul says, "Now concerning virgins I do not have a command from the Lord, but I am giving an opinion as one shown mercy by the Lord to be trustworthy." (1 Cor. 7:25) "But in my opinion she is happier if she remains as she is, and I think that I too have the Spirit of God." (1 Cor. 7:40) Paul's point is clear; he, too, is inspired and moved along by the Holy Spirit. Paul's direction was "God-breathed" and so was Scripture, having the same authority as the rest of those Scriptures. – 2 Peter 3:15-16.

CHAPTER III What Do We Know About Books, Reading, and Writing, Literacy In Early Christianity?

Books, Reading, and Writing; Literacy In Early Christianity

EDWARD D. ANDREWS

Before delving into the discussion, we should mention the severe difficulty of defining what literacy was in the ancient Roman Empire of the first three centuries of Christianity and how literate the populace was.

Full Illiteracy: This one has *no* reading or writing *skills*, no math skills, and is incapable of signing his name for daily living and employment beyond fundamental manual labor. He would work as fruit and vegetable picking, handling materials or low-level tools, manual digging or building, farming, or working in large workshops that produced items such as dishes or pots, as well as household slaves.

Fragmentary Literacy: (inconsistent or incomplete in some areas) The *very basic ability* to understand spoken words, a *very basic grasp* of written words, *very basic math skills* (buying in the marketplace), and the ability to sign one's name for daily living and employment. He would work as a manual laborer in the marketplace, not requiring math, a shop assistant that performs manual labor, or a soldier.

Fundamental Literacy: The *essential ability* to understand spoken words, an *elementary grasp* of written words, *necessary* math skills and the ability to sign one's name, and the *ability* to read and write simple words for daily living and employment, such as work as a craftsman, works in the marketplace, or soldier.

Functional Literacy: This one has the *competent ability* to understand spoken words, a *beginner-intermediate level grasp* of written words, and the ability to prepare *necessary documents* for daily living and employment tasks that require reading skills beyond a basic level. He is a semiliterate writer who is untrained in writing but can read or write simple sentences and take on some basic jobs, such as a copyist or scribe.

Proficient Literacy: This one is a *highly skilled* person, who can understand spoken words, and has an *intermediate-advanced level grasp* of written words. He has the *proficient ability* to prepare short texts for daily living and employment tasks that require reading skills at the *intermediate* level. He is a literate writer who is trained in writing and can take on jobs, such as a copyist or scribe, tax collector, or clerk.

Full Literacy: This one is a *highly skilled expert* who can understand spoken words, an *advanced level grasp* of written words. He has the *professional ability* to prepare long texts for daily living and employment tasks that require reading skills at the *advanced* level. He is a fully literate writer who is professionally trained in writing and can take on jobs, such as a copyist or scribe, a tax collector, teacher, lawyer, or a clerk, to high-ranking positions like Senators.

Rome was a complex society. Levels of literacy were fluid because of the conditions of the day being as culturally and ethnically diverse as it was. From the first century to the fourth century, the Roman Empire was as culturally and ethnically diverse as New York City and its five boroughs: the Bronx, Brooklyn, Manhattan, Queens, and Staten Island. A person's literacy level to carry out different job functions and skills for daily living and employment would not be the same in Nazareth as would have been the case in Rome. The need or desire for literacy would not be as crucial in Nazareth as it would have been in Rome. As we will see, the need or desire for literacy **was likely <u>not</u> as critical** to the pagan as it would have been to the Jew or the Christian.

Therefore, when we look at all of the evidence over the next two chapters, we will discover that literacy on all levels was more prominent than historians have long held. They have felt literacy in ancient Rome was no greater than 10-20 percent. It is clear that a *far greater proportion* of the Roman Empire's population from the days of Jesus Christ to the time of Constantine the Great could make use of their skills in understanding the spoken word, grasping the written word, math skills, and writing. The Roman world was in this time that we speak of overflowing with documents, a range of literacies as we can see from above, as well as different literary genres: historical, religious, military, commercial, poetry, and so on. These were distinguished by the social location of those who possessed them, by the method in which they were produced, the material used to receive the writing, the publication, circulation, languages, kinds of text, and those who used them.

The city of Rome was founded in 753 B.C.E., some 750 years before Jesus was born. The Roman citizens had long believed that reading and writing strengthened them. It gave them confidence that their rulers were not going to take advantage of them. It is a given that as an empire grows, what is expected out of its subjects grows exponentially as well. When a state bureaucracy develops, documents grow right alongside it, and the people have no choice but to become *functionally literate.*[98]

Based on what you will learn over the next two chapters, consider the accuracy of the following quote from Dr. Bart D. Ehrman, a prominent scholar of early Christianity, and the history of the New Testament's Greek manuscripts.

> The best and most influential study of literacy in ancient times, by Columbia University professor William Harris, indicates that at the very best of times and places—for example, Athens at the height of the classical period in the fifth century B.C.E.— literacy rates were rarely higher than 10–15 percent of the population. To reverse the numbers, this means that under the best of conditions, 85–90 percent of the population could not read or write. In the first Christian century, throughout the Roman Empire, the literacy rates may well have been lower.[99]

On this, early Christianity and New Testament Textual scholar Larry Hurtado writes, "A few decades ago, it became fashionable in some scholarly circles, including NT/Christian Origins, to hold the view that in the Roman period there was an extremely low level of literacy, and that only elite levels of society had that skill. One still sees this view touted today (typically by those echoing what they believe to be authoritative pronouncements on the matter by others). But a number of studies show that such generalizations are simplistic and that "literacy" was both more diverse and much more widely distributed than some earlier estimates. The earlier claims of an extremely low level of literacy resurfaced in some comments, so I take the time to draw attention to some previous postings on the subject. Likewise, various studies have rightly corrected the older (early 20th century) notion that early Christian circles were composed of slaves and unlearned nobodies. The pioneering study by Edwin Judge, *The Social Pattern of Christian*

---

[98] Mary Beard; et al, *Literacy In the Roman World* (Ann Arbor, MI: Journal of Roman Archaeology, 1991), 11.

[99] Bart D. Ehrman, *MISQUOTING JESUS: The Story Behind Who Changed the Bible and Why* (New York, NY: Harper One, 2005), 37-38

Groups in the First Century (1960), was followed by a number of works focused on the social description of early Christian groups." – *Larry Hurtado's Blog.*[100]

Literacy in the First Century

Craig A. Evans writes, "In recent years, a number of scholars have suggested that Jesus could not read and that in all likelihood none of his disciples could read either. They maintain this because of studies that have concluded that rates of literacy in the Roman Empire were quite low, and that Jesus and his earliest followers were probably not exceptions."[101] We will see this is not the case below. But for now, let it be said that we cannot take aggregate data and apply it to individuals. In other words, we cannot say that the literacy level in the Roman Empire of the first four centuries of our Common Era is less than ten percent; therefore, Jesus, the apostles, and the New Testament authors were illiterate. This is especially true when we can extrapolate insights from the data that we have. This is not the case. This would be like saying the average income for Columbus, Ohio is 52,000 dollars a year, so John Smith, who lives in Columbus, makes 52,000 dollars a year. You cannot apply that aggregate data to individuals unless you have direct information, such as tax records of that specific person.

How can we, modern readers, know so much about letters from the ancient Roman Empire? We have two different sources that provide us some insight into the writer and his letters. Lucius, or Marcus Annaeus Seneca, known as **Seneca the Elder** (54 B.C.E. – 39 C.E.), was a Roman rhetorician[102] and writer, born of a wealthy equestrian family of Cordoba Hispania. Seneca lived through the reigns of three significant emperors: Augustus, Tiberius, and Caligula. For our purpose here, we are particularly interested in his letters, which were published; i.e., someone paid to have a scribe produce a copy of them. As was the case with many antiquity works, the process was repeated frequently throughout the centuries. Today, we have critical editions of them.

Our other source for insight into the development of the letter-writing process is found in ordinary people's letters, uncovered by archaeologists. These were never published, as they were simply discarded after they served their purpose. In many cases, in order to save costs, these writers would

---

[100] Retrieved Tuesday, March 26, 2019 (Larry Hurtado's Blog Comments on the New Testament and Early Christianity (and related matters)

https://larryhurtado.wordpress.com/2018/11/01/literacies-in-the-roman-world/

[101] Craig A. Evans, *JESUS AND HIS WORLD: The Archaeological Evidence* (Louisville, KY: Westminster John Knox Press, 2012), Loc. 1403-1406, KDP.

[102] A rhetorician is a speaker whose words are primarily intended to impress or persuade.

simply flip a letter over and use the other side for something else. Many such letters ended up in the garbage dumps. However, some recipients of these letters valued them, so they stored them as though they were a treasure. Therefore, when archaeologists uncovered homes, these letters would be found within the ruins of the home.

In some cases, they were even buried with the deceased because they were so valued. Hundreds of thousands of letters have been discovered over the past century by archaeologists. These were the work of ordinary folk, writing about everyday things. On the subjects of an empire learning a language so as not to be exploited by a powerful kingdom, Gregory Wolf writes,

> This is wonderfully illustrated by the Roman Empire by the personal archive of the Jewish woman named Babatha, found in the Cave of Letters on the shore of the Dead Sea and dating to the early second century C.E.[103] Babatha's papers comprised thirty-five documents written in Greek, Nabatean, and Aramaic or a mixture of these languages, with occasional transliterated Latin terms for Roman institutions. The archive included documents relating to the sale of land, dates and probably also wine, various marriage contracts and probably details of a dowry, a bequest, a court summons, various notices of deposits and loans, a court summons and a deposition, petitions, and an extract from the minutes of the council of Petra relating to the guardianship of her son. Much of this was generated by private transactions-both commercial and disputes arising from her complicated family life. But it was the recourse to law, and to civic and provincial administration, that generated this mass of material, which she kept with her until her death in the disturbances arising from the Bar Kokhba war.[104]

Most of us have heard of Marcus Tullius Cicero, or simply Cicero (106 B.C.E. – 43 B.C.E.), a Roman philosopher, politician, lawyer, orator, political theorist, consul, and constitutionalist. He came from a wealthy municipal family in Rome. In his everyday affairs, he penned letters to correspond with others. However, while Cicero was writing letters to one person, he knew that others would also be reading them. Therefore, he took advantage of these opportunities to use writing to communicate points persuasively, using

---

[103] N. Lewis 1989.

[104] William A Johnson; Holt N Parker. Ancient Literacies: The Culture of Reading in Greece and Rome (Kindle Locations 655-659). Kindle Edition.

logic and reason, philosophical arguments, and the like. His letters grew from concise messages to far longer, intricate rhetorical notes.

We find yet another famous Roman named Seneca in the days of the apostle Paul. He was the second son of Seneca the Elder. Lucius Annaeus Seneca, or simply **Seneca the Younger** (c. 4 B.C.E. – 65 C.E.), was a Roman Stoic philosopher, statesman, and dramatist, i.e., a very famous, skilled, and compelling, and competent speaker. As for written works, Seneca is known for twelve philosophical essays, 124 letters to Lucilius Junior, nine tragedies, and an uncertain satire. Seneca was a representative of the Silver Age of Latin literature. In his letters to his friend Lucilius, dealing with moral issues, he delved into philosophical ideas, setting aside the straightforward and bare letters of the day for something far more complex.

As we have seen, the apostle Paul used personal letters and letter carriers as a substitute until he could visit churches and key people. He produced through his scribe Tertius 433 verses, 7,111 words in the book of Romans, which would have taken two days to copy. Like the skilled rhetoricians before him, Paul knew that many others would be reading his letters. In fact, he urged them to do so. – Colossians 4:16.

We should note that the level of literacy in the first century is a somewhat subjective measurement because of the limited available evidence and one's interpretation of that evidence. Consider as an analogy the historian today compared to the historian during the first few centuries of Christianity. Today, we can cover almost anything that goes on in life, from the most insignificant to the most noteworthy. In the United States, we may watch live on television or a laptop as some firefighters in New Zealand rescue a puppy trapped in a storm drain. Then again, we can observe a 9.0 earthquake as it hits Japan, causing the deaths of over 15,000 people.

What about the first few centuries of Jesus, the apostles, and the earliest Christians? The coverage of people, places, and events is not even remotely comparable. The range of coverage at that time was of the most prominent people, like Seneca the Elder, Cicero, Seneca the Younger, Mark Antony, and Augustus, i.e., the emperor of Rome, senators, generals, the wealthy, with very little press being given to the lower officials, let alone the lower class. We do not have much information on Pontius Pilate at all, but what we do have is an exception to the rule.

History from antiquity, then, is recoverable but incomplete due to the limited extent and frequently tendentious nature of the sources. Ancient historiography, more than its modern counterpart, is to a greater degree approximate or provisional. A new discovery may alter previous perceptions. Until the discovery of Claudius's Letter to the Alexandrians, written on his accession in 41 but lost until modern times, that emperor's steely resolve could not have been guessed. In short, evidence from Greco-Roman antiquity is fragmentary, generally devoted to "important" people and events and its texts overtly "interpreted."[105]

According to E. Randolf Richards, literacy in the first century was determined by reading, not writing.[106] The need for writing today is far greater than antiquity. Richards offers an excellent analogy when he says, "I am right handed, so to pen a long paper with my left hand would be quite difficult, and not very legible. The man of antiquity would write with the same difficulty because the need to write was so seldom."[107] This author finds this to be true of himself, now that we have entered an era of texting and typing. I have not written a paper by hand in many years. When I fill out a form or even sign my name, I struggle to write because it is seldom required. Many have argued that the lower class of antiquity was almost entirely illiterate. However, recent research shows that this was not the case,[108] as literacy was more of an everyday need than they had thought.[109]

Richard's definition of literacy is too simplistic because defining literacy among historians has been plagued by many different definitions. It is also relative to the person determining how the word should be defined. For some historians of the first three centuries of Christianity under the Roman Empire, literacy could refer to any ancient person who merely could write one's name. For another, as Richard's suggested, it might be one who can read but cannot write. Then, again, it could be a semiliterate writer who is untrained in writing but could prepare short documents, to a literate writer who has had experience in making lengthy documents and understands what he is writing, to the professional who is paid to write for others. The literacy

---

[105] Paul Barnett, *The Birth of Christianity: The First Twenty Years* (After Jesus, Vol. 1) Grand Rapids, MI: Wm. B. Eerdmans, 2005, 13.

[106] E. Randolph Richards, *PAUL AND FIRST-CENTURY LETTER WRITING: Secretaries, Composition and Collection* (Downers Grove, IL: IVP Academic, 2004), 28.

[107] E. Randolph Richards, *PAUL AND FIRST-CENTURY LETTER WRITING: Secretaries, Composition and Collection* (Downers Grove, IL: IVP Academic, 2004), 28.

[108] "Throughout the Hellenistic and Roman world the distinction prevailed in that there were educated people who were proficient readers and writers, less educated ones who could read but hardly write, some who were readers alone, some of them only able to read slowly or with difficulty and some who were illiterate." – Millard, Alan Reading and Writing in the Time of Jesus (Sheffield, Sheffield Academic Press, 2000), p. 154

[109] Exler, Form. P. 126 warns, "The papyri discovered in Egypt have shown that the art of writing was more widely, and more popularly, known in the past, than some scholars have been inclined to think." For example, see PZen. 6, 66, POxy. 113,294, 394, 528, 530, 531 and especially 3057.

levels that were laid out at the beginning of this chapter cover the different levels of literacy in early Christianity.

In passing, I will mention something that few Christian historians or textual scholars will address, **the gift of languages**. An extraordinary gift conveyed through the Holy Spirit to a number of disciples starting at Pentecost 33 C.E. that made it possible for them to speak or otherwise glorify God in a tongue in addition to their own that they had never known prior to being given this gift. Therefore, Christians would have been greatly appreciative of the ability to be miraculously able to speak a foreign language in the Roman Empire. In conjunction with this, we must also remember that Christianity grew out of a melting pot of languages: Hebrew, Aramaic, Greek, Latin, Coptic, and Syriac (an Aramaic dialect). Thus, when we think about it, the first and second century Jewish Christians **in Palestine** may be quite familiar with Hebrew, Greek, and even Aramaic but be illiterate when it comes to Latin. On the other hand, the Gentile Christian may be very familiar with Greek, somewhat familiar with Hebrew, and a little familiar with Aramaic but possess the fundamental ability to understand spoken words and have an elementary grasp of written words when it comes to Latin. Then, **in Rome**, the Gentile and Jewish Christians might be literate when it comes to Latin and be quite familiar with Greek, yet be wholly illiterate when it comes to Hebrew and Aramaic.

Even though Greek was very much used **in Egypt**, the need to have a translation in the native language of the growing Egyptian Christian population would come. Coptic was a later form of the ancient Egyptian language. In the late first or early second century C.E., a Coptic alphabet was developed using somewhat modified Greek letters (majuscules and seven characters from the demotic,[110] representing Egyptian sounds the Greek language did not have). At least by the end of the second or the beginning of the third century (c. 200 C.E.), translators produced the first translation of parts of the New Testament, which was published for Egypt's Coptic natives. Various Coptic dialects were used in Egypt, and in time, the Egyptian Christians had different Coptic versions made. Therefore, In the Egyptian part of the Roman Empire, the Christian may be literate in Coptic but struggles with Greek. And whether the Egyptian Christian is Gentile or Jew, he may or may not have any working knowledge when it comes to Hebrew or Aramaic.

Syria was a region with Mesopotamia to its East, with the Lebanon Mountains on the West, the Taurus Mountains to its North, Palestine, and

---

[110] Demotic is a simplified form of Egyptian hieroglyphics. Hieroglyphics is a writing system that uses symbols or pictures to denote objects, concepts, or sounds.

the Arabian Desert to its south. Syria played a very prominent role in the early growth of Christianity. The city of Antioch in Syria was the third-largest city in the Roman Empire. Luke tells us of "those who were scattered because of the persecution that occurred in connection with Stephen [shortly after Pentecost, yet just before the conversion of Paul in 34 or 35 C.E.] made their way to Phoenicia and Cyprus and **Antioch**, speaking the word to no one except to Jews alone. But there were some of them, men of Cyprus and Cyrene, **who came to Antioch** [of Syria] and began speaking to the Greeks also, preaching the Lord Jesus." (Ac 11:19-20, bold mine) Because of the thriving interest of the Gospel manifested in Antioch, where many Greek-speaking people were becoming believers, the apostles in Jerusalem sent Barnabas. He then called Paul in from Tarsus to help. (Ac 11:21-26) Both Barnabas and Paul remained there for a year, teaching the people. Antioch became the center for the apostle Paul's missionary journeys.

Also, "the disciples were first called Christians in Antioch." (Ac 11:26) While the New Testament letters were written in Koine Greek, the universal language of the Roman Empire, Latin being the official language, it was thought best to **translate the New Testament books into Syriac in mid-second century C.E.** as Christianity spread throughout the rest of Syria.

However, for the sake of discussion, let us assume that literacy was very low among the lower class and even relatively low among the upper class, who had the ability to pay for the service. What does this say about individual Christians throughout the Roman Empire? It is believed that more than 30–40 million people lived in the combined eastern and western Roman Empire (50–200 C.E.). Now, assume that the literacy rate is statistically low in a specific area or a particular city, like Rome (slave population). Does this mean that everyone is illiterate in that region or city? Do we equate the two? If we accept the belief that the lower class were likely to be illiterate, meaning that they could not write or struggled to write, what does this really mean for individuals or Christianity? Very little, because if 40-100 million people live throughout the Roman Empire and one million were Christians by 125-150 C.E., we are only referring to one or two percent of the population. There is no way to arrive at a specific statistical level of literacy for this small selection in a time when history focused on the prominent. If a person from that period said anything about the lower class, this was only based on the sphere of whom he knew or what he had seen in his life. This would be very limited when compared to the whole. The last 20 years or so have seen many new directions in the field of literacy in the ancient world. Johnson and Parker offer the following.

> The moment seems right, therefore, to try to formulate more interesting, productive ways of talking about the conception and

construction of 'literacies' in the ancient world—literacy not in the sense of whether 10 percent or 30 percent of people in the ancient world could read or write, but in the sense of text-oriented events embedded in particular sociocultural contexts. The volume in your hands [*ANCIENT LITERACIES*] was constructed as a forum in which selected leading scholars were challenged to rethink from the ground up how students of classical antiquity might best approach the question of literacy, and how that investigation might materially intersect with changes in the way that literacy is now viewed in other disciplines. The result is intentionally pluralistic: theoretical reflections, practical demonstrations, and combinations of the two share equal space in the effort to chart a new course. Readers will come away, with food for thought of many types: new ways of thinking about specific elements of literacy in antiquity, such as the nature of personal libraries, or the place and function of bookshops in antiquity; new constructivist questions, such as what constitutes reading communities and how they fashion themselves; new takes on the public sphere, such how literacy intersects with commercialism, or with the use of public spaces, or with the construction of civic identity; new essentialist questions, such as what "book" and "reading" signify in antiquity, why literate cultures develop, or why literate cultures matter.[111]

Books, Reading, and Writing; Literacy and Early Jewish Education

The priests of Israel (Num. 5:23) and leading persons, such as Moses (Ex. 24:4), Joshua (Josh. 24:26), Samuel (1 Sam 10:25), David (2 Sam. 11:14-15), and Jehu (2 Ki 10:1, 6), were capable of reading and writing. The Israelite people themselves generally could read and write, with few exceptions. (Judges 8:14; Isa. 10:19; 29:12) Even though Deuteronomy 6:8-9 is used figuratively, the command to write the words of the Law on the doorposts of their house and their gates implied that they were literate. Yes, it is true that even though Hebrew written material was fairly common, few Israelite inscriptions have been discovered. One reason for this is that the Israelites did not set up many monuments to admire their accomplishments. Thus, most of the writing, including the thirty-nine Hebrew Old Testament books of the Bible, was primarily done with ink on papyrus or parchment. Most did not survive the damp soil of Palestine. Nevertheless, the Hebrew Old

---

[111] William A. Johnson; Holt N. Parker, *Ancient Literacies: The Culture of Reading in Greece and Rome* (Oxford, United Kingdom: Oxford University Press, 2011), 3-4.

Testament Scriptures were preserved by careful, meticulous copying and recopying throughout the centuries.

During the first seven years of Christianity (29 – 36 C.E.), three and a half with Jesus' ministry and three and a half after his ascension, only Jewish people became disciples of Christ and formed the newly founded Christian congregation. In 36 C.E., the first gentile was baptized: Cornelius.[112] From that time forward, Gentiles came into the Christian congregations. However, the church still mainly consisted of Jewish converts. What do we know of the Jewish family as far as their education? Within the nation of Israel, everyone was strongly encouraged to be literate. Again, the texts of Deuteronomy 6:8-9 and 11:20 were figurative (not to be taken literally). However, we are to ascertain what was meant by the figurative language, and that meaning is what we take literally.

Deuteronomy 6:8-9 Updated American Standard Version (UASV)

[8] You shall bind them [God's Word] as a sign on your hand and they shall be as frontlets bands between your eyes.[113] [9] You shall write them on the doorposts of your house and on your gates.

Deuteronomy 11:20 Updated American Standard Version (UASV)

[20] You shall write them on the doorposts of your house and on your gates,

The command to bind God's Word "as a sign on your hand" denoted constant remembrance and attention. The command that the Word of God was "to be as frontlet bands between your eyes" meant that the Law should be kept before their eyes constantly, so that wherever they looked, whatever was before them, they would see the law before them. They would be biblically minded, that is, having a biblical worldview. Therefore, while figurative, these texts implied that Jewish children grew up being taught how to read and write. The Gezer Calendar (ancient Hebrew writing), dated to the 10th-century B.C.E., is believed by some scholars to be a schoolboy's memory exercise.

The Jewish author Philo of Alexandria (20 B.C.E.–50 C. E.), a Hellenistic Jewish philosopher whose first language was Greek, had this to say about Jewish parents and how they taught their Children the Law and how to read it. Philo stated, "All men guard their own customs, but this is especially true of the Jewish nation. Holding that the laws are oracles

---

[112] Cornelius was a centurion, an army officer in charge of a unit of foot soldiers, i.e., in command of 100 soldiers of the Italian band.

[113] I.e. on your forehead

vouchsafed by God and having been trained [*paideuthentes*] in this doctrine from their earliest years, they carry the likenesses of the commandments enshrined in their souls."[114] This certainly involved the ability to read and write at a competent level. Philo also wrote, "for parents, thinking but little of their own advantage, think the virtue and excellence of their children the perfection of their own happiness, for which reason it is that they are anxious that they should obey the injunctions which are laid upon them, and that they should be obedient to all just and beneficial commands; for a father will never teach his child anything which is inconsistent with virtue or with truth."[115] Again, it needs to be repeated that in the nation of Israel, some 1,550 years before Philo, everyone was strongly encouraged to be literate. (Deut. 4:9; 6:7, 20, 21; 11:19-21; Ps 78:1-4) The father to the children and prophets, Levites, especially the priests, and other wise men served as teachers. Fathers taught their sons a trade, while mothers taught their daughters domestic skills. Fathers also taught their children the geography of their land, as well as the rich history. Philo informs us of the Jewish people of his day, saying that it is the father, who is responsible for educating the children academically, philosophically, physically, as well as moral instruction and discipline.

Josephus (37 – 100 C.E.), the first-century Jewish historian, writes, "Our principle care of all is this, to educate our children well; and we think it to be the most necessary business of our whole life to observe the laws that have been given us, and to keep those rules of piety that have been delivered down to us."[116] Even allowing for an overemphasis for apologetic purposes; clearly, Jesus was carefully grounded in the Word of God (Hebrew Old Testament), as was true of other Jews of the time. Josephus also says, "but for our people, if anybody do but ask any one of them about our laws, he will more readily tell them all than he will tell his own name, and this in consequence of our having learned them immediately as soon as ever we became sensible of anything, and of our having them, as it were engraven on our souls. Our transgressors of them are but few; and it is impossible, when any do offend, to escape punishment."[117] He also says: "[the Law] also commands us to bring those children up in learning [*grammata paideuein*] and to exercise them in the laws, and make them acquainted with the acts of their predecessors, in order to their imitation of them, and that they may be

---

[114] Peder Borgen, *Philo of Alexandria: An Exegete for His Time* (Leiden, Boston: Brill, 1997), 187.

[115] Charles Duke Yonge with Philo of Alexandria, *The Works of Philo: Complete and Unabridged* (Peabody, MA: Hendrickson, 1995), 590–591.

[116] Flavius Josephus and William Whiston, *The Works of Josephus: Complete and Unabridged* (Peabody: Hendrickson, 1987), 777.

[117] Flavius Josephus and William Whiston, *The Works of Josephus: Complete and Unabridged* (Peabody: Hendrickson, 1987), 805.

nourished up in the laws from their infancy, and might neither transgress them, nor yet have any pretense for their ignorance of them."[118] Again, this clearly involves, at a minimum, the ability to read and write at a competent level.

From the above, we find that the Jewish family education revolved around studying the Mosaic Law. If their children were going to live by the Law, they needed to know what it says, as well as understand it. If they were going to know and understand the Law, this would require reading it and hopefully applying it. Emil Schurer writes: "All zeal for education in the family, the school and the synagogue aimed at making *the whole people a people of the law.* The common man too was to know what the law commanded, and not only to know but to do it. His whole life was to be ruled according to the norm of the law; obedience thereto was to become a fixed custom, and departure therefrom an inward impossibility. On the whole this object was to a great degree attained."[119] Scott writes that "from at least the time of Ezra's reading of the law (Neh. 8), education was a public process; study of the law was the focus of Jewish society as a whole. It was a lifelong commitment to all men. It began with the very young. The Mishnah[120] requires that children be taught 'therein one year or two years before [they are of age], that they may become versed in the commandments.' Other sources set different ages for beginning formal studies, some as early as five years."[121]

It may be that both Philo and Josephus are presenting their readers with an idyllic picture, and what they have to say could possibly refer primarily to wealthy Jewish families who could afford formal education. However, this would be shortsighted, for the Israelites had long been a people who valued the ability to read and write competently. In the apocryphal account of 4 Maccabees 18:10-19, a mother addresses her seven sons, who would be martyred, reminding them of their father's teaching. There is nothing in the account to suggest that they were from a wealthy family. Herein the mother referred to numerous historical characters throughout the Old

---

[118] Flavius Josephus and William Whiston, *The Works of Josephus: Complete and Unabridged* (Peabody: Hendrickson, 1987), 807.

[119] Emil Schürer, *A History of the Jewish People in the Time of Jesus Christ, Second Division.*, vol. 4 (Edinburgh: T&T Clark, 1890), 89–90.

[120] The Mishnah was the primary body of Jewish civil and religious law, forming the first part of the Talmud.

[121] Mishnah *Yoma* 8:4

Julius J. Scott Jr., *Jewish Backgrounds of the New Testament* (Grand Rapids, MI: Baker Academic, 1995), 257.

Testament and quoted from multiple books – Isaiah 43.2; Psalm 34:19; Proverbs 3:18; Ezekiel 37:3; Deuteronomy 32:39.

Jesus would have received his education from three sources. As was made clear from the above, Joseph, Jesus' stepfather, would have played a major role in his education. Paul said that young Timothy was trained in "the sacred writings" by his mother, Eunice, and his grandmother Lois. (2 Tim. 1:5; 3:15) Certainly, if Timothy received education in the law from his mother because his father was a Greek (Acts 16:1), no doubt Jesus did as well after Joseph died.

Jesus would have also received education in the Scriptures from the attendant at the synagogue. In the first-century C.E., the synagogue was a place of instruction, not a place of sacrifices. The people carried out their sacrifices to God at the temple. The exercises within the synagogue covered such areas as praise, prayer, and recitation, and reading of the Scriptures, in addition to expository preaching. – Mark 12:40; Luke 20:47

> Before any instruction in the holy laws and unwritten customs are taught... from their swaddling clothes by parents and teachers and educators to believe in God, the one Father, and Creator of the world. (Philo *Legatio ad Gaium* 115.)

The Mishnah tells us the age that this formal instruction would have begun, "At five years old one is fit for the scripture... at thirteen for the commandments." (Mishnah *Abot* 5.21.) Luke 4:20 tells of the time Jesus stood to read from the scroll of Isaiah in the synagogue in Nazareth, and once finished, "he rolled up the scroll and gave it back to the attendant." An attendant such as this one would have educated Jesus, starting at the age of five. As Jesus grew up in Nazareth, he "increased in wisdom and in stature and in favor with God and man." (Lu 2:52) Jesus and his half-brothers and sisters would have been known to the people of the city of Nazareth, which was nothing more than a village in Jesus' day. "As was his custom, [Jesus] went to the synagogue on the Sabbath day," each week. (Matt. 13:55, 56; Lu. 4:16) While Jesus would have been an exceptional student, unlike anything that the Nazareth synagogue would have ever seen, we must keep in mind that the disciples would have been going through similar experiences as they grew up in Galilee. Great emphasis was laid on the need for every Jew to have an accurate knowledge of the Law. Josephus wrote,

> for he [God] did not suffer the guilt of ignorance to go on without punishment, but demonstrated the law to be the best and the most necessary instruction of all others, permitting the people to leave off their other employments, and to assemble together for the hearing of the law, and learning it exactly, and this not once or

twice, or oftener, but every week; which thing all the other legislators seem to have neglected."[122]

The high priest questioned Jesus about his disciples and his teaching. Jesus answered him, "I have spoken openly to the world. I have always taught in synagogues and in the temple, where all Jews come together. I have said nothing in secret." (John 18:19-20) We know that another source of knowledge and wisdom of Jesus came from the Father. Jesus said, "My teaching is not mine, but his who sent me," i.e., the Father. – John 7:16

Mark 1:22 Updated American Standard Version (UASV)	Mark 1:27 Updated American Standard Version (UASV)
22 And they were **astounded**[123] **at his teaching**, for he taught them as **one who had authority**, and not as the scribes.	27 And they were all **astonished**,[124] so that they questioned among themselves, saying, "What is this? A new teaching **with authority**! ..."

At first, in the days of Ezra and Nehemiah, the priests served as scribes. (Ezra 7:1-6) The scribes referred to here in the Gospel of Mark are more than copyists of Scripture. They were professionally trained scholars who were experts in the Mosaic Law. As was said above, a great emphasis was laid on the need for every Jew to have an accurate knowledge of the Law. Therefore, those who gave a great deal of their life and time to acquire an immense amount of knowledge were admired, becoming scholars, forming a group separate from the priests, creating a systematic study of the law, as well as its exposition, which became a professional occupation. By the time of Jesus, these scribes were experts in more than the Mosaic Law (entire Old Testament actually) as they became experts on the previous experts from centuries past, quoting them in addition to quoting Scripture. This is like an attorney in the United States citing the United States Supreme Court case law before a judge. In other words, if there was any Scriptural decision to be made, these scribes quoted previous experts in the law, i.e., their comments on the law, as opposed to quoting applicable Scripture itself. The scribes were among the "teachers of the law," also referred to as "lawyers." (Lu 5:17;

---

[122] Flavius Josephus and William Whiston, *The Works of Josephus: Complete and Unabridged* (Peabody: Hendrickson, 1987), 805.

[123] **Astounded**: (Gr. *ekplēssō*) This is one who is extremely astounded or amazed, so much so that they lose their mental self-control, as they are overwhelmed emotionally.–Matt. 7:28; Mark 1:22; 7:37; Lu 2:48; 4:32; 9:43; Ac 13:12.

[124] **Astonished**: (Gr. *thambeō;* derivative of *thambos*) This is one who is experiencing astonishment, to be astounded, or amazed as a result of some sudden and unusual event, which can be in a positive or negative sense.–Mark 1:27; 10:32; Lu 4:36; 5:9; Acts 3:10.

11:45) The people were **astonished** and **amazed** at Jesus' **teaching** and **authority** because he did not quote previous teachers of the law but rather referred to Scripture alone as his authority, along with his exposition.

Jesus' Childhood Visits to Jerusalem

Only one event from Jesus' childhood is given to us, and it is found in the Gospel of Luke. It certainly adds weighty circumstantial evidence to the fact that Jesus could read and, therefore, was literate.

Luke 2:41-47 Updated American Standard Version (UASV)

[41] Now His parents went to Jerusalem every year at the Feast of the Passover. [42] And <u>when he [Jesus] was twelve years old</u>, they went up according to the custom of the feast. [43] And after the days were completed, while they were returning, the boy Jesus stayed behind in Jerusalem. And his parents did not know it, [44] but supposing him to be in the company, they went a day's journey; and they began looking for him among their relatives and acquaintances, [45] and when they did not find him, they returned to Jerusalem, looking for him. [46] Then, it occurred, after three days they <u>found him in the temple</u>, sitting in the midst of the teachers and **listening** to them and **questioning them**. [47] And all those listening to him were **amazed at his understanding** and his answers.

This was no 12-year-old boy's questions of curiosity. The Greek indicates that Jesus, at the age of twelve, did not ask childlike questions, looking for answers, but was likely challenging the thinking of these Jewish religious leaders.

This incident is far more magnificent than one might first realize. Kittel's *Theological Dictionary of the New Testament* helps the reader to appreciate that the Greek word *eperotao* (to ask, to question, to demand of), for "questioning" was far more than the Greek word erotao (to ask, to request, to entreat), for a boy's curiosity. *Eperotao* can refer to questioning, which one might hear in a judicial hearing, such as a scrutiny, inquiry, counter questioning, even the "probing and cunning questions of the Pharisees and Sadducees," for instance, those we find at Mark 10:2 and 12:18-23.

The same dictionary continues: "In [the] face of this usage it may be asked whether . . . [Luke] 2:46 denotes, not so much the questioning curiosity of the boy, but rather His successful disputing. [Verse] 47 would fit in well with the latter view." Rotherham's translation of verse 47 presents it as a dramatic confrontation: "Now all who heard him were beside themselves, because of his understanding and his answers." Robertson's Word Pictures in the New Testament says that their constant amazement means, "they stood out of themselves as if their eyes were bulging out."

After returning to Jerusalem, and after three days of searching, Joseph and Mary found young Jesus in the temple, questioning the Jewish religious leaders, at which "they were astounded." (Luke 2:48) Robertson said of this, "second aorist passive indicative of an old Greek word [*ekplesso*]), to strike out, drive out by a blow. Joseph and Mary 'were struck out' by what they saw and heard. Even they had not fully realized the power in this wonderful boy."[125] Thus, at twelve years old, Jesus, only a boy, is already evidencing that he is a great teacher and defender of truth. BDAG says, "to cause to be filled with amazement to the point of being overwhelmed, amaze, astound, overwhelm (literally, Strike out of one's senses).[126]

Some 18 years later, Jesus again confronted the Pharisees with these types of interrogative questions, so much so that not "anyone [of them] dare from that day on to ask him any more questions." (Matthew 22:41-46) The Sadducees fared no better when Jesus responded to them on the subject of the resurrection: "And no one dared to ask him any more questions." (Luke 20:27-40) The scribes were silenced just the same after they got into an exchange with Jesus: "And from then on no one dared ask him any more questions." (Mark 12:28-34) Clearly, this insight into Jesus' life and ministry provides us with evidence that he could read very well and likely write. There is the fact that Jesus was also divine. However, he was also fully human, and he grew, progressing in wisdom, because of his studies in the Scriptures.

Luke 2:40, 51-52 Updated American Standard Version (UASV)

[40] And the child continued growing and became strong, **being filled with wisdom**. And the favor of God was upon him. [51] And he went down with them and came to Nazareth, and he continued in subjection to them; and his mother treasured all these things in her heart. [52] And Jesus kept **increasing in wisdom** and stature, and in favor with God and men.

Jesus was often called "Rabbi," which was used in a real or genuine sense as "teacher." (Mark 9:5; 11:21; 14:45; John 1:38, 49 etc.) We find "*Rabbo(u)ni*" (Mark 10:51; John 20:16) as well as its Greek equivalents, "schoolmaster" or "instructor" (*epistata*; Luke 5:5; 8:24, 45; 9:33, 49; 17:13) or "teacher" (*didaskalos*; Matt. 8:19; 9:11; 12:38; Mark 4:38; 5:35; 9:17; 10:17, 20; 12:14, 19, 32; Luke 19:39; John 1:38; 3:2). Jesus used these same terms

---

[125] A.T. Robertson, Word Pictures in the New Testament (Nashville, TN: Broadman Press, 1933), Lk 2:48.

[126] William Arndt, Frederick W. Danker and Walter Bauer, A Greek-English Lexicon of the New Testament and Other Early Christian Literature, 3rd ed. (Chicago: University of Chicago Press, 2000), 308.

for himself, as did his disciples, even his adversaries, and those with no affiliation.

Another inference that Jesus was literate comes from his constant reference to reading Scripture when confronted by the Jewish religious leaders: law students, Pharisees, Scribes, and the Sadducees. Jesus said, "**Have you not read** what David did when he was hungry, and those who were with him ... Or **have you not read in the Law** how on the Sabbath the priests in the temple profane the Sabbath and are guiltless? (Matt. 12:3, 5; reference to 1 Sam 21:6 and Num 28:9) Again, Jesus responded, "**Have you not read** that he who created them from the beginning made them male and female." (Matt. 19:3; a paraphrase of Gen 1:27) Jesus said to them, "Yes; **have you never read**, "'Out of the mouth of infants and nursing babies you have prepared praise'?" (Matt. 21:16; quoting Psa. 8:2) Jesus said to them, "**Have you never read in the Scriptures**: "'The stone that the builders rejected has become the cornerstone; this was the Lord's doing, and it is marvelous in our eyes'? (Matt. 21:42; Reference to Isaiah 28:16) Jesus said to him, "**What is written in the Law? How do you read it**?" (Lu. 10:26) Many of Jesus' references or Scripture quotations were asked in such a way to his opponents; there is little doubt Jesus himself had read them. When Jesus asked in an interrogative way, "have you not read," it was taken for granted that he had read them. Jesus referred to or quoted over 120 Scriptures in the dialogue that we have in the Gospels.

> The data that have been surveyed are more easily explained in reference to a literate Jesus, a Jesus who could read the Hebrew Scriptures, could paraphrase and interpret them in Aramaic and could do so in a manner that indicated his familiarity with current interpretive tendencies in both popular circles (as in the synagogues) and in professional, even elite circles (as seen in debates with scribes, ruling priests and elders). Of course, to conclude that Jesus was literate is not necessarily to conclude that Jesus had received formal scribal training. The data do not suggest this. Jesus' innovative, experiential approach to Scripture and to Jewish faith seems to suggest the contrary.[127]

How did Jesus gain such wisdom? Jesus, although divine, was not born with this exceptional wisdom that he demonstrated at the age of twelve and kept increasing. It was acquired. (Deut. 17:18-19) This extraordinary wisdom was no exception to the norm, not even for the Son of God himself. (Luke 2:52) Jesus' knowledge was acquired by his studying the Hebrew Old

---

[127] Craig A. Evans, *JESUS AND HIS WORLD: The Archaeological Evidence* (Louisville, KY: Westminster John Knox Press, 2012), Loc. 1872.

Testament, enabling him to challenge the thinking of the Jewish religious leaders with his questions at the age of twelve. Therefore, Jesus had to be very familiar with the Hebrew Old Testament and the skill of reasoning from the Scriptures.

Books, Reading, and Writing; the Literacy Level of the Apostle Peter and John

Acts 4:13 Updated American Standard Version (UASV)	Acts 4:13 New American Standard Bible (NASB)
[13] Now when they saw the boldness of Peter and John, and perceived that **they were <u>uneducated</u>[128]** and untrained men, they were astonished, and they recognized that they had been with Jesus.	[13] Now as they observed the confidence of Peter and John and understood that **they were <u>uneducated</u> and untrained men**, they were amazed, and *began* to recognize them as having been with Jesus.

How are we to understand the statement that Peter and John **were uneducated**? (ESV, NASB, HCSB, LEB, UASV, and others) [*unlettered* (YLT) or *unlearned* (ASV)] This did not necessarily mean that they could not read and write, as the letters that were penned by these apostles (or their secretaries) testify that they could. This means that they were not educated in higher learning of the Hebrew schools, such as studying under someone like Gamaliel, as was the case with apostle Paul (Ac 5:34-39; 22:3).[129] The Greek words literally read καταλαβομενοι [having perceived] οτι [that] ανθρωποι [men] αγραμματοι [unlettered] εισιν [they are] και [and] ιδιωται [untrained]. This means that the disciples were not educated in rabbinic schools. It did not mean that they were illiterate. In other words, they lacked scribal training. In addition, ιδιωται [untrained], simply means that in comparison to professionally trained scribes of their day, they were not specialists, i.e., were not trained or expert in the scribal duties. This hardly constitutes the idea that they were illiterate.

It was the same reason that the Jewish religious leaders were surprised by the extensive knowledge that Jesus had. They said of him, "How is it that this man has learning when he has never studied?" (John 7:15) This is our best Scriptural evidence that Jesus could read. Let us break it down to what the religious leaders were really saying of Jesus. They asked πως [how] ουτος [this one] γραμματα [letters/writings] οιδεν [has known] μη [not] μεμαθηκως

---

[128] Or *unlettered* (YLT) that is, not educated in the rabbinic schools; not meaning illiterate.

[129] Gamaliel was a Pharisee and a leading authority in the Sanhedrin, as well as a teacher of the law, of which Acts says, Paul was "educated at the feet of Gamaliel according to the strict manner of the law of our fathers." (Ac 22:3)

[have learned]. First, this is a reference to the fact that Jesus did not study at the Hebrew schools, i.e., scribal training. In other words, 'how does this one [Jesus] have knowledge of letters/writings, when he has not studied at the Hebrew schools. This question means more than Jesus' ability to read because Jewish children were taught to read, as we saw above.

Another example is Luke 4:16-30, which says that he "came to Nazareth, where he had been brought up. And as was his custom, he went to the synagogue on the Sabbath day, and he stood up to read. And the scroll of the prophet Isaiah was given to him. He unrolled the scroll and found ..." (Lu 4:16-17) Jesus was able to take the scroll of Isaiah and read what is now known as Isaiah 61:1-2. While the parallel account in Mark 6:1-6 does not refer to Jesus reading this text, scholars have long known that the gospel writers shared the events through their separate viewpoints, i.e., they drew attention to what stood out to them and what served their purpose for writing their Gospel accounts.

From the first to the fourth century, we find public writings in and throughout all cities within the Roman Empire. It encompasses inscriptions, which are "dedications, lists of names, imperial decrees, statements or reminders of law, quotations of famous men, and even rather pedestrian things, such as directions. Many gravestones and tombs are inscribed with more than the deceased's name; some have lengthy, even poetic obituaries; others have threats and curses against grave robbers (literate ones, evidently!). The impression one gains is that everybody was expected to be able to read; otherwise, what was the point of all of these expensive inscriptions, incised on stone?"[130] This impression does not end with inscriptions because archaeology can conclude that between the fourth and sixth centuries C.E., hundreds upon hundreds of thousands of documents came out of Oxyrhynchus, just one city, based on the more than 500 thousand documents found in their garbage dumps. Of these, five hundred thousand documents, they were discovered in the first three meters that ran nine meters deep, as the bottom six meters the sand was damp from the seepage from a nearby canal. We could extrapolate that if all nine meters were salvageable, we might have 1.5 million documents available to us.

The **Library of Celsus** (45 – ca. 120 C.E.) is an ancient Roman building in Ephesus (completed in 135 C.E.) containing 12,000 scrolls. The library was also built as a monumental tomb for Celsus. He is buried in a stone coffin beneath the library. The **Ancient Library of Alexandria**, Egypt (third-century to 30 B.C.E.), was one of the largest and most significant libraries of

[130] Craig A. Evans, *JESUS AND HIS WORLD: The Archaeological Evidence* (Louisville, KY: Westminster John Knox Press, 2012), Loc. 1418, KDP.

the ancient world. Most of the books were kept as papyrus scrolls. King Ptolemy II Philadelphus (309 – 246 B.C.E.) is believed to have set 500,000 scrolls as a library goal. Apparently, by the first century C.E., the library contained one million scrolls. The **Library of Pergamum** (Asia Minor) was one of the most important libraries in the ancient world. It is said to have housed roughly 200,000 volumes. Historical records say that the library had a large central reading room. We have not even mentioned Rome, Athens, Corinth, Antioch (Syria), and the rest. The Mediterranean world from Alexander the Great (356 – 323 B.C.E.) to Constantine the Great (272-337 C.E.), some 700 years, saw hundreds of major libraries and thousands of moderate to minor ones, with hundreds of millions of documents being written and read. Indeed, this does not suggest illiteracy but literacy.

Some point out that "Celsus,[131] the first writer against Christianity, makes it a matter of mockery, that labourers, shoemakers, farmers, the most uninformed and clownish of men, should be zealous preachers of the Gospel."[132] Paul explained it this way: "For consider your calling, brothers: not many of you were wise according to worldly standards, not many were powerful, not many were of noble birth. But God chose what is foolish in the world to shame the wise; God chose what is weak in the world to shame the strong." (1 Cor. 1:26-27) It seems that these so-called illiterate Christians, which they were not, were able to grow from 120 in Jerusalem about 33 C.E., to some one million by 125-150 C.E., a mere 92-117 years later. This growth in the Christian population all came about because they effectively evangelized, using the Septuagint (Greek Old Testament). They were so effective with the Septuagint that the Jews abandoned it and went back to the Hebrew Old Testament.

In any case, Celsus was an enemy of Christianity. Also, as was stated above, what Celsus observed was only within the sphere of his personal experiences. How many Christians could he have known out of almost a million at the time of his writing? Moreover, although not highly educated in schools, it **need not** be assumed that most or all of the early Christians were entirely illiterate, but rather a good number of them could read and write (with difficulty). Many had a *very basic* ability to understand spoken words, a *very basic* grasp of written words, *very basic* math skills (buying in the marketplace), and the ability to sign one's name for daily living and employment.

---

[131] This Celsus was a second-century Greek philosopher and opponent of early Christianity, who should not be confused with the previously mentioned Celsus, Roman Senator Tiberius Julius Celsus Polemaeanus.

[132] *The History of the Christian Religion and Church, During the Three First Centuries,* by Augustus Neander; translated from the German by Henry John Rose, 1848, p. 41

Let us return to Peter and John. For the sake of argument, we will assume that literacy was between five and ten percent, with most readers being men. We will accept that Peter and John were entirely illiterate in the sense the modern historian believes it to be true (even though they likely were not). The time of the statement in Acts about the two apostles being **"uneducated"** (i.e., unlettered) was about 33 C.E.[133] Peter would not pen his first letter for about 30 more years. Throughout those 30 years, Peter progressed spiritually, maturing into the position of being one of the leaders of the entire first-century Christianity. A few years later, Peter and John were viewed as developing and growing into their new position as leaders in the Jerusalem congregation; as Paul said of them, "James and Cephas and John, who seemed to be pillars" of the Christian community. On the other hand, John did not pen his books until about 60 years after Acts 4:13. Are we to assume that he, too, had not grown in 60 years? Could education in the first century have become more accessible?

The Birth of Koine Greek

After Alexander the Great's conquests and the extension of Macedonian rule in the fourth-century B.C.E, a transferal of people from Greece proper to the small Greek communities in the Middle East took place. Throughout what became known as the Hellenistic period, the Attic dialect, spoken by the educated classes and the traders and many settlers, became the language common to all the Middle East. From about 300 B.C.E. to about 500 C.E. was the age of Koine, or common Greek, a combination of different Greek dialects of which Attic was the most significant. Koine soon became the universal language. It had a tremendous advantage over the other languages of this period in that it was almost universally used. "Koine" means the "common" language or dialect common to all. The Greek vocabulary of the Old Testament translation, the Septuagint, was the Koine of Alexandria, Egypt, from 280 to 150 B.C.E. Everett Ferguson writes,

> Literacy became more general, and education spread. Both abstract thought and practical intelligence were enhanced in a greater proportion of the population. This change coincided with the spread of Greek language and ideas, so that the level and extent of communication and intelligibility became significant.[134]

---

[133] B.C.E. means "before the Common Era," which is more accurate than B.C. ("before Christ"). C.E. denotes "Common Era," often called A.D., for *anno Domini,* meaning "in the year of our Lord."

[134] Everett Ferguson, *Backgrounds of Early Christianity* (Grand Rapids, MI: Wm. B. Eerdmans, 2003), 14.

Education was voluntary, but elementary schools at least were widespread. The indications, especially on the evidence of the papyri, are that the literacy rate of Hellenistic and early Roman times was rather high, probably higher than at any period prior to modern times. Girls as well as boys were often included in the elementary schools, and although education for girls was rarer than for boys, it could be obtained. The key for everyone was to get what you could on your own.[135]

By the time we enter the first-century C.E., the era of Jesus and the apostles, Koine Greek had become the international language of the Roman Empire. The Bible itself bears witness to this; e.g., when Jesus was executed by the Roman Pontius Pilate, the inscription above his head was in Hebrew, the language of the Jews, in Latin, Rome's official language. It was also in Greek, the language spoken on the streets of Alexandria to Jerusalem, to Athens, Rome, and the rest of the Empire. (John 19:19- 20; Acts 6:1) Acts 9:29 informs us that Paul was preaching in Jerusalem to Greek-speaking Jews. As we know, Koine, a well-developed tongue by the first-century C.E., would be the tool that would facilitate the publishing of the 27 New Testament books.

Books, Reading, and Writing; Archaeological Evidence for Literacy In Early Christianity

Archaeologists have discovered hundreds of thousands of examples of graffiti on the outsides of buildings throughout the ancient Roman world, over 11,000 in Pompeii alone.

---

[135] Everett Ferguson, *Backgrounds of Early Christianity* (Grand Rapids, MI: Wm. B. Eerdmans, 2003), 111.

Graffiti and Literacy in Early Christianity

Pompeii was a prosperous populace (15,000), economically diverse ancient Roman city near modern Naples in Italy's Campania region. Over 11,000 graffiti samples, etched into the plaster or painted on the walls, in both public and private places, have been uncovered in the excavations of Pompeii. Archaeologists have been studying and recording graffiti in Pompeii since the 1800s.

Mount Vesuvius blew a column of gas, magma, and debris for thirty-six hours that literally darkened the sky as though it were night, which caused a dreadful rain of ash and lapilli (small lava rock fragments ejected from a volcano). It only took two days until Pompeii, and an enormous rural area was covered with a thick layer, with the average depth of about eight feet **[2.5 m]**. The earth continued to be shaken by violent tremors that released a massive cloud of poisonous gases into the air. These gases were invisible but deadly, which covered the city, bringing death. As Pompeii was being buried, the small Roman town Herculaneum vanished instantly, being preserved more or less intact. "Lava flowed down on Herculaneum, submerging that town under a mass of mud and volcanic debris to a depth that reached twenty-two meters [72 feet] near the shore."[136]

VI.13.6 Pompeii. Painting of two gods with graffiti inscriptions, found on front exterior wall between entrances 6 and 7.

---

[136] Dell 'Orto; Luisa Franchi, *Riscoprire Pompei* (Rediscovering Pompeii) Italy: L'Erma di Bretschneider, 1990, 131.

A fresco showing the baker Terentius Neo and his wife, from Pompeii: "This remarkable portrait on the wall of a bakery in first-century Pompeii depicts the proprietor holding a book roll and his wife holding a stylus and a diptych made of two waxed wooden tablets. The stylus tablets are for taking notes; the book roll represents the finished, polished text. The portrait proclaims the literacy of this otherwise modest couple."[137]

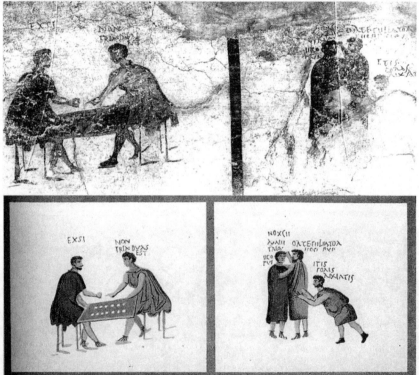

CIL IV, 03494 National Archaeological Museum of Naples (inv. N. 111482), Scenes of osteria, Pompeian fresco (50 x 205 cm) from the Caupona of Salvius (VI, 14, 35-36) with "comics."

[137] Craig A. Evans, *JESUS AND HIS WORLD: The Archaeological Evidence* (Louisville, KY: Westminster John Knox Press, 2012), Loc. 1462, KDP.

www.commons.wikimedia.org.

These buried cities have helped us understand the ancient Roman world better, and specifically, it's Graffiti that has enabled us to understand its literary level better. The Graffiti of the ancient Roman world was **writing** in charcoal, scratched with a stylus or stick, painted with a brush, **or drawings** scribbled, scratched, or painted with a brush on a wall or other surface in a public place. In the ancient world of the first-century Roman Empire, graffiti was a valued form of expression, which was even interactive. It should not be confused with the modern-day criminal defacement we now see in most of our modern cities. There are dialogues where one passage answers another. These responses take the forms of greetings, insults, prayers, etc.

Successus textor amat coponiaes ancilla(m) nomine Hiredem quae quidem illum non curat sed ille rogat illa com(m)iseretur scribit rivalis vale	**TRANSLATION**: Successus the weaver is in love with the slave of the Innkeeper, whose name is Iris. She doesn't care about him at all, but he asks that she take pity on him. A rival wrote this

A response to this translates to: You're so jealous you're bursting. Don't tear down someone more handsome – a guy who could beat you up and who is good-looking.[138]

CIL IV, 10237 A graffito from Pompeii shows musicians, the emperor, and a fight between a murmillō and a secūtor.

---

[138] Benefiel, Rebecca R. "Dialogues of Ancient Graffiti in the House of Maius Castricius in Pompeii." American Journal of Archaeology 114.1 (2010): 59-101. Web. 3 Nov. 2015.

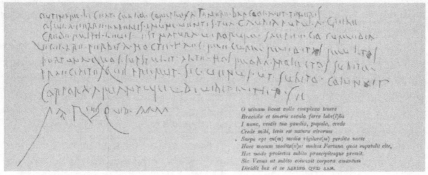

O utinam liceat collo complexa tenere
Bracciola et teneris oscula ferre lab(e)llis
I nunc, ventis tua gaudia, pupule, crede
Crede mihi, levis est natura virorum
Saepe ego cu(m) media vigilare(m) perdita nocte
Haec mecum medit(n)s: multos Fortuna quos supstulit alte,
Hos modo proiectos subito praecipitesque premit.
Sic Venus ut subito coniunxit corpora amantum
Dividit lux et se ... QVID AAM.

1CIL 4.5296, transcribed in the Corpus Inscriptionum Latinarum. A poem of graffiti on the wall of a hallway in Pompeii. It is discovered in 1888 as one of the longest and most elaborate surviving graffiti texts from the town.

C.I.L. IV 4091
QVIS AMAT VALEAT PEREAT QVI
NESCIT AMARE BIS TANTI PEREAT
QVISQVIS AMARE VETAT

CIL IV, 4091 "Whoever loves, let him flourish, let him perish who knows not love, let him perish twice over whoever forbids love"

As we have already seen from above and others not mentioned herein, some scholars have attempted to downplay the importance of the texts of the Greek New Testament within early Christianity. Instead, they argue that the oral gospel played a far more critical, dominant role. This is primarily supported by the long-held belief that the vast majority of those in the ancient Roman world could not read and write. Many scholars throughout the twentieth century have argued that the low literacy level is evidence that the early Christians did not place a significant value on the texts of the New Testament. On this, Alan Millard, professor of Hebrew and ancient Semitic languages, writes, "Another authority stated, 'there was a gap of several

130

decades between the public ministry of Jesus and the writing down of his words by the authors of the Gospels. During this time, what was known about Jesus was handed on orally.'" The Jesus Seminar, fifty critical Biblical scholars and one-hundred laymen founded in 1985 by Robert Funk, even argue that Jesus' early disciples "were technically illiterate."[139]

From the last forty to fifty years, the evidence supports that people of all sorts knew how to read and write in the first century. The Hebrew, Aramaic, and Greek languages were common at all levels of society during Jesus' life and ministry and the apostle's lifetime. The argument that the Gospels came out of an utterly illiterate society is false because the evidence tells another story entirely, as reading and writing would be pretty common throughout the Roman Empire. In almost every circumstance, there would be people who could write something that someone tells them, be it for their personal use or the benefit of another.

C.I.L. IV 5092
AMORIS IGNES SI SENTIRES MVLIO
MAGI PROPERARES VT VIDERIS VENEREM
DILIGO IVVENEM (PVERVM) VENVSTVM ROGO PVNGE IAMVS
BIBISTI IAMVS PRENDE LORA ET EXCVTE
POMPEIOS DEFER VBI DVLCIS EST AMOR
MEVS ES

CIL IV, 5092 Graffiti from Pompeii, in verse. The writer, burned by the flames of love, incites the mule driver to stop drinking and goad the mules to get to Pompeii first, where a handsome boy, whose writer is in love, awaits him, and where love is sweet.

For example, consider the commonness of graffiti in Pompeii and throughout the Roman Empire. The elites that argue for orality do not include this kind of evidence in the discussion, which they should, but it would detract from their literacy theme, impacting the production, publication, and distribution of a written text. Think about graffiti by its very nature cannot be derived from the wealthy, prominent Roman society

---

[139] Alan Millard, *READING AND WRITING IN THE TIME IF JESUS* (New York, NY: NYU Press, 2000), 185.

members. Who would argue that such memorable writers as Vergil (or Virgil), Horace, Catullus, Propertius, Tibullus, and Ovid were found scribbling on the side of some public building? On this, Kristina Milnor writes, "The corpus of Pompeian wall writings, moreover, has been seen as a window onto the language of everyday life in the ancient Roman world, one of our few opportunities to read words written by ordinary people performing an activity (writing graffiti) that we in the modern-day do not associate with the cultural elite."[140]

As Milnor rightly points out, the graffiti is not by the hands of the elite writers but rather by ordinary everyday people. She makes the acute observation that the prominent Latin poets of the day had mixed feelings and concerns about producing their book that they knew would be read and reread, which meant being copied and copied, and copies of copies being copied. They knew this also meant that human error would creep into the work, and copyists may even take liberties. Moreover, these published authors knew that they also faced public criticism. In contrast, the graffiti authors knew their work was an autograph and never had to face any production, publication, distribution issues, or even critical reviews. The author of a graffito simply concerned himself with the **technical** aspects of his written work: its properties and techniques, as seen from a literary and language perspective. In many cases, the Latin poet's work may become known throughout the entire empire, while the graffito author is simply a local phenomenon.

We need to view graffiti in the light of all written works that impacted the ancient Roman culture of the day. Some might mistakenly believe that graffiti was at the bottom of the written record spectrum. However, we might place the graffiti above the daily writings of advertisements for rental properties, shopping lists, or signs throughout the city offering public information to the passerby. We might even place the graffiti on the same level as the local newspaper or something like the tabloid magazine of the first century C.E., with writers showing much interest in the classics, who dabbled in poetry and mythology, as well as local gossip, with a mixture of advertisements. While it is true that the messages were likely more impactful on the urban level, let's not think the elites were any less impacted by the graffiti than the elites of today and TMZ. The readers were incidental in nature, happening upon the graffiti, not seeking it out like a published book. However, the workers of the elites likely communicated these things to their employers or masters if the subject or context was relevant. There is nothing to say that when a wealthy person walked the streets through the shops, they

---

[140] William A. Johnson; Holt N. Parker, *Ancient Literacies: The Culture of Reading in Greece and Rome* (Oxford: Oxford University Press, 2011), 291.

never paused to read the graffiti. The general conclusion is "It seems clear that a significant percentage of wall writers and readers were literate in Greek, although the common practice of transliteration suggests that there may have been more speakers than writers/readers."[141]

While we have focused on the public places of Pompeii and the Roman empire as a whole, graffiti can also be found in the catacombs and on various early Christian monuments. Throughout the Roman Empire of the first three centuries of Christianity, graffiti could have been in the millions engraved into or painted on the walls, floors, and engraved on tombstones. Craig A. Evans informs us that Israel was not exempt from graffiti, stating, "There are many examples in Israel too, though not nearly as 'colourful' as those preserved on the scorched walls of Pompeii and Herculaneum. At the very least these graffiti and inscriptions attest to a crude literacy that reached all levels of society." Evans cites Rock Inscriptions and Graffiti Project (3 vols, SBLRBS 28, 29, 31; Atlanta: Scholars Press, 1992-4), "Stone and his colleagues catalogued some 8,500 inscriptions and graffiti found in southern Israel: the Judean desert, the desert of the Negev and Sinai. The inscriptions are in several languages, including Hebrew, Aramaic, Greek, Latin, Nabatean, Armenian, Georgian, Egyptian hieroglyphs, and others. Not many date to late antiquity, because, unlike the graffiti and inscriptions of Pompeii and Herculaneum, the graffiti and inscriptions in the deserts of Israel were exposed to the eroding elements."[142] The graffiti help us to illustrate literacy and the literary sources of the life of the early Christians.

C.I.L. IV 8364
SECVNDVS
PRIME SVAE VBI
QVE ISSE SALVTE
ROGO DOMINA VT ME AMES

CIL IV, 8364 Pompeyan inscription Translation: ""I subscribe to your dear Prima in every place a cordial greeting, I beg of you, my mistress, to love me."

---

[141] William A. Johnson; Holt N. Parker, *Ancient Literacies: The Culture of Reading in Greece and Rome* (Oxford: Oxford University Press, 2011), 295.

[142] Craig A. Evans, *Jesus and His World: The Archaeological Evidence* (Westminster: John Knox Press, 2012), Loc. 3317, KDP.

Public Writing

Theodotus Inscription to Greek-Speaking Jews: The inscription reads: "Theodotus son of Vettenus, priest and synagogue-president, son of a synagogue-president and grandson of a synagogue-president, has built the synagogue for the reading of the Law and the teaching of the Commandments, and (he has built) the hostelry and the chambers and the cisterns of water in order to provide lodgings for those from abroad who need them—(the synagogue) which his fathers and the elders and Simonides had founded."[143]

The text was carved on a limestone slab measuring 72 cm (28 inches) in length and 42 cm (17 inches) in width. It was discovered early in the 20th century on the hill of Ophel in Jerusalem. The inscription, written in Greek, refers to a priest, Theodotus. It has been dated to shortly before the destruction of Jerusalem in 70 C.E. It is evident that there were Greek-speaking Jews in Jerusalem in the first century C.E. (Ac 6:1) Some believe that the writing is referring to "the synagogue of the Freedmen (as it was called)," The inscription also references that Theodotus, as well as his father Vettenus and his grandfather, had the title *archisynagogos* (**leader of a synagogue**, local ruler of the community),[144] a title that used a number of

---

[143] G. Ernest Wright, *Biblical Archaeology* (London, United Kingdom: Gerald Duckworth & Co, 1962), 240.

[144] James Swanson, *Dictionary of Biblical Languages with Semantic Domains: Greek (New Testament)* (Oak Harbor: Logos Research Systems, Inc., 1997).

times in the Greek New Testament. – Mark 5:22, 35-36, 38; Luke 8:49; 13:14; Acts 13:15; 18:8, 17, etc.

There has been a countless number of archaeological finds that seem to suggest that many within the Roman Empire could read. Throughout the Roman Empire, we find hundreds if not thousands of public inscriptions like the Theodotus Inscription shown above. These inscriptions range from a list of names, general public information, imperial decrees, laws and regulations, quotations from famous people, as well as directions or distances from one place to another. In addition, even in the graveyards and the tombs, we find far more inscribed on the gravestones than merely the names of the deceased. On these tombstones, we find graffiti as mentioned above but also an inscription on the stone itself, such as threats and curses against any suspecting grave robbers who might happen upon their burial site. Indeed, it seems that they believed that the lowest criminal elements of the day could read. The impression from all of this public writing is that the public as a whole could read; otherwise, what is the point of spending all of the time and money so that a mere 5-10 percent of 100-150 million people could read it.

Literacy and the Literature from Egyptian Garbage Heaps

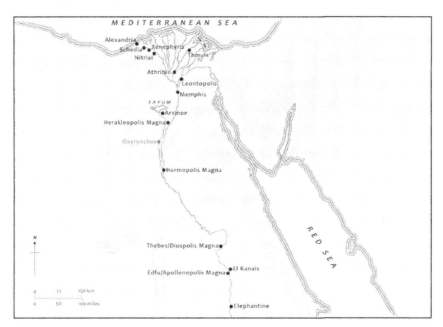

Beginning in 1778 and continuing to the end of the 19th century, many papyrus texts were accidentally discovered in Egypt that dated from 300

B.C.E. to 500 C.E., almost 500 thousand documents in all. About 130 years ago, there began a systematic search. At that time, a continuous flow of ancient texts was being found by the native fellahin, and the Egypt Exploration Society, a British non-profit organization, founded in 1882, realized that they needed to send out an expedition team before it was too late. They sent two Oxford scholars, Bernard P. Grenfell and Arthur S. Hunt, who received permission to search the area south of the farming region in the Faiyūm district. Grenfell chose a site called Behnesa because of its ancient Greek name, Oxyrhynchus. A search of the graveyards and the ruined houses produced nothing. The only place left to search was the town's garbage dumps, which were some 30 feet [9 m] high. It seems to Grenfell and Hunt that all was lost but they decided to try.

Grenfell (left) and Hunt (right) in about 1896

In January 1897, a trial trench (excavation or depression in the ground) was dug, and it only took a few hours before ancient papyrus materials were found. These included letters, contracts, and official documents. The sand had blown over them, covering them, and for nearly 2,000 years, the dry climate had served as a protection for them.

Illustrates excavations at Oxyrhynchus

It took only a mere three months to pull out and recover almost two tons of papyri from Oxyrhynchus. They shipped twenty-five large cases back to England. Over the next ten years, these two courageous scholars returned each winter to grow their collection. They discovered ancient classical writing, royal ordinances and contracts mixed in with business accounts, private letters, shopping lists, and fragments of many New Testament manuscripts.

Of what benefit were all these documents? Foremost, the bulk of these documents were written by ordinary people in Koine (common) Greek of the day. Many of the words used in the marketplace, not by the elites, appeared in the Greek New Testament Scriptures, which awakened scholars to the fact that Biblical Greek was not some unique Greek. Instead, it was the ordinary language of the common people, the man on the street in the marketplace. Thus, a clearer understanding of Biblical Greek emerged by comparing how the words had been used in these papyri. At the time of this writing, less than ten percent of these papyri have been published and studied. As was stated earlier, most of the papyri were found in the top 10 feet 93 m] of the garbage heap because the other 20 feet [6 m] had been ruined by water from a nearby canal. If we look at it, this will mean that the 500 thousand documents found could have been 1.5 – 2 million in total. Then, we must ponder just how many documents must have come through Oxyrhynchus that were never discarded in the dumps.

We have almost a half-million papyrus documents (likely there were millions more that did not survive) in garbage dumps in the dry sands of Oxyrhynchus, Egypt. This is but one city in the entirety of the Roman Empire. Are we to believe that Oxyrhynchus is the exception, and some of the biggest cities, such as Rome, Corinth, Athens, Pergamum, Ephesus,

Smyrna, Antioch, Jerusalem, Alexandria, and Carthage, which numbered anywhere from one hundred thousand to over a million in their population, did not have equal or greater writings discarded in their dumps? Then we should consider the temples and the libraries that boasted about tens of thousands of books. Reportedly, by the first century C.E., the Alexandrian library housed one million scrolls. In fact, Mark Antony took 200,000 scrolls from the library at Pergamum to replenish the Alexandrian library for Cleopatra. Because of moisture damage and being written on perishable material, we cannot discover the documents of these centers of education as we have in Egypt's dry sands. Yet, should we for a moment believe that their garbage dumps saw any fewer books that were discovered at Oxyrhynchus, Egypt?

Clearly, the tremendous amount of document discoveries begs for widespread literacy, not low levels. We are not trying to overturn the apple cart here. Historians' common consensus is that in the Roman Empire, the first three centuries of Christianity were 5-10 percent literate, and they were male. We **are _not_** trying to suggest that widespread means the 80-90 percent literacy but instead at least 40-50 percent, if not more. We think of the immense production of the twenty-seven New Testament books of the first century and the Apostolic Fathers in the late first and early second centuries, as well as the Apologists from near the middle of the second century through its end. Then, we consider the publication of these books, the copying of these books, and their circulation, and we conclude that the use of these books in the early Christian Church is apparent. All of the available evidence clearly shows some level of literacy within Christianity, but it cannot offer us the exact extent. We would argue the percentage be broken down instead of trying to suggest a one-size-fits-all.

Full Illiteracy (20%): This one has no reading or writing skills, no math skills, and is incapable of signing his name for daily living and employment beyond fundamental manual labor. He would work as fruit and vegetable picking, handling materials or low-level tools, manual digging or building, farming, or working in large workshops that produced items such as dishes or pots, as well as household slaves.

Fragmentary Literacy (40): (inconsistent or incomplete in some areas) The very basic ability to understand spoken words, a very basic grasp of written words, very basic math skills (buying in the marketplace), and the ability to sign one's name for daily living and employment. He would work as a manual laborer in the marketplace, not requiring math, a shop assistant that performs manual labor, or a soldier.

Fundamental Literacy (20): The basic ability to understand spoken words, an elementary grasp of written words, basic math skills and the ability to sign one's name, and the ability to read and write simple words for daily living and employment, such as work as a craftsman, works in the marketplace, or soldier.

Functional Literacy (15%): This one has the competent ability to understand spoken words, a beginner-intermediate level grasp of written words, and the ability to prepare basic documents for daily living and employment tasks that require reading skills beyond a basic level. He is a semiliterate writer who is untrained in writing but has the ability to read or write simple sentences and take on some basic jobs, such as a copyist or scribe.

Proficient Literacy (3%): This one is a highly skilled person, who can understand spoken words, and has an intermediate-advanced level grasp of written words. He has the proficient ability to prepare short texts for daily living and employment tasks that require reading skills at the intermediate level. He is a literate writer who is trained in writing and can take on jobs, such as a copyist or scribe, a tax collector, or a clerk.

Full Literacy (2%): This one is a highly skilled expert who can understand spoken words, an advanced level grasp of written words. He has the professional ability to prepare long texts for daily living and employment tasks that require reading skills at the advanced level. He is a fully literate writer who is professionally trained in writing and can take on jobs, such as a copyist or scribe, a tax collector, teacher, lawyer, or a clerk, to high-ranking positions like Senators.

CHAPTER IV The Reading Culture of Early Christianity

There is evidence of universality in the early orthodox Christian manuscripts. While the Roman society elite preferred the roll or scroll for their pagan literature, the Christians preferred the codex book form. This is even the case with the roll or scroll being preferred for apocryphal apostate Christian literature as opposed to the codex. Except for **P²²** (John 15:25–16:2, 21–32), all of the third/fourth-century canonical gospel manuscripts were papyrus codices. Going back to the second/third centuries, we also find that the Gospel codices were given some special status, as they were all produced in standard sizes that were smaller than the other canonical NT books. The gospels were 11.5–14 cm in width and height at least 3 cm higher than width, while other NT books were 12–14 cm in width and height not quite twice that. Even so, while the other NT books might have been a little taller, they all were easily carried.[145] The codex came to be used toward the end of the first century, and the Christians commonly used it after the first century.[146] The evidence for such a conclusion comes from our earliest Christian manuscripts that are still in existence, which were produced in codex form. The manuscripts include the Old Testament that the Christians used and the New Testament texts and the Apostolic Fathers, the Apologists, and other early Church Fathers.

---

[145] Charles E. Hill; Michael J. Kruger, *THE EARLY TEXT OF THE NEW TESTAMENT* (Oxford, United Kingdom: Oxford University Press, 2012), 38.

[146] T. C. Skeat, *Zeitschrift für Papyrus und Epigraphic* 102 (1994): 263–68.

Another piece of evidence of universality in the early orthodox Christian manuscripts was the *nomina sacra* (Lat. "sacred names"), which were contractions and abbreviations of several frequently occurring divine names or titles in the early texts, the Greek counterparts of God, Lord, Jesus, Christ, Son, Spirit, David, Cross, Mother, Father, Israel, Savior, Man, Jerusalem, and Heaven.[147] Early on, there was universality with the four divine names or titles God, Jesus, Christ, and Lord. Later they added the other sacred names above. Even how the sacred names were to be contracted in the manuscripts was standardized and universal. Early on, it was decided that regardless of whether sacred names were used in a sacred or mundane way, they were to be contracted. For example, whether the Greek *kurios* (Lord) was used about the Son Jesus (sacred) as opposed to the master of a household (mundane/non-sacred), it was to be contracted. Another example of whether the Greek *pater* (Father/father) was used about the Father (sacred) or a father in some narrative or parable (mundane/non-sacred), it was to be contracted. For example, in **P**[66] (c. 200 C.E.),[148] *kurios* ("Lord") is contracted through the entire manuscript, whether it was sacred or mundane in its use. We have the same situation with *pneuma* (spirit) in **P**[75] (c. 175-225 C.E.),[149] even when referring to an unclean spirit. This is evidence of a universal, systematic approach to the Christian canonical books, which shows a concern for the accuracy of the content and the handiness, convenience, and portability of the New Testament books in the latter half of the second-century C.E.[150]

---

[147] Bruce Manning Metzger, *Manuscripts of the Greek Bible: An Introduction to Palaeography* (New York, NY: Oxford University Press, 1981), 36-37.

[148] CONTENTS: John 1:1–6:11; 6:35–14:26, 29–30; 15:2–26; 16:2–4, 6–7; 16:10–20:20, 22–23; 20:25–21:9, 12, 17.

[149] CONTENTS: Luke 3:18–22; 3:33–4:2; 4:34–5:10; 5:37–6:4; 6:10–7:32, 35–39, 41–43; 7:46–9:2; 9:4–17:15; 17:19–18:18; 22:4–24:53; John 1:1–11:45, 48–57; 12:3–13:1, 8–10; 14:8–29; 15:7–8.

[150] What we have learned here and in the whole of THE TEXT OF THE NEW TESTAMENT undermine what secular scholars such as Walter Bauer, Robert A. Kraft, and agnostic Bart D. Ehrman maintain. These argue that **Gnosticism** (a false philosophy, speculation, and pagan mysticism of apostate Christianity), **Montanism** (a heresy based on the teachings of the charismatic prophet Montanus), and **Marcionism** (condemned as a Christian heresy that rejected the Old Testament) were just alternative forms of Christianity, just as organized and fast-growing if not faster. They have maintained, moreover, that the form of Christianity in Rome prevailed in the fourth century and became the standard, causing these groups and others to be seen as apostate forms of Christianity. This is not the case. First, the early evidence is that these groups were only tiny apostate offshoots of true Christianity, who broke away, abandoning the truth. Second, they were busy arguing amongst themselves over doctrine, as opposed to making disciples. Third, the apocryphal non-canonical Gospel of Thomas, the Gospel of Mary, the Gospel of Peter, the so-called Egerton Gospel, and the Gospel of Judas were composed in the second century C.E. by no apostle or anyone associating directly with Jesus, not to mention that they all indicate that they were private manuscripts, having no earmarks that they were meant to be universal. Finally, if these heresies and their apocryphal writings were just as far-reaching as Orthodox Christianity, why are there no citations of them in the second/third century apostolic fathers? Only the Gospel of Thomas has two early third-century citations. If they were as impactful as the canonical gospels, they should have been cited as much. The early papyri do not support Walter Bauer, Robert A. Kraft, and Bart D. Ehrman in their views of early Christianity.

141

The Reading Culture of Early Christianity

Textual scholar Larry Hurtado[151] borrows an approach from William A. Johnson in his book *Readers and Reading Culture in the High Roman Empire: A Study of Elite Communities*. I would like to take the liberty of borrowing this concept as well. Johnson, under the heading, CONTEXTUALIZING READING COMMUNITIES, writes, "The more proper goal, as I [Johnson] have argued, is to understand the particular reading cultures that obtained in antiquity, rather than to try to answer decontextualized questions that assume in 'reading' a clarity and simplicity it manifestly does not have." (Johnson 2012 (Reprint), 14) Johnson focuses his reading culture on "'the reading of Greek literary prose texts by the educated elite during the early empire (first and second centuries AD)'" (Hill and Kruger 2012, 49), just one of many surrounding reading cultures of the time. We are going to focus our attention on the reading culture of early Christianity, namely, the first three centuries. Just as the manuscript evidence above gave us proof of a universal approach of early Christianity to the publication of their canonical books, showing concern for the accuracy of the content, this will be an extension of that.

What made Johnson's work so appealing for Hurtado is the Roman elite reading culture, and how he demonstrated that their approach was actually designed to keep out anyone who could not handle the difficulty with which their reading community functioned. The Roman literary world had long had word separation within their texts. Still, in the second and third centuries, the Roman world's elite reading culture returned to *scriptio continua* (Lat. for "continuous script"), a writing style without spaces or other marks between the words and sentences. This choice of writing style over others that were current and common, with spaces between words and sentences as well as punctuation, diacritical marks that indicate how words are to be pronounced, and distinguished letter case, is evidence that they were putting up roadblocks to keep the uneducated out of their elite reading culture.

This is even further evidenced when they ignored the codex and stayed with the rolls or scrolls, which were held horizontally, with the text being read vertically. The text was in "columns ranging from 4.5 to 7.0 centimeters in width, about 15–25 letters per line, left and right justification, and about 15–25 centimeters in height, with about 1.5–2.5 centimeters spacing between columns. The letters were carefully written, calligraphic in better quality manuscripts, but with no spacing between words, little or no punctuation, and no demarcation of larger sense-units. The strict right-hand justification was achieved by 'wrapping' lines (to use a computer term), ending each line

---

151   Charles E. Hill; Michael J. Kruger, *THE EARLY TEXT OF THE NEW TESTAMENT* (Oxford, United Kingdom: Oxford University Press, 2012), 49.

either with a given word or a syllable and continuing with the next word or syllable on the next line, the column 'organized as a tight phalanx of clear, distinct letters, each marching one after the other to form an impression of continuous flow, the letters forming a solid, narrow rectangle of written text, alternating with narrower bands of white space'."[152]

Another feature of this elite reading culture was that they cared deeply about the elegant and beautiful or artistic handwriting that was pleasing to the eyes but not as reader-friendly as the rounded, unadorned writing in the Christian texts. Indeed, the elite reading culture cared about the accuracy of the content in their documents as well, but it took a backseat to visually stimulating handwriting. The reader had the task of bringing to life this text with no sense breaks or punctuation.

The early codex manuscripts present us a picture of early Christianity that was a book-buying, book-reading, and book-publishing culture unlike no other, as they turned to the book form, i.e., the codex, finding it handy, convenient, and portable. Matthew, Mark, Luke, John, Paul, Peter, James, and Jude were moved along by the Holy Spirit, penning their books. The writings were then delivered and distributed by a trusted traveling companion, who then read it aloud to the Christian congregation(s).

Paul, in his final greeting to the Ephesians, writes, "But that you also may know about my affairs, as to how I am doing, Tychicus, the beloved brother and faithful minister in the Lord, will make everything known to you. whom I have sent to you for this very purpose, that you may know the things about us, and he may encourage your hearts." (Eph. 6:21-22) Paul tells the Christians in Colossae, "All my affairs Tychicus, my beloved brother, and faithful minister and fellow slave in the Lord will make known to you. I have sent him to you for this very purpose, that you may know how we are and that he may encourage your hearts." (Col. 4:7-8) The first Christians were encouraged to read the Scriptures during their religious services and to discuss them. – 1 Corinthians 14:26; Ephesians 5:18-19; Colossians 3:16; 1 Timothy 4:13; See Matthew 24:15; Mark 13:14; Revelation 1:3.

The members of these early Christian congregations were from a wide-ranging spectrum; the poor, slaves, freedman (emancipated from slavery), male and female, old and young, children, workers, business owners, landowners, and even some from the wealthy segment of society. Generally, the day's influential political leaders and the very wealthy were missing from these Christian meetings. The apostle Paul encouraged Timothy, "devote yourself to the **public reading** of Scripture, to exhortation, to teaching." (1

---

[152] Charles E. Hill; Michael J. Kruger, THE EARLY TEXT OF THE NEW TESTAMENT (Oxford, United Kingdom: Oxford University Press, 2012), 50.

Tim 4:13) Writing about 155 C.E., Justin Martyr says of the weekly Christian meetings, "And on the day called Sunday, all who live in cities or in the country gather together to one place, and the memoirs of the apostles or the writings of the prophets are read, as long as time permits; then, when the reader has ceased, the president verbally instructs and exhorts to the imitation of these good things.[153]

Gamble says that Justin Martyr's words suggest typical weekly Christian meetings in mid-second century Asia Minor and Rome. Scholars agree that reading Scripture at Christian meetings, offering an exposition of what had been read, was common and likely universal in Justin's day, the practice originating with the first-century Christians.[154] By the end of the first century, every Christian community in the then-known world likely had as many of the New Testament books as were available (excluding the Gospel of John, his three epistles, and the book of Revelation, since they were written between 95-98 C.E.). Also, they would have had Old Testament books as well. These congregations would have had several readers who were responsible for the congregation's library.

Further, many Christians themselves could probably read. In addition, likely, these assigned readers were also serving as scribes. In some cases, these readers/scribes would probably have had the same training as the Jewish Sopherim (scribes), meaning that they possessed excellent reading, copying, translating, and interpreting skills. It might even have been that these were Jewish converts to Christianity, very familiar with the synagogue practice of copying manuscripts, studying the texts, and reading and interpreting the texts. As Comfort points out, 'the relationship between scribes and readers is found in the subscription to 1 Peter and to 2 Peter in P[72], wherein both places, it says, "Peace to the one having written [i.e., the scribe] and to the one having read [i.e., the lector].' As such, the scribe of P[72] was asking for a blessing of God's peace on the scribe [presumably himself] and on the lector. As such, the scribe knew that the publication of 1 Peter and 2 Peter was dependent on the twofold process—the copying of the text and the oral reading of it."[155]

---

[153] Justin Martyr, "The First Apology of Justin," in *The Apostolic Fathers with Justin Martyr and Irenaeus*, ed. Alexander Roberts, James Donaldson, and A. Cleveland Coxe, vol. 1, The Ante-Nicene Fathers (Buffalo, NY: Christian Literature Company, 1885), 186.

[154] Henry Y. Gamble, *Books and Readers in the Early Church: A History of Early Christian Texts* (New Haven, CT, New Haven University Press, 1995), 151-2.

[155] Philip Comfort, *Encountering the Manuscripts: An Introduction to New Testament Paleography & Textual Criticism* (Nashville, TN: Broadman & Holman, 2005), 52.

When we look at the evidence for the first three centuries of Christianity, we find that most early Christians were from a lower social stratum, a minority from the middle class, and a minute few from society's upper classes.[156] It would seem that the early Christian manuscripts were prepared for the early Christian reading culture. We have already spoken at length about the book form of the codex instead of the roll or scroll with its continuous text. Unlike the elite reading culture that Johnson surveyed, the Christian reading culture was not aiming for what was pleasing to the eyes, i.e., elegant handwriting. The highest priority was creating a text that was accurate in content and reader-friendly. While the elite reading culture during this same period was creating texts designed to keep the uneducated out (too overwhelming for the average reader), the Christian texts were prepared in such a way that they placed fewer demands on the reader (more Christians could reach out to be readers), so as to bring this to a more diverse audience. If we are to fully understand early Christianity, the early reading culture, and their view of their text, we need at look to the early papyri and scribal activity, the patristic quotations, and any early attitudes expressed about textual transmission.

Literacy in the Roman Empire and the Early Church

The question of reading, writing, and literacy levels in the Roman Empire and the early Church is not as settled or decided as secular scholarship might like us to believe. We can start by noting that there is a difference between what we deem literate today and the Roman Empire's situation and the first three centuries of the Church. Being literate today means reading and writing, while literacy in the Roman Empire mainly applied to those who could read. The ability to write was not necessarily assumed.[157] Secular sources suggest that the Greco-Roman world's literacy level was rarely, if ever, more than twenty percent. Scholars argue that the average was possibly not much more than ten percent in the Roman Empire. They point out that it varied within different regions, which would be true for any period. They further argue that in the western province's literacy never rose above five percent.[158] Some Bible scholars are unfamiliar with the reading culture of early Christianity.

---

[156] Charles E. Hill; Michael J. Kruger, *THE EARLY TEXT OF THE NEW TESTAMENT* (Oxford, United Kingdom: Oxford University Press, 2012), 55.

[157] See Eric A. Havelock, The Literate Revolution in Greece and its Cultural Consequences (Princeton, N.J.: Princeton University Press, 1982), 38-59.

[158] William V. Harris, *Ancient literacy* (Harvard University Press, 1989) 328.

In many cases, the scholars fail to mention the overabundance of evidence for a literate culture between 50 B.C.E. and 325 C.E. There is considerable evidence that the early Christians' literacy rates were higher than those of the Roman Empire in general. Bible scholar Christopher D. Stanley offers us the **commonly accepted misconception** about the literacy level among the early Christians:

> Literacy levels were low in antiquity, access to books was limited, and most non-Jews had little or no prior knowledge of the Jewish Scriptures. Of course, Gentile Christians who had been Jewish sympathizers (Luke's "God-fearers") would have been exposed to the Jewish Scriptures, but we have no reason to think that their literacy levels differed appreciably from their contemporaries.[159]

In the Greco-Roman world, education was voluntary. Nevertheless, we do know that elementary schools were widespread. The archaeological evidence, especially the papyri, actually points to a higher literacy rate in the Hellenistic-Roman world than at any other time outside modern history. We have already spoken at length on the literacy level of early Christianity in the previous chapter and will briefly look at more evidence here in this chapter.

THE DAILY NEWSPAPER OF ROME

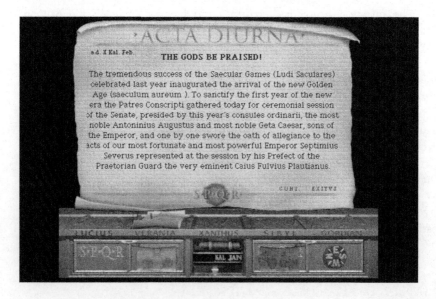

---

[159] Christopher D. Stanley, *Arguing with Scripture: The Rhetoric of Quotations in the Letters of Paul* (London; New York: T&T Clark, 2004), 3.

From the days of Gaius Octavius, who became the first emperor of Rome (after that known as Caesar Augustus), to almost two centuries after the execution of Christ (59 B.C.E. to 222 C.E.), the Roman Empire published and distributed a regular news publication for the city of Rome. The Latin phrase *Acta Diurna* (Daily Acts/Events or Daily Public Records) were Rome's official notices, a sort of Daily Roman Times. Much of the news out of the city of Rome was also published broadly across the Empire as well.[160] Acta Diurna introduced the expression "publicare et propagare," meaning, "Make public and propagate." The expression was placed at the end of the news release to both Roman citizens and non-citizens. There was a daily *papyrus* newspaper, which informed all who could read of the daily events. It was distributed throughout Rome in such places as the public bathhouses,[161] as well as message boards.

Pliny the Elder (23 C.E. – 79 C.E.) was a Roman author, naturalist, natural philosopher, and naval and army commander. Pliny informs us that there were different grades of papyrus, such as the low-grade Saitic paper, so-called from the city of that name in Lower Egypt, as well as the taeniotic paper, possibly from Alexandria.[162] These low-grade papyruses were likely used for public notices, which would also explain why we have never discovered a single piece of the Acta Diurna (Daily Events). This Daily Newspaper of Rome covered such vital information as royal or senatorial decrees and events, military and political news, deaths, crimes, trials, as well as economic insights. It also offered social information like weddings and divorces, births, festivals, astrology, human-interest stories, and even gossip. On this, Brian J. Wright said,

> The Latin term *Acta* in its broadest sense means 'the things that have been done,'[163] or more simply, 'events'. Without any additional qualifiers, these events could – and did – include public and private activities; secular and sacred matters; government and civilian affairs. With additional qualifiers, these events had a narrower and even more specialized meaning. The *Acta Militaria* refers to published military events,[164] the *Acta Senatus* indicates

---

[160] Propertius 2.7.17–18; Pliny the Elder, *Naturalis historia* 35.2.11; *Epigrams* 7.17; *Epigrams* 5.5; *Tristia* 4.9.20-25; *Tristia* 4.10.130.

[161] The largest of these was the Baths of Diocletian, which could hold up to 3,000 bathers.

[162] Pliny, *Natural History*, book 13, ch, 23

[163] John Percy Vyvian Dacre and Andrew William Lintott, 'Acta', in *The Oxford Classical Dictionary*, 4th ed., ed. Simon Hornblower and Antony Spawforth (Oxford: UP, 2012), 10.

[164] The first-century papyrus PSI 13.1307 is one example. For further details, see J. F. Gilliam, 'Notes on PSI 1307 and 1308', Classical Philology 47.1 (1952), 29-31. Cf. Sergio Daris, 'Osservazioni AD alcuni papyri di carattere militare', *Aegyptus* 38 (1958), 151-58, esp. 157-58; Sergio Daris, 'Note di lessico e di onomastica militare', *Aegyptus* 44 (1964), 47-51. For other examples from inscriptions and ancient

published senatorial events,[165] and the *Acta Triumphorum* denotes the published triumphs of emperors.[166] The main qualifier for the purposes of this study is diurna, which simply means 'daily.' Thus, the Acta Diurna represents published 'daily events.'[167] Though there are no authentic fragments of these specific kinds of acta,[168] and thus no physical features to discuss, there are ample references to them in ancient authors (again, by various nomenclature). Both Tacitus and Suetonius used these Acta as sources for information about the Empire's earlier emperors when they were writing their histories of Rome.[169] (B. J. Wright 2017)[170]

Moreover, it should be noted that the Roman *Acta Diurna* (Daily Acts/Events or Daily Public Records) was not the only newspaper of its kind during this period of 59 B.C.E. to about 222 C.E. Around 225 C.E., we find a Roman official ordering several mayors in the Hermopolite region of Egypt to post copies of his letter 'in well-known places so that all may be aware of his pronouncements' (P. Oxy. 2705). When we consider these things at face

---

authors see M. Léon Renier, *Inscriptions Romaines de l'Algérie* (Paris: Imprimerie Impériale, 1855); J. F. Gilliam, 'Some Military Papyri from Dura', in *Yale Classical Studies: Volume 11*, ed. Harry M. Hubbell (New Haven, CT: Yale University Press, 1950), 171-252, esp. 209–252.

[165] The bulletin of daily news was almost exclusively a private affair before Julius Caesar made it regular and official in 59 BC. Although private publications continued, he ordered that these occasionally published *Acta* were to be published daily for mass consumption under the authority of the government from the court reporters' notes (e.g. Seneca the Younger *Apocolocyntosis* 9). After Julius Caesar's death, a custom arose that future emperors (and their magistrates every January) were to swear to keep and respect all previous *Acta Senatus* from their predecessors (e.g. Dio Cassius 47.48; cf. 37.20); with a few exceptions (e.g. Dio Cassius 56.33). For inscriptional evidence of how emperors dealt with the *acta* of their predecessors, see Benjamin Wesley Kicks, 'The Process of Imperial Decision-Making from Augustus to Trajan' (Ph.D. dissertation, Rutgers, 2011), 86-91, the case study regarding the *Epistula Domitiani ad Falerienses*. For additional details and texts, see, among others, William Smith, William Wayte, and G. E. Marindin, eds., *A Dictionary of Greek and Roman Antiquities* (London: John Murray, 1890); Harry Thurston Peck, ed., *Harper's Dictionary of Classical Literature and Antiquities* (New York: Cooper Square, 1965), 14-15.

[166] *Pliny,* Naturalis historia. *37.6.*

[167] Too much emphasis should not be placed on the word 'daily' since it is possible that it could mean 'everyday' events, as in 'current events.'

[168] I say 'authentic' here because some forgeries have been published. For example, eleven fragments of the *Acta Diurna* were published in 1615 by Pighius, and defended by Dodwell. Though the fragments were exposed as a fifteenth century forgery (by Wesseling, Ernesti et al.), some scholars still attempted to defend their authenticity at least as far as 1844; with Lieberkühn. For more details and background to this story, see Wilhelm Sigismund Teuffel, *A History of Roman Literature: Volume One, The Republican Period*, trans. Wilhelm Wagner (London: George Bell and Sons, 1873), 381. Cf. Hermann L. G. Heinze, ' *De Spuriis Actorum Diurnorum Fragmentis Undecim: Fasciculus Prior'* (Ph.D. dissertation, University of Greifswald, 1860), 11-24; Andrew Lintott, 'Acta Antiquissima: A Week in the History of the Roman *Republic,'* Papers of the British School at Rome *54 (1986), 213-28.

[169] A. W. Mosley, 'Historical Reporting in the Ancient World', *NTS* 12.1 (1965), 10-26.

[170] Brian J. Wright, *COMMUNAL READING IN THE TIME OF JESUS: A Window Into Christian Reading Practices* (Minneapolis, MN: Fortress Press, 2017)

Brian J. Wright, *Communal Reading in the Time of Jesus: A Window into Early Christian Reading Practices* (Minneapolis: Fortress Press, 2017).

value, they indicate that notices were being written so that the populace could be updated about current affairs by reading them, not having them read to them.

We can conclude from these facts that reading, writing, and disseminating information were far more extensive than has long been held, with a much higher basic literacy level. This then adds to our understanding of the writing, publication, and distribution of the Greek New Testament letters read in the Christian congregations throughout the Roman Empire (Col. 4:46; 1 Thess. 5:27; 1 Tim. 4:13; Jam. 1:1; Rev. 1:3). Evidence indicates a far higher level of basic literacy throughout the Roman Empire than thought. The same and even more so can be said of the Christians who originated primarily as Jewish converts and prided themselves on their being taught to read and write in their youth, enabling them to read and write. Then we must consider that they also had the Great Commission to evangelize to the whole inhabited earth (Matt. 24:14; 28:19-20; Ac 1:8). As a result, it is no exaggeration to say that Christians were able to take over the Roman power that had a military unlike any other up to that time by growing the faith in a pagan world. They went from 120 disciples at Pentecost in 33 C.E. to over one million disciples about a century later. It has been estimated that by 325 C.E., there were some seven million Christians in the Roman Empire, and as many as two million had been martyred for their faith.

Richard Bauckham writes,

> John and his readers lived in a world in which God's name was not hollowed, his will was not done, and evil ruled through the oppression and exploitation of the Roman system of power.[171]

Rodney Stark informs us,

> Christianity **did not** grow because of miracle working in the marketplaces (although there may have been much of that going on), or because Constantine said it should, or even because the martyrs gave it such credibility. It grew because Christians constituted an intense community, able to generate the "invincible obstinacy" that so offended the younger Pliny but yielded immense religious rewards. And the primary means of its growth was through the united and motivated efforts of the growing numbers

---

[171] Richard Bauckham, *The Theology of the Book of Revelation* (NTT, Cambridge, UK: Cambridge University Press, 1993, 40.

of Christian believers, who invited their friends, relatives, and neighbors to share the "good news."[172]

Jewish education under this same period was significantly different as to the content, though, in some respects, they had stages similar to Greco-Roman education. The primary objective of Jewish education was knowledge of the Hebrew Scriptures. The parents were their Jewish children's first and primary educators, especially their earlier elementary education in reading, writing, and understanding the Torah (2 Tim 1:5; 3:14-15). We read briefly of young Jesus as he grew up in Nazareth. He would have received his education from three sources: Joseph, Jesus' stepfather, would have played a significant role in his education. Paul said that young Timothy was trained in "the sacred writings" by his mother, Eunice, and his grandmother Lois (2 Tim. 1:5; 3:15). Indeed, if Timothy received education in the Scriptures from his mother though his Father was a Greek (Acts 16:1), no doubt Jesus did as well from Joseph during his childhood. Jesus would have also received education in the Scriptures from the attendant at the synagogue, a place of instruction.

We know that another source of knowledge and wisdom for Jesus was the divine Father. Jesus said, "My teaching is not mine, but his who sent me," i.e., the Father (John 7:16) Mark 1:22 reads, "And they were **astounded at his teaching**, for he taught them as **one who had authority**, and not as the scribes."

The third-century Rabbi Judah b. Tema outlines the stages of Jewish education. "At five years old *one is fit* for the Scripture, at ten years for Mishnah, at thirteen for the commandments, at fifteen for Talmud, at eighteen for marriage, at twenty for retribution (a vocation)."[173] Again, the home was the primary place of Jewish education in reading, writing, and memorizing the Hebrew Scriptures. There were several primary schools in Jerusalem in the first century, but it was not until the second century C.E. that they grew more numerous outside of Jerusalem. Children began their studies as early as age 4-5 in primary school **Beth Sefer** ("house of reading"). Both boys and girls could attend the class in the synagogue or an adjoining room.[174]

---

[172] Rodney Stark, *The Rise of Christianity: A Socialist Reconsiders History* (Princeton, NJ: Princeton University Press, 1996), 208.

[173] Robert Henry Charles, ed., *Pseudepigrapha of the Old Testament*, vol. 2 (Oxford: Clarendon Press, 1913), 710.

[174] Everett Ferguson, *Backgrounds of Early Christianity* (Grand Rapids, MI: Wm. B. Eerdmans, 2003), 112.

First-century Jewish historian Josephus (30-100 C.E.) said of the Jewish life, "Our principle care of all is this, to educate our children well."[175] In speaking of what the Mosaic Law commands, he wrote, "It also commands us **to bring those children up in learning** and to exercise them in the laws, and make them acquainted with the acts of their predecessors, in order to their imitation of them, and that they may be nourished up in the laws from their infancy, and might neither transgress them nor yet have any pretense for their ignorance of them."[176] We have even more texts, especially from the later Rabbis, which make similar statements. If we take these comments at face value, it is evidence of a reading culture among the Jews that is undoubtedly higher than that of the Roman Empire, which was undoubtedly higher than the secular sources claim.

Five hundred years from now, what if we were to ask the historian, "how well could the Amish in America read and write?" It would be challenging to be accurate because they teach themselves. It is 2021, and they have one-room county schoolhouses with chalkboards, which remind us of the pioneer days in America or some Laura Ingalls Wilder novels. The historian might find slate chalkboards and tablets that are blank, so they could only guess at the level of reading and writing. Would it surprise anyone that this highly religious community, who value the ability to read their religious books, very similar to the first-century Jewish community, can speak two to three languages (Dutch or German and English), as well as read and write thoroughly?

When we see signs of a reading environment, it suggests a populace with at least a basic reading level. In the first-century C.E. Roman Empire, there were hundreds of public inscriptions of dedications, imperial decrees, lists of names, laws, and regulations, and even directions. Even the gravestones of the time were meant to do more than mark the name of the person. Some had lines of poetry; others had threats and curses for any who even thought of robbing the graves. The painstaking time taken to publish these things indicates the expectation that the public can read them, even lowly grave robbers.

We have such enormous quantities of written material that suggests a much higher literacy level than most are willing to accept. Only ten percent of the Oxyrhynchus papyri have been investigated, but they offer insight that indicates a more literate society, not less. Many men and women who wrote

[175] Flavius Josephus and William Whiston, *The Works of Josephus: Complete and Unabridged* (Peabody: Hendrickson, 1987).

[176] Flavius Josephus and William Whiston, *The Works of Josephus: Complete and Unabridged* (Peabody: Hendrickson, 1987).

had scribes pen their words, suggesting that they were literate by what they said, while their signatures at the end of letters shows only that some of them had poor penmanship. We should not judge their literacy level by the limitations of their handwriting. We must remember, in that period, that it was reading that dictated one's level of literacy. Moreover, it isn't easy to make judgment calls when many likely could write. Still, the challenging task was usually given to scribes because who wants to go through such an aggravation if they can afford to do otherwise.

We also have the Vindolanda Writing Tablets. "The writing tablets are perhaps Vindolanda's greatest discovery and have been previously voted by experts and the public alike as 'Britain's Top Treasure.' Delicate, wafer-thin slivers of wood covered in spidery ink writing, the tablets were found in the oxygen-free deposits on and around the floors of the deeply buried early wooden forts at Vindolanda and are the oldest surviving handwritten documents in Britain. Like postcards from the past, the tablets allow a rare insight into the real lives of people living and working at Vindolanda near Hadrian's Wall nearly 2000 years ago. They provide a fascinating and compelling insight into private and military lives from a very different time but are hauntingly familiar, covering matters from birthdays through to underpants! Have we changed that much in two millennia?"[177]

The Vindolanda Writing Tablets, like the papyri in the dry sands of Oxyrhynchus, offer us insights into the literacy of the Roman officers who we would expect to be literate but also indicate the literacy of the low-ranking soldiers, wives, friends, and servants. The handwriting of these tablets ranges from writing that is barely legible to the professional hand. We have to ask ourselves the same question: if these common soldiers had some basic writing skills, some even to the document hand level, and even a few at the professional hand, what are we to think of the literacy level of the Roman Empire?[178] Must we keep disputing the obvious? If the evidence suggests, as it does, a far higher literacy level than a mere 5-10 percent throughout the Roman Empire, what are we to expect from the Christian community that grew out of the Jewish populace that so valued reading, writing, and memorization, that was commissioned with evangelizing the entire inhabited earth?

---

[177] Vindolanda Writing Tablets - Roman Vindolanda and Roman .., https://www.vindolanda.com/roman-vindolanda/writing-tablets (accessed March 23, 2017).

[178] (Bowman 1998, 82-99)

CHAPTER V

The Early Christian's View of the Integrity of the Greek New Testament Books

Saints Peter and Paul, from a Catacomb by Anonymous. Paul Joseph De Mola, published on 09 May 2013 under the following license: CC BY-SA

Paul was the author of fourteen letters within the Greek New Testament.[179] Paul's earliest letters were 1 Thessalonians (50 C.E.), 2 Thessalonians (51 C.E.), Galatians (50-52 C.E.), 1&2 Corinthians (55 C.E.), Romans (56 C.E.), Ephesians, Philippians, Colossians, Philemon (60-61 C.E.), Hebrews (61 C.E.), 1 Timothy, and Titus (61-64 C.E.). 2 Timothy was penned last, about 65 C.E. This means that the apostle Peter could have been aware of at least thirteen out of fourteen Pauline letters at the time of his penning 2 Peter in 64 C.E., in which he writes,

2 Peter 3:15-16 Updated American Standard Version (UASV)

[15] and regard the patience of our Lord as salvation; just as also **our beloved brother Paul**, according to the wisdom given him, wrote to you, [16] as also **in all his letters**, speaking in them of these things, in which are some things hard to understand, which the untaught and unstable distort,

---

[179] This author accepts that Paul is the author of the book of Hebrews. For further information see the CPH Blog article, Who Authored the Book of Hebrews: A Defense for Pauline Authorship

https://christianpublishinghouse.co/2016/11/02/who-authored-the-book-of-hebrews-a-defense-for-pauline-authorship/

as they do also **the rest of the <u>Scriptures</u>**, to their own destruction. [bold is mine]

Notice that Peter speaks of Paul's letters, referring to them as a collection. Thus, Peter is our earliest reference to Paul's letters that were gathered together as a collection. Peter also states that the letters were viewed as being on equal footing with the Hebrew Scriptures when he says that "the untaught and unstable distort" Paul's letters as they do "the rest of the Scriptures." Günther Zuntz was certain that there was a full collection of Pauline letters by 100 C.E. (Zuntz 1953, 271-272) In 65 C.E.,[180] Peter could say of Paul, "in all his letters," and his readers would know who Paul was and of Paul's many letters. Also, his readers would have accepted the idea that Paul's letters were equal to the Hebrew Scriptures, which indicates that they were being collected among the churches.

1 Timothy 5:18 Updated American Standard Version (UASV)

[18] For **the Scripture says**, "You shall not muzzle the ox while he is threshing," and "The laborer is worthy of his wages." [bold is mine]

Notice that Paul says, "the Scripture says" (λέγει γὰρ ἡ γραφή), just before he quotes from two different Scriptures. The first half of the quote, "You shall not muzzle the ox while he is threshing," is from Deuteronomy 25:4. The Second half, "The laborer is worthy of his wages." seems to be from Luke 10:7. Here Paul is doing exactly what Peter did in the above at 2 Peter 3:16, placing the Gospel of Luke on par with the Hebrew Scriptures.

---

[180] 2 Peter generally is wrongly dated to about 100-125 C.E. (e.g. **J. N. D. Kelly**, A *Commentary on the Epistles of Peter and of Jude: Introduction and Commentary*; **J. D. Mayor**, the *Epistle of St. Jude and the Epistle of Second Peter*; **D. J. Harrington**, Jude and 2 Peter). Other Bible scholars date 2 Peter to 80-90 C.E. (e.g., **R. Bauckham** *Jude, 2 Peter*; **B. Reicke**, *The Epistle of James, Peter and Jude*). We should begin with a date of about 64 C.E. for 2 Peter. Then, the Greek makes it apparent that the author is a contemporary of the apostle Paul because it suggests that Paul is speaking to the churches at the time of this writing. The Greek ἐν πάσαις ἐπιστολαῖς λαλῶν ("*in all letters [he] speaking*") strongly implies such. The author of the document says that he is "Simon Peter, a bond-servant and apostle of Jesus Christ" (2 Pet. 1:1, NASB). He refers to this as "the second letter I am writing to you" (2 Pet. 3:1, NASB). The author clearly states that he was an eyewitness to the transfiguration of Jesus Christ, at which only Peter, James, and John were present (Matt. 17:1-13; Mark 9:1-13; Lu 9:28–36; See 2 Pet. 1:16-21). The author mentions that Jesus foretold his death, "knowing that the laying aside of my *earthly* dwelling is imminent, as also our Lord Jesus Christ has made clear to me" (2 Pet. 1:14; John 21:18, 19.). The argument that the style is different from 1 Peter is moot because the subject and the purpose in writing were different. The implication of the phrases "in all *his* letters" and "the rest of the Scriptures" is that many of Paul's letters (thirteen of them) were viewed as "Scripture" by the first-century Christian congregation and should not be "twisted" or "distorted." In addition, Second Peter was regarded as canonical by a number of authorities prior to the Third Council of Carthage (i.e., Irenaeus of Asia Minor c. 180 C.E., Origen of Alexandria c. 230 C.E., Eusebius of Palestine c. 320 C.E., Cyril of Jerusalem c. 348 C.E., Athanasius of Alexandria c. 367 C.E., Epiphanius of Palestine c. 368 C.E., Gregory Nazianzus of Asia Minor c. 370 C.E., Philaster of Italy c. 383 C.E., Jerome of Italy c. 394 C.E., and Augustine of N. Africa c. 397 C.E.).

Some have tried to dismiss 1 Timothy 5:18 by saying that Paul was just quoting oral tradition, but that can hardly be the case when he says, "**the Scripture says**," which requires a written source, and it happens that we have such a source: The Gospel of Luke. Luke was written about 56-58 C.E. in Caesarea, and First Timothy was written about 61-64 C.E. in Macedonia. Then, there is the fact that Luke was a faithful traveling companion and co-worker of the apostle Paul. Luke was one of Paul's closest traveling companions from about 49 C.E. until Paul's martyrdom. The Gospel of Luke was written just after the two of them returned from Paul's third missionary journey. At the same time, Paul was imprisoned for two years at Caesarea, after which Paul was transferred to Rome in about 58 C.E. Other "scholars believe Luke wrote his Gospel and the book of Acts while in Rome with Paul during the apostle's first Roman imprisonment. Apparently, Luke remained nearby or with Paul also during the apostle's second Roman imprisonment. Shortly before his martyrdom, Paul wrote that 'only Luke is with me' (2 Tim. 4:11)."[181] Either way, Luke was a very close co-worker with Paul for almost twenty years. In fact, Luke's writing shows evidence of Paul's influence (Lu 22:19-20; 1 Cor. 11:23-25). We must remember that Luke was a first-rate historian, as well as being inspired. He says he "investigated everything carefully from the beginning, to write it out" (Lu 1:3). Regardless, the apostle Paul had access to Luke's Gospel for many years before penning 1 Timothy, where it appears that he made a direct quote from what we know now as Luke 10:7, referring to it as Scripture.

The use of the well-known phrase, "**it is written**," further confirms the authority of the New Testament books. We understand that when this phrase is used, it is a reference to the Scriptures of God, the inspired Word of God. It should be noted that the gospel writers themselves use the phrase "**it is written**" some forty times when referring to the inspired Hebrew Scriptures.

The *Epistle of Barnabas* dates after the destruction of the Second Temple in 70 C.E., but it dates before the Bar Kochba Revolt of 132 C.E. At Barn 4:14, we read, "let us be on guard lest we should be found to be, as **it is written**, 'many called, but few chosen.'"[182] Immediately after using the phrase "it is written," Barnabas quotes Jesus' words found in Matthew 22:14, "For many are called, but few are chosen."

The *Letter of Polycarp to the Philippians* dates to about 110 C.E. Poly 12:1 reads, "For I am convinced that you are all well trained in the sacred

---

[181] T. R. McNeal, "Luke," ed. Chad Brand et al., *Holman Illustrated Bible Dictionary* (Nashville, TN: Holman Bible Publishers, 2003), 1056–1057.

[182] Michael William Holmes, *The Apostolic Fathers: Greek Texts and English Translations*, Third ed. (Grand Rapids, MI: Baker Books, 2007), 373.

Scriptures and that nothing is hidden from you (something not granted to me). Only, as it is said in these Scriptures, 'be angry but do not sin,' and 'do not let the sun set on your anger.' Blessed is the one who remembers this, which I believe to be the case with you."[183] The first phrase, "be angry but do not sin," is a quotation from Ephesians 4:26, where Paul is quoting Psalm 4:5. However, the latter part of the quote, "do not let the sun set on your anger" is Paul's words alone. It is clear here that Polycarp is referring to both the Psalm and the book of Ephesians when he writes, "it is said in these Scriptures."

Clement of Rome (c. 30-100 C.E.) penned two books: we focus on the second, *An Ancient Christian Sermon* (2 Clement), which dates to about 98-100 C.E. II Clement 2:4 reads, "And another Scripture says, 'I have not come to call the righteous, but sinners.'"[184] Here Clement is quoting Mark 2:17 or Matt. 9:13, which is likely the earliest quotation of a New Testament passage as Scripture. In the Gospel of Mark and Matthew, Jesus is quoted as saying, "I came not to call the righteous, but sinners." II Clement 14:2 reads, "But if we do not do the will of the Lord, we will belong to those of whom the Scripture says, 'My house has become a robbers' den'" which is a quote from Matthew 21:13, Mark 11:17, and Luke 19:46, where Jesus himself is quoting Jeremiah 7:11 after cleansing the temple of greedy merchants.

Indeed, we can garner from this brief look at early Christianity's view of Scriptures that the New Testament books were placed on the same footing as the Hebrew Scriptures quite early, starting with Peter's words about the apostle Paul's letters. Again, Justin Martyr tells us that at the early Christian meetings, "the memoirs of the apostles or the writings of the prophets are read, as long as time permits; then, when the reader has ceased, the president verbally instructs and exhorts to the imitation of these good things" (1 Apology 67).[185] Ignatius of Antioch (c. 35-108 C.E.), Theophilus of Antioch (d. 182 C.E.), and Tertullian (c. 155-240 C.E.) also spoke of the Prophets, the Law, and the Gospels as equally authoritative.

---

[183] Ibid., 294.

[184] Ibid., 141.

[185] Justin Martyr, "The First Apology of Justin," in *The Apostolic Fathers with Justin Martyr and Irenaeus*, ed. Alexander Roberts, James Donaldson, and A. Cleveland Coxe, vol. 1, The Ante-Nicene Fathers (Buffalo, NY: Christian Literature Company, 1885), 186.

The Early Christian View of the Integrity of the Greek New Testament Originals

If the early Christians' view of the New Testament books were on the same footing as the Hebrew Scriptures, then we would see them guarding the New Testament's integrity in the same way the Old Testament authors and the scribes in ancient Israel guarded the Hebrew Old Testament.

Deuteronomy 4:2 Updated American Standard Version (UASV) ² You shall **not add to** the word which I am commanding you, **nor take away** from it, that you may keep the commandments of Jehovah your God which I command you.	**Deuteronomy 12:32** Updated American Standard Version (UASV) ³² "Everything that I command you, you shall be careful to do; you shall **not add to** nor **take away from** it.

There indeed were severe consequences, even death to some, if scribes or copyists were to add to or take away from God's Word, disregarding these warnings. Eugene H. Merrill observes, "There is a principle of canonization here as well in that nothing is to be added to or subtracted from the word. This testifies to the fact that God himself is the originator of the covenant text and only he is capable of determining its content and extent."[186]

Proverbs 30:6 Updated American Standard Version (UASV)

⁶ **Do not add to** his words,

    lest he reprove you and you be found a liar.

This is an ongoing command about God's words that we had just seen above given to the Israelites in Deuteronomy 4:2 and 12:32. There is no need to add to or take away from God's Word, for it is sufficient. Bible commentator Duane A. Garrett, an expert on the book of Proverbs, tells us that "Verse 6 is an injunction against adding to God's words similar to the injunctions found in Deut. 12:32 and Rev 22:18. It is noteworthy that this text does not warn the reader not to reject or take away from divine revelation; it is more concerned that no one supplements it. This is, therefore, not a warning to the unbelieving interpreter but rather to the believer. The temptation is to improve on the text, if not by actually adding new material then by interpreting it in ways that make more of a passage's teaching than is

---

186 Eugene H. Merrill, *Deuteronomy*, vol. 4, The New American Commentary (Nashville: Broadman & Holman Publishers, 1994), 229.

really there. It is what Paul called "going beyond what is written" – 1 Corinthians 4:6.[187]

The Jewish people's attitude and their Hebrew Scriptures can be summed up in the words of Josephus, the first-century (37 – c.100 C.E.) Jewish historian wrote, "We have given practical proof of our reverence for our own Scriptures. Although such long ages have now passed, no one has ventured either to add, remove, or alter a syllable. It is an instinct with every Jew, from the day of his birth, to regard them as the decrees of God, to abide by them, and, if need be, cheerfully to die for them."[188] The longstanding view of the Jews toward the Hebrew Scriptures is fundamental, especially given what the apostle Paul wrote to the Roman Christian congregation. The apostle says, the Jews "were entrusted with the sayings[189] of God." – Romans 3:1-2.

Galatians 3:15 Updated American Standard Version (UASV)

[15] Brothers, I speak according to man:[190] even though it is only a man's covenant, yet when it has been ratified, **no one sets it aside or adds conditions to it**.

The letter from Paul to Galatians was penned about **50-52 C.E.** Here Paul's words in dealing with the covenant to Abraham and his descendants echo the words from the Law of Moses at Deuteronomy 4:2, when he says, "no one sets it aside or adds conditions to it," i.e., "not add to… nor take away." The covenant word of God was not to be altered.

Revelation 22:18-19 Updated American Standard Version (UASV)

[18] I testify to everyone who hears the words of the prophecy of this book: if anyone **adds to them**, God will add to him the plagues which are written in this book; [19] and if anyone **takes away from** the words of the book of this prophecy, God will take away his part from the tree of life and out of the holy city, which are written in this book.

Apostle John's letter to the seven congregations was penned about 95 C.E. Kistemaker, and Hendriksen wrote, "The solemn warning not to add to or detract from the words of this book is common in ancient literature. For instance, Moses warns the Israelites not to add to or subtract from the

---

[187] Duane A. Garrett, *Proverbs, Ecclesiastes, Song of Songs*, vol. 14, The New American Commentary (Nashville: Broadman & Holman Publishers, 1993), 237.

[188] Josephus, *The Life/Against Apion*, vol. 1, LCL, ed. by H. St. J. Thackeray (Cambridge, MA: Harvard University Press, 1976), pp. 177–181.

[189] **Sayings**: (Gr. *logia, on* [only in the plural]) A saying or message, usually short, especially divine, gathered into a collection–Acts 7:38; Romans 3:2; Hebrews 5:12; 1 Peter 4:11.

[190] Or *in terms of human relations*; or *according to a human perspective*; or *using a human illustration*

decrees and laws God gave them (Deut. 4:2; 12:32). This formula was attached to documents much the same as copyright laws protect modern manuscripts. In addition, curses were added in the form of a conditional sentence, 'If anyone adds or takes away anything from this book, a curse will rest upon him.' Paul wrote a similar condemnation when he told the Galatians that if anyone preached a gospel which was not the gospel of Christ, 'let him be eternally condemned' (Gal. 1:6–8). Now Jesus pronounces a curse on anyone who distorts his message."[191]

The Didache (The Teaching of the Twelve Apostles) dates to about 100 C.E. At 4:13, it reads, "You must not forsake the Lord's commandments, but must guard what you have received, neither adding nor subtracting anything."[192] This author is drawing on the command in Deuteronomy 4:2 and 12:32.[193] The point here is that while the author uses "the Lord" (i.e., Jehovah, that is, the Father) in Deut. 4:2, 12:32, he is actually referring to Jesus' teaching found in the Gospels. Therefore, the Gospels and, more specifically, Jesus' teaching are equal to the Hebrew Scriptures.

Papias of Hierapolis, about 135 C.E., records what he had to tell about the details surrounding each apostles' personal life and ministry. Papias 3:3-4 says, "I will not hesitate to set down … everything I carefully learned then from the elders and carefully remembered, guaranteeing their truth. For unlike most people, I did not enjoy those who have a great deal to say, but those who teach the truth. Nor did I enjoy those who recall someone else's commandments, but those who remember the commandments given by the Lord to the faith and proceeding from the truth itself. And if by chance someone who had been a follower of the elders should come my way, I inquired about the words of the elders—what Andrew or Peter said, or Philip, or Thomas or James, or John or Matthew or any other of the Lord's disciples."[194]

Papias says of Mark's Gospel: "Mark, having become Peter's interpreter, wrote down accurately everything he remembered." Further confirming the Gospel's accuracy, Papias continues: "Consequently Mark did nothing wrong in writing down some things as he remembered them, for he **made it his**

---

[191] Simon J. Kistemaker and William Hendriksen, *Exposition of the Book of Revelation*, vol. 20, New Testament Commentary (Grand Rapids: Baker Book House, 1953–2001), 594.

[192] Michael William Holmes, *The Apostolic Fathers: Greek Texts and English Translations*, Third ed. (Grand Rapids, MI: Baker Books, 2007), 351.

[193] (LXX 13:1.)

[194] Michael William Holmes, *The Apostolic Fathers: Greek Texts and English Translations*, Third ed. (Grand Rapids, MI: Baker Books, 2007), 735.

one concern **not to omit** anything which he heard **or to make any false statement in** them."[195] This is an apparent reference to Deuteronomy 4:2 while referencing Mark's Gospel, again showing that Christians viewed the New Testament books as being equal to the Hebrew Scriptures. Papias offers testimony that Matthew initially penned his Gospel in the Hebrew language. Papias says, "So Matthew composed the oracles in the Hebrew language, and each person interpreted them as best he could."[196] As the overseer of Hierapolis in Asia Minor, Papias was able to inquire and carefully learn from the elders throughout the church at the time, establishing the authenticity and divine inspiration of the New Testament. Sadly, though, only scanty fragments of the writings of Papias survived.

The *Epistle of Barnabas,* dated about 130 C.E., declares, "You shall guard what you have received, **neither adding nor subtracting** anything" (Barn 19:11).[197] Here again, Barnabas is drawing on Deuteronomy 4:2 as he expresses his concern about the Word of God, as he speaks about "the way of light" in chapter 19 of his letter, making multiple references to New Testament teachings and principles.

Dionysius of Corinth wrote in about 170 C.E. about those who had dared to alter his own writings. He writes, "For I wrote letters when the brethren requested me to write. And these letters the apostles of the devil have filled with tares [false information], **taking away some things and adding others**, for whom a woe is in store. It is not wonderful, then, if some have attempted to adulterate the Lord's writings when they have formed designs against those which are not such."[198] Here, Dionysius refers to Deuteronomy 4:2 and 12:32, noting the curse or woe that is in store for altering his own writings, and all the more so for daring to alter the Scriptures themselves. The reference to adulterating "the Lord's writings" is a reference to the New Testament writings – "A probable, though not exclusive, reference to Marcion, for he was by no means the only one of that age that interpolated and mutilated the works of the apostles to fit his theories. Apostolic works—true and false—circulated in great numbers and were

---

[195] Ibid, 739-40.

[196] Ibid, 741.

[197] Ibid, 437.

[198] Dionysius of Corinth, "Fragments from a Letter to the Roman Church," in *Fathers of the Third and Fourth Centuries: The Twelve Patriarchs, Excerpts and Epistles, the Clementina, Apocrypha, Decretals, Memoirs of Edessa and Syriac Documents, Remains of the First Ages*, ed. Alexander Roberts, James Donaldson, and A. Cleveland Coxe, trans. B. P. Pratten, vol. 8, The Ante-Nicene Fathers (Buffalo, NY: Christian Literature Company, 1886), 765.

made the basis for the speculations and moral requirements of many of the heretical schools of the second century."[199]

If there were no significant concerns over the New Testament originals' integrity, we would not see early church leaders showing such respect. The principle of not adding nor taking away found in Deuteronomy 4:2 and 12:32 can be applied to just one word or even a single number. We have the case of Irenaeus in about 180 C.E., who complained about the number 666 found in Revelation 13:18 that had been changed to 616. Irenaeus wrote, "Such, then, being the state of the case, and this number being found **in all the most approved and ancient copies** [of the Apocalypse], and those men who saw John face to face bearing their testimony [to it]; while reason also leads us to conclude that the number of the name of the beast, [if reckoned] according to the Greek mode of calculation by [the value of] the letters contained in it, will amount to six hundred and sixty and six."[200] The passage ἐν πᾶσι τοῖς σπουδαίοις καὶ ἀρχαίοις ἀντιγράφοις ("in all the most approved and ancient copies") shows that by then the autographs of the New Testament were not available, with various readings creeping into the manuscripts of the canonical books.

Irenaeus went on to let those guilty of willfully adding to or taking away from the Scriptures know that there will be severe punishment. He wrote, "Now, as regards those who have done this in simplicity, and without evil intent, we are at liberty to assume that pardon will be granted them by God. But as for those who, for the sake of vainglory, lay it down for certain that names containing the spurious number are to be accepted, and affirm that this name, hit upon by themselves, is that of him who is to come; such persons shall not come forth without loss, because they have led into error both themselves and those who confided in them. Now, in the first place, it is loss to wander from the truth, and to imagine that as being the case which is not; then again, as there shall be no light punishment [inflicted] **upon him who either** <u>adds</u> **or** <u>subtracts</u> **anything from the Scripture**."[201] Here Irenaeus is referring to John's warning in Revelation 22:18.

[199] Philip Schaff and Henry Wace, eds., *Eusebius: Church History, Life of Constantine the Great, and Oration in Praise of Constantine*, vol. 1, A Select Library of the Nicene and Post-Nicene Fathers of the Christian Church, Second Series (New York: Christian Literature Company, 1890).

[200] Irenaeus of Lyons, "Irenæus Against Heresies," in *The Apostolic Fathers with Justin Martyr and Irenaeus*, ed. Alexander Roberts, James Donaldson, and A. Cleveland Coxe, vol. 1, The Ante-Nicene Fathers (Buffalo, NY: Christian Literature Company, 1885), 558.

[201] Irenaeus of Lyons, "Irenæus Against Heresies," in *The Apostolic Fathers with Justin Martyr and Irenaeus*, ed. Alexander Roberts, James Donaldson, and A. Cleveland Coxe, vol. 1, The Ante-Nicene Fathers (Buffalo, NY: Christian Literature Company, 1885), 559.

Again, the *Letter of Polycarp to the Philippians,* dating to about 110 C.E., reads at 7:1, "For everyone who does not confess that Jesus Christ has come in the flesh is antichrist [cf. 1 John 4:2-3]; and whoever does not acknowledge the testimony of the cross is of the devil [cf. 1 John 3:8]; and **whoever twists the sayings of the Lord** to suit his own sinful desires and claims that there is neither resurrection nor judgment—well, that person is the first-born of Satan."[202] Of course, "the sayings of the Lord" come from the Gospels. Therefore, Polycarp was declaring a warning to anyone who would alter the Gospels. Some would argue that Polycarp was referring to oral traditions when he used the term "the sayings of the Lord" (τὰ λόγια τοῦ κυρίου), but this simply is not the case, since in the next verse he refers to these "sayings" (κυρίου) again and then quotes Matthew 6:13 and 26:41, where we find Matthew recording Jesus' sayings.

We could cite many more quotations from early church leaders about their concern for their integrity of the New Testament originals. However, we can see from our limited look at early Christianity's view of the Scriptures that the New Testament books were placed on the same footing as the Hebrew Scriptures from the very beginning. When we look at the first three centuries of Christianity, we find that the manuscripts were prepared for Christians' reading culture, who prioritized publishing and distributing a text that was accurate in content and reader-friendly. The Christian texts were prepared in such a way as to place the least demand on the reader to bring the Scriptures to a more diverse audience.

Clearly, Paul and Peter showed concern for their writings and equating NT books other than their own with the Hebrew Scriptures in authority. Early on, the church leaders were very concerned about preserving the integrity of the original, down to the individual words. The papyri of the first three centuries after Christ **provides evidence** that most scribes (copyists) also cared about preserving their exemplars' integrity and did not seek to change or alter the wording. On the other hand, we would be misleading others and ourselves if we were to deny that a small minority of the copyists did freely choose to make alterations—as Colwell said for example, that the scribe of **P[45]** worked "without any intention of exactly reproducing his source. He writes with great freedom, harmonizing, smoothing out, substituting almost whimsically." However, the scribe who worked on **P[75]** was a "disciplined scribe who writes with the intention of being careful and accurate." Then again, Colwell said that **P[66]** reflects "a scribe working with the intention of making a good copy, falling into careless errors, … but also

---

[202] Michael William Holmes, *The Apostolic Fathers: Greek Texts and English Translations*, Third ed. (Grand Rapids, MI: Baker Books, 2007), 289.

under the control of some other person, or second standard, ... It shows the supervision of a foreman, or a scribe turned proofreader."[203]

Generally speaking, the early scribes were very concerned about the accuracy of their copying. Still, while some were more successful than others, every one of them—due to human imperfection—made some transcriptional errors at times, which were **unintentional** (Matt. 27:11; Mark 6:51; 10:40; Rom. 5:1; Eph. 1:15; 1 Thess. 2:7; Heb. 12:15). We can also attribute human imperfection to **intentional changes,** *purposeful* scribal alterations, such as *conflation* (Luke 24:53; John 1:34; Rom. 3:32), *interpolation* (Mark 9:29; Lu 23:19, 34; Rom. 8:1; 1 Cor. 15:51), and attempts to clarify the meaning of a text (1 Cor. 3:3) or to enhance a doctrinal position (1 John 5:7).

We can say that **on the whole**, the early church leaders valued the integrity of the original, and the scribes valued the integrity of the exemplars which they were copying. In fact, the high value placed on the integrity of the original ironically led to some erroneous changes because scribes were prone at times to correct what they believed to be mistakes within the sacred text. Many modern textual scholars will tell their readers that the early copying period was "'free,' 'wild,' 'in a state of flux,' 'chaotic,' 'a turbid textual morass.'" (Hill and Kruger 2012, 10) The truth was actually the opposite. The church leaders valued the originals above all else, and the scribes saw their exemplars as master copies of those originals and reverentially feared to make any mistakes.

The goal of textual scholarship since the days of Erasmus in the sixteenth century has been to get back to the original, preserving the exact wording of the original twenty-seven New Testament books penned by Matthew, Mark, Luke, John, James, Jude, Peter, and Paul. However, this has not always proved to be the case with recent scholarship. Philip W. Comfort has been one of the leading outspoken proponents of the traditional goal of reconstructing the exact wording of the originals, and I quote the following observation by Comfort at length:

> The time gap between the autographs and the earliest extant copies is quite close—no more than 100 years for most of the books of the New Testament. Thus, we are in a good position to recover most of the original wording of the Greek New Testament. Such optimism was held by the well-known textual critics of the nineteenth century—most notably, Samuel Tregelles, B. F. Westcott, and F. J. A. Hort, who, although acknowledging that we may never recover all of the original text of the

---

[203] Ernest Colwell, "Method in Evaluating Scribal Habits: A Study of P45, P66, P75," in *Studies in Methodology in Textual Criticism of the New Testament,* New Testament Tools and Studies 9 (Leiden: Brill, 1969), 114–21.

New Testament books with absolute certainty, believed that the careful work of textual criticism could bring us extremely close. In the twentieth century, two eminent textual critics, Bruce Metzger and Kurt Aland, affirmed this same purpose, and were instrumental in the production of the two critical editions of the Greek New Testament that are widely used today.

Tregelles, Hort, Metzger, and Aland, as well as Constantine von Tischendorf, the nineteenth-century scholar who famously discovered Codex Sinaiticus, all provided histories of the transmission of the New Testament text and methodologies for recovering the original wording. Their views of textual criticism were derived from their actual experience of working with manuscripts and doing textual criticism in preparing critical editions of the Greek New Testament. Successive generations of scholars, working with ever-increasing quantities of manuscripts (especially earlier ones) and refining their methodologies, have continued with the task of recovering the original wording of the Greek New Testament.

By contrast, a certain number of textual critics in recent years have abandoned the notion that the original wording of the Greek New Testament can ever be recovered. Let us take, for example, Bart Ehrman (author of *The Orthodox Corruption of Scripture*) and David Parker (author of *The Living Text of the Gospels*). Having analyzed their positions, J. K. Elliott writes, "Both [men] emphasize the living and therefore changing text of the New Testament and the needlessness and inappropriateness of trying to establish one immutable original text. The changeable text in all its variety is what we textual critics should be displaying" (1999, 17). Elliott then speaks for himself on the matter: "Despite my own published work in trying to prove the originality of the text in selected areas of textual variation, ... I agree that the task of trying to establish the original words of the original authors with 100% certainty is impossible. More dominant in text critics' thinking now is the need to plot the changes in the history of the text" (1999, 18).

Not one textual critic could or would ever say that any of the critical editions of the Greek New Testament replicates the original wording with 100 percent accuracy. But an accurate reconstruction has to be the goal of those who practice textual criticism as classically defined. To veer from this is to stray from the essential task of textual criticism. It is an illuminating exercise "to plot the changes in the history of the text," but this assumes a known starting point. And what can that starting point be if not the original text? In analyzing Ehrman's book, *The Orthodox Corruption of Scripture*, Silva notes this same paradox: "Although this book is appealed to in support of blurring the notion of an original text, there is hardly a page in that book that does not in fact mention such a text or assume its accessibility …. Ehrman's book is unimaginable unless he can identify an initial form of the text that can be differentiated from a later alteration" (2002, 149). In short, one cannot speak about the text being corrupted if there is not an original text to be corrupted.

I am not against reconstructing the history of the text. In fact, I devoted many years to studying all the early Greek New Testament manuscripts (those dated before A.D. 300) and compiling a fresh edition of them in The Text of the Earliest New Testament Greek Manuscripts (coedited with David Barrett). This work provides a representative sampling of New Testament books that were actually read by Christians in the earliest centuries of the church. But whatever historical insights we may gain by studying the varying manuscript traditions as texts unto themselves, this is no reason to abandon the goal of producing the best critical edition possible, one that most likely replicates the original wording. Thus, I echo Silva's comments entirely, when he says: "I would like to affirm—not only with Hort, but with practically all students of ancient documents—that the recovery of the original text (i.e., the text in its initial form, prior to the alterations produced in the copying process) remains the primary task of textual criticism" (2002, 149).[204]

The author of this work would echo the words of Silva and Comfort in that the primary task of a textual scholar is the process of attempting to ascertain the original wording of the original text that was published by Matthew, Mark, Luke, John, James, Jude, Peter, and Paul. Even if we acknowledge that we can never say with absolute **certainty** that we have established the original wording one hundred percent, this should always be the goal. Imagine any other field in life, the **certainty** of a successful heart transplant by a surgeon, the **certainty** of astronauts going to the moon and back, or just the certainty that our automobile will get us to our destination, and the like. Do we want a heart surgeon who aims for eighty-percent certainty in a successful operation on us? Most objective textual scholars would agree that between the 1881 Westcott and Hort text and the Nestle-Aland/United Bible Societies Greek text, we are in the very high nineties, if not ninety-nine percent mirror-like reflection of the original wording of the twenty-seven New Testament books. Of course, the ongoing objective is to reach one hundred percent even if it is not achievable.

---

[204] Philip Comfort, NEW TESTAMENT TEXT AND TRANSLATUION COMMENTARY: Commentary on the variant readings of the ancient New Testament manuscripts and how they relate to the major English translations (Carol Stream, ILL: Tyndale House Publishers, Inc., 2008), Page xi.

CHAPTER VI

The Early Christian Copyists

Today, about two billion people call themselves Christians who own or are aware of the Bible. Most are unaware of just how that book came down to them, yet many, if not most, would acknowledge that it is inspired by God and free of errors and contradictions. In this chapter, we will take a brief look at how the early Christians went about the work of making copies of what would become known as New Testament books, books that they felt were Scripture, just like the inspired Hebrew Scriptures. Such background cannot only build confidence that we have been carrying the very Word of God, but it also allows us to do as the apostle Peter said, to 'be prepared to make a defense to anyone who asks you for a reason for the hope that is in you.' (1 Pet 3:15) One might say that the 140+ New Testament papyrus manuscripts known today are hardly a notable amount.[205] Most of those are regarded as

---

[205] First, there are close to one million papyrus fragments in various libraries throughout the world that have not yet been published. Since only about one percent of all papyri have been published (about 10,000), there is a very high degree of probability that some of the remainders will be NT fragments. The last NT papyrus to be published was papyrus 141 or P[141], a third-century (200-300 C.E.) fragment of Luke 2:32-34, 40-42; 24:22-28, 30-38 housed at Papyrology Rooms, Sackler Library, Oxford, UK. Therefore, when we speak of how many have survived, we can understand that the question is not that easy to answer.

NT scholars use the term "extant" to describe MSS that have survived. It means that some have survived and are known to exist. With that definition, you might think that 140 is the number. However, there is a slight problem with that, too. Some fragments, such as P64 and P[67], were later determined to belong to the same manuscript. This happens a few times for NT MSS, but mostly for minuscules (of which we now have extant about 2900). However, most scholars do not wrestle with such details.

the earliest witnesses to the original text of the Greek New Testament. When we consider that the ancients wrote on perishable materials, we understand why relatively few manuscripts have been preserved to our day.

Further, early Christianity suffered much persecution. Both emperors, Nero (64 C.E.) and Domitian (95 C.E.) persecuted Christians, but this likely did not significantly affect the survival of manuscripts. However, throughout the second and third centuries C.E., other Roman Emperors persecuted Christians on an empire-wide scale, which substantially affected manuscript survival.

Many scholars tend to speak disapprovingly of the work of the early Christian copyists. First, they maintain that copyists were not concerned with the importance of accurately copying the manuscripts, resulting in many mistakes. Second, they claim that most of the copyists were untrained in the practice of making copies, resulting in more copyist errors. Third, they say that the copyists were taking liberties by freely changing words, clauses, even whole sentences, omitting and inserting to improve the account, and at times to strengthen orthodoxy. However, as we have seen and will see shortly, this observation is not the case. We do not claim the early copyists or any copyists, for that matter, were error-free or that they were inspired, moved along by the Holy Spirit, producing a full inerrant copy, as they were not. However, professional and semi-professional scribes copied many of the early New Testament manuscripts, with most being done by copyists who, at a minimum, had experience making documents.[206] Nevertheless, there undoubtedly were copyists with no training at all who did copy some manuscripts.

Therefore, some of the early Christian copyists because they were untrained in the task of making copies, did make errors. However, were these errors noteworthy? No. Again, we can say that the vast majority of the Greek text from the early papyri until the Byzantine text, about **92.6 percent**, is not affected by variants. "The stability of the New Testament text under

---

Therefore, most simply round the number to 5,500 NT Greek manuscripts instead of totaling the catalog entries that come out to 5,898.

As for dates, the papyri range in date from early second century C.E. to early seventh century C.E. I have worked up a chart of all NT MSS through the 8th century: as much as 43% of all the verses of the NT are attested by the end of the third century in the extant papyri.--Dr. Daniel B. Wallace of The Center for the Study of New Testament Manuscripts.

[206] C. H. Roberts wrote, "In the second century, locally produced texts such as the scrap of *The Shepherd* [of Hermas] on the back of a document from the Fayum or the Baden Exodus-Deuteronomy might be carefully collated and corrected; the numerous duplications and omissions of the first hand of the Chester Beatty Numbers-Deuteronomy codex were put right by the corrector. This scrupulous reproduction of the text may be a legacy from Judaism and reminds us that no more in this period than in any other does quality of book production go hand in hand with quality of text." (C. H. Roberts, Manuscript, Society, and Belief in Early Christian Egypt 1979, 22)

consideration, from the early papyri to the Byzantine text, achieves an average of 92.6 percent."[207] Of the **small amount** of the text affected by variants, the vast majority are minor slips of the pen, such as misspelling words. Also, they are minor intentional changes, e.g., using a synonym in place of the word in the text, using a pronoun for a noun, and spelling the same word differently. With these insignificant mishaps, we are sure what the original reading is in these places.

On this, Metzger writes, "The *Alexandrian text,* which Westcott and Hort called the *Neutral text* (a question-begging title), is usually considered to be the best text and the most faithful in preserving the original. Characteristics of the Alexandrian text are brevity and austerity. It is generally shorter than the text of other forms, and it does not exhibit the degree of grammatical and stylistic polishing that is characteristic of the Byzantine type of text.[208] So, momentarily moving away from the early Alexandrian papyrus manuscripts and comparing the Alexandrian text-type and the Byzantine text-type, even they "actually exhibit a remarkable degree of agreement, perhaps as much as 80 percent!"[209] Maurice A. Robinson and William G. Pierpont have estimated that the Alexandrian text-type and the Byzantine text-type agreement to be about 90 percent.[210] Of our **small amount**, an infinitesimal (very small) number of variants is difficult in establishing the original reading. Lastly, there are negligible (very scarce) variants where we would say that we are uncertain about the original reading. However, these latter two categories affect no doctrine; moreover, variant readings can be placed in a footnote, giving the reader access to the original using either the main text or the footnote.

One may wonder why more Old and New Testament manuscripts have not survived. Really, the better question would be, how come so many of our Bible manuscripts survived in comparison to ancient secular manuscripts? The primary materials used to receive writing in ancient times were perishable papyrus and parchment. It must be remembered that the Christians suffered intense persecution during intervals in the first 300 years from Pentecost 33 C.E. With this persecution from the Roman Empire came many orders to

---

[207] K. Martin Heide, "Assessing the Stability of the Transmitted Texts of the New Testament and the Shepherd of Hermas," in *The Reliability of the New Testament: Bart D. Ehrman and Daniel B. Wallace in Dialogue,* ed. Robert B. Stewart (Minneapolis: Fortress, 2011), 138.

[208] Bruce Manning Metzger, United Bible Societies, *A Textual Commentary on the Greek New Testament, Second Edition a Companion Volume to the United Bible Societies' Greek New Testament (4th Rev. Ed.)* (London; New York: United Bible Societies, 1994), xix.

[209] Kurt and Barbara Aland, *THE TEXT OF THE NEW TESTAMENT: An Introduction to the Critical Editions and to the Theory and Practice of Modern Textual Criticism* (Grand Rapids, MI: Wm. B. Eerdmans Publishing Co., 1995), 28.

[210] Maurice A. Robinson and William G. Pierpont, *The New Testament in the Original Greek: Byzantine Textform,* 2005 (Southborough, MA: Chilton, 2005), 584.

destroy Christian texts. In addition, these texts were not stored in such a way as to secure their preservation. They were actively used by the Christians in the congregation and were subject to wear and tear.

Furthermore, moisture is the enemy of papyrus, and it causes them to disintegrate over time. This is why, as we will discover, the papyrus manuscripts that have survived have come from the dry sands of Egypt. Moreover, it seems not to have entered the early Christians' minds to preserve their documents because their solution to the loss of manuscripts was just to make more copies. Fortunately, making copies transitioned to the more durable animal skins, which would last much longer. Those that have survived, especially from the fourth century C.E. and earlier, are the path to restoring the original Greek New Testament.[211]

Both papyrus and parchment jeopardized the survival of the Bible because they were perishable materials. Papyrus, the weakest of the two, can tear and discolor. Because of moist climates, a sheet of papyrus can decay to the point where it is nothing more than a handful of dust. We must remember papyrus is a plant, and when the scroll has been stored, it can grow mold and rot from dampness. It can even be eaten by starving rodents or insects, especially white ants (i.e., termites) when buried. When some of the manuscripts were first discovered early on, they were exposed to excessive light and humidity, hastening their deterioration.

While parchment is far more durable than papyrus, it will also perish in time if mishandled or exposed to the elements (temperature, humidity, and light) over time.[212] Parchment is made from animal skin, so it too is also a victim of insects. Hence, when it comes to ancient records, Everyday Writing in the Graeco-Roman East states, "survival is the exception rather than the rule."[213] Think about it for a moment; the Bible and its special revelation could have died from decay in the elements.

Old Testament Textual scholars Brotzman and Tully write, "Writing is central to the theology of the OT because it is through writing that God's mighty acts, covenant relationship with his people, and subsequent expectations are passed down to future generations. The first occurrence of the verb 'to write' in the OT is found in Exod. 17:14 when YHWH tells Moses to write down his promise that he will utterly blot out the memory of Amalek. YHWH says that Moses must then 'place' it in the ears of Joshua.

---

[211] Cf. J. H. Greenlee, *Introduction to New Testament Textual Criticism* (Peabody: Hendrickson, 1995), 11.

[212] For example, the official signed copy of the U.S. Declaration of Independence was written on parchment. Now, less than 250 years later, it has faded to the point of being barely legible.

[213] Roger S. Bagnall, *The Oxford Handbook of Papyrology* (Oxford Handbooks) Oxford, NY: Oxford University Press, 2009, 140.

The point here is that the written word would serve as a reminder of what God had promised. In 24: 4, Moses writes down all the words of YHWH's covenant with Israel and then reads it to the people (24: 7). That writing served as a witness to what God had done and the necessity of response on their part. It was intended for all people, not just the elites, including future generations yet to be born. A few verses later, in 24:12, God has written down the stipulations of the covenant, which are for the instruction of the people. Just these three examples illustrate the central place of writing in the theological foundation of the nation of Israel. It is the written word that allows future generations access to former words and deeds which would otherwise be lost to them. This is so critical that each king was to have a copy of the Torah and was to read from it all the days of his life that he might learn to fear YHWH (Deut. 17: 18– 19). Texts such as Deut. 6, Josh. 4, and Ps. 78 emphasize the necessity of YHWH's people instructing future generations about the character, power, deeds, and expectations of YHWH; the failure to remember would certainly result in apostasy and destruction."[214]

Brotzman and Tully go on to say, "Those who argue for widespread literacy usually point to the relative ease of using a syllabic alphabet in contrast to the hundreds of signs in other ancient writing systems. In addition, there are a number of references in the Bible to average, everyday people, reading and writing. Although he argues that literacy was not widespread, Menahem Haran mentions the following examples. In Deut. 6:9 every Israelite is commanded to write the words of the law on the doorposts of houses and gates. In Deut. 24: 1– 3 there is a reference to a (hypothetical) man writing a bill of divorce for his wife. In Judg. 8: 14 the young man from Succoth could write down the names of seventy-seven men for Gideon (Haran, 'On the Diffusion of Literacy and Schools in Ancient Israel,' in Congress Volume: Jerusalem 1986, ed. J. A. Emerton, VTSup 40 [Leiden: Brill, 1988], 81– 82). Archaeologists have also found many inscribed seals, receipts for payment, and even an inscription on a tomb warning would-be thieves of the consequences for breaking and entering. This might suggest that even thieves were literate. Demsky and Bar-Ilan argue that the hundreds of seals with writing (rather than pictures), the ubiquity of vulgar script identifying the owner of everyday objects, inscriptions by and for craftsmen and farmers, and writing that popularized the message of the prophets all point to common literacy in ancient Israel (" Writing in Ancient Israel," 15– 16).[215]

---

[214] Ellis R. Brotzman; Eric J. Tully, Eric Old Testament Textual Criticism: A Practical Introduction (p. 15). Baker Publishing Group. Kindle Edition.

[215] IBID.

The Mosaic Law commanded every future king, "And when he sits on the throne of his kingdom, he shall write for himself in a book a copy of this law, approved by the Levitical priests." (Deuteronomy 17:18) Moreover, the professional copyist of the Hebrew Old Testament made so many manuscripts, by the time of Jesus and the apostles, throughout all of Israel and even into distant Macedonia, there were many copies of the Scriptures in the synagogues. (Luke 4:16, 17; Acts 17:11) How did our Hebrew Old Testament and Greek New Testament survive the elements to the point where there are far more of them than any other ancient document. For example, there are 5,898 New Testament manuscripts in the original Greek alone that have been cataloged.[216]

New Testament scholar Philip W. Comfort writes, "Jews were known to put scrolls containing Scripture in pitchers or jars to preserve them. The Dead Sea scrolls found in jars in the Qumran caves are a celebrated example of this. The Beatty Papyri were very likely a part of a Christian library, which was hidden in jars to be preserved from confiscation during the Diocletian persecution."[217] Christianity was initially made up of Jewish Christians only for the first seven years (29-36 C.E.), with Cornelius being the first Gentile baptized in 36 C.E. Much of early Christianity (33-350 C.E.) was made up of Jewish Christians, who evidently carried over the tradition of putting "scrolls containing Scripture in pitchers or jars in order to preserve them." For this reason, some of our earliest Bible manuscripts have been discovered in unusually dry regions, in clay jars, and even dark closets and caves.

The result is that the New Testament has been preserved in over **5,898** complete or fragmented Greek manuscripts and some 10,000 Latin manuscripts, and 9,300 manuscripts in various other ancient languages, including Syriac Slavic, Gothic, Ethiopic, Coptic, and Armenian. Some of these are about 2,000 years old—**the end of the excursion**.

---

[216] While at present here in 2020, there are 5,898 manuscripts. There are **140 listed Papyrus** manuscripts, 323 Majuscule manuscripts, 2,951 Minuscule manuscripts, and 2,484 Lectionary manuscripts, bringing the total cataloged manuscripts to 5,898 manuscripts. However, you cannot simply total the number of cataloged manuscripts because, for example, $P^{11/14}$ are the same manuscript but with different catalog numbers. The same is true of $P^{33/5}$, $P^{4/64/67}$, $P^{49/65}$ and $P^{77/103}$. Now this alone would bring our 140 listed papyrus manuscripts down to 134. Then, we turn to one example from our majuscule manuscripts where clear 0110, 0124, 0178, 0179, 0180, 0190, 0191, 0193, 0194, and 0202 are said to be part of 070. A minuscule manuscript was listed with five separate catalog numbers for 2306, which then have the letters a through e. Thus, we have the following GA numbers: 2306 for 2306a, and 2831- 2834 for 2306b-2306e.' – (Hixon 2019, 53-4) The problem is much worse when we consider that there are 323 Majuscule manuscripts and then far worse still with a listed 2,951 Minuscule and 2,484 Lectionaries. Nevertheless, those who estimate a total of 5,300 (Jacob W. Peterson, Myths and Mistakes, p. 63) 5,500 manuscripts (Dr. Ed Gravely / ehrmanproject.com/), 5,800 manuscripts (Porter 2013, 23), it is still a truckload of evidence far and above the dismal number of ancient secular author books.

[217] Philip Wesley Comfort and David P. Barrett, *The Text of the Earliest New Testament Greek Manuscripts* (Wheaton, IL: Tyndale House, 2001), 158.

Public Reading Indicates the Importance of New Testament Books

Public reading is yet another necessary inference that the first-century Christian congregation valued the books that were being produced by the New Testament authors Matthew, Mark, Luke, John, Paul, Peter, James, and Jude.

Matthew 24:15 Updated American Standard Version (UASV)

15 "Therefore when you see the abomination of desolation,[218] which was spoken of through Daniel the prophet, standing in the holy place (let the reader understand),

This parenthetical "let the reader understand" is a reference to a public reader within the congregations.

1 Timothy 4:13 Updated American Standard Version (UASV)

13 Until I come, devote yourself to the public reading of Scripture, to exhortation, to teaching

Only the privileged owned scrolls of the Holy Scriptures. Most Christians in the first century gained access to God's Word, as Paul explains here in his first letter to Timothy, by "the public reading of Scripture." Public reading was a major part of Christian meetings, a traditional practice of the Jews from Moses's time, and one which was carried over to the Christian congregation. – Acts 13:15; 15:21; 2 Corinthians 3:15.

Revelation 1:3 Updated American Standard Version (UASV)

3 Blessed is the one who reads and those who hear the words of the prophecy, and who keep what is written in it, for the time is near.

This reference to "he who reads and those who hear" is to the public reader and his audience in each of the seven mentioned congregations. Another factor is how the writers of the Christian Greek Scriptures viewed their own published works.

2 Peter 3:16 Updated American Standard Version (UASV)

16 as also in all his letters, speaking in them of these things, in which are some things hard to understand, which the untaught and unstable distort, **as**

---

[218] **Abomination of Desolation:** (Gr. *bdelugma eremoseos*) An expression by Jesus recorded in Mathew 24:15 and Mark 13:14 referring to Daniel 11:31 and 12:11. *Bdelugma* refers to something that is an abomination, unclean, which horrifies clean persons, leaving them disgusted. *Eremoseos* has the sense of an extensive desolating act or destruction, which caused total ruin, leaving no place for shelter.

they do also the rest of the Scriptures, to their own destruction. (Bold added.)

Here, about 64 C.E., we have the apostle Peter, who has just canonized Paul's letters, grouping them together as a collection. This is evidence of their being viewed as having authority. At 2 Timothy 3:16 and 2 Peter 1:20, the apostles Paul and Peter respectively appear to be referring to both the Hebrew Old Testament and the Greek Christian writings as [Greek *graphe*] "Scripture." Note that Peter is comparing Paul's letters to *"the rest of the Scriptures."* What exactly does that mean?

Both Jesus and the Christian Greek Scriptures writers often used the Greek word *graphe* in their references to Moses' writings and the prophets, viewing them as having authority from God, being inspired. Many times, Jesus designates these Old Testament books as a whole as *graphe*, i.e., "Scripture." (Matthew 21:42; 22:29; Mark 14:49; John 5:39; Acts 17:11; 18:24, 28) At other times, the singular for "Scripture" was used when quoting a specific text to make a point, referring to it as a part of the whole of writings encompassing our 39 books of the Hebrew Old Testament. (Rom. 9:17; Gal. 3:8) Still, at other times *graphe* is used in a single text reference, such as Jesus' reference when dealing with the Jewish religious leaders: "Have you not read this [*graphe*] Scripture: 'The stone that the builders rejected has become the cornerstone.'" (Mark 12:10) Jesus' use of *graphe* in such an authoritative and traditional way only strengthens the point that immediately, the New Testament authors' writings were viewed as *graphe*, namely, Scripture.

From an Oral Gospel to the Written Record

Jesus had commanded his disciples to, "'Go therefore and make disciples of all the nations, baptizing them in the name of the Father and the Son and the Holy Spirit, teaching them to observe all that I commanded you; and look, I am with you always, even to the end of the age.'" (Matt 28:19-20) How then was this gospel (good news) to be made known?

> During the forty-day period between Jesus' resurrection and his ascension, Jesus instructed his disciples in the teaching of the gospel. Accordingly, he prepared them for the tremendous task that awaited them on and after Pentecost.[219]

There were only ten days after Jesus' ascension to Pentecost, when "they were all filled with the Holy Spirit." Jesus put it this way, in his words, it being

---

[219] Simon J. Kistemaker and William Hendriksen, vol. 17, New Testament Commentary: Exposition of the Acts of the Apostles, New Testament Commentary (Grand Rapids: Baker Book House, 1953-2001), 47-48.

only "a few days." This time would have been filled with the process of replacing Judas Iscariot, prayer, and the established gospel message, which would be the official oral message until it was deemed necessary to have a written gospel some 10 to 15 years later. According to Scripture, the gospel message was quite simple: 'Christ died for our sins, was buried, and he was resurrected on the third day.' – 1 Corinthians 15:1-8

1 Corinthians 15:1-2 Updated American Standard Version (UASV)

15 Now I make known to you, brothers, the gospel which I proclaimed to you, which you have also received, in which you also stand, ² by which you are also being saved, if you hold fast to the message I proclaimed to you, unless you believed in vain.

By the time of the destruction of Jerusalem by General Titus of Rome (70 C.E.), all of the Greek New Testament books had been written, except for those penned by the apostle John. The Gospel of Matthew was penned first, published between 45 and 50 C.E. The Gospel of Luke was written about 56-58 C.E., and the Gospel of Mark between 60 to 65 C.E. Matthew, Mark, and Luke are known as the Synoptic Gospels, as they are similar in content. At the same time, John chose to convey other information, perhaps because he wrote his gospel to the second generation of Christians in about 98 C.E. Luke informs us of how the first Christians received the gospel message. Very few translations make explicit the exact process.

Luke 1:1-4 Updated American Standard Version (UASV) [220]

¹ Inasmuch as many have undertaken to compile a narrative of the things that have been fulfilled among us, ² just as they were handed down to us by those who from the beginning were eyewitnesses and servants of the word, ³ It also seemed good to me, since I have carefully investigated everything from the very first, to write an orderly account for you, most excellent Theophilus, ⁴ so that you may know the certainty concerning the things about which you were **taught orally** [κατηχέω katēcheō].

Acts 18:24-25 Updated American Standard Version (UASV)

²⁴ Now a Jew named Apollos, an Alexandrian by birth, came to Ephesus. He was an eloquent man, competent in the Scriptures. ²⁵ This man had been **orally** [κατηχημένος katēchēmenos] **instructed** in the way of the Lord, and being fervent in spirit, he spoke and taught accurately the things concerning Jesus, knowing only the baptism of John.

---

[220] The Updated American Standard Version (UASV) is under production by Christian Publishing House. It is by permission that we use these next few verses before it is published, as their rendering better conveys the original Greek.

Galatians 6:6 Updated American Standard Version (UASV)

The one who is **orally** [κατηχούμενος katēchoumenos] **taught** the word must share all good things with the one who teaches.

We can see clearly from the above that both Theophilus and Apollos received the initial gospel message orally, just as all Christians did in the early years. Even after the written gospels were available, the gospel of Jesus was still taught by oral instruction (κατηχέω katēcheō). In time, it was deemed necessary for a written record, which is why Luke gives for his Gospel. This was not to discount what Theophilus had been orally taught but rather to give credence to that oral message that he had already received. Of course, the New Testament was not limited to these gospels.

The publishing of these New Testament books in written form would have come about in the following stages:

(1) the inspired author certainly would have used a well-trusted, skilled Christian scribe to take down what he was inspired to convey, *some believe* by shorthand;[221]

(2) The scribe would then make a rough draft *if it had been taken* by shorthand.[222] If shorthand had not been used, this first copy would have been the rough draft;

(3) this draft would then be read by both the scribe and author, making corrections because the copyist, though professional or at least skillful at making documents, was not inspired;

(4) after that, the scribe would make what is known as the autograph, original, or initial text, to be signed by the author,

(5) which would then be used as the official exemplar to make other copies.

---

[221] "I Tertius, who wrote this letter, greet you in the Lord." (Rom. 16:22) "By Silvanus, a faithful brother as I regard him, I have written briefly to you, exhorting and declaring that this is the true grace of God. Stand firm in it." (1 Pet. 5:12)

[222] Again, there is the **slight possibility** of Tertius or other Bible author's scribes taking it down in shorthand and after that making out a full draft, which would have been reviewed by both Paul and Tertius. This is only the case if it is comparable to what a modern-day court reporter does. In some sense, they are taking down whoever is speaking down in shorthand. Imagine a courtroom where you have a witness talking fast, the prosecution interrupts, the defense jumps in with his rebuttal and the judge snaps his ruling, and the witness resumes his or her account of things. All of that is taken down explicitly word for word in shorthand, and if ever turned into longhand, it would be exactly what was said, down to the uh and um common in speech. So, if the shorthand of the day had that kind of capability; then, it is conceivable. We must remember these are the Bible author's dictated words to the scribe based on their inspiration, not the word choice or writing style of the scribe.

Both Tertius and Silvanus were very likely skilled Christian scribes who assisted the New Testament authors. (Rom. 16:22; 1 Pet. 5:12) It is unlikely that Paul personally wrote any of his letters that were of great length. It is clear that Peter used the trained Silvanus to pen his first letter. Some scholars have suggested, the second letter was possibly the result of Jude's copyist skills. Why? Some as it is remarkably similar in style to the letter by Jude. They say that this may explain the differences in style between First and Second Peter. We should emphasize that this is not logical. It *is not possible* nor *reasonable* that the inspired author would give his skilled Christian scribe some latitude to serve as a coauthor regarding word choices or writing style, as some have suggested. There is **no Scriptural support** to suggest that the Bible authors' scribes were inspired and moved along by the Holy Spirit. Therefore, there must be different reasons why the writing style differs between First and Second Peter, such as the subject and the purpose in writing were different, because Peter is the author of both letters.

The Christian's Use of the Codex

Going back to the first-century once again, let us take a moment to deal with the invention of the codex. Was it the first-century Christians who invented the codex, or at least put it on the stage of the world scene?

The writing tablet of ancient times was made from two flat pieces of wood, held together by a thong hinge, which looks something like our modern book. It had its limits because of the impracticality of fastening more than a few such tablets together. The center of the tablet pages was slightly hollowed to receive a wax coating. A stylus was the standard instrument used to write on these waxed tablets. The stylus was made of metal, ivory, or bone and was sharpened to a point on one side while having a rounded knob on the other for erasing and making corrections. This was the oldest form of writing for the Greeks, who borrowed it from the Hittites. History and evidence credit the Romans with replacing the wooden tablet with the parchment notebook. The apostle Paul is the only Greek writer of the first-century C.E. to mention the parchment notebook.

2 Timothy 4:13 Updated American Standard Version (UASV)

13 When you come, bring the cloak that I left behind in Troas with Carpus, and the scrolls, especially the parchments. [Gr., *membranai*, parchment notebooks]

However, it should be recognized that the parchment notebook was not used for literature in the first two centuries before the Christian era (B.C.E.); this was done with the roll or scroll. Even though the codex was commonly used for books, the first indication that it was going to displace the roll came toward the end of the first century C.E. (Roberts and Skeat, The Birth of the Codex 1987, 24) Thus, again, the Jews of the late first century C.E. and after that used scrolls, while the Christians used codices. However, many of the first Christians were Jewish and likely read their Old Testament from a scroll. Before becoming a Christian, the apostle Paul was a Pharisee and would have used scrolls. However, at least until about the end of the first century C.E., Christians used scrolls primarily.

Only a handful of manuscripts of the New Testament that are still in existence were written on scrolls (P^{13}, P^{18}, and P^{98}). However, these were written on the backs of other writings, so they were not composed in scroll form. P^{22} was written on a roll, and we await more research there, as it is a peculiarity among the group of papyri. All other New Testament manuscripts were written on codices. There is evidence that the second-century Christians were trying to set themselves apart from the Jews, so they likely made the transition partly because they wished to be different. We say in part because it is quite evident that the first Christians grouped their writings together, the Gospels and Paul's letters. The codex afforded them the means of doing this, while a scroll of the gospels would have been far too long and bulky, and finding a portion of desired text would have been difficult at best. For example, P^{46}, dating to about 150 C.E., contained ten of Paul's letters. P^{45} dates to about 225 C.E. and originally included all four Gospels and the book of Acts. In the end, it can be said that the Christians adopted the codex (1) to be different from the Jews, (2) to have the Gospels and the Apostle Paul's letters all in one book, and (3) because of the ease of being able to find a portion of text, and this made the spread of the good news much more convenient.

We do learn a good deal from the New Testament. The apostle Peter writes, "... just as our beloved brother Paul also wrote to you according to the wisdom given him, as he does in all his letters when he speaks in them of these matters ...." (2 Pet 3:15-16, about 64 C.E.) This shows how early Paul's letters were grouped together. The apostle John wrote, "Though I have much to write to you, I would rather not use paper and ink. Instead, I hope to come to you and talk face to face so that our joy may be complete." (2 John 12, about 98 C.E.) We see from this that John used papyrus in writing to a sister congregation. The Greek word *chartou* means "papyrus," "a sheet of paper." The apostle Paul wrote Timothy and asked him, "when you come, bring the cloak that I left with Carpus at Troas, also the books [likely scrolls of OT books], and, above all, the parchments [codices]." (2 Tim 4:13, about 65 C.E) While it is thought by most scholars that Paul was talking about two different items here, it is quite possible that he was referring to only one, which is Skeat's position. Let us look at the verse again:

When you come bring ... the books, especially the parchments.

When you come, bring ... the books, that is my parchment notebooks.

If the second version above is correct, Paul hoped to obtain some of his notebooks, possible rough drafts that he had left behind. The Old Testament books could have been located right where he was, but he would have been highly interested in unpublished works that he wanted to get out before his execution. Of course, this latter thought is the formation of judgments based on incomplete or inconclusive information. However, one thing is sure that either Paul was asking for codices in complete book form or notebook form. This indicates that Paul was the first to have his books collected into codex form, and we can conclude that the Christians were using the codex at the end of the first century.

The Trustworthiness of Early Copyists

In his *Methods in Establishing the Nature of Text-Types*, E. C. Colwell notes: "the overwhelming majority of readings were created before the year 200. But very few, if any, text-types were established by that time." (p. 55) In *The Bodmer and Mississippi Collection*, G. D. Kilpatrick says, "Apart from errors which can occur anywhere as long as books are copied by hand, almost all variants can be presumed to have been created by A.D. 200." (p. 42) And Kurt and Barbara Aland say, "practically all the substantive variants in the text of the New Testament are from the second century ..." – *The Text of the New Testament*, 295.

Lee McDonald states,

"Many mistakes in the manuscripts were made and subsequently transmitted in the churches. This suggests that these documents were not generally recognized as Scripture until the end of the second century C.E. Scribal attempts at improvements in the text occurred regularly, and apparently, no attempts were made to stop this activity until the fourth century, when more stability in the text of the NT began to take place."[223]

Throughout much of the twentieth century, it was common to form three conclusions about the earliest copyists and their work:

(1) The first three centuries saw copyists who were semiliterate and unskilled in the work of making copies.

---

[223] L. M. McDonald, The Biblical Canon (Peabody, Mass.: Hendrickson, 2007), 359. A similar argument is made by G. M. Hahneman, The Muratorian Fragment and the Development of the Canon (Oxford: Clarendon, 1992), 96; D. W. Riddle, 'Textual Criticism as a Historical Discipline', ATR 18 (1936): 227; and Parker, The Living Text, 202–5.

(2) Copyists in these early centuries felt as though the end was nigh, so they took liberties with the text in an attempt to strengthen orthodoxy.

(3) In the early centuries, manuscripts could be described as "free," "wild," "in a state of flux," "chaotic," "a turbid textual morass," i.e., a "free text" (so the Alands).

Number (1) in the above would undoubtedly lead to many unintentional changes, while number (2) would escalate intentional changes. J. Harold Greenlee had this to say:

> In the very early period, the NT writings were more nearly "private" writings than the classics . . . the classics were commonly, although not always, copied by professional scribes, the NT books were probably usually copied in the early period by **Christians who were not professionally trained** for the task, and **no corrector** was employed to check the copyist's work against his exemplar (the MS from which the copy was made) …. It appears that a copyist sometimes even took liberty to add or change minor details in the narrative books on the basis of personal knowledge, alternative tradition, or a parallel account in another book of the Bible …. **At the same time, the importance of these factors in affecting the purity of the NT text <u>must not be exaggerated</u>**. The NT books doubtless came to be considered as "literature" soon after they began to be circulated, with attention to the precise wording required when copies were made.[224] (Bold and underline mine)

Greenlee had not changed his position 14 years later when he wrote the following:

> The New Testament, on the other hand, was probably copied during the earliest period mostly by ordinary Christians **who were not professional scribes** but who wanted a copy of the New Testament book or books for themselves or for other Christians.[225] (Bold mine)

The Alands, in their *Text of the New Testament,* saw the New Testament books as not being canonical, i.e., not viewed as Scripture in the first few centuries, so the books were subject to changes. They wrote, "not only every

---

[224] J. Harold Greenlee, Introduction to New Testament Textual Criticism (Revised Edition, 1995), 51–52.

[225] J. Harold Greenlee, The Text of the New Testament: From Manuscript to Modern Edition (2008), 37.

church but each individual Christian felt 'a direct relationship to God.' Well into the second century, Christians still regarded themselves as possessing inspiration equal to that of the New Testament writings which they read in their worship service." Earlier the Alands had written, "That was all the more true of the early period when the text had not attained canonical status, especially in the early period when Christians considered themselves filled with the Spirit." They claimed that "until the beginning of the fourth century the text of the New Testament developed freely."[226]

Generally, once an established concept is set within the world of textual scholars, it is not easily displaced. During the start of the 20th century (1900–1940), there were a handful of papyri discovered that obviously represented the work of a copyist who had no training. It is during this time that Sir Frederic Kenyon, director and principal librarian of the British Museum for many years, said,

> The early Christians, a poor, scattered, often **illiterate** body, looking for the return of the Lord at no distant date, **were not likely to care** sedulously for minute accuracy of transcription or to preserve their books religiously for the benefit of posterity.[227]

The first papyri discovered (P[45], P[46], P[66]) showed this possibly could be the case. Professional scribes copied P[46] and P[66]. P[45] contains much of the Gospels and Acts, and it varies with each biblical book. Comfort informs us that "P[45] (Gospels and Acts) may have also been done by professionals—at least, they display the reformed documentary hand."[228] However, Barbara Aland says that "P[45] has a great number of singular readings."[229] On the origin of these singular readings, E. C. Colwell comments:

> As an editor the scribe of P[45] wielded a sharp axe. The most striking aspect of his style is its conciseness. The dispensable word is dispensed with. He omits adverbs, adjectives, nouns, participles, verbs, personal pronouns—without any compensating habit of addition. He frequently omits phrases and clauses. He prefers the simple to the compound word. In short, he favors brevity. He

---

[226] Kurt and Barbara Aland, *THE TEXT OF THE NEW TESTAMENT: An Introduction to the Critical Editions and to the Theory and Practice of Modern Textual Criticism* (Grand Rapids, MI: Wm. B. Eerdmans Publishing Co., 1995), 295, 69.

[227] F. Kenyon, Our Bible and the Ancient Manuscripts (1895), 157.

[228] Philip Wesley Comfort and David P. Barrett, *The Text of the Earliest New Testament Greek Manuscripts* (Wheaton, IL: Tyndale House, 2001), 159. See also Kenyon, *The Chester Beatty Biblical Papyri*, fasc. 2.1, *Gospels and Acts, Text*, 13–14.

[229] Barbara Aland, *The Significance of the Chester Beatty in Early Church History, in:* The Earliest Gospels *ed. Charles Horton, London 2004, p. 110.*

shortens the text in at least fifty places in singular readings alone. But he does not drop syllables or letters. His shortened text is readable.[230]

So, it would seem that P[45], which came to light when it was purchased from some dealer in **1930-31**, was the predominant factor for the negative view of the copyist in early Christianity. However, as more papyri became known, especially after the discovery of P[75] in the **1950s** in Pabau, Egypt, it proved to be just the opposite. P[75] is generally described as "the most significant"[231] papyrus of the Greek New Testament to be discovered. These new discoveries prompted Sir Frederic Kenyon to write,

> We must be content to know that the general authenticity of the New Testament text has been remarkably supported by the modern discoveries which have so greatly reduced the interval between the original autographs and our earliest extant manuscripts, and that the differences of reading, interesting as they are, do not affect the fundamental doctrines of the Christian faith.[232]

Even though many textual scholars were crediting the Alands' *The Text of the New Testament* with their description of the text as "free," that was not the entire position of the Alands. True, they spoke of the different text styles such as the "normal," "free," "strict," and the "paraphrastic." However, like Kenyon, they saw a need based on the evidence, which suggested a rethinking of how the evidence should be described:

> Our research on the early papyri has yielded unexpected results that require a change in the traditional views of the early text. We have inherited from the past generation the view that the early text was a "free" text, and the discovery of the Chester Beatty papyri seemed to confirm this view. When P[45] and P[46] were joined by P[66] sharing the same characteristics, this position seemed to be definitely established. P[75] appeared in contrast to be a loner with its "strict" text anticipating Codex Vaticanus. Meanwhile the other witnesses of the early period had been ignored. It is their collations which have changed the picture so completely.[233]

---

[230] Ernest Cadman Colwell, "Scribal Habits in the Early Papyri: A Study in the Corruption of the Text," in: "The Bible in Modern Scholarship" ed. J. P. Hyatt, New York: Abingdon Press 1965, p.383.

[231] Aland and Aland, *The Text of the New Testament* (1989), p. 244

[232] F. Kenyon, Our Bible and the Ancient Manuscripts (1962), 249.

[233] Kurt and Barbara Aland, *THE TEXT OF THE NEW TESTAMENT: An Introduction to the Critical Editions and to the Theory and Practice of Modern Textual Criticism* (Grand Rapids, MI: Wm. B. Eerdmans Publishing Co., 1995), 93-95.

While we have said this previously, it bears repeating that *some* of the earliest manuscripts we now have indicate that a professional scribe copied them.[234] *Many* of the other papyri confirm that a semi-professional scribe copied them, while *most* of these early papyri give evidence of being produced by a copyist who was literate and experienced. Therefore, either literate or semi-professional copyists did the vast majority of our early papyri, with some being done by professionals. As it happened, the few poorly copied manuscripts became known first, establishing a precedent that was difficult for some to discard when the enormous amount of evidence came forth that showed just the opposite.

Distribution of Papyri by Century and Type				
DATE	ALEX	WEST	CAES	BYZ
100-150/175 C.E.	7Q4? 7Q5? $P^{4/64/67}$ P^{32} P^{46} P^{52} P^{66} P^{75} $P^{77/103}$ P^{101} P^{87} P^{90} P^{98} (bad shape, differences) P^{109} (too small) P^{118} (too small) P^{137} 0189 P. Oxyrhynchus 405 P. Egerton 2	P^{104}	0	0
175-250 C.E.	P^{1} P^{5} P^{13} P^{20} P^{23} P^{27} P^{30} P^{35} P^{39} P^{40} P^{45} P^{47} $P^{49/65}$ P^{71} P^{72} P^{82} P^{85} P^{95} P^{100} P^{106} P^{108} P^{110} P^{111} P^{113} P^{115} P^{121} (too small) P^{125} P^{126} (too small) P^{133} P^{136} 0220 0232 P. Oxyrhynchus 406 P. Egerton 3	P^{29} (Metzger Western & Aland Free; too small to be certain) P^{38} P^{48} P^{69} 0171 0212 (mixed) P^{107} (Independent)	0	0

---

[234] Some may argue that we can only be confident that we have good manuscripts of an "early" form of the text but not necessarily of the originally published text. This hypothesis cannot be disproven. However, I think it is highly doubtful for four reasons: (1) The intervening time between the publication date of various New Testament books (from AD 60–90) and the date of several of our extant manuscripts (from AD 100–200) is narrow, thereby giving us manuscripts that are probably only three to five "manuscript generations" removed from the originally published texts. (2) We have no knowledge that any of these manuscripts go back to an early "form" that postdates the original publications. (3) We are certain that there was no major Alexandrian recension in the second century. (4) Text critics have been able to detect any other second-century textual aberrations, such as the D-text, which was probably created near the end of the second century, not the beginning. Thus, it stands to reason that these "reliable" manuscripts are excellent copies of the authorized published texts." (P. Comfort, Encountering the Manuscripts: An Introduction to New Testament Paleography and Textual Criticism 2005, 269)

250-300 C.E.	P8 P9 P12 P15 P16 P17 P18 P19 P24 P28 P50 P51 P53 P70 P78 P80 P86 P88 P89 (too small) P91 P92 P114 P119 P120 P129 (too small) P131 P132 too small) P134 0162 0207 0231 P. Antinoopolis 54	P37 (Free, mostly Western)	0	0
290-390 C.E.	P3 P6 P7 P10 P21 P54 P62 P81 P93 P94 P102 (too small) P117 (too small) P122 (too small) P123 P127 P130 (too small) P139 (too small) 057 058 059 / 0215 071 0160 0163 0165 0169 0172 0173 0175 0176 0181 0182 0185 0188 0206 0214 0217 0218 0219 0221 0226 0227 0228 0230 0242 0264 0308 0312 P. Oxyrhynchus 4010 P. Oxyrhynchus 5073	P21 (mixed) P25 (independent) P112 (independent) P127 (independent; like no other)	0	0
4th / 5th Century C.E.	P11 P14 P33/P58 P56 P57 P63 P105 (too small) P124 0254			069 P. Oxyrhynchus 1077?

Also, as we noted earlier, textual scholars such as Comfort[235] and others believe that the very early Alexandrian manuscripts that we now possess are a reflection of what would have been found throughout the whole of the Greco-Roman Empire from about 85–275 C.E. So these early papyri can play a major role in our establishing the original readings. While this is true, it might not be in the way that one might think. Have the early papyri made a difference in the critical text of the New Testament? Maurice A. Robinson has estimated that the current Nestle-Aland 28th edition of 2012 is 99.5 percent the same as the 1881 Westcott and Hort's edition of the Greek New Testament. From the Westcott and Hort Greek text of 1881 to the 25th edition of the Nestle-Aland Greek New Testament Text of 1963, the

---

[235] Philip W. Comfort, The Quest for the Original Text of the New Testament (Eugene, Oregon: Wipf and Stock Publishers, 1992).

critical texts were essentially based on the accumulated evidence from the days of Desiderius Erasmus in 1516, 1522 up unto the 19th/early 20th century. In other words, the codices manuscripts, with Codex Vaticanus (c. 300–325 C.E.) and Codex Sinaiticus (c. 330–360), were leading the way. Again, there were no significant changes from 1881 to the 2012 28th edition of the Nestle-Aland Text. However, that is, in fact, what makes the early papyri majorly important, extremely significant, very consequential, considerable evidence for establishing the original Greek New Testament. It simply gives validity to those who had placed much trust in the great majuscules.

However, Epp asks, "If Westcott-Hort did not utilize papyri in constructing their NT text, and if our own modern critical texts, in fact, are not significantly different from that of Westcott-Hort, then why are the papyri important after all?"[236] From there, Epp goes on to strongly advise that the papyri should play an essential role in three areas: **(1)** "to isolate the earliest discernable text-types, **(2)** assisting "to trace out the very early history of the NT text," and, **(3)** "Finally, the papyri can aid in refining the canons of criticism—the principles by which we judge variant readings—for they open to us a window for viewing the earliest stages of textual transmission, providing instances of how scribes worked in their copying of manuscripts."[237] We should add that the early papyri have changed textual scholars' and committees' decisions so that they have not retained Westcott and Hort's readings at times. Again, there has been little change between the Westcott and Hort Greek New Testament 1881 and the 2012 28th edition of the Nestle-Aland Greek New Testament. The early papyri (1) have reinforced what we already knew to be original and (2) helped us improve the critical text ever slightly.

To offer just one example, both Metzger and Comfort inform us that the papyri's external evidence resulted in the change in the NU text, adopting the reading that was also in the Textus Receptus, as opposed to what was in the Westcott and Hort text.

Matthew 26:20 (WH)	Matthew 26:20 (TRNU)
[20] μετα των δωδεκα μαθητων	[20] μετα των δωδεκα
With the twelve disciples	With the twelve

---

[236] The New Testament Papyrus Manuscripts in Historical Perspective, in To Touch the Text: Biblical and Related Studies in Honour of Joseph A. Fitzmyer, S. J. (ed. Maurya P. Horgan and Paul J. Kobelski; New York: Crossroad, 1989), 285 (there italicized) repr. in Epp, Perspectives, 338.

[237] Ibid., 288

Metzger writes, "As is the case in 20:17,[238] the reading μαθηταί after οἱ δώδεκα is doubtful. In the present verse [26:20] the weight of the external evidence seems to favor the shorter reading." (B. M. Metzger, A Textual Commentary on the Greek New Testament 1994, 53) Comfort in his *New Testament Text and Translation* writes, "Even though both P[37] and P[45] are listed as 'vid,' it is certain that both did not include the word μαθητων because line spacing would not accommodate it. P[37] has the typical abbreviation for 'twelve,' as ιβ; and P[45] has it written out as [δω]δεκα. P[64+67] is less certain, but line lengths of the manuscript suggest that it reads ‾ιβ (see *Texts of Earliest MSS*, 69)." Comfort more explicitly explains what Metzger hinted at; "The testimony of the papyri (with B and D) created a change in the NU text. Prior to NA26, the NU text included the word μαθητων ("disciples"). But the early evidence shows that this must have been a later addition." Comfort continues, "Such an addition is not necessary in light of the fact that Jesus' closest followers were often designated by the gospel writers as simply "the twelve." (P. W. Comfort 2008, 77)

Again, many textual scholars before 1961 believed that the early copyists of the New Testament papyri were among the untrained in making documents (P[45], P[46], P[47]; P[66] and P[72] in 2 Peter and Jude) and that the papyri were texts in flux.[239] It was not until the discovery of P[75] and other papyri that textual scholars began to think differently. Nevertheless, the attitude of the 1930s through the 1950s is explained well by Kurt and Barbara Aland:

> Of special importance are the early papyri, i.e., of the period of the third/fourth century. As we have said, these have an inherent significance for the New Testament textual studies because they witness to a situation before the text was channeled into major text types in the fourth century. Our research on the early papyri has yielded unexpected results that require a change in the traditional views of the early text. We have inherited from the

---

[238] 20:17 τοὺς δώδεκα [μαθητάς] {C}

Although copyists often add the word μαθηταίto the more primitive expression οἱ δώδεκα (see Tischendorf's note *in loc.* and 26.20 below), a majority of the Committee judged that the present passage was assimilated to the text of Mark (10:32) or Luke (18:31). In order to represent both possibilities it was decided to employ square brackets. (B. M. Metzger, A Textual Commentary on the Greek New Testament 1994, 42)

On 20:17, Comfort writes, "Either reading could be original because they both have good support and because the gospel writers alternated between the nomenclature 'the twelve disciples' and 'the twelve.'" (P. W. Comfort 2008, 60)

[239] Kurt and Barbara Aland write, "By the 1930s the number of known papyri had grown to more than forty without any of them arousing any special attention, despite the fact that many of them were of a quite early date. (Aland and Aland, The Text of the New Testament 1995, 84)

past generation the view that the early text was a "free" text,[240] and the discovery of the Chester Beatty papyri seemed to confirm this view. When P[45] and P[46] were joined by P[66] sharing the same characteristics, this position seemed to be definitely established. (Aland and Aland, The Text of the New Testament 1995, 93)

Before P[75] and other early papyri, scholars were under the impression that scribes must have used untrained copyists' manuscripts to make a recension (critical revision, i.e., revised text); and this, according to scholars before 1961, was how Codex Vaticanus (B) came about. In 1940, Kenyon inferred the following:

> During the second and third centuries, a great variety of readings came into existence throughout the Christian world. In some quarters, considerable license was shown in dealing with the sacred text; in others, more respect was shown to the tradition. In Egypt, this variety of texts existed, as elsewhere; but Egypt (and especially Alexandria) was a country of strong scholarship and with a knowledge of textual criticism. Here, therefore, a relatively faithful tradition was preserved. About the beginning of the fourth century, a scholar may well have set himself to compare the best accessible representatives of this tradition, and so have produced a text of which B [Codex Vaticanus] is an early descendant.[241]

While Kenyon was correct about the manuscripts coming up out of Egypt being a reasonably pure text, he was certainly mistaken when he suggested that Codex Vaticanus was the result of a critical revision by early scribes. P[75] put this theory to rest. The Agreement between P[75] and codex B is 92% in John and 94% in Luke. However, Porter has it at about 85% agreement. Zuntz, on the other hand, went a little further than Kenyon did. Kenyon believed that the critical text had been made in the early part of the fourth century, leading to Codex Vaticanus. Zuntz believed similarly but felt that the recension[242] began back in the mid-second century and was a process that ran up into the fourth-century. Zuntz wrote:

---

[240] Early manuscripts (from before the fourth century) are classified by the Alands as "strict," "normal," or "free." The "normal" text "transmitted the original text with the limited amount of variation." Then, there is the "free" text, "characterized by a greater degree of variation than the 'normal' text." Finally, there was the "strict" text, "which reproduced the text of its exemplar with greater fidelity (although still with certain characteristic liberties), exhibiting far less variation than the 'normal' text." (Aland 1987, 93)

[241] F. Kenyon, "Hesychius and the Text of the New Testament," in *Memorial Lagrange* (1940), 250.

[242] **Recension**: a revision of the Greek NT combining various sources. The term has particular relevance to Lucian, a presbyter of Antioch, who was martyred in 312. In the traditional criticism of Westcott and Hort, Lucian produced the recension that came to be called the Byzantine Text (among

The Alexander correctors strove, in ever repeated efforts, to keep the text current in their sphere free from the many faults that had infected it in the previous period and which tended to crop up again even after they had been obelized [i.e., marked as spurious]. These labours must time and again have been checked by persecutions and the confiscation of Christian books, and counteracted by the continuing currency of manuscripts of the older type. Nonetheless they resulted in the emergence of a type of text (as distinct from a definite edition) which served as a norm for the correctors in provincial Egyptian scriptoria. The final result was the survival of a text far superior to that of the second century, even though the revisers, being fallible human beings, rejected some of its own correct readings and introduced some faults of their own.[243]

P[75] and other early papyri, as we can see from the above, influenced the thinking of Kurt Aland. While he said, "We have inherited from the past generation the view that the early text was a 'free' text," he was one of those saying that very thing. However, as he would later say, "Our research on the early papyri has yielded unexpected results that require a change in the traditional views of the early text." P[75] greatly affected the Alands: "P[75] shows such a close affinity with the Codex Vaticanus that the supposition of a recension of the text at Alexandria, in the fourth century, can no longer be held."[244] Gordon Fee clearly states that there was no Alexandrian recension before P[75] (175-225 C.E.) and the time of Codex Vaticanus (350 C.E.), as he commented that P[75] and Vaticanus "seem to represent a 'relatively pure' form of preservation of a 'relatively pure' line of descent from the original text."[245] New Testament textual scholarship has been aware that P75 is an extremely accurate copy for many decades now. Of the copyist behind P[75], Colwell said, "his impulse to improve style is for the most part defeated by the obligation

---

other names) and was adopted by the church. There is no absolute proof of the recension, the theory of which rests largely on references to it by Jerome. Even assuming the veracity of the theory; however, the value of it has been called into question in modern research. The Byzantine Text does not appear to have reached a consistent form until after the ninth century.

[243] G. Zuntz, *The Text of the Epistles* (1953), 271–272.

[244] Kurt Aland, "The Significance of the Papyri for New Testament Research" in *The Bible in Modern Scholarship* (1965), 336.

[245] Gordon Fee, "P75, P66, and Origen: The Myth of Early Textual Recension in Alexandria" in *New Dimensions in New Testament Study* (1974), 19–43.

to make an exact copy."[246] Colwell went on to comment on the work of that scribe:

> In P[75] the text that is produced can be explained in all its variants as the result of a single force, namely the disciplined scribe who writes with the intention of being careful and accurate. There is no evidence of revision of his work by anyone else, or in fact of any real revision, or check.... The control had been drilled into the scribe before he started writing.[247]

We do not want to leave the reader with the impression that P[75] is perfect, as it is not. On this Comfort says,

> The scribe had to make several corrections (116 in Luke and John), but there was no attempt 'to revise the text by a second exemplar, and indeed no systematic correction at all.'[248] The scribe of P[75] shows a clear tendency to make grammatical and stylistic improvements in keeping with the Alexandrian scriptorial tradition, and the scribe had a tendency to shorten his text, particularly by dropping pronouns. However, his omissions of text hardly ever extend beyond a word or two, probably because he copied letter by letter and syllable by syllable.[249]

As the early Nestle Greek critical text moved from edition to edition, the influence of the New Testament papyri increased. The son of Eberhard Nestle, Erwin, added a full critical apparatus in the thirteenth edition of the 1927 Nestle Edition. It was not until 1950 that Kurt Aland began to work on the text that would eventually become known as the Nestle-Aland text. He would begin to add even more evidence from papyri to the critical apparatus of the twenty-first edition. At Erwin Nestle's request, he looked over and lengthened the critical apparatus, adding far more manuscripts. This ultimately led to the 25th edition of 1963. The most significant papyri and recently discovered majuscules (i.e., 0189), a few minuscules (33, 614, 2814), and rarely also lectionaries were also considered. However, while the critical apparatus was being added to and even altered, the text of the Nestle-Aland was not changed until the 26th edition (1979). Many of these changes to the

---

[246] Ernest C. Colwell, "Method in Evaluating Scribal Habits: A Study of P45, P66, P75," in *Studies in Methodology in Textual Criticism of the New Testament*, New Testament Tools and Studies 9 (Leiden: Brill, 1969), 121.

[247] Ibid., 117

[248] James Ronald Royse, "Scribal Habits in Early Greek New Testament Papyri" (Ph.D. diss., Graduate Theological Union, 1981), 538–39.

[249] (Comfort and Barret, The Text of the Earliest New Testament Greek Manuscripts 2001, 506)

text were a direct result of the papyri. In the 2012 28th edition of the Nestle Aland Greek Text, there were only 34 changes to the text, all of which were in the General Epistles (James-Jude). The 27th edition of the NA was the same as the 26th edition of 1979, which would mean that in 33 years up unto 2012, with many new manuscript discoveries and much research, very little has needed to be changed, even very little change with the 1881 WH Greek New Testament text. It bears repeating that Robinson[250] has estimated that the 27th edition of the NA Greek New Testament text is 99.5% the same as the 1881 WH Greek New Testament text. There were only 34 changes between the 27th edition and the 2012 28th NA Greek New Testament text. The NA is still 99.5% the same as the 1881 WH Greek New Testament text.

Returning to the First Century

The writers of the 27 books comprising the Christian Greek Scriptures were Jews.[251] (Romans 13:1-2) These men were apostles, intimate traveling companions of the apostles, or were picked by Christ in a supernatural way, such as the apostle Paul. Being Jewish, they would have viewed the Old Testament as being the inspired, inerrant Word of God. Paul said, "all Scripture is inspired by God" (2 Timothy 3:16). These authors of the 27 New Testament books would have viewed the teachings of Jesus, or their books were expounding on his teachings, as Scripture as well as the Old Testament. The teachings of Jesus came to most of these New Testament writers personally from Jesus, being taught orally; after that, they would be the ones who published what Jesus had said and taught orally. When it came time to be published in written form, it should be remembered that Jesus had promised them, "The Helper, the Holy Spirit, whom the Father will send in my name, he will teach you all things and **bring to your remembrance** all that I have said to you." – John 14:26

The early first-century Christian copyists were very much aware of the Jewish scribes' traditions in meticulously copying their texts. It bears repeating that most of Christianity throughout most of the first century was Jewish. These copyists would have immediately understood that they were copying sacred texts. In fact, the early papyri show evidence of shared features with the Jewish Sopherim, men who copied the Hebrew Scriptures

---

[250] Maurice A. Robinson and William G. Pierpont, *The New Testament in the Original Greek: Byzantine Textform*, 2005 (Southborough, MA: Chilton, 2005), 551.

[251] Some believe that Luke was a Gentile, basing this primarily on Colossians 4:11, 14. Because Paul first mentioned "the circumcision" (Col 4:11) and thereafter talked about Luke (Col 4:14), the inference is drawn that Luke was not of the circumcision and therefore was not a Jew. However, this is by no means decisive. Romans 3:1-2 says, "Jews were entrusted with the whole revelation of God." Luke is one of those to whom such inspired revelations were entrusted.

from the time of Ezra in the fifth-century B.C.E. to Jesus' day and beyond. They were meticulous and were terrified of making mistakes.[252] We will find common features when we compare the Jewish Greek Old Testament with the Christian Greek Scriptures, such as an enlarged letter at the beginning of each line and the invention of the nomen sacrum[253] to deal with God's personal name. Marginal notes, accents, breathing marks, punctuation, corrections, double punctuation marks (which indicate the flow of text)—all of these show adoptions of scribal practices of the Sopherim by Jewish Christian writers and scribes.

There are, unfortunately, fierce critics who reject any claims of accuracy and reliability for these early manuscripts. Former evangelical Christian, now agnostic New Testament Bible scholar, Dr. Bart Ehrman writes,

> Not only do we not have the originals, we don't have the first copies of the originals. **We don't even have copies of the copies of the originals, or copies of the copies of the copies of the originals.** What we have are copies **made later—much later**. In most instances, they are copies made many *centuries* later. And these **copies all differ from one another, in many thousands of places**. As we will see later in this book, these copies **differ from one another in so many places that we don't even know how many differences** there are. Possibly it is easiest to put it in comparative terms: **there are more differences among our manuscripts than there are words in the New Testament**.[254] (Bold mine)

As we read these remarks, it is easy to get a sense of hopelessness because "all feels lost, for there is certainly no way to get back to the originals." Correct? Ehrman has had a long history of creating hopelessness for his readers as he carries on his alleged truth quest. He asserts that even in the very few places that we might be sure about the *wording*, we cannot be certain about the *meaning*.

---

[252] It is true that they took some liberties with the text, but these few places were the exception to the rule. They intentionally altered some passages that appeared to show irreverence for God or one of his spokespersons.

[253] Nomina sacra (singular: nomen sacrum) means "sacred names" in Latin, and can be used to refer to traditions of abbreviated writing of several frequently occurring divine names or titles in early Greek manuscripts, such as the following:

Lord ($\overline{KC}$), Jesus ($\overline{IH}, \overline{IHC}$), Christ ($\overline{XP}, \overline{XC}, \overline{XPC}$), God ($\overline{\Theta C}$), and Spirit ($\overline{\Pi NA}$).

[254] Bart D. Ehrman, *MISQUOTING JESUS: The Story Behind Who Changed the Bible and Why* (New York, NY: Harper One, 2005), 10.

Blinded by Misguided Perceptions

Ehrman clearly has been immensely impacted because we do not have the originals or immediate copies. Here we have a world-renowned textual and historian of early Christianity, emphasizing that we do not have the originals nor the direct copies. Ehrman informs his readers: (1) we do have copies of the copies of the originals, or copies of the copies of the copies of the originals, and (2) there are so many copyist errors, it is virtually impossible to get back to the Word of God at all. Even if by some stroke of good fortune, we cannot know the meaning with assurance. Ehrman is saying to the lay reader: we can no longer trust the text of the Greek New Testament as the Word of God. If so, we would have to conclude that all translations are untrustworthy as well.

Ehrman has misrepresented the evidence[255] available to us and has exaggerated the negative to his readers to the detriment of the positive in New Testament textual criticism. Mark Minnick assesses it nicely: "Doesn't the existence of these variants undermine our confidence that we have the very words of God inspired? No! The fact is that because we know of them and are careful to preserve the readings of every one of them, *not one word of God's word has been lost to us.*"[256] The wealth of manuscripts that we have for establishing the original Greek New Testament is overwhelming compared to other ancient literature. We can only wonder what Ehrman does with an ancient piece of literature that has only one copy, and that copy is hundreds or even over a thousand years removed from the time of the original.

Consider a few examples. Before beginning, it should be noted that some of the classical authors are centuries removed, and some are many centuries before the first century New Testament era, which is a somewhat unfair comparison. Why would that be unfair? Because the copying practices in the sixth to the first century B.C.E. were not as productive compared to the First to the fifth century C.E. See the chart below.[257]

---

[255] The argument from Ehrman that we do not even have "copies of the copies of the copies of the originals" is just misinformation. We have 15 early papyri manuscripts that date within decades of the orifinals (100-150/175 C.E.). And we have another 35 early papyri manuscripts that are within a few decades of those (175-250 C.E.).

[256] Mark Minnick, "Let's Meet the Manuscripts," in *From the Mind of God to the Mind of Man: A Layman's Guide to How We Got Our Bible,* eds. James B. Williams and Randolph Shaylor (Greenvill, SC: Ambassador-Emerald International, 1999), p. 96.

[257] The concept of this chart is taken from *The Bibliographical Test Updated - Christian Research ...* http://www.equip.org/article/the-bibliographical-test-updated/ May 04, 2017. However, some adjustments have been made as well as footnotes added.

The New Testament Compared to Classical Literature

Author	Work	Writing Completed	Earliest MSS	Years Removed	Number of MSS
Homer	*Iliad*	800 B.C.E.	3rd century B.C.E.[258]	500	1,757
Herodotus	*History*	480–425 B.C.E.	10th cent. C.E.	1,350	109
Sophocles	*Plays*	496–406 B.C.E.	3rd cent. B.C.E.[259]	100-200	193
Thucydides	*History*	460–400 B.C.E.	3rd cent. B.C.E.[260]	200	96
Plato	*Tetralogies*	400 B.C.E.	895 C.E.	1,300	210
Demosthenes	*Speeches*	300 B.C.E.	Fragments from 1st cent. B.C.E.	200	340
Caesar	*Gallic Wars*	51-46 B.C.E.	9th cent. C.E.	950	251
Livy	*History of Rome*	59 B.C.E.–17 C.E.	5th cent. C.E.	400	150
Tacitus	*Annals*	100 C.E.	9th-11th cent. C.E.	750–950	33
Pliny, the Elder	*Natural History*	49–79 C.E.	5th cent. C.E. fragment	400	200
Eight Greek NT Authors	27 Books	50 – 98 C.E.	110-150 C.E.	12-52	5,898

The Greek New Testament evidence, as we've mentioned previously, is over 5,898 Greek NT manuscripts. This is made up of 140+ papyri, 323 majuscules, 2,951 minuscules, and 2,484 lectionaries[261] that have been

---

[258] There are a number of fragments that date to the second century B.C.E. and one to the third century B.C.E., with the rest dating to the ninth century C.E. or later.

[259] Most of the 193 MSS date to the tenth century C.E., with a few fragments dating to the third century B.C.E.

[260] Some papyri fragments date to the third century B.C.E.

[261] Of the 5,898 Greek NT manuscripts cataloged, 83 percent of them date after 1000 C.E., with 17% (889 manuscripts) dating from the second to the tenth century. Between the second to the tenth century, we find in whole or in part 365 Gospels, 112 Acts and Catholic Epistles, 158 Epistles of Paul, 33 Revelation, and 313 lectionaries. The Gospel of Mark is the least attested **prior to the fourth century**, with chapters 2, 3, 10, and 13-16 having no representation at all. The Gospel of Mark is only represented in (P45), but about 78% of the Gospel is missing, and the fragment P137, a codex, written on both sides with text from the first chapter of the Gospel of Mark; verses 7-9 on the recto side and 16-18 on the verso side. The Gospel of John on the other hand, prior to the fourth century it is very well attested, with only 14 verses not being covered between chapters 16 and 20. The Gospel of John is found in some of the earliest and most significant manuscripts (P45 P66 P75).

cataloged.[262] We also have over 9,284 versions and over 10,000 Latin manuscripts, not to mention an innumerable amount of church fathers' quotations. This places the Greek New Testament in a class by itself because no other ancient document is close to this. However, there is even more. Again, there are 60 Greek papyri and five majuscules manuscripts that date to the second and third centuries C.E. Moreover, these early papyri manuscripts are from a region in Egypt that appreciated books as literature and were copied by semi-professional and professional scribes or highly skilled copyists. This region produced what is known as the most accurate and trusted manuscripts.

Were the Scribes in the Early Centuries Amateurs?

We could **go on nearly forever** talking about specific places in which the texts of the New Testament came to be changed, either accidentally or intentionally. As I have indicated, the examples are **not just in the hundreds but in the thousands**. The examples given are enough to convey the general point, however: there are lots of differences among our manuscripts, differences created by scribes who were reproducing their sacred texts. **In the early Christian centuries, scribes were amateurs** and as such were more inclined to alter the texts they copied—or more prone to alter them accidentally—than were scribes in the later periods who, starting in the fourth century, began to be professionals.[263] [Bold mine]

Let us take just a moment to discuss Ehrman's statement, "**in the early Christian centuries, scribes were amateurs....**" In this book, we established just the opposite. Literate or semi-professional copyists did the

---

[262] While at present here in 2020, there are 5,898 manuscripts. There are **140 listed Papyrus** manuscripts, 323 Majuscule manuscripts, 2,951 Minuscule manuscripts, and 2,484 Lectionary manuscripts, bringing the total cataloged manuscripts to 5,898 manuscripts. However, you cannot simply total the number of cataloged manuscripts because, for example, P[11/14] are the same manuscript but with different catalog numbers. The same is true of P[33/5], P[4/64/67], P[49/65] and P[77/103]. Now this alone would bring our 140 listed papyrus manuscripts down to 134. Then, we turn to one example from our majuscule manuscripts where clear 0110, 0124, 0178, 0179, 0180, 0190, 0191, 0193, 0194, and 0202 are said to be part of 070. A minuscule manuscript was listed with five separate catalog numbers for 2306, which then have the letters a through e. Thus, we have the following GA numbers: 2306 for 2306a, and 2831- 2834 for 2306b-2306e.' – (Hixon 2019, 53-4) The problem is much worse when we consider that there are 323 Majuscule manuscripts and then far worse still with a listed 2,951 Minuscule and 2,484 Lectionaries. Nevertheless, those who estimate a total of 5,300 (Jacob W. Peterson, Myths and Mistakes, p. 63) 5,500 manuscripts (Dr. Ed Gravely / ehrmanproject.com/), 5,800 manuscripts (Porter 2013, 23), it is still a truckload of evidence far and above the dismal number of ancient secular author books.

[263] Bart D. Ehrman, *MISQUOTING JESUS: The Story Behind Who Changed the Bible and Why* (New York, NY: Harper One, 2005), 98.

vast majority of our early papyri, with some being done by professionals. As it happened, the few poorly copied manuscripts became known first, establishing a precedent that was difficult for some to discard when the truckload of evidence came forth that showed just the opposite. (P. Comfort 2005, 18-19)

Ehrman is misrepresenting the situation to his readers when he states, "We don't even have copies of the copies of the originals or copies of the copies of the copies of the originals." The way this is worded, he is saying that we do not have copies that are three or four generations removed from the originals. Ehrman cannot know this because we have 50 copies that are 20 to 150 years removed from the death of the apostle John in 100 C.E. There is the possibility that any of these could be a third or fourth generation removed copies. Furthermore, they could have been copied from a second or third generation. Therefore, Ehrman is misstating the evidence.

Let us do another short review of the two most significant manuscripts: P75 and Vaticanus 1209 (B). P75 is also known as Bodmer 14, 15. As has already been stated, papyrus is writing material used by the ancient Egyptians, Greeks, and Romans made from the pith of the stem of a water plant. These are the earliest witnesses to the Greek New Testament. P75 contains most of Luke and John, dating from 175 C.E. to 225 C.E Vaticanus is designated internationally by the symbol "B" (and 03) and is known as an uncial manuscript written on parchment. It is dated to the beginning of the fourth-century C.E. [c. 300-325] and originally contained the entire Bible in Greek. At present, Vaticanus' New Testament is missing parts of Hebrews (Hebrews 9:14 to 13:25), all of First and Second Timothy, Titus, Philemon, and Revelation. Initially, this codex probably had approximately 820 leaves, of which 759 remain.

What kind of weight or evidence do these two manuscripts carry in the eyes of textual scholars? Vaticanus 1209 is a crucial source for our modern translations. When determining an original reading, this manuscript can stand against other external evidence that would seem to the non-professional to be much more significant. P75 also one of the weightiest manuscripts we have and is virtually identical to Vaticanus 1209, which dates 175 to 125 years later than P75. When textual scholars B. F. Westcott and F. J. A. Hort released their critical text in 1881, Hort said that Vaticanus preserved "not only a very ancient text but a very pure line of a very ancient text." (Westcott and Hort 1882, 251) Later, scholars argued that Vaticanus was a scholarly recension: a critical revision or edited text. However, P75 has vindicated Westcott and Hort because of its virtual identity with Vaticanus; it establishes that Vaticanus is essentially a copy of a second-century text. It is a copy of the original text, except for a few minor points.

Kurt Aland[264] wrote, "P75 shows such a close affinity with the Codex Vaticanus that the supposition of a recension of the text at Alexandria, in the fourth century, can no longer be held."[265] David C. Parker[266] says of P75 that "it is extremely important for two reasons: "like Vaticanus, it is carefully copied; it is also very early and is generally dated to a period between 175 and 225. Thus, it pre-dates Vaticanus by at least a century. A careful comparison between P75 and Vaticanus in Luke by C.M. Martini demonstrated that P75 was an earlier copy of the same careful Alexandrian text. It is sometimes called proto-Alexandrian. It is our earliest example of a controlled text that was not intentionally or extensively changed in successive copying. Its discovery and study have provided proof that the Alexandrian text had already come into existence in the third century." (Parker 1997, 61) Let us look at a few more textual scholars' remarks: J. Ed Komoszewski, M. James Sawyer, and Daniel Wallace.

Even some of the early manuscripts show compelling evidence of being copies of a much earlier source. Consider again Codex Vaticanus, whose text is very much like that of P75 (B and P75 are much closer to each other than B is to [Codex Sinaiticus]). Yet the papyrus is at least a century older than Vaticanus. When P75 was discovered in the 1950s, some entertained the possibility that Vaticanus could have been a copy of P75, but this view is no longer acceptable since the wording of Vaticanus is certainly more primitive than that of P75 in several places.' They both must go back to a still earlier common ancestor, probably one that is from the early second century.[267]

Comfort comments on how we can know that Vaticanus is not a copy of P75: "As was previously noted, Calvin Porter clearly established the fact that P75 displays the kind of text that was used in making codex Vaticanus. However, it is unlikely that the scribe of B used P75 as his exemplar because the scribe of B copied from a manuscript whose line length was 12–14 letters per line. We know this because when the scribe of Codex Vaticanus

---

[264] (1915 – 1994) was Professor of New Testament Research and Church History. He founded the Institute for New Testament Textual Research in Münster and served as its first director for many years (1959–83). He was one of the principal editors of The Greek New Testament for the United Bible Societies.

[265] K. Aland, "The Significance of the Papyri for New Testament Research," 336.

[266] Professor of Theology and the Director of the Institute for Textual Scholarship and Electronic Editing at the Department of Theology and Religion, University of Birmingham. Scholar of New Testament textual criticism and Greek and Latin paleography.

[267] J. ED Komoszewski; M. James Sawyer; Daniel B Wallace, *Reinventing Jesus* (Grand Rapids, MI, 2006), 78.

made large omissions, they were typically 12–14 letters long.[268] The average line length for P[75] is about 29–32 letters per line. Therefore, the scribe of B must have used a manuscript like P[75], but not P[75] itself."[269]

Ehrman suggests that the early Christians were not concerned about the integrity of the text, its preservation of accuracy. Let us consult the second-century evidence by way of Tertullian.[270]

> Come now, you who would indulge a better curiosity, if you would apply it to the business of your salvation, run over the apostolic churches, in which the very thrones[271] of the apostles are still pre-eminent in their places,[272] in which their own **authentic writings** are read, uttering the voice and representing the face of each of them severally.[273] (Bold mine)

What did Tertullian mean by "authentic writings"? If he was referring to the Greek originals, and it seems that he was, according to the Latin, it is an indication that some of the original New Testament books were still in existence at the time of his penning this work. However, let us say that it is simply referring to well-preserved copies. In any case, this shows that the Christians valued the preservation of accuracy.

We need to visit an earlier book by Ehrman for a moment, *Lost Christianities*, in which he writes, "In this process of recopying the document by hand, what happened to the original of 1 Thessalonians? For some unknown reason, it was eventually thrown away, burned, or otherwise destroyed. Possibly, it was read so much that it simply wore out. The early Christians **saw no need to preserve it** as the 'original' text. They had copies of the letter. Why keep the original?" (B. D. Ehrman 2003, 217) Bold is mine.

Here Ehrman is arguing from silence. We cannot read people's minds today, let alone read the minds of persons 2,000 years in the past. It is known that congregations valued Paul's letters, and Paul exhorted them to share the letters with differing congregations. Paul wrote to the Colossians, and in what we know as 4:16, he said, "And when this letter has been read among you,

---

[268] Brooke F. Westcott and Fenton J. A. Hort, *Introduction to the New Testament in the Original Greek* (New York: Harper & Bros., 1882; reprint, Peabody, Mass.: Hendrickson, 1988), 233–34.

[269] (Comfort and Barret, The Text of the Earliest New Testament Greek Manuscripts 2001)

[270] Tertullian (160 – 220 C.E.), was a prolific early Christian author from Carthage in the Roman province of Africa.

[271] Cathedrae

[272] Suis locis praesident.

[273] Alexander Roberts, James Donaldson and A. Cleveland Coxe, The Ante-Nicene Fathers Vol. III: Translations of the Writings of the Fathers Down to A.D. 325 (Oak Harbor: Logos Research Systems, 1997), 260.

have it **also read in the church of the Laodiceans**; and see that you also read the letter from Laodicea." The best way to facilitate this would be to send someone to a congregation, have them copy the letter, and bring it back to their home congregation.

On the other hand, someone could make copies of the letter in the congregation that received it and deliver it to interested congregations. In 1 Thessalonians, the congregation that Ehrman is talking about here, at chapter five, verse 27, Paul says, "I put you under oath before the Lord to **have this letter read to all the brothers**." What did Paul mean by "all the brothers"? It could be that he meant it to be used like a circuit letter, circulated to other congregations, giving everyone a chance to hear the counsel. It may merely be that, with literacy being so low, Paul wanted a guarantee that all were going to get to listen to the letter's contents, and he simply meant for every brother and sister locally to have a chance to hear it in the congregation. Regardless, even if we accept the latter, the stress that was put on the reading of this letter shows the weight that these people were placed under concerning Paul's letters.[274] In addition, Comfort comments on how Paul and others would view apostolic letters:

> Paul knew the importance of authorized apostolic letters, for he saw the authority behind the letter that came from the first Jerusalem church council. The first epistle from the church leaders who had assembled at Jerusalem was the prototype for subsequent epistles (see Acts 15). It was authoritative because it was apostolic, and it was received as God's word. If an epistle came from an apostle (or apostles), it was to be received as having the imprimatur [**approval**/authority] of the Lord. This is why Paul wanted the churches to receive his word as being the word of the Lord. This is made explicit in 1 Thessalonians (2:13), an epistle he insisted had to be read to all the believers in the church (5:27). In the Second Epistle to the Thessalonians, Paul indicated that his epistles carry the same authority as his preaching (see 2:15). Paul also told his audience that if they would read what he had written, they would be able to understand the mystery of Christ, which had been revealed to him (see Eph. 3:1–6). Because Paul explained the

---

[274] The exhortation ἐνορκίζω ὑμᾶς τὸν κύριον ἀναγνωσθῆναι τὴν ἐπιστολὴν πᾶσιν τοῖς ἀδελφοῖς ("I adjure you by the Lord that this letter be read aloud to all the brothers [and sisters]"), is stated quite strongly. ἐνορκίζω takes a double accusative and has a causal sense denoting that the speaker or writer wishes to extract an oath from the addressee(s). The second accusative, in this case τὸν κύριον ("the Lord"), indicates the thing or person by whom the addressees were to swear. The forcefulness of this statement is highly unusual, and in fact it is the only instance in Paul's letters where such a charge is laid on the recipients of one of his letters.—Charles A. Wanamaker, The Epistles to the Thessalonians: A Commentary on the Greek Text (Grand Rapids, Mich.: W.B. Eerdmans, 1990), 208-09.

197

mystery in his writings (in this case, the encyclical epistle known as "Ephesians"), he urged other churches to read this encyclical (see Col. 4:16). In so doing, Paul himself encouraged the circulation of his writings. Peter and John also had publishing plans. Peter's first epistle, written to a wide audience (the Christian diaspora in Pontus, Galatia, Cappadocia, Asia, Bithynia—see 1 Pet. 1:1), was a published work, which must have been produced in several copies from the onset, to reach his larger, intended audience. John's first epistle was also published and circulated— probably to all the churches in the Roman province of Asia Minor. First John is not any kind of occasional epistle; it is more like a treatise akin to Romans and Ephesians in that it contains John's full explanation of the Christian life and doctrine as a model for all orthodox believers to emulate. The book of Revelation, which begins with seven epistles to seven churches in this same province, must have also been inititally published in seven copies, as the book circulated from one locality to the next, by the seven "messengers" (Greek *anggeloi*—not "angels" in this context). By contrast, the personal letters (Philemon, 1 and 2 Timothy, Titus, 2 John, 3 John) were not originally "published"; therefore, their circulation was small. Second Peter also had minimal circulation in the early days of the church. Because of its popularity, the book of Hebrews seemed to have enjoyed wide circulation—this was promoted by the fact that most Christians in the East thought it was the work of Paul and therefore was included in Pauline collections (see discussion below). The book of Acts was originally published by Luke as a sequel to his Gospel (see Acts 1:1–2). Unfortunately, in due course, this book got detached from Luke when the Gospel of Luke was placed in one-volume codices along with the other Gospels.[275]

Peter, as we have seen, also had this to say about Paul's letters: "there are some things in them [Paul's letters] that are hard to understand, which the ignorant and unstable twist to their own destruction, **as they do the other Scriptures**." (2 Pet 3:16) Peter viewed Paul's letters as being on the same level as the Old Testament, which was referred to as Scripture. In the second century (about 135 C.E.), Papias, an elder of the early congregation in Hierapolis, made the following comment.

I will not hesitate to set down for you, along with my interpretations, everything I carefully learned then from the elders

---

[275] Philip Comfort, *Encountering the Manuscripts: An Introduction to New Testament Paleography & Textual Criticism* (Nashville, TN: Broadman & Holman, 2005), 17.

and carefully remembered, guaranteeing their truth. For unlike most people I did not enjoy those who have a great deal to say, but those who teach the truth. Nor did I enjoy those who recall someone else's commandments, but those who remember the commandments given by the Lord to the faith and proceeding from the truth itself. In addition, if by chance someone who had been a follower of the elders should come my way, I inquired about the words of the elders--what Andrew or Peter said, or Philip, or Thomas or James, or John or Matthew or any other of the Lord's disciples, and whatever Aristion and the elder John, the Lord's disciples, were saying. For I did not think that information from books would profit me as much as information from a living and abiding voice.[276]

As an elder in the congregation at Hierapolis in Asia Minor, Papias was an unrelenting researcher and thorough information compiler; he exhibited great indebtedness for the Scriptures. Papias determined correctly that any doctrinal statement of Jesus Christ or his apostles would be far more appreciated and respected to explain than the unreliable statements found in the written works of his day. We can compare Jude 1:17, where Jude urges his readers to preserve the words of the apostles.

Therefore, the notion that the "early Christians saw no need to preserve it as the 'original' text" is far too difficult to accept when we consider the above. Moreover, imagine a church in middle America being visited by Billy Graham. Now imagine that he wrote them a warm letter, but one also filled with some stern counsel. Would there be little interest in the preservation of those words? Would they not want to share it with others? Would other churches not be interested in it? The same would have been even truer of early Christianity receiving a letter from an apostle like Peter, John, or Paul. There is no doubt that the "original" wore out eventually. However, they lived in a society that valued the preservation of the apostle's words, and it is far more likely that it was copied with care, to share with others, and to preserve. Moreover, let us acknowledge that their imperfections took over as well. Paul would have become a famous apostle who wrote a few churches, and there were thousands of churches toward the end of the first century. Would they have not exhibited some pride in the fact that they received a letter from the famous apostle Paul, who was martyred for the truth? Ehrman's suggestions are reaching and contrary to human nature.

---

[276] Michael W. Holmes, *The Apostolic Fathers: Greek Texts and English Translations,* 3rd Edition (Grand Rapids, MI: Baker Academic. 2007), 565.

However, Ehrman may not have entirely dismissed the idea of getting back to the original if he had agreed with Metzger in their coauthored fourth edition of *The Text of the New Testament*. Metzger's original comments from previous editions are repeated there as follows.

> Besides textual evidence derived from New Testament Greek manuscripts and from early versions, the textual critic compares numerous scriptural quotations used in commentaries, sermons, and other treatises written by early church fathers. Indeed, so extensive are these citations that if all other sources for our knowledge of the text of the New Testament were destroyed, they would be sufficient alone for the reconstruction of practically the entire New Testament.[277]

How are we to view the patristic citations? Let us look at another book for which Ehrman was coeditor and a contributor with other textual scholars: *The Text of the New Testament in Contemporary Research* (1995). The following is from Chapter 12, written by Gordon Fee (*The Use of the Greek Fathers for New Testament Textual Criticism*).

> In NT textual criticism, patristic citations are ordinarily viewed as the third line of evidence, indirect and supplementary to the Greek MSS, and are often therefore treated as of tertiary importance. When properly evaluated, however, patristic evidence is of primary importance, for both of the major tasks of NT textual criticism: in contrast to the early Greek MSS, the Fathers have the potential of offering datable and geographically certain evidence. (B. D. Ehrman 1995, 191)

To conclude, we have established that Ehrman has painted a picture that is not quite the truth of the matter for the average churchgoer while saying something entirely different for textual scholars. Moreover, he does not help the reader appreciate just how close the New Testament manuscript evidence is to the time of the original writings compared to manuscripts of other ancient works. Many ancient works are few in number and hundreds, if not a thousand years removed.

In addition, Ehrman has exaggerated the variants in the Greek New Testament manuscripts by **not** qualifying the level of variants. In other words, he has not explained how he counts them to obtain such high numbers. Moreover, Ehrman's unqualified statement, "in the early Christian centuries, scribes were amateurs," has been discredited as well. Either literate

---

[277] Bruce M. Metzger; Bart D. Ehrman, *THE TEXT OF THE NEW TESTAMENT: Its Transmission, Corruption, and Restoration*, 4th ed. (New York, NY: Oxford University Press, 2005), 126.

or semi-professional copyists did **the vast majority** of the early papyri, with some being done by professionals.

As mentioned earlier, E. C. Colwell states: "the overwhelming majority of readings were created before the year 200. But very few, if any, text-types were established by that time." G. D. Kilpatrick says, "Apart from errors which can occur anywhere as long as books are copied by hand, almost all variants can be presumed to have been created by A.D. 200." And Kurt and Barbara Aland say, "practically all the substantive variants in the text of the New Testament are from the second century ..."

I do not see how this is even possible to make such claims. That would mean the Byzantine readings, almost all of them as the above scholar's claim, are before 200 A.D. Even James R. Royse, in his Scribal Habits in Early Greek New Testament Papyri, quotes these comments without denying the possibility. (p. 20 ftn. 68) Wouldn't the following papyri pre-200 A.D. (P52 P32 P46 P66 P75 P77/103 P87 P90 P104 P137) have to contain almost all of these variant readings (hundreds of thousands) to make such claims. When looking at the three biggest pre-200 A.D. papyri (P46 P66 P75) two were done by professional scribes. Everyone knows about (P75) and Zuntz said that (P46) was a representative of "a text of the superior, early-Alexandrian type." (Zuntz, Text of the Epistles, 25) "According to recent studies done by Berner[278] and Comfort,[279] it seems evident that P66 has preserved the work of three individuals: the original scribe, a thoroughgoing corrector (*diorthōtēs*), and a minor corrector."[280] The Alands list P66 as Category I, which means it is important when considering textual problems and viewed by many scholars as a good representation of the autograph based on early dating. P66 is very close to P75, B, and 016.

If we set aside the Aland's "substantive variants" because we do not know what they mean by "substantive." Nevertheless, in the case of all three quotes (Colwell, Kilpatrick, and the Alands) combined with Royse not rejecting it after having quoted them as well, they seem to simply be saying **almost all** textual variants were in existence before 200 A.D. It would seem that there would have to be some manuscript evidence to make such a claim, as this would mean that we would have many, many thousands of Byzantine readings in our Alexandrian papyri before 200 A.D.

---

[278] Karyn Berner, "Papyrus Bodmer II, P66: A Reevaluation of the Correctors and Corrections," (master's thesis, Wheaton College, 1993).

[279] Philip W. Comfort, "The Scribe as Interpreter: A New Look at New Testament Textual Criticism according to Reader-Reception Theory" (D.Litt. et Phil. diss., University of South Africa, 1996).

[280] Philip Wesley Comfort and David P. Barrett, *The Text of the Earliest New Testament Greek Manuscripts* (Wheaton, IL: Tyndale House, 2001), 376.

Daniel B. Wallace, professor of New Testament Studies at Dallas Theological Seminary, founder and executive director of the Center for the Study of New Testament Manuscripts, and author of Greek Grammar Beyond the Basics writes in his article, *The Majority Text Theory*, that "Sturz pointed out 150 distinctively Byzantine readings found in the papyri. This claim that the Byzantine text is early because it is found in the papyri (Sturz's central thesis) has become the basis for hyperbolic claims by MT advocates. Cf. Hodges, "Defense," 14; Pickering, *Identity*, 41-42; Willem Franciscus Wisselink, *Assimilation as a Criterion for the Establishment of the Text: A Comparative Study on the Basis of Passages from Matthew, Mark and Luke* (Kampen: Uitgeversmaatschappij J.H. Kok 1989), 32-24; Maurice A. Robinson and William G. Pierpont, *The New Testament in the Original Greek according to the Byzantine/Majority Textform* (Atlanta: Original Word, 1991), xxiv-xxvii. But the evidence that Sturz presents is subject to three criticism: (1) Many of his readings have substantial support from other text types and are thus not distinctively Byzantine (cf. Fee's review of Sturz [240-41]; conceded by Sturz [personal conversation, 1987]), (2) the existence of a Byzantine *reading* in early papyri does not prove the existence of the Byzantine *text type* in early papyri, and (3) whether the agreements are genetically significant or accidental is overlooked (as even Wisselink admits [*Assimilation*, 33]). In my examination of Sturz's list, I found only eight Byzantine-papyrus alignments that seemed to be genetically significant; six were not distinctively Byzantine (Luke 10:21; 14:3, 34; 15:21; John 10:38; 19:11). Sturz's best case was in Phil 1:14 (the omission of του θεου)—a reading adopted in NA²⁷/*UBSGNT⁴*. When these factors are taken into account, the papyrus-Byzantine agreements become an insufficient base for the conclusions that either Sturz or the MT advocates build from it. For a balanced review of Sturz, see Michael W. Holmes, *TrinJ* n.s. 6 (1985): 225-228.—The Majority Text Theory: History, Methods, and Critique in The Text of the New Testament in Contemporary Research Author: Daniel B. Wallace, note is #35 on pp. 718-19.

CHAPTER VII

The Original Text or the Earliest Text of the New Testament

This chapter may be somewhat controversial because many modern textual scholars are not certain (sure or confident) that we can get back to the original text. Recently, Dr. Daniel B. Wallace, professor of New Testament Studies at Dallas Theological Seminary, founder and executive director of the Center for the Study of New Testament Manuscripts, wrote in the Foreword of MYTHS AND MISTAKES In New Testament Textual Criticism, "The new generation of evangelical scholars is **far more comfortable with ambiguity and uncertainty** than previous generations."[281] (Bold mine) Modern-day scholarship and even the branch of textual studies should be deemed 'the **ambiguity and uncertainty** of the modern Bible scholar.' The uncertainty and ambiguity are of their own making by abandoning the objective documentary approach for a subjective reasoned eclecticism approach.

The most used and referred to is reasoned eclecticism, which is supposed to view all the evidence internal and external objectively. And

---

[281] Elijah Hixon and Peter J. Gurry, *MYTHS AND MISTAKES In New Testament Textual Criticism* (Downer Groves, IL: InterVarsity Press, 2019), xii.

maybe it **mostly** did up until about the 1990s. Now, reasoned eclecticism[282] is almost entirely looking at internal evidence, not paying too much attention to the external manuscripts. For the textual scholar, generally speaking, all manuscripts are considered equal. Comfort writes about textual methods after the days of Westcott and Hort, "Left without a solid methodology for making external judgments, textual critics turned more and more to internal evidence."[283]

This author's approach and Philip W. Comfort, Dr. Don Wilkins of the NASB is the **Documentary Approach**. Earlier manuscripts usually have better readings by this standard. However, textual mixture or contamination is always assumed for modern-day textual scholars who have twisted reasoned eclecticism. In the minds of many or most textual critics, internal evidence should prevail over documentary when the two are in opposition. For Tregelles, Hort, Colwell, Comfort, myself (Edward D. Andrews), and Wilkins and some others, we maintain that superior documentary evidence should prevail over internal unless internal evidence is extremely significant in overruling it. We believe in looking at both internal and external evidence but give a slight weightiness to the manuscripts that have earned it. When a manuscript is consistently presenting superior readings elsewhere, it should be preferred when it's reading in a passage that seems, in some way, inferior to that of lesser manuscripts.

Those who practice textual criticism know this all too well. The situation then becomes one of emphasis. Does one give more weight to documentary evidence or to internal consideration? Scholars such as Tregelles, Hort, and Colwell (see comments below) **place more emphasis on the documents**. I tend to follow their lead. Other scholars, such as Kilpatrick, Boismard, and Elliott, place more emphasis on internal criticism, such that they advocate "thorough-going eclecticism" (see a good article on this by Elliott 2002, 101–124). Other scholars practice reasoned

---

[282] **Reasoned Eclecticism**: the method of textual criticism that aims to give about equal weight to external and internal evidence (cf. "Eclecticism"). It is also called the local-genealogical method as developed by Kurt and Barbara Aland. Variant readings are evaluated on a case-by-case basis. The extent to which external evidence, e.g. the age of important manuscripts, is taken into account can be difficult to judge.

[283] Philip W. Comfort, *New Testament Text and Translation Commentary: Commentary on the Variant Readings of the Ancient New Testament Manuscripts and How They Relate to the Major English Translations* (Carol Stream, IL: Tyndale House Publishers, Inc., 2008), xiii.

eclecticism, as explained by Holmes. Among those are Aland and Metzger, though each has his own emphasis.[284] (bold mine)

Refining the Documentary Approach

All textual critics—including those working with the classics—implement both external and internal criticism in selecting the reading which is most likely original. And all textual critics must do this on a variant-unit by variant-unit basis. Some give priority of place to internal over external evidence; others do the opposite. The editors of NU demonstrate that they tried to do both; this can be seen in Metzger's discussions in *A Textual Commentary on the Greek New Testament*. However, it is my observation that the resultant eclectic text exhibits too much dependence on internal evidence, emphasizing the "local" aspect of the "local-genealogical" method, to use Aland's language. This means that the decision making, on a variant-unit by variant-unit basis, produced a text with an uneven documentary presentation. Furthermore, the committee setting, with members voting on each significant textual variant, cannot help but produce a text with uneven documentation. All eclectic texts reconstruct a text that no ancient Christian actually read, even though they approach a close replication of the original writings. However, the NU edition's eclecticism extends even to following different manuscripts within the same sentence.

In my view, an eclectic approach that gives greater weight to external (documentary) evidence is best. Such an approach labors to select a premier group of manuscripts as the primary witnesses for certain books and/or sections of the New Testament, not for the entire New Testament, since each book of the New Testament was, in its earliest form, a separate publication. Once the best manuscripts for each book or group of books in the New Testament are established, these manuscripts need to be pruned of obvious errors and singular variants. Then these should be the manuscripts used for determining the most likely original wording. The burden of proof on textual critics is to demonstrate that the best manuscripts, when challenged by the testimony of other witnesses, do *not* contain the original wording. The part of this process that corresponds to Aland's "localness" (internal evidence) is that the text must be determined on a variant-unit basis. However, my view of the "genealogical" (external evidence) aspect is that it must be preestablished for an entire book and not re-created verse by verse, which results in a

---

[284] Philip W. Comfort, *New Testament Text and Translation Commentary: Commentary on the Variant Readings of the Ancient New Testament Manuscripts and How They Relate to the Major English Translations* (Carol Stream, IL: Tyndale House Publishers, Inc., 2008), xv.

very uneven documentary presentation. Of course, internal criticism will have to come into play when documentary evidence is evenly divided, or when some feature of the text strongly calls for it. And, on occasion, it must be admitted that two (or more) readings are equally good candidates for being deemed the original wording.[285] (See chapter XVI The Practice of Textual Criticism to Determine the Original Reading, where Philip Comfort will expand on his preference for favoring documentary evidence.)

Some renowned NT textual scholars from the 1700s to the 21st century who personally worked with the manuscripts would be J. J. Griesbach (1745–1812), Karl Lachmann (1793-1851), to Samuel Tregelles (1813–1875), to Constantin von Tischendorf (1815–1874), to Westcott (1825 – 1901) and Hort (1828 – 1892), Bruce M. Metzger (1914 – 2007), to the Nestles and Alands of the Nestle Aland Text. These had methods of deciding the original reading and working with the manuscripts personally, making critical texts for our modern-day Bible translations.

Philip Comfort has maintained decades of consistency with his approach to New Testament Textual Criticism. The difference between him and most other textual scholars today is stated by Dr. Stanley E. Porter, who says "that Comfort is one of few that I know of who has actually examined and published a major work in which he contends that he has examined the entire range of early New Testament manuscripts."[286] Many modern-day textual scholars have the mental disposition described by Dr. Daniel Wallace in the Foreword of *Myths and Mistakes in New Testament Textual Criticism*; modern evangelical scholars are "**far more comfortable with ambiguity and uncertainty** than previous generations." (bold and underline mine) Now that we have established the lenses from which much of modern textual scholars focus let's return to this chapter's subject. Should we be interested in attempting to ascertain the original word of the **original text** or the words of the **earliest text** of the New Testament?

Again, when we use the term "original" reading or "original" text in this publication, it is a reference to the exemplar manuscript by the New Testament author (e.g., Paul) and his secretary (e.g., Tertius)–if he used one– from which other copies were made for publication and distribution to the Christian communities. While this chapter focuses on the textual criticism

---

[285] Philip W. Comfort, *New Testament Text and Translation Commentary: Commentary on the Variant Readings of the Ancient New Testament Manuscripts and How They Relate to the Major English Translations* (Carol Stream, IL: Tyndale House Publishers, Inc., 2008), xv–xvi.

[286] Stanley E. Porter, (2013) "Recent efforts to Reconstruct Early Christianity on the Basis of its Payrological Evidence" in *Christian Origins and Graeco-Roman Culture*, Eds Stanley Porter and Andrew Pitts, Leiden, Brill, 76.

process, its primary focus is the early text of the New Testament, namely, the first three centuries of Christianity. In other words, we will be considering the text of the New Testament from the middle of the first century up to the close of the fourth century C.E.

Whether in commentaries, the footnotes within our Bibles, or from the pastor on Sunday, we have all read or heard something like "the *original* Greek word …" For example, the *original* Greek word here is *hagiazo,* meaning "to set apart to a sacred use" (Matt. 6:9). The *original* Greek word here is *kleros* and is related to the word *kleronomia,* "inheritance" (Col. 1:12; 1 Pet. 5:3). Perhaps the author or pastor is trying to provide a little Bible background, such as pointing out that the cubit is the *original* Greek word *pechus* in Matthew 6:27, which literally means "forearm." The publication or pastor may be emphasizing the nuances of different words for Christian services, such as the *original* Greek verb *diakoneo* (Matt. 20:26). One original Greek verb may emphasize the *subjection* that is involved in serving, such as a slave (*douleuo;* Col. 3:24), another could be the *sacredness* of service (*latreuo;* Matt. 4:10), while another might be focused on the *public nature* of the service provided (*leitourgeo;* Acts 13:2).

When incorporating a source, the author or pastor may mention *Mounce's Complete Expository Dictionary of Old & New Testament Words,* for example. It will be used to explain the original Greek word, such as *epikaleo,* which means "*to receive an appellation* or *surname … to call upon, invoke … to appeal to.*"[287] Paul used this same word when he declared, "I appeal to Caesar!" (Acts 25:11) A common way of expressing it is, "in the original Greek, this term basically "denotes" (the meaning, especially a specific or literal one) or "connotes (to imply or suggest something in addition to the literal or main meaning)." When Paul wrote about "the mind of the spirit," he used an *original* Greek word that **denotes** 'a way of thinking' or 'mindset.' The *original* Greek word for our English transliteration "amen," **connotes** 'certainty,' 'truthfulness,' 'faithfulness,' and 'absence of doubt.' We can see that getting back to the word in the *original* language can add considerable insight into the Scriptures. Therefore, our getting back to the actual words of the *original* language that the New Testament Bible author penned is, rightly so, the goal of some remaining textual scholars. We need the original words before we can translate or interpret the Scriptures. If scholars want to pursue insights into the sociohistorical approach to New Testament Textual Studies, to follow the scribal traditions and the transmission history of the Greek within each text-type of the family of manuscripts and where they grew up in order to have a better understanding of the social history of early Christianity, so

---

[287] William D. Mounce, *Mounce's Complete Expository Dictionary of Old & New Testament Words* (Grand Rapids, MI: Zondervan, 2006), 1152.

be it. However, to do so, one must have the starting point of the original reading to evaluate the motivation behind the variants.

The importance of the actual words is consistently evident when we examine the text of the original. Let's look at one example: a story that we all know. On the return trip home after the festivals in Jerusalem, Joseph and Mary thought that Jesus was somewhere with the family, so at first, his not being present was no cause for alarm. Three days later, when Mary and Joseph came back to Jerusalem to find Jesus, he was in the temple, "sitting amid the teachers and listening to them and **questioning them**" (Luke 2:44-46, UASV). Other translations read, "Listening to them and **asking them questions**" (RSV, NASB, ESV, LEB, and HCSB). However, that rendering does not capture the original language word.

Luke 2:46 English Standard Version (ESV)	Luke 2:46 New American Standard Bible (NASB)	Luke 2:46 Updated American Standard Version (UASV)
[46] After three days they found him in the temple, sitting among the teachers, listening to them and **asking them questions**.	[46] Then, after three days they found Him in the temple, sitting in the midst of the teachers, both listening to them and **asking them questions**.	[46] Then, it occurred, after three days they found him in the temple, sitting in the midst of the teachers and listening to them and **questioning them**.

This was no 12-year-old boy asking questions out of curiosity. The Greek word *erotao* simply means to "ask," "question," and is a synonym of *eperotao*. The latter of the two was used by Luke and is much more demanding. It means "to ask a question, to question, interrogate someone, questioning as used in judicial examination" and, therefore, could include counter questioning. Therefore, at the age of twelve, Jesus did not ask childlike questions looking for corresponding answers but was likely challenging the thinking of these Jewish religious leaders. What was the response of those Jewish religious leaders? The account says, "And all those listening to him **were amazed** at his understanding and his answers. When they [the parents] saw him, they **were astounded**[288] ..." – Luke 2:47.

---

[288] **Astounded**: (ἐκπλήσσω ekplēssō) This is one who is extremely astounded or amazed, so much so that they lose their mental self-control, as they are overwhelmed emotionally. – Matt. 7:28; Mark 1:22; 7:37; Lu 2:48; 4:32; 9:43; Ac 13:12.

What Is Meant by 'Establishing the Original Text'?

Because the terms *original* and *autograph* are used interchangeably, it can cause confusion at times if not differentiated. As was explained in the introduction, the **Autograph**[289] (self-written) was the text actually written by a New Testament author, or the author and scribe as the author dictated to him. If the scribe was taking down dictation (Rom. 16:22; 1 Pet. 5:12), he might have done so in shorthand.[290] Whether by shorthand or longhand, we can assume that both the scribe and the author would check the scribe's work. The author would have authority over all corrections since the Holy Spirit did not move the scribe. The finished product would be the autograph if the inspired author wrote everything down as the Spirit moved him. This text is also often referred to as the **Original**. Hence, again, the terms *autograph* and *original* are often used to have the same meaning. Sometimes textual critics prefer to make a distinction, using "original" as a reference to the text that is correctly attributed to a biblical author. This is a looser distinction, one that does not focus on the process of how a book or letter was written. Once more, the term "original" reading or "original" text in this publication is a reference to the exemplar manuscript by the New Testament author (e.g.,

---

[289] **Autograph**: The autograph (self-written) was the text actually written by a New Testament author, or the author and scribe as the author dictated to him. If the scribe was taking it down in dictation (Rom: 16:22; 1 Pet: 5:12), he might have done so in shorthand. Whether by shorthand or longhand, we can assume that both the scribe and the author would check the scribe's work. The author would have authority over all corrections since the Holy Spirit did not move the scribe. If the inspired author wrote everything down himself as the Spirit moved him, the finished product would be the autograph. This text is also often referred to as the original. Hence, the terms *autograph* and *original* are often used interchangeably. Sometimes textual critics prefer to make a distinction, using "original" as a reference to the text that is correctly attributed to a biblical author. This is a looser distinction, one that does not focus on the process of how a book or letter was written.

[290] "The usual procedure for a dictated epistle was for the amanuensis to take down the speaker's words (often in shorthand) and then produce a transcript, which the author could then review, edit, and sign in his own handwriting. Two New Testament epistles provide the name of the amanuensis: Tertius for (Romans 16:22) and Silvanus (another name for Silas) for 1 Peter 5:12" Philip Comfort, *Encountering the Manuscripts: An Introduction to New Testament Paleography & Textual Criticism* (Nashville, TN: Broadman & Holman, 2005), 06.

However, the author of this book qualifies Comfort's comments. Again, there is the **slight possibility** of Tertius or other Bible author's scribes taking it down in shorthand and after that making out a full draft, which would have been reviewed by both Paul and Tertius. This is only the case if it is comparable to what a modern-day court reporter does. In some sense, they are taking down whoever is speaking down in shorthand. Imagine a courtroom where you have a witness talking fast, the prosecution interrupts, the defense jumps in with his rebuttal and the judge snaps his ruling, and the witness resumes his or her account of things. All of that is taken down explicitly word for word in shorthand, and if ever turned into longhand, it would be exactly what was said, down to the uh and um common in speech. So, if the shorthand of the day had that kind of capability; then, it is conceivable. We must remember these are the Bible author's dictated words to the scribe based on their inspiration, not the word choice or writing style of the scribe.

Paul) and his secretary (e.g., Tertius) from which other copies were made for publication and distribution of the Christian communities.

An original is what the author was inspired, moved along by the Holy Spirit to write either by himself or in conjunction with a scribe (Paul and Tertius; Peter and Silvanus). When they were done, it is possible that Tertius, who was not inspired, made a scribal error that Paul would fix, not years later but at once. Once it was what Paul was explicitly inspired to write, it was published, put out into the public, sent to the recipient. It is not an original if anyone copied it even a month later at the congregation it was sent to, whether that copyist made a mistake or did not make a mistake. It is a copy of the original. And if a year from then a congregation used that copy of an original to make a copy, this second copy is not a copy of the original. It is a copy of a copy of the original. There is only one original, the one published by the author.

Some readers may find it disconcerting that those ancient copies of the New Testament are not inspired, and thousands of variations crept into them over the first fourteen centuries. However, this is not the complete picture because we have the next five centuries of restoration work done by hundreds of renowned textual scholars worldwide. If asked, "Are our copies inspired, without error?" the short answer would have to be **no**. But what if we have the exact wording of the original by way of restoration?

If we can get back to the exact words written in the original 27 books that were first published, would we not have an exact copy of the inspired original? We know that 2 Timothy 3:16 informs us, "all Scripture is inspired by God," meaning that the actual words in the autographs were a product of inspiration. Moreover, the inspired authors were, as 2 Peter 1:21 informs us, "men [who] spoke from God as the Holy Spirit carried them along." Nevertheless, if dictation were the process of composition for some New Testament books, they would have still needed to be checked for scribal errors because the amanuensis, i.e., the author's scribe (secretary), was not moved along by Holy Spirit in the same sense. Therefore, the author would review the dictated draft if he used a scribe, making corrections necessary. Depending on the length (e.g., 1 Peter (1,160 words) vs. Romans (7,000 words), the scribe would make a corrected copy or use the corrections within the original, which would become the officially published edition, which, if approved by the author, would have been signed by the author. Therefore, the original text that we are interested in duplicating is the one that was handed over by the author to be read in the churches and copied by others. In the final analysis, a textual committee, e.g., NA28/UBS5, has the potential to give us the exact wording of the original in the main text. In a few cases, maybe the original reading is in the textual apparatus (footnote) and would, in essence, be giving us the restored edition of the original. Even so, I would argue that between the Westcott and Hort 1881 critical text and the 2012 Nestle-Aland critical text, we have a 99.99% restoration. Most good literal translations will have readings of the alternative reading anyway, so the reader is not going to miss out on the actual original reading. It is highly improbable that it would alter what we already have if we discovered an original manuscript of any book.

Today we have a storehouse of external evidence: original language manuscripts, versions, apostolic quotations, and lectionaries that take us ever closer to the recovery of the original. Textual scholar Paul D. Wegner, author of *A Student's Guide to Textual Criticism of the Bible*, has addressed this for both the Old and the New Testaments:

> Careful examination of these manuscripts has served to strengthen our assurance that our Modern Greek and Hebrew texts are very close to the original autographs, even though we do not have those autographs. (2006, 301)[291]

The traditional goal of scholars within textual criticism has been to get back to the *original* by applying the rules and principles of textual criticism. These rules and principles go back to the early textual scholars such as Johann Jakob Griesbach (1745-1812),[292] Friedrich Constantin von Tischendorf (1815-1874), Brook Foss Westcott (1825-1901, Fenton John Anthony Hort (1828-1892), Frederick G. Kenyon (1863-1952), Kirsopp Lake (1872-1946), Eberhard Nestle (1851-1913),[293] and his son Erwin Nestle (1883-1972). Kurt Aland (1915-1994) is the lynchpin between the older generation of textual scholars and modern textual scholarship. Bruce M. Metzger (1914-2007), Ernest Cadman Colwell (1901-1974), Jacob Harold Greenlee (1918-2015), Gordon D. Fee (1934-), and Philip W. Comfort (1950-) join Aland, among many, many others.

J. Harold Greenlee wrote, "Textual criticism is the study of copies of an ancient writing to try to determine the exact words of the text as the author

---

[291] Paul D. Wegner, *A Student's Guide to Textual Criticism of the Bible* (InterVarsity Press, Downers Grove 2006), 301.

[292] J. J. Griesbach is the one who really laid the foundation for the rules and principles for New Testament textual criticism.

[293] In 1898, Eberhard Nestle published a significant handbook of textual criticism, and in 1898 published the first edition of a Greek New Testament under the title Novum Testamentum Graece cum apparatu critico ex editionibus et libris manu scriptis collecto. The text of this Greek New Testament was a combination of the editions of Constantin von Tischendorf, The New Testament in the Original Greek of Westcott and Hort, and the edition of Richard Francis Weymouth. Wherever two of these three editions agree, this was the preferred reading by Nestle.

originally wrote them."[294] This is the fundamental thought found in almost all introductory-intermediate textbooks on textual criticism throughout the twentieth century. The traditional approach was to look at all of the evidence, internal (largely contextual) and external (e.g., dating and established trustworthiness). However, the priority or weight in determining the original reading was given to the oldest manuscripts, displaying the more challenging (harder) readings, contributing to their trustworthiness. Most modern critical texts were the product of this approach. However, the Alands and others have shifted the emphasis to internal evidence instead of external evidence.[295]

Hundreds of textual scholars realize that without knowing what the original words of the original text were; then, there is no way to accurately translate the Scriptures, interpret the Scriptures, or defend the Scriptures. As Hill and Kruger put it,

> While the complexities in recovering the original text need to be acknowledged, that is a separate question from whether the concept of an original text is incoherent and should therefore be abandoned as a goal of the discipline. Unfortunately, these two questions are often mingled together without distinction. Although recovering the original text faces substantial obstacles (and therefore the results should be qualified), there is little to suggest that it is an illegitimate enterprise. If it were illegitimate, then we would expect the same would be true for Greek and Roman literature outside the New Testament. ... Recognizing the historical value of such scribal variations need not be set in opposition to the goal of recovering the original text. These two aspects of textual criticism are complementary, not mutually exclusive. Indeed, it is only when we can have some degree of assurance regarding the original text that we are even able to recognize that later scribes occasionally changed it for their own theological purposes. Without the former we would not have the latter. – (Hill and Kruger 2012, Loc. 233-250 KDP)

---

[294] Greenlee, J. Harold (2008). *The Text of the New Testament, From Manuscript to Modern Edition* (p. 2). Baker Publishing Group. Kindle Edition.

[295] External evidence is manuscript evidence: its date, geographical location, and relationship to other known manuscripts. Textual scholars generally prefer the readings supported by the Alexandrian family of witnesses. The Byzantine family of manuscripts tends to be rejected because of its being less trustworthy, but most critics now grant that it should still be considered.

Those Who Doubt the Recovery

Many scholars today believe that recovering the complete original Greek New Testament is outside the realm of possibility. Lee Martin MacDonald writes, "The traditional goal of textual criticism has been to establish the 'original' or earliest possible biblical text, but the overwhelming number of textual variants and the overlapping of several textual traditions make that goal a significant if not impossible challenge. Some scholars continue in the hope of recovering the originals and eliminating all ambiguities in the present texts, but they appear to be in the minority."[296]

MacDonald's comments are on point, and it is likely even graver than he has remarked. However, his comment about "the traditional goal of textual criticism" being "to establish the 'original' or [italics mine] the earliest possible biblical text" is not exactly the longstanding traditional objective. It was, in fact, "to establish the original"–**not** "the earliest possible biblical text." There is a number who remain in that group of scholars who aim at establishing the original.[297] I again go to Daniel Wallace, in the Foreword of MYTHS AND MISTAKES, who writes, "The new generation of evangelical scholars is far **more comfortable with ambiguity and uncertainty** than previous generations."[298] (Page xii)

The traditional goal of the 19th century and early 20th-century textual scholars was to make the critical text a mirror image of the "original text." This was their goal even if they were aware that it would never be a one-hundred-percent success. In fact, we can go back to Richard Bentley (1662-1742), who believed, in reality, that he could establish the original text in the majority of places where variants existed. The goal of the contemporary textual scholar is to get back to the "initial text." In the Editio Critica Maior (ECM), a critical edition of the Greek New Testament, we find that the "initial text is the form of a text that stands at the beginning of a textual tradition."[299] According to Gerd Mink, "the initial text preceded the textual tradition and has not survived in any manuscript." He goes on to say, "We cannot know this text with certainty but can only reconstruct it

---

[296] L. M. McDonald, *Forgotten Scriptures: The Selection and Rejection of Early Religious Writings* (Louisville: Westminster John Knox Press, July 13, 2009), 184.

[297] Again, when we employ the term "original" reading or "original" text in this publication, it is a reference to the exemplar manuscript composed by the New Testament author (e.g., Paul) and recorded by his secretary (e.g., Tertius), if he used one, from which all other copies ultimately were derived for publication and distribution to the Christian communities.

[298] Elijah Hixon and Peter J. Gurry, *MYTHS AND MISTAKES In New Testament Textual Criticism* (Downer Groves, IL: InterVarsity Press, 2019), xii.

[299] ECM/1–2Peter, 23*n. 4

hypothetically."[300] He also says, "The initial text is not identical with the original, the text of the author. Between the autograph and the initial text, considerable changes may have taken place which may not have left a single trace in the surviving textual tradition."[301] In short, the general, basic consensus is that the "initial text" is the earliest possible text for each of the twenty-seven books of the New Testament.

Early Christianity gave rise to what is known as "local texts." Christian congregations in and near cities, such as Alexandria, Antioch, Constantinople, Carthage, or Rome, were making copies of the Scriptures in the form that would become known as a text-type. In other words, manuscripts grew up in certain areas, just like a human family, becoming known as their text-type (family of manuscripts), having their own characteristics. The reality is not as simple as this because there are mixtures of text types within each text type. However, each text type resembles itself more than it does the others. It should also be remembered that most of our extant manuscripts are identical in more than seventy-five percent of their texts. Thus, the percentage of variant readings identifies a manuscript as a particular text type, i.e., "agreement in error" or variation from the original.

Therefore, for many years, the process of classifying manuscripts has been to classify them as a particular text type, such as Alexandrian, Western, Caesarean, or Byzantine. However, these days are fading because technology has allowed the textual scholar to carry out a more comprehensive comparison of all readings in all manuscripts, possibly making all previous classifications meaningless or nearly so. This new method is known as The Coherence-Based Genealogical Method (CBGM), which will be explained at great length in the forthcoming book by Dr. Don Wilkins in 2022.[302] In this method, an "initial text" is "relatively close to the form of the text from which the textual tradition of a New Testament book has originated." (Stephen C. Carlson)[303] In addition, "D. C. Parker's essay asserts the impossibility of the attempt to recover a single original text, and hence the editor or critic must

---

[300] This presentation is based on lectures given by the author at the Münster Colloquium on the Textual History of the Greek New Testament

http://www.uni-muenster.de/INTF/Colloquium2008_programme.pdf

[301] Gerd Mink, "Problems of a Highly Contaminated Tradition, the New Testament: Stemmata of Variants as a Source of a Genealogy for Witnesses," in Studies in Stemmatology, vol. 2 [ed. Pieter van Reenen, August den Hollander, and Margot van Mulken; Amsterdam: John Benjamins, 2004], 25).

[302] For now, read Dr. Wilkins' 120+ page article here on CBGM: https://bit.ly/3sflrOM

[303] http://textualcriticism.scienceontheweb.net/RECON/Carlson-CBGM1.html

be content with the text from which the readings in the extant manuscripts are genealogically descended (p. 21)."[304]

Believing that We Can Establish the Original

B. F. Westcott and F. J. A. Hort believed that they had established the original text with their *New Testament in the Original Greek* (1881). They write, "This edition is an attempt to present exactly the original words of the New Testament, so far as they can be determined from surviving documents."[305] We notice that Westcott and Hort qualified their goal with "as far as can be determined from surviving documents." The producers of the 5th edition of the *Greek New Testament,* United Bible Societies' Corrected Edition (2014)[306], and Kurt and Barbara Aland in their 28th edition of the *Nestle-Aland Greek New Testament* (2012)[307] believe that these critical texts are the most anyone has achieved in establishing the original.[308] However, it must be said that the NA28 has been shifted to the goal of establishing the "initial text." Westcott and Hort looked to the **earliest manuscripts** of their day as their foundation for the original text and considered internal evidence. The Alands, while appreciating the early texts, did move away to the reasoned eclectic approach, an approach that focuses more heavily on internal evidence rather than external evidence.[309] Nevertheless, their clearly stated goal was "an assurance of certainty in establishing the original text."[310] Sadly, as MacDonald said above, many modern textual scholars have abandoned the hope of ever establishing the original text or accepting that the above-mentioned critical

---

[304] The Textual History of the Greek New Testament: Changing Views in Contemporary Research (Peter Rodgers Review) ..., http://peter-rodgers.com/#articles (accessed July 7, 2014).

[305] B. F. Westcott; F. J. A. Hort, *The New Testament In the Original Greek,* Cambridge/London, 1881.

[306] Referred to as UBS5

[307] Referred to as NA28. It should be noted that the Greek text of the NA28 and the UBS5 are exactly the same, but their apparatuses are different. The NA28 is more for the scholar, the pastor, and the Bible student and deals with far more variants and offers more evidence for each variant, while the UBS5 is more for the Bible translator and includes only variants deemed important to Bible translation.

[308] Aland and Aland in their book, *The Text of the New Testament,* make the clear statement that the text of the Greek New Testament, United Bible Societies (UBS3) and the Nestle-Aland Greek New Testament (NA26) "comes closer to the original text of the New Testament than did Tischendorf or Westcott and Hort not to mention von Soden." (Aland and Aland, The Text of the New Testament 1995, 24)

[309] This approach addresses textual criticism by looking to internal and external evidence. However, many who use this approach do lean too heavily on internal evidence. In addition, while they value early manuscripts, they choose the best reading from a consideration of all manuscripts, believing that any of them can carry the original, avoiding preferences.

[310] Kurt and Barbara Aland, *THE TEXT OF THE NEW TESTAMENT: An Introduction to the Critical Editions and to the Theory and Practice of Modern Textual Criticism* (Grand Rapids, MI: Wm. B. Eerdmans Publishing Co., 1995), 291-2.

texts might live up to that claim. I personally find it ironic that the idea of establishing the original text became less and less of concern to the textual scholar over the 20th century as liberal-progressive scholarship consumed conservative scholarship throughout that same century. The reader must determine his own view as to whether there is any correlation.

On the objective of getting back to the original, the authors of *The Early Text of the New Testament* wrote, "However, while the complexities in recovering the original text need to be acknowledged, that is a separate question from whether the concept of an original text is incoherent and should, therefore, be abandoned as a goal of the discipline. Unfortunately, these two questions are often mingled together without distinction. Although recovering the original text faces substantial obstacles (and therefore, the results should be qualified), there is little to suggest that it is an illegitimate enterprise. If it were illegitimate, then we would expect the same would be true for Greek and Roman literature outside the New Testament. Are we to think that an attempt to reconstruct the original word of Tacitus, or Plato, or Thucydides is misguided? Or that it does not matter? Those who argue that we should abandon the concept of an original text for the New Testament often give very little (if any) attention to the implications of such an approach for classical literature."[311]

Westcott and Hort sought to establish the original text by choosing what they felt was the most faithful text or family of texts, the Alexandrian family (especially the Codex Vaticanus, designated B), and worked from there to establish their critical text. Again, modern scholarship has abandoned both the idea of establishing the original and choosing a trusted text or family of texts as a foundation. Since the mid-19th century, they have been using "eclecticism," now known as "reasoned eclecticism."[312] In this, all manuscripts are placed on equal footing. They simply look to all text types and decide which variant gave rise to all others, assigning more weight to internal evidence than to the external evidence of manuscripts. The last couple of decades have seen the growth of the newest form of NTTC, The Coherence-Based Genealogical Method (CBGM).

Philip Comfort, the author of *Encountering the Manuscripts: An Introduction to New Testament Paleography and Textual Criticism* (2005), has **not** abandoned the possibility of establishing the original text. Comfort finds this hope in the very earliest papyri and the Alexandrian text. He believes that the very early

---

[311] Charles E. Hill; Michael J. Kruger, *THE EARLY TEXT OF THE NEW TESTAMENT* (Oxford, United Kingdom: Oxford University Press, 2012), 4.

[312] Nonetheless, the oldest manuscripts, which are of the Alexandrian text-type, seem to be the favored, and text of the United Bible Society, 5th ed. and Nestle-Aland, 28th ed. has an Alexandrian disposition.

Alexandrian (Egyptian) text represents what the whole of the Christian writings must have looked like at that time. Writings of the early church fathers such as Irenaeus, Marcion, and Hippolytus reflect the Alexandrian form of the text. New Testament textual scholar Larry W. Hurtado holds this position as well. We will quote his position extensively.

> All indications are that early Christians were very much given to what we today would call "networking" with one another, and that includes translocal efforts. Indeed, the Roman period generally was a time of impressive travel and translocal contacts, for trading, pilgrimages, and other purposes.[313] Eldon Epp has marshaled evidence that the early Christian papyri, mainly from Egypt, reflect "extensive and lively interactions between Alexandria and the outlying areas, and also between the outlying areas [of Egypt] and other parts of the Roman world ... and ... the wide circulation of documents in this early period."[314] In another essay, Epp also demonstrated how readily people expected to send and receive letters all across the Roman Empire, reflecting more broadly a "brisk 'intellectual commerce' and dynamic interchanges of people, literature, books, and letters between Egypt and the vast Mediterranean region."[315]
>
> In illustration of this, note that we have at least three copies of the Shepherd of Hermas that are dated to the late second/early third century, at most only a few decades later than the composition of this text. Thus, this Roman-provenance writing made its way to Egypt very quickly and was apparently received positively. Even more striking is the appearance of a copy of Irenaeus's Against Heresies that has been dated to the late second or early third century. Again, within a very short time, we have a

---

[313] See Lionel Casson, Travel in the Ancient World (London: Allen & Unwin, 1974); and Richard Bauckham's discussion in his essay, "For Whom Were the Gospels Written?" in The Gospels for All Christians: Rethinking the Gospel Audiences, ed. Richard Bauckham (Grand Rapids: Eerdmans, 1998), 32 (9-48).

[314] Eldon Jay Epp, "The Significance of the Papyri for Determining the Nature of the New Testament Text in the Second Century: A Dynamic View of Textual Transmission," in Gospel Traditions in the Second Century: Origins, Recensions, Text, and Transmission, ed. William L. Petersen (Notre Dame: University of Notre Dame Press, 1989), 81 (71-103).

[315] Eldon Jay Epp, "New Testament Papyrus Manuscripts and Letter Carrying in Greco-Roman Times," in The Future of Early Christianity: Essays in Honor of Helmut Koester, ed. Birger A. Pearson (Minneapolis: Fortress Press, 1991), 55 (35-56). As another particular piece of evidence of Christian networking across imperial distances, Malcolm Choat pointed me to a third-century letter sent from an unknown individual Christian in Rome to fellow Christians in Egypt (P. Amherst 1.3), requesting certain financial transactions. For discussion see Charles Wessely, "Les plus anciens monuments du Christianisme ecrits sur papyrus," Patrologia Orientalis, Tomas Quartus (Paris: Librairie de Paris, 1908), 135-38.

writing composed elsewhere (Gaul) finding its way to Christians in Oxyrhynchus (about 120 miles south of Cairo). We could also note the several early copies of writings of Melito of Sardis (Roman Asia Minor). In short, the extant manuscript evidence fully supports the conclusion that the Oxyrhynchus material reflects a broad, translocal outlook.

... We shall explore the implications of the papyrus evidence, on the working assumption that though largely of Egyptian provenance, these early Christian papyri reflect attitudes, preferences, and usages of many Christians more broadly in the second and third centuries. We turn now to consider what we might infer from the list of textual witnesses provided to us in these papyri.[316]

Distribution of Papyri Witnesses for Each New Testament Book

NT Book	Total	Early	NT Book	Total	Early
Matthew	23	11	1 Timothy	0	0
Mark	3	2	2 Timothy	0	0
Luke	10	6	Titus	2	1
John	30	19	Philemon	2	1
Acts	14	7	Hebrews	8	4
Romans	10	5	James	6	4
1 Corinthians	8	3	1 Peter	3	1
2 Corinthians	4	2	2 Peter	2	1

---

[316] Larry W. Hurtado, *The Earliest Christian Artifacts: Manuscripts and Christian Origins* (Grand Rapids: William B. Eerdmans, 2006), 26-27.

Galatians	2	1	1 John	2	1
Ephesians	3	3	2 John	1	0
Philippians	3	2	3 John	1	0
Colossians	2	1	Jude	3	2
1 Thessalonians	4	3	Revelation	7	4
2 Thessalonians	2	2			

It appears that some of the answers to establishing the original text of the Christian Greek Scriptures lie within the Westcott and Hort approach. Fifteen papyrus manuscripts date from about 100–200 C.E. As of 2021, a **total of 141 NT papyri** are known, although some of the numbers issued were later considered to be fragments of the same original manuscript (e.g., P4/64/67 P77/103 P49/65). It is from these manuscripts, especially the earliest ones, that we are going to be **aided** in establishing the original text.[317] Tregelles (1813-75), Tischendorf (1815-74), and Westcott (1825-1901) and Hort (1828-92) hung their textual hats on the two best manuscripts of their day, i.e., Sinaiticus (c. 360) and Vaticanus (c. 350), both of the Alexandrian text-type.

P75 (c.175–225) contains most of Luke and John and has vindicated Westcott and Hort for their choice of Vaticanus as the premium manuscript for establishing the original text. After careful study of P75 against the Vaticanus Codex, scholars have found that they are just short of being identical. In his introduction to the Greek text, Hort argues that the Vaticanus Codex is a "very pure line of very ancient text."[318]

Those who have abandoned all hope of such a venture would argue differently, saying, "oldest is not necessarily best." For these scholars, the original reading could be found in any manuscript. This is true to a degree. They continue with the approach that the reading that produced the other

---

[317] It should be noted that Andrews is not arguing for setting aside all manuscripts except the early papyri. Rather, he is merely suggesting that our best evidence lies within these early papyri.

[318] B. F. Westcott and F. J. A. Hort, Introduction [and] Appendix, Vol. 2 of *New Testament in the Original Greek* (London: Macmillan and Company, 1881), 251.

readings is likely the original. While on the surface, this sounds great, it is not as reliable a principle as one might think. On this issue, Comfort writes:

> For example, two scholars, using this principle to examine the same variant, may not agree. One might argue that a copyist attempting to emulate the author's style produced the variant; the other could claim the same variant has to be original because it accords with the author's style. Or, one might argue that a variant was produced by an orthodox scribe attempting to rid the text of a reading that could be used to promote heterodoxy or heresy; another might claim that the same variant has to be original because it is orthodox and accords with Christian doctrine (thus a heterodoxical or heretical scribe must have changed it). Furthermore, this principle allows for the possibility that the reading selected for the text can be taken from any manuscript of any date. This can lead to subjective eclecticism.[319]

When we look deeper into reasoned eclecticism and the local-genealogical method,[320] we find that they lean more heavily on the internal evidence side than external evidence. This author's position is that the greater weight should be placed on the external evidence if we are to recover the original text. This is not to say that we do not consider internal evidence because we should. Westcott and Hort held this position as well. They wrote, "Documentary attestation has been in most cases allowed to confer the place of honour as against internal evidence." (Westcott and Hort 1882, 17) Ernest Colwell, who was of the same mindset, suggested in 1968 that we needed to get back to Westcott and Hort's principles. Sadly, textual scholarship has mostly strayed from those principles.

The Early Text of the New Testament

We have already discussed the level of skilled copying of the early papyri, Alexandria, Egypt's scribal practices have played a significant role in this. As historical records have shown, Alexandria had an enormous Jewish population. We can imagine a large, predominately Jewish, Christian congregation early on as the gospel made its way throughout that land. This congregation would have maintained deep ties with their fellow Christians in Jerusalem and Antioch. Then, the Didaskelion catechetical school of Alexandria had some of the most influential Church Fathers as head

---

[319] Philip Wesley Comfort, *The Quest for the Original Text of the New Testament* (Grand Rapids, MI: Baker House, 1992), 29-39.

[320] This method holds that a variant can be established as original and can come from any given manuscript(s).

instructors. As has already been noted, Pantaenus took over and was in charge from about 160–180 C.E., Clement being his greatest student, and Origen, who brought this school to Caesarea in 231, establishing a second school and scriptorium.

As the Greek Septuagint originated from Alexandria, and the vast majority of the earliest New Testament papyri also had their origins in Egypt (Fayum and Oxyrhynchus), it is quite clear that the above-mentioned Church Fathers would have accessed the Septuagint and the Christian Greek Scriptures in their writings and evangelistic work. Origen, who learned from both Clement and Pantaenus, wrote more than any of the earliest Christian leaders, and his writings are a reflection of the early New Testament papyri, as is true with Clement and his writings. Considering that Clement studied under Pantaenus, it is not difficult to surmise that his writings would also reflect the early New Testament papyri. Therefore, it truly is not unreasonable to suggest that going in reverse chronologically: Origen, Clement, Pantaenus, and those who studied with Pantaenus and brought him into Christianity from Stoic philosophy, were using Alexandrian family texts-types that were mirror-like reflections of the original texts of the Christian Greek Scriptures. The church historian Eusebius helps us to appreciate just how early this school was; note how he expresses it:

> About the same time, a man most distinguished for his learning, whose name was Pantaenus, governed the school of the faithful. There had been a school of sacred learning *established there from ancient times* [italics mine], which has continued down to our own times, and which we have understood was held by men able in eloquence and the study of divine things. The tradition is that this philosopher was then in great eminence, as he had been first disciplined in the philosophical principles of those called Stoics.[321]

We have learned thus far that in the second and third centuries C.E., Alexandria's scholarship and scribal practices had a tremendous impact on all of Egypt as far south as Fayum and Oxyrhynchus. This means that the standard text of the Christian Greek Scriptures reflecting the originals came up out of Egypt during the second century. The Alexandrian Library had been a force for influencing rigorous scholarship and setting high standards from the third century B.C.E. onward. Is it a mere coincidence that the four greatest libraries and learning centers were located in the very places that Christianity had its original growth: Alexandria, Pergamum near Ephesus, Rome, and Antioch? Their book production would greatly influence the congregations within these cities and nearby ones.

---

[321] Eusebius, *Ecclesiastical History* 5:10:1.

The Impact of the Early Papyri

Some improvements can be made to these critical texts because the editors of the 26th to 28th editions of the Nestle-Aland text made revisions setting the text further apart from the Westcott and Hort text of 1881. The 1881 WH Greek NT text is 99.5% the same as the 2012 NA Greek text. Yet, the committee for the NA28 NT Greek text has ignored the testimony of the earliest manuscripts and Codex Vaticanus and has rejected many readings by relegating them to the margin, or the critical apparatus, leaving an inferior reading in the main text. It is as Comfort says in his *New Testament Text and Translation Commentary*:

> …the resultant eclectic text exhibits too much dependence on internal evidence, emphasizing the 'local' aspect of the 'local-genealogical' method, to use Aland's language. This means that the decision-making, on a variant-unit-by-variant-unit basis, produced a text with an uneven documentary presentation. Furthermore, the committee setting, with members voting on each significant textual variant cannot help but produce a text with uneven documentation. All eclectic texts reconstruct a text that no ancient Christian actually read, even though they approach a close replication of the original writings. However, the NU edition's eclecticism extends even to following different manuscripts within the same sentence.[322]

Comfort goes on to say,

In conclusion, my preference for emphasizing the documentary method in making text-critical choices is revealed in the fact that I decide against many choices made by the editors of the NU text. The reader may see these decisions in the following notes:

Matthew 3:16; 4:24; 5:28; 8:21; 9:14, 26; 12:47; 13:35b; 14:16, 27, 30; 15:6b, 14; 17:9; 18:15; 19:22; 21:44; 25:6; 27:49

Mark 3:32; 6:51; 7:4; 15:12; 16:8 [ending to Mark]

Luke 3:22a; 8:43; 14:17; 17:24; 20:9; 22:43–44

John 1:34; 3:31–32; 5:44; 6:14; 7:9; 7:53–8:11; 9:4, 38–39a; 10:8, 16, 18; 11:45–46; 13:2a, 2c, 32; 16:23; 20:31; 21:18

Acts 3:6; 7:13, 38; 9:12; 16:12

---

[322] Philip W. Comfort, *New Testament Text and Translation Commentary: Commentary on the Variant Readings of the Ancient New Testament Manuscripts and How They Relate to the Major English Translations* (Carol Stream, IL: Tyndale House Publishers, Inc., 2008) XV.

Romans 3:4; 7:17; 8:11a, 23; 11:17; 12:14; 15:33 [placement of doxology]

1 Corinthians 1:14; 3:13; 4:2; 7:7, 15; 8:3a, 3b; 9:9b; 10:2; 12:10

2 Corinthians 4:5b; 5:3, 12

Galatians 1:3, 6, 15a; 2:12a, 12b; 3:21a

Ephesians 1:1b, 15, 18; 3:19; 4:24, 28; 5:2a, 20; 6:12a, 19

Philippians 3:3, 7, 10, 12a

Colossians 2:7a, 10, 13, 23; 3:6, 22b, 23; 4:8, 12

1 Thessalonians 3:2, 13; 5:4, 9

2 Thessalonians 2:13; 3:6

2 Timothy 3:15

Philemon 25

Hebrews 1:8; 3:2; 4:3a; 7:4, 28; 9:1, 19; 11:4; 12:1, 3, 4; 13:15, 21c, 24, 25a

James 1:17; 2:3; 4:14a; 5:4

1 Peter 1:12b; 2:21; 3:14, 18; 4:11; 5:8, 10b, 10c

2 Peter 1:3; 2:6a; 3:18b

1 John 3:23a; 5:20b

2 John 8

Jude 5

Revelation 1:6b; 9:12–13a, 13b; 11:8; 12:8a, 10; 13:18; 14:3a, 5; 15:3, 6; 16:5b; 18:2, 3; 19:11[323]

The Reliability of the Early Text

Even though many textual scholars credited Aland's *The Text of the New Testament* with their description of the text as "free," that was not the entire position of the Alands. They did describe different texts' styles, such as "at least normal," "normal," "free," and "strict," seemingly to gauge or weigh the textual faithfulness of each manuscript. However, like Kenyon, they saw a need based on the evidence, which suggested a rethinking of how the evidence should be described,

---

[323] Philip W. Comfort, *New Testament Text and Translation Commentary: Commentary on the Variant Readings of the Ancient New Testament Manuscripts and How They Relate to the Major English Translations* (Carol Stream, IL: Tyndale House Publishers, Inc., 2008), 883–884.

We have inherited from the past generation the view that the early text was a 'free' text, and the discovery of the Chester Beatty papyri seemed to confirm this view. When P^{45} and P^{46} were joined by P^{66} sharing the same characteristics, this position seemed to be definitely established. P^{75} appeared in contrast to be a loner with its "strict" text anticipating Codex Vaticanus. Meanwhile the other witnesses of the early period had been ignored. It is their collations which have changed the picture so completely.[324]

While we have said a couple of times now, it bears repeating, as *some* of the earliest manuscripts that we now have evidence that a professional scribe copied them. *Many* of the other papyri confirm that a semiprofessional scribe copied them, while *most* of these early papyri give evidence of being produced by a copyist who was literate and experienced. Therefore, either literate or semiprofessional copyists did the vast majority of the early extant papyri, with some being done by professionals. As it happened, the few poorly copied manuscripts became known first, establishing a precedent that was difficult for some to shake when the enormous amount of evidence emerged that showed just the opposite.

After a detailed comparison of the papyri, Kurt and Barbara Aland concluded that these manuscripts from the second to the fourth centuries are of three kinds (at least normal, normal, free, and strict). "It is their collations which have changed the picture so completely." (p. 93)

1. Normal Texts: The normal text is a relatively faithful tradition (e.g., P^{52}, which departs from its exemplar only occasionally, as do New Testament manuscripts of every century. It is further represented in P^4, P^5, P^{12}(?), P^{16}, P^{18}, P^{20}, P^{28}, P^{47}, P^{72} (1, 2 Peter), and P^{87}.[325]

2. Free Texts: This is a text dealing with the original text in a relatively free manner with no suggestion of a program of standardization (e.g., p^{45}, p^{46}, and p^{66}), exhibiting the most diverse variants. It is further represented in P^9 (?), P^{13}(?), P^{29}, P^{37}, P^{40}, P^{69}, P^{72} (Jude), and P^{78}.[326]

3. Strict Texts: These manuscripts transmit the text of the exemplar with meticulous care (e.g., P^{75}) and depart from it only rarely. It is further represented in P^1, P^{23}, P^{27}, P^{35}, P^{36}, P^{64+67}, P^{65}(?), and P^{70}.[327]

---

[324] Kurt and Barbara Aland, *THE TEXT OF THE NEW TESTAMENT: An Introduction to the Critical Editions and to the Theory and Practice of Modern Textual Criticism* (Grand Rapids, MI: Wm. B. Eerdmans Publishing Co., 1995), 93-95.

[325] Ibid., 95

[326] Ibid., 59, 64, 93

[327] Ibid., 64, 95

Bruce M. Metzger (1914 – 2007) was an editor with Kurt and Barbara Aland of the United Bible Societies' standard Greek New Testament and the Nestle-Aland Greek New Testament. In his *A Textual Commentary on the Greek New Testament*, Second Edition (1971, 1994), and other works, we have his view of the Alexandrian text-type as follows.

> The *Alexandrian text,* which Westcott and Hort called the *Neutral text* (a question-begging title), is usually considered to be the best text and the most faithful in preserving the original. Characteristics of the Alexandrian text are brevity and austerity. That is, it is generally shorter than the text of other forms, and it does not exhibit the degree of grammatical and stylistic polishing that is characteristic of the Byzantine type of text. Until recently, the two chief witnesses to the Alexandrian text were codex Vaticanus (B) and codex Sinaiticus (ℵ), parchment manuscripts dating from about the middle of the fourth century. With the acquisition, however, of the Bodmer Papyri, particularly P[66] and P[75], both copied about the end of the second or the beginning of the third century, evidence is now available that the Alexandrian type of text goes back to an archetype that must be dated early in the second century. The Sahidic and Bohairic versions frequently contain typically Alexandrian readings.

It is best if textual scholars focus their attention on the categories the Alands set out instead of their over-generalization that the early period of copying was "uncontrolled" and "free." The Alands' rating system consisted of "at least normal," "normal," "strict," and "free," designed to evaluate the textual faithfulness of each manuscript. It seems that these terms were meant to gauge the level of control that the scribe showed in copying his exemplar. Manuscripts labeled "at least normal" referred to a copyist who at least gave some consideration to his task, namely, producing an accurate copy of the exemplar. "Normal," on the other hand, referred to a copyist who permitted what was deemed a normal number of variants within copying of the exemplar. Therefore, "strict" referred to a scribe who allowed very few variants in his copy of the exemplar. Lastly, "free" refers to a copyist who showed almost no regard for being faithful to the exemplar he was copying.

It behooves the textual scholar to pay much attention to the study of scribal habits, which began with Ernest Colwell in 1969, who analyzed the scribal habits in P45, P66, and P75 examining their singular readings.[328]

---

[328] Ernest C. Colwell, "*Method in Evaluating Scribal Habits: A Study of P45, P66, P75*," in *Studies in Methodology in Textual Criticism of the New Testament,* New Testament Tools and Studies 9 (Leiden: Brill, 1969).

Singular readings are variant readings found only in the manuscript being examined, not in any other extant documents. By studying these singular readings of a particular manuscript, we see into the habits of that scribe, namely, his pattern of textual variations, his interactions with the text. Colwell's investigation was followed by a much more extensive study of singular readings by James Royse of the same manuscripts some twelve years later.[329] Then, we had Philip Comfort in his doctoral dissertation in 1997.[330] Comfort explains that his objective was "to determine what it was in the text that prompted the scribes of P45, P66, and P75 to make individual readings." Comfort suggests that we forgo the categories of the Alands and "that textual critics could use the categories "reliable," "fairly reliable," and "unreliable" to describe the textual fidelity of any given manuscript." This author would agree. Moreover, he shows "that many of the early papyri are 'reliable,' several 'fairly reliable,' and a few 'unreliable.'" Comfort then logically explains, "One of the ways of establishing reliability (or lack thereof) is to test a manuscript against one that is generally proven for its textual fidelity. For example, since many scholars have acclaimed the textual fidelity of P75 (both for intrinsic and extrinsic reasons), it is fair to compare other manuscripts against it in order to determine their textual reliability."[331]

How do we know that the critical texts NA28 and the UBS5 are reliable? In 1989, Eldon J. Epp noted that the papyri had added virtually no new substantial variants to the variants already known from our later manuscripts.[332] Even with the discovery of many other papyri over the last 25 years, the situation has remained the same. It can be said that after 135 years of early manuscript discoveries since Westcott and Hort of 1881, the above critical editions of the Greek New Testament have gone virtually unchanged. Hill and Kruger go on to say, "It also means that the fourth-century 'best texts,' the 'Alexandrian' codices Vaticanus and Sinaiticus, have roots extending throughout the entire third century and even into the second."[333]

---

[329] James Ronald Royse, "*Scribal Habits in Early Greek New Testament Papyri*" (Ph.D. diss., Graduate Theological Union, 1981). According to Royse, this investigation of singular readings does not apply to lectionaries, patristic sources, and versions, just New Testament papyri, uncials, and minuscules.

[330] Philip Comfort, "*The Scribe as Interpreter: A New Look at New Testament Textual Criticism according to Reader Reception Theory*," D. Litt. et Phil, dissertation, University of South Africa (1997).

[331] Philip Comfort, *Encountering the Manuscripts: An Introduction to New Testament Paleography & Textual Criticism* (Nashville, TN: Broadman & Holman, 2005), 268.

[332] E. J. Epp, 'The Significance of the Papyri for Determining the Nature of the New Testament Text in the Second Century: A Dynamic View of Textual Transmission', in W. L. Petersen, ed., *The Gospel Traditions in the Second Century* (Notre Dame: University of Notre Dame Press, 1989), 101.

[333] Charles E. Hill; Michael J. Kruger, THE EARLY TEXT OF THE NEW TESTAMENT (Oxford, United Kingdom: Oxford University Press, 2012), 5-6.

The most reliable of the earliest texts are P[1], P[4, 64, 67], P[23], P[27], P[30], P[32], P[35], P[39], P[49, 65], P[70], P[75], P[86], P[87], P[90], P[91], P[100], P[101], P[106], P[108], P[111], P[114], and P[115]. The copyists of these manuscripts allowed very few variants in their copies of the exemplars.[334] They had the ability to make accurate judgments as they went about their copying, resulting in superior texts. Whether their copying skills resulted from their belief that they were copying a sacred text or their training cannot be known. It could have been a combination of both. These papyri are of great importance when considering textual problems and are considered by many textual scholars to be a good representation of the original wording of the text that the biblical author first published. Still, "many of these manuscripts contain singular readings and some 'Alexandrian' polishing, which needs to be sifted out." (P. Comfort 2005, 269) Nevertheless, again, they are the best texts and the most faithful in preserving the original. While it is true that some of the papyri are mere fragments, some contain substantial portions of text. We should note too that text types really did not exist per se in the second century, and it is a mere convention to refer to the papyri as Alexandrian, since the best Alexandrian manuscript, Vaticanus, did exist in the second century by way of P[75].[335] It is not that the Alexandrian text existed, but rather P[75]/Vaticanus evidence that some very strict copying with great care was taking place.[336] Manuscripts that were not of this caliber of strict and careful copying were the result of scribal errors and scribes taking liberties with the text. Therefore, even though P[5] may be categorized as a Western text type, it is more a matter of negligence in the copying process.

---

[334] In 1988, the Alands, in the second edition of *The Text of the New Testament* (93-95), categorized thirty of the forty-four earliest manuscripts (40 papyri and 4 parchment) as "at least normal," "normal," and "strict," with the other fourteen being categorized as "free" or "like Codex Bezae (D)." At that time, the Alands did not rate P[90] [2nd], P[92], [3rd/4th] and P[95] [3rd], likely because they had only recently been discovered. However, we now have the Aland classification of "strict."

[335] The Coherence Based Genealogical Method, which was developed by Gerd Mink and assists scholars in developing genealogical trees of manuscripts, will be discussed in far greater detail in the forthcoming release, *An Essential Investigation of the Coherence-Based Genealogical Method*, in 2020 by Dr. Don Wilkins: but we should note here that it has no relation to the traditional text-type model. It is for this reason that scholars such as Holger Strutwolf have suggested that we abandon any references to the manuscripts by the tradition text-types.

[336] "What we do know, from the manuscript evidence, is that several of the earliest Christian scribes were well-trained scribes who applied their training to making reliable texts, both of the Old Testamfent and the New Testament. We know that they were conscientious to make a reliable text in the process of transcription (as can be seen in manuscripts like P[4+64+67] and P[75]), and we know that others worked to rid the manuscript of textual corruption. This is nowhere better manifested than in P[66], where the scribe himself and the *diorthotes* (official corrector) made over 450 corrections to the text of John. As is explained in the next chapter, the *diorthotes* of P[66] probably consulted other exemplars (one whose text was much like that of P[75]) in making his corrections. This shows a standard Alexandrian scriptoral practice at work in the reproduction of a New Testament manuscript." (P. Comfort, Encountering the Manuscripts: An Introduction to New Testament Paleography and Textual Criticism 2005, 264)

Strict	At Least Normal	Normal	Free	Like D
𝔓1, 𝔓23, 𝔓27, 𝔓35, 𝔓39, 𝔓64/67, 𝔓65(?), 𝔓70, 𝔓75, 𝔓77, 𝔓102, 𝔓103, 𝔓104, 𝔓106, 𝔓108, 𝔓109, 𝔓111	𝔓15, 𝔓22, 𝔓30, 𝔓32, 𝔓49, 𝔓53	𝔓4, 𝔓5, 𝔓12(?), 𝔓16, 𝔓18, 𝔓20, 𝔓28, 𝔓47, 𝔓52, 𝔓72 (1, 2 Pet.), 𝔓87, 𝔓90, 𝔓101, 𝔓107	𝔓45, 𝔓46, 𝔓66, 𝔓9(?), 𝔓13(?), 𝔓29, 𝔓37, 𝔓40, 𝔓69, 𝔓72(Jude), 𝔓78, 𝔓95	𝔓38, 𝔓48
Early Uncials 0220	0162, 0189		0171	

The Aland Classification of Papyri as of 2002

As Hill and Kruger put it, "if one accepts the Alands' analyses, in 2002, forty out of fifty-five (or just under 73 percent) of the earliest NT manuscripts had Normal to Strict texts, and fifteen (or just over 27 percent) had Free to Like D texts. The single largest category, consisting of eighteen out of fifty-five (or nearly a third) of the earliest manuscripts, is the category of Strict text."[337] Therefore, it would be difficult to follow in the footsteps of previous authors who cite the Alands as their source in describing the early period of copying the Greek New Testament as "free," or "wild," "in a state of flux," "chaotic," "a turbid textual morass," and so on.

The Primary Task of a Textual Scholar

The long-held task of the textual scholar has been to recover the original reading. Samuel Prideaux Tregelles (1813-1875) stated that the objective "of all textual criticism is to present an ancient work, as far as possible, in the very words and form in which it proceeded from the writer's own hand. Thus, when applied to the Greek New Testament, the result proposed is to give a text of those writings, as near as can be done on existing evidence, such as they were when originally written in the first century."[338] B. F. Westcott (1825-1901) and F. J. A. Hort (1828-1892) said it was their goal "to present exactly the original words of the New Testament, so far as they can now be determined from surviving documents."[339] Throughout the twentieth century, leading textual scholars such as Bruce M. Metzger (1914-2007) and Kurt Aland (1915-1994) had the same goals for textual criticism. Griesbach (1745-1812), Tregelles, Tischendorf (1815-1874), Westcott and Hort, Metzger, Aland, and other prominent textual scholars since the days of

---

[337] Charles E. Hill; Michael J. Kruger, *THE EARLY TEXT OF THE NEW TESTAMENT* (Oxford, United Kingdom: Oxford University Press, 2012), 5-6.

[338] Tregelles, *An Account of the Printed Text of the Greek New Testament,* 174.

[339] Westcott and Hort, *Introduction to the New Testament in the Original Greek,* 1.

Erasmus (1466-1536) all gave their lives to the restoration of the Greek New Testament.

However, sadly, "more dominant in text critics' thinking now is the need to plot the changes in the history of the text."[340] While Bart Ehrman, David Parker, and J. K. Elliot are correct that we could never restore or establish the authors' original words of the twenty-seven Greek New Testament books **beyond question**, it should remain the goal, as opposed to the pessimistic attitude of late. If we sidestep the traditional goal of textual criticism, we are really abandoning textual criticism itself. While the textual scholar wants to track down the variants to the text through the centuries, this can only be done by realizing there was a beginning, i.e., the twenty-seven original texts. How does one identify an alteration in the text without knowing from what it was altered? While the NA28/UBS5 critical edition cannot be considered a 100% reproduction of the twenty-seven original books, textual scholarship should always work in that direction, or otherwise, what is the purpose? The author of this publication is in harmony with the words of Paul D. Wegner, who writes, "Textual criticism is foundational to exegesis and interpretation of the text: we need to know what the wording of the text is before we can know what it means."[341]

The sad situation is that textual scholarship as a whole is unwittingly or knowingly moving the goalposts for some unknown reason. In textual criticism, it is now the earliest knowable text. In biblical hermeneutics, it is dissecting a text until you no longer have the Word of God but rather the word of man, and a jumbled word at that. Bible translation goes beyond what the Word of God is in the receptor language (e.g., English, Spanish, German) into what the translator thinks the original author meant. How is it possible for **so few** to see the danger of what is happening? What has happened right before our eyes are

- the goal of an early text, not the original,

- Bible books by unknown authors, not the ones bearing their name,

- with Jesus, not saying half of what the Gospels claim he said, in mini commentary,

- and interpretive translations by translators that are of the biblical criticism mindset.

---

[340] J. K. Elliott, "The International Greek New Testament Project's Volumes on the Gospel of Luke: Prehistory and Aftermath," NTTRU 7, 17.

[341] Paul D. Wegner, *A Student's Guide to Textual Criticism of the Bible: Its History, Methods & Results* (Downers Grove, IL: InterVarsity Press, 2006), 230.

CHAPTER VIII

How Did the Spread of Early Christianity and the Persecution of the Early Church Impact the Text of the New Testament?

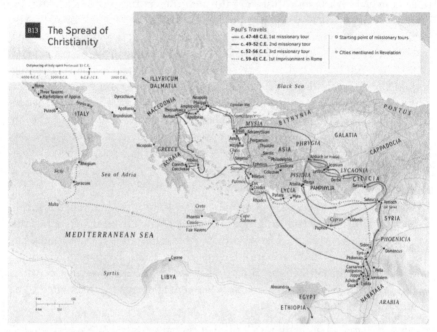

The Foretold Apostasy

Within just a few short decades after the apostle John's death, divisions were already evident among the early Christians. Historians Will and Ariel Durant write: "Celsus [Greek Philosopher and second-century opponent of Christianity] himself had sarcastically observed that Christians were 'split up into ever so many factions, each individual desiring to have his own party.' About 187 AD, Irenaeus listed twenty varieties of Christianity; about 384 AD Epiphanius counted eighty." (*The Story of Civilization: Part III, Caesar and Christ*) The first-century Christianity that Jesus Christ started, and the apostles grew went from 120 Christians in the upper room of Pentecost 33 C.E. to shortly over one million by 130 C.E. This was accomplished in a world of only one hundred million in population.

2 Thessalonians 2:1a, 3 Updated American Standard Version (UASV)

2 Now we request you, brothers, with regard to the coming of our Lord Jesus Christ … ³ Let no one deceive you in any way, for it will not come unless **the apostasy comes first**, and the man of lawlessness is revealed, the son of destruction,

Apostasy: (Gr. *apostasia*) The term literally means "to stand away from" and is used to refer to ones who 'stand away from the truth.' It is abandonment, a rebellion, an apostasy, a refusal to accept or acknowledge true worship. In Scripture, this is used primarily concerning the one who rises up in defiance of the only true God and his people, working in opposition to the truth. – Ac 21:21; 2 Thess. 2:3.

Concerning this text, New Testament scholar Knute Larson writes, "Before that great day comes, Paul declared, the **rebellion** must occur. The word used here is *apostasia*, or apostasy. Before the day of the Lord, there will be a great denial, a deliberate turning away by those who profess to belong to Christ. It will be a rebellion. Having once allied themselves with Christ, they will abandon him. Within the recognized church there will come a time when people will forsake their faith. Throughout history there have been defections from the faith. But the apostasy about which he wrote to the Thessalonians would be of greater magnitude and would signal the coming of the end."[342]

DIVERSITY OF BIBLICAL INTERPRETATION
DIVERSITY OF CHRISTIAN BELIEFS

In his forward to R. C. Sproul's Knowing Scripture, J. I. Packer observes that Protestant theologians are in conflict about biblical interpretation. To illustrate the diversity of biblical interpretations, William Yarchin pictures a shelf full of religious books saying different things, but all claiming to be faithful interpretations of the Bible. Bernard Ramm observed that such diverse interpretations underlie the "doctrinal variations in Christendom." A mid-19th century book on biblical interpretation observed that even those who believe the Bible to be "the word of God" hold "the most discordant views" about fundamental doctrines." Below are just a few examples.

Four Views of Hell	Four Views of Salvation	Two Views of Inspiration	Three Views of Atonement
Four Views of creation	Four Views of Eternal Security	Four Views of Inspiration	Four Views of Works in Final Judgment
Four Views of Inerrancy	Four Views of Sanctification	Two Views of Fasting	Four Views of the Book of Revelation
Two Views of Christology	Three Views of Image of God	Three Views of Grace	Three Views of Human Constitution
Four Views of Providence	Two Views of Lord's Supper	Four Views of Free Will	Two Views of Charismatic Gifts
Two Views of Baptism	Three Views of Jesus' Return	Two Views of Sabbath	Four Views of Predestination
Three Views of Purgatory	Four Views of the Church	Four Views of End Times	Four Views of Christian Spirituality
Four Views of Antichrist	Three Views of Neutrality	Three Views of Heaven	Two Views of Foreknowledge

---

[342] Knute Larson, *I & II Thessalonians, I & II Timothy, Titus, Philemon*, vol. 9, Holman New Testament Commentary (Nashville, TN: Broadman & Holman Publishers, 2000), 105–106.

The apostle Paul says to the Ephesian elders, there is but "one Lord, one faith, one baptism." (Eph. 4:5) Paul penned those words about 60 C.E., and he was informing them that there was but one Christian faith. Yet, today we see more varieties of Christian faith than we care to count (41,000+), all claiming that they are the truth and the way. Whenever a brave soul dares to be truthful and brings up doctrinal differences (views or beliefs) and different conduct standards, he is shouted down as an alarmist. They claim that most of these denominations are the same on the essential doctrines, i.e., the salvation doctrines. This is not true and attempts to hide the truth because even the salvation doctrines have three to five different interpretations. Regardless, we must concern ourselves with a crucial question from Jesus Christ, "when the Son of Man comes, will he find faith on earth?" (Lu 18:8) This is a whole other discussion. We will only concern ourselves with how these divisions came about in the first place.

The blame lies with Satan and his proxies from the moment he contemplated a rebellion. Many atrocities were at his hand in the 4,000-year history down to Christ as well. Returning to our first century, Satan attempted to have Jesus killed as a baby. He tempted Jesus in the wilderness after his baptism. He attempted persecution right from the start. Peter wrote, "Be sober-minded; be watchful. Your adversary, the devil, prowls around like a roaring lion, seeking someone to devour." (1 Pet. 5:8) Initially, the persecution of this young Christian body came from Jewish religious leaders, and then from the Roman Empire itself. With "all authority in heaven" (Matt. 28:20), Jesus watched on, as the Holy Spirit guided and directed them, this infancy Christian congregation endured the best that Satan and his henchman had to offer. (See Rev. 1:9; 2:3, 19) As we know from Scripture, Satan is not one to give up, so he devised a new plan, divide and conquer. Yes, he would cause divisions within the Christian congregation. Satan broke out the ultimate weapon— **the apostasy**. We need not believe that all of a sudden, the apostasy came into the Christian congregation. No, he made sure that he had warned them while he was here on earth of what was to come, and after his ascension, Jesus was watching from heaven as his apostles made the young Christian congregation aware of what was coming and when it was getting started. – Colossians 1:18

In the Greek New Testament, the noun "apostasy" (Gr., *apostasia*) has the sense of "desertion, abandonment or rebellion." (Acts 21:21) There it predominantly is alluding to abandonment, a drawing away from or abandoning of pure worship.

"[Jesus] Be Aware of False Prophets . . .

[Peter] There Will Be False Teachers Among You."

Matthew 7:15 Updated American Standard Version (UASV)

15 "Beware of the false prophets, who come to you in sheep's clothing, but inwardly are ravenous wolves.

Jesus was well aware of what Satan would try to accomplish step-by-step and that divisions through those from within were on the list. New Testament scholar Stuart K. Weber says, "Jesus had an important reason for inserting the wolf metaphor (Acts 20:27–31)—to alert his listeners to the danger of a false prophet. If the false prophets were thought of as a source of bad fruit, then the disciples might think it was enough simply to recognize and ignore the false prophet, refusing to consume his bad fruit, and awaiting God's judgment on him. But the wolf metaphor attributes a more active and malicious motive to the false prophet. He is actually an enemy of the sheep and, if not confronted, will get his way by destroying the sheep." (Weber 2000, 101)

Weber mentions Acts 20:28-30, where Paul, about **56 C.E.**, warned the Ephesian elders,

Acts 20:28-30 Updated American Standard Version (UASV)

28 Pay careful attention to yourselves and to all the flock, in which the Holy Spirit has made you overseers, to care for the congregation of God, which he obtained with the blood of his own Son.* 29 I know that after my departure fierce wolves will come in among you, not sparing the flock; 30 and **from among your own selves** men will arise, **speaking twisted things**, to **draw away the disciples after them**.

* Lit *with the blood of his Own.*

Yes, these, who standoff from the Truth and the Way, would not be seeking their own disciples, but instead, they would be seeking, to draw away the disciples after them." i.e., the disciples of Christ. Jesus was well aware that the easiest way to defeat any group is to divide them, and so was Satan, who had been watching humanity for over 4,000 years, and especially the Israelites (Isaac and Ishmael / Jacob and Esau / Israel and Judah), as "Satan disguises himself as an angel of light. So, it is no surprise if his servants also disguise themselves as servants of righteousness. – 2 Corinthians 11:14-15.

The apostle Peter also spoke of these things about **64 C.E.**, "there will be false teachers among you, who will secretly bring in destructive heresies … in their greed they will exploit you with false words." (2 Pet. 2:1, 3) These abandoned the faithful words, became false teachers, rising within the Christian congregation, sharing their corrupting influence, intending to hide, disguise, or mislead.

These dire warnings by Jesus and the New Testament Authors began in the first century C.E. Yes, they started small but burst forth on the scene in the second century.

"[Paul says it] Is Already at Work"

About **51 C.E.**, some 18-years after Jesus' death, resurrection, and ascension, division was already starting to creep into the faith, "the mystery of lawlessness is already at work." (2 Thess. 2:7) Yes, the power of **the man of lawlessness** was already present, which is the power of Satan, the god of this world (2 Cor. 4:3-4), and his tens of millions of demons, are hard at work behind the scenes.

There were even some divisions beginning as early as **49 C.E.**, when the elders wrote a letter to the Gentile believers, saying,

Acts 15:24 Updated American Standard Version (UASV)

24 Since we have heard that some went out from among us and troubled you with words, unsettling your souls,343 although we gave them no instructions,

Here we see that some *within* were very vocal about their opposition to the direction the faith was heading. Here, it was over whether the Gentiles needed to be circumcised, suggesting that they must be obedient to the Mosaic Law. – Ac 15:1, 5.

As the years progressed throughout the first-century, this divisive "talk [would] spread like gangrene." (2 Tim. 2:17, **c. 65 C.E.**) About **51 C.E.**, They had some in Thessalonica, at worst, going ahead of, or at best, misunderstanding Paul, and wrongly stating by word and a bogus letter "that the day of the Lord has come." (2 Thess. 2:1-2) In Corinth, about **55 C.E.**, "some of [were saying] that there is no resurrection of the dead. (1 Cor. 15:12) About **65 C.E.**, some were "saying that the resurrection has already happened. They [were] upsetting the faith of some." – 2 Tim 2:16-18.

Throughout the next three decades, no inspired books were written. However, by the time of the Apostle John's letter-writing days of 96-98 C.E., he tells us, "Now many antichrists have come. Therefore, we know that it is the last hour." (1 John 2:18) These are ones "who deny that Jesus is the Christ," and those who do not confess "Jesus Christ has come in the flesh is from God." – 1 John 2:22; 4:2-3.

---

343 This means that some left the Christian faith and were trying to subvert (undermine) others' faith. Some within the congregation were expressing their conflicting beliefs. Here it was over the issue of Gentile Christians needing to be circumcised and whether Christians needed to observe the Mosaic Law.

From 33 C.E. to 100 C.E., the apostles served Christ as a restraint against "the apostasy" that was coming. Paul stated in 2 Thessalonians 2:7, "For the mystery of lawlessness is already at work. Only he [Apostle by Christ] who now restrains it [the apostasy] will do so until he **[apostles]** is out of the way." 2 Thessalonians 2:3 said, "Let no one deceive you in any way **[misinterpretation or false teachers of Paul's first letter]**. For that day **[presence, parousia (second coming) of Christ]** will not come, unless the apostasy comes first, and the man of lawlessness **[likely one person, or maybe an organization/movement, empowered by Satan]** is revealed, the son of destruction."

We must keep in mind that the meaning of any given text is what the author meant by the words he used, as it should have been understood by his audience and had some relevance/meaning for his audience. The rebellion [apostasy] began slowly in the first century and would break forth after the last apostle's death, i.e., John. As a historian, Ariel Durant informed us earlier, by 187 C.E., there were 20 varieties of Christianity, and by 384 C.E., there were 80 varieties of Christianity. Christianity would become one again, a universal religion, i.e., Catholicism.

Gnostic Belief

Marcion (85-c.160) was a semi-Gnostic, who believed that the teachings of Jesus were irreconcilable with the actions of the God of the Old Testament. He viewed the God of the Old Testament, Jehovah, to be vicious, violent, and cruel, an oppressor who gave out material rewards to those worshiping him. In contrast, Marcion described the New Testament God, Jesus Christ, as a perfect God, the God of unadulterated love and compassion, of kindness, and quickness to forgive.

Montanus (late second century) was a "prophet" from Asia Minor who believed that their revelation came directly from the Holy Spirit, which superseded the authority of Jesus, Paul, Peter, John, James, anyone really. They believed in the imminent return of Christ and the setting up of the New Jerusalem in Pepuza. They believed that the apostle and prophets had the power to forgive sin. He was more concerned about Christian conduct than Christian doctrine, wanting to get back to the first century's Christian values. However, he took this to the extreme, just as John Calvin would some 1,300 years later in the 16th century. Montanism was a movement focused on prophecy, especially the founder's views, being seen as the light for their time.

Valentinus (c.100-c.160) was a Greek poet who founded his school in Rome and was the most prominent early Christian gnostic theologian. He claimed that though Jesus' heavenly (spiritual) body was from Mary, he was not actually born from her. This belief came about because Gnostics viewed all matter as evil. Therefore, if Jesus had really been a natural human person with a physical body, he would have been evil. Another form of Gnosticism was Docetism, which claimed that Jesus Christ was not a natural person, i.e., it was a mere appearance and illusion, which would have included his death and resurrection.

Manes (c. 216-274) was the prophet and the founder of Manichaeism, a gnostic religion. He sought to combine elements of Christianity, Buddhism, and Zoroastrianism, based on a rigid dualism of good and evil, locked in an eternal struggle. He believed that salvation is possible through education, self-denial, fasting, and chastity. He also believed that he was an "apostle of Jesus Christ" (Ramsey 2006, 272) although, strictly speaking, his religion was not a movement of Christian Gnosticism in the earlier approach.

Beginning with the Council of Nicaea in 325 C.E., Emperor Constantine legalized Christianity to reunite the empire. He fully understood that religious division was a threat to the continuation of the Roman Empire. However, Emperor Theodosius I (347 – 395 C.E.) banned paganism and imposed Christianity as the State religion of the Roman Empire. The Roman Catholic Church can trace its existence back to the council of Nicaea in 325 C.E. at best. Protestantism had its beginnings in the Reformation of the 16th century. However, there were quarrels within Catholicism for a thousand years.

Returning to the First Century Once More

The early Christian congregations were not isolated from one another. The Roman roads and maritime travel connected all the regions from Rome to Greece, Asia, Syria and Palestine, and Egypt.[344] Following the days of Pentecost 33 C.E., Jewish or Jewish proselyte Christians returned to Egypt with the good news of Christ (Acts 2:10). Three years after that, the Ethiopian eunuch traveled home with the good news as well (Acts 8:26–39). Apollos of Alexandria, Egypt, a renowned speaker, left Egypt with the knowledge of John the Baptizer and arrived in Ephesus in about 52 C. E. (Acts 18:24-25) The apostle Paul traveled approximately 10,282 miles throughout the Roman Empire establishing congregations.[345] The apostles were a restraint to the apostasy and division within the whole of the first-century Christian congregation (2 Thess. 2:6-7; 1 John 2:18). It was not until the second century

---

[344] People of the first three centuries sent and received letters and books from all over the Roman Empire. Hurtado has given us two examples: the Shepherd of Hermas was written in Rome and found its way to Egypt within a few decades; Irenaeus' Against Heresies was written in Gaul and made it to Egypt (Oxyrhynchus) within short order.

[345] http://orbis.stanford.edu/

that the next generation of Christian leaders gradually caused divisions.[346] However, the one true Christianity that Jesus started, and the apostles established was spiritually healthy, active, and able to defend against Gnosticism, Roman persecution, and Jewish opposition.

Map 21

The Spread of the Gospel
to Asia and Europe

It is conceivable that by 55 C.E., there would have been a thriving congregation in Alexandrian Egypt, with its huge Jewish population.[347] "Now those who had been scattered because of the persecution that arose over Stephen went through as far as Phoenicia and Cyprus and Antioch, speaking the word to no one except Jews" (Acts 11:19). While this indicates traveling north to Antioch, it does not negate traveling south to Egypt. Antioch is obviously mentioned because it played a significant role as a commencement for first-century Christianity, particularly for the apostle Paul.

The Coptic Church claims the Gospel writer Mark as its founder and first patriarch. Tradition has it that he preached in Egypt just before the middle of the first century. At any rate, Christianity spread to Egypt and North Africa at an early date. It became a prominent religious center, with a

---

[346] This apostasy and divisiveness did not just come into the Christian congregation from nowhere. It started developing in the first century but was restrained by apostolic authority.

[347] Macquarie University, *Ancient History Documentary Research Center* (AHDRC), Papyri from the Rise of Christianity in Egypt (PCE),

http://www.anchist.mq.edu.au/doccentre/PCEhomepage.html.

noted scholar named Pantaenus, who founded a catechetical school in Alexandria, Egypt, about 160 C.E. In about 180 C.E., another leading scholar, Clement of Alexandria, took over his position. Clement put this religious, educational institution on the map as a possible center for the whole of the Christian church throughout the Roman Empire. The persecution that came circa the year 202 C.E. forced Clement to flee Alexandria, but one of the most noted scholars of early Christian history, Origen, replaced him. In addition, Origen took this scholarly environment to Caesarea in 231 C.E. and started yet another prominent school and scriptorium (i.e., a room for copying manuscripts).

What does all this mean? While we cannot know absolutely, textual scholar Philip W. Comfort[348] and others believe that the very early Alexandrian manuscripts that we now possess are a reflection of what would have been found throughout the whole of the Greco-Roman Empire about 125–300 C.E. If we were to discover other early manuscripts from Antioch, Constantinople, Carthage, or Rome, they would be very similar to the early Alexandrian manuscripts. This means that these early manuscripts are a primary means of establishing the original text, and we are in a far better position today than were Westcott and Hort in 1881. Even still, there is a 99.5% agreement between the Westcott and Hort critical text and the 2012 Nestle-Aland 28th edition critical text. This emphasizes what a tremendous job Westcott and Hort had done when we consider all the early second and third century New Testament papyri discovered in the 20th century, and yet so few changes.

We can also assume an effort on the part of copyists to preserve the originals unchanged because the authors themselves spoke of their writings as authoritative and said that no one should alter what they had published or taught. The apostle Paul wrote to the Galatians that they should consider as "accursed" anyone (even angels) who proclaimed a gospel contrary to the one they had preached. (Gal. 1:6-9) Paul went on to write, "the gospel that was preached by me is not according to man [I.e., human origin]. For I neither received it from man, nor was I taught it, but I received it through a revelation [Lit., uncovering; disclosure] of Jesus Christ." (Gal. 1:11-12) The apostle Paul charged that 'the Corinthian Christians had put up with false teachers, readily enough, who proclaim another Jesus and another gospel.' (2 Cor. 11:3-4) Paul, Silvanus (one of Paul's secretaries, scribe), and Timothy wrote to the Thessalonians that they constantly thanked God that when the Thessalonians received the word of God, which they had heard from them, they accepted it not as the word of men, but for what it really was, the **word of God**. (1

---

[348] Philip W. Comfort, *The Quest for the Original Text of the New Testament* (Eugene, Oregon: Wipf and Stock Publishers, 1992).

Thess. 2:3) Paul then closed that letter by commanding them "by the Lord, have this letter read aloud to all the brothers." (1 Thess. 5:27) In 2 Thessalonians, Paul 'requested that they not be quickly shaken from their composure or be disturbed either by a spirit or a word or a letter as if from us.' (2:2) Paul closed the letter with a greeting in his own hand to authenticate it. (3:17) Lastly, John closed the book of Revelation to warn everyone about adding to or taking away from what he had written therein. (Rev. 22:18-19) The New Testament authors were well aware that future scribes could intentionally alter the Word of God, so they warned them of the consequences.

Let's look at yet another author of the New Testament. The apostle Peter wrote about **64 C.E.,**

2 Peter 1:12-18 Updated American Standard Version (UASV)

[12] Therefore, I will always be ready to remind you of these things, though you know them and are established in the truth that is present with you. [13] I consider it right, as long as I am in this tabernacle,[349] to stir you up by way of reminder, [14] knowing that the putting off of my tabernacle[350] is soon,[351] just as also our Lord Jesus Christ made clear to me. [15] So I will make every effort so that after my departure, you may be able to recall these things for yourselves.[352]

Prophetic Word Made More Sure

[16] For we did not follow cleverly devised myths when we made known to you the power and coming[353] of our Lord Jesus Christ, but we were eyewitnesses of his majesty. [17] For when he received honor and glory from God the Father, and the voice was brought[354] to him by the Majestic Glory, "This is my beloved Son, with whom I am well pleased," [18] and we ourselves

---

[349] Or *earthly dwelling* or *tent*; that is, *his earthly body*

[350] Or *earthly dwelling* or *tent*; that is, *his earthly body*

[351] Or *is coming swiftly*

[352] Lit *to call these things to remembrance*

[353] **Presence; Coming**: (Gr. *parousia*) The Greek word which is rendered as "presence" is derived from *para*, meaning "with," and *ousia*, meaning "being." It denotes both an "arrival" and a consequent "presence with." Depending on the context, it can mean "presence," "arrival," "appearance," or "coming." In some contexts, this word is describing the presence of Jesus Christ in the last days, i.e., from his ascension in 33 C.E. up unto his second coming, with the emphasis being on his second coming, the end of the age of Satan's reign of terror over the earth. We do not know the day nor the hours of this second coming. (Matt 24:36) It covers a marked period of time with the focus on the end of that period. – Matt. 24:3, 27, 37, 39; 1 Cor. 15:23; 16:17; 2 Cor. 7:6-7; 10:10; Php 1:26; 2:12; 1 Thess. 2:19; 3:13; 4:15; 5:2.

[354] Or *borne* or *made*

heard this very voice brought from heaven, when we were with him on the holy mountain.

Peter was making it clear that he was sharing firsthand accounts and not devised tales. Like the other New Testament authors, Peter warned his readers of false teachers, who corrupted the truth and distorted the Scriptures, such as Paul's letters. Like Paul and John, Peter warned that this would be done to the offenders' own destruction.

2 Peter 3:15-16 Updated American Standard Version (UASV)

[15] and regard the patience of our Lord as salvation; just as also our beloved brother Paul, according to the wisdom given him, wrote to you, [16] as also in all his letters, speaking in them of these things, in which are some things hard to understand, which the untaught and unstable distort, as they do also the rest of the Scriptures, to their own destruction.

Yes, "It is especially interesting that Peter writes of the distortion of Paul's letters along with 'the other Scriptures.' The implication is that the letters of Paul were already regarded as Scripture at the time Peter wrote."[355] Verse 16 shows that Peter

> ...is aware of several Pauline letters. This knowledge again raises the dating issue. We know that Paul himself on one occasion had requested that churches share his letters: 'After this letter has been read to you, see that it is also read in the church of the Laodiceans and that you, in turn, read the letter from Laodicea' (Col 4:16). However, it is a big jump in time from Colossians to the first concrete evidence we have of people who know more than one letter. This evidence shows up in *1 Clement*, who not only knows Romans but can also write to the Corinthians, 'Take up the epistle of the blessed Apostle Paul' (*1 Clem.*[356] 47:1). It appears later in *2 Clement* and in Ignatius's *Ephesians*.[357] Thus, we are on solid ground when we accept that a collection of the Pauline letters existed by the end of the first century.[358] It is also likely that some Pauline letters circulated independently of a collection (which is what

---

[355] Allen Black and Mark C. Black, *1 & 2 Peter*, The College Press NIV Commentary (Joplin, MO: College Press Pub., 1998), 2 Pe 3:16.

[356] *1 Clem. First Epistle of Clement to the Corinthians*

[357] Ignatius, *Eph.* 12:2, refers to Paul, "who in all his Epistles makes mention of you in Christ Jesus." (Although one wonders how Ignatius thought the Ephesians were mentioned in every Pauline letter he knew.) On the evidence for 2 Clement's knowledge of a collection, see Karl P. Donfried, *The Setting of Second Clement in Early Christianity* (NovTSup 38; Leiden: E. J. Brill, 1974), 93–95.

[358] Jack Finegan, "The Original Form of the Pauline Collection," *HTR* 49 (1956) 85–104. See also Walter Schmithals, "Zur Abfassung und ältesten Sammlung der pauli nischen Hauptbriefe" ["On the Composition and Earliest Collection of the Major Epistles of Paul"], *ZNW* 51 (1960) 225–45.

one would expect as one church hears that another has a letter that might prove helpful in their situation),[359] and that there were collections of a few Pauline letters before there was a collection of all of his letters.[360] All of this is quite logical since Paul was a valued teacher in his circle of communities and, as he left an area and especially as he died, his letters were his continuing voice. Thus churches would share letters and, as they obtained funds (a few hundred dollars to a couple thousand dollars in today's money), they would make copies. Copies would turn into collections, especially since it was possible to use one scroll for several of the shorter letters. Probably by the end of the first century, the complete collection (i.e., all extant letters) was circulating to at least a limited degree (remember, these copies did not come cheap). The issue is which stage in this process 2 Peter is indicating.[361]

This author would argue that the stage to which Peter was referring was the time when "there were collections of a few Pauline letters before there was a collection of all of his letters." It is most likely that Peter's first letter was written about 62-64 C.E., while **Peter's second letter was written about 64 C.E.**[362] At the time Peter penned his second letter, several of Paul's letters from the 50s and early 60s was available to Peter (Romans [56], 1 & 2 Corinthians [55], Galatians [50-52], and 1 & 2 Thessalonians [50-51]). He could have had access to those from the early 60s as well (Ephesians [60-61], Philippians [60-61], Colossians [60-61], Titus [61-64], Philemon [60-61], and Hebrews [61]). The only clearly unavailable ones would have been 1 & 2 Timothy [61, 64] and possibly Titus [61-64]. Thus, from Peter's reference to "in all his [Paul's] letters, speaking in them of these things," we garner several insights. It highly suggests (1) there were collections of Paul's letters, (2) Peter and the early church viewed them as "Scripture" in the same sense as the Old Testament Scriptures, (3) they were not to be changed, and (4) that apostolic authors' written works were being collected and preserved for posterity.

Second-Century Manuscripts: Once we enter the second century, almost all firsthand witnesses of Jesus Christ would have died, and most of the younger traveling companions, fellow workers, and students of the apostles would be advancing into old age. However, some, like Polycarp, was born to Christian parents about 69 C.E. in Asia Minor in Smyrna. As he grew into a man, he

---

[359] Harry Gamble, "The Redaction of the Pauline Letters and the Formation of the Pauline Corpus," *JBL* 94 (1971) 403–18.

[360] Mary Lucetta Mowry, "The Early Circulation of Paul's Letters," *JBL* 63 (1944) 73–86.

[361] Peter H. Davids, *The Letters of 2 Peter and Jude*, The Pillar New Testament Commentary (Grand Rapids, MI: William B. Eerdmans Pub. Co., 2006), 302–303.

[362] Clinton E. Arnold, *Zondervan Illustrated Bible Backgrounds Commentary: Hebrews to Revelation.*, vol. 4 (Grand Rapids, MI: Zondervan, 2002), 153.

became known for his kindness, self-discipline, compassionate treatment of others, and thorough study of God's Word. Soon enough, he became an elder in the Christian congregation at Smyrna. Polycarp was very fortunate to live in a time when he was able to learn from the apostles themselves. In fact, the apostle John was one of his teachers.

By any standard, Polycarp must be reckoned as one of the more notable figures in the early postapostolic church. Already bishop of Smyrna in Asia Minor when his friend and mentor, Ignatius of Antioch [c. 35 C.E. – c. 108 C.E.], addressed one of his letters to him (ca. A.D. 110; cf. above, p. 131), he died a martyr's death (see the *Martyrdom of Polycarp*) several decades later at age eighty-six (ca. 155–160), having served as bishop for at least forty and possibly sixty or more years. Irenaeus (who met Polycarp as a child) and Eusebius both considered him a significant link in the chain of orthodox apostolic tradition. His life and ministry spanned the time between the end of the apostolic era and the emergence of catholic [i.e., universal] Christianity, and he was deeply involved in the central issues and challenges of this critical era: the growing threat of persecution by the state, the emerging Gnostic movement (he is particularly known for his opposition to one of the movement's most charismatic and theologically innovative teachers, Marcion), the development of the monepiscopal form of ecclesiastical organization, and the formation of the canon of the New Testament. Polycarp's only surviving document[363] is a letter to the Philippians, written in response to a letter from them (cf. 3.1; 13.1). It reveals, in addition to a direct and unpretentious style and a sensitive pastoral manner, a deep indebtedness to the Scriptures (in the form of the Septuagint) and early Christian writings, including *1 Clement* (with which Polycarp seems to be particularly familiar).[364] While apparently no New Testament books are cited as 'Scripture' (the reference to Ephesians in 12.1 is a possible exception), the manner in which Polycarp refers to them indicates that he viewed them as authoritative documents.[365]

---

[363] The attempt by H. von Campenhausen ("Polykarp und die Pastoralen," repr. *Aus der Frühzeit des Christentums* [Tübingen: Mohr/Siebeck, 1963], 197–252) to show that Polycarp also authored the pastoral Epistles has met with little acceptance.

[364] Schoedel (*Polycarp*, 4–5) suggests that it is "fairly certain" that the letter "reflects more or less direct contact" with the following writings: Psalms, Proverbs, Isaiah, Jeremiah, Ezekiel, Tobit, Matthew, Luke, Acts, Romans, 1–2 Corinthians, Galatians, Ephesians, Philippians, 1–2 Timothy, 1 John, 1 Peter, and *1 Clement*. Metzger (*Canon*, 61–62) adds to the New Testament list 2 Thessalonians and Hebrews while deleting Acts and 2 Corinthians.

[365] Michael William Holmes, *The Apostolic Fathers: Greek Texts and English Translations*, Third ed. (Grand Rapids, MI: Baker Books, 2007), 272–273.

Christ "gave gifts to men." "He gave some as apostles, and some as prophets, and some as evangelists, and some as shepherds and teachers." (Eph. 4:8, 11-13) The Father moved these inspired ones along by the Holy Spirit, as they set forth God's Word for the Christian congregation, "to stir [them] up by way of reminder," repeating many things already written in the Scriptures (2 Pet. 1:12-13; 3:1; Rom 15:15). Thus, we have internal New Testament evidence from Second Peter circa 64 C.E. that "there were collections of a few Pauline letters before there was a collection of all of his letters." Outside of Scripture, we find evidence of a collection of at least ten Pauline letters that were collected together by 90-100 C.E.[366] We can be certain that the early Christians were collecting the inspired Christian Scriptures as early as the middle of the first century C.E. to the early second century C.E.

Clement of Rome (c. 96 C.E.) was acquainted with Paul's letter to the church at Corinth and said that Paul wrote under the inspiration of the Spirit. Thus, we have Clement of Rome (c. 30-100 C.E.), Polycarp of Smyrna (69-155 C.E.), and Ignatius of Antioch (c. 35 C.E. – c. 108 C.E.), who wove Scripture of the Greek New Testament into their writings, showing their view of them as inspired Scripture. Justin Martyr, who died about 165 C.E., used the expression "it is written" when quoting from Matthew. Theophilus of Antioch, who died about 181 C.E., declared, "concerning the righteousness which the law enjoined, confirmatory utterances are found both with the prophets and in the Gospels because they all spoke inspired by one Spirit of God."[367] Theophilus then used such expressions as "**says the Gospel**" (quoting Matt, 5:28, 32, 44, 46; 6:3) and "**the divine word** gives us instructions, in order that "we may lead a quiet and peaceable life."[368] And it teaches us to render all things to all,[369] "honour to whom honour, fear to whom fear, tribute to whom tribute; to owe no man anything, but to love all."[370]

---

[366] Jack Finegan, "The Original Form of the Pauline Collection," *HTR* 49 (1956) 85–104. See also Walter Schmithals, "Zur Abfassung und ältesten Sammlung der pauli nischen Hauptbriefe" ["On the Composition and Earliest Collection of the Major Epistles of Paul"], *ZNW* 51 (1960) 225–45.

[367] Theophilus of Antioch, "Theophilus to Autolycus," in *Fathers of the Second Century: Hermas, Tatian, Athenagoras, Theophilus, and Clement of Alexandria (Entire)*, ed. Alexander Roberts, James Donaldson, and A. Cleveland Coxe, trans. Marcus Dods, vol. 2, The Ante-Nicene Fathers (Buffalo, NY: Christian Literature Company, 1885), 114.

[368] 1 Tim. 2:2

[369] Rom. 13:7, 8

[370] Theophilus of Antioch, "Theophilus to Autolycus," in *Fathers of the Second Century: Hermas, Tatian, Athenagoras, Theophilus, and Clement of Alexandria (Entire)*, ed. Alexander Roberts, James Donaldson, and A. Cleveland Coxe, trans. Marcus Dods, vol. 2, The Ante-Nicene Fathers (Buffalo, NY: Christian Literature Company, 1885), 115.

Once we reach the middle to the end of the second century C.E., it comes down to whether those who came before **would stress the written documents as Scripture by**

- the apostles, who had been personally selected by Jesus (Matthew, John, and Peter),

- Paul, who was later chosen as an apostle by the risen Jesus himself,

- the half-brothers of Jesus Christ (James and Jude),

- as well as Mark and Luke, who were close associates and traveling companions of Paul and Peter.

We can see from the above that this essentially was the case. We know that significant church leaders across the Roman Empire had done just that. We know, for example, that Irenaeus of Asia Minor (180 C.E.) fully accepted 25 of 27 books of the New Testament but had some doubt about Hebrews and uncertainty about James. We know that Clement of Alexandria (190 C.E.) fully accepted 26 of 27 books of the New Testament but may not have been aware of 3 John. We know that Tertullian of North Africa (207 C.E.) fully accepted 24 of 27 books but may not have been aware of 2 and 3 John or Jude. We know that Origen of Alexandria (230 C.E.) and Eusebius of Palestine (320 C.E.) fully accepted all 27 books of the New Testament. It has been estimated that by the close of the second century C.E., there were over 60,000 copies of significant parts of the Greek New Testament in existence. This would be an enormous number, even if only one in every fifty professing Christians possessed a copy.

However, would there be evidence that these church leaders, going back to the apostles' days, would influence the copyists? Moreover, were the copyists' professionals? In other words, even if some of the copyists did not see the documents as Scripture, would the church leaders and long-standing traditions motivate them to copy the documents with accuracy? In addition, would the professional scribe copy accurately even if he did not view them as Scripture? And if the scribe did view the texts as Scripture, the inspired Word of God, was it plenary inspiration (every word), or that the meaning was inspired? Generally speaking, from what we know about the Alexandrian scribes, they would have sought to reproduce an accurate copy regardless of their views. We can say that other scribes saw the message as inspired; thus, their focus was not on retaining every word or word order. It seems that they felt they could alter the words without damaging the intended meaning of the author. These copyists added and removed words here and there, rearranged words, and substituted words, presumably hoping to improve the text but not intending to alter the meaning. It also must be acknowledged that some untrained copyists produced inaccurate copies, regardless of how they viewed the text.

Then, some scribes willfully altered the text, intending to improve it. Some were seeking to harmonize the gospel accounts. An extreme example would be Tatian, a noteworthy, apologetic writer of the second century C.E. In an account of his conversion to nominal Christianity, Tatian states, "I sought how I might be able to discover the truth," which points to his intent. About 170 C.E., Tatian compiled a harmonized account of the life and ministry of Jesus Christ, combining the four Gospels into a single narrative (Diatessaron means "of the four"). Another who willfully revised the New Testament was Lucian of Antioch (c. 240-312 C.E.). Lucian produced the Syrian text, renamed the Byzantine text. About 290 C.E., some of his associates made various subsequent alterations, deliberately combining elements from earlier text types. This text was adopted about 380 C.E. At Constantinople, it became the predominant form of the New Testament throughout the Greek-speaking world. The text was also edited, with parallel accounts harmonized, grammar corrected, and abrupt transitions modified to produce a smooth text. As a result, this was not a faithfully accurate copy. However, others willfully altered the text to have it support their doctrinal position. Marcion (c. 85-c. 160 C.E.), a semi-Gnostic of the second century C.E., is a leading example. In fact, the idea of forming a catalog of authoritative Christian writings did not come to mind until Marcion. One such catalog was the Muratorian Fragment, Italy (170 C.E.) The list shows 24 books of the New Testament were accepted without question as Scriptural and canonical, some uncertainty about 2 Peter, and Hebrews and James were not listed, possibly unknown. In the end, we must admit that there were heretics who altered the text to align with their doctrinal positions and Orthodox Christians who also altered the text to strengthen their doctrinal beliefs.

We must keep in mind that we are dealing with an oral society. Therefore, the apostles, who had spent three and a half years with Jesus, first published the Good News orally. The teachers within the newly founded Christian congregations would repeat this information until it was memorized. After that, those who had heard this gospel would, in turn, share it with others (Acts 2:42, Gal 6:6). In time, they would see the need for a written record, so Matthew, Luke, Mark, and John would pen the Gospels, and other types of New Testament books would be written by Paul, James, Peter, and Jude. From the first four verses of Luke, we can see that **Theophilus**[371] was being given a written record of what he had already

---

[371] **Theophilus** means "friend of God," was the person to whom the books of Luke and Acts were written (Lu 1:3; Ac 1:1). Theophilus was called "most excellent," which may suggest some position of high rank. On the other hand, it simply may be Luke offering an expression of respect. Theophilus had

245

been taught orally. In verse 4, Luke says to Theophilus, "[My purpose is] that you may know the exact truth about the things you have been taught."

The appearance of the written record did not mean the end of the oral publication. Both oral and written would be used together. Most did not read the written records themselves, as they would hear them read in the congregational meetings by the lector. Paul and his letters came to be used in the same way, as he traveled extensively but was just one man and could only be in one place at a time. It was not long before he took advantage of the fact that he could be in one place and dispatch letters to other locations through his traveling companions. These traveling companions would not only deliver the letters but would know the issues well enough to address questions that might be asked by the leaders of the congregation to which they had been dispatched. In summary, the first century saw the life and ministry of Jesus Christ, the Son of God, and his death, resurrection, and ascension. After that, his disciples spread this gospel orally for at least 15 years before Matthew penned his gospel. The written was used in conjunction with the oral message.

In the first-century C.E., the Bible books were being copied individually. In the late first century or the beginning of the second century, they began to be copied in groups. At first, it was the four gospels and then the book of Acts with the four gospels and a collection of the Apostle Paul's writings. Each of the individual books of the New Testament was penned, edited, and published between 44 and 98 C.E. A group of the apostle Paul's letters and the gospels were copied and published between 90 and 125 C.E. The entire 27 books of the New Testament were not published as a whole until about 290 to 340 C.E.

Thus, we have the 27 books of the New Testament that were penned individually in the second half of the first century. Each of these would have been copied and recopied throughout the first century. Copies of these copies would, of course, be made as well. Some of the earliest manuscripts that we now have indicate that a professional scribe copied them. Many of the other papyri provide evidence that a semi-professional hand-copied them, while most of these early papyri give proof of being made by a copyist who was literate and experienced at making documents. Therefore, either literate or semi-professional copyists produced the vast majority of our early papyri, with some being made by professionals. The first century Christians carried out their evangelism with a sense of urgency because the great apostasy was on the horizon, not so much that the end was nigh. So, yes, the spread of

---

initially been orally taught about Jesus Christ and his ministry. Thereafter, it seems that the book of Acts, also by Luke, confirms that he did become a Christian. The Gospel of Luke was partially written to offer Theophilus assurances of the certainty of what he had already learned by word of mouth.

Christianity definitely impacted our efforts to ascertain the original wording of the original text. The early Christians were seeking to evangelize the world because of the foretold apostasy that was coming. They viewed the twenty-seven New Testament books as inspired in the same way the Jews considered the thirty-nine Old Testament books as inspired. Again, literate or semi-professional copyists produced the vast majority of our early papyri, with some being made by professionals.

How did the Persecution of Early Christians Impact the Scriptures?

Jesus had told his followers, "'a slave is not greater than his master.' If they persecuted me, they will also persecute you. If they kept my word, they will keep yours also.'" (John 15:20) Indeed, the growth of Christianity from 120 disciples on Pentecost 33 C.E. to over one million by the middle of the second century was a frightening thought to the pagan mind as well as Judaism. Thus, shortly after the death and resurrection of Jesus Christ, the pagan population, Judaism, and the Roman government began the very persecution of which Jesus had warned. However, in the fourth century, under the Roman Emperor Diocletian, a program of persecution began with the intent of wiping out Christianity. In 303 C.E., Diocletian spread a series of progressively harsh edicts against Christians. This brought about what some historians have called "The Great Persecution."

Diocletian's first edict ordered the burning of copies of the Scriptures and the destruction of Christian houses of worship. Harry Y. Gamble writes, "Diocletian's edict of 303 ordering the confiscation and burning of Christian books is itself important evidence, in both its assumptions and results. At the start of the fourth century, Diocletian took it for granted that every Christian community, wherever it might be, had a collection of books and knew that those books were essential to its viability." (Gamble 1995, 150) Church historian Eusebius of Caesarea, in his *Ecclesiastical History*, reported, "all things in truth were fulfilled in our day when we saw with our very eyes the houses of prayer cast down to their foundations from top to bottom, and the inspired and sacred Scriptures committed to the flames in the midst of the market-places." (Cruse 1998, VIII, 1. 9-11.1) The Christians who were most affected by the persecution lived in Palestine, Egypt, and North Africa. In fact, just three months after Diocletian's edict, the mayor of the North African city of Cirta, which was destroyed at the beginning of the 4th century and was rebuilt by the Roman Emperor Constantine the Great, is said to have ordered the Christians to give up all of their "writings of the law" and "copies of scripture." It is quite clear that Diocletian and local leaders' intent was to wipe out the Word of God.

The authorities had many Christians who obeyed the decrees by handing over their copies of the Scriptures. Nevertheless, some refused to give up their copies of God's Word. Bishop Felix of Thibiuca (d. 303 C.E.) in Africa was martyred during the Great Persecution alongside Audactus, Fortunatus, Januarius, and Septimus.[372] Felix resisted the command of the local magistrate Magnillian (Lat. *Magnillianus*) to surrender his congregation's copies of the Christian Scriptures. One account had Felix and the others being taken to Carthage and decapitated on July 15, 303 C.E. Other Christian leaders deceived the leaders by handing in their pagan writings, safeguarding their Scriptures.

The Diocletian persecution was, in the end, unsuccessful. Many Christian libraries escaped the persecution of Diocletian. Today, the Beatty and Bodmer papyri, two of the best collections that we have extant survived the fires. Alfred Chester Beatty (1875-1968), at the age of 32, had amassed a fortune. As a collector of books, he had over 50 papyrus codices, both religious and secular, which are dated earlier than the fourth century C.E. There are seven consisting of portions of Old Testament books, and three consisting of portions of the New Testament (P^{45} c. 250, P^{46} c. 175–225, and P^{47} c. 250-300). Martin Bodmer (1899-1971) was also a wealthy collector who discovered twenty-two papyri in Egypt in 1952, which contained parts of the Old and New Testaments, as well as other early Christian literature. Particularly noteworthy are the New Testament Bodmer papyri, which consists of P^{66} dating to c. 200 C.E. and P^{75} dating to c. 175 C.E. Many in rural Egypt would have heard of the persecution in Alexandria, likely making great efforts to remove their manuscripts from their congregations, hiding them until the oppression was lifted.

The men who were known as the *readers* in the early Christian congregations, who read from the Scriptures during the meeting, carried the burden of preserving the Word of God beyond maintaining accurate copies.[373] They also would have guarded them during times of persecution. Because of the mass persecution against Alexandria, Egypt,[374] we owe the primary preservation of our New Testament manuscripts to those congregations within rural Egypt. During times of persecution, manuscripts would not have been housed in the facilities of the congregation but instead would have been hidden in homes. Because of Egypt's dry sands, the professional scribal practices, and the courage of the Christians, we owe the

---

[372] These men may have been deacons but, apart from their joint martyrdom with Felix, more about their identities is unknown at the time of this writing.

[373] Some may have been scribes as well but not all. Retaining accurate, fresh copies for the congregation entailed reaching out to scribes or scriptoriums, to acquire copies for their congregation.

[374] This is not to say that no manuscripts survived the persecution in Alexandria; it is possible that some came through the flames.

Egyptian Christians for the preservation of the New Testament and the original *words* that made up the New Testament. Let's look at the manuscripts copied right after the Diocletian persecution (Codex Vaticanus and Sinaiticus c. 350 C.E.). They are reflective of the manuscripts from rural Egypt that survived, such as **P**[5] [225 C.E.] from Oxyrhynchus, Egypt, **P**[4, 64, 67] [150-175 C.E.] from Coptos, **P**[13] [225-250 C.E.] from Oxyrhynchus, and **P**[46] [150 C.E.] from Fayum, **P**[66] [150 C.E.] from Jabal Abu Mana **P**[75] [175-225 C.E.] from Abu Mana, **P**[133] [225-250 C.E.] from Oxyrhynchus, **P**[137] [175-225 C.E.] from Egypt, **P**[138] [225-250 C.E.] from Oxyrhynchus, and many more.

We know that by the time we get to the era of the Diocletian persecution (February 23, 303 – July 25, 306.), the authorities were well aware that there were still many copies of the New Testament throughout the Roman Empire. Otherwise, there would have been no need on February 24, 303 for Diocletian's first "Edict against the Christians" to be published. Diocletian thought he could eradicate Christianity by destroying its sacred writings. After the persecution of Diocletian and Constantine succeeding his father on July 25, 306, Constantine immediately ended any ongoing persecutions and offered Christians complete restitution of what they had lost under the persecution. When Constantine issued the Edict of Milan of **313 C.E.**, Christianity was legalized in the Roman Empire. At that point, the church would have seen the need to dramatically increase the number of copies of the Scriptures. Now that Christianity was no longer being persecuted, Christian scribes could openly make copies of the New Testament manuscripts.

In **331 C.E.**, Constantine ordered Eusebius to prepare fifty copies of the entire Bible on prepared parchment for distribution to the churches he intended to build in Constantinople. (Eus., Vit. Const. 4.36.2) From this small order placed by Constantine, we can only imagine how many copies had been made in the churches throughout the entire Roman Empire. It has been estimated that there were some fifteen hundred to two thousand manuscripts of the Greek New Testament copied in the fourth century C.E. (J. Duplacy) While we certainly took a loss in the number of copies that may have come down to us today as a result of ongoing sporadic persecution of Christianity in those first two and a half centuries after the death of the apostle Paul at the hands of the Roman Emperor Nero in about 65 C.E. up unto Diocletian (303-306 C.E.), there is little doubt that the storehouse of Greek original language manuscripts (5,898) that we do possess are an envy of the secular historians, who have next to nothing in comparison.

CHAPTER IX

What Were the Scribal Tendencies or Habits of the Early Copyists?

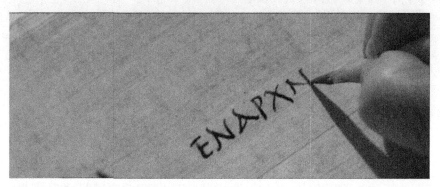

As noted elsewhere, the textual scholar looks at two forms of evidence: *external* (manuscripts) and *internal* (what the author or scribe wrote). Internal evidence concerns what might have led to scribal errors. Therefore, we will discuss scribal practices and tendencies to get an image of how the Word of God came down to us through the work of copyists. In another chapter, The Practice of Textual Criticism to Determine the Original Reading, we will deal with scribal tendencies as well.

The originals were completely accurate and without error of any kind. We know that the men who penned the twenty-seven New Testament books "were carried along by the Holy Spirit." (2 Pet. 1:21) However, as has been made clear from the outset, we do not have the originals, so we are dependent on the work of the copyists from the first to the sixteenth centuries. Therefore, it is prudent on our part to analyze the practices of the scribes, the habits or tendencies of the scribes. Some of the scribal tendencies have led to certain kinds of variants within our copies of the text of the New Testament. If we are aware of the causes of errors as the text is being copied, we will be better equipped to ascertain which reading is the original. The New Testament textual scholar aims to ascertain what the original words were in the original text. If we can fully grasp how scribes went about their work in copying the text (scribal habits), again, we are in a better position at being able to restore the original words of the Greek text.

We have long had the text-critical principle *lectio brevior potior or*, "the shorter reading is preferred."[375] This has long been the mantra of textual scholars because they have long held that scribes tended to add to the text they were copying, not omit. James R. Royse, in his extensive study of the scribal habits in the early New Testament papyri, coined a new text-critical principle, which he has called *lectio longior potior or*, "the longer reading is preferred." Royse wrote: "there has been (it seems) a failure to explore the problem of scribal habits for the text of the New Testament in the best possible case, namely, where the Vorlage of an extant manuscript is also known to be extant. In such a situation, we can virtually look over the scribe's shoulder and compare the text he is copying with his result."[376]

We will indeed find studies where some scribes tended to add while others omitted. Therefore, the wise course of action is that we not entirely abandon "the shorter reading is preferred" or "the longer reading is preferred," but rather, we should remain alert to either possibility and make neither a diehard rule.[377] Therefore, the length of a reading should not be the determining factor in determining the original reading.[378] There are going to be different scribes who possess different scribal habits, even though some basic habits should be considered in a general sense. Many factors go into each and every scribe and his copying work. We must consider his work experience. Was he a professional scribe, a literate scribe who had experience in preparing documents and literature, or a literate scribe who has had experience in preparing documents only? Or was he a semiliterate writer who was untrained in making documents, and how familiar was he with the language?

Scribes who are unfamiliar with the language that they are copying may copy exceptionally well, being incredibly accurate for the most part. This is because they have a minimal idea of what the text says or no idea at all, so there is no temptation to take liberties with the text. Therefore, the scribe being unfamiliar with the language has no actual ability to add or omit any words intentionally. However, when they come to a difficulty, they may produce an obvious error, a nonsense error. There needs to be more research into the scribal habits of those who were copying a language with which they were unfamiliar.

---

[375] James R. Royse, *Scribal Habits in Early Greek New Testament Papyri* (NTTSD 36; Atlanta: Society of Biblical Literature, 2008), 732.

[376] Royse, Scribal Habits, 34.

[377] Stephen C. Carlson, *The Text of Galatians and Its History* (WUNT 2:385; Tübingen: Mohr Siebeck, 2015), 90.

[378] Peter Malik, *P. Beatty III* (P47): The Codex, Its Scribe, and Its Text (NTTSD 52; Leiden: Brill, 2017), 114–15.

On the other hand, scribes who are pretty familiar with the language they were copying, we can find these scribes making errors that evidence they know the language, such as adding and omitting words. They tend to make what they perceive to be corrections to their text. The scribe familiar with the language will make some substitutions, perceived corrections but few nonsense errors. In other words, some were prone to take liberties with the text, either adding to it or omitting from it. All of these things are to be expected because each scribe is an individual with different abilities and different motivations or views of the work that they were doing.

Types of Scribal Errors

The errors within our texts of the New Testament are of two kinds: those that were accidental and those that were intentional. We will cover a few of those that are encountered most often.

Accidental Errors

Word Divisions: We have to remember that there were no spaces between the words early on, nor were there accents or breathing marks.

Codex Vaticanus (c. 300-325 C.E.) and Codex Sinaiticus (330-360 C.E.)

1 Timothy 3:16 has ομολογουμενωςμεγα, so how are we to understand it? How is it to be divided? Do we have "ομολογουμενως μεγα" ("confessedly great"), or do we have "ομολογουμεν ως μεγα" ("we acknowledge how great")?

Similar Endings (Homoeoteleuton)

The scribe's eyes skipped from a letter or word to the same letter(s) or word down the page, leaving out a line or two in the transcription.

ελλ-
ΒΕΝΛΕΤΟΥϹΛΡΤΟΥϹ [ΟΙΣ]ΚΛΙΕ
ΥΧΛΡΙϹΤΗϹΛϹΛΙΕΛωΚΕΝΤΟΙϹ
ΜΛΘΗΤΛΙϹΟΙΛΕΜΛΘΗΤΛΙΤΟΙϹ
ΛΝΛΚΕΙΜΕΝΟΙϹΟΜΟΙωϹΚΛΙΕΚ
ΤωΝ ΟΨΛΡΙωΝ ΟϹΟΝ ΗΘΕΛΟΝ

Single Writing (Haplography)

The scribe essentially wrote once what should have been written twice. Codex Vaticanus has an omission at John 17:15. The scribe working on the Vaticanus would have likely had an exemplar that looked similar to the following image, with the following arrangement of lines.

ΟΥΚΕΡωΤωΙΝΛΛΡΗϹΛΥΤΟΥϹΕΚΤΟΥ
ΚΟϹΜΟΥΛΛΛΙΝΛΤΗΡΗϹΗϹΛΥΤΟΥϹΕΚΤΟΥ
ΠΟΝΗΡΟΥ

John 17:15: I do not pray that you should take them out of the world, but that you should keep them out of the evil one.

Double Writing (Dittography): in this case, the scribe wrote a letter or word twice instead of once. The phrase "Great is Artemis of the Ephesians" appears twice in Codex Vaticanus, whereas it only appears once in other manuscripts.

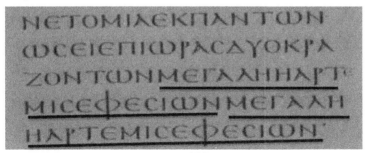

Acts 19:34: But when they recognized that he was a Jew, for about two hours they all cried out with one voice, "Great is Artemis of the Ephesians!" "Great is Artemis of the Ephesians!"

Change of Place (Metathesis)

The scribe changed the order of the letters or words.

ΕΥΑΓΓΕΛΙΟΝ ΚΑΤΑ ΜΑΡΚΟΝ 14:65 Tyndale House Greek New Testament

καὶ (and) ἤρξαντό (they began) τινες (some) ἐμπτύειν (to spit) αὐτῷ (on him) καὶ (and) περικαλύπτειν (to cover) αὐτοῦ (his) τὸ πρόσωπον (face) καὶ (and) κολαφίζειν (to strike) αὐτὸν (him) καὶ (and) λέγειν (to say) αὐτῷ (to him) προφήτευσον (prophesy) καὶ (and) οἱ ὑπηρέται (the servants) ῥαπίσμασιν (with blows) αὐτὸν (him) **ἔλαβον** (they took).

ΚΑΤΑ ΜΑΡΚΟΝ 14:65 1550 Stephanus New Testament

και (and) ηρξαντο (they began) τινες (some) εμπτυειν (to spit) αυτω (on him) και (and) περικαλυπτειν (to cover) το προσωπον (the face) αυτου (of him) και (and) κολαφιζειν (to strike) αυτον (him) και (and) λεγειν (to say) αυτω (to him) προφητευσον (prophesy) και (and) οι υπηρεται (the servants) ραπισμασιν (with blows) αυτον (him) **εβαλλον** (they struck).

An example of metathesis is found in Mark 14:65. Some manuscripts read "ελαβον" (WHNU), which is translated "received" while others have "εβαλλον" (Byz. Text), which is translated "struck." We find the two readings as follow:

Mark 14:65 Updated American Standard Version (UASV)

65 And some began to spit on him and to cover his face and to strike him with their fists, and to say to him "Prophesy!" And the court attendants **received** him with slaps in the face.

Mark 14:65 King James Version (KJV)

65 And some began to spit on him, and to cover his face, and to buffet him, and to say unto him, Prophesy: and the servants did **strike** him with the palms of their hands.

Itacism (Similar Iota Sound): the scribe confused Greek vowels and diphthongs[379] because they sounded alike early on as they had a similar pronunciation to the letter iota. The Greek transliteration of the diphthongs

---

[379] A diphthong is a complex vowel sound in which the first vowel gradually moves toward a second vowel so that both vowels form one syllable, e.g., "a" and "I" in "rail"

would be *ai* as in aisle, *ei* as in eight, *oi* as in oil, *and ui* as in suite. This often resulted in confusion of Greek pronouns. Though not cases of itacism per se, confusion also resulted from other vowels that tended to be pronounced alike. An especially interesting example is found in Romans 5:1.

ΠΡΟΣ ΡΩΜΑΙΟΥΣ 5:1 Tyndale House Greek New Testament

Δικαιωθέντες (Having been justified) οὖν (therefore) ἐκ (from) πίστεως (faith) εἰρήνην (peace) **ἔχωμεν** (let us have) πρὸς (with) τὸν θεὸν (God) διὰ (through) τοῦ κυρίου (the Lord) ἡμῶν (our) Ἰησοῦ (Jesus) χριστοῦ (Christ).

ΠΡΟΣ ΡΩΜΑΙΟΥΣ 5:1 1550 Stephanus New Testament

δικαιωθεντες (having been justified) ουν (therefore) εκ (from) πιστεως (faith) ειρηνην (peace) **εχομεν** (let us have) προς (with) τον θεον (God) δια (through) του κυριου (the Lord) ημων (our) ιησου (Jesus) χριστου (Christ).

Romans 5:1 Updated American Standard Version (UASV)

5 Therefore, having been justified by faith, **we have** peace with God through our Lord Jesus Christ,

Westcott and **H**ort (WH) and The Greek New Testament chose the variant reading εχωμεν, a subjunctive, i.e., a grammatical mood that expresses doubts, wishes, and possibilities because it has excellent textual support (ℵ* A B* C D K L 33 81 it[d], [g] vg syr[p], [pal] copbo arm eth al). On the other hand, the **N**estle-Aland and the **U**nited Bible Societies and the Greek-English New Testament Interlinear preferred the internal evidence of the indicative reading, εχομεν,[380] the basic mood of verbs in ordinary objective statements because the context has Paul stating a fact of what they now have since they have been justified by faith. In other words, Paul was **not** exhorting his listeners to have peace with God. In addition, it should be noted that there was a discovery of an earlier manuscript in the middle of the twentieth-century which had εχομεν, Uncial 0220[vid], dating to about 300 C.E., and it is of the Alexandrian family, penned in a Reformed Documentary hand. The reader will notice the superscript "vid" beside the Gregory-Aland number. Vid is short for Latin *videtur*, meaning, "It seems so." The scribal abbreviation (siglum) is an indication that a reading is uncertain for some reason, e.g. there may be a lacuna, i.e., a gap or place where something is missing in the manuscript.

Unfortunately, the Greek verb εχομεν has broken letters where there is a hole in the manuscript. Where this missing section is we find the "ε" of our

---

[380] (ℵ[a] B[3] G[gr] P Ψ 0220[vid] 88 326 330 629 1241 1739 Byz Lect it[61vid?] syr[h] cop[sa] al)

verb, but the "χομεν" is no longer there. Textual scholar William Hatch examined the manuscript, observing,

> The first three letters of the verb stood at the end of the line, and a small hole in the vellum has destroyed the χ and the letter which followed it. However, the letter after χ must have been an o, because the above-mentioned hole does not occupy enough space to contain the letters χ and ω. On the other hand, the space would be completely filled by an χ and an o. Moreover, a little ink can be seen at the top and right hand side of the hole, and this seems to be the remainder of a letter with a closed top. Hence, the letter must have been an o and not an ω. [This] fragment is the earliest known witness for εχομεν in Romans 5:1, and thus the indicative in this verse is attested by a goof text which antedates the earliest testimony for the subjunctive. (Hatch 45, 83)

Uncial 0220 (Romans 4:23-5:3; 5:8-13) c. 300 C.E.

Comfort writes,

> "The reading with an indicative ("we have peace") suits the context better than the subjunctive ("let us have peace" or "let us be at peace"). Paul was speaking of what the believers have received as a result of being justified: They have peace with God and access to him through the Lord Jesus Christ. It does not seem likely that Paul was urging the believers to "be at peace with God" (see NJBmg). If so, it is more likely that he would have used a

different verb, ποιησωμεν ("let us make"). However, the translators of the neb adopted the variant reading because they viewed εχωμεν as introducing the first of three hortative clauses, followed by καυχωμεθα ("let us boast"—if taken as a subjunctive and not an indicative) in both 5:2 and 5:3 (see Tasker 1964, 434). However, it is more likely that all three predicates are indicatives, stating that we have peace with God and, as such, are boasting in the hope of glory and in our sufferings, which intensify our hope.[381]

Metzger writes,

> Although the subjunctive ἔχωμεν (ℵ* A B* C D K L 33 81 it[d,] vg syr[p,] cop[bo] arm eth *al*) has far better external support than the indicative ἔχομεν (ℵ B³ G[gr] P Ψ 0220[vid] 88 326 330 629 1241 1739 *Byz Lect* it[61?] syr[h] cop[sa] *al*), a majority of the Committee judged that internal evidence must here take precedence. Since in this passage it appears that Paul is not exhorting but stating facts ("peace" is the possession of those who have been justified), only the indicative is consonant with the apostle's argument. Since the difference in pronunciation between o and ω in the Hellenistic age was almost non-existent, when Paul dictated ἔχομεν, Tertius, his amanuensis (16:22), may have written down ἔχωμεν. (For another set of variant readings involving the interchange of o and ω, see 1 Cor 15.49.)[382]

Intentional Errors

Unintentional errors are understandable. However, we struggle to appreciate how and why a scribe would intentionally alter the text, especially if he is a Christian who is copying the New Testament. While the intentional errors are far less than the **un**intentional in number, there are still enough to be of concern, and they are the more important kind. Nevertheless, they are solvable, so we need not fret over their impact on the New Testament. Besides, these are not intentional errors by heretics, who were placing destructive variants within the text. In every case of which we are aware, the copyist did them with good intentions.

---

[381] Philip W. Comfort, *New Testament Text and Translation Commentary: Commentary on the Variant Readings of the Ancient New Testament Manuscripts and How They Relate to the Major English Translations* (Carol Stream, IL: Tyndale House Publishers, Inc., 2008), 444.

[382] Bruce Manning Metzger, United Bible Societies, *A Textual Commentary on the Greek New Testament, Second Edition a Companion Volume to the United Bible Societies' Greek New Testament (4th Rev. Ed.)* (London; New York: United Bible Societies, 1994), 452.

In some cases, it was to fix what the copyist perceived to be grammatical errors or to harmonize one gospel with another. In other cases, it was combining two different readings because the scribe could not decide which was the original or misunderstanding a marginal note and entering it into the text, and in very few cases making a change to strengthen a doctrinal belief. We are going to offer an example for each of these.

Spelling and Grammar Changes

The scribe believed that he was correcting an ordinary error and was under the impression that he was improving the text.

Spelling

ΕΥΑΓΓΕΛΙΟΝ ΚΑΤΑ ΜΑΘΘΑΙΟΝ 1:7-8 Tyndale House Greek New Testament

7 Σολομὼν (Solomon) δὲ (and) ἐγέννησεν (begot) τὸν Ῥοβοάμ (Rehoboam)· Ῥοβοὰμ (Rehoboam) δὲ (and) ἐγέννησεν (begot) τὸν Ἀβιά (Abijah)· Ἀβιὰ (Abijah) δὲ (and) ἐγέννησεν (begot) τὸν **Ἀσάφ** (Asaph)· 8 **Ἀσὰφ** (Asaph) δὲ (and) ἐγέννησεν (begot) τὸν Ἰωσαφάτ (Jehoshaphat)· Ἰωσαφὰτ (Jehoshaphat) δὲ (and) ἐγέννησεν (begot) τὸν Ἰωράμ (Joram)· Ἰωρὰμ (Joram) δὲ (and) ἐγέννησεν (begot) τὸν Ὀζείαν (Uzziah)·

ΚΑΤΑ ΜΑΤΘΑΙΟΝ 1:7-8 1550 Stephanus New Testament

7 σολομων (Solomon) δε (and) εγεννησεν (begot) τον ροβοαμ (Rehoboam) ροβοαμ δε (and Rehoboam) εγεννησεν (begot) τον αβια (Abijah) αβια δε (and Abijah) εγεννησεν (begot) τον **ασα** (Asa) 8 **ασα** δε (and Asa) εγεννησεν (begot) τον ιωσαφατ (Jehoshaphat) ιωσαφατ δε (and Jehoshaphat) εγεννησεν (begot) τον ιωραμ (Joram) ιωραμ δε (and Joram) εγεννησεν (begot) τον οζιαν (Uzziah)

In Matthew 1:7–8, we have the name *Asaph* (᾿Ασάφ), which is found in more than a few older manuscripts (P[1vid], ℵ, B, f[1] f[13] 700 1071, etc.), in Eastern versions (cop arm eth). However, later copyists believed that they were making a correction to the text by changing it to *Asa* (᾿Ασά), the king of Judah (1 Kings 15:9–24) (L, W, Δ, etc.). Textual scholarship is almost certain that the original reading was (᾿Ασάφ). Moreover, Asaph has the best documentary support. P1, an Alexandrian MS dating to about 250 C.E., is shown with a vid siglum because a small fragment which showed the second occurrence of the name Asaph went missing shortly after its discovery. However, the original photograph of the manuscript shows this portion.

Asa was the third king of Judah. He was the son of Abijam and the grandson of Rehoboam. (1 Ki 15:8-10) Here we have a problem since the best documentary evidence supports the incorrect spelling (Asaph). Therefore, do we have an accidental corruption, or do we have intentional or unintentional confusion? Comfort writes, "Apparently Matthew wrote Ἀσάφ, following a spelling he copied from a genealogical record other than that found in most copies of the Septuagint (which read Ἀσά). Later Scribes changed it to "Asa," probably because they did not want readers to think this king was the Psalmist "'Asaph.'" (P. W. Comfort 2008, 3) In other words, Comfort is suggesting that the inspired Matthew, who was being moved by Holy Spirit, penned the incorrect spelling. Therefore, if Matthew used Asaph, it would mean he was either mistaken, or he did it for some unknown reason.

Bruce M. Metzger wrote, "Since, however, the evangelist may have derived material for the genealogy, not from the Old Testament directly, but from subsequent genealogical lists, in which the erroneous spelling occurred, the Committee saw no reason to adopt what appears to be a scribal emendation in the text of Matthew." (TCGNT, 2) If Matthew did as Comfort and Metzger suggest, it would still mean that he erroneously chose the incorrect spelling. As Metzger mentions, Lagrange[383] objects and in his commentary prints Asa in the text of Matthew. He states, "Literary criticism is not able to admit that the author, who could not have drawn up this list without consulting the Old Testament, would have taken the name of a psalmist in place of a king of Judah. It is necessary, therefore, to suppose that Ἀσάφ is a very ancient [scribal] error." (p. 5) Yes, there is no way that Matthew, under inspiration, chose the incorrect spelling of Asaph. He penned Asa. Early on, a scribal error of Asaph must have entered the text, which later copyists corrected. This verse receives scant attention but has great significance. If Asaph is the original reading, then Matthew 1:7 is in error.

In our pursuit of knowledge and understanding, we do not want to take the approach that many scholars have succumbed to, i.e., being so involved in analyzing the text that they see it as of human origin alone. Because of their presupposition, they set aside the fact that these men were moved by Holy Spirit. We, as conservative Christians, are not ashamed or embarrassed and do not feel the need to apologize to others because we see the Bible authors as inspired, producing fully inerrant manuscripts.

---

[383] Marie-Joseph Lagrange (1855 – 1938) was a Catholic priest in the Dominican Order, who penned an influential handbook of textual theory and method as related to the textual criticism of the New Testament.

Presuppositions are what we think, feel, and others have said and what we have read. Scholars see presuppositions as something we need to be cautious of because they can interject subjectivity into our analysis, whether we are trying to determine what the author meant or the original reading of the text. It is virtually impossible to come to the Bible text without some pre-understanding or presuppositions, however. As Christian students of God's Word, there are certain presuppositions that we are never to set aside, nor should we be ashamed or embarrassed about them, nor do we need to apologize to others. We do our investigations and analyses of the Bible with the presupposition that the Bible (1) is the inspired Word of God, (2) is fully inerrant in the originals, and (3) is made up of sixty-six books.

Grammar

The copyists attempt to correct a perceived grammatical or syntactical problem.

REVELATION 1:4 2020 *Greek-English New Testament Interlinear* (GENTI)

Grace   to you   and   peace   from   [God or Lord]   the (one)being   and the (one) was   and the (one)   coming.
4 χάρις ὑμῖν καὶ εἰρήνη ἀπὸ **[θεοῦ or Κυρίου]**   ὁ ὢν καὶ ὁ ἦν καὶ ὁ ἐρχόμενος,

In Revelation 1:4, the grammar rules are that the genitive case should follow the Greek preposition *απο*, but John has an article in the nominative case instead. Scribes, over the years had tried to alleviate this perceived grammatical problem. The two most famous were to use God or Lord in the genitive case.

Removal of Perceived Discrepancies

Mark 1:2-3 (UASV)	**Malachi 3:1** (UASV)	**Isaiah 40:3** (UASV)
² ² As it is written in Isaiah the prophet;[384] "Behold, I send my messenger before your face,	³ 3 "Look! **I am sending my messenger, and he will prepare a way before me.**[386] And suddenly the true Lord, whom you are seeking, will come to	³ A voice of one calling out, In the wilderness, "prepare the way of Jehovah; make straight in the desert a highway for our God.

---

[384] Some manuscripts that carry no textual weight have *in the prophets*; however, the first part of Mark's quote is actually from Malachi 3:1, the second portion from Isaiah 40:3, which makes it easy to see why some copyist would have altered "Isaiah the prophet." Comfort suggests that Mark's attributing all of it to Isaiah may have been because his Roman audience would likely be more familiar with Isaiah. Regardless, Mark does not acknowledge any Deutero-Isaiah.

[386] John the Baptizer was the 'messenger who cleared up or prepared the way.' (Matt. 11:10-11)

who will prepare your way,[385]

³ the **voice of one crying in the wilderness**:

'Make ready the way of the Lord,
make his paths straight.'"

his temple; and the messenger of the covenant will come, in whom you take delight. Look, he will certainly come," says Jehovah of armies.

Mark says, "As it is written in Isaiah the prophet." However, the quotation in verses 2 and 3 of Mark chapter 1 is made up of two different verses: Malachi 3:1 and Isaiah 40:3. Therefore, it is easy to see why the scribes chose to alter this verse to read, "As it is written in the prophets." "Isaiah the prophet" is found in the earliest Alexandrian and Western witnesses, while "the prophets" is found in the Byzantine text. The harder reading, "Isaiah the prophet," is preferred because there is reason to change to "the prophets," but no rational reason for changing from "the prophets" to "Isaiah the prophet." The other textual principle also supports this: "The reading that the other reading(s) most likely came from is likely the original."

Harmonization (Parallel Passages)

This is usually an intentional change. We most often find this taking place in what is known as the Synoptic Gospels because they are similar: Matthew, Mark, and Luke. For example, we have Matthew 19:17 parallel to Mark 10:18. As we can see below, a scribe felt the need to harmonize Matthew 19:17 with Mark 10:18.

MATTHEW 19:17 2020 *Greek-English New Testament Interlinear* (GENTI)

17 εἷς ἐστιν ὁ ἀγαθός·
There is one who is good
א B (D) L Θ (f1) ita,d copbo

Byz. Text Οὐδεὶς ἀγαθός εἰ μὴ εἷς ὁ θεός
No one is good, except one, God
C W f13 33 Maj syrh,p copsa

Mark 10:18 Updated American Standard Version (UASV)

¹⁸ And Jesus said to him, "Why do you call me good? No one is good except God alone.

---

[385] In fulfillment of Malachi 3:1, John the Baptizer appeared as the messenger who prepared the way for the Father by way of the Son who had been given all authority in heaven and on earth, to get the Jews ready for the coming of Jesus Christ.—Matt. 11:10-11; 28:18-20; Mark 1:1-4; Lu 7:27-28.

If the reading at Matthew 19:17 found in the Byzantine Text, "No one is good, except one, God," were the original, there is no good reason for a scribe to alter it to the more ambiguous one. Why do we say ambiguous? We do so because the reading "there is one who is good" has been interpreted by some as Jesus speaking of himself. However, others, such as this author, view Jesus as speaking of the Father.

So, if the Byzantine reading were original in Matthew, it is difficult to imagine why copyists would have altered it to a more obscure one. In contrast, scribal assimilation to Synoptic parallels frequently occurs.

The conflation of Variant Readings

Here the scribe combines two or more variants into one reading.

As an example, we have Luke 24:53, αἰνοῦντες [praising] καὶ εὐλογοῦντες [blessing].

Luke 24:53 (GENTI WHNU)

[53] και ησαν δια παντος εν τω ιερω **ευλογουντες** τον θεον

Luke 24:53 (Byz)

[53] και ησαν διαπαντος εν τω ιερω **αινουντες** και **ευλογουντες** τον θεον αμην

Luke 24:53 (UASV)

[53] and were continually in the temple **blessing** God.

Luke 24:53 (KJV)

[53] And were continually in the temple, **praising** and **blessing** God. Amen.

The readings αἰνοῦντες καὶ εὐλογοῦντες (A C2 K W X Δ Θ Ψ *f* 1 *f* 13 33) and εὐλογοῦντες καὶ αἰνοῦντες (eth) are certainly conflations, arising from combinations of εὐλογοῦντες (P75 ℵ B C* L syrs, pal copsa, bo geo) and αἰνοῦντες (D ita, b, d. e. ff2, l, r1 Augustine). In trying to ascertain the original reading, we must first look at the external evidence. Clearly, the witnesses for εὐλογοῦντες are far superior to that of the conflations, as well as being diversified.

Second, we must consider the internal evidence, such as the context, what the author may or may not have done, in addition to what a copyist may or may not have done. Therefore, this analysis starts with questions e.g. what would Luke likely have written? Do we assume that since Luke used εὐλογεῖν twelve times, while he only used αἰνεῖν in three other passages, he likely chose to use εὐλογεῖν here? Alternatively, do we look at the fact that in the next century εὐλογεῖν became a select term for praising God among the Christians, and so assume that the copyists chose to replace αἰνεῖν with εὐλογεῖν, pointing go αἰνεῖν as the original? Then, looking at the context, because εὐλογεῖν was present in verses 50 and 51, does it not seem likely that Luke would use the same term here in verse 53? On the other hand, were the copyists moved to use the same verb, so that they replaced αἰνεῖν with εὐλογεῖν? Then again, were the copyists seeking to differentiate the disciples from Jesus, suggesting that they replaced εὐλογοῦντες with αἰνοῦντες?

In the end, the internal evidence is not clear enough to make a decision, but combined with the external evidence, we can be almost certain that εὐλογοῦντες was the original reading, which some the copyists changed to αἰνοῦντες. Then later copyists, to avoid discarding the original verb, conflated the reading by combining the two, i.e., **praising** [**αινουντες**] and **blessing** [**ευλογουντες**] God.

Theological Changes

In these cases, a scribe was trying to strengthen a doctrinal position by altering a passage to support the doctrine. Some examples would be Acts 20:28, Romans 9:5, and 1 Timothy 3:16.

Acts 20:28a Care for the Church of God

What exactly do we mean by faithful, and faithful to what or whom? By faithful, we mean unwavering to the original, to the author himself. However, there are times when textual scholars or committees choose a reading that is unfaithful to the original text. Obviously, theological bias should not affect a scribe's activity, nor that of the textual scholar, or the translation committee that brings us our English translation.

Acts 20:28 Revised Standard Version (RSV)	**Acts 20:28** New Living Translation (NLT)
28 Take heed to yourselves and to all the flock, in which the Holy Spirit has made you overseers, to care for the church of God which he obtained with the blood of <u>his</u> own Son.	28 So guard yourselves and God's people. Feed and shepherd **God**'s flock, his church, purchased with his own blood, over which the Holy Spirit has appointed you as elders.

263

Acts 20:28: The RSV reads that the church was purchased with "the blood of his [God's] own Son." On the other hand, the NLT reads that the church was purchased with "God's . . . own blood." Before we can begin determining which of these two renderings is correct, it should be noted that we have two textual problems within this verse.

ACTS 20:28 1881 (GENTI WH-NU)

Pay careful attention to yourselves and to all the flock, in which you the spirit the holy put
28 προσέχετε ἑαυτοῖς καὶ παντὶ τῷ ποιμνίῳ, ἐν ᾧ ὑμᾶς τὸ πνεῦμα τὸ ἅγιον ἔθετο
overseers, to shepherd the congregation of the God,
ἐπισκόπους, ποιμαίνειν **τὴν ἐκκλησίαν τοῦ θεοῦ**, ...

ΠΡΑΞΕΙΣ ΤΩΝ ΑΠΟΣΤΟΛΩΝ 20:28 1550 Stephanus New Testament (TR1550)

Pay careful attention therefore to yourselves and to all the flock, in which you the spirit the holy put
28 προσέχετε **οὖν**, ἑαυτοῖς καὶ παντὶ τῷ ποιμνίῳ, ἐν ᾧ ὑμᾶς τὸ πνεῦμα τὸ ἅγιον ἔθετο
overseers, to shepherd the congregation of the God.
ἐπισκόπους, ποιμαίνειν **τὴν ἐκκλησίαν τοῦ θεοῦ**, ...

TR WH NU TGNT τὴν ἐκκλησίαν τοῦ θεοῦ
"the church of God"
א B 614. 1175. 1505 vg syr bo[ms]; Cyr

Variant 1 την εκκλησιαν του κυριου
"the church of the Lord"
P[74] A C* D E Ψ 33. 453. 945. 1739. 1891. 2818 gig p sy[hmg] co; Ir[lat] Lcf

Variant 2 την εκκλησιαν του κυριου και του θεου
"the church of the Lord and God"
C[3] L 323. 1241 Maj

As we can see from the above Acts 22:28a has three different readings, two different variants, within the Greek New Testament manuscripts: Reading "the church of God," variant (1) "the church of the Lord", and variant (2) "the church of the Lord and God". WHNU has the better manuscript support and is the choice of the Textus Receptus of 1551 as well. The expression "the church of the Lord" is found nowhere in the New Testament. "the church of God" is found eleven times, all by the Apostle Paul and Luke, the writer of Acts, who was Paul's traveling companion.

The question of what reading led to the other in this case will be discussed in two parts. There is no doubt that variant (2) is simply a conflation (combination of the text reading and variant (1)). If "the church

264

of the Lord" were the original reading, it could have been that a copyist familiar with Paul made the change to "the church of God." On the other hand, if "the church of God" were the original reading, there is a slight chance that a copyist was influenced by the Greek Old Testament (Septuagint) and changed it to "the church of the Lord."

However, the essential text-critical principle, 'the more difficult reading is to be preferred' (more challenging to understand (i.e., accept)), seems to be most helpful. This principle is also related to the dominant principle, "the reading that led to the others is the original," as the copyist would have changed to an easier reading. Basically, it is common sense that scribes make difficult readings easier to understand rather than do the reverse with easy readings. There is no doubt that "the church of God" is the more difficult reading. Why? The following clause (which will be dealt with shortly) could have been taken as "which he purchased with his own blood." This would almost certainly cause pause for any copyist, asking himself, "Does God have blood?" Thus, the original was "the church of God", which was changed to "the church of the Lord", because the idea that God had blood would have been repugnant. All things considered (internal and external evidence), the reading most likely original is "the church of God."

Acts 20:28b With the Blood of His Own Son

Acts 20:28b has two different readings within the Greek New Testament Manuscripts:

Acts 20:28 Updated American Standard Version (UASV)
[28] Pay careful attention to yourselves and to all the flock, in which the Holy Spirit has made you overseers, to care for the congregation of God, which he obtained **with the blood of his own Son**.

Acts 20:28 King James Version (KJV)
[8] Take heed therefore unto yourselves, and to all the flock, over the which the Holy Ghost hath made you overseers, to feed the church of God which he hath purchased **with his own blood**.

Acts 20:28 Revised Standard Version (RSV)

[28] Take heed to yourselves and to all the flock, in which the Holy Spirit has made you overseers, to care for the church of God which he obtained **with the blood of his own Son**.

Acts 20:28 Lexham English Bible (LEB)

[28] Be on guard for yourselves and for all the flock among which the Holy Spirit has appointed you *as* overseers, to shepherd the church of God which he obtained **through the blood of his own *Son*.**

ACTS 20:28 1881 (WH-NU GENTI)

<small>Pay careful attention to yourselves and to all the flock, in which you the spirit the holy put</small>
28 προσέχετε ἑαυτοῖς καὶ παντὶ τῷ ποιμνίῳ, ἐν ᾧ ὑμᾶς τὸ πνεῦμα τὸ ἅγιον ἔθετο
<small>overseers, to shepherd the congregation of the God,</small>
ἐπισκόπους, ποιμαίνειν τὴν ἐκκλησίαν τοῦ θεοῦ,
<small>which he purchased by the blood of the own [son].</small>
ἣν περιεποιήσατο διὰ **τοῦ αἵματος τοῦ ἰδίου.**

ACTS 20:28 1550 Stephanus New Testament (TR1550)

<small>Pay careful attention therefore to yourselves and to all the flock, in which you the spirit the holy put</small>
28 προσέχετε **οὖν,** ἑαυτοῖς καὶ παντὶ τῷ ποιμνίῳ, ἐν ᾧ ὑμᾶς τὸ πνεῦμα τὸ ἅγιον ἔθετο
<small>overseers, to shepherd the congregation of the God.</small>
ἐπισκόπους, ποιμαίνειν τὴν ἐκκλησίαν τοῦ θεοῦ,
<small>which he purchased with the of his own blood.</small>
ἣν περιεποιήσατο διὰ **τοῦ ἰδίου αἵματος.**

WH NU GENTI ἣν περιεποιήσατο διὰ τοῦ αἵματος τοῦ ἰδίου

"which he [God] purchased with the blood of his own [Son]"

$\mathfrak{P}^{74}$ ℵ A B C E Ψ 33 1739 ($\mathfrak{P}^{41}$ D add εαυτω after περιεποιησατο)

variant/TR ην περιεποιησατο δια του ιδιου αιματος

"which he [God] purchased with his own blood"

Maj

The WHNU GENTI text reading for Acts 20:28b has the best manuscript evidence by far and judging from this we can be certain beyond a reasonable doubt (BRD) that it is the original reading. Therefore, we will not use space debating the two but will spend our time determining how it should be understood.

In his *Textual Commentary,* Bruce Metzger has this to say:

> This absolute use of ὁ ἴδιος ["his Own"] is found in Greek papyri as a term of endearment referring to near relatives.[387] It is possible, therefore, that "his Own" (ὁ ἴδιος) was a title that early Christians gave to Jesus, comparable to "the Beloved" (ὁ ἀγαπητός); compare Ro 8:32, where Paul refers to God "who did not spare τοῦ ἰδίου υἱοῦ" ["his own Son"] in a context that clearly alludes to Gn 22:16, where the Septuagint has ἀγαπητοῦ υἱοῦ ["beloved Son"].

> The reading ἰδίου αἵματος is supported by many of the Byzantine witnesses that read the conflation κυρίου καὶ θεοῦ in the preceding variant. It may well be, as Lake and Cadbury point out,

---

[387] James Hope Moulton, *Prolegomena,* p. 90; and Moulton and Milligan, *Vocabulary, s. v.*

that after the special meaning of ὁ ἴδιος ["his Own"] (discussed in the previous comment) had dropped out of Christian usage, τοῦ ἰδίου ["of his own"] of this passage was misunderstood as a qualification of αἵματος ("his own blood"). "This misunderstanding led to two changes in the text: τοῦ αἵματος τοῦ ἰδίου ["the blood of his own"] was changed to τοῦ ἰδίου αἵματος ["his own blood"] (influenced by Heb. ix. 12?), which is neater but perverts the sense, and θεοῦ was changed to κυρίου by the Western revisers, who doubtless shrank from the implied phrase 'the blood of God.' "[388] (TCGNT, 427)

J. H. Moulton in *A Grammar of New Testament Greek*, Vol. 1 (Prolegomena), 1930 ed., p. 90, says,

> "Before leaving ἴδιος [*idios*] something should be said about the use of ὁ ἴδιος [*ho idios*] without a noun expressed. This occurs in Jn 111 131, Ac 423 2423. In the papyri, we find the singular used thus as a term of endearment to near relations . . . . In Expos. VI. iii. 277 I ventured to cite this as a possible encouragement to those (including B. Weiss) who would translate Acts 20:28 'the blood of one who was his own.'"

The different renderings are as follows:

- "care for the church of God"

  (1) "which he [God] purchased with the blood of his own Son"

  (2) "which he [God] purchased with his own blood"

In the end, we must draw the conclusion from all of the evidence; the 1952, 1971 Revised Standard Version (RSV), the 2012 Lexham English Bible (LEB), and the 2021 Updated American Standard Version (UASV) has followed the evidence with its rendering: "Take heed to yourselves and to all the flock, in which the Holy Spirit has made you overseers, to care for the church of God which he obtained with the blood of his own Son." On the other hand, it seems that the New Living Translation publisher or committee has allowed theological bias to affect their translation choices: "So guard yourselves and God's people. Feed and shepherd God's flock, his church, purchased with his own blood, over which the Holy Spirit has appointed you as elders." Robert H. Stein said in a lecture at Southern Baptist Theological Seminary, 'God does not need our help [in translation]. Simply render it as it should be, whether it supports your position or not.'

---

[388] *The Beginnings of Christianity*, vol. iv, p. 261.

- Be honest in all things

- Follow the truth regardless

- Obey God, not man

If textual scholars and translators obey all three of those principles, then fine, if the text, translation, or interpretation supports our specific doctrinal view. If it does not, fine. A so-called central doctrine does not hang in the balance based on one Bible verse.

The original wording in Acts 20:28b is "which he [God] purchased with the blood of his own [Son]" (ἣν περιεποιήσατο διὰ τοῦ αἵματος τοῦ ἰδίου), which is found in the early good documentary witnesses P[74] ℵ A B C E Ψ 33 1739 and accepted by GENTI WH TGNT SBLGNT. We have **a variant**, "which he [God] purchased with his own blood" (ην περιεποιησατο δια του ιδιου αιματος), which is found in the Maj text and the TR.

1 Timothy 3:16 He Was Manifested in the Flesh

1 TIMOTHY ´ 3:16 (WH NU GENTI) **[BRD]** All modern-day translations

and   confessedly   great   is   the of the reverence well   mystery;   Who
16 καὶ ὁμολογουμένως μέγα ἐστὶν τὸ τῆς εὐσεβείας μυστήριον· Ὃς
was   manifested in   flesh,   was vindicated in   Spirit,   was seen to   angels,   was preached in
ἐφανερώθη ἐν σαρκί, ἐδικαιώθη ἐν πνεύματι, ὤφθη ἀγγέλοις, ἐκηρύχθη ἐν
nations,   was believed in   world,   was taken up in   glory.
ἔθνεσιν, ἐπιστεύθη ἐν κόσμῳ, ἀνελήμφθη ἐν δόξῃ.

ℵ* A* C* F G 33 Didymus

variant 1 ὃ εφανερωθη
"which was manifested"
D*

variant 2/TR θεος εφανερωθη
"God was manifested"
ℵ^c A^c C^2 D^2 Ψ 1739 Maj

1 Timothy 3:16 King James Version	1 Timothy 3:16 Updated American Standard Version	1 Timothy 3:16 English Standard Version	1 Timothy 3:16 Christian Standard Bible
[16] … God was manifest in the flesh, …	[16] … He was manifested in the flesh, …	[16] … He was manifested in the flesh, …	[16] … He was manifested in the flesh, …

"who [or he who] was manifested in the flesh" was the original reading based on the earliest and best manuscripts (ℵ* A* C*), as well as F G 33 Didymus. There are two other variant readings, "which" (D*) and "God" (ℵc Ac C2 D2 Ψ 1739 Maj). Using Comfort's system, "A superscript c or numbers designate corrections made in the manuscript. An asterisk designates the original, pre-corrected reading." The witnesses (manuscripts) that support "who" or "he who" is very weighty. We can see from the above that many manuscripts made what they perceived to be a correction in their manuscript, which clearly comes across as a scribal emendation. Indeed, the pronoun "who" is a reference to Jesus Christ.

List of Greek *Nomina Sacra*

English Meaning	Greek Word	Nominative (Subject)	Genitive (Possessive)
God	Θεός	$\overline{\Theta\Sigma}$	$\overline{\Theta Y}$
Lord	Κύριος	$\overline{K\Sigma}$	$\overline{KY}$
Jesus	Ἰησοῦς	$\overline{I\Sigma}$	$\overline{IY}$
Christ/Messiah	Χριστός	$\overline{X\Sigma}$	$\overline{XY}$
Son	Υἱός	$\overline{Y\Sigma}$	$\overline{YY}$
Spirit/Ghost	Πνεῦμα	$\overline{\Pi NA}$	$\overline{\Pi N\Sigma}$
David	Δαυίδ	$\overline{\Delta A\Delta}$	
Cross/Stake	Σταυρός	$\overline{\Sigma T\Sigma}$	$\overline{\Sigma TY}$
Mother	Μήτηρ	$\overline{MHP}$	$\overline{MH\Sigma}$
God Bearer i.e. Mother of God	Θεοτόκος	$\overline{\Theta K\Sigma}$	$\overline{\Theta KY}$
Father	Πατήρ	$\overline{\Pi HP}$	$\overline{\Pi P\Sigma}$
Israel	Ἰσραήλ	$\overline{IH\Lambda}$	
Savior	Σωτήρ	$\overline{\Sigma HP}$	$\overline{\Sigma P\Sigma}$
Human being/Man	Ἄνθρωπος	$\overline{ANO\Sigma}$	$\overline{ANOY}$
Jerusalem	Ἰερουσαλήμ	$\overline{IAHM}$	
Heaven/Heavens	Οὐρανός	$\overline{OYNO\Sigma}$	$\overline{OYNOY}$

This simply solved textual issue caused many problems in the nineteenth century and really with the King James Version Onlyist, and it still does today. The Bible scholars entered the fray because they thought the textual scholars undermined their doctrine that God became man. The early argument by some textual scholars as to how the variant **2/TR** came about was that the Greek word translated "God," which was abbreviated to the nomen sacrum (sacred name) **ΘC,** had initially looked like the Greek word **OC,** which means "who" or "he who." They argued that a horizontal stroke showed faintly through from the other side of the vellum manuscript page, and a later hand added a line across the top, which turned the word **OC** ("who") into the nomen sacrum contraction **ΘC** ("God"). However, it seems highly unlikely as Comfort comments: "how several fourth- and fifth-century scribes, who had seen thousands of nomina sacra, would have made this mistake." This author would agree with Comfort that it was clearly a doctrinal motivation, wanting it to read, "God was manifest in the flesh."[389]

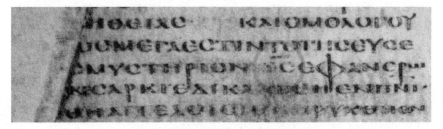

Codex Alexandrinus, 1 Timothy 3:16-4:3 theos

Metzger rates "He was manifested in the flesh" as certain, saying,

The reading which, on the basis of external evidence and transcriptional probability, best explains the rise of the others is ὅς. It is supported by the earliest and best uncials (ℵ* A*vid C* Ggr) as well as by 33 365 442 2127 syrhmg, goth ethpp Origenlat Epiphanius Jerome Theodore Eutherius Cyril Cyrilacc. to Ps-Oecumenius Liberatus. Furthermore, since the neuter relative pronoun ὅ must have arisen as a scribal correction of ὅς (to bring the relative into concord with μυστήριον), the witnesses that read ὅ (D* itd, ·, vg Ambrosiaster Marius Victorinus Hilary Pelagius Augustine) also indirectly presuppose ὅς as the earlier reading. The Textus Receptus reads θεός, with ℵc (this corrector is of the twelfth century) A² C² Dc K L P Ψ 81 330 614 1739 *Byz Lect* Gregory-Nyssa Didymus Chrysostom Theodoret Euthalius and later Fathers. Thus, no uncial (in the first hand) earlier than the eighth or ninth century (Ψ) supports θεός; all ancient versions presuppose ὅς or ὅ; and no patristic writer prior to the last third of the fourth century testifies

---

[389] Philip W. Comfort, New Testament Text and Translation Commentary: Commentary on the Variant Readings of the Ancient New Testament Manuscripts and How They Relate to the Major English Translations (Carol Stream, IL: Tyndale House Publishers, Inc., 2008), 662–663.

to the reading θεός. The reading θεός arose either (*a*) accidentally, through the misreading of ος as ΘΣ, or (*b*) deliberately, either to supply a substantive for the following six verbs, or, with less probability, to provide greater dogmatic precision.[390]

Early on, Johann Jakob Wettstein (1693-1754) noted that **ΘC** originally looked like **OC**, but felt that a horizontal stroke had faintly shown through the other side of the uncial manuscript page, indicating a later hand adding a horizontal line to **OC** and giving us the contraction **ΘC** ("God"). However, this author believes that Comfort made a valid point above, looking at his words more fully, "It is difficult to imagine how several fourth- and fifth-century scribes, who had seen thousands of nomina sacra, would have made this mistake. It is more likely that the changes were motivated by a desire to make the text say that it was "God" who was manifested in the flesh." (P. W. Comfort 2008, 663) If we believe that doctrinal considerations were not behind the scribal changes, all we have to do is investigate what took place when it was understood that the actual reading was "**He who** was manifested in the flesh," as opposed to "**God** was manifested in the flesh." The battle in the nineteenth century was as though the loss of the reading in the Textus Receptus (θεός KJV) would undermine the doctrine of the Trinity. Doctrinal motivations have always played a role in copying the Bible, but the truth is that these are actually few in number. Considering the number of manuscripts that were copied, if these kinds of changes were a major problem, we should see more of them.

1 John 5:7 Testimony Concerning the Son of God

1 JOHN 5:7-8 2020 *Greek-English New Testament Interlinear* (GENTI & WH NU TGNT) **[BRD]**

Because three are the (ones) bearing witness, the spirit and the water and the blood, and

7 ὅτι τρεῖς εἰσὶν οἱ μαρτυροῦντες, **8** τὸ πνεῦμα καὶ τὸ ὕδωρ καὶ τὸ αἷμα, καὶ

the three into the one (thing) are

οἱ τρεῖς εἰς τὸ ἕν εἰσιν.

1 JOHN 5:7-8 1550 Stephanus New Testament (TR1550)

of in

Because three are the (ones) bearing witness, the heavens the Father the Word and the

7 ὅτι τρεῖς εἰσὶν οἱ μαρτυροῦντες, εν τω ουρανω ο πατηρ ο λογος και το

Holy Spirit and these the three one are and three there are who bear witness in

αγιον πνευμα και ουτοι οι τρεις εν εισιν **8** και τρεις εισιν οι μαρτυρουντες εν

the earth the Spirit and the water and the blood and the three to the one are

τη γη το πνευμα και το υδωρ και το αιμα και οι τρεις εις το εν εισιν

---

[390] Bruce Manning Metzger, United Bible Societies, *A Textual Commentary on the Greek New Testament, Second Edition a Companion Volume to the United Bible Societies' Greek New Testament (4th Rev. Ed.)* (London; New York: United Bible Societies, 1994), 573–574.

1 John 5:7-8 Updated American Standard Version (UASV)	1 John 5:7-8 English Standard Version (ESV)
[7] For there are three that testify: [8] the Spirit and the water and the blood; and the three are in agreement.	[7] For there are three that testify: [8] the Spirit and the water and the blood; and these three agree.

1 John 5:7-8 King James Version (KJV)

[7] For there are three that bear record in heaven, the Father, the Word, and the Holy Ghost: and these three are one. [8] And there are three that bear witness in earth, the Spirit, and the water, and the blood: and these three agree in one.

GENTI WH NU TGNT SBLGNT ὅτι τρεῖς εἰσιν οἱ μαρτυροῦντες, [8] τὸ πνεῦμα καὶ τὸ ὕδωρ καὶ τὸ αἷμα, καὶ οἱ τρεῖς εἰς τὸ ἕν εἰσιν.

"For there are three that testify: [8] the Spirit and the water and the blood; and the three are in agreement."
א A B (Ψ) Maj syr cop arm eth it

Variant/TR οτι τρεις εισεν οι μαρτυρουντες εν τω ουρανω, ο πατηρ, ο λογος και το αγιον πνευμα, και ουτοι οι τρεις ἕν εισιν. [8] και τρεις οι μαρτυρουντες εν τη γη, το πνευμα και το υδωρ και το αιμα, και οι τρεις εις το ἕν εισιν.

"Because there are three that bear record in heaven, the Father, the Word, and the Holy Ghost: and these three are one. [8] And there are three that bear witness in earth, the Spirit, and the water, and the blood: and these three agree in one."

(61 629 omit και ουτοι οι τρεις ἕν εισιν) 88 221[v.r.] 429 636[v.r.] 918 2318 it[l.] vg[mss]Speculum (Priscillian Fulgentius)

NOTE: When there is a superscript א* This siglum refers to the original before it has been corrected. The superscript [1]א This siglum refers to the corrector who worked on the manuscript before it left the scriptorium. The superscript [2]א refers to correctors in the 6th and 7th century C.E., who altered the text to conform more with the Byzantine text. The superscript [v.r.] refers to a variant reading listed in a manuscript.

The original wording in 1 John 5:7-8 is "For there are three that testify: ⁸ the Spirit and the water and the blood; and the three are in agreement." (ὅτι τρεῖς εἰσιν οἱ μαρτυροῦντες, ⁸ τὸ πνεῦμα καὶ τὸ ὕδωρ καὶ τὸ αἷμα, καὶ οἱ τρεῖς εἰς τὸ ἕν εἰσιν), which is found in very good early documentary witnesses א A B, as well as (Ψ) Maj, numerous early versions syr cop arm eth it, and GENTI WH NU TGNT SBLGNT. We have **a variant (TR)**, "Because there are three that bear record in heaven, the Father, the Word, and the Holy Ghost: and these three are one. ⁸ And there are three that bear witness in earth, the Spirit, and the water, and the blood: and these three agree in one." (οτι τρεις εισεν οι μαρτυρουντες εν τω ουρανω, ο πατηρ, ο λογος και το αγιον πνευμα, και ουτοι οι τρεις ἕν εισιν. ⁸ και τρεις οι μαρτυρουντες εν τη γη, το πνευμα και το υδωρ και το αιμα, και οι τρεις εις το ἕν εισιν) in some late manuscripts (61 629 omit και ουτοι οι τρεις ἕν εισιν) 88 221ᵛ·ʳ· 429 636ᵛ·ʳ· 918 2318 and the TR.

If this passage had been in the original, there is no good reason why it would have been removed either accidentally or intentionally. None of the Greek church fathers quote this passage, which they certainly would have during the Trinitarian controversy. (Sabellian and Arian). This interpolation is not in any of the ancient versions, such as Syriac, Coptic, Armenian, Ethiopic, Arabic, Slavonic, and the Old Latin in its early form, or Jerome's Latin Vulgate. Intrinsically, the interpolation "makes an awkward break in the sense" as Metzger points out.

Some three hundred years after the apostle John completed the last books of the New Testament (c. 98 C.E.), a writer (c. 400 C.E.) seeking to strengthen the Trinitarian doctrine added the addition (interpolation) to 1 John 5:7: "in heaven, the Father, the Word, and the Holy Ghost: and these three are one." This statement was not in the original text. "From the sixth century onwards," says the leading New Testament textual scholar of the twentieth century Bruce Metzger, those words were "found more and more frequently in manuscripts of the Old Latin and of the [Latin] Vulgate."

The utter enormous number of manuscripts that we possess today actually helps textual scholars to detect errors. The spurious words of 1 John 5:7 crept into what would become the most influential English Bible in history, the King James Version! However, as textual scholars began to discover other manuscripts, it was revealed that this interpolation was not found in any Greek manuscript prior to the fourth-century. Bruce Metzger wrote: "The passage [at 1 John 5:7] is absent from the manuscripts of all ancient versions (Syriac, Coptic, Armenian, Ethiopic, Arabic, Slavonic), except the Latin." Based on this, revised editions of the King James Version

273

(ERV, ASV, RSV, NRSV, NASB, ESV, HCSB.CSB, and the UASV) and other Bibles (NIV, TNIV, NEB, REB, NJB, NAB, NLT, TEV, NET, and many others) have removed the erroneous phrase.

1 John 5:7 Codex Vaticanus (c. 300-325 C.E.)

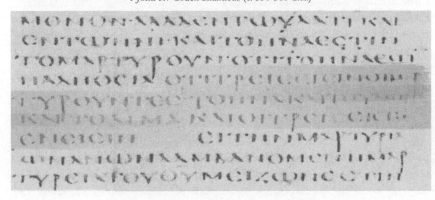

1 John 5.7 Codex Sinaiticus (c. 330-360 C.E.)

1 John 5.7 Codex Alexandrinus (c. 400-440 C.E.)

274

On this Philip W. Comfort writes,

John never wrote the following words: "in heaven, the Father, the Word, and the Holy Spirit: and these three are one. And there are three that bear witness in earth." This famous passage, called "the heavenly witness" or Comma Johanneum, came from a gloss on 5:8 which explained that the three elements (water, blood, and Spirit) symbolize the Trinity (the Father, the Word [Son], and the Spirit).

This gloss had a Latin origin (as did the one in 5:20—see note). The first time this passage appears in the longer form (with the heavenly witness) is in the treatise Liber Apologeticus, written by the Spanish heretic Priscillian (died ca. 385) or his follower, Bishop Instantius. Metzger said, "apparently the gloss arose when the original passage was understood to symbolize the Trinity (through the mention of the three witnesses: the Spirit, the water, and the blood), an interpretation which may have been written first as a marginal note that afterwards found its way into the text" (TCGNT). The gloss showed up in the writings of Latin fathers in North Africa and Italy (as part of the text of the Epistle) from the fifth century onward, and it found its way into more and more copies of the Latin Vulgate. (The original translation of Jerome did not include it.) "The heavenly witnesses" passage has not been found in the text of any Greek manuscript prior to the fourteenth century, and it was never cited by any Greek father. Many of the Greek manuscripts listed above (in support of the variant reading) do not even include the extra verbiage in the text but rather record these words as a "variant reading" (v.r.) in the margin.

Erasmus did not include "the heavenly witnesses" passage in the first two editions of his Greek New Testament. He was criticized for this by defenders of the Latin Vulgate. Erasmus, in reply, said that he would include it if he could see it in any one Greek manuscript. In turn, a manuscript (most likely the Monfort Manuscript, 61, of the sixteenth century) was especially fabricated to contain the passage and thereby fool Erasmus. Erasmus kept his promise; he included it in the third edition. From there it became incorporated into TR and was translated in the KJV. Both KJV and NKJV have popularized this expanded passage. The NKJV translators included it in the text, knowing full well that it has no place there. This is evident in their footnote: "Only four or five very late manuscripts contain these words in Greek." Its inclusion in the text demonstrates their commitment to maintain the KJV heritage.

Without the intrusive words the text reads: "For there are three that testify: the Spirit, the water, and the blood; and the three are in agreement" (NIV). It has nothing to do with the Triune God, but with the three critical phases in Jesus' life where he was manifested as God incarnate, the Son of God in human form. This was made evident at his baptism (= the water), his death (= the blood), and his resurrection (= the Spirit). At his baptism, the man Jesus was declared God's beloved Son (see Matt 3:16–17). At his crucifixion, a man spilling blood was recognized by others as "God's Son" (see Mark 15:39). In resurrection, he was designated as the Son of God in power (see Rom 1:3–4). This threefold testimony is unified in one aspect: Each event demonstrated that the man Jesus was the divine Son of God.[391]

In verse 7 of 1 John 5, after μαρτυροῦντες ("testify"), the Textus Receptus adds, ἐν τῷ οὐρανῷ, ὁ Πατήρ, ὁ Λόγος, καὶ τὸ Ἅγιον Πνεῦμα· καὶ οὗτοι οἱ τρεῖς ἕν εἰσι ("in heaven, the Father, the Word, and the Holy Ghost: and these three are one"). In verse 8, the Textus Receptus has καὶ τρεῖς εἰσιν οἱ μαρτυροῦντες ἐν τῇ γῇ ("And there are three that bear witness in earth"). There is no doubt that these words are an interpolation in the text, which textual scholarship has long known.

These additional words are found in only Greek manuscripts, the earliest being from the tenth century. Metzger comments:

> After μαρτυροῦντες, the Textus Receptus adds the following: ἐν τῷ οὐρανῷ, ὁ Πατήρ, ὁ Λόγος, καὶ τὸ Ἅγιον Πνεῦμα· καὶ οὗτοι οἱ τρεῖς ἕν εἰσι. (8) καὶ τρεῖς εἰσιν οἱ μαρτυροῦντες ἐν τῇ γῇ. That these words are spurious and have no right to stand in the New Testament is certain in the light of the following considerations.... The passage is absent from every known Greek manuscript except eight, and these contain the passage in what appears to be a translation from a late recension of the Latin Vulgate. Four of the eight manuscripts contain the passage as a variant reading written in the margin as a later addition to the manuscript." (TCGNT, 649)

In addition, the interpolation was not quoted by any of the Greek Fathers. Certainly, had they been aware of the passage, there is little doubt that they would have referenced it repeatedly in the fourth-century Trinitarian

---

[391] Philip W. Comfort, New Testament Text and Translation Commentary: Commentary on the Variant Readings of the Ancient New Testament Manuscripts and How They Relate to the Major English Translations (Carol Stream, IL: Tyndale House Publishers, Inc., 2008), 785.

debates. Metzger tells us that "Its first appearance in Greek is in a Greek version of the (Latin) Acts of the Lateran Council in 1215." (TCGNT, 649)

The interpolation is also missing from all the manuscripts of the ancient versions (Syriac, Coptic, Armenian, Ethiopic, Arabic, and Slavonic), except the Latin. However, it is not found in Old Latin in its earliest form (Tertullian Cyprian Augustine). Moreover, it is not present in "the Vulgate (*b*) as issued by Jerome (codex Fuldensis [copied a.d.541–46] and codex Amiatinus [copied before A.D. 716]) or (*c*) as revised by Alcuin (first hand of codex Vallicellianus [ninth century])." (TCGNT, 649)

This interpolation had its beginning in Latin, in the treatise Liber Apologetics, which was written by the Spanish heretic Priscillian (d. c. 385), bishop of Ávila, or his follower, Bishop Instantius. Metzger writes, "Apparently the gloss arose when the original passage was understood to symbolize the Trinity (through the mention of three witnesses: the Spirit, the water, and the blood), an interpretation that may have been written first as a marginal note that afterward found its way into the text. In the fifth century the gloss was quoted by Latin Fathers in North Africa and Italy as part of the text of the Epistle, and from the sixth century onwards it is found more and more frequently in manuscripts of the Old Latin and of the Vulgate." (TCGNT, 649)

Consider this: if these interpolations were original, there would be no reason to remove them, and they would be found in our earliest and best manuscripts, as well as hundreds of years of later copies. Moreover, there would be no reason for their being missing from the versions, either.

Both a Science and an Art

We said at the outset that New Testament textual criticism is both a science and an art. Throughout almost all of this book, we have addressed the science aspect, in that we have spoken of and applied many of the rules and principles. However, we will offer one verse here where the art aspect comes into play; we must not be rigid in applying the rules and principles. It is important that we must be balanced.

Mark 1:41 Was Jesus "Moved with Pity" or "Moved with Anger"?

MARK 1:41 2019 *Greek-English New Testament Interlinear* (TR WH NU GENTI) [BRD]

And having been moved with pity having stretched out the   hand   of him he touched and is saying to him I am willing,

41 καὶ σπλαγχνισθεὶς ἐκτείνας τὴν χεῖρα αὐτοῦ ἥψατο καὶ λέγει αὐτῷ Θέλω,

be   cleansed;

καθαρίσθητι·

MARK 1:41 1550 Stephanus New Testament (TR)

And having been moved with compassion having stretched out the   hand   of him   he touched   and   is saying to him

41 καὶ σπλαγχνισθεὶς ἐκτείνας τὴν χεῖρα αὐτοῦ ἥψατο καὶ λέγει αὐτῷ

I am willing, be   cleansed;

Θέλω, καθαρίσθητι·

TR WH NU GENTI σπλαγχνισθεὶς ἐκτείνας τὴν χεῖρα αὐτοῦ ἥψατο

"being compassionate he stretched out his hand and touched [the man]"

א A B C L W f[1,] 33 565 700 syr cop Diatessaron

variant οργισθεις εκτεινας την χειρα αυτου ηψατο

"being angry he stretched out his hand and touched [the man]"

D it

Mark 1:41 Updated American Standard Version (UASV)	Mark 1:41 Lexham English Bible (LEB)
[41] At that he was **moved with pity** [*splanchnon*], and he stretched out his hand and touched him, and said to him, "I want to! Be made clean."	[41] And **becoming angry [*orgistheis*]**, he stretched out his hand *and* touched *him*, and said to him, "I am willing; be made clean."

This text is considered difficult because one is compelled to think contrary to the leading internal textual principle: *Which reading is it that the other reading(s) most likely came from?* It is easy to see how "moved with anger" would have been changed to "moved with pity." In that case, the scribe would have been softening the reading. It is very difficult to understand why a scribe would be tempted to change "moved with pity" to "moved with anger." On the other hand, the external textual evidence for "moved with pity" is very weighty, while the evidence for "moved with anger" has no real weight at all.

People define textual criticism as both a science and art because as a science, it has rules and principles, while as an art, balance is required in the application of those rules and principles. The rule of which reading is it that the others came from is not to be rigidly applied; there are times when it can possibly be overruled when the evidence supports such a decision, as in this case.

First, the Western text **D**, which displays the reading "moved with anger," is notorious for having "significant" changes to the text. Comfort and Metzger, as well as others, offer a very plausible reason as to why the scribe may have chosen to do so. "He may have decided to make Jesus angry with the leper for wanting a miracle–in keeping with the tone of voice Jesus used in 1:43 when he sternly warned the leper." (P. W. Comfort 2008, 98) However, as Comfort goes on to point out, this would have been a misunderstanding on the part of the scribe because Jesus was not warning him about seeking a miracle; it was instead "a warning about keeping the miracle a secret." Another possible motive for the scribe to alter the text to the harder reading is that he may have felt the man was slow to believe that Jesus was serious about healing him. (v. 40) Moreover, why would scribes soften the text here from "moved with anger" to "moved with pity" but not do the same at Mark 3:12 and 10:14?

Scribal Tendencies or Habits

When we discuss scribal tendencies or habits, it should always be qualified as "speaking generally." That is, these are tendencies that we can attribute in a general way. *Generally*, if a reading seems more difficult or awkward, the easier reading would **not** be preferred because the scribe likely changed the reading to make it easier to understand. *Generally*, the **shorter reading is preferred if** it is determined that it was intentional because a scribe tended to add to the text to clarify it, as opposed to adding to it by mistake. *Generally*, the **longer reading is preferred if** it is determined that the change came about unintentionally. In this case, a scribe would tend to omit a word or phrase by accident instead of intentionally adding. The same is true if a scribe intentionally omitted a word or phrase due to perceived contradictions or awkwardness. For example, a scribe may have willfully removed or altered a verse repeating one of the previous verses. However, this analysis of scribal tendencies is in no way set in stone. Each scribe likely had their own tendencies, so they must be evaluated on their work, with the above tendencies as foundational knowledge. Colwell's conclusions on scribal tendencies in select papyri are revealing:

(1) **P**[45] gives the impression of a scribe who writes without any intention of exactly reproducing his source. He writes with great freedom - harmonizing, smoothing out, substituting almost whimsically. There is no evidence of control by a second party (fewer than three singular readings per hundred are corrected), nor in fact of external controls of any kind.

(2) **P**[66] seems to reflect a scribe working with the intention of making a good copy, falling into careless errors, particularly the error of dropping a letter, syllable, a word, or even a phrase where it is doubled, but also under the control of some other person, or second standard so that the corrections which are made are usually corrections to a reading read by a number of other witnesses. Nine out of ten nonsense readings are corrected, and two out of three of his singular readings. In short, **P**[66] gives the impression of being the product of a scriptorium, i.e., a publishing house. It shows the supervision of a foreman or of a scribe turned proofreader.

(3) In **P**[75], the produced text can be explained in all its variants as the result of a single force, namely the disciplined scribe who writes intending to be careful and accurate. There is no evidence of revision of his work by anyone else, or in fact of any real revision, or check. Only one out of five of his singular readings (including nonsense readings) is corrected. The control had been drilled into the scribe before he started writing.

(4) In summary, **P**[75] and **P**[66] represent a controlled tradition; **P**[45] represents an uncontrolled tradition. **P**[75] and **P**[45] are, according to their own standards, careful workmen. **P**[66] is careless and ineffective - although he is the only calligrapher of the three. He uses up his care, his concern, in the production of beautiful letters. (E. C. Colwell 1969, p. 117-118)

We also find many comments in the TCGNT as to what a scribe might have done or might have not done, with reasons as to why or why not. For example:

- In the present passage, not only do the earlier representatives of several text-types support γένεσις, but **the tendency of copyists would have been** to substitute a word of more specialized meaning for one that had been used in a different sense in ver. 1. (TCGNT, Matt 1:18)

- It is difficult to decide which is the original reading. On the one hand, **the prevailing tendency of scribes was** to expand either Ἰησοῦς or Χριστὸς by the addition of the other word. (TCGNT, Matt 1:18)

- **Copyists who** remembered the parallel account in Mk 2:18 transformed the statement into a question. (TCGNT, Matt 1:18)

- The distinctively Lukan clause assigning the reason for the permanence of the house ("because it had been well built"), which corresponds to the earlier statement concerning the builder's industry ("dug deep, and laid the foundation upon rock"), was supplanted by **copyists who preferred** the reason given by Matthew ("for it was founded upon the rock," Mt 7:25). (TCGNT, Luke 6:48)

- it is also **possible that copyists omitted**[392] the clause in order to draw attention to what was taken as the primary element in Jesus' reply. (TCGNT, John 21:23)

Canons of Criticism

There have been Canons of Criticism or Canons of Textual Criticism for centuries, being refined with each new generation of textual scholars, adding to them and determining how they are to be applied. "Canon" in this context means a general rule, principle, or standard applied by the critic to ascertain the original reading. One of the earliest of these canons came from Johann Albrecht Bengel (1687–1752), who, in 1734, published an edition of the Greek New Testament. In his commentary, Bengel introduced the rule of preferring harder reading, which would become very influential in the centuries to come. He wrote, *proclivi scriptioni praestat ardua,* "Before the easy reading, stands the difficult."[393] Bengel himself had twenty-seven canons that he observed in his work as a textual scholar.

One of the most influential textual scholars of all time was Johann Jakob Griesbach (1745–1812), who published several editions of the Greek New Testament. He would establish fifteen rules of textual criticism, refining and improving upon his predecessors. Among them were,[394]

(1) The shorter reading, if not wholly lacking the support of old and weighty witnesses, is to be preferred over the more verbose; **for scribes**

---

[392] Bold in this section is mine.

[393] "Critical Rules of Johann Albrecht Bengel." Bible-researcher.com. Retrieved 08-03-2014.

[394] We will offer his entire first canon in the chapter, The Arrival of the Critical Text, which deals with the history of the critical text.

were much more prone to add than to omit. They hardly ever leave out anything on purpose, but they added much.

(2) The more difficult and more obscure reading is preferable to that in which everything is so plain and free of problems that every scribe is easily able to understand it. Because of their obscurity and difficulty, chiefly unlearned scribes were vexed by those readings.

(3) The harsher reading is preferable to that which instead flows pleasantly and smoothly in style.

(4) The more unusual reading is preferable to that which constitutes nothing unusual.

1881 is the best-known year in all textual criticism. It is the year that Brooke Foss Westcott (1825–1901) and Fenton J. A. Hort (1828–1892) published the most significant critical Greek New Testament text. There were nine critical rules of Westcott and Hort. We will discuss them more fully in the chapter, The Arrival of the Critical Text. Three of those rules are (1) The reading is less likely to be original, showing a disposition to smooth away difficulties. (2) Readings are approved or rejected because of the quality, and not the number, of their supporting witnesses. (3) The reading is to be preferred that most fitly explains the existence of the others.

External: The Canons of Criticism are subjective in that each textual scholar chooses to what degree they are obeyed, at least in practice if not formally. If taken rigidly, without being qualified, the canons may even seem to contradict each other sometimes. In addition, some textual scholars may give more weight to certain manuscript families, while others feel that they are all equal. Any two scholars who prefer the Alexandrian family may not give it the same weight or select different manuscripts when there is a split within the family. We have already dealt with how doctrinal positions affected the scribes, and sometimes this is the case with the textual scholar or the Bible translator.

Internal: At the same time, there are differences in how internal evidence is viewed because internal canons are even more affected by subjectivity. Any two textual scholars looking at a text, both having full and accurate knowledge of the principles, may very well disagree. For example, they may be grappling with the principle of *consideration of the author's style and vocabulary*. The first scholar may argue that the variant is original because it accords with the author's style. The second scholar may argue that the variant is not original because the copyist was trying to imitate the author when he interjected the variant.

External versus Internal: Then, there is the issue of internal evidence in opposition to external. For example, Reasoned Eclecticism is supposed to give balanced consideration to internal and external evidence. However, in practice, preference usually goes to internal evidence. The Nestle-Aland Greek New Testament 28th Edition is the standard text today. In this author's opinion, its readings are based too much on internal evidence, and it is inconsistent in the use of documentary evidence.[395]

Indeed, there will never be 100 percent agreement on every textual issue, but we must ask, what can be taken away from the above? It seems that our focus needs to be on individual scribal tendencies while appreciating general scribal tendencies as well, such as those mentioned above. Nevertheless, when we have a document that just does not have enough of the scribe's work to formulate sound insights into his tendencies, we must lean on what we know of the scribes of that era, in general, and our documentary evidence. While individual scribes will have their own tendencies, they will also have others that are shared by those who work in the scribal community. It is like any other field of specialty (lawn care workers, dentists, mental health workers, teachers, and the like). If we were to look across many different cultures worldwide, there would be certain tendencies that all share as they carry out their work. Nevertheless, each person within these specialized fields would have their own way of carrying out the work unique to them as individuals.

We have *A Textual Commentary of the Greek New Testament* by Bruce Metzger, *New Testament Text and Translation Commentary* by Philip W. Comfort, and even *The New Testament in the Original Greek*, by Westcott and Hort, vol. 2, among others. This author is building a free online *New Testament Textual Commentary*.[396] In these textual commentaries, we discover many reasons why a copyist has done this or that or failed to do this or that. However, in my view, the reader is not given evidence that supports the textual scholar's suggested reasons as to why a copyist did or did not do something. When we think of the principle of external evidence, we know that witnesses must be "weighed not counted." This approach needs to be adopted with internal evidence: we must weigh the errors in each manuscript, and each copyist of a manuscript needs to be profiled, producing a brief description that summarizes the copyist's patterns of mistakes. If textual scholars had access to profiles of the copyists who produced manuscripts, by which they were making decisions, it would offer them greater insight for determining the original reading.

---

[395] See Matthew 3:16; 4:24; 5:28; 8:21; 9:14, 26; 12:47; Mark 3:32; 6:51; 7:4; Luke 8:43; 14:17; 22:43-44; John 1:34; 3:31; Acts 16:12; Romans 11:17; 1 Corinthians 4:2; 2 Corinthians 5:3, 12; Galatians 1:3, 6; 2 Tim 3:5; James 5:4, to mention just a few.

[396] https://christianpublishinghouse.co/category/nt-textual-commentary/

CHAPTER X

Tracing the Script: Paleography and the Text of the New Testament

Materials for Receiving Writing

Introduction to Writing Materials in the Ancient World

Paleography, the study of ancient handwriting, is an essential discipline for understanding and analyzing the text of the New Testament. By examining the styles, materials, and techniques used in creating manuscripts, paleography allows scholars to date and categorize the texts, establish their authenticity, and trace the development and transmission of the New Testament over time. This knowledge is crucial for textual criticism, as it helps identify variations and potential scribal errors in the manuscripts.

In the ancient world, various materials were used for writing purposes, each with its unique properties and limitations. The choice of material depended on factors such as availability, cost, and the intended purpose of the document. Here, we provide an overview of the primary writing materials used during the time of the New Testament's composition and transmission.

1. **Papyrus**: Papyrus was the most common writing material in the ancient Mediterranean world, particularly in Egypt, where it was made from the pith of the papyrus plant. Papyrus sheets were created by placing strips of pith side by side and overlaying them with another layer of strips laid perpendicularly. The two layers were then pressed and dried, forming a sturdy writing surface. Papyrus was relatively cheap and widely available, making it an ideal material for the dissemination of the New Testament texts.

2. **Parchment and Vellum**: Parchment, made from animal skins (usually calf, sheep, or goat), provided a more durable and expensive alternative to papyrus. Vellum, a term often used interchangeably with parchment, specifically refers to a high-quality, fine-grained parchment made from the skins of young animals. Parchment and vellum were more resilient to moisture and wear, which made them suitable for preserving valuable texts, such as copies of the New Testament intended for long-term use.

3. **Ostraca**: Ostraca, or potsherds, were broken pieces of pottery or limestone used for writing short notes, receipts, or informal correspondence. While they were not typically used for writing New Testament texts, they provide valuable insight into the everyday language and writing practices of the ancient world.

4. **Inscriptions on Stone and Metal**: Permanent records or commemorations, such as monumental inscriptions or public decrees, were often engraved on stone or metal surfaces. These materials were not used for writing New Testament texts but do serve as important sources for understanding the historical and cultural context in which the New Testament was written and transmitted.

In conclusion, the study of writing materials in the ancient world is an essential component of paleography and the analysis of the New Testament text. Understanding the properties and limitations of these materials helps scholars to better interpret the manuscripts and reconstruct the history of the New Testament's transmission.

Papyrus: The Most Common Material for Early New Testament Texts

Papyrus, the most prevalent writing material in the early centuries of the New Testament's composition and transmission, played a crucial role in the preservation and dissemination of its texts. Derived from the pith of the papyrus plant (Cyperus papyrus), this material was especially popular in Egypt due to its abundance and cost-effectiveness. Papyrus' widespread use, coupled with its durability under the region's dry climate, enabled a substantial number of early New Testament manuscripts to survive, allowing scholars to study and analyze these ancient texts.

Papyrus Manufacturing: Creating papyrus sheets involved several steps. First, the pith of the papyrus plant was cut into thin strips. These strips were then placed side by side, with their edges slightly overlapping, to form a layer. Another layer of strips was laid perpendicularly over the first, and the two layers were soaked in water, pressed, and dried to create a firm, flat surface. The final product was polished using a smooth stone or shell to create a more uniform writing surface. Papyrus sheets could be joined together by gluing their edges to form a continuous roll (known as a scroll) or by stacking and binding them to create a codex, an early form of the modern book.

Papyrus in New Testament Manuscripts: The majority of the earliest surviving New Testament manuscripts are written on papyrus. Some of these papyri date back to the 2nd and 3rd centuries CE, providing valuable insight into the early transmission and textual history of the New Testament. Among the most significant papyrus collections are the Chester Beatty Papyri, which include portions of the Gospels, Acts, Pauline Epistles, and Revelation, and the Bodmer Papyri, containing substantial sections of the Gospels of John and Luke, as well as other New Testament writings.

Writing on Papyrus: Scribes typically wrote on the recto (front) side of papyrus sheets, where the horizontal fibers provided a smoother writing surface. The ink was made from a mixture of soot or other pigments, gum, and water. Scribes used reed pens with split nibs to write, and the script could vary from formal, carefully executed styles to more informal and rapidly written cursive hands. In some instances, scribes wrote on both the recto and verso (back) sides of the papyrus, known as an opisthograph. This practice was more common in the case of codices than scrolls.

Limitations and Preservation of Papyrus: While papyrus was relatively inexpensive and widely available, it had its limitations. Papyrus sheets were susceptible to damage from humidity, insects, and physical wear. Consequently, many papyrus manuscripts have only partially survived or are fragmented. The dry climate of Egypt, however, has helped preserve numerous papyrus texts, including early New Testament manuscripts, which are invaluable resources for textual scholars.

In conclusion, papyrus played a significant role in the early transmission of the New Testament texts. Its widespread use and accessibility facilitated the copying and circulation of these writings throughout the ancient world. The surviving papyrus manuscripts provide essential evidence for the textual history of the New Testament and offer scholars a window into the early Christian communities and their practices.

Parchment and Vellum: Durable Alternatives to Papyrus

As the study of the New Testament manuscripts progressed, two additional writing materials, parchment and vellum, emerged as important alternatives to papyrus. These materials offered greater durability, making them suitable for preserving sacred texts and other significant writings for posterity.

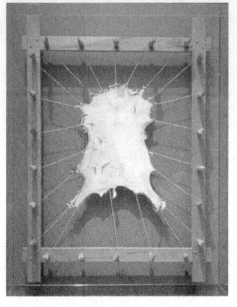

Parchment: A Durable Writing Material Parchment, made from the cleaned and treated skins of animals, such as sheep, goats, and calves, was a more resilient alternative to papyrus. The production process involved soaking the animal skins in lime, stretching them on a wooden frame, and scraping off any remaining hair and tissue. The skins were then treated with a pumice stone to create a smooth writing surface.

The advantages of parchment over papyrus included its greater flexibility, strength, and resistance to moisture. Parchment could also be written on both sides, making it more efficient for creating larger volumes. Due to its durability, parchment eventually became the preferred writing material for many scribes, particularly for copying and preserving religious texts such as the New Testament.

Vellum: A High-Quality Form of Parchment: Vellum is a refined form of parchment made from the skins of young, often stillborn, animals, typically calves. The manufacturing process was similar to that of parchment, but the result was an even smoother, finer, and more supple writing surface. Vellum was considered a luxury material due to its high quality and the scarcity of suitable skins. Consequently, it was often reserved for the most important texts, including illuminated manuscripts and deluxe editions of sacred works.

Parchment and Vellum in New Testament Manuscripts: Some of the most well-known New Testament manuscripts, including Codex Sinaiticus, Codex Vaticanus, and Codex Alexandrinus, were written on parchment. These codices contain substantial portions or even the entirety of the New Testament and have been essential for understanding the textual history of these writings.

The transition from papyrus to parchment and vellum took place gradually, as scribes recognized the benefits of these more durable materials. By the 4th century CE, parchment had become the dominant writing material for New Testament texts, with vellum reserved for the most exquisite copies.

In conclusion, parchment and vellum provided more durable and long-lasting alternatives to papyrus in the production and preservation of New Testament manuscripts. Their use allowed for the creation of high-quality, resilient copies of sacred texts, which have become invaluable resources for textual scholars and paleographers studying the history and development of the New Testament.

Ostraca: Potsherds as Writing Surfaces

In the context of the New Testament and paleography, ostraca provide another form of writing material, distinct from papyrus, parchment, and vellum. Ostraca are broken pieces of pottery or ceramic, known as potsherds, used as a writing surface in ancient times. Though not as common or prestigious as papyrus, parchment, or vellum, ostraca held unique advantages and has contributed valuable insights into the textual history of the New Testament.

The Lachish Ostraca

Lachish, 605–539 BC

Ostracon: potsherd with writing

Found in the Israelite city of Lachish

Written before Nebuchadnezzar's Judah conquest

The Use of Ostraca in Antiquity: Ostraca were widely used in the ancient world, particularly in Egypt, Greece, and the Near East. They were an affordable and readily available alternative to more expensive writing materials. Pottery was a common household item, and broken pieces were easily repurposed for writing.

In ancient societies, ostraca were utilized for various purposes, such as receipts, tax records, lists, letters, and even literary texts. These fragments often contained brief texts or notes, and their durability ensured they could survive for centuries.

Ostraca and the New Testament: While the majority of New Testament manuscripts were written on papyrus, parchment, or vellum, some New Testament texts have been discovered on ostraca. These instances are relatively rare, but they offer additional evidence for the textual history of the New Testament and the dissemination of its message.

For example, a 3rd-century ostracon from Egypt contains a portion of the Gospel of John (John 2:11-22), providing valuable insight into the text's transmission during this period. Another ostracon, dated to the 5th century, features a fragment of the Gospel of Matthew (Matthew 27:62-64).

Although ostraca are not as common as other writing materials for preserving New Testament texts, their existence demonstrates the wide variety of materials used by ancient scribes to record and transmit the Christian message. Ostraca also provide paleographers with unique opportunities to study ancient handwriting styles, as the texts inscribed on these potsherds were often more informal and less polished than those found on more expensive writing materials.

In conclusion, ostraca serve as a crucial resource in the study of the New Testament's textual history and paleography. These potsherds, though less common than other writing materials, offer unique insights into the transmission and dissemination of the New Testament in antiquity. They reveal how ancient scribes used various materials to ensure the preservation and communication of the Christian message, and they provide valuable information for scholars studying the development of ancient handwriting styles.

Inscriptions on Stone and Metal: Permanent Records

In the study of the New Testament and paleography, inscriptions on stone and metal hold a significant place as enduring records from antiquity. Although such inscriptions are not as common as papyrus, parchment, or vellum for preserving New Testament texts, they offer valuable insights into the cultural, historical, and linguistic context in which the early Christian texts were produced and circulated.

Inscriptions on Stone: Stone inscriptions were widely used in the ancient world for various purposes, including commemorative monuments, public records, legal documents, and religious texts. Because stone is a durable material, many inscriptions have survived the ravages of time and offer scholars important information about the societies that created them.

In the context of the New Testament, stone inscriptions are particularly useful for understanding the linguistic environment in which the texts were written. For instance, inscriptions featuring the Greek language and Koine dialect provide essential background information for the study of the New Testament, as they help scholars understand the vocabulary, grammar, and syntax employed by the authors.

Potsherd with an Aramaic inscription mentioning allocation of barley to a person named Hatt for a camel and two donkeys

Baked clay, ink ; Tel Arad, Israel ; 5th–4th century BCE

IAA 1987-1857

חרס עם כתובת ארמית התצייחת הקצאת שעורה לאדם בשם חט עבור גמל ושני חמורים

Moreover, stone inscriptions related to early Christianity, such as epitaphs, dedicatory inscriptions, and monumental texts, shed light on the beliefs, practices, and social dynamics of the early Christian communities. Although direct quotations from the New Testament are rare in stone inscriptions, they do provide indirect evidence for the circulation and impact of the Christian message.

Inscriptions on Metal: Metal inscriptions, though less common than those on stone, also hold significance for the study of the New Testament and paleography. Metals such as bronze, silver, and gold were used for inscribing important texts, often for ceremonial or religious purposes.

In the context of the New Testament, metal inscriptions offer valuable insights into the social and cultural milieu of the early Christian communities. For example, inscriptions on metal objects like cups, plates, or plaques provide information about the religious practices and rituals of the early Christians. Additionally, metal inscriptions may also offer clues about the linguistic environment and the transmission of Christian texts.

In conclusion, inscriptions on stone and metal, while not directly preserving New Testament texts, play a crucial role in the study of the New Testament's historical and linguistic context. These permanent records offer valuable information about the ancient societies that produced and circulated the Christian message, and they provide essential background knowledge for scholars examining the text and paleography of the New Testament.

Other Writing Materials: Wax Tablets and Wooden Boards

Besides papyrus, parchment, vellum, ostraca, and inscriptions on stone and metal, other writing materials such as wax tablets and wooden boards also played a role in the ancient world, including in the context of the New Testament and early Christian communities. While these materials may not have been commonly used for preserving the biblical text, they were essential for everyday communication, education, and record-keeping in antiquity.

Wax Tablets: Wax tablets were a popular and reusable writing surface in the ancient Mediterranean world. These tablets consisted of a wooden frame filled with a layer of beeswax. Using a stylus, writers could inscribe their messages onto the wax surface, and the text could be easily erased by smoothing the wax for reuse.

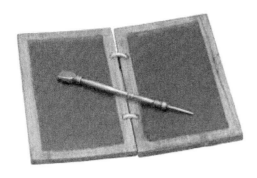

Wax tablets were frequently employed for various purposes, such as taking notes, composing drafts, keeping records, and teaching children to write. In the context of the New Testament, it is likely that some of the authors and their scribes may have used wax tablets for composing drafts or taking notes before transcribing the final version onto more durable materials like papyrus or parchment.

Although no New Testament texts have been preserved on wax tablets, these materials provide valuable insights into the writing practices and the educational system of the ancient world. Furthermore, the use of wax tablets illustrates the importance of writing and literacy in the early Christian communities and the broader Greco-Roman society.

Wooden Boards: Wooden boards, also known as wooden tablets, were another writing material used in antiquity. These boards were typically made of thin, smooth wooden panels, often joined together by cords or hinges to form a booklet or diptych. The wooden surface could be used for writing directly with ink, or it could be covered with a thin layer of gesso or another material to create a more receptive surface for writing.

Wooden boards were employed for a variety of purposes, such as legal documents, personal correspondence, and literary texts. Some early Christian texts, known as the "wooden codices," have been found written on wooden boards, although none of them are part of the New Testament canon.

In the study of the New Testament and paleography, the use of wooden boards demonstrates the variety of writing materials available in antiquity and provides insights into the writing practices of the early Christian communities. While papyrus, parchment, and vellum were the primary materials for preserving the biblical text, wax tablets and wooden boards played essential roles in everyday communication, education, and record-keeping in the ancient world.

Writing Utensils

The Reed Pen: The Main Writing Tool for Papyrus and Parchment

In the ancient world, the reed pen was the primary writing tool used for inscribing texts on papyrus and parchment. The pen's widespread use and its role in the transmission of the New Testament text make it an essential element to consider when studying paleography and the textual history of the biblical writings.

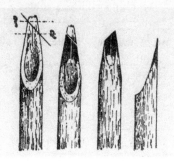

The Reed Pen: The reed pen was typically made from the stem of a reed plant, such as the Phragmites or Arundo species, which grew abundantly in the marshy areas around the Mediterranean, especially in Egypt. The reed's hollow stem would be cut, shaped, and sharpened at one end to form a nib. The nib was split, allowing it to hold ink, which would then be transferred onto the writing surface when pressure was applied.

The reed pen was a versatile and durable writing tool, and its nib could be sharpened and reshaped multiple times before the pen was discarded. These pens were relatively cheap and easy to produce, making them the preferred writing instrument for the majority of scribes and writers in the ancient world.

Using the Reed Pen for Writing on Papyrus and Parchment: The reed pen was well-suited for writing on both papyrus and parchment due to its flexibility and adaptability. When writing on papyrus, scribes would use the pen to apply ink along the horizontal fibers of the papyrus sheet, which allowed for smooth and even writing. On parchment, the pen could be used to write on both the smooth, flesh side and the rougher, hair side of the animal skin.

In the context of the New Testament, it is likely that the authors and their scribes used reed pens to inscribe the biblical text onto papyrus and parchment manuscripts. The use of the reed pen contributed to the unique features of ancient handwriting, such as letterforms and ligatures, which are essential aspects of paleographical analysis.

The reed pen played a crucial role in the transmission of the New Testament text and the broader world of ancient writing practices. Its widespread use and adaptability to various writing surfaces, including papyrus and parchment, make it an indispensable element in the study of paleography and the textual history of the New Testament.

The Metal Stylus: For Inscriptions and Wax Tablets

While the reed pen was the primary writing tool for papyrus and parchment, the metal stylus played a significant role in the ancient world for inscribing texts on other surfaces, such as stone, metal, and wax tablets. Understanding the metal stylus's use and its impact on writing practices is essential in the study of paleography and the textual history of the New Testament.

The Metal Stylus: The metal stylus was a writing instrument typically made of bronze, iron, or sometimes bone. It had a pointed end for writing and a flat end, called a spatula, for erasing or smoothing the writing surface. The pointed end of the stylus was used to inscribe or engrave text onto surfaces like stone, metal, or wax-covered wooden tablets.

Inscriptions on Stone and Metal Inscriptions on stone and metal were common forms of communication and record-keeping in the ancient world. They were used to create permanent records, such as commemorative inscriptions, official documents, and epitaphs. The metal stylus was the primary tool for engraving these inscriptions. Although the New Testament texts were not typically inscribed on stone or metal, studying these inscriptions can provide insights into the broader context of writing practices and language usage in the ancient world.

Wax Tablets: Wax tablets were another popular writing surface in the ancient world, especially for temporary records or drafts. These tablets typically consisted of a wooden frame filled with a layer of wax, and the metal stylus was used to write on the wax surface. The flat end of the stylus could be used to smooth the wax and erase the text, allowing the tablet to be reused multiple times.

While wax tablets were not commonly used for transmitting the New Testament text, they may have been employed for drafting or taking notes before the final text was written on papyrus or parchment. Studying the use of wax tablets can provide valuable insights into the writing practices and methodologies of the authors and scribes involved in producing the New Testament.

In conclusion, the metal stylus played a crucial role in the transmission of written texts in the ancient world, particularly for inscriptions and writing on wax tablets. Although it was not the primary writing tool for the New Testament, understanding its use and impact on writing practices enhances our knowledge of paleography and the textual history of the biblical writings.

Ink: Composition and Varieties

In the context of paleography and the textual history of the New Testament, understanding the composition and varieties of ink used in ancient writings is essential. Ink played a crucial role in the transmission of the New Testament texts, as it was the primary medium used to write on materials like papyrus and parchment.

Ink Composition: Ancient ink was typically composed of two main components: a colorant and a binder. The colorant provided the ink with its distinctive color, while the binder helped the ink adhere to the writing surface.

Colorants were usually derived from natural sources, such as minerals, plants, and even animal byproducts. The most common colorant for ink in the ancient world was carbon black, which was produced by grinding soot or charcoal into a fine powder. Other colorants, such as red ochre, were also used occasionally.

Binders were typically derived from plant gums or other organic materials, such as egg whites, animal glues, or honey. These substances helped to bind the colorant particles together and ensure that the ink adhered to the writing surface.

Ink Varieties: There were several different types of ink used in the ancient world, depending on the specific requirements of the writing project and the materials available.

1. **Carbon Ink**: This was the most common type of ink used in the ancient world, particularly for writing on papyrus and parchment. Carbon ink was made by combining carbon black with a binder, such as gum arabic or another plant gum. The ink was water-soluble, which made it relatively easy to produce and use. Most of the New Testament manuscripts were written using carbon ink.

2. **Iron Gall Ink**: Iron gall ink was another popular ink variety, especially in later periods. It was made by combining iron salts with tannic acids derived from oak galls or other plant materials. The resulting ink was dark blue-black and had a higher resistance to fading and water damage than carbon ink. However, iron gall ink could be corrosive, causing damage to the writing surface over time. Some later New Testament manuscripts were written using iron gall ink.

3. **Metal-based Inks**: Inks made from metal compounds, such as copper or lead salts, were occasionally used in ancient writings. These inks were more durable and resistant to fading but were less common due to their higher cost and limited availability.

Understanding the composition and varieties of ink used in ancient writings is crucial for paleography and the study of the New Testament textual history. The choice of ink and its properties could impact the longevity, readability, and preservation of the biblical texts, providing valuable insights into the writing practices and transmission of the New Testament manuscripts.

Brushes and Chisels: Tools for Stone and Metal Inscriptions

While the primary focus of New Testament textual criticism is on manuscripts written on papyrus, parchment, and other organic materials, stone and metal inscriptions also played a role in the transmission and preservation of texts in the ancient world. These inscriptions were created using different tools and techniques than those employed on more fragile writing surfaces. Brushes and chisels were the primary tools used for creating inscriptions on stone and metal surfaces.

1. **Brushes**: For inscriptions on stone, brushes were often used to apply paint or ink to the surface. These brushes were typically made from animal hair, plant fibers, or reeds, and were attached to wooden or bone handles. The brushes allowed scribes to create smooth, flowing lines, making them suitable for a wide range of lettering styles. Although the paint or ink used for inscriptions on stone would eventually fade or wear away over time, the brushstrokes could leave subtle traces in the stone's surface, providing valuable evidence for paleographers studying ancient writing practices.

2. **Chisels**: For more permanent inscriptions on stone or metal surfaces, chisels were employed to carve the text directly into the material. These chisels were made of metal, typically bronze or iron, and had a sharp, wedge-shaped tip. To create an inscription, the

chisel was placed against the surface, and a mallet was used to strike the handle, driving the chisel into the material and carving out the desired letter forms.

There were various types of chisels used for different purposes. For example, flat chisels were used for creating straight lines and broad strokes, while curved chisels were used for carving rounded letters and intricate designs. In some cases, a scribe would first sketch the outline of the letters using a brush or a sharp stylus, then use the chisel to carve the final inscription.

Stone and metal inscriptions played a significant role in preserving texts and commemorating important events, laws, or religious dedications in the ancient world. While the New Testament was primarily transmitted through manuscripts on papyrus and parchment, the study of inscriptions on stone and metal can provide valuable insights into the wider context of ancient writing practices, scripts, and languages. Understanding the tools and techniques used to create these inscriptions, such as brushes and chisels, is essential for paleographers and New Testament textual scholars as they seek to reconstruct the history of the biblical text.

Book Forms

The Scroll: The Ancient Standard

Before the advent of the codex, the most common book form in the ancient world was the scroll. Scrolls were used for literary, religious, and official documents, and were a prominent feature of the cultural and intellectual life of the ancient Mediterranean world. Understanding the nature and role of scrolls in antiquity is essential for a comprehensive understanding of the textual transmission and history of the New Testament.

1. **Composition of Scrolls**: Scrolls were made by attaching sheets of writing material, such as papyrus or parchment, together in a long strip. Papyrus scrolls were the most common type in the eastern Mediterranean, while parchment scrolls were more common in the western regions. The sheets were typically glued or sewn together, and the completed scroll could range from a few inches to several feet in length, depending on the content.

2. **Writing and Reading Scrolls**: Text was written on one side of the scroll, in columns running parallel to the short edges of the sheets. The reader would unroll the scroll with one hand while rolling it up with the other, exposing the text column by column. This method of reading limited the reader's ability to access specific parts of the text easily, making scrolls less convenient for reference purposes than the later codex format.

3. **Storage and Preservation**: Scrolls were typically stored in protective cylindrical containers, often made of leather, wood, or metal. They were shelved or stacked horizontally in libraries and archives, with labels attached to the containers to identify the contents. Scrolls were susceptible to damage from moisture, insects, and general wear and tear, which is why so few ancient scrolls have survived to the present day.

4. **Scrolls in Early Christianity**: The New Testament documents were initially written and circulated as scrolls, although the exact form and size of these scrolls remain a matter of scholarly debate. The use of scrolls in early Christianity is confirmed by several New Testament passages (e.g., Luke 4:17, 2 Timothy 4:13, Revelation 5:1). The transition from scrolls to the codex format, which eventually became the standard for Christian texts, occurred gradually over the course of the second and third centuries CE.

The study of ancient scrolls is crucial for understanding the early transmission of the New Testament text. By examining the physical characteristics, writing techniques, and methods of production and circulation of scrolls, paleographers and textual scholars can gain valuable insights into the origins and development of the New Testament documents and the broader literary culture in which they were produced.

The Codex: A Revolutionary Format Developed by Christians

The codex, which eventually replaced the scroll as the primary form of book in the ancient world, had a significant impact on the preservation and transmission of the New Testament text. Developed by early Christians, the codex provided numerous advantages over the scroll, ultimately leading to its widespread adoption throughout the Christian world and beyond.

1. **Origins and Development of the Codex**: The codex format emerged in the first and second centuries CE, with early Christians being among the first to adopt and popularize its use. The exact reasons for this adoption remain debated among scholars; however, it is likely that the codex offered practical advantages for the compilation, organization, and accessibility of Christian texts, such as the Gospels and the letters of Paul.

2. **Structure and Composition of the Codex**: The codex consists of individual sheets of writing material, such as papyrus or parchment, which are folded and bound together along one edge. The sheets, known as leaves or folios, are then cut or trimmed to create a book with pages that can be easily turned and accessed. Text is written on both sides of the leaves, maximizing the use of available writing space.

3. **Advantages of the Codex**: The codex format offers several significant advantages over the scroll, including easier navigation and reference, greater durability, and more efficient use of writing materials. The codex allows for random access to specific passages or sections, making it an ideal format for studying, teaching, and preaching. Furthermore, the bound structure of the codex provides better protection for the written text, contributing to the improved preservation of many early Christian manuscripts.

4. **Impact on the Transmission of the New Testament**: The adoption of the codex format by early Christians had a lasting impact on the preservation and transmission of the New Testament text. As the codex became the standard format for Christian texts, it facilitated the compilation and organization of the various New Testament writings into a single volume. This not only aided in the development of the New Testament canon but also contributed to the widespread dissemination and standardization of the text throughout the Christian world.

The codex format, developed and popularized by early Christians, played a crucial role in shaping the textual history of the New Testament. By examining the physical characteristics, writing techniques, and production methods of early Christian codices, paleographers and textual scholars can gain valuable insights into the early transmission and reception of the New Testament documents, as well as the broader development of the book as a cultural and technological innovation.

EXCURSION: The Early Christian Codex

Before the advent of the printed book, literary works were recorded on scrolls made of either animal skins or papyrus sheets. These scrolls were long and narrow, measuring around 20-30 feet in length and 9-10 inches in height. To form a scroll, multiple sheets were fastened together and written on in columns, which formed the pages. The word "volume" comes from the Latin word for something that is rolled up or revolves around rollers. Jesus himself would have been familiar with this form of book, as he was handed a scroll of the prophet Isaiah in the synagogue of Nazareth.

However, over time, a new format for recording information emerged called the codex. The word "codex" comes from the Latin word for "tree trunk," as early versions of the codex were made of wooden tablets with raised rims, coated in wax and written on with a stylus. By the fifth century BCE, these wooden tablets had evolved into multi-leaf tablets bound together with strings passing through pierced holes. Because they looked like a tree trunk when bound together, they were called a codex.

Carrying around these heavy and unwieldy wooden tablets was not ideal, and so the search began for a lighter and more flexible material. The Romans developed the parchment notebook, an intermediate step between the tablet and the later book-form codex. As the style and material of the original tablet changed, it became a problem to know what to call the new format. The Latin word "membranae" was used to describe the parchment notebook, and Paul even used this word when requesting "the scrolls, especially the parchments [membranas]." It is believed that Paul used a Latin word because there was no Greek equivalent to describe what he was calling for. Later, the word "codex" was transliterated into the Greek language to refer to the book.

Christians Develop the Codex: The development of the codex, a book format that replaced the traditional scroll, is a topic of much interest to scholars. Evidence gathered to date places the rise of the codex alongside the increasing use of vellum in the fourth century CE, according to F.G. Kenyon, a manuscript keeper at the British Museum. However, until the discovery of numerous papyrus manuscripts in Egypt and the Dead Sea region in recent years, there was little evidence of papyrus codices, as papyrus requires a dry climate to survive.

Most striking is the fact that nearly all the Christian-era Bible manuscripts found on papyrus are in codex form, suggesting that the codex was regarded as especially suitable for Christian writings. This is in contrast to classical writings, which continued to be circulated in scrolls for a long time. A survey of pagan literature from the second century CE revealed only about 2.4% codices to rolls, with only one later manuscript of the Psalms in roll form. In contrast, all Biblical manuscripts assigned to the second century are codices.

Today, over a hundred and forty-four Bible codices on papyrus, some just fragments, written before the end of the fourth century, are scattered throughout museums and collections worldwide. This evidence suggests that Christians abandoned the roll form early on, in favor of the more versatile and practical codex format.

Second Century Bible Manuscripts: Determining the age of an ancient manuscript can be challenging, as very few dates are prominently displayed on the manuscript. However, paleography, the art of studying the writing, form, and style of a manuscript, can provide clues to its age. Minute features such as spaces between words, punctuation, and abbreviations can help experts date a manuscript to within forty or fifty years. Tables of typical letters have been drawn up from non-literary papyri, such as receipts, letters, petitions, and leases, that give exact dates and provide a good basis for comparison.

For example, the fragment of John's Gospel known as P[52] has distinctive features such as a hook or flourish added to some strokes, certain marks omitted, a special type of cross-stroke, and rounded letters that are all typical of early second-century writers. While not all experts agree, most of them have assigned two dozen papyrus codices to the second century CE based on paleography.

These early Greek New Testament papyri and Septuagint Greek version of the Hebrew Scriptures are recognized internationally and given numbers on the Gregory-von Dobschütz and Rahlfs lists, respectively. Each manuscript also bears a collection name and number to identify where it was found or to whom it belongs. These second-century codices are of great importance due to their early date and early codex form.

Making a Codex: When examining early codices, several interesting features can be noticed. Early codices were often made up of one enormous quire, or a group of sheets folded together, resulting in narrow columns of writing compared to the wider outer leaves. However, it was later found that quires consisting of four or five sheets, or eight to ten leaves, were more convenient.

Different methods of laying down the sheets reveal personal preferences. Each sheet consists of two layers of papyrus fiber glued together crosswise, so the side showing the horizontal layer is known as the recto, while the side displaying the vertical layer of fibers is the verso. The method of laying down the sheets would alter the appearance when the codex was opened. A recto page might face a verso page, but some might prefer to have recto facing recto and verso facing verso.

Some early codices with two narrow columns of writing to a page were likely copied from rolls with as little disarrangement of the original layout as possible. Conversely, when the back of an old roll containing an epitome of Livy was reused, an economical Christian copied from a codex of Hebrews and even inserted the page numbers. Such a reused roll is called an opisthograph. These factors reveal the personal preferences and practical considerations of those making codices.

Why the Codex Was Preferred: The codex, or book format, was preferred over the traditional roll for several reasons. First, the codex allowed for convenient compilation of texts, such as putting all four Gospels in one book, which would not be practical as a single roll due to its length. Additionally, the codex allowed for quick reference to specific texts, which was important to early Christians who used their Scriptures extensively. Even pocket-sized codices have been discovered, demonstrating the value of portability.

Another benefit of the codex was its protection of the inspired books of Scripture. When several of Paul's epistles were bound together in one codex, it established a link between the various writings and made it more difficult for unrecognized works to be inserted into the collection. The adoption of the codex for the Septuagint version of the Hebrew Scriptures also shows that it was frequently used and not considered inferior to newer writings.

The universal use of the codex in Christian circles in the second century suggests that its adoption must have gone back to the first century. This could explain the loss of the ending of Mark's Gospel, which could have been lost with the last leaf of a codex, whereas in a roll, the beginning would be more likely to suffer damage. Additionally, the codex was cheaper, as both sides of the papyrus sheet were used. These factors demonstrate why the codex was preferred and became the dominant book format over the traditional roll.

As the Greek New Testament began to take shape, it is possible to imagine the scene. Matthew, known for his meticulous record-keeping as a tax collector, likely continued this habit when he began writing his Gospel. His notes may have initially been made in a parchment notebook, which would then be compiled into a codex. As other Gospels were completed, they would be added to Matthew's Gospel to form a collection.

As demand for copies of the Gospels grew, the codex format would become more prevalent. Copies would be widely circulated, with pocket codices making it possible for traveling ministers like Paul, Timothy, and Titus to carry the Scriptures with them. Upon returning to congregations, these ministers would likely commend those using the newly received codices while still encouraging those using the traditional roll format.

The prevalence of the second-century codex provides important insights into the early Christian community. Firstly, it supports the authenticity of the Bible as the gap between the time of the apostles and the earliest surviving manuscripts is greatly reduced. Secondly, it highlights the eagerness of early Christians to make the Scriptures widely available, reducing the cost of books so that everyone could have access to them. Lastly, the codex shows us how important it was for early Christians to be able to quickly and easily locate specific passages within their copies of the Scriptures. As modern believers, we can learn from the example of these enthusiastic early Christians by regularly studying our own Bibles and carefully examining them to confirm our faith.

END OF EXCURSION

The Transition from Scroll to Codex: Factors and Implications

The transition from the scroll to the codex format played a pivotal role in the preservation and transmission of the New Testament text. This shift involved a complex interplay of cultural, technological, and religious factors, ultimately leading to widespread adoption of the codex by early Christians and transforming the way texts were produced, circulated, and consumed in the ancient world.

1. **Technological Advancements**: The development of the codex format was facilitated by advances in the production of writing materials, such as papyrus and parchment. These materials were more durable and flexible than those used for scrolls, making them better suited for folding, binding, and cutting into the pages of a codex.

2. **Practical Benefits**: The codex format offered several practical advantages over the scroll, including easier navigation and reference, more efficient use of writing materials, and greater durability. These benefits made the codex an appealing option for early Christians, who were eager to share and study their sacred texts.

3. **The Role of Early Christians**: Early Christians played a crucial role in popularizing the codex format. They were among the first to recognize its potential for organizing, preserving, and disseminating their sacred writings, such as the Gospels and the letters of Paul. The adoption of the codex by early Christians helped to establish it as the standard format for Christian texts and contributed to its eventual acceptance by other religious and secular communities.

4. **Canonical Implications**: The transition from scroll to codex facilitated the compilation and organization of the various New Testament writings into a single volume. This process not only aided in the development of the New Testament canon but also contributed to the standardization and widespread dissemination of the text throughout the Christian world.

5. **Impact on Textual Scholarship**: The shift from scroll to codex had significant implications for the study of the New Testament text. The increased durability and accessibility of the codex format contributed to the preservation of many early Christian manuscripts, providing valuable resources for modern textual scholars. Furthermore, the codex format allowed for the development of more consistent and standardized methods of copying and transmitting the text, which can help scholars reconstruct the original wording of the New Testament and trace its textual history.

In conclusion, the transition from scroll to codex was a transformative event in the history of the New Testament text, driven by a combination of technological advancements, practical benefits, and the influence of early Christians. By embracing the codex format, early Christians played a crucial role in shaping the textual history of the New Testament and laid the groundwork for the development of the book as a cultural and technological innovation.

Other Book Forms: Tablets, Diptychs, and Collections

In addition to scrolls and codices, the ancient world saw the development and use of various other book forms for preserving and transmitting texts. These alternative formats played a role in shaping the textual history of the New Testament and provided insight into the diverse methods of communication and documentation during that time.

1. **Tablets**: Before the widespread use of papyrus and parchment, clay and wax tablets were commonly used for writing in the ancient world. These tablets were often made of wooden boards covered with a layer of wax, providing a reusable surface for inscribing text with a metal stylus. Tablets were used for various purposes, including recording notes, legal documents, and even literary works. While not directly related to the New Testament, tablets demonstrate the diversity of writing materials and methods available in the ancient world.

2. **Diptychs**: Diptychs consisted of two hinged tablets, typically made of wood, ivory, or metal, and often adorned with intricate carvings or artwork. These were used for various purposes, such as writing letters, creating lists, or commemorating important events. Some early Christian texts, like letters and homilies, might have been written on diptychs before being copied onto more permanent materials like parchment or papyrus.

3. **Collections**: In addition to individual book forms, collections of texts were also common in the ancient world. These could include sets of scrolls, bundles of codices, or even groups of inscriptions or ostraca. Collections played an essential role in the development and organization of the New Testament canon, as early Christians gathered and compiled various sacred writings into a coherent body of literature.

4. **The Relationship to the New Testament**: While the New Testament was primarily transmitted through scrolls and codices, these other book forms provide valuable context for understanding the broader literary and cultural environment of early Christianity. By examining these alternative formats, scholars can gain insight into the diverse methods of documentation, communication, and textual transmission available to early Christians, shedding light on the ways

in which the New Testament texts were produced, circulated, and preserved.

In summary, the diverse range of book forms, including tablets, diptychs, and collections, played a role in shaping the textual history of the New Testament and provided valuable context for understanding the literary and cultural environment of early Christianity. By examining these alternative formats, scholars can better appreciate the variety of methods and materials used for communication and documentation in the ancient world, offering important insights into the development and transmission of the New Testament texts.

Handwriting Styles

The Professional Bookhand: Some of the early manuscripts of the New Testament were produced by skilled professionals who were able to create literary texts. One such example is the Gospel codex known as P4+64+67, which displays expert calligraphy, paragraph markings, double-columns, and punctuation. The papyrologist C. H. Roberts noted that the text was divided into sections according to a system found in other manuscripts, indicating that this characteristic was not specific to Egypt. Other professionally produced manuscripts with skilled calligraphy include P30, P39, P46, P66, P75, P77+P103, P95, and P104. These manuscripts demonstrate the high level of skill and attention to detail required to create such works, and attest to the importance and value placed on the written word by early Christians. The existence of these manuscripts also confirms the authenticity of the biblical text and its importance in the early Christian community.

Reformed Documentary Hand: Many of the early New Testament manuscripts were written in what is called "the reformed documentary hand," indicating that the scribe knew they were working on a manuscript that was not just a legal document but a literary work. The style of writing exhibits a competent level of calligraphy that was likely the work of experienced scribes, whether Christian or not. It is assumed that these scribes may have been employed to make copies for individual Christians or for a Christian congregation. Among the extant papyri that predate 300 CE, there are at least fifteen "reformed documentary" New Testament manuscripts, according to estimation. These manuscripts include P1, P30, P32, P35, P38, P45, P52, P69, P87, P90, P100, P102, P108, P109, and P110.

Documentary Hand: It seems that a number of the earliest New Testament manuscripts were not produced by professionals in the book trade, but by people within communities who were used to writing documents. Manuscripts with a "documentary" hand are less uniform in appearance than those produced by professionals, with letters on each line not necessarily keeping an even line across the page. Documentary texts will often have larger letters at the beginning of each line or section, sporadic punctuation, numerical abbreviations, and spaces between words or groups of words.

Many of these manuscripts were likely produced by churchmen or women who had been trained in writing documents and then applied those skills to making copies of Scripture for specific individuals or for their congregations. It's possible that many of these scribes were church lectors, whose job was to keep copies of Scripture, make new ones as needed, and prepare the text for reading to the congregation.

Nearly half of the early New Testament papyri (27 in total) are "documentary," according to my study. These include P5, P13, P15+P16, P17, P20, P23, P27, P28, P29, P37, P47, P48, P49+65, P50, P53, P70, P80, P91, P92, P101, P106, P107, P108, P111, P113, and P114.

Common Hand: The "common" hand refers to a writing style that indicates the scribe had little to no formal training in writing Greek. It can be difficult to distinguish between a "documentary" hand and a "common" hand, but a common hand is usually more crude and less uniform in appearance. Examples of manuscripts produced in a common hand include P9, which contains a portion of 1 John, and P78, which is an amulet. Interestingly, many of the manuscripts containing the book of Revelation exhibit a common hand, such as P18, P24, and P98. It is unclear if this is simply a coincidence or if it indicates that Revelation was not being read in the churches and therefore not being copied by trained scribes.

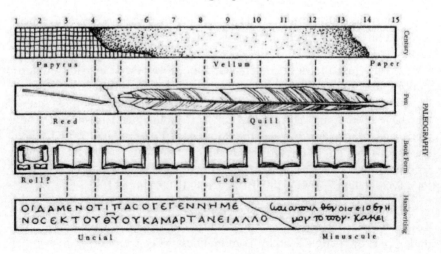

Uncial Script: The Early Majuscule Style

The development of different handwriting styles played a significant role in the transmission and preservation of the New Testament texts. One of the earliest and most significant writing styles employed in the copying of the Greek New Testament was the uncial script, which emerged as the predominant majuscule (or uppercase) style.

1. **Characteristics of Uncial Script**: Uncial script was characterized by its clear and distinct letterforms, written with a rounded, capital style. The letters were usually separated from each other and did not have connecting strokes or ligatures. This made the text easier to read, as each letter was distinct and stood on its own. Uncial script also lacked punctuation, word spacing, and diacritical marks, which were later added to the text by scholars to aid in reading and understanding.

2. **Development and Use**: Uncial script developed around the 3rd century CE and continued to be widely used until the 9th century CE. The script was especially popular among Christian scribes, who used it for copying biblical texts, including the Greek New Testament. The earliest and most important uncial manuscripts of the New Testament, such as Codex Vaticanus, Codex Sinaiticus, and Codex Alexandrinus, were written in this script.

3. **Significance for New Testament Textual Criticism**: The uncial script played a crucial role in the transmission and preservation of the New Testament texts. The script's clarity and distinct letterforms facilitated accurate copying, reducing the likelihood of transcriptional errors. Additionally, the uncial script's widespread use among early Christian scribes means that many of the oldest and most valuable New Testament manuscripts were written in this style. These manuscripts serve as vital sources for scholars engaged in textual criticism, helping to reconstruct the original text and trace the development of variant readings.

In conclusion, the uncial script was an essential handwriting style employed in the early transmission of the New Testament. Its clear and distinct letterforms facilitated accurate copying, and its widespread use among early Christian scribes resulted in the preservation of many important manuscripts. The study of uncial script and its use in New Testament manuscripts is crucial for understanding the development and transmission of the biblical text and remains a vital area of focus for textual criticism.

Minuscule Script: The Emergence of Lowercase Letters

The evolution of handwriting styles had a significant impact on the transmission and preservation of the New Testament texts. As the uncial script began to decline, a new writing style known as minuscule script emerged and became the primary script for Greek manuscripts from the 9th century CE onwards. The minuscule script introduced lowercase letters to the Greek alphabet and greatly influenced the way texts were copied and read.

1. **Characteristics of Minuscule Script**: Minuscule script is characterized by its smaller, more compact letterforms, which were written using a combination of uppercase (majuscule) and lowercase (minuscule) letters. The script utilized ligatures, connecting letters to form a continuous flow of text, resulting in a more efficient and faster writing style. Minuscule script also introduced word spacing, punctuation, and diacritical marks, making the text more accessible and easier to read.

2. **Development and Use**: Minuscule script developed around the 9th century CE and quickly gained popularity due to its efficiency and readability. The script became the standard for Greek manuscripts, including those of the New Testament. Notable minuscule manuscripts of the New Testament include Minuscule 1 (also known as Codex Basiliensis) and Minuscule 2 (also known as Codex Angelicus).

3. **Significance for New Testament Textual Criticism**: The minuscule script played a vital role in the transmission and preservation of the New Testament texts during the Byzantine period. Its efficient and readable nature allowed for the production of a large number of manuscripts, which increased the availability of the biblical texts to a broader audience. As a result, the majority of surviving New Testament manuscripts are written in minuscule script. These manuscripts serve as important sources for textual critics, enabling them to reconstruct the original text and identify the development of variant readings.

In summary, the minuscule script was a significant handwriting style in the transmission of the New Testament. Its efficiency and readability facilitated the production of numerous manuscripts and contributed to the widespread dissemination of biblical texts. The study of minuscule script and its use in New Testament manuscripts is essential for understanding the development and transmission of the biblical text and remains an important area of focus for textual criticism.

Cursive Script: A Faster Writing Style

Cursive script, also known as cursiva, is another handwriting style that emerged in the ancient world and played a role in the transmission of the New Testament texts. This script was developed primarily for speed and efficiency, and it was often used for everyday writing, including personal letters, business transactions, and informal documents.

1. Characteristics of Cursive Script: Cursive script is characterized by its rapid, flowing letterforms that are connected to each other, allowing the scribe to write quickly without lifting the writing instrument from the surface. The script exhibits a high degree of ligatures, abbreviations, and shorthand symbols, which further increased its writing speed. However, this efficiency came at the cost of legibility, making cursive script more challenging to read than other handwriting styles such as uncial or minuscule script.

2. Development and Use: Cursive script developed alongside other handwriting styles, such as uncial and minuscule scripts, and was used predominantly for informal and everyday writing purposes. It was not commonly used for copying the New Testament texts, but some cursive manuscripts have been identified, such as 𝔓66 (Papyrus 66), a fragmentary copy of the Gospel of John dating from around the 2nd century CE. This manuscript is written in a semi-cursive script, exhibiting both cursive and formal letterforms.

3. Significance for New Testament Textual Criticism: Although cursive script is not as prevalent in New Testament manuscripts as uncial or minuscule script, it still offers valuable insights into the transmission and preservation of the biblical texts. The study of cursive script can help textual critics understand the writing practices, scribal habits, and abbreviations used in the ancient world, which can aid in identifying and evaluating variant readings in the New Testament manuscripts.

In conclusion, cursive script is an important handwriting style in the study of the New Testament's textual history. Although it was not as widely used for copying biblical texts, its use in certain manuscripts and everyday writing offers insights into the scribal practices and the transmission of the New Testament. The study of cursive script remains a valuable area of focus for textual criticism, contributing to our understanding of the development and preservation of the biblical text.

Ligatures and Abbreviations: Space-saving Techniques

Ligatures and abbreviations are important aspects of ancient handwriting styles, including those used in the transmission of the New

Testament text. These techniques served as space-saving methods that allowed scribes to fit more content onto limited writing surfaces, such as papyrus, parchment, or ostraca.

1. **Ligatures**: A ligature is the combination of two or more letters into a single, connected character. Ligatures were employed to save space and increase writing speed by reducing the number of strokes needed to form each word. They are commonly found in various ancient scripts, including uncial, minuscule, and cursive writing styles. Ligatures can sometimes make reading ancient texts more difficult, as the combination of letters can alter the appearance of individual characters.

2. **Abbreviations**: Abbreviations were widely used in ancient manuscripts to conserve space on writing materials and to increase writing efficiency. They were especially common in the New Testament texts, where certain words or phrases appeared frequently. One notable example is the use of nomina sacra, sacred names or terms that were abbreviated in the manuscripts by writing the first and last letters of a word, followed by a horizontal line above the letters to indicate the abbreviation. Common examples of nomina sacra include abbreviations for words such as "God," "Jesus," "Christ," and "Lord."

3. **Significance for New Testament Textual Criticism**: The study of ligatures and abbreviations in the ancient handwriting styles is crucial for textual critics working with New Testament manuscripts. Understanding these space-saving techniques helps scholars to accurately decipher, transcribe, and analyze the text. Additionally, the analysis of ligatures and abbreviations can provide insights into the scribal habits, practices, and preferences of the scribes who copied the New Testament texts. This information can contribute to the process of evaluating and comparing different manuscripts and assessing the reliability of the transmitted text.

In summary, ligatures and abbreviations are essential aspects of ancient handwriting styles that played a crucial role in the transmission of the New Testament texts. The study of these space-saving techniques is vital for textual critics, as it helps to accurately read and analyze the manuscripts, providing valuable insights into the scribal practices and preferences of the ancient scribes. By understanding these techniques, textual critics can make more informed decisions when evaluating and comparing different manuscripts, ultimately contributing to our knowledge of the history and preservation of the New Testament text.

Decorative Elements and Illuminations: The Artistry of Manuscripts

While the primary purpose of New Testament manuscripts was to preserve and transmit the sacred text, the artistry and craftsmanship involved in their production were also significant. Decorative elements and illuminations added beauty, elegance, and visual impact to the manuscripts, demonstrating the reverence and devotion of the scribes and patrons who commissioned them.

1. **Decorative Elements**: Decorative elements in New Testament manuscripts could include ornamental designs, such as intricate patterns, flourishes, or borders that adorned the text. These embellishments often enhanced the appearance of the manuscript, making it more aesthetically pleasing and engaging. Decorative elements could also serve practical purposes, such as helping to organize the text by visually separating sections, chapters, or paragraphs.

2. **Illuminations**: Illuminated manuscripts are those that feature elaborate illustrations, often in gold, silver, or vibrant colors, which were intended to enhance the text and its meaning. These illuminations could depict scenes from the biblical narrative, portray religious figures, or represent symbolic imagery. Illuminated manuscripts were typically produced for wealthy patrons or religious institutions, as the materials and labor required for their creation were expensive and time-consuming. The level of skill and artistry involved in creating illuminations reflected the importance placed on the sacred text and its preservation.

3. **Significance for New Testament Textual Criticism**: The study of decorative elements and illuminations in New Testament manuscripts provides insight into the cultural, artistic, and religious contexts in which these texts were created. Examining these artistic features can help scholars to better understand the motivations and intentions of the scribes and patrons responsible for producing the manuscripts. Furthermore, the presence of unique decorative elements or illuminations can sometimes aid in the identification of specific scribal traditions or artistic schools, which can be useful for dating and attributing manuscripts.

In conclusion, decorative elements and illuminations in New Testament manuscripts represent the artistry and devotion that went into preserving and transmitting the sacred text. These artistic features not only added visual appeal to the manuscripts but also provided valuable context and meaning to the biblical narrative. The study of these elements is essential for textual critics, as it sheds light on the cultural, artistic, and religious influences that shaped the production and preservation of the New Testament text, ultimately enriching our understanding of its history and development.

Evolution of Handwriting Styles: Regional and Chronological Variations

The study of handwriting styles in New Testament manuscripts is an essential aspect of paleography, as it helps scholars to date, classify, and trace the development of the text through time and space. Handwriting styles in the New Testament manuscripts evolved over centuries, reflecting regional and chronological variations that offer valuable insights into the cultural, artistic, and linguistic contexts in which these texts were created.

1. **Regional Variations**: Throughout the history of New Testament textual transmission, different regions developed distinct handwriting styles due to geographical, cultural, and linguistic factors. For example, Byzantine minuscule script was prevalent in the Eastern Mediterranean, while Insular script was characteristic of manuscripts produced in the British Isles. Studying these regional variations can help scholars to trace the movement of manuscripts, identify scribal traditions, and understand the cultural influences that shaped the transmission of the New Testament text.

2. **Chronological Variations**: Over time, handwriting styles in New Testament manuscripts evolved, reflecting changes in artistic trends, writing materials, and tools. For instance, the transition from uncial to minuscule script occurred around the 9th century, coinciding with the rise of the Carolingian Renaissance and the spread of parchment as a writing material. These chronological variations can be crucial for dating manuscripts, as well as tracing the development of scribal practices and textual traditions over time.

3. **Interactions Between Regional and Chronological Variations**: Regional and chronological variations in handwriting styles often intersected and influenced one another. For example, the development of minuscule script in the Byzantine Empire eventually spread to other regions, where it was adapted and modified to suit local artistic and linguistic preferences. By analyzing these interactions, scholars can better understand the complex processes of cultural exchange and adaptation that shaped the transmission and preservation of the New Testament text.

In summary, the evolution of handwriting styles in New Testament manuscripts is a critical aspect of paleography that provides insight into the regional and chronological variations that influenced the text's development. By examining these variations, scholars can trace the movement of manuscripts, identify scribal traditions, and gain a deeper understanding of the cultural, artistic, and linguistic contexts that shaped the New Testament text. This knowledge is essential for textual critics, as it helps to illuminate the history and development of the sacred text, ultimately enriching our understanding of its origins and transmission.

Introduction to Paleography: The Art and Science of Deciphering Ancient Manuscripts

Paleography is the study of ancient handwriting, which involves the art and science of deciphering, analyzing, and understanding ancient manuscripts. It plays a crucial role in the field of New Testament textual criticism, as it aids scholars in determining the age, origin, and authenticity of manuscripts. By examining the scripts, styles, and materials used in ancient documents, paleographers can piece together the historical context and development of New Testament texts.

1. **Analyzing Handwriting Styles**: Paleographers closely examine the handwriting styles, letterforms, and other distinctive features in manuscripts to identify specific periods and regions. By studying the evolution and variations of writing styles, they can establish a relative chronology for the manuscripts and, in some cases, narrow down the possible dates of composition.

2. **Identifying Scribal Practices**: Scribes often had their unique habits, including spelling, punctuation, and abbreviations. Paleographers can identify individual scribes or scriptoria (writing centers) by recognizing these patterns, which can provide insight into the transmission and provenance of New Testament texts.

3. **Understanding Manuscript Materials and Techniques**: Analyzing the writing materials (such as papyrus, parchment, or ink) and techniques (like the use of pens, brushes, or chisels) can offer valuable information about the production and conservation of ancient manuscripts. It can also reveal the social, economic, and cultural context of the time and place in which the texts were created.

4. **Deciphering Damaged or Obscured Texts**: Paleographers employ various methods to read damaged or faded manuscripts, including the use of advanced imaging technology, chemical treatments, or digital enhancements. By recovering lost or hidden

text, they can contribute to a more accurate reconstruction of the original New Testament writings.

5. **Assessing Authenticity and Reliability**: Paleographical analysis can help scholars differentiate between authentic manuscripts and forgeries or determine the reliability of a text by evaluating the competence and care of the scribe. This is particularly important when comparing different manuscript traditions or weighing the value of variant readings in the process of textual criticism.

In conclusion, paleography plays an essential role in the study of the New Testament by providing a deeper understanding of the manuscripts' historical context, development, and transmission. By deciphering ancient manuscripts, paleographers contribute invaluable information to the field of New Testament textual criticism, helping scholars reconstruct the most accurate text possible and understand the rich history of these sacred writings.

The Development of Greek Script: From Uncials to Severe Style

There are four distinct styles of handwriting used in early Christianity that are relevant to New Testament paleography. These styles include the Roman Uncial, Biblical Uncial, Decorated Rounded Uncial, and Severe (or Slanted) style. It should be noted, however, that these styles are not always clearly distinct, and there is often a blending of features between them. Additionally, it is difficult to pinpoint exactly when each style emerged, as there was a lot of overlap and evolution between them. Nonetheless, each style has its own unique features and a general chronology for their popularity and eventual disappearance.

The Emergence and Characteristics of the Roman Uncial Script

Paleography scholars have determined that the Roman Uncial script emerged shortly after the conclusion of the Ptolemaic period in 30 BC. Consequently, the early Roman Uncial can be traced back to around 30 BC, and its usage can be observed throughout the first two to three centuries of the Common Era. When examining the Roman Uncial script, one can identify specific attributes that set it apart from the manuscripts of the preceding Ptolemaic period.

In contrast to the Ptolemaic manuscripts, the Roman Uncial script exhibits a more rounded and smoother appearance in the formation of its letters. Additionally, the script tends to be larger in size. Another distinguishing feature of the Roman Uncial script is the presence of decorative serifs in several, but not all, letters. This is in contrast to the Decorated Rounded style, which focuses on ensuring that the decorations are uniformly rounded and abundant.

The Evolution from Roman Uncial to Biblical Uncial The Roman Uncial script is considered a precursor to the Biblical Uncial script, with the latter evolving from the former. Consequently, some paleographers may use the terms "Roman Uncial" and "Biblical Uncial" interchangeably. However, there are subtle differences between the two styles. The Biblical Uncial script typically displays minimal or no decoration and exhibits noticeable shading, which is characterized by the deliberate alternation of thick and thin pen-strokes in relation to the angle at which the pen contacts the writing surface.

An Exemplary Roman Uncial Manuscript: P46 Sir Frederic Kenyon, a renowned paleographer, identified P46 as a prime example of a New Testament manuscript written in the Roman Uncial script. According to Kenyon, the editor of the editio princeps, the letters in P46 demonstrate an early Roman Uncial style characterized by well-formed lettering consistent with the Roman period. For further information, refer to the discussion on P46 in a future chapter.

The Biblical Uncial Handwriting Style (AKA Biblical Majuscule)

The Biblical Uncial, also known as the Biblical Majuscule, is a type of handwriting characterized by large, separate, unconnected uncial letters. This term was first used by Grenfell and Hunt to describe the handwriting found in specific biblical texts but was later extended to include any manuscript exhibiting this particular style, regardless of content. In this form of writing, letters maintain a bilinear appearance, conforming to imaginary upper and lower lines, and there is a purposeful alternation of thick vertical and thin horizontal strokes. Rectangular strokes exhibit right-angled shapes, while circular letters are truly circular rather than oval. The Biblical Uncial style does not include ligatures (connected letters) or ornamentation at the end of strokes, such as serifs and blobs.

This writing style began to emerge in the first century CE. Some paleographers have identified P. Herculaneum 1457, a manuscript from Herculaneum dated before 79 CE, as an early example of the Biblical Uncial. Other notable instances of this style can be seen in P. London II 141, a document dated to 88 CE, and in several Roman Uncial manuscripts from the second century. G. Cavallo, in his extensive work Richerche sulla Maiuscola Biblica, argues that the Biblical Uncial style took definitive shape in the middle to late second century CE, based on the dating of several significant manuscripts.

Early New Testament manuscripts written in the Biblical Uncial style include P4+64+67, P30, P35, P39, P40, P70, P95, 0162, and 0189. Each of these manuscripts exhibits the key features of the Biblical Uncial style, such as bilinearity, the alternation of thick and thin strokes, and the absence of ligatures and ornamentation. As paleographers continue to study these texts and their handwriting, our understanding of the development and significance of the Biblical Uncial style in the broader context of ancient manuscript production will only deepen.

Decorated Rounded Uncial: A Handwriting Style in Early Christian Manuscripts

The Decorated Rounded Uncial is a distinct handwriting style that was prevalent during the early period of the Christian church. This style features serifs or decorative roundels at the end of each vertical stroke. Some scholars, such as Schubart, believe that this style dates back to the last century of the Ptolemaic period (first century BC) and lasted until the end of the first century CE. Others, like Turner, argue that the style extended to the end of the second century, and possibly even into the early third century.

The debate over whether the Decorated Rounded Uncial represents a single style or a single feature of multiple styles continues, but the fact remains that manuscripts featuring this style of handwriting are easily recognizable. Several existing examples of dated manuscripts (i.e., manuscripts with specific dates) showcasing this style fall within the period of 100 BC to 150 CE.

A notable concentration of dated manuscripts featuring the Decorated Rounded Uncial style can be found between 100 BC and 100 CE, with evidence suggesting that this time frame may extend to 150 CE. However, there are few dated documents beyond 150 CE that display this style. E. G. Turner points to P. Oxyrhynchus 3093 (dated 217 CE) and P. Oxyrhynchus 3030 (dated 207 or 211 CE) as rare late examples of this style.

While the Decorated Rounded Uncial may have been more common in the late first century and the second century, many scholars have hesitated to assign these dates to New Testament manuscripts featuring the style. Nevertheless, several New Testament manuscripts displaying the Decorated Rounded Uncial style, such as P32, P66, P90, and P104, likely belong to the period prior to 150 CE.

In conclusion, the Decorated Rounded Uncial is an important handwriting style that significantly influenced early Christian manuscripts. By examining the historical context and time frames of these manuscripts, scholars can gain valuable insights into the development and transmission of early Christian texts.

The Development and Characteristics of the Severe Style in Greek Handwriting

Over time, formal Greek handwriting experienced a transition from its traditional upright form during the Ptolemaic and Roman periods to a more slanted style. When the handwriting is upright, it features right angles and rounded curves. However, when the handwriting is slanted, the broad letters emphasize angularity, and the curves resemble ellipses. This style also combines both narrow and broad letters. As such, Turner referred to it as Formal Mixed, while Schubart named it Strenge Stil, or Severe Style. Turner believed that no effort was made in documents to differentiate between broad and narrow letters before Hadrian's age (117-138 CE). Nonetheless, G. Cavallo's work, "Libri scritture scribi a Ercolano," contradicts this view by demonstrating that documents exhibiting wide and narrow letters were present in Herculaneum prior to the second century.

Several second-century, third-century, and early fourth-century manuscripts with established dates showcase the Severe Style:

1. **P. Giss. 3 (117 CE)**: Celebratory libretto for Hadrian's accession, displaying the broad, slanting style that later became popular.

2. **P. Michigan 3 (second half of the second century)**: Dated solidly due to the verso's documentary text with a 190 CE date.

3. **P. Oxyrhynchus 2341 (202 CE)**: A legal proceeding record with a certain date.

4. **P. Florentine II. 108 (circa 200 CE)**: A manuscript of Homer's Iliad III, part of the Heroninos archive, dating to around 260 AD, with literary texts written approximately 50 years earlier.

5. P. **Rylands I. 57 (circa 200 CE)**: A Demosthenes manuscript, De Corona, also from the Heroninos archive.

6. **P. Florentine II. 259 (circa 260 CE)**: A letter in the Heroninos archive written in a professional hand resembling the common literary style of the time.

7. **P. Oxyrhynchus 2098 (first half of the third century)**: A manuscript featuring Herodotus, book 7, with a verso land survey dated to Gallienus' reign (253-268 CE).

8. **P. Oxyrhynchus 1016 (early to middle third century)**: A difficult-to-date Phaedres manuscript, written on the verso of a land register with an uncertain Roman emperor's 13th year.

9. **P. Oxyrhynchus 223 (early third century)**: A Homer manuscript (Iliad V), written on the verso of a document with Oxyrhynchite provenance, dated 186 CE.

10. **P. Herm. Rees 5 (circa 325 CE)**: A letter addressed to a known scholasticus (government official) from the 320s of the fourth century.

Early New Testament manuscripts that display the Severe (slanted) style include P13, P45, P48, P49, P110, and P115.

Dating New Testament Manuscripts: Methods and Challenges

Determining the Age of Manuscripts: Criteria and Considerations

Before delving into the identification of the earliest New Testament manuscripts, it is essential to establish the criteria used for dating these manuscripts. These criteria include archaeological evidence, codicology, comparative palaeography, and the evolution of nomina sacra. Among these, comparative palaeography is the most intricate, warranting a more in-depth discussion. In this context, the focus will be on determining the dates for literary texts based on dated documentary manuscripts and examining comparative morphology, which refers to the study of comparable handwriting styles.

1. **Archaeological Evidence**: This criterion involves assessing the physical context in which a manuscript was discovered, such as the location, associated artifacts, and stratigraphic information. These factors can provide valuable information about the manuscript's age.

2. **Codicology**: Codicology is the study of ancient manuscripts as physical objects, including their construction, materials, and format. Examining these aspects can reveal clues about the time and place of a manuscript's creation, as well as its cultural and historical context.

3. **Comparative Palaeography**: Comparative palaeography is the study of ancient handwriting styles and their development over time. By comparing the script of a manuscript with other known examples from various periods, scholars can narrow down the time frame in which it was likely written. This approach comprises two main aspects:

a. **Dating Literary Texts Based on Documentary Manuscripts**: Literary texts can be challenging to date because they often lack explicit historical or chronological context. However, scholars can estimate their age by comparing them with documentary manuscripts that have known dates, such as legal documents or official records. By identifying similarities in handwriting styles between the literary and documentary texts, researchers can establish a more accurate date for the literary work.

b. **Comparative Morphology**: This aspect of comparative palaeography involves analyzing and comparing the specific forms and shapes of letters used in different manuscripts. By identifying similarities and differences in handwriting styles across various texts, scholars can trace the evolution of these styles and establish a more precise chronology for the manuscripts in question.

4. **Evolution of Nomina Sacra**: Nomina sacra refers to the abbreviated forms of sacred names used in early Christian manuscripts. These abbreviations evolved over time, with distinct patterns emerging during specific periods. By analyzing the nomina sacra used in a manuscript, scholars can gain insight into its age and context.

In conclusion, determining the age of ancient manuscripts is a complex task that requires careful consideration of various criteria, including archaeological evidence, codicology, comparative palaeography, and the evolution of nomina sacra. By taking these factors into account, scholars can arrive at a more accurate and comprehensive understanding of the historical context and chronology of these important texts.

Assessing Manuscript Ages through Archaeological Evidence and Other Criteria

The initial method employed in dating a manuscript involves examining archaeological evidence. External and circumstantial factors can aid scholars in determining the age of manuscripts. For instance, the terminus ante quem (latest possible date) for the Herculaneum manuscripts is 79 CE, corresponding to Mount Vesuvius' eruption, while for the Dead Sea Scrolls, it is 70 CE, when the Qumran caves were abandoned. As Scanlin notes, the

Qumran community was destroyed during the Jewish war and Roman invasion around 70 CE. Assuming that the Dead Sea Scrolls discovered near the Qumran settlement were products of this community, the latest possible date for the manuscripts hidden in the nearby caves would be 70 CE. However, it is important to acknowledge that not all Dead Sea Scroll manuscripts may have originated from the Qumran community, as the caves could have been utilized by other Jews to hide manuscripts at different times. Nevertheless, very few scholars would date any of the Dead Sea Scrolls beyond the mid-first century AD, based on both archaeological and paleographical grounds.

The New Testament papyrus manuscript P4+P64+P67 cannot be dated later than 200 CE, as it was used in strips (potentially as binding) for a third-century codex of Philo. A certain period must be allowed for a well-crafted codex to have been used extensively before being torn up and repurposed as binding. The Gospel harmony manuscript 0212 cannot be dated later than 256 CE and is likely dated around 230 CE, as it was found in the filling of an embankment constructed in 256 CE. A nearby Christian house, which existed from 222 to 235 CE, was destroyed when the embankment was built.

Regrettably, most manuscripts cannot be dated based on archaeological evidence alone, as the surrounding circumstances are often unclear or ambiguous. Therefore, when dating the majority of biblical manuscripts, paleographers rely on additional criteria, such as codicology and comparative palaeography, which also encompass comparative stylistics and morphology.

Codicology and Its Influence on Manuscript Dating

Codicology, as explored in a previous chapter, refers to the study of codices, which were in use before the end of the first century AD. The codex was the exclusive book form employed by Christians for copying biblical texts. As such, any New Testament codex manuscript could date as far back as the late first century. The understanding of the codex's dating grew more refined during the latter half of the twentieth century, as an increasing number of papyri were published. Paleographers in the early twentieth century often regarded the codex as a late second-century or early third-century invention, which led them to hesitate in dating Christian manuscripts earlier than the third century. This was the case with Grenfell and Hunt, who assigned numerous third- and fourth-century dates to Christian Old Testament and New Testament manuscripts, despite the handwriting clearly belonging to an earlier era.

Advancements in knowledge about the codex's origins have prompted paleographers to reconsider and redate many of these manuscripts to earlier periods. This redating process is examined on a manuscript-by-manuscript basis in the following discussion.

Comparative Paleography: A Comprehensive Overview

Comparative paleography plays a crucial role in dating biblical manuscripts, which are primarily literary texts. Unlike documentary texts, which often contain explicit or implicit dates, literary manuscripts rarely, if ever, bear dates. Thus, paleographers rely on comparative analysis to determine the dates of these manuscripts.

One method involves examining literary texts written on the recto (the primary, higher-quality side of a papyrus or parchment leaf) with dated documentary texts on the verso (the secondary side). The date of the documentary text serves as the terminus ante quem (latest possible date) for the literary text. The time difference between the two could be significant, as the literary text would have likely been in use for an extended period before being repurposed for documentary use.

Conversely, if a literary text is written on the verso of a dated documentary text, the date of the documentary text serves as the terminus post quem (earliest possible date) for the literary text. The time between the two is typically shorter, as the document would have been deemed less valuable and quickly repurposed for literary use.

The primary method for dating New Testament manuscripts is comparing their handwriting with that of dated documentary texts. A secondary method involves comparing the handwriting of undated literary texts with literary manuscripts bearing dates due to their association with documentary texts on either the recto or verso. Since several New Testament papyrus manuscripts feature a documentary hand, it is possible to find comparable dated documentary manuscripts.

While dating literary texts by comparing them to other literary texts involves a degree of subjectivity, it remains an essential practice in paleography. The proposed date for the earliest New Testament manuscripts is often based on a comparative analysis of various dated documentary manuscripts and literary texts. However, factors such as the scribe's age or the time of a particular writing style's emergence can influence the date of a manuscript, potentially altering it by 25 to 50 years.

To account for such factors, it is advisable to date manuscripts within a 50-year range, offering both an early and a later date. Despite the inherent subjectivity in comparative analysis, paleographers seek to determine a manuscript's date by employing comparative morphology—a study of letter forms. This approach focuses on the overall resemblance between texts rather than matching individual letter forms, as was the practice in the past.

Comparative Stylistics: A Basic Analysis

Paleographers also employ comparative stylistics to date manuscripts by identifying the prevalent handwriting style during a specific time period. By comparing a manuscript to others with established dates, a paleographer can determine whether the manuscript exhibits early or late features of that period. In the following discussion, we will examine four distinct styles: Roman Uncial, Biblical Uncial, Decorated Rounded, and Severe (Slanting) Style. Several Christian manuscripts from both the Old Testament and New Testament display one of these styles.

Renowned papyrologists like Roberts and Turner have identified scribal tendencies during the first three centuries AD. They note that scribes in the first and second centuries tended to align their letters with an imaginary top line. Most bookhands exhibit bilinearity, striving to align letters with both imaginary top and bottom lines. Slanting handwriting emerged in the second century, while other second-century features include the final nu on a line replaced with an extending overbar over the last letter, a small omicron in documentary hands becoming prominent in third-century literary hands, and angular letters in the late second and early third centuries. There was also a tendency for documentary scribes to enlarge the first letter of each line or each new section in documentary and Greek biblical manuscripts from the first century AD onwards.

Additional Features for Dating Manuscripts: Paleographers may consider ink color when estimating a manuscript's date. Lustrous black ink, or carbon ink, is typically earlier than brown ink, which often derives from an iron salt or other chemical compound and usually indicates a date post-300 CE. The distinction between black and brown ink is significant for dating P15 and P16. Meanwhile, metallic ink typically suggests a later date, though P. Oxyrhynchus 2269, written in metallic ink, is dated 269 CE.

Turner also identified another feature that emerged in the early third century: the use of a separating apostrophe between double consonants. Some paleographers have taken this observation as fact, using it to date manuscripts with this feature as post-200 CE. However, it is important to consider that the presence of this specific feature could actually indicate an earlier date for its emergence, rather than redating the manuscript itself.

For instance, the Egerton Gospel, initially dated by many scholars to around 150 CE, should maintain that date despite the presence of the separating apostrophe. Similarly, the date for P52 should remain as early

324

second century. Other manuscripts dated before 200 CE also exhibit the apostrophe or hook between double consonants, such as BGU iii 715.5 (101 CE), P. Petaus 86 (= P. Michigan 6871) (185 CE), SPP xxii 3.22 (second century), and P. Berol. 9570 + P. Rylands 60 (dated by the editors of the editio princeps to around 200, and by Cavallo to around 50). These examples serve as further evidence that the presence of this specific feature could predate the early third century.

Evolution of Nomina Sacra and Dating New Testament Manuscripts

The nomina sacra, or sacred names, underwent an evolutionary process. Initially, the divine names Kurios (Lord), Iesous (Jesus), Christos (Christ), and Theos (God) were given special written representations. As will be discussed later, the divine title Pneuma (Spirit) was also included early in the textual transmission process. Other early nomina sacra included Stauros (cross) and Stauromai (crucify). Over time, additional nomina sacra were incorporated, such as Huios (Son), Pater (Father), Anthropos (man), Israel, Ierosalem (Jerusalem), and Ouranos (heaven).

One might assume that fewer nomina sacra indicate an earlier manuscript. T. C. Skeat, for instance, used this rationale to date P4+64+67 to the second century. However, the second-century manuscript P66 contains more nomina sacra, similar to those found in the Chester Beatty VI, dated to the early to mid-second century. Hunger used the similarity of nomina sacra in P66 and Chester Beatty VI to argue for P66's second-century date.

English Meaning	Greek Word	Nominative (Subject)	Genitive (Possessive)
God	Θεός	Θ̄Σ̄	Θ̄Ȳ
Lord	Κύριος	Κ̄Σ̄	Κ̄Ȳ
Jesus	Ἰησοῦς	Ῑ̄Σ̄	Ῑ̄Ȳ
Christ/Messiah	Χριστός	Χ̄Σ̄	Χ̄Ȳ
Son	Υἱός	Ῡ̄Σ̄	Ῡ̄Ȳ
Spirit/Ghost	Πνεῦμα	Π̄Ν̄Ᾱ	Π̄Ν̄Σ̄
David	Δαυίδ	Δ̄ᾹΔ̄	
Cross/Stake	Σταυρός	Σ̄Τ̄Σ̄	Σ̄Τ̄Ȳ
Mother	Μήτηρ	Μ̄Η̄Ρ̄	Μ̄Η̄Σ̄
God Bearer i.e. Mother of God	Θεοτόκος	Θ̄Κ̄Σ̄	Θ̄Κ̄Ȳ
Father	Πατήρ	Π̄Η̄Ρ̄	Π̄Ρ̄Σ̄
Israel	Ἰσραήλ	Ῑ̄Η̄Λ̄	
Savior	Σωτήρ	Σ̄Η̄Ρ̄	Σ̄Ρ̄Σ̄
Human being/Man	Ἄνθρωπος	ᾹΝ̄Ο̄Σ̄	ᾹΝ̄Ο̄Ȳ
Jerusalem	Ἰερουσαλήμ	Ῑ̄Λ̄Η̄Μ̄	
Heaven/Heavens	Οὐρανός	Ō̄ῩΝ̄Ο̄Σ̄	Ō̄ῩΝ̄Ο̄Ῡ

Using nomina sacra to date New Testament manuscripts is challenging because their evolution began in the first century, possibly when the New Testament books were first written, and continued into the second century. By the mid-second century, many divine names were represented as nomina sacra. Some names were consistently written as nomina sacra, while others, like Son and Father, were inconsistently represented in the same manuscript. This inconsistency suggests an ongoing evolutionary process for these titles, which became more fixed as nomina sacra in the third century.

Nomina Sacra Mark 1.1 Codex Sinaiticus

For instance, the second-century manuscript P4+64+67 does not use nomina sacra for Son and Father. In other notable second-century manuscripts, such as P46, P66, and P75, "Son" and "Father" are sometimes written as nomina sacra and other times not. In most third-century manuscripts, these titles are consistently treated as nomina sacra. Consequently, a manuscript with inconsistent representation of Father and Son or without nomina sacra for these titles should be considered for a second-century date, such as P45.

Nomina Sacra Mark 1.1 Codex Vaticanus

Another example is P46, which displays both nomina sacra and full written forms for all names of the Trinity (Father, Son, and Spirit). Notably, the scribe did not consistently use the nomen sacrum for Pneuma (Spirit) as expected. This suggests that the title was not yet fixed as a nomen sacrum when P46 was created and may indicate an early date for the manuscript.

Additionally, the suspended and short contracted forms likely preceded the longer contracted form. The question remains whether the fuller form developed later or concurrently with the shorter form. Some scholars believe the suspended form of Iesous (Jesus), IH, was the earliest, but this is uncertain.

In conclusion, using nomina sacra forms to date manuscripts is challenging. However, the presence or absence of specific nomina sacra and fluctuations in usage within a manuscript (as seen in P46) can provide valuable insights for dating purposes.

The Role of Paleography in Textual Criticism: Establishing Manuscript Relationships

Paleography, the study of ancient handwriting, plays a crucial role in textual criticism, the field of analyzing and evaluating the manuscripts of a text to establish its most accurate and reliable version. In the context of biblical studies, textual criticism involves examining the thousands of handwritten copies of biblical texts to reconstruct the original text as closely as possible. Paleography is essential in this process for several reasons:

1. **Dating Manuscripts**: One of the primary objectives of paleography is to date manuscripts based on their handwriting styles. By analyzing the evolution of letter shapes, ligatures, punctuation, and other scribal features, paleographers can estimate the age of a manuscript. Accurate dating of manuscripts is crucial for textual criticism, as it helps scholars establish a chronological order and determine which manuscripts are closer to the original text.

2. **Identifying Scribes and Scriptoria**: Paleography enables scholars to identify the scribes who copied manuscripts or the scriptoria (writing centers) where they were produced. Analyzing specific scribal habits, such as spelling tendencies, letter formations, and

decorative elements, can reveal connections between different manuscripts. Identifying scribes and scriptoria helps textual critics understand the transmission of texts and trace the lineage of various manuscript families.

3. **Establishing Manuscript Relationships**: Paleography can uncover relationships between manuscripts by highlighting similarities in handwriting styles, layouts, and other scribal features. These similarities may suggest that two or more manuscripts share a common ancestor or belong to the same textual tradition. Establishing manuscript relationships is essential for creating a stemma (family tree) of the manuscripts, which allows textual critics to reconstruct the original text more accurately.

4. **Detecting Corrections and Alterations**: Paleographers can identify corrections, alterations, or additions made by scribes or later editors by examining the manuscript's handwriting. These changes can offer insights into the textual history and the scribes' understanding of the text. Identifying such alterations aids textual critics in determining which readings are more likely to be original and which are later modifications.

5. **Evaluating Manuscript Authenticity**: Paleography can help determine the authenticity of a manuscript. Forgeries or modern reproductions may exhibit anachronistic handwriting features or other inconsistencies that reveal their true nature. By analyzing the handwriting of a manuscript, paleographers can confirm or disprove its authenticity, ensuring that textual critics only work with genuine manuscripts in their analysis.

6. **Contributing to the Critical Apparatus**: The critical apparatus is an essential tool for textual critics, presenting variant readings from different manuscripts and providing information about their sources. Paleography contributes to the apparatus by offering detailed descriptions of the manuscripts' handwriting, enabling textual critics to make informed decisions about the weight and reliability of specific readings.

In summary, paleography plays a vital role in textual criticism by dating manuscripts, identifying scribes and scriptoria, establishing manuscript relationships, detecting corrections and alterations, evaluating manuscript authenticity, and contributing to the critical apparatus. Through these functions, paleography enables textual critics to reconstruct the original text more accurately and gain a deeper understanding of the textual history and transmission.

Analyzing Scribal Habits and Tendencies: Insights into the Transmission of the Text

Textual criticism, the discipline of studying and evaluating the manuscripts of a text to establish its most accurate and reliable version, relies heavily on understanding the habits and tendencies of the scribes who copied these manuscripts. By analyzing scribal habits, textual critics can gain valuable insights into the transmission of the text, manuscript relationships, and the reliability of specific readings. This essay will discuss various aspects of scribal habits and tendencies and their significance in the field of textual criticism.

Scribal Tendencies: An Overview

Scribes were responsible for manually copying texts before the invention of the printing press. During the process of copying, scribes could introduce unintentional errors or deliberate changes to the text. Some of the common scribal habits and tendencies include:

1. **Spelling and Orthography**: Scribes often had personal preferences or regional variations in spelling, which can help identify their origin or distinguish between different manuscript traditions. Consistent spelling mistakes or deviations from standard orthography may indicate a scribe's level of education or familiarity with the language of the text.

2. **Letter Formation and Abbreviations**: The way a scribe forms individual letters or employs abbreviations can provide clues about their training, scriptorium, or the time period in which they were active. Certain letter formations or abbreviations can be characteristic of specific regions or periods, helping to date and localize a manuscript.

3. **Punctuation and Layout**: Punctuation marks and layout choices, such as paragraph divisions, line breaks, and indentation, can reveal a scribe's understanding of the text or their adherence to a specific textual tradition. Consistent patterns in punctuation and layout across multiple manuscripts may suggest a common ancestor or shared scribal training.

4. **Corrections and Alterations**: Scribes sometimes corrected their work or made alterations to the text, either while copying or after completing the manuscript. These corrections can offer insights into the textual history and the scribes' comprehension of the text.

5. **Marginal Annotations and Glosses**: Scribes occasionally added annotations, glosses, or other supplementary material in the margins or between lines of the text. These additions can provide valuable context for understanding the text or reveal the scribe's interpretation of specific passages.

6. **Decorative Elements and Colophons**: Scribes often included decorative elements, such as initial letters, illustrations, or ornamental borders, in their manuscripts. Colophons, or notes at the end of a manuscript containing information about the scribe, date, or place of production, can also provide essential information about the manuscript's history and provenance.

Significance of Scribal Habits in Textual Criticism

1. **Dating Manuscripts**: By examining scribal habits and tendencies, textual critics can approximate the age of a manuscript. Certain letter formations, abbreviations, or decorative elements can be characteristic of specific time periods, helping scholars to date manuscripts more accurately.

2. **Identifying Scribes and Scriptoria**: Analyzing scribal habits can reveal the identity of individual scribes or the scriptoria where they were trained or worked. Recognizing specific scribal tendencies across different manuscripts can help scholars trace the lineage of various manuscript families and better understand the transmission of the text.

3. **Establishing Manuscript Relationships**: Scribal habits and tendencies can highlight similarities between manuscripts, suggesting that they share a common ancestor or belong to the same textual tradition. Establishing manuscript relationships allows textual critics to create stemmata (family trees) of the manuscripts, contributing to a more accurate reconstruction of the original text.

4. **Evaluating the Reliability of Readings**: By examining scribal habits, textual critics can assess the reliability of specific readings. For instance, if a scribe consistently makes certain types of errors, a textual critic can determine whether a variant reading in a manuscript is likely the result of an error or an intentional alteration. Understanding the tendencies of a particular scribe can help scholars weigh the evidence for different readings and make more informed decisions about the most likely original text.

5. **Identifying Intentional Changes and Editorial Practices**: Analyzing scribal habits and tendencies can help distinguish between unintentional errors and deliberate changes to the text. Scribes sometimes made purposeful alterations to clarify, harmonize, or otherwise modify the text. Recognizing these intentional changes can provide valuable information about the editorial practices and theological perspectives of the scribes or their communities, which in turn can shed light on the broader context of the text's transmission and reception.

6. **Tracing the Evolution of Textual Features**: Scribal habits can offer insights into the development of specific textual features, such as punctuation, orthography, or abbreviations. By studying the patterns of these features in different manuscripts, scholars can trace their evolution over time and better understand the history of the text and its transmission.

7. **Understanding the Social and Cultural Context of Manuscript Production**: Studying scribal habits and tendencies can also reveal information about the social and cultural context of manuscript production. For example, analyzing the materials, techniques, or artistic styles employed by scribes can help scholars uncover information about the economic and cultural conditions of the time, the influence of different artistic and intellectual traditions, or the educational background of the scribes themselves.

In conclusion, the analysis of scribal habits and tendencies is a crucial aspect of textual criticism, providing valuable insights into the transmission of the text, the reliability of specific readings, and the relationships between manuscripts. By examining the various characteristics of scribes and their work, scholars can better understand the history, context, and evolution of the texts they study. This knowledge, in turn, allows textual critics to reconstruct the most accurate and reliable version of the text, ensuring its continued preservation and understanding for future generations.

Notable New Testament Manuscripts: A Paleographic Perspective

The study of New Testament manuscripts from a paleographic perspective allows scholars to analyze the physical features of these manuscripts, such as the style of handwriting, ink, and parchment, in order to date them and establish their relationships to one another. Throughout the centuries, numerous notable New Testament manuscripts have been discovered, each possessing unique characteristics that provide insights into the text's transmission and development. This essay will examine several of these significant manuscripts and their implications from a paleographic viewpoint.

1. **P52 (Rylands Library Papyrus P52)**: P52 is a small fragment of the Gospel of John, discovered in Egypt and dated to the first half of the 2nd century CE. It is currently the earliest known New Testament manuscript, with its early date offering important evidence for the early circulation of the Gospel of John. Paleographically, P52 is written in a script known as Roman uncial, characterized by its use of capital letters with minimal separation between words. Its early date and script type highlight the rapid spread of Christianity and its texts during the 2nd century.

2. **P66 (Bodmer Papyrus II)**: P66 is dated to 110-150 CE. It is a papyrus codex containing a large portion of the Gospel of John. It is an essential witness to the text, as it predates many other manuscripts containing the same gospel. Paleographically, P66 displays a professional and elegant style of Greek handwriting, showcasing the scribe's skill and the importance placed on the production of Christian texts. Its well-preserved state provides essential information on the text's early form and offers insights into the scribal practices of the time.

3. **P45 (Chester Beatty I)**: P45 is dated to 175-225 CE. It is a papyrus codex containing portions of the four canonical gospels and Acts of the Apostles. It is one of the earliest witnesses to the text of these books, offering a glimpse into the early stages of the New Testament canon. Paleographically, P45 exhibits a script known as severe (slanting) style, characterized by its slanted, angular letterforms. The scribe's use of this particular style suggests a high level of skill and emphasizes the manuscript's importance within the Christian community.

4. **P46 (Chester Beatty II)**: P46 is a papyrus codex from 110-150 CE, containing a majority of Paul's letters, making it one of the oldest and most extensive collections of these texts. Paleographically, P46 is written in a professional and elegant script, with carefully executed letterforms and ligatures. The high quality of the script indicates the value placed on the Pauline epistles and their role within the early Christian community.

5. **P75 (Bodmer Papyrus XIV–XV)**: P75 is a papyrus codex from 175-225 CE, containing substantial portions of the Gospels of Luke and John. It is considered one of the most important witnesses to

these texts, as it predates many other manuscripts and provides crucial information about their early form. Paleographically, P75 displays a careful and deliberate script, with the scribe taking great care to ensure the accuracy and legibility of the text. This attention to detail speaks to the importance of these gospels within the Christian community and the care taken to preserve them.

6. **Codex Sinaiticus (ℵ)**: Codex Sinaiticus, discovered in the 19th century at the Monastery of Saint Catherine in Sinai, is a 4th-century Greek codex (330-360 CE) that contains the earliest complete copy of the New Testament, as well as a substantial portion of the Greek Old Testament. Paleographically, Codex Sinaiticus is written in a script known as biblical uncial, characterized by its use of large, rounded capital letters and clear separation between words. The high quality of the script and the care taken in its production suggest the significant role that the codex played within the early Christian community. The Codex Sinaiticus is of immense value to textual critics, as it offers a complete and early witness to the New Testament text and sheds light on the development of the canon.

7. **Codex Vaticanus (B)**: Codex Vaticanus, housed in the Vatican Library, is another 4th-century Greek codex (300-330 CE), containing almost the entire Bible. Like Codex Sinaiticus, it is an essential witness to the text of the New Testament and the development of the canon. Paleographically, Codex Vaticanus is written in a script similar to that of Codex Sinaiticus, utilizing biblical uncial with well-executed and rounded letterforms. The elegance and care displayed in its production highlight the importance of the text to the Christian community of the time.

8. **Codex Alexandrinus (A)**: Codex Alexandrinus, now in the British Library, is a 5th-century Greek codex containing the entire Bible. It is considered one of the most important witnesses to the text of the New Testament, alongside Codex Sinaiticus and Codex Vaticanus. Paleographically, Codex Alexandrinus is written in a script known as decorated rounded style, which is characterized by its use of large, rounded letterforms with decorative elements. The style and quality of the script emphasize the manuscript's significance within the Christian tradition.

9. **Codex Bezae (D)**: Codex Bezae, housed in Cambridge University Library, is a 5th-century Greek and Latin diglot (dual-language) codex containing the Gospels and Acts of the Apostles. It is known for its unique and variant readings, providing valuable insights into the transmission and development of the New Testament text.

Paleographically, Codex Bezae is written in a script known as Latin uncial, characterized by its use of capital letters, decorative elements, and occasional ligatures. The bilingual nature of the manuscript and the care taken in its production underscore the significance of the text within the Christian community.

10. **Codex Ephraemi Rescriptus (C)**: Codex Ephraemi Rescriptus, housed in the Bibliothèque nationale de France, is a 5th-century Greek palimpsest (a manuscript in which the original text has been overwritten) containing portions of the Bible. The overwritten text includes substantial sections of the New Testament, making it an important witness to the early text. Paleographically, Codex Ephraemi Rescriptus is written in a script similar to that of Codex Sinaiticus and Codex Vaticanus, utilizing biblical uncial with rounded letterforms. The manuscript's status as a palimpsest highlights the challenges faced in preserving ancient texts and the lengths to which scribes went to conserve valuable materials.

In conclusion, the study of notable New Testament manuscripts from a paleographic perspective offers invaluable insights into the transmission, development, and preservation of the text. These manuscripts, ranging from small fragments like P52 to complete codices like Codex Sinaiticus, serve as essential witnesses to the early stages of the New Testament and provide a deeper understanding of the textual history and the evolution of the Christian canon. Furthermore, the analysis of scribal practices, handwriting styles, and the physical features of these manuscripts enables scholars to date them and establish relationships, ultimately enhancing our understanding of the rich and complex history of the New Testament.

The Intersection of Paleography, Codicology, and Papyrology: A Multidisciplinary Approach

The study of ancient manuscripts is a complex and multidimensional field, requiring the collaboration and integration of various disciplines to gain a comprehensive understanding of these invaluable historical resources. Three key disciplines that intersect in the study of ancient manuscripts are paleography, codicology, and papyrology. Each of these fields contributes its unique expertise and methodologies, allowing for a holistic analysis of the manuscripts, their contents, and the historical context in which they were produced.

1. **Paleography**: Paleography is the study of ancient and historical handwriting, focusing on the analysis of scripts, letterforms, and writing styles. Paleographers examine the physical features of a

manuscript, such as the type of script, the arrangement of text on the page, and the use of abbreviations or punctuation. Through these analyses, paleographers can establish the date and provenance of a manuscript, as well as determine the scribal habits and tendencies of its scribe. In addition, paleography plays a crucial role in the reconstruction of the text, as the identification of specific handwriting styles can help in establishing relationships between manuscripts and understanding the transmission of the text.

2. **Codicology**: Codicology is the study of the physical structure and material aspects of a manuscript, such as its binding, format, and layout. Codicologists analyze the materials used in the production of a manuscript, including the type of writing surface (e.g., parchment, papyrus, or paper), the ink, and the techniques employed in its creation. These analyses can provide insights into the historical context of a manuscript, its function within the community, and the socio-economic status of its patron or owner. Moreover, codicology contributes to our understanding of the development and evolution of the book as a physical object, including its transition from scroll to codex format and the various binding techniques used over time.

3. **Papyrology**: Papyrology is the study of ancient texts written on papyrus; a writing material made from the pith of the papyrus plant. Papyrologists focus on deciphering and interpreting papyri, which often contain literary, documentary, or administrative texts from the ancient world. Papyri are valuable sources of information on various aspects of ancient life, such as religion, law, administration, and daily life. Papyrology, as a discipline, shares some similarities with paleography and codicology, as it also involves the analysis of handwriting, textual content, and the physical properties of the writing material.

The intersection of paleography, codicology, and papyrology in the study of ancient manuscripts allows for a multidisciplinary approach that combines the expertise and methodologies of each field. This collaborative approach enables scholars to gain a more comprehensive understanding of the manuscripts, their historical context, and their significance within the communities that produced and used them. By examining the physical properties, handwriting styles, and content of the manuscripts, researchers can uncover valuable information about the transmission of texts, the development of the book as a physical object, and the socio-cultural context in which these manuscripts were created and used. Ultimately, the integration of paleography, codicology, and papyrology enriches our understanding of the rich and complex history of ancient manuscripts and the people who created them.

Paleographic Advances and Discoveries: New Techniques and Technologies

In recent years, paleographic research has benefited from significant advances and discoveries, driven by the development of new techniques and technologies. These innovations have not only enhanced our ability to analyze and understand ancient manuscripts, but also opened up new avenues for research and collaboration in the field of paleography.

1. **Digital Paleography**: One of the most significant advancements in paleography has been the widespread adoption of digital tools and methods. High-resolution digital imaging allows for the creation of detailed, accurate reproductions of manuscripts, which can be easily accessed, shared, and analyzed by researchers around the world. Digital images can be enhanced, manipulated, or layered to reveal hidden or faint text, enabling paleographers to decipher previously unreadable passages or identify corrections and alterations made by scribes. Digital paleography also allows for the creation of interactive databases and repositories, which can be used to compare manuscripts, identify common features, and establish relationships between texts.

2. **Multispectral Imaging**: Multispectral imaging is a non-invasive imaging technique that captures images of a manuscript at different wavelengths of light. This method can reveal text that is invisible to the naked eye, such as text that has faded or been erased, or ink that has reacted with the writing surface over time. Multispectral imaging has been instrumental in the discovery of previously unknown texts or the recovery of lost information from damaged or deteriorated manuscripts.

3. **Machine Learning and Artificial Intelligence**: Machine learning and artificial intelligence (AI) have also emerged as valuable tools in paleographic research. By training algorithms to recognize specific handwriting styles, letterforms, or other features, researchers can automate the analysis of large collections of manuscripts, expediting the process of dating and cataloging texts. AI-driven tools can also help identify scribal habits and tendencies, revealing unique characteristics of individual scribes and potentially uncovering previously unknown connections between manuscripts.

4. **Collaborative Research Platforms**: The development of online collaborative platforms has facilitated communication and cooperation between researchers across disciplines and geographical boundaries. These platforms allow paleographers to share their findings, contribute to ongoing research projects, and access resources such as databases, digital repositories, and scholarly publications. In turn, this increased connectivity has led to the formation of international research networks and collaborations, driving the growth of interdisciplinary projects and fostering innovation in the field.

5. **3D Imaging and Virtual Reality**: 3D imaging and virtual reality technologies have the potential to revolutionize the way we study and experience ancient manuscripts. By creating three-dimensional, interactive models of manuscripts, researchers can examine the physical structure, layout, and material properties of a text in ways that were previously impossible. Virtual reality platforms can also be used to recreate historical environments or simulate the experience of reading a manuscript in its original context, providing valuable insights into the cultural and social significance of these texts.

These advances in paleographic research have not only improved our understanding of ancient manuscripts but have also expanded the possibilities for future discoveries and innovations in the field. As new techniques and technologies continue to emerge, they will undoubtedly reshape the landscape of paleography, offering exciting opportunities for scholars to uncover the hidden secrets of our written past.

The Future of Paleography in New Testament Studies: Challenges and Prospects

The future of paleography in New Testament studies is filled with both challenges and prospects. As scholars continue to uncover, analyze, and interpret ancient manuscripts, the field of paleography will play an increasingly vital role in our understanding of the historical and textual context of the New Testament. Despite the many advances in recent years, the field is not without its obstacles. In this discussion, we will explore some of the key challenges and opportunities that lie ahead for paleography in New Testament studies.

1. **Access to Manuscripts**: One of the primary challenges faced by paleographers is gaining access to manuscripts, many of which are scattered across libraries, archives, and private collections around the world. In some cases, political instability, legal restrictions, or

institutional barriers may prevent scholars from studying these valuable resources. The digitization of manuscripts has made it easier to share and access high-quality images of texts, but the process of digitization itself can be time-consuming and costly, particularly for fragile or damaged manuscripts. As a result, there is a need for continued investment in digitization projects and initiatives to improve access to these crucial resources.

2. **Interdisciplinary Collaboration**: As our understanding of ancient manuscripts evolves, so too does the need for interdisciplinary collaboration. Paleographers must work closely with experts in related fields, such as codicology, papyrology, linguistics, archaeology, and computer science, to develop innovative research methods and draw upon diverse perspectives. Building strong networks and fostering collaboration between scholars from various disciplines will be crucial to advancing our knowledge of the New Testament and its textual history.

3. **Training and Education**: The specialized nature of paleography means that there is a need for ongoing training and education for scholars entering the field. As new techniques and technologies are developed, researchers must continually update their skills and knowledge to stay at the forefront of their discipline. This may involve creating and participating in workshops, conferences, and online courses, as well as promoting the study of paleography at the undergraduate and graduate levels.

4. **Technological Innovation**: The future of paleography in New Testament studies will be shaped by the continued development and adoption of new technologies. Machine learning, artificial intelligence, and advanced imaging techniques have already made significant contributions to the field, but there is still much room for growth and innovation. Researchers must continue to explore the potential of these tools and develop new methods for analyzing and interpreting ancient texts.

5. **Preservation and Conservation**: The physical preservation and conservation of ancient manuscripts is an ongoing challenge for paleographers and institutions alike. As many manuscripts are fragile and susceptible to deterioration, it is essential to invest in conservation efforts to ensure their long-term survival. This may involve the development of new preservation techniques or the creation of climate-controlled environments for storing and displaying manuscripts.

In conclusion, the future of paleography in New Testament studies holds many exciting prospects, but also poses significant challenges. By addressing these challenges and capitalizing on new opportunities, researchers can continue to deepen our understanding of the New Testament and its historical context. As paleography continues to evolve and adapt to new technologies and methodologies, it will remain a vital and dynamic field within the broader landscape of biblical studies.

CHAPTER XI

The Sources of New Testament Textual Criticism

If we are to be able to evaluate the readings of the manuscripts that we have, we must be familiar with the manuscripts themselves. Moreover, we must understand how they are connected by their likenesses and differences. Westcott and Hort wrote concerning internal manuscript evidence, "The first step toward obtaining a sure foundation is a consistent application of the principle that KNOWLEDGE OF DOCUMENTS SHOULD PRECEDE FINAL JUDGMENT UPON READINGS."[397]

The textual scholar has three sources that enable him to carry out his work of establishing which reading of any given text is the original:

(1) the Greek manuscripts include the papyri, the uncial manuscripts, the minuscule manuscripts, and the lectionaries.

(2) the versions or the translations into other languages, and

(3) the quotations of the New Testament by the apostolic fathers (e.g., Clement of Rome, Ignatius of Antioch, Polycarp of Smyrna, Hermas, and Papias), the apologists (e.g., Justin Martyr, Clement of Alexandria, Tertullian, etc.), and later church fathers.

---

[397] B.F. Westcott and F.J.A Hort, Introduction to the New Testament in the Original Greek, Vol. II, (New York, Harper and Brothers, 1882), 31.

Before delving into the sources of the New Testament, we must again make mention of Kurt and Barbara Aland. New Testament manuscripts in Greek can be categorized into five categories, according to their assessment in *The Text of the New Testament*.[398] Kurt Aland (1915 – 1994) was a German theologian and Biblical scholar who specialized in New Testament textual criticism. He founded the Institut für neutestamentliche Textforschung (Institute for New Testament Textual Research) in Münster, where he served as its first director for many years (1959–83). In 1983, Barbara Aland became director. The Alands were two of the principal editors of the Nestle-Aland Novum Testamentum Graece (Greek New Testament) for the Deutsche Bibelgesellschaft and The Greek New Testament for the United Bible Societies. Their five categories of manuscripts follow.

Description of Categories

Category I – Alexandrian Text-type

Manuscripts of a very special quality should always be considered in establishing the original text. The papyri and uncials through the third/fourth century also belong here automatically; one may say because they represent the text of the early period (if they offer no significant evidence, they are bracketed).

Category II – Egyptian Texts

Manuscripts of a special quality but distinguished from manuscripts of category I by the presence of alien influences (particularly of the Byzantine text), and yet of importance for establishing the original text.

Category III – Mixed Texts

These manuscripts are of a distinctive character with an independent text, usually important for establishing the original text but particularly important for the history of the text (e.g., f^1, f^{13}).

Category IV – Western Text-type

These are manuscripts of the D (Codex Bezae) text.

Category V – Byzantine Text-type

Manuscripts with a purely predominately Byzantine text.

After a detailed comparison of the papyri, the Alands concluded that these manuscripts from the second to the fourth centuries are of three kinds

---

[398] Kurt and Barbara Aland, *The Text of the New Testament*, Second Edition (Grand Rapids: William B Eerdmans Publishing, 1987), 121.

(Normal, Free, and Strict). "It is their collations which have changed the picture so completely." (p. 93)

1. Normal Texts: The normal text is a relatively faithful tradition (e.g., P^{52}), which departs from its exemplar only occasionally, as do New Testament manuscripts of every century. It is further represented in P^4, P^5, P^{12}(?), P^{16}, P^{18}, P^{20}, P^{28}, P^{47}, P^{72} (1, 2 Peter), and P^{87}.[399]

2. Free Texts: This is a text dealing with the original text in a relatively free manner with no suggestion of a program of standardization (e.g., p^{45}, p^{46}, and p^{66}), exhibiting the most diverse variants. It is further represented in P^9(?), P^{13}(?), P^{29}, P^{37}, P^{40}, P^{69}, P^{72} (Jude), and P^{78}.[400]

3. Strict Texts: These manuscripts transmit the text of the exemplar with meticulous care (e.g., P^{75}) and depart from it only rarely. It is further represented in P^1, P^{23}, P^{27}, P^{35}, P^{39}, P^{64+67}, P^{65}(?), and P^{70}.[401]

Bruce M. Metzger (1914 – 2007) was an editor with Kurt and Barbara Aland of the United Bible Societies' standard Greek New Testament and the Nestle-Aland Greek New Testament. We will also borrow a few paragraphs from one of his publications, *A Textual Commentary on the Greek New Testament, Second Edition* (1971, 1994), so we have an additional understanding of these text-types.

> The *Alexandrian text,* which Westcott and Hort called the *Neutral text* (a question-begging title), is usually considered to be the best text and the most faithful in preserving the original. Characteristics of the Alexandrian text are brevity and austerity. That is, it is generally shorter than the text of other forms, and it does not exhibit the degree of grammatical and stylistic polishing that is characteristic of the Byzantine type of text. Until recently the two chief witnesses to the Alexandrian text were codex Vaticanus (B) and codex Sinaiticus (ℵ), parchment manuscripts dating from about the middle of the fourth century. With the acquisition, however, of the Bodmer Papyri, particularly P^{66} and P^{75}, both copied about the end of the second or the beginning of the third century, evidence is now available that the Alexandrian type of text goes back to an archetype that must be dated early in the second century. The Sahidic and Bohairic versions frequently contain typically Alexandrian readings.

---

[399] Ibid., 95

[400] Ibid., 59, 64, 93

[401] Ibid., 64, 95

The so-called *Western text,* which was widely current in Italy and Gaul as well as in North Africa and elsewhere (including Egypt), can also be traced back to the second century. It was used by Marcion, Tatian, Irenaeus, Tertullian, and Cyprian. Its presence in Egypt is shown by the testimony of P[38] (about A.D. 300) and P[48] (about the end of the third century). The most important Greek manuscripts that present a Western type of text are codex Bezae (D) of the fifth century (containing the Gospels and Acts), codex Claromontanus (D) of the sixth century (containing the Pauline epistles), and, for Mark 1:1 to 5:30, codex Washingtonianus (W) of the fifth century. Likewise the Old Latin versions are noteworthy witnesses to a Western type of text; these fall into three main groups, the African, Italian, and Hispanic forms of Old Latin texts.

The chief characteristic of Western readings is fondness for paraphrase. Words, clauses, and even whole sentences are freely changed, omitted, or inserted. Sometimes the motive appears to have been harmonization, while at other times it was the enrichment of the narrative by the inclusion of traditional or apocryphal material. Some readings involve quite trivial alterations for which no special reason can be assigned. One of the puzzling features of the Western text (which generally is longer than the other forms of text) is that at the end of Luke and in a few other places in the New Testament certain Western witnesses omit words and passages that are present in other forms of text, including the Alexandrian. Although at the close of the last century certain scholars were disposed to regard these shorter readings as original (Westcott and Hort called them "Western non-interpolations"), since the acquisition of the Bodmer Papyri many scholars today are inclined to regard them as aberrant readings (see the Note on Western Non-Interpolations, pp. 164–166).

In the book of Acts the problems raised by the Western text become most acute, for the Western text of Acts is nearly ten percent longer than the form that is commonly regarded to be the original text of that book. For this reason, the present volume devotes proportionately more space to variant readings in Acts than to those in any other New Testament book, and a special Introduction to the textual phenomena in Acts is provided (see pp. 222–236).

An Eastern form of text, which was formerly called the *Caesarean* text,[402] is preserved, to a greater or lesser extent, in several Greek manuscripts (including Θ, 565,700) and in the Armenian and Georgian versions. The text of these witnesses is characterized by a mixture of Western and Alexandrian readings. Although recent research has tended to question the existence of a specifically Caesarean text-type,[7] the individual manuscripts formerly considered to be members of the group remain important witnesses in their own right.

Another Eastern type of text, current in and near Antioch, is preserved today chiefly in Old Syriac witnesses, namely the Sinaitic and the Curetonian manuscripts of the Gospels and in the quotations of Scripture contained in the works of Aphraates and Ephraem.

The *Byzantine text,* otherwise called the *Syrian text* (so Westcott and Hort), the *Koine text* (so von Soden), the *Ecclesiastical text* (so Lake), and the *Antiochian text* (so Ropes), is, on the whole, the latest of the several distinctive types of text of the New Testament. It is characterized chiefly by lucidity and completeness. The framers of this text sought to smooth away any harshness of language, to combine two or more divergent readings into one expanded reading (called conflation), and to harmonize divergent parallel passages. This conflated text, produced perhaps at Antioch in Syria, was taken to Constantinople, whence it was distributed widely throughout the Byzantine Empire. It is best represented today by codex Alexandrinus (in the Gospels; not in Acts, the Epistles, or Revelation), the later uncial manuscripts, and the great mass of minuscule manuscripts. Thus,

John Rylands Library Papyrus P52, recto

[402] For a summary of the chief research on the so-called Caesarean text, see Metzger, "The Caesarean Text of the Gospels," *Journal of Biblical Literature,* lxiv (1945), pp. 457–489, reprinted with additions in Metzger's *Chapters in the History of New Testament Textual Criticism* (Leiden and Grand Rapids, 1963), pp. 42–72.

except for an occasional manuscript that happened to preserve an earlier form of text, during the period from about the sixth or seventh century down to the invention of printing with moveable type (a.d.1450–56), the Byzantine form of text was generally regarded as *the* authoritative form of text and was the one most widely circulated and accepted.[403]

The Importance of the Papyrus Manuscripts

The earliest sources for the Greek New Testament are the papyri in codex (book-like) form. Of course, this designation came from the medium on which they were inscribed. At present, there have been over one hundred of these discovered, with sixty-two of these manuscripts dating between 100 – 300 C.E. These biblical papyri range from a tiny fragment to codices, which may be incomplete, but still contain large portions of several New Testament books. They are noted in literature with the Black letter character, also known as Gothic script 𝔓, or by an upper- or lowercase "P" followed by a superscript Arabic number. (e.g., 𝔓[52], 𝔓[66], and 𝔓[75]).

Image of the front (recto) of Papyrus 1

P[1] (Papyrus 1 – P. Oxy. 2)

Contents: Matt. 1:1–9, 12, 14–20
Date: 250 C.E.
Discovered: Oxyrhynchus, Egypt
Housing Location: University of Pennsylvania Museum (E 2746)
Physical Features: The manuscript is a fragment of one leaf, one column per page; 12 cm x 25 cm; 37–38 lines per page; reformed documentary hand. The words are written continuously without separation. There are no accents or breathings marks. The nomina sacra are written in abbreviated forms:

IC XC YC ΠNA KΣ [404]

---

[403] *Bruce M. Metzger, A Textual Commentary on the Greek New Testament, Second Edition,* © *1994 Deutsche Bibelgesellschaft, Stuttgart.* Used by permission.

[404] B. P. Grenfell & A. S. Hunt, *Oxyrhynchus Papyri I* (London, 1898), p. 4.

Luke 6:4-16

Textual Character: The copyist of P¹ stayed faith to the very reliable exemplar that he was using. P¹ has a close agreement with the Alexandrian family where there are major variants, particularly Codex Vaticanus, from which it scarcely differs.[405]

$P^{4/64/67}$ (Papyrus 4/64/67 – Suppl. Gr. 1120/Gr. 17/P. Barcelona 1)

P^4

Contents: Luke 1:58–59; 1:62–2:1, 6–7; 3:8–4:2, 29–32, 34–35; 5:3–8; 5:30–6:16

Date: 150–175 C.E.

Discovered: Coptos, Egypt in 1889

Housing Location: Paris, Bibliothèque Nationale, Suppl. Gr. 1120

Physical Features: P⁴ is one the earliest manuscripts of the Gospel of Luke and contains extensive sections of the first six chapters: 1:58-59; 1:62-2:1; 2:6-7; 3:8-4:2; 4:29-32, 34-35; 5:3-8; 5:30-6:16

Textual Character: P⁴ is of the Alexandrian text-type and agrees with P⁷⁵ and B 93 percent of the time. The copyist of P⁴ was likely a professional scribe. "P⁴ and P⁷⁵ are identical in forty complete verses, with only five significant exceptions (Luke 3:22, 36; 5:39; 6:11, 14)."[406] Comfort and Barret in their book *Text of the Earliest NT Greek Manuscripts* inform us that P⁴ came from the same codex as P⁶⁴/⁶⁷.

The Common Identity of P4, P64, and P67

Textual scholars acknowledge that P64 and P67 come from the same manuscript. But few have recognized that renowned papyrologist Colin Roberts identified the Lucan manuscript P4 as also belonging to the same codex. Roberts, who is best known for his dating of the Johannine manuscript P52 to the early second century, was both the editor of P64 and the scholar who first

---

[405] Philip W. Comfort and David P. Barrett, *The Text of the Earliest New Testament Greek Manuscripts*. Wheaton, Illinois: Tyndale House Publishers Incorporated, 2001, p. 39

[406] Ibid. p. 43

identified P67 as belonging to the same manuscript. This same papyrologist was convinced that P4 also came from the same codex. Speaking of P4, P64, and P67, he wrote:

There can in my opinion be no doubt that all these fragments come from the same codex which was reused as packing for the binding of the late third century codex of Philo (= H. 695). An apparent discrepancy was that Ἰησοῦς appeared as ΙΣ in the Paris fragments and as τ̅η̅ in the Oxford fragments; the correct reading in the latter, however, is ΙΣ, as can be checked in the photograph.

Roberts made the above statement in his 1977 lecture to the British Academy. Ten years later, in his publication *The Birth of the Codex*, he still affirmed that P4, P64, and P67 are parts of the same Gospel codex. To my knowledge, he never changed his opinion. The only scholar I know of who changed his mind on this matter is Kurt Aland. In 1963, he listed P4 as separate from P64/P67. In 1965, he suggested that P4 belonged to the same codex as P64 and P67, but thereafter, he never refers to them as belonging to the same codex. P4 is always listed separately from P64/P67 in Aland's publications. But I cannot find a reason for the change.

In the 1965 article about new papyrus manuscripts of the New Testament, Kurt Aland presented the position that P4 probably belonged to the same codex as P64 and P67. The only hesitancy Aland had in affirming a complete identification is that the color of P64 was much lighter than that of P4. Otherwise, with respect to all other paleographic features, Aland noted that P64/P67 bears a remarkable similarity to P4. Following Aland's lead, the papyrologist Joseph van Haelst also identified P4 as probably belonging to the same manuscript as P64 and P67.

Thus, the common identity of the three papyri needs to be reexamined and reaffirmed, which can be done by showing common provenance for the manuscripts and shared paleographic features. This discussion will then lead naturally to the dating of these manuscripts.[407]

---

[407] Philip Wesley Comfort and David P. Barrett, *The Text of the Earliest New Testament Greek Manuscripts* (Wheaton, IL: Tyndale House, 2001), 45–47.

P⁶⁴

Papyrus 64 "Magdalen"

Contents: Matthew 3; 5; 26

Date: 150–175 C.E.

Discovered: Coptos, Egypt

Housing Location: Barcelona, Fundación Sant Lluc Evangelista, Inv. Nr. 1; Oxford, Magdalen College, Gr. 18

Physical Features: The fragments have writing on both sides, which indicates that they came from a codex as opposed to a scroll.

Textual Character: P⁶⁴ is of the Alexandrian text-type, evidencing a strong affinity with Alexandrian features, "agreeing slightly more with ℵ than with B."[408]

P⁶⁷

Contents: Matt. 3:9, 15; 5:20–22, 25–28

Date: 150–175 C.E.

Discovered: Coptos, Egypt

Housing Location: Barcelona, Fundación Sant Lluc Evangelista, Inv. Nr. 1; Oxford, Magdalen College, Gr. 18

Physical Features: The fragments have writing on both sides, codex style.

Textual Character: P⁶⁷ is of the Alexandrian text-type, evidencing a strong affinity with Alexandrian features, determined by Roca-Puig to have a close affinity to ℵ.[409] Comfort and Barret show that this P⁴/⁶⁴/⁶⁷ has affinities with a number of the late 2nd century papyri.[410] Comfort says, "T. C. Skeat[411] makes a convincing case for the claim that P⁴/P⁶⁴/P⁶⁷ once belonged to a

---

[408] Ibid., pp. 50–53

[409] Ibid., pp. 50–53

[410] P. Oxy. 224, 661, 2334, 2404 2750, P. Ryl. 16, 547, and P. Vindob G 29784

[411] Colin H. Roberts and T. C. Skeat, *The Birth of the Codex* (London: Oxford University Press for the British Academy, 1987), 40–41, 65.

348

four-Gospel codex. This would make P⁴/P⁶⁴/P⁶⁷ the earliest extant four-Gospel codex." In reference to their common identity, Roberts wrote of P⁴, P⁶⁴, and P⁶⁷:

> There can in my opinion be no doubt that all these fragments come from the same codex which was reused as packing for the binding of the late third-century codex of Philo (= H. 695). An apparent discrepancy was that 'Ιησοῦς appeared as $\overline{IC}$,] in the Paris fragments and as $\overline{ιη}$ in the Oxford fragments; the correct reading in the latter, however, is $\overline{IC}$, as can be checked in the photograph.[412]

Roberts made the above statement at a lecture to the British Academy in 1977. In 1987, he reaffirmed that this was still his position in his publication, *The Birth of the Codex*. There is nothing on record that suggests Roberts ever changed his position that P⁴, P⁶⁴, and P⁶⁷ are parts of the same Gospel codex.

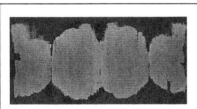

Folios 13-14 with part of the Gospel of Luke

P⁴⁵ (P. Chester Beatty I)

Contents: It contains sections within Matthew 20-21 and 25-26; Mark 4-9 and 11-12; Luke 6-7 and 9-14; John 4-5 and 10-11; and Acts 4-17.

Date: 200 – 225 C.E.

Discovered: Its origin is possibly the Fayum or ancient Aphroditopolis (modern Atfih) in Egypt (see Comfort, 157-9).

Housing Location: It is currently housed at the Chester Beatty Library, except for one leaf containing Matt. 25:41-26:39, which is at the Österreichische Nationalbibliothek, Vienna (Pap. Vindob. G. 31974). It was purchased by Chester Beatty of Dublin, Ireland, in 1931.

Physical Features: It has portions of thirty pages, but it is estimated that the original codex had 224 pages. Comfort tells us, "The first and last pages are blank and unnumbered, but pagination numbers are extant for 193 and 199. Approximately 20 cm broad x 25 cm high (5–6 cm thick, without binding); an average of 36–37 lines per page." (Comfort and Barrett, 155)

---

[412] Colin H. Roberts, *Manuscript, Society, and Belief in Early Christian Egypt*, Schweich Lectures 1977 (London: Oxford University Press for the British Academy, 1979), 13.

Textual Character: P45 is an eclectic text-type and a Category I. The Gospel of Mark reflects the Caesarean family, while the other Gospels reflect a mixture of Western and Alexandrian. The book of Acts largely reflects the Alexandrian family, with some minor variants from the Western family.

A folio from P46 containing 2 Corinthians 11:33-12:9. As with other folios of the manuscript, text is lacunose at the bottom.

P46

Contents: P46 contains most of the Pauline epistles, though with some folios missing. It has (in order) "the last eight chapters of Romans; all of Hebrews; virtually all of 1–2 Corinthians; all of Ephesians, Galatians, Philippians, Colossians; and two chapters of 1 Thessalonians. All of the leaves have lost some lines at the bottom through deterioration."[413]

Date: 150 C.E.[414]

Discovered: Comfort says, "the Fayum, Egypt, or perhaps in the ruins of a church or monastery near Atfih (ancient Aphroditopolis)." (p. 203)

Housing Location: Ann Arbor, Mich.: The University of Michigan, Special Collections Library (P. Mich. inv. 6238).

Physical Features: In the original form, it would have had 52 folios,[415] which equals 104 leaves, 208 pages. However, in its current condition, 9 folios are missing. It is 15 cm x 27 cm, with 25–31 lines per page, a single column of 26 – 32 lines of text per page. Its pagination is 1 – 199.[416] P46 was written by a professional scribe.

---

[413] Michael Marlowe, Papyrus 46; http://www.bible-researcher.com/papy46.html

[414] Thus, it is my opinion that P46 belongs to an era after a.d.81–96 (the era posited by Kim)— perhaps the middle of the second century.

Dating P46 to this era allows some time for the formation of the Pauline corpus to have occurred and for an archetypal collection to have been produced and to circulate in Egypt. Zuntz figured that an archetypal Pauline corpus was formed by A.D. 100 in Alexandria.⁶ Thus, an Alexandrian copy such as P46 could have been produced shortly thereafter and been used by Egyptian Christians in Alexandria and other nearby towns such as Aphroditopolis …. (Comfort and Barret, The Text of the Earliest New Testament Greek Manuscripts 2001)

[415] A folio is sheet of papyrus, parchment, or paper folded once to give two leaves or four pages.

[416] Pagination is page numbers, i.e., the sequential numbers given to pages in a book or document, and is one of the signs of a professional scribe.

Textual Character: P⁴⁶ is an Alexandrian text-type / Category I. It is similar to Minuscule 1739.

Papyrus 47: Rev. 13:16-14:4

P⁴⁷

Contents: Rev. 9:10–11:3; 11:5–16:15; 16:17–17:2.

Date: 250 – 300 C.E.

Discovered: P⁴⁷ (along with P⁴⁵ and P⁴⁶) it was discovered in the Fayum of Egypt or perhaps in the ruins of a church or monastery near Atfih, ancient Aphroditopolis.[417]

Housing Location: Dublin, Ireland: Chester Beatty Library.[418]

Physical Features: P⁴⁷ has thirty leaves (60 pages); 14 cm x 24 cm; 26–28 lines per page. It was written in a documentary hand.[419] Comfort states, "The consistent abbreviation of numerals shows that the scribe was practiced at making documents. A second corrector (c2) made some additional corrections and darkened many letters."[420]

---

[417] Comfort and Barret, *The Text of the Earliest NT MS*, 335.

[418] "Liste Handschriften". Münster: Institute for New Testament Textual Research. Retrieved 26 August 2011.

[419] A documentary hand is the work of one, who has the basic understanding and skills in preparing documents.

[420] Comfort and Barret, *The Text of the Earliest NT MS*, 335.

Textual Character: P⁴⁷ is an Alexandrian text-type Category I. It most closely resembles Sinaiticus but is similar to two other manuscripts of Revelation: P¹⁸ (250-300) and P²⁴ (c. 300). Kenyon was first to examine the manuscript, saying, "It is on the whole closest to ℵ and C, with P next, and A rather further away."⁴²¹ However, after further investigation of P⁴⁷, it has

John 18:31–33, 37–38

been shown that it "is allied to ℵ, but not to A or to C, which are of a different text type."⁴²² Comfort says, "We know that A, C, and P¹¹⁵ ... form one early group for Revelation, while P⁴⁷ and ℵ form another."⁴²³

P⁵²

Contents: John 18:31–33, 37–38.

Date: 100 – 125 C.E.⁴²⁴

Discovered: Fayum or Oxyrhynchus, Egypt, believed to have been circulated in both areas.

Housing Location: John Rylands Library in Manchester, England.

Physical Features: One leaf; 18 cm x 22 cm; 18 lines per page; written in a reformed documentary hand.

Textual Character: P⁵² is hardly enough to suggest which text type it belongs to. The Alands list it as Category I, or what they call "normal."⁴²⁵

---

⁴²¹ Frederic G. Kenyon, *The Chester Beatty Biblical Papyri,* fasc. 3.1,*Pauline Epistles and Revelation, Text* (London: Emery Walker, 1934), xiii.

⁴²² Aland and Aland, *Text of the New Testament,* 59.

⁴²³ Comfort and Barret, *The Text of the Earliest NT MS,* 335.

⁴²⁴ "This dating is derived from comparing P52 to manuscripts such as P. Fayum 110 (A.D. 94), the Egerton Gospel (A.D. 130–150), P. Oslo 22 (a.d.127), P. London 2078 (reign of Domitian, A.D. 81–96), and P. Berolinenses 6845 (ca. A.D. 100). Though each of these manuscripts bears significant resemblance to P52, P. Berolinenses 6845 is the closest parallel, in Roberts's opinion. Another manuscript shares many similarities with P52, P. Oxy. 2533. The editors of P. Oxy. 2533 said that its handwriting could be paralleled with first-century documents, but since it had the appearance of being second century, they assigned it a second-century date. Thus, both P. Oxy. 2533 and P52 can safely be dated to A.D. 100–125. However, its comparability to manuscripts of an even earlier period (especially P. Berol. 6845), pushes the date closer to a.d. 100, plus or minus a few years. This is extremely remarkable, especially if we accept the consensus dating for the composition of the Fourth Gospel: A.D. 80–85. This would mean that P52 may be only twenty years removed from the original." – (Comfort and Barret, The Text of the Earliest New Testament Greek Manuscripts 2001)

⁴²⁵ Aland and Aland, *Text of the New Testament,* 99.

P[52] is the oldest manuscript of the New Testament known today. It measures 2 1/2 by 3 1/2 inches and contains only a few verses of the fourth gospel, John 18:31-33 (recto, the front), 37, and 38 (verso, the back). Bernard P. Grenfell acquired it around 1920, yet it went unnoticed until 1934, when paleographer C. E. Roberts noticed that it contained the Gospel of John. Roberts had evaluated the fragment, dating it to the beginning of the second century C.E. While other paleographers disagreed, other renowned scholars reached the same conclusion, including Frederic Kenyon, W. Schubart, Harold I. Bell, Adolf Deissmann, Ulrich Wilcken, and W. H. P. Hatch. P[52] is very important because It establishes that the Gospel of John was written in the first century.[426]

First page, showing John 1:1-13 and the opening words of v.14

P[66]

Contents: John 1:1–6:11; 6:35–14:26, 29–30; 15:2–26; 16:2–4, 6–7; 16:10–20:20, 22–23; 20:25–21:9, 12, 17. Does not include the pericope of the adulteress (7:53–8:11), earliest witness not to include this spurious passage.

Date: 150 C.E.

Discovered: Jabal Abu Mana.

Housing Location: Bodmer Library, Geneva.

Physical Features: 39 folios, equaling 78 leaves, 156 pages; 14.2 × 16.2 cm; 15-25 lines per page; pagination numbers from 1 to 156. The handwriting suggests that it was the work of a professional scribe.

Textual Character: P[66] is a free text, with both Alexandrian and Western elements. In recent studies, Berner[427] and Comfort[428] maintain that P[66] has preserved the work of three individuals: the original scribe (professional), a thoroughgoing corrector (*diorthōtēs*), and a minor corrector. However, in studies that are more recent James Royse argues that, aside from

---

[426] Professor Ferdinand Christian Baur (1792 – 1860) argued that the apostle John did not write the Gospel of John in the last days of the first-century, but rather about 160 C.E. P[52] was found in Egypt, far from Ephesus, the home congregation of John. The fact that it is dated to about 110-125 C.E., and had circulated as far down as Egypt, establishes that it was written in the first century.

[427] Karyn Berner, "Papyrus Bodmer II, P66: A Reevaluation of the Correctors and Corrections," (master's thesis, Wheaton College, 1993).

[428] Philip W. Comfort, "The Scribe as Interpreter: A New Look at New Testament Textual Criticism according to Reader-Reception Theory" (D.Litt. et Phil. diss., University of South Africa, 1996).

the possible exception of John 13:19, the corrections are all by the hand of the original professional scribe.[429]

The manuscript also contains, consistently, the use of Nomina Sacra. For example, in at least ten places one finds "[t]he common symbol ..., the staurogram, which is made up of the superimposed letters tau (T) and rho (P) as an abbreviation for *stauros / stauroō*."[430] The Staurogram was initially used as an abbreviation for the Greek words (σταύρος) *stauros* and (σταυρόω) *stauroō* in very early NT MSS, such as P[45], P[66] and P[75], somewhat like a nomen sacrum.[431]

Two sides of the Papyrus Bodmer VIII

P[72]

Contents: 1 Peter 1:1–5:14; 2 Peter 1:1–3:18; Jude 1–25.

Date: c. 300 C.E.

Discovered: uncertain.

Housing Location: Cologny / Geneva, Switzerland; Vatican City, Bibl. Bodmeriana; Bibl. Vaticana.

Physical Features: P[72] is "three parts of a 72-page codex; 14.5 cm x 16 cm; 16–20 lines per page. 1 and 2 Peter are paginated 1–36; Jude is paginated 62–68."[432] It is in the documentary hand, meaning a person who was trained in preparing documents copied it. The manuscript contains "several marginal topical descriptors, each beginning with περι." (Ibid.) The nomina sacra are used. This document also contains the Nativity of Mary, the apocryphal correspondence of Paul to the Corinthians, the eleventh Ode of Solomon, Melito's Homily on the Passover, a fragment of a hymn, the Apology of Phileas, and Psalms 33 and 34.

Textual Character: P[72] is of the Alexandrian text-type and the Alands have it as Category I. It is a free text, with certain uniqueness, often lacking careful attention in the transcription of a moderately reliable exemplar. P[72] resembles P[50].

---

[429] James R. Royse, Scribal Habits in Early Greek New Testament Papyri (Atlanta: Society of Biblical Literature, 2008), 409-21.

[430] Eerdmans and Brill *The Encyclopedia of Christianity* (2005) Volume 3, Page 637

[431] Hutado, Larry (2006). "The staurogram in early Christian manuscripts: the earliest visual reference to the crucified Jesus?" In Kraus, Thomas. *New Testament Manuscripts*. Leiden: Brill. pp. 207–26

[432] (Comfort and Barret, The Text of the Earliest New Testament Greek Manuscripts 2001, 479)

P⁷⁵

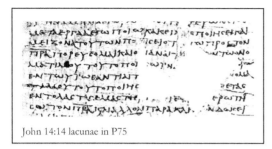

John 14:14 lacunae in P75

Contents: Luke 3:18–22; 3:33–4:2; 4:34–5:10; 5:37–6:4; 6:10–7:32, 35–39, 41–43; 7:46–9:2; 9:4–17:15; 17:19–18:18; 22:4–24:53; John 1:1–11:45, 48–57; 12:3–13:1, 8–10; 14:8–29; 15:7–8. It does not contain the adulterous story found at John 7:53–8:11.[433]

Date: 175 – 225 C.E.

Discovered: Pabau, Egypt.

Housing Location: Cologne-Geneva, Switzerland: Bibliotheca Bodmeriana.

Physical Features:

Textual Character: P⁷⁵ is Alexandrian text-type and the Alands have it as Category I, strict text. The text is closer to Codex Vaticanus than to Codex Sinaiticus. It agrees with P¹¹¹ (200-250).

It bears repeating what we discussed on pages 53 and 74 ff. P⁷⁵ (c.175–225) contains most of Luke and John and has vindicated Westcott and Hort for their choice of Vaticanus as the premium manuscript for establishing the original text. After careful study of P⁷⁵ against Vaticanus, scholars found that they are just short of being identical. In his introduction to the Greek text, Hort argued that Vaticanus is a "very pure line of very ancient text."[434] Of course, Westcott and Hort were not aware of P⁷⁵ that would be published in 1961, about 80 years later.

The discovery of P⁷⁵ proved to be the catalyst for correcting the misconception that early copyists were predominately unskilled. As we established earlier, either literate or semi-professional copyists produced the vast majority of the early papyri, and some were copied by professionals. The few poorly copied manuscripts simply became known first, giving the impression that was difficult for some to discard when the enormous amount of evidence surfaced that showed just the opposite. Of course, the discovery of P⁷⁵ has also had a profound effect on New Testament textual criticism because of its striking agreement with Codex Vaticanus.

---

[433] The manuscripts Codex Sinaiticus, Codex Vaticanus, and P⁶⁶ support this omission.

[434] B. F. Westcott and F. J. A. Hort, Introduction [and] Appendix, Vol. 2 of *New Testament in the Original Greek* (London: Macmillan and Company, 1881), 251.

Papyri 100 – 300[435]

Papyri	Content	Date	Text-Type
Papyrus 1 (P. Oxy. 2)	Matt. 1:1–9, 12, 14–20	250	Alexandrian / Category I Strict Text / reliable
Papyrus 4/64/67	**P[4]** Luke 1:58–59; 1:62–2:1, 6–7; 3:8–4:2, 29–32, 34–35; 5:3–8; 5:30–6:16 **P[64]** Matt. 3; 5; 26 **P[67]** Matt. 3:9, 15; 5:20–22, 25–28	**P[4]** 150–175 **P[64]** 150–175 **P[67]** 150–175	**P[4]** Alexandrian / Category I Normal Text / Reliable **P[64]** Alexandrian / Category I Strict Text / Reliable **P[67]** Alexandrian / Category I Strict Text / Reliable
Papyrus 5 (P. Oxy. 208, 1781)	John 1:23–31, 33–40; 16:14–30; 20:11–17, 19–20, 22–25	225-250	Western / Category I Normal Text / Fairly Reliable
Papyrus 9 (P. Oxy. 402)	1 John 4:11–12, 14–17	3rd Century	Alexandrian / Category I Free Text[436] / Unreliable
Papyrus 12	Heb. 1:1	285–300	Alexandrian / Category I Normal Text
Papyrus 13 (P. Oxy. 657)	Heb. 2:14–5:5; 10:8–22; 10:29–11:13; 11:28–12:17	225-250	Alexandrian / Category I Free Text / Reliable
Papyrus 15/16 (P. Oxy. 1008, 1009)	**P[15]** 1 Cor. 7:18–8:4 **P[16]** Phil. 3:10–17; 4:2–8	275-300	**P[15/16]** Alexandrian / Category I Normal Text / Fairly Reliable
Papyrus 17	Heb. 9:12–19	275-300	Alexandrian / Category II

[435] Information within the chart comes from Philip Comfort's *The Text of the Earliest New Testament Greek Manuscripts* (2001), Kurt and Barbara Aland's *The Text of the New Testament* (1987) Categories, at least normal, strict, and free belong to the Alands, while reliable, fairly reliable, and unreliable belong to comfort. Cf. chart above, p. 76.

[436] Somewhat carelessly written.

(P. Oxy. 1078)			
Papyrus 18 (P. Oxy. 1079)	Rev. 1:4–7	250-300	Alexandrian / Category I Normal Text / Fairly Reliable
Papyrus 20 (P. Oxy. 1171)	James 2:19–3:9	3rd century	Alexandrian / Category I Normal Text / Reliable
Papyrus 22 (P. Oxy. 1228)	John 15:25–16:2, 21–32	Middle 3rd century	Alexandrian / Category I Normal Text / Fairly Reliable
Papyrus 23 (P. Oxy. 1229)	James 1:10–12, 15–18	c. 200	Alexandrian / Category I Strict Text / fairly reliable
Papyrus 24 (P. Oxy. 1230)	Rev. 5:5–8; 6:5–8	c. 300	Alexandrian /Category I
Papyrus 27 (P. Oxy. 1355)	Rom. 8:12–22, 24–27; 8:33–9:3, 5–9	3rd century	Alexandrian / Category I Strict Text / Reliable
Papyrus 28 (P. Oxy. 1596)	John 6:8–12, 17–22	275-300	Alexandrian / Category I Normal Text / Reliable
Papyrus 29 (P. Oxy. 1597)	Acts 26:7–8, 20	200-225	Alexandrian / Category I Free Text
Papyrus 30 (P. Oxy. 1598)	1 Thess. 4:12–13, 16–17; 5:3, 8–10, 12–18, 25–28; 2 Thess. 1:1–2; 2:1, 9–11	200-225	Alexandrian / Category I Normal Text / Reliable
Papyrus 32	Titus 1:11–15; 2:3–8	150-200	Alexandrian / Category I Normal Text / Reliable
Papyrus 35	Matt. 25:12–15, 20–23	3rd century	Alexandrian / Category I Strict Text / Reliable
Papyrus 37	Matt. 26:19–52	225-275	Alexandrian / Category I Free Text[437] / fairly Reliable

---

[437] P37 frequently agrees with P45. In a dissertation study under Barbara Aland, Kyoung Shik Min developed a category called "Transmission Quality," which sorts out the errors attributed to the individual scribe. In this study, Min concludes that P37 produced a "free" text, but that the scribe's exemplar was a

Papyrus 38	Acts 18:27–19:6, 12–16	200-225	Alexandrian / Category IV Free Text[438]
Papyrus 39 (P. Oxy. 1780)	John 8:14–22	200-250	Alexandrian / Category I Strict Text / Reliable
Papyrus 40	Rom. 1:24–27; 1:31–2:3; 3:21–4:8; 6:2–5, 15–16; 9:17, 27	3rd century	Alexandrian / Category I Free Text[439] / fairly Reliable
Papyrus 45	Gospels, Acts	200-225	Midway between Alexandrian and Western in Luke and John[440] / Category I Free Text / Unreliable
Papyrus 46	Most of Paul's epistles, excluding the Pastorals	150	Alexandrian / Category I Free Text / reliable - Fairly Reliable
Papyrus 47	Rev. 9:10–11:3; 11:5–16:15; 16:17–17:2	250-300	Alexandrian / Category I Normal Text / Fairly Reliable
Papyrus 48	Acts 23:11–17, 25–29	3rd century	Alexandrian /Category IV Free Text[441]
Papyrus 49/65	P[49] Eph. 4:16–29; 4:31–5:13 P[65] 1 Thess. 1:3–2:1, 6–13	250	Alexandrian / Category I P[49] Normal Text P[65] Strict Text[442] / Reliable
Papyrus 50	Acts 8:26–32; 10:26–31	c. 300	Alexandrian / Category III
Papyrus 52	John 18:31–33, 37–38	110 – 125	Alexandrian / Category I Normal Text[443]

"normal" text. – Kyoung Shik Min, Die *früheste Überlieferung des Matthäusevangeliums* (Berlin and New York: Walter de Gruyter, 2005).

[438] Related to D.

[439] Carelessly written, category I because of date.

[440] It is not possible to assign any text-type to Matthew in P[45]. (Hill and Kruger 2012, 91)

[441] Related to D.

[442] Too brief for certainty.

[443] Category I because of age.

Papyrus 53	Matt. 26:29–40; Acts 9:33–10:1	250	In Matt independent, in Acts Alexandrian / Category I At Least Normal Text / Fairly Reliable
Papyrus 66	John 1:1–6:11; 6:35–14:26, 29–30; 15:2–26; 16:2–4, 6–7; 16:10–20:20, 22–23; 20:25–21:9, 12, 17. Does not include the pericope of the adulteress (7:53–8:11), Earliest witness not to include this spurious passage	150	Alexandrian / Category I Free Text / reliable
Papyrus 69 (P. Oxy. 2383)	Luke 22:40, 45–48, 58–61	250	Alexandrian / Category IV Very Free Text[444] / Unreliable
Papyrus 70 (P. Oxy. 2384)	Matt. 2:13–16; 2:22–3:1; 11:26–27; 12:4–5; 24:3–6, 12–15	275-300	Alexandrian / Category I Strict Text/ fairly Reliable
Papyrus 72	1 Peter 1:1–5:14; 2 Peter 1:1–3:18; Jude 1–25	c. 300	Alexandrian / Category I Normal Text[445] Reliable 1 Peter / Unreliable 2 Peter and Jude
Papyrus 75	Luke 3:18–22; 3:33–4:2; 4:34–5:10; 5:37–6:4; 6:10–7:32, 35–39, 41–43; 7:46–9:2; 9:4–17:15; 17:19–18:18; 22:4–24:53; John 1:1–11:45, 48–57; 12:3–13:1, 8–10; 14:8–29; 15:7–8. Does not include 7:53–8:11, making it the second earliest witness (next to P66) not to include this spurious passage.	175 – 225	Alexandrian / Category I Strict Text / Reliable
Papyrus 77/103	Matt. 23:30–39 (P. Oxy. 2683 + 4405); Matt. 13:55–57; 14:3–5 (P. Oxy. 4403)	150-200	Alexandrian / Category I P[77] Strict[446] / Reliable

---

[444] Characteristic of precursors of the D-text; therefore, Category IV.

[445] 1, 2 Peter normal text, Jude free text, both with certain peculiarities

[446] In 1988, in *The Text of the New Testament*, P[77] was said by the Alands to be "at least normal" by a "careless scribe" (p. 101). However, in 2002 Barbara Aland classified P[77] as strict, which would agree with Comfort, who says that it was produced by a trained scribe. It is believed that P[103] belongs to the same codex as P[77], which is why Comfort came to a different conclusion. Comfort says that the additional fragments affirm the proto-Alexandrian character of the manuscript, showing more agreement with ℵ than with B. Both papyrus fragments also confirm that the manuscript was produced by a trained

(P. Oxy. 2683 + 4405)			
Papyrus 78 (P. Oxy. 2684)	Jude 4–5, 7–8	c. 300	Alexandrian / Category I Free Text / Unreliable
Papyrus 80	John 3:34	250	Alexandrian / Category I[447]
Papyrus 86	Matt. 5:13–16, 22–25	c. 300	Alexandrian / Category II Reliable
Papyrus 87	Philem. 13–15, 24–25	150	Alexandrian / Category I Normal Text / Reliable
Papyrus 90 (P. Oxy. 3523)	John 18:36–19:7	150-200	Alexandrian / Category I fairly Reliable
Papyrus 91	Acts 2:30–37; 2:46–3:2	250	Alexandrian / Category I Reliable
Papyrus 92	Eph. 1:11–13, 19–21; 2 Thess. 1:4–5, 11–12	300	Alexandrian / Reliable
Papyrus 95	John 5:26–29, 36–38	3rd century	Alexandrian / Category I
Papyrus 98	Rev. 1:13–2:1	2nd century	The fragment is a badly damaged text Fairly Reliable
Papyrus 100 (P. Oxy. 4449)	James 3:13–4:4; 4:9–5:1	275-325	Alexandrian / Reliable
Papyrus 101 (P. Oxy. 4401)	Matt. 3:10–12; 3:16–4:3	3rd century	Alexandrian / Normal Text / Reliable
Papyrus 102 (P. Oxy. 4402)	Matt. 4:11–12, 22–23	c. 300-325	Alexandrian / Strict Text
Papyrus 104 (P. Oxy. 4404)	Matt. 21:34–37, 43, 45(?)	125	Category I Reliable

scribe. (p. 610) According to Roberts, P[77] was written "in an elegant hand [and] has what was or became a standard system of chapter division, as well as punctuation and breathing marks."

[447] Category I because of date.

Papyrus 106 (P. Oxy. 4445)	John 1:29–35, 40–46	200-250	Alexandrian / Category I Strict Text / Reliable
Papyrus 107 (P. Oxy. 4446)	John 17:1–2, 11	200-250	Normal Text / Reliable?
Papyrus 108 (P. Oxy. 4447)	John 17:23–24; 18:1–5	c. 200	Alexandrian / Fairly Reliable
Papyrus 109 (P. Oxy. 4448)	John 21:18–20, 23–25	150-200	Strict Text
Papyrus 110 (P. Oxy. 4494)	Matt. 10:13–15, 25–27	250-300	Alexandrian / Free Text Unreliable
Papyrus 111 (P. Oxy. 4495)	Luke 17:11–13, 22–23	200-250	Alexandrian / reliable
Papyrus 113 (P. Oxy. 4497)	Rom. 2:12–13, 19	3rd century	Alexandrian / Strict Text
Papyrus 114 (P. Oxy. 4498)	Heb. 1:7–12	3rd century	Strict Text / Reliable
Papyrus 115 (P. Oxy. 4499)	Rev. 2:1–3, 13–15, 27–29; 3:10–12; 5:8–9; 6:5–6; 8:3–8, 11–13; 9:1–5, 7–16, 18–21; 10:1–4, 8–11; 11:1–5, 8–15, 18–19; 12:1–5, 8–10, 12–17; 13:1–3, 6–16, 18; 14:1–3, 5–7, 10–11, 14–15, 18–20; 15:1, 4–7	250-300	Alexandrian / Category I Reliable
Papyrus 118	Romans 15:26-27,32-33; 16:1,4-7,11-12	3rd century	Uncertain
Papyrus 119	John 1:21-28,38-44	3rd century	Alexandrian
Papyrus 121	John 19:17-18,25-26	3rd century	Uncertain
Papyrus 125	1 Peter 1:23-2:5; 7-12	3rd/4th cent.	Alexandrian
Papyrus 137	Mark 1:7-9; 1:16-18	175-225	Uncertain
Papyrus Antinoopolis 2.54	Matt. 6:10–12	3rd century	uncertain

361

Early Uncials	Content	Date	Text-Type
0162 (P. Oxy. 847)	John 2:11–22	c. 300	Alexandrian / Category I Agrees with P[66] and P[75], and B
0171 (PSI 2.124)	Matt. 10:17–23, 25–32; Luke 22:44–50, 52–56, 61, 63–64	c. 300	Western / Category IV Reformed Documentary Hand
0189 (P. Berlin 11765)	Acts 5:3–21	175-252	Alexandrian / Normal Text Reformed Documentary Hand
0220	Rom. 4:23–5:3, 8–13	c. 300	Alexandrian / Category I Reformed Documentary Hand

Papyri 300 - 600

Papyri	Content	Date	Text-Type
Papyrus 6	John 10-11 †; First Epistle of Clement	4th century	Alexandrian text-type
Papyrus 7	Luke 4 †	4th–6th century	Alexandrian text-type
Papyrus 8	Acts 4-6 †	4th century	Alexandrian text-type
Papyrus 10	Romans 1 †	4th century	Alexandrian text-type
Papyrus 17	Hebrews 9 †	4th century	Alexandrian text-type
Papyrus 19	Gospel of Matthew 10-11 †	4th–5th century	Alexandrian text-type
Papyrus 21	Matthew 12:24-33 †	4th century	mixed
Papyrus 24	Revelation 5-6 †	4th century	Alexandrian text-type

Papyrus 25	Matthew 18-19 †	4th century	Diatesaric text[448]
Papyrus 50	Acts 8:26-32; 10:26-31	3rd-4th century	mixed
Papyrus 57	Acts 4:36-5:2.8-10	4th-5th century	Alexandrian text-type
Papyrus 62	Matthew 11:25-30, Book of Daniel 3:51-53 and Odae	4th century	Alexandrian text-type
Papyrus 71	Matthew 19:10-11, 17-18	4th century	Alexandrian text-type
Papyrus 81	1 Peter 2:20-3:1, 4-12	4th century	Alexandrian text-type
Papyrus 82	Luke 7:32-34, 37-38	4th-5th century	Alexandrian text-type
Papyrus 85	Revelation 9:19-10:2, 5-9	4th-5th century	Alexandrian text-type
Papyrus 86	Matthew are verses 5:13-16, 22-25	4th century	Alexandrian text-type
Papyrus 88	Mark 2:1-26	4th century	Mixed; Category III
Papyrus 105	Matthew 27:62-64; 28:2-5	5th/6th century	Strict Text
Papyrus 110	Gospel of Matthew 10:13-15, 25-27	4th century	Alexandrian text-type
Papyrus 112	Acts 26:31-32; 27:5-7	5th century	Free Text
Papyrus 116	Hebrews 2:9-11; 3:3-6	6th century	Uncertain
Papyrus 117	2 Corinthians 7:6-8,9-11	4th / 5th-century	Uncertain
Papyrus 120	John 1:25-28,38-44	4th century	Alexandrian

---

[448] The Diatessaron is the most prominent early gospel harmony, and was created by Tatian, an Assyrian early Christian apologist and ascetic. Tatian sought to combine all the textual material he found in the four gospels—Matthew, Mark, Luke, and John—into a single coherent narrative of Jesus's life and death. However, and in contradistinction to most later gospel harmonists, Tatian appears not to have been motivated by any aspiration to validate the four separate canonical gospel accounts; or to demonstrate that, as they stood, they could each be shown as being without inconsistency or error. – Wikipedia.

Papyrus 122	John 21:11-14,22-24	4th / 5th century	Alexandria
Papyrus 123	1 Corinthians 14:31-34; 15:3-6	4th century	Alexandrian
Papyrus 124	2 Corinthians 11:1-4; 6-9	6th century	Alexandrian
Papyrus 125	1 Peter 1:23-2:5; 7-12	3rd / 4th century	Alexandrian
Papyrus 126	Hebrews 13:12-13.19-20	4th century	Uncertain
Papyrus 127	Acts 10-12, 15-17	5th century	Uncertain
Papyrus 128	John 9:3–4, 12:16–18	6th / 7th century	Uncertain

Greek Uncial Manuscripts of the New Testament

This category can be somewhat confusing because the papyrus manuscripts were written in uncial letters.[449] However, "uncial" is a term used to designate only the parchment manuscripts, written in uncial letters. Papyrus was used for penning literary works for a very long time, while parchment was used for business papers, notebooks, and the first drafts of an author's works. Some very significant Bible manuscripts extant today were originally penned on parchment.

Parchment began to displace papyrus in writing manuscripts from about the fourth century to the fifteenth century C.E. Even though papyrus was used by secular literature up to the seventh century, Christians started using the parchment as early as the second century, with continued growth into the third, and almost completely by the fourth century. Constantine the Great ordered 50 copies of the Bible, commissioned in 331, which were produced in the Greek language and on parchment. Constantin von Tischendorf, the discoverer of Codex Sinaiticus, believed that Sinaiticus and Vaticanus were among these fifty Bibles prepared by Eusebius in Caesarea. However, Metzger writes, "there are, however, one or two indications which point to Egypt as the place of origin of Codex Vaticanus, and the type of text found

---

[449] Uncial is a letter of the kind used in Greek and Latin manuscripts written between the 3rd and 10th centuries that is similar to a modern capital letter, but more rounded. I use "uncial" because it has been the common term, and out of personal habit; "majuscule" is preferred by many textual critics.

in both codices is unlike that by Eusebius."[450] The Institute for New Testament Textual Research (INTF)[451] reports 322 uncial manuscripts of the Greek New Testament, dating from the fourth century C.E. to the tenth-century C.E.

In 325 C.E., Emperor Constantine legalized Christianity, giving it equal status to the pagan religions. It was then much easier to have manuscripts copied. Christianity had been treated like a dissident, rebellious, seditious, and destabilizing movement up until this time. Christians were persecuted and martyred on the grounds that their beliefs destabilized the pagan religions of the Roman government, thus calling the empire itself into question. Constantine's actions made it possible for Christians to worship and to copy their manuscripts freely.

The Greek uncial manuscripts of the New Testament are different from other ancient New Testament texts for the following reasons:

- The New Testament papyri were written on papyrus and are generally earlier (1st – 4th centuries C.E.)

- The New Testament minuscule, as the name indicates, were written in minuscule letters and generally later (9th – 15th centuries C.E.)

- Lectionaries were usually written in minuscule (but some in uncial) letters and generally later, on parchment, papyrus, or paper (from the 6th century)

- The uncials were written in majuscule letters on parchment (1st – 10th centuries)

In 1751, textual scholar Johann Jakob Wettstein (1693-1754) was aware of only twenty-three uncial codices of the Greek New Testament. A little over 100 years later, in 1859, renowned textual scholar Constantin von Tischendorf (1815-1874) had brought the number of uncial codices to sixty-four. Some sixty years later, in 1909, Caspar René Gregory (1846-1917) identified 161 uncial codices. Some 210 years from Wettstein, in 1963, Kurt Aland (1915-1994) increased the count to 250 uncial codices. In 1989, the second edition of Kurt and Barbara Alands' publication *The Text of the New Testament*, the authors listed 299 uncial codices.

Wettstein gave us one of the modern methods of classifying these uncial codices. He used the Latin capital letters to identify the uncials. For example, Codex Alexandrinus was given the letter "A," Codex Vaticanus was

---

[450] Metzger, Bruce M. (1992). *The Text of the New Testament: Its Transmission, Corruption, and Restoration* (in English) (3rd ed.). New York – Oxford: Oxford University Press. pp. 7-8.

[451] www.uni-muenster.de/INTF/

designated "B," with Codex Ephraemi being given the designation "C," and Codex Bezae was classified with "D." The last letter to be used by Wettstein in the classification uncial codices was "O." As time passed, the number of uncial manuscripts became larger than the Latin alphabet, so future textual scholars exhausted the Greek and Hebrew alphabets. It was Caspar René Gregory who moved on to assign manuscripts numerals that began with an initial 0. Codex Sinaiticus received the number 01, Alexandrinus received 02; Vaticanus was given 03, Ephraemi was designated with 04, and Bezae received the number 05, to mention just a few. By the time of Gregory's death in 1917, the number had reached 0161, with Ernst von Dobschütz increasing the number of uncials codices to 0208 by 1993. As of June 1, 2010, the number of codices had reached 0323 in the Gregory-Aland system, a forgotten 4th- or 5th-century Greek fragment of the Gospel of John in the Syrus Sinaiticus,[452] dating paleographically to 300-499 C.E., cataloged by the Institute for New Testament Textual Research (INTF) in Münster, Germany.[453]

Important Uncial Manuscripts

Codex Sinaiticus (01, ℵ) alone has a complete text of the New Testament. It is dated to c. 330–360 C.E.

---

[452] "That the famous Syrus Sinaiticus contains not only the Old Syriac Gospels, but also other palimpsest leaves, among them four leaves of a Greek codex of John's Gospel, is not a secret. Nevertheless, for 120 years, this Greek fragment, though probably contemporary with the great uncials, was not registered in any list of NT manuscripts and, as a result, completely neglected." – https://bibil.unil.ch/bibil/public/indexSimpleSearch.action

[453] http://ntvmr.uni-muenster.de/liste/

The Codex Sinaiticus Project has described the Sinaiticus as "one of the most important books in the world."[454] F. J. A. Hort felt that Codex Vaticanus and Codex Sinaiticus (as well as a few other early manuscripts) represented a text that reflected the original writing. Textual scholars have repeatedly told the story of how Constantin von Tischendorf rediscovered Codex Sinaiticus. We might begin with a short biography. Tischendorf was born in Lengenfeld, Saxony, near Plauen, in the year 1815. In 1834, he was educated in Greek at the University of Leipzig, and largely influenced by Georg Benedikt Winer. He soon took a special interest in New Testament criticism. However, Tischendorf became troubled by higher criticism of the Bible, which was at the root of German theologians' efforts to undermine the Greek New Testament as not authentic. To the contrary, Tischendorf was certain that a

Tischendorf in 1841

study of early manuscripts would enable textual scholars to restore the originals. Accordingly, he went on a quest to research all known manuscripts himself, believing that he would find others throughout his travels.

Tischendorf spent four years searching through some of the finest libraries in Europe. In May of 1844, he reached the Monastery of St. Catherine, located 4,500 feet above the Red Sea in Sinai. Gaining access to this impregnable fortress sanctuary was by way of a basket being lowered by a rope through a small opening in the wall.

Tischendorf was given permission to search their three libraries, which produced nothing noteworthy for some days. Then, as he was about to give up and continue his journey, he caught sight of exactly what he was looking for: ancient parchments, which filled a large basket in the main library hall. Likely shocking him to his very core, he listened as the librarian told him that they were going to be burned as two full baskets had already met the same fate. He spent hours on the manuscript, poring over the details, and Tischendorf was shocked to find 129 leaves from the oldest manuscript that he had ever seen. It was a Greek translation of parts of the Hebrew Scriptures. The librarian gave him 43 sheets but denied him the rest.

Tischendorf came back in 1853 when he found a mere fragment of the same manuscript that we now know dates to c. 330–360 C.E. He "deposited

---

[454] http://codexsinaiticus.org/en/

in the library of the University of Leipzig, in the shape of a collection which bears his name, fifty manuscripts, some of which convinced him that the manuscript originally contained the entire Old Testament, but that the greater part had been long since destroyed."[455] Codex Sinaiticus most likely consisted of 730 leaves. It was written in Greek uncial. Some six years later, Tischendorf returned to visit the monks at Mount Sinai for the third time. Just before he was scheduled to leave, he was shown the leaves that he had saved from the fire some fifteen years earlier and many others. They consisted of the entire Greek New Testament and part of a Greek translation of the Hebrew Old Testament.

Eventually, Tischendorf was given permission to take the manuscript to Cairo, Egypt, to make a copy. Ultimately, he carried the manuscript to the czar of Russia, to whom it was presented as a gift from the monks. Today, it can be found in the British Museum alongside Codex Alexandrinus. Modern textual scholars have identified at least three scribes (A, B, and C) who worked on codex Sinaiticus, with at least seven correctors (a, b, c, ca, cb, cc, e).[456] James H. Ropes describes the quality of Codex Sinaiticus:

Codex Sinaiticus is carelessly written, with many lapses of spelling due to the influence of dialectal and vulgar speech and many plain errors and crude vagaries. Omissions by homeoteleuton abound, and there are many other careless omissions. All these gave a large field for the work of correctors, and the manuscript does not stand by any means on the same level of workmanship as B.[457]

A two-thirds portion of the codex was held in the National Library of Russia from 1859 until 1933

Public Domain, https://commons.wikimedia.org/w/index.php?curid=480037

It can still be said that Codex Sinaiticus is considered fairly reliable as a witness to the New Testament text. However, it is true that the scribe of

[455] When Were our Gospels Written? - Christian Classics .., http://www.ccel.org/ccel/tischendorf/gospels.ii.iii.html (accessed March 28, 2016).

[456] Aland, Kurt; Barbara Aland (1995). *The Text of the New Testament: An Introduction to the Critical Editions and to the Theory and Practice of Modern Textual Criticism, trans. Erroll F. Rhodes.* Grand Rapids, Michigan: William B. Eerdmans Publishing Company. p. 107.

[457] James H. Ropes, "Vol. III: The Text of Acts," *The Beginnings of Christianity, Part I: Acts of the Apostles,* ed. F. J. Foakes Jackson and Kirsopp Lake (London: Macmillan, 1926), p. xlviii.

Sinaiticus was not as careful as the scribe of the Vaticanus. Not only was he more inclined to errors, but to creative corrections as well. F. J. A. Hort offered a comparison between the scribe of Vaticanus (B) and the scribe of the Sinaiticus (ℵ): "Turning from B to ℵ, we find ourselves dealing with the handiwork of a scribe of a different character. The omissions and repetitions of small groups of letters are rarely to be seen, but on the other hand, all the ordinary lapses due to rapid and careless transcription are more numerous, including substitutions of one word for another.… The singular readings are very numerous, especially in the Apocalypse, and scarcely ever commend themselves on internal grounds. It can hardly be doubted that many of them are individualisms of the scribe himself."[458]

Codex Alexandrinus (02, A) contains a complete text of the New Testament, minus Matthew 1:1-25:6; John 6:50 -8:52; and 2 Corinthians 4:13-12:6.

Alexandrinus is one of the four Great uncial codices. It is one of the earliest and most complete uncial manuscripts, along with Sinaiticus and Vaticanus.

Codex Alexandrinus resided in Alexandria for a number of years, the city from which it received its name. Thereafter, in 1621, Patriarch Cyril Lucar took it to Constantinople.[459] It would later be given to Charles I of England in 1627, which was too late for it to be used in the 1611 King James Version. In 1757, George II presented it to the National Library of the British Museum. Alexandrinus was the best manuscript in Britain until 1933,[460] when the British government purchased ℵ for the British Museum for £100,000.

---

[458] Westcott and Hort, *Introduction to the New Testament in the Original Greek*, 246–47.

[459] Tregelles, Samuel Prideaux (1856). *An Introduction to the Critical study and Knowledge of the Holy Scriptures*. London. p. 152.

[460] In 1875 Scrivener called it, "[t]his celebrated manuscript, by far the best deposited in England". *Scrivener, Frederick Henry Ambrose (1875). Six Lectures on the Text of the New Testament and the Ancient Manuscripts which contain it. London: Deighton, Bell & Co. p. 51.*

Of possibly 820 original leaves of Alexandrinus, 773 have been preserved, 639 of the Old Testament and 134 of the New. The physical features are as follows:

- **Dimensions:** 320 x 280 mm (text space: 240 x 205 mm). Two columns, generally of 50 or 51 lines; each line usually contains from 20 to 25 letters, but more are often inserted by compression at the end of the line.

- **Foliation:** ff. 144 (+ two unfoliated modern parchment flyleaves: one at the beginning and one at the end; f. 1 is a parchment flyleaf).

- **Collation:** Gatherings originally of eight leaves, numbered at the top of the first page; rebound in modern times in gatherings of six leaves.

- **Script:** Uncial. Written probably by three different hands (III, IV, and V in Milne and Skeat 1938); punctuation by the original scribes.

- **Binding:** Post-1600; gold-tooled leather with the royal arms of England and initials 'CR'.[461]

The beginning lines of each book are written in red ink, and a larger letter is set into the margin marks sections within the book. There are no accents or breathing marks by the original hand. However, there are a few by a later hand. The first hand wrote the punctuation.[462] The letters in codex Alexandrinus are larger than those in the Vaticanus. While there are no spaces between the words, there are some pauses by way of a dot between the words. The swapping of vowels of similar sounds is quite frequent in codex Alexandrinus. There is an affinity to increase the size of the first letter of each sentence. The letters N and M are sometimes confused. The letter combination ΓΓ is exchanged for ΝΓ. Codex Alexandrinus has capital letters to indicate new sections and is the oldest manuscript to do so. Alexandrinus has many iotacisms and other cases of the confusion of vowel sounds, e.g. αι in place of ε, ει for ι and η for ι. However, the number of iotacisms is no greater than other manuscripts from that period. There are many corrections that have been made in Alexandrinus, some of which come from the original scribe. However, most by far come from later hands. The corrected portions of the text agree with codices D, N, X, Y, Γ, Θ, Π, Σ, Φ and the vast majority of the minuscule manuscripts.[463]

---

[461] Digitized Manuscripts — British Library ... - bl.uk, http://www.bl.uk/manuscripts/FullDisplay.aspx?ref=Royal_MS_1_d_viii8 (accessed April 11, 2016).

[462] Bruce M. Metzger, *Manuscripts of the Greek Bible: An Introduction to Greek Palaeography* (Oxford, NY: Oxford University Press, 1991), 86.

[463] Ibid., 86.

The Greek text of the codex is of mixed text-types. On this Metzger writes, "In the Gospels, it is the oldest example of the Byzantine type of text, which is generally regarded as an inferior form of text. In the rest of the New Testament (which may have been copied by the scribe from a different exemplar from that which he employed for the text of the Gospels), it ranks along with B and ℵ as representative of the Alexandrian type of text."[464]

Codex Vaticanus (03, B) contains the Gospels, Acts, the General Epistles, the Pauline Epistles, the Epistle to the Hebrews (up to Hebrews 9:14, καθα[ριεί); it lacks 1 and 2 Timothy, Titus, Philemon, and Revelation. It is written on 759 leaves of vellum and is dated to c. 300–325 C.E.

Arguably, one could say that codex Vaticanus is the most valuable witness that we have for the Greek New Testament.[465] It is of course, named Vaticanus because it has been stored in the Vatican library from a time prior to 1475.[466] For centuries, the Vatican authorities kept the B (03) a private treasure and discouraged work on it by outside scholars. Paul D. Wegner writes, "At the beginning of the nineteenth century, Napoleon carried off this codex to Paris with other manuscripts as a war prize, but on his death in 1815, it was returned to the Vatican library. Constantine von Tischendorf applied for and finally obtained permission to·see the manuscript in order to collate difficult passages. He copied out or remembered enough of the text to be able to publish an edition of Vaticanus in 1867. Later that century (1868–1881) the Vatican published a better copy of the codex, but in 1889–

[464] Bruce M. Metzger, *The Text of the New Testament: Its Transmission, Corruption, and Restoration (3rd ed.)* (Oxford, NY: Oxford University Press, 1992), 47.

[465] Kurt Aland; Barbara Aland, *The Text of the New Testament: An Introduction to the Critical Editions and to the Theory and Practice of Modern Textual Criticism*, trans. Erroll F. Rhodes (Grand Rapids, Michigan: William B. Eerdmans Publishing Company, 1995), 109.

[466] Ibid. 47

1890 a complete photographic facsimile of this manuscript superseded all earlier attempts."[467]

The writing in codex Vaticanus is "small and delicate majuscules, perfectly simple and unadorned"[468] as Metzger put it. The Greek runs continuously, with no separation between the words, and all letters are an equal distance from one another so that to the modern eye, each line looks like one long word. Some scholars feel that Vaticanus is a little earlier than Sinaiticus because of it having no ornamentation at all, while others feel that Vaticanus and Sinaiticus were among the fifty manuscripts ordered by Constantine the Great. However, Skeat goes a step further, arguing that Vaticanus was to be a part of the fifty manuscripts but was a reject, "for it is deficient in the Eusebian canon tables and has many corrections by different scribes.[469] Whether Skeat is correct or not, codex Vaticanus is one of the most important manuscripts for the text of the Septuagint and especially the Greek New Testament.

Tischendorf claimed that codex Vaticanus was copied by three scribes (A, B, C), suggesting that two worked on the Old Testament while the third copied the entire New Testament.[470] Kenyon accepted Tischendorf's view, while T. C. Skeat, who had an opportunity to do a more extensive examination of the codex, contested the position of a third scribe (C) and argued that there were only two scribes, both working on the Old Testament (A and B), and one of them copying the entire New Testament (B).[471] Other paleographers agree with Skeat. Scribe (A) wrote Genesis through 1 Kings (pp 41–334) and Psalms through Tobias (pages 625–944). Scribe (B) wrote 1 Kings through 2 Esdra (pp 335–624), Hosea through Daniel (pp 945–1234), and the entire New Testament.[472] One corrector worked on Vaticanus soon after its writing, and another corrector from the 10th or 11th century worked on the manuscript. The latter corrector traced over the faded letters with fresh ink. However, he also omitted words and letters he judged to be wrong and added accent and breathing marks. Vaticanus is a representative of the Alexandrian text-type, the Alands placing it in Category I, "manuscripts of a very special quality which should always be considered in establishing the

---

[467] Paul D. Wegner, *A Student's Guide to Textual Criticism of the Bible: Its History Methods & Results* (Downers Grove, IL: InterVarsity Press, 2006), 260.

[468] Bruce M. Metzger, *The Text of the New Testament: Its Transmission, Corruption, and Restoration (4th ed.)* (Oxford, NY: Oxford University Press, 1992), 67.

[469] Ibid. 48.

[470] Constantin von Tischendorf, *Editio octava critica maior*, ed. C. R. Gregory (Lipsiae 1884), 360.

[471] Kurt Aland; Barbara Aland, *The Text of the New Testament: An Introduction to the Critical Editions and to the Theory and Practice of Modern Textual Criticism, trans. Erroll F. Rhodes* (Grand Rapids, Michigan: William B. Eerdmans Publishing Company, 1995), 109.

[472] H.J.M. Milne & T.C. Skeat, "Scribes and Correctors" (British Museum: London 1938).

original text …. B is by far the most significant of the uncials." (Aland and Aland, The Text of the New Testament 1995, 109, 109)

Codex Ephraemi (04, C) dates to the fifth century C.E., with 209 leaves surviving, of which 145 contain material from every New Testament book except Second Thessalonians and Second John. It is a noted palimpsest, i.e. a manuscript written over a partly erased older manuscript in such a way that the old words can be read beneath the new. Codex Ephraemi is about 12 inches by 9 inches (31 cm by 23 cm), and it is the earliest example of a manuscript containing just one column of writing on each page.

The Scriptural text that had appeared on this fifth-century codex was removed in the twelfth century, being written over with a Greek translation of thirty-eight sermons of the Syrian scholar Ephraem. It was not until the end of the seventeenth century that textual scholars noticed the Bible text beneath. While there was some progress made over the years in trying to decipher the text that lay beneath, it was difficult because of the faint and unclear condition of the ink that had been erased, not to mention the ragged state of many of the leaves, and the other text that overlapped with the original text. In an effort to read the text, some chemicals were applied to the manuscript. Eventually, most textual scholars of the time felt that the erased text was beyond recovery.

However, a name that we have heard before, Konstantin von Tischendorf, went to work on Codex Ephraemi in the early 1840s. It took Tischendorf two years, but he eventual deciphered the manuscript. How was he able to succeed where others had failed? Tischendorf had a good eye for the Greek uncial script and was blessed with excellent eyesight. Moreover, he discovered that if he held the parchment up to the light, the erased text was legible enough for him to make it out. Today scholars would use infrared, ultraviolet, and polarized light to illuminate the ancient text.

Metzger says that even "though the document dates from the fifth century, its text is of less importance than one might assume from its age. It seems to be compounded from all major text types, frequently agreeing with secondary Alexandrian witnesses and those of the later Koine or Byzantine type, which most scholars regard as the least valuable. Two correctors, referred to as C² or Cᵇ and C³ or Cᶜ, have corrected the manuscript. The former probably lived in Palestine in the sixth century, and the latter seems to have done his work in Constantinople in the ninth century."[473] Today, Codex Ephraemi is kept in the National Library in Paris, France.

Codex Bezae (05, Dᵉᵃ) dates to about 400 C.E., consisting of 406 leaves. It contains most of the four Gospels and Acts, with a small fragment of Third John. The codex is about ten by eight inches (25 by 20 cm), and it is an early example of a bilingual text, with Greek on the left page and Latin on the right. Theodore Bezae presented it to the University of Cambridge in 1581.

Paul D. Wegner observes that Bezae "is written in 'sense lines' so that some sentences are short and others long depending on the thought in the line. There is one column per page. The codex includes the Gospels (in Western order, i.e., Mt, Jn, Lk, Mk), Acts, and a short fragment of 3 John. It was found in 1562 at Lyons, France, by Theodore Beza, the successor of John Calvin at Geneva, who presented it to Cambridge University in 1581 (thus it is sometimes called 'Codex Cantabrigiensis')."

Codex Bezae is most likely a copy of a papyrus manuscript with an early text. It is similar to P²⁹ (Alexandrian, Western, Category I), P³⁸ (Western text-type, Category IV), and P⁴⁸, (Western text-type, Category IV), papyri dating to the third or fourth centuries. The first three lines of each book are in red

[473] Bruce M. Metzger; Bart D. Ehrman, *The Text of the New Testament: Its Transmission, Corruption, and Restoration (4ᵗʰ ed.)* (Oxford, NY: Oxford University Press, 1992), 68.

letters, and black and red ink alternate the title of books. Between the sixth and twelfth centuries, some eleven people have corrected the manuscript (G, A, C, B, D, E, H, F, J[1], L, K).[474] Of this manuscript, Metzger writes, "No known manuscript has so many and such remarkable variations from what is usually taken to be the normal New Testament text. Codex Bezae's special characteristic is the free addition (and occasional omission) of words, sentences, and even incidents."[475] For example, Luke 23:53 reads in the NASB (NA text), "And he took it down and wrapped it in a linen cloth, and laid Him in a tomb cut into the rock, where no one had ever lain." Bezae adds the words, "And after he [Jesus] was laid [in the tomb], he [Joseph of Arimathea] put before the tomb a [great] stone which twenty men could scarcely roll." Acts 19:9 reads in the NASB (NA text), "But when some were becoming hardened and disobedient, speaking evil of the Way before the people, he [Paul] withdrew from them and took away the disciples, reasoning daily in the school of Tyrannus." To this Bezae adds "from eleven o'clock to four," which is doubtful because of the heat at that time of day. Codex Bezae is the principal representative of the Western text.

Greek Uncial Manuscripts

#	Sign	Name	Date	Content
01	א	Sinaiticus	4th	A complete text of the New Testament
02	A	Alexandrinus	5th	It contains a complete text of the New Testament, minus Matthew 1:1-25:6; John 6:50 -8:52; 2 Corinthians 4:13-12:6
03	B	Vaticanus	4th	Gospels, Acts, the General Epistles, the Pauline Epistles, the Epistle to the Hebrews (up to Hebrews 9:14, καθα[ριει); it is lacking 1 and 2 Timothy, Titus, Philemon, and Revelation

---

[474] David C. Parker, *Codex Bezae: An Early Christian Manuscript and its Text*, Cambridge University Press, 1992, ss. 35-43, 123-163.

[475] Bruce M. Metzger; Bart D. Ehrman, The Text of the New Testament: Its Transmission, Corruption, and Restoration (4th ed.) (Oxford, NY: Oxford University Press, 1992), 68.

#	Sign	Name	Date	Content
04	C	Ephraemi	5th	Every New Testament book except Second Thessalonians and Second John
05	D^ea	Bezae	5th	In both Greek and Latin, most of the four Gospels and Acts, with a small fragment of 3 John
06	D^p	Claromontanus	6th	Pauline epistles
07	E^c	Basilensis	8th	Gospels
08	E^a	Laudianus	6th	Acts of the Apostles
09	F^c	Boreelianus	9th	Gospels
010	F^p	Augiensis	9th	Pauline epistles
011	G^c	Seidelianus I	9th	Gospels
012	G^p	Boernerianus	9th	Pauline epistles
013	H^c	Seidelianus II	9th	Gospels
014	H^a	Mutinensis	9th	Acts of the Apostles
015	H^p	Coislinianus	6th	Pauline Epistles
016	I	Freerianus	5th	Pauline epistles
017	K^c	Cyprius	9th	Gospels
018	K^ap	Mosquensis	9th	Acts, Paul, James, 1 Peter, 2 Peter, 1 John, 2 John, 3 John, Jude
019	L^c	Regius	8th	Gospels

#	Sign	Name	Date	Content
020	L^{ap}	Angelicus	9th	Acts, Paul
021	M	Campianus	9th	Gospels
022	N	Petropolitanus Purp.	6th	Gospels
023	O	Sinopensis	6th	Gospel of Matthew
024	P^c	Guelferbytanus A	6th	Gospels
025	P^{apr}	Porphyrianus	9th	Acts, Paul, James, 1 Peter, 2 Peter, 1 John, 2 John, 3 John, Jude, Rev
026	Q	Guelferbytanus B	5th	Luke 4,6,12,15,17–23; John 12,14
027	R	Nitriensis	6th	Gospel of Luke
028	S	Vaticanus 354	**949**	Gospels
029 = [0113=0125=0139]	T	Borgianus	5th	Luke — John
030	U	Nanianus	9th	Gospels
031	V	Mosquensis II	9th	Gospels
032	W	Washingtonianus	5th	Gospels
033	X	Monacensis	10th	Gospels
034	Y	Macedoniensis	9th	Gospels
035	Z	Dublinensis	6th	Matt 1–2,4–8,10–15,17–26
036	Γ	Tischendorfianus IV	10th	Gospels

#	Sign	Name	Date	Content
037	Δ	Sangallensis	9th	Gospels
038	Θ	Coridethianus	9th	Gospels
039	Λ	Tischendorfianus III	9th	Luke, John
040	Ξ	Zacynthius	6th	Gospel of Luke †[476]
041	Π	Petropolitanus	9th	Gospels
042	Σ	Rossanensis	6th	Matthew, Mark
043	Φ	Beratinus	6th	Matthew, Mark
044	Ψ	Athous Lavrensis	9th/10th	Gospels, Acts, Paul
045	Ω	Athous Dionysiou	9th	Gospels

Uncials 046-0323

#	Name	Date	Content
046	Vaticanus 2066	10th	Book of Revelation
047	—	8th	Gospels
048	Vaticanus 2061	5th	Acts, James, 1 Peter, 2 Peter, 1 John, 2 John, 3 John, Jude, Paul
049	—	9th	Acts, James, 1 Peter, 2 Peter, 1 John, 2 John, 3 John, Jude, Pauline epistles
050	—	9th	Gospel of John

---

[476] In textual criticism and in some editions of works written before the invention of printing, daggers are used to enclose text that is believed not to be original. – Paul D. Wegner (2006). A student's guide to textual criticism of the Bible. InterVarsity Press. p. 194

#	Name	Date	Content
051	Ath. Pantokratoros	10th	Book of Revelation
052	Ath. Panteleimonos	10th	Book of Revelation
053	—	9th	Gospel of Luke
054	Codex Barberini	8th	Gospel of John
055	—	11th	Gospels
056	—	10th	Acts, Pauline epistles
057	—	4th/5th	Acts of the Apostles
058	—	4th	Gospel of Matthew 18
059=0215	—	4th/5th	Gospel of Mark
060	—	6th	Gospel of John 14
061	—	5th	1 Timothy
062	—	5th	Epistle to the Galatians
063=0117	—	9th	Luke, John
064 =074 =090	—	6th	Matthew 27, Mark
065	—	6th	Gospel of John
066	—	6th	Acts of the Apostles
067	—	6th	Matthew, and Mark
068	—	5th	Gospel of John 16

#	Name	Date	Content
069	—	5th	Gospel of Mark 10–11
070 =0110 =0124=017 8=0179 =0180=019 0=0191 =0193=019 4=0202	—	6th	Luke, and John
071	—	5th/6th	Gospel of Matthew 1, 25
072	—	5th/6th	Gospel of Mark 2–3
073=084	—	6th	Gospel of Matthew 14–15 †
074	—	6th	Matt. 25, 26, 28, Mark 1, 2, 5 †
075	—	10th	Pauline epistles
076	—	5th/6th	Acts of the Apostles 2
077	—	5th	Acts of the Apostles 13
078	—	6th	Matt, Luke, John
079	—	6th	Gospel of Luke
080	—	6th	Gospel of Mark 9–10
081	Tischendorfianus II	6th	2 Corinthians 1–2
082	—	6th	Epistle to the Ephesians 4
083 =0112=235	—	5th/6th	John 1–4, Mark 14–16 Mark 13
084	—	6th	Gospel of Matthew 15 †

#	Name	Date	Content
085	—	6th	Gospel of Matthew 20, 22
086	—	6th	Gospel of John 1, 3–4
087=092b	—	6th	Matt 1–2, 19, 21; John 18; Mark 12
088	—	5th/6th	1 Cor. 15:53–16:9, Tit 1:1–13
089=092a	—	6th	Gospel of Matthew 26:2–19
090	—	6th	Matt 26, 27; Mark 1–2 †
091	—	6th	John 6
092a, 092b	—	6th	Matt 26:4–7.10-12
093	—	6th	Acts 24–25, 1 Pet 2–3
094	—	6th	Gospel of Matthew 24:9–21
095=0123	—	8th	Acts of the Apostles 2–3 †
096	—	7th	Acts of the Apostles 2, 26
097	—	7th	Acts of the Apostles 13
098	—	7th	2 Corinthians 11
099	—	7th	Gospel of Mark 16
0100=0195	—	7th	Gospel of John 20
0101	—	8th	Gospel of John 1
0102=0138	—	7th	Gospel of Luke 3–4

#	Name	Date	Content
0103	—	7th	Gospel of Mark 13–14
0104	—	6th	Matthew 23 †; Mark 13–14 †
0105	—	10th	Gospel of John 6–7
0106=0119	Tischendorfianus I	7th	Matthew 12–15 †
0107	—	7th	Matt 22–23; Mark 4–5
0108	—	7th	Gospel of Luke 11
0109	—	7th	Gospel of John 16–18
0110	—	6th	Gospel of John
0111	—	7th	2 Thess. 1:1–2:2
0112	—	5th/6th	Gospel of Mark 14–16
0113=029	—	5th	Gospel of Luke 21 Gospel of John 1
0114	—	8th	Gospel of John 20 †
0115	—	9th/10th	Gospel of Luke 9–10 †
0116	—	8th	Matt 19–27; Mark 13–14;Luke 3–4 †
0117	—	9th	Gospel of Luke †
0118	—	8th	Gospel of Matthew 11 †
0119	—	7th	Gospel of Matthew 13–15 †
0120	—	8th	Acts of the Apostles

#	Name	Date	Content
0121a	—	10th	1 Corinthians †
0121b	Codex Ruber	10th	Epistle to the Hebrews †
0122	—	10th	Galatians †; Hebrews †
0123	—	8th	Acts of the Apostles 2–3 †
0124	See 070	6th	—
0125	See 029	5th	—
0126	—	8th	Gospel of Mark 5–6
0127	—	8th	Gospel of John 2:2–11
0128	—	9th	Gospel of Matthew 25:32–45
0129=0203	—	?	1 Peter †
0130	Sangallensis 18	9th	Mark 1–2, Luke 1–2 †
0131	—	9th	Gospel of Mark 7–9 †
0132	—	9th	Gospel of Mark 5 †
0133	Blenheimius	9th	Matthew †; Mark †
0134	—	8th	Gospel of Mark 3 †; 5 †
0135	—	9th	Matthew, Mark, Luke
0136=0137	—	9th	Gospel of Matthew 14; 25–26 †
0137	—	9th	Gospel of Matthew 13 †

#	Name	Date	Content
0138	—	7th	Gospel of Matthew 21:24–24:15
0139	See 029	5th	—
0140	—	10th	Acts of the Apostles 5
0141	—	10th	Gospel of John †
0142	—	10th	Acts, Paul, James, 1 Peter, 2 Peter, 1 John, 2 John, 3 John, Jude
0143	—	6th	Gospel of Mark 8 †
0144	—	7th	Gospel of Mark 6 †
0145	—	7th	Gospel of John 6:26–31
0146	—	8th	Gospel of Mark 10:37–45
0147	—	6th	Gospel of Luke 6:23–35
0148	—	8th	Gospel of Matthew 28:5–19
0149 = 0187	—	6th	Gospel of Mark 6 †
0150	—	9th	Pauline epistles
0151	—	9th	Pauline epistles
0152	Talisman	—	—
0153	Ostracon	—	2 Cor. 4:7; 2 Timothy 2:20
0154	—	9th	Gospel of Mark 10, 11
0155	—	9th	Gospel of Luke 3, 6

#	Name	Date	Content
0156	—	6th	2 Peter 3
0157	—	7th/8th	1 John 2
0158	—	5th/6th	Epistle to the Galatians 1
0159	—	6th	Epistle to the Ephesians 4–5
0160	—	4th/5th	Gospel of Matthew 26
0161	—	8th	Gospel of Matthew 22
0162	—	3rd/4th	Gospel of John 2:11–22
0163	—	5th	Book of Revelation 16
0164	—	6th/7th	Gospel of Matthew 13
0165	—	5th	Acts of the Apostles 3–4
0166	—	5th	Acts 28 James 1:11
0167	—	7th	Gospel of Mark
0168	—	8th	Gospels †
0169	—	4th	Book of Revelation 3–4
0170	—	5th/6th	Gospel of Matthew 6 †
0171	—	3rd/4th	Matthew 10; Luke 22
0172	—	5th	Epistle to the Romans 1–2 †
0173	—	5th	Epistle of James 1 †

#	Name	Date	Content
0174	—	5th	Epistle to the Galatians 2:5–6
0175	—	5th	Acts of the Apostles 6 †
0176	—	4th/5th	Epistle to the Galatians 3 †
0177	—	10th	Gospel of Luke 1–2 †
0178 = 070	—	6th	Gospel of Luke 16:4-12
0179 = 070	—	6th	Gospel of Luke 21:30-22:2
0180 = 070	—	6th	Gospel of John 7:3-12
0181	—	4th/5th	Gospel of Luke 9–10
0182	—	5th	Gospel of Luke 19
0183	—	7th	Gospel of Luke 9–10
0184	—	6th	Gospel of Mark 15
0185	—	4th	1 Corinthians 2, 3
0186	—	5th/6th	2 Corinthians 4 †
0187	—	6th	Gospel of Mark 6
0188	—	4th	Gospel of Mark 11
0189	—	2nd/3rd	Acts of the Apostles 5:3–21
0190 = 070	—	6th	Gospel of Luke 10:30-39
0191 = 070	—	6th	Gospel of Luke 12:5-14

#	Name	Date	Content
0192 = *ℓ 16 04*	—	—	—
0193 = 070	—	6th	Gospel of John 3:23-32
0194 = 070	—	6th	—
0195	—	7th	Gospel of John 20 †
0196	—	9th	Matthew 5, Luke 24
0197	—	9th	Gospel of Matthew 20; 22
0198	—	6th	Epistle to the Colossians 3
0199	—	6th/7th	1 Corinthians 11
0200	—	7th	Gospel of Matthew 11
0201	—	5th	1 Corinthians 12; 14
0202	—	6th	Gospel of Luke 8–9 †
0203	—	9th	—
0204	—	7th	Gospel of Matthew 24
0205	—	8th	Epistle to Titus
0206	—	4th	1 Peter 5
0207	—	4th	Book of Revelation 9:2–15
0208	—	6th	Col 1–2, 1 Thess. 2

#	Name	Date	Content
0209	—	7th	Rom. 14:9-23; 16:25-27; 15:1-2; 2 Cor. 1:1-15; 4:4-13; 6:11-7, 2; 9:2-10:17; 2 Pet 1:1-2, 3
0210	—	7th	John 5:44; 6:1-2, 41-42
0211	—	7th	Gospels
0212	Dura Parchment 24	3rd	Diatessaron
0213	—	5th/6th	Gospel of Mark 3
0214	—	4th/5th	Gospel of Mark 8
0215	—	5th/6th	Gospel of Mark 15:20–21,26-27
0216	—	5th	Gospel of John 8–9
0217	—	5th	Gospel of John 11–12
0218	—	5th	Gospel of John 12
0219	—	4th/5th	Epistle to the Romans 2–9
0220	—	3rd/4th	Epistle to the Romans 4:23–5:3; 5:8–13
0221	—	4th	Epistle to the Romans 5–6
0222	—	4th	1 Corinthians 9
0223	—	6th	2 Corinthians 1–2
0224	—	5th/6th	2 Corinthians 4 †
0225	—	6th	2 Corinthians 5–6, 8

#	Name	Date	Content
0226	—	5th	1 Thessalonians 4:16–5:5
0227	—	5th	Epistle to the Hebrews 11
0228	—	4th	Epistle to the Hebrews 12
0229	—	8th	Book of Revelation 18, 19
0230	—	4th	Epistle to the Ephesians 6
0231	—	4th	Gospel of Matthew 26–27
0232	—	5th/6th	2 John 1–5, 6–9
0233	—	8th	Gospels
0234	—	8th	Matthew 28; John 1
0235	—	5th/6th	Gospel of Mark 13
0236	—	5th	Acts of the Apostles 3
0237	—	6th	Gospel of Matthew 15
0238	—	8th	Gospel of John 7
0239	—	7th	Gospel of Luke 2
024	—	5th	Epistle to Titus 1
0241	—	6th	1 Timothy 3–4
0242	—	4th	Gospel of Matthew 8–9; 13
0243	—	10th	1 Cor 13-2 Cor 13

#	Name	Date	Content
0244	—	5th	Acts of the Apostles 11–12
0245	—	6th	1 John 3–4
0246	—	6th	Epistle of James 1
0247	—	5th/6th	1 Peter 5; 2 Peter 1
0248	—	9th	Gospel of Matthew
0249	—	10th	Gospel of Matthew 25
0250	Climaci Rescriptus	8th	Gospels †
0251	—	6th	3 John 12–15; Jude 3–5
0252	Barcilonensis 6	5th	Epistle to the Hebrews 6 †
0253	—	6th	Gospel of Luke 10:19–22
0254	—	5th	Galatians 5:13–17
0255	—	9th	Gospel of Matthew 26; 27
0256	—	8th	Gospel of John 6
0257	—	9th	Matthew 5–26; Mark 6–16
0258	—	?	Gospel of John 10
0259	—	7th	1 Timothy 1
0260	—	6th	Gospel of John 1
0261	—	5th	Galatians 1; 4
0262	—	7th	1 Timothy 1

#	Name	Date	Content
0263	—	6th	Gospel of Mark 5
0264	—	5th	Gospel of John 8
0265	—	6th	Gospel of Luke 7
0266	—	6th	Gospel of Luke 20
0267	Barcelonensis 16	5th	Gospel of Luke 8
0268	—	7th	Gospel of John 1
0269	—	9th	Gospel of Mark 6
0270	—	5th/6th	1 Corinthians 15
0271	—	9th	Gospel of Matthew 12
0272	—	9th	Gospel of Luke 16–17; 19
0273	—	9th	Gospel of John 2–3†; 4†; 5–6†
0274	—	5th	Gospel of Mark 6–10†
0275	—	7th	Gospel of Matthew 5
0276	—	8th	Gospel of Mark 14–15
0277	—	7th/8th	Gospel of Matthew 14
0278	—	9th	Pauline epistles
0279	—	8th/9th	Gospel of Luke 8; 2
0280	—	8th	Pauline epistles
0281	—	7th/8th	Gospel of Matthew 6–27 †
0282	—	6th	Epistle to Philemon 2; 3 †
0283	—	9th	Gospel of Mark †
0284	—	8th	Matthew 26; 27; 28 †

#	Name	Date	Content
0285	—	6th	Pauline epistles †
0286	—	6th	Matt. 16:13–19; John 10:12–16
0287	—	9th	Gospels †
0288	—	6th	Gospel of Luke †
0289	—	7th/8th	Romans — 1 Corinthians
0290	—	9th	Gospel of John 18:4–20:2
0291	—	7th/8th	Gospel of Luke 8–9
0292	—	6th	Gospel of Mark 6–7
0293	—	7th/8th	Gospel of Matthew 21; 26
0294	—	7th/8th	Acts of the Apostles 14–15
0295	—	9th	2 Corinthians 12:14–13:1
0296	—	6th	2 Cor. 7; 1 John 5
0297	—	9th	Gospel of Matthew 1; 5
0298	—	8th/9th	Gospel of Matthew 26
0299	—	10th/11th	Gospel of John 20:1–7
0300	—	6th/7th	Gospel of Matthew 20:2–17
0301	—	5th	Gospel of John 17:1–4
0302	—	6th	Gospel of John 10:29–30
0303	—	7th	Gospel of Luke 13:17–29
0304	—	9th	Acts of the Apostles 6:5–7:13
0305	—	?	Gospel of Matthew 20
0306	—	9th	Gospel of John 9

#	Name	Date	Content
0307	—	7th	Matt 11–12; Mark 11–12; Luke 9–10,22
0308	—	4th	Book of Revelation 11
0309	—	6th	Gospel of John 20
0310	—	10th	Epistle to Titus 2:15–3:7
0311	—	8th/9th	Epistle to the Romans 8:1–13
0312	—	3rd/4th	Gospel of Luke 5; 7
0313	—	5th	Gospel of Mark 4:9.15
0314	—	6th	Gospel of John 5:43
#	Name	Date	Content
0315	—	4th/5th	Mark 2:9.21.25; 3:1–2
0316	—	7th	Epistle of Jude 18–25
0317	—	7th?	Gospel of Mark 14
0318	—	7th	Gospel of Mark 9–14
0319 (D^{abs1})	Sangermanensis	9th/10th	Pauline epistles
0320 (D^{abs2})	Waldeccensis	10th	Ephesians 1:3–9; 2:11–18
0321		5th	Matt 24:37-25; 1:32-45; 26:31-45
0322		8th/9th	Gospel of Mark 3; 6
0323	Syrus Sinaiticus	4th/5th	Gospel of John 7:6–15 ; 9:17–23

Minuscule Manuscripts

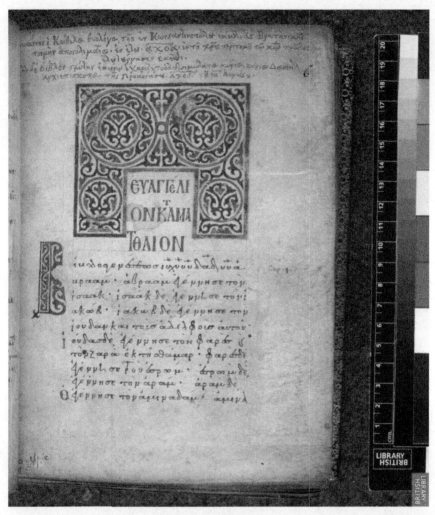

The minuscule script was a style of Greek writing used as a book hand during the ninth and tenth centuries in Byzantine manuscripts. The minuscule took the place of the Greek uncial, third and ninth centuries C.E. that resembles a modern capital letter but is more rounded. The minuscule differed from the uncial in that it used smaller letters, which were more round and more connected letters, as well as a large number of ligatures. Most of the minuscules were written on parchment. It was not until the twelfth century that paper began to be used. These forms came about through earlier informal cursive writing. There are at present 2,882 minuscule texts, made in a running style of writing. These were written during the period from the ninth-century C.E. to the inception of the printing press in 1455. The following is a chart showing the differences between the letter formats.

Majuscule	Uncial	Cursive	Minuscule	Minuscule with ligatures	Modern lower case
A	Λ	λυατα	δωϡα	α αϳ αϙ ϳα μα ϱϥ	α
B	B	υ&3βυ	βεββυ		β
Γ	Γ	ⲅⲅγ	ⲅⲅγ	γ ⲅ̃ ϳ ϟ	γ
Δ	Δ	δϟλϟλ	λⲁⲋ	δ δα ϟϟ ϟϟ	δ
E	E	ετεϲϐδ	ϐεϟϲε	ε ϥ δϐ ϟ ⲅϳ	ε
Z	Z	ⲍⲍⲋⲋ	ⲍⲍⲋⲍⲋ		ζ
H	H	ⲡⲡⲕⲕ	ⲕⲕⲏⲛ	η ⲓⲱ ϟ ϟϟ	η
Θ	Θ	θⲩⲇⲗ	θϙϙ	θ ϟ ϟϟ ϟϟⲟ	θ
I	I	ⲓ	ⲓⲩ ⲓ		ι
K	K	ⲕⲕⲕⲕ	ⲕⲕⲕⲏ	κ κα κϟⲩ κϟⲩ	κ
Λ	λ	λⲩⲗ	λⲗⲩⲩ	λ ϟ ϟϟ ϟϐ	λ
M	M	ⲩⲩⲕ	ⲙⲙⲙⲩ	μ μϟⲩ μϟⲩ ⲩϟ	μ
N	N	ⲛⲕⲛⲙ	ⲛⲛγⲩⲕ	ν ⲟⲩ ϟⲩ ϟ ⲧϟⲩ	ν
Ξ	Σ	Ξϟ?ϟ	ϟϟⲈⲈ		ξ
O	O	ⲟϟⲟ	ⲟ	ⲟ ϟϟ κϟ ϟⲟ ϟ	ο
Π	Π	ⲡⲡⲛⲱ	π ⲱ ⲱ	π ⲟϟ ϟ ⲁⲱ	π
P	P	ρϟϟⲉ	ρⲉⲉρρ	ρ ϟⲩ ϟⲩ ⲟⲩϟα	ρ
Σ	C	ⲩⲥⲟ	ⲉⲥⲟⲩⲟⲉ	σ ϟⲁⲋ ⲟϟ ⲟⲩⲱ	σ
T	T	ⲧⲧγⲩ	ϟⲧⲗⲗ	τ ϟ ⲧⲟ ⲧϟ ϟ ϟ	τ
Υ	Υ	ⲩⲅ	ⲩⲅⲩⲓ	υ ϟ ⲓⲱ ⲓⲋ	υ
Φ	Φ	φⲧϟ	φ ϟ	φ ϟⲓ ϟⲟ φ	φ
X	X	χ	ⲭϟⲭ		χ
Ψ	Ψ	ϟⲧ	Ψⲯⲯ		ψ
Ω	ⲱ	ⲱφⲟⲟ	ⲱⲱⲱⲟⲟ	ⲱ ϟⲩ ϟⲱ ϟⲟ	ω

395

Important Minuscule Manuscripts

Family 1

Kirsopp Lake c. 1914

Family 1 was discovered in 1902 when Kirsopp Lake (1872–1946) identified this text family, which included 1, 118, 131, 209. Family 1 is a group of Greek manuscripts of the gospels, dating from the 12th to the 15th century. It is symbolized as f^1; however, it is also known as "the Lake Group." Textual scholars now consider 205, 205[abs], 872 (Mark only), 884 (in part), 1582, 2193, and 2542 (in part) to be members of Family 1. Metzger says that after analyzing the Gospel of Mark, indications are that this family often agrees with **Codex Koridethi**, also named *Codex Coridethianus*, designated by Θ, 038, or Theta (in the Gregory-Aland numbering), going back to the type of text in Caesarea in the third and fourth centuries.[477] Dutch scholar Desiderius Erasmus used manuscript 1 along with a handful of others to produce the first Greek New Testament.

Minuscule_1_(GA)_f_265_v

Family 1 or the Lake Group of manuscripts placed the interpolation story of the Adulteress, also known as the Pericope Adulterae (John 7:53-8:11), after John 21:25. It is a later addition to the Gospel John and not a part of the original. Family 1 also includes the longer ending of Mark (16:9-20), which is also a second-century addition. Additional evidence against the long conclusion of Mark's Gospel is the fact that manuscripts 1 and 1582 contain a scholion (scribal note) that brings into question its authenticity: Εν τισι μεν των αντιγραφων εως ωδε πληρουται ο ευαγγελιστης εως ου και Ευσεβιος ο Παμφιλου εκανονισεν εν πολλοις δε και ταυτα φερεται. ("In some of the copies, the evangelist is fulfilled until here, until

---

[477] Bruce M. Metzger; Bart D. Ehrman, *The Text of the New Testament: Its Transmission, Corruption, and Restoration (fourth Ed.)*, (New York: Oxford University Press, 2005), p. 87.

which point also Eusebius Pamphili made his canons. But in many these [following] things also are extant.")[478]

Family 13

In 1868, William Ferrar of Dublin University discovered four manuscripts belonging to the same text type or family, which include 13, 69, 124, and 346. Because 13 was the first manuscript, the group became known

as family 13 (f[13]); however, it is also known as the Ferrar Group, which now include 13, 69, 124, 230, 346, 543, 788, 826, 828, 983, 1689, and 1709, dating between the eleventh and fifteenth centuries.[479] This family exhibits unique variant readings, such as placing the story of the adulterous woman (John 7:53-8:11) after Luke 21:38, or elsewhere in Luke's Gospel rather than in the Gospel of John. The text of Luke 22:43-44 is placed after Matthew 26:39. The text of Matthew 16:2b–3 is absent. Barbara Aland, Klaus Wachtel, and others at the Institute for New Testament

Minuscule 13 Ending of Mark

Textual Research (Institut für Neutestamentliche Textforschung, INTF) suggest that some of these manuscripts from family 13 (Ferrar Group) are more comparable to the majority Byzantine Text, and, therefore, should not be included in this family at all.

---

[478] Kirsopp Lake, *Codex 1 of the Gospels and its Allies*, Texts and Studies 1902, s. 92.

[479] Bruce M. Metzger; Bart D. Ehrman, *The Text of the New Testament: Its Transmission, Corruption, and Restoration (fourth Ed.)*, (New York: Oxford University Press, 2005), p. 87.

Minuscule 16

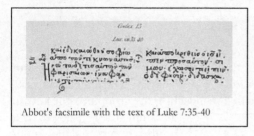

Abbot's facsimile with the text of Luke 7:35-40

This is a Diglot of Greek-Latin in the minuscule script of the New Testament on 361 parchment leaves, dated paleographically to the 14th century.[480] The minuscule is about 12.4 by 9.9 inches (31.6 cm by 25.2 cm). It has full notes written in the margin (i.e., marginalia) and was arranged for liturgical use. Minuscule 16 was "written in four different colors: the narrative in vermilion, the words of Jesus and angels in crimson, Old Testament quotes and the words of the disciples in blue, and the words of the Pharisees, the centurion, Judas Iscariot, and Satan in black. Presently the manuscript is housed in the Bibliothèque Nationale, Paris."[481] The four gospels are almost complete within the text. However, it has lacunae (gaps in the text) in Mark 16:14-20. Minuscule 16 is written in two columns per page, 26 lines per page.[482] The Greek portion of the text is mixed, but it is largely the Byzantine text-type.

Minuscule 28

The manuscript contains the text of the four Gospels on 292 parchment leaves. It is about 9.09 by 7.4 inches (31.6 cm by 25.2 cm), dated by paleographers to the eleventh century C.E., with numerous lacunae. The text is written in one column per page, 19 lines per page.[483] The words are continuous without any separation. Metzger would agree that the letters were "written carelessly by an ignorant scribe;"[484] however, he goes on to say that it "contains many noteworthy readings, especially in Mark, where its text is akin to the Caesarean type,"[485] and the Byzantine text-type in the rest of the

---

[480] Aland, K.; M. Welte; B. Köster; K. Junack (1994). *Kurzgefasste Liste der griechischen Handschriften des Neues Testaments* (2 ed.). Berlin, New York: Walter de Gruyter. p. 47.

[481] Paul D. Wegner, *A Student's Guide to Textual Criticism of the Bible: Its History, Methods and Results*, (Downers Grove: InterVarsity Press, 2006), p. 266.

[482] Liste; Münster: Institute for New Testament Textual Research. Retrieved 05-09-2016.

[483] Ibid.

[484] Frederick Henry Ambrose Scrivener; Edward Miller (1894). *A Plain Introduction to the Criticism of the New Testament* (4 ed.). London: George Bell & Sons. p. 194.

[485] Bruce M. Metzger; Bart D. Ehrman, *The Text of the New Testament: Its Transmission, Corruption, and Restoration (fourth Ed.)*, (New York: Oxford University Press, 2005), p. 87.

Gospels. The initial letters of minuscule 28 are in color. The Alands placed it in Category V.[486]

Minuscule 33

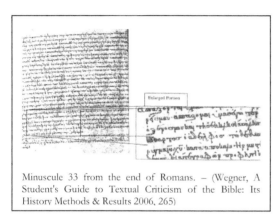

Minuscule 33 from the end of Romans. – (Wegner, A Student's Guide to Textual Criticism of the Bible: Its History Methods & Results 2006, 265)

Wegner says, the "text of this manuscript (33) is very similar to that of Codex Vaticanus, and since the time of Johann G. Eichhorn in the early nineteenth century, it has been nicknamed 'the Queen of the Cursives.'"[487] Minuscule 33 contains some of the Prophets of the Old Testament and the entire New Testament minus the book of Revelation by John. It contains 143 parchment leaves. It is about 14.8 by 9.8 inches (31.6 cm by 25.2 cm), having one column per page with lines ranging from 48-52. It is dated by paleographers to the nine century C.E., with three lacunae in the Gospel of Mark and the Gospel of Luke (Mark 9:31-11:11; 13:11-14:60; Luke 21:38-23:26).[488] Metzger says that 33 is an excellent representative of the Alexandrian type of text, but it also shows the influence of the Koine or Byzantine type, particularly in Acts and the Pauline epistles."[489] The text is divided into chapters, with the numbers given in the margins and chapter titles at the top of the pages. The order of books is as follows: the Gospels, Acts, James, First and Second Peter, First, Second, and Third John, Jude, Romans, First and Second Corinthians, Galatians, Ephesians, Philippians, Colossians, First and Second Thessalonians, Hebrews, First and Second Timothy, Titus and Philemon, but the book of Revelation missing. The book of Romans ends as follows, 16:23; 16:25-27; 16:24, similar to Codex Porphyrianus and minuscules 104, 256, 263, 365, 436, 459, 1319, 1573, and 1852.

---

[486] Kurt Aland; Barbara Aland (1995). *The Text of the New Testament: An Introduction to the Critical Editions and to the Theory and Practice of Modern Textual Criticism.* Erroll F. Rhodes (trans.). Grand Rapids: William B. Eerdmans Publishing Company. p. 129.

[487] Paul D. Wegner, *A Student's Guide to Textual Criticism of the Bible: Its History, Methods and Results*, (Downers Grove: InterVarsity Press, 2006), p. 266.

[488] Caspar René Gregory, (1900). *Textkritik des Neuen Testamentes.* Leipzig: J.C. Hinrichs. p. 136.

[489] Bruce M. Metzger; Bart D. Ehrman, *The Text of the New Testament: Its Transmission, Corruption, and Restoration (fourth Ed.)*, (New York: Oxford University Press, 2005), p. 88.

Minuscule 61

Codex Montfortianus, also known as minuscule 61, is a minuscule Greek manuscript of the New Testament on paper. It is dated to about 1520 and is now at the Trinity College, Dublin. Minuscule 61 contains the entire New Testament. It has one column per page, 21 lines per page, on 455 paper leaves. It is about 6.2 by 4.7 inches (15.8 cm by 12 cm). The Gospels and Acts are of the Byzantine text-type, which the Alands place in Category V. It is a mixed text in the Pauline epistles and General epistles, placed in Category III.

Minuscule 69 (GA) 14b

Minuscule 69

Codex Leicester or Codex Leicestrensis, also known as minuscule 69, is a minuscule Greek manuscript of the New Testament on paper and parchment leaves (91 parchments and 122 paper). It is dated to the 15th century and is now at Leicester, in the East Midlands of England. Minuscule 69 contains the entire New Testament with four lacunae (Matthew 1:1-18:15; Acts 10:45-14:17; Jude 7-25; Revelation 19:10-22:21), on 213 leaves, about 14.9 by 10.6 inches (37.8 cm by 27 cm). The Gospels are of the Caesarean text-type (Category III), the rest of the books being of a Byzantine text-type (Category V).

Minuscule 81

Minuscule 81 is a minuscule Greek manuscript of the New Testament on parchment. It is dated to 1044 and is now at the British Library in Alexandria. It is about 7.09 by 5.0 inches (18 cm by 12.6 cm). Minuscule 81 contains almost a complete text of the book of Acts and the Epistles on 282 parchment leaves, with some lacunae (Acts 4:8-7:17; 17:28-23:9), having one column per page, 23 lines per page, in small letters. The Alands place it in Category II, of the Alexandrian text-type, with some Byzantine readings.

Metzger says, "It is one of the most important of all minuscule manuscripts."[490]

Minuscule 157

Minuscule 157

Minuscule 157 is a minuscule Greek manuscript of the New Testament on vellum. According to the colophon (i.e. details in books), it is dated to the year 1122, and it is now at the Vatican Library. It contains a complete text of the four Gospels on 325 parchment leaves, having one column per page, 22 lines per page, about 7.3 by 5.4 inches (18.6 cm by 13.6 cm). Its readings often agree with Codex Bezae. However, it is a mixture of text-types with a strong Alexandrian element. The Alands placed it in Category III. At the end of each Gospel, it is stated that it was written in 1122. It was penned "for the Emperor John II Comnenus (1118-43)."[491]

Ancient Versions

A version is a translation of the Bible from Hebrew, Aramaic, and Greek into another language. Actually, the entire Bible has been translated into over 450 languages, although sections of the Bible have been translated into more than 2,000 languages.

Bible translation in part or whole from the original languages into another language has been going on for some 2,200 years and has allowed literally millions of people, who might otherwise have been deprived of God's Word, to have access to it. The early versions of the Bible were no different from the original language copies in their production; they too had to be written by hand on papyrus or animal skin. However, since the invention of the printing press in 1455, the number of versions has grown astronomically, in much greater quantities in comparison to their ancient counterparts. Not all versions have been prepared directly from the Hebrew or Greek Bible texts; some are based on earlier translations.

---

[490] Ibid. 86

[491] Ibid. 86

The Septuagint

The Septuagint is the customary term for the Old Greek translation of the Hebrew Scriptures. I mention it here in a book about NT textual criticism because it was usually the source of quotations found in the New Testament. The word "Septuagint" means "seventy" and is frequently shortened by using the Roman numeral LXX, which is a reference to the tradition that 72 Jewish translators (rounded off to 70) produced the version in the time of Ptolemy II Philadelphus (285-246 B.C.E.). The first five books of Moses were done around 280 B.C.E. The rest was completed by 150 B.C.E. As a result, the name Septuagint came to denote the complete Hebrew Scriptures translated into Greek.

There are currently over **2000 classified manuscripts** of the Greek **Septuagint**. The Septuagint is the oldest translation from the original language of biblical Hebrew, and it has more significant deviations from the Masoretic Text (MT) than all other versions combined. The Pentateuch (Genesis – Deuteronomy) was translated first between 280-240 B.C.E. The rest of the books were translated between 240-150 C.E. Later, translators used OG Original Greek Pentateuch as a lexicon to have Greek equivalents for certain Hebrew words. If you see the siglum OG Original Greek, this is scholars trying to distinguish between the original translation of the Septuagint (280-150 B.C.E.) from the later translations and revisions. The name Septuagint can refer to the original translation from the Hebrew into Greek, and sometimes the term is used to refer to all later Greek translations and revisions. Some making translations of the Hebrew text into Greek had access to the OG translation and were aware of the differences with the standardized Hebrew text. So, some endeavored to make corrections in the Greek text to bring it in alignment with the protomasoretic text. Others, instead, attempted to do what they felt was a better translation than the translators of the OG translation.

The **kaige revision**, or simply **kaige**, is the group of **revisions** to the Septuagint made in order to more closely align its translation with the proto-Masoretic Hebrew. ... The individual **revisions** characteristic of **kaige** were first observed by Dominique Barthélemy in the Greek Minor Prophets Scroll from Nahal Hever. The kaige revision wrote out the Tetragrammaton, God's personal name (JHVH), in Paleo-Hebrew script. The kaige revision is, at times, also called kaige-Theodotion because it has shared readings with Theodotion. This is a good place to explain that the Jews loved the Greek Septuagint, and they initially saw it as being just as inspired as the original Hebrew books were. However, the Christians were drawn to the Septuagint as well. In the late first century and second century, these Christians used the Greek Septuagint apologetically in debates with Jews. Well, the Jews grew suspicious of the Greek Septuagint that they once saw inspired. They dropped the Greek Septuagint and returned to their Hebrew text, which ended up being a good thing. This also brought about three different Greek translations that rival each other.

Aquila of Sinope was a translator of the Hebrew *Bible* into *Greek*, a Jewish proselyte, and disciple of Rabbi Akiva. **Aquila**, also called Akilas, (flourished 2nd-century C.E.), a scholar who in about 150 C.E. completed an extremely literal translation into **Greek** of the Old Testament; it replaced the **Septuagint** (q.v.) among Jews and was used by the Church Fathers Origen in the 3rd century and St. … Jerome in the 4th and 5th centuries. It was so literal that he would use the same Greek word for the same Hebrew word in every instance even if the context demanded otherwise. Without having knowledge of the Hebrew text that lies behind it it is very much difficult to understand.

Symmachus (/ˈsɪməkəs/; **Greek**: Σύμμαχος "ally"; fl. … late 2nd century) was a Samaritan that converted to Judaism, who would then translate the Old Testament into **Greek**. His translation was included by Origen in his Hexapla and Tetrapla, which compared various versions of the Old Testament side by side with the **Septuagint**. It is thought that he used Aquila in his efforts to make his translation but unlike Aquila, he sought to be more varied in his use of the vocabulary to communicate more clearly in Greek.

Theodotion (/ˌθiːəˈdoʊʃən/; **Greek**: Θεοδοτίων, gen.: Θεοδοτίωνος; died c. 200) was a Hellenistic Jewish scholar, perhaps working in Ephesus, who in c. 150 CE translated the Hebrew **Bible** into **Greek**. … In the 2nd century, **Theodotion's** text was quoted in The Shepherd of Hermas and in Justin Martyr's Dialogue with Trypho. The literalness of his version was between Aquila and Symmachus. He left some difficult Hebrew words untranslated. Many believe that he was also using the kaige revision mentioned above because many of his readings were actually known before he lived.

Origen (184-253 C.E.) brings us to the next stage in the history of the Greek OT. The Hexapla (Ancient *Greek*: Ἑξαπλᾶ, "sixfold") is the term for a critical edition of the Hebrew *Bible* … *Origen's* eclectic recension of the *Septuagint* had a significant influence on the Old Testament text in several important manuscripts, such as the Codex Sinaiticus and Codex Vaticanus. The original work, which is said to have had about 6000 pages (3000 parchment sheets) in 15 volumes and which probably existed in only a single complete copy, seems to have been stored in the library of the bishops of Caesarea for some centuries, but it was destroyed during the Muslim invasion of 638 at the latest. The first column was the Hebrew text. The second column was a transliteration of the Hebrew text in Greek letters. The third column contained Aquila's version, the fourth Symmachus's, the fifth Origen's own revision of the Septuagint text, and the final column Theodotion's version. Origen's fifth column contained obelus symbols in the text to mark readings that were found in the Greek version but not the Hebrew and asterisk symbols for omissions from the Greek that were in Hebrew. This revision of the Greek text was so significant that it "dominated the subsequent history of the [Septuagint]." In spite of the importance of Origen's work, today, we only have fragments of partial copies. 19 It can be consulted in the classic edition by Frederick Field. – Brotzman, Ellis R.; Tully, Eric J.. Old Testament Textual Criticism: A Practical Introduction (p. 70). Baker Publishing Group.

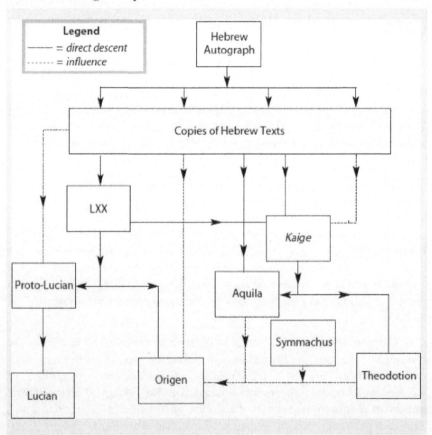

Ellis Brotzman Chart On History of Greek Septuagint, p. 71. ORIGINAL IMAGE Source: Karen H. Jobes and Moisés Silva, Invitation to the Septuagint, 2nd ed. (Grand Rapids: Baker Academic, 2015), 49.

Lucian of Antioch (240-312 C.E.) is credited with a critical recension of the text of the *Septuagint* and the *Greek* New Testament, which was later used by Chrysostom and the later *Greek* fathers, and which lies at the basis of the textus receptus. "This revision was a stylistic update of an existing Greek text that was not Origen's edition in the fifth column of the Hexapla. Like Theodotion, it contains distinctive readings that were known long before Lucian lived in the fourth century. We call this earlier Greek text proto-Lucian. The Lucianic revision tends to fill in gaps in the Greek text (in comparison with the Hebrew MT), adds clarifying elements, and corrects grammatical difficulties. It is a full text and less woodenly literal than the previous translations and revisions."[492]

Ellis R. Brotzman,

Therefore, there were five stages in the development of the Septuagint as a group of Greek translations. First, there was an original translation (Old Greek) of the Pentateuch and then the rest of the OT. Second, there were early revisions of the Greek text (proto-Lucian and kaige-Theodotion). Third, the translations/revisions of Aquila, Symmachus, and Theodotion were completed. Fourth, Origen included the preceding work along with his own revision in the Hexapla. Finally, Lucian completed a new revision (see image above). The Septuagint "was produced by many people unknown to us, over two or three centuries, and almost certainly in more than one location. Consequently, the Greek OT does not have the unity that the term the Septuagint might imply."[493]

Acts 8:26-38 Updated American Standard Version (UASV)

[26] But an angel of the Lord spoke to Philip saying, "Get up and go south to the road that descends from Jerusalem to Gaza." (This is a desert road.) [27] And he rose and went. And there was an Ethiopian, a eunuch, a court official of Candace, queen of the Ethiopians, who was in charge of all her treasure, who had come to worship in Jerusalem, [28] and he was returning and sitting in his chariot, and was reading the prophet Isaiah. [29] And the Spirit said to Philip, "Go over and join this chariot." [30] So Philip ran to him and heard him reading Isaiah the prophet and asked, "Do you understand what you are reading?" [31] And he said, "How can I, unless someone guides me?" And he invited Philip to come up and sit with him. [32] Now the passage of the Scripture that he was reading was this:

"He was led as a sheep to slaughter
and like a lamb before its shearer is silent,

---

[492] Ellis R. Brotzman; Eric J. Tully, Old Testament Textual Criticism: A Practical Introduction (pp. 70-71). Baker Publishing Group.

[493] Ellis R. Brotzman; Eric J. Tully, Old Testament Textual Criticism: A Practical Introduction (pp. 71-72). Baker Publishing Group.

so he opens not his mouth.
33 In his humiliation was taken away.
Who can describe his generation?
For his life is taken away from the earth."[494]

34 And the eunuch answered Philip and said, "I beg you, of whom does the prophet say this? Of himself or of someone else?" 35 Then Philip opened his mouth, and beginning from this Scripture he declared to him the good news about Jesus. 36 And as they went along the road they came to some water; and the eunuch said, "Look! Water! What prevents me from being baptized?" 37—[495] 38 And he commanded the chariot to stop, and they both went down into the water, Philip and the eunuch, and he baptized him.

The Eunuch court official to whom Philip preached was an influential man in charge of the treasury of the queen of Ethiopia. He was a proselyte (convert) to the Jewish religion who had come to Jerusalem to worship God. He had been reading aloud from the scroll of Isaiah (53:7-8 as our English Bible has it sectioned) and was puzzled as to whom it was referring; however, Philip explained the text, and the official was moved to the point of being baptized. The Eunuch was not reading from the Hebrew Old Testament; he was reading from the Greek translation, i.e., the Greek Septuagint. This work was very instrumental to both Jews and Christians in the Greek-speaking world in which they lived.

On this Kenneth O. Gangel **writes, "8:34–35.** Not only did the eunuch invite Philip to sit with him and explain the text, but he asked the very questions that lead to an introduction of the Savior. Could Philip have begun somewhere in Deuteronomy or Job and explained the new covenant gospel to this man? Quite probably. God made it much easier. Jesus had repeatedly quoted portions of Isaiah 53 as being fulfilled in his death (Matt. 8:17; John 12:38; Luke 22:37), and the disciples certainly passed that information on to the Christians in the early church. With joy Philip explained, and with joy Luke recorded this good man hearing for the first time the **good news about Jesus**. Can we conceive of a modern parallel to this incident? Picture yourself waiting in the departure lounge of an airport. A stranger sitting next to you has an open Bible on his lap. He may not be reading aloud, but his finger moves along the lines as he ponders the words. You glance over and discover

---

[494] A quotation from Isaiah 53:7–8

[495] The earliest and best Greek manuscripts (P[45, 74] ℵ A B C) as well as 33 81 614 vg syr[p.h] cop[sa,bo] eth Chrysostom Ambrose do not contain vs 37, while other manuscripts 4[mg] (E 1739 it syr[h**] Irenaeus Cyprian) contain, And Philip said, "If you believe with all your heart, you may." And he replied, "I believe that Jesus Christ is the Son of God." If this were apart of the original, there is no good reason why it would be missing in so many early witnesses and versions. This is a classic example of a scribe taking liberties with the text by answering the Eunuch's question ("Look! Water! What prevents me from being baptized?") with ancient Christian baptismal practices from a later age.

he's in John 3 rapidly approaching verse 16. God prompts you to speak, and you say something like, 'How unusual to find someone reading a Bible in an airport; isn't that third chapter wonderful?' The stranger turns to you and replies, 'It is interesting; but I'm stumped on this sixteenth verse. What exactly does it mean to believe in Jesus and have eternal life?' Could you handle that situation without a seminary degree? Any serious Christian would offer a prayer of thanks and plunge in with a simple explanation of the gospel."[496]

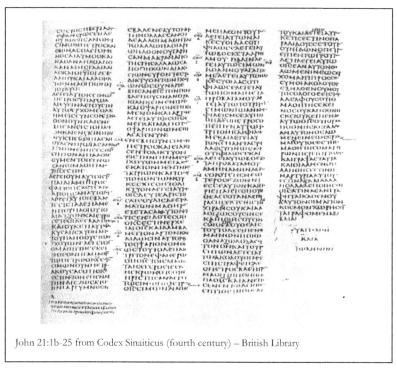

John 21:1b-25 from Codex Sinaiticus (fourth century) – British Library

What contributed to the Hebrew Old Testament's being translated into Greek, and when and how did it occur? What was the need that brought about the Septuagint? How has it affected the Bible throughout these last 2,200 years? What impact does the Septuagint still have on the translator today?

[496] Kenneth O. Gangel, *Acts*, vol. 5, Holman New Testament Commentary (Nashville, TN: Broadman & Holman Publishers, 1998), 127.

The Greek-Speaking Jews and the Septuagint

In 332 B.C.E., Alexander the Great had just finished destroying the Phoenician city of Tyre and was then entering Egypt, but was received as a great deliverer, not as a conqueror. It was here that he would find the city of Alexandria, bringing humankind one of the great learning centers of all time in the ancient world. The result of Alexander's conquering much of the then-known world was the spread of Greek culture and the Greek language. Alexander himself spoke Attic Greek, which was the dialect that spread throughout the territories that he conquered. As the Attic dialect spread, it interacted with other Greek dialects and the local languages, resulting in what we call Koine Greek or common Greek spreading throughout this vast realm.

By the time of the third century B.C.E., Alexandria had a large population of Jews. King Nebuchadnezzar of Babylon destroyed Jerusalem and exiled its people to Babylon centuries before. Many Jews had fled to Egypt at the time of the destruction. The returning Jews in 537 were scattered throughout southern Palestine, migrating to Alexandria after it was founded. The need for a Greek translation of the Hebrew Scriptures arose among the Jews in their worship services and education within the Jewish community of Alexandria.

Many of the Jews in Alexandria could no longer understand the Hebrew language, with others simply letting it go out of use. Most could only speak the common Greek of the Mediterranean world. However, they remained Jews in custom and culture and wanted to be able to understand the Scriptures that affected their everyday lives and worship. Therefore, the time was right for the production of the first translation of the Hebrew Scriptures.

Aristobulus of Paneas (c. 160 B.C.E.) wrote that the Hebrew law was translated into Greek, being completed during the reign of Ptolemy Philadelphus (285-246 B.C.E.). We cannot be certain as to what Aristobulus meant by the term "Hebrew law." Some have suggested that it encompassed only the Mosaic Law, the first five books of the Bible, while others suggested that it was the entire Hebrew Scriptures.

Useful in the First Century

The Septuagint was put to use at great length by Greek-speaking Jews both prior to and throughout first century Christianity. Just after Jesus ascension, at Pentecost 33 C.E., countless numbers of Jews gathered in Jerusalem for the Passover and Festival of Weeks, coming from such places as the districts of Asia, Egypt, Libya, Rome, and Crete, places where Greek was spoken. There is little doubt that they were using the Septuagint in their services. (Acts 2:9-11) As a result, the Septuagint played a major role in spreading the Gospel message in the Jewish and proselyte communities. To see an example, we can look at the account of Stephen.

Acts 6:8-10 Updated American Standard Version (UASV)

⁸ And Stephen, full of grace and power, was performing great wonders and signs among the people. ⁹ But some men from what was called the Synagogue of the Freedmen, both Cyrenians and Alexandrians, and some from Cilicia and Asia, rose up and disputed with Stephen. ¹⁰ But they were not able to withstand the wisdom and the Spirit with which he was speaking.

In his defense, Stephen gave a long history of the Israelite people, and at one point he said,

Acts 7:12-14 Updated American Standard Version (UASV)

¹² But when Jacob heard that there was grain in Egypt, he sent our fathers the first time. ¹³ On the second visit Joseph made himself known to his brothers, and the family of Joseph became known to Pharaoh. ¹⁴ And Joseph sent and summoned Jacob his father and all his kindred, <u>seventy-five souls in all</u>.

This account comes from Genesis 46:27, which reads, "All the persons of the house of Jacob who came into Egypt <u>were seventy</u>." The Hebrew Old Testament reads seventy, but it is the Septuagint that reads seventy-five. Therefore, Stephen was referencing the Septuagint in his defense before the synagogue of the Freedmen.

The Apostle Paul traveled more than 20,000 miles on his missionary tours, which brought him into contact with devout Greeks (Gentiles) who worshiped God. (Acts 13:16, 26; 17:4). They became worshipers of God because they had access to the Septuagint. The Apostle Paul used the Septuagint quite often in his ministry and his letters. – Genesis 22:18; Galatians 3:8.

The Greek New Testament contains about 320 direct quotations, as well as a combined 890 quotations and paraphrases from the Hebrew Old Testament. Most of these are from the Septuagint. Therefore, those Septuagint quotations and paraphrases became a part of the inspired Greek New Testament. Jesus had said, "you will be my witnesses in Jerusalem and in all Judea and Samaria, and to the end of the earth." (Acts 1:8) He had also foretold, "this gospel of the kingdom will be proclaimed throughout the whole world." (Matt 24:14) In order for this to take place, it had to be translated into other languages.

Still Beneficial Today

The Septuagint's great purpose today is to shed light on textual variants that crept into the Hebrew Old Testament text, as it was being copied throughout the centuries. An example of this can be found at Genesis 4:8, which reads:

Genesis 4:8 Updated American Standard Version (UASV)

⁸ Cain said to Abel his brother. "Let us go out into the field."⁴⁹⁷ And it came about when they were in the field, that Cain rose up against Abel his brother and killed him.

The portion in the brackets "let us go out to the field" is not in the tenth century C.E. Hebrew manuscripts. However, it is found in the earlier Septuagint manuscripts (4th cent C.E.) and the Samaritan Pentateuch,⁴⁹⁸ the Peshitta,⁴⁹⁹ and the Vulgate.⁵⁰⁰ **First**, the Hebrew that is used to introduce speech [way*yomer*, "and he said"] is in the Hebrew text, "Cain Spoke." However, there is no speech that follows in the Hebrew text. Many scholars argue that these words were in the original Hebrew text but were omitted accidentally very early. **Second**, on the other hand, a few others argue that the Hebrew construction found here is used in three other passages with nothing being said, so the more difficult and shorter reading is original, which would mean that the Greek translators added the words to complete the meaning. This author prefers the first textual argument, along with the majority of scholars. Herein, we see how the Septuagint can help in identifying textual errors that may have crept into the Hebrew text over centuries of copying.

The Septuagint continues to be very much important today and is used by textual scholars to help uncover copyists' errors that **might have** crept into the Hebrew manuscripts either intentionally or unintentionally. However, it cannot do it alone without the support of other sources. While the Septuagint is the second most important tool after the original language texts for ascertaining the original words of the original Hebrew text, it is also true that the LXX translators took liberties at times, embellishing the text, deliberate changes, harmonizations, and completing of details. Even so, it

---

⁴⁹⁷ This phrase is not present in the Hebrew, nor is it in the NASB; it is supplied in other versions *Samaritan, Septuagint, Syriac,* and the *Vulgate*

⁴⁹⁸ This version only encompasses the first five books and is really a transliteration of the Hebrew text into Samaritan script, developed from the ancient Hebrew script.

⁴⁹⁹ The Syriac version of the Bible, written around the 4th century.

⁵⁰⁰ A Latin version of the Bible produced by Saint Jerome in the 4th century.

should be noted that the Septuagint manuscript of **Aquila** (Codex X), **Symmachus** (also Codex X), and **Theodotion** also read "according to the number of the sons of Israel."

Brotzman and Tully write,

> The earliest of these rival versions (ca. 150 CE) was produced by **Aquila**, a Jewish proselyte and disciple of Rabbi Akiva. The most noteworthy characteristic of his version is its **extreme literalness**. He translates the same Hebrew word with the same Greek word, even if the word is not really appropriate in the context, and **preserves the same word order as the Hebrew text**. … **Symmachus** was a Samaritan who converted to Judaism and worked at the end of the first century CE. 11 He probably based his work on that of Aquila, but he is much more versatile in his use of vocabulary in order to communicate clearly in Greek. Symmachus adapts Hebrew idioms to Greek usage and does not always use the same Greek word to translate each occurrence of a particular Hebrew word. He may have been attempting to avoid the absurdities of Aquila's version and to create something much more readable. … The third rival version of the second century CE was produced by **Theodotion**. He came from Ephesus in Asia Minor and was also a convert to Judaism. Theodotion worked at the end of the second century CE and produced a version located between Aquila and Symmachus in terms of formal correspondence to the Hebrew text (see fig. 4.1 below). He often leaves difficult Hebrew words and constructions untranslated. Some of Theodotion's distinctive readings were known long before he lived. Therefore, it is likely that he was updating the kaige revision mentioned above. For this reason, and due to confusion and uncertainty of the relationship, some scholars reject this as a distinct translation and refer to it as kaige-Theodotion.[501]

The primary weight of external evidence generally goes to the original language manuscripts. The **Codex Leningrad B 19A** and the **Aleppo Codex** are almost always preferred. In the Biblia Hebraica Stuttgartensia (BHS; critical edition of the Hebrew Bible), 90 percent is without a significant variation. Of the 10 percent that does exist, a very small percentage of that impacts its meaning. In almost all of these minimal textual variants, we can ascertain the original wording of the original text with certainty. Yes, it is rare to find a substantive variant among manuscripts of the Hebrew Bible.

---

[501] Ellis R. Brotzman; Eric J.Tully. Old Testament Textual Criticism: A Practical Introduction (p. 68-69). Baker Publishing Group.

The **Codex Leningrad B 19A** dating to about (1008 C.E.) and the **Aleppo Codex** from about (930 C.E.) were produced by the Masoretes, who are the most by far extremely disciplined copyists of all time. Their scribal practices date back to about the year 500 C.E. In fact, by the second century C.E., a particular text entire Hebrew Bible became the generally accepted standard text, which is often referred to as the Proto-Masoretic text, as it preceded the work of the Masoretes and, it already had the basic form of the Masoretic text that was to come. These subtle differences in the Masoretic manuscripts are almost exclusively spelling differences, which also included vocalization, the presence or absence of the conjunction wāw, and other features that in no way impact the meaning of the text. In Old Testament Textual Criticism, the Masoretic text is our starting point and should only be abandoned as a last resort. While it is true that the Masoretic Text is not perfect, there needs to be a heavy burden of proof in we are to go with an alternative reading. All of the evidence needs to be examined before concluding that a reading in the Masoretic Text is corrupt.

These Masoretes were early Jewish scholars who were the successors to the Sopherim, in the centuries following Christ, who produced what came to be known as the Masoretic Text. The Masoretes were well aware of the alterations made by the earlier Sopherim. Rather than simply remove the alterations, they noted them in the margins or at the end of the text. These marginal notes came to be known as the Masora. Between the 6th and 10th centuries C.E., the Masoretes set up a vowel point and accent mark system. (e.g., אִשָּׁה ishshah *woman, wife, female*) In the image of the Aleppo Codex above, all of the vowels appear below the line except *Cholam* ( ), which is placed above, and *Shuruk* ( ), which appears in the bosom of *Waw* (ו = *u*). This would help the reader to pronounce the vowel sounds properly, meaning that there would be a standard and no need to have the pronunciation handed down by oral tradition. Because the Masoretes saw the text as sacred, it needed to be repeated; they made no changes to the text itself but chose to record notes within the margins of the text. Unlike the Sopherim before them, they did not take any textual liberties. Moreover, they drew attention to any textual issues, correcting them within the margins. Many places within the Hebrew Old Testament text was far more of a difficult reading to the Masoretes than what we find in Deuteronomy 32:8, yet they made no changes in the text, but rather if there was an alternative reading that they deemed the original reading, they placed this in the margins of the text.

As Paul D. Wegner writes,

The job of the textual critic is very similar to that of a detective searching for clues as to the original reading of the text. It is reminiscent of the master detective Sherlock Holmes who could determine a number of characteristics of the suspect from the slightest of clues left at the crime scene. In our case, the "crime scene" is the biblical text, and often we have far fewer clues to work from than we would like. Yet the job of the textual critic is extremely important, for we are trying to determine the exact reading of a text in order to know what God has said and expects from us.[502]

Patristic Quotations from New Testament Authors

Another primary source for recovery the original text of the New Testament is the enormous number of quotations from the early Christian writers (apologetic works, epistles, commentaries, sermons, and the like). "**Apostolic Fathers**" is the descriptive term used for churchmen who wrote about Christianity in the late first and early second centuries. Some of them were Clement of Rome, Ignatius, Polycarp, Hermas, and Papias. From near the middle of the second century to its end, churchmen became prominent who are now called "**Apologists.**". They wrote in defense of Christianity against hostile philosophies prevalent in the Roman world of that time and apostate forms of Christianity that were beginning to develop. Among the best known were Marcion, Justin Martyr, Tatian, Athenagoras, Theophilus, and Clement of Alexandria. Tertullian was an Apologist who wrote in Latin. Then, we have the "**Church Fathers**," prominent theologians and Christian philosophers who lived between the second and fifth centuries. We have writings from Hippolytus of Rome, Origen of Alexandria and Caesarea, Eusebius of Caesarea, Hilary of Poitiers, Lucifer of Cagliari, Athanasius of Alexandria, Ephrem the Syrian, Gregory of Nazianzus, Gregory of Nyssa, Ambrose of Milan, and many others.

It is commonly said that these quotations are so extensive that the entire New Testament could be reconstructed without the use of the manuscripts.[503] While this is basically true, the statement is not meant to suggest that a critical text based on these early patristic quotations would be reflective of the original to the extent of what we have today by way of the Greek manuscripts.

---

[502] Paul D. Wegner, A Student's Guide to Textual Criticism of the Bible : Its History, Methods & Results (Downers Grove, Ill.: InterVarsity Press, 2006), 22-23.

[503] (Greenlee, Introduction to New Testament Textual Criticism 1995, 46) (Metzger and Ehrman, The Text of the New Testament: Its Transmission, Corruption, and Restoration (4th Edition) 2005, 124) (Wegner, A Student's Guide to Textual Criticism of the Bible: Its History Methods & Results 2006, 237)

It is meant to convey the enormous amount of quotations that are available to textual scholarship.

Patristic quotations require more analysis than the manuscripts, bearing in mind several questions. Was the quotation a direct quote of a Greek manuscript? Alternatively, was it a paraphrase, even an allusion to the Greek text? On the other hand, was it a quote, paraphrase, or an allusion from a version, i.e., a secondary source? The writer may have had several different sources lying before him at the time, so these possibilities must be considered. Patristic quotations are also to be investigated under the same principles and rules that are applied to the primary sources. Regardless of how difficult the task is, however, patristic quotations play an essential role in determining an original reading and weighing the primary texts' importance. On this, the Alands writes,

> Establishing the New Testament text of the Church Fathers has a strategic importance for textual history and criticism. It shows us how the text appeared at particular times and in particular places: this is information we can find nowhere else. With a Greek manuscript there is no way of knowing the age of the exemplar it was copied from, nor when we know the provenance of a manuscript (as we do in exceptional instances) is there any way of knowing the provenance of its exemplar, which is even more important. Only the papyri from the early period before A.D. 300 may be relied on for such information, but these are relevant only to developments in Egypt when it was hardly a leading province of the Church. For an appreciation of the development of the text in the major church centers of the period they are useless. Many important tasks challenge us here. With more adequate information about the Church Fathers' text of the New Testament we would have firmer guidelines for a history of the text.[504]

Just as we do not have the autographs of the New Testament authors themselves, we do not have the autographs of the early Christian writers either. Therefore, we must broach the same question: has the coping of the early Christian writer, who quoted the New Testament author, been altered in any way? For that reason, here too, we must establish through the manuscripts whether the copyist has intentionally or unintentionally altered his work. Therefore, these manuscripts also must undergo the rigors of textual criticism to determine as much as possible the original wording of the early Christian's quotation of the New Testament author.

---

[504] Aland and Aland, *Text of the New Testament,* pp. 172–73.

After we have established the above, believing that we do have the original words of the early Christian writer, we must ask, did the writer intend to quote the New Testament author verbatim, or was he simply paraphrasing? Thus, we would need to have the original words of the New Testament author. In addition, we would need a list of all New Testament variants. We would have to have a good knowledge of the early Christian's tendencies and the context in which he wrote. For example, if the quote is quite lengthy, it is more likely that the early Christian writer was copying from his text verbatim. However, even if we discover that the writer was merely paraphrasing or loosely quoting the NT author, it is still beneficial on many levels. Maybe a reference to a word, phrase, sentence, or verse has little or no manuscript support from the early papyri. Maybe the quote is verbatim enough to establish that later copyists took liberties with the New Testament author's writing by adding or deleting something.

Apostolic Fathers

Clement of Rome: (d. 100 C.E.) Bishop or overseer of Rome, one of the earliest sources of writings on Christianity. Of his epistle, Michael W. Holmes writes, "1 Clement is one of the earliest—if not the earliest—extant Christian documents outside the New Testament. Written in Rome around the time that John was composing the Book of Revelation on the island of Patmos, it reveals something of both the circumstances and the attitudes of the Roman Christians, circumstances, and attitudes that differ dramatically from those of their Christian sisters and brothers in Asia Minor to whom Revelation was addressed."[505] Few details are known about Clement's life, and most information comes from tradition.

There is a second letter of Clement, actually a sermon, that was once attributed to Clement of Rome but no longer. First Clement is a letter written to the Corinthian congregation, the same one to whom Paul wrote two letters in 55 C.E., some forty years earlier. Paul, in his first letter, had dealt with factions in the congregation, a serious case of immorality, and the congregation was seeking answers to questions like religiously divided

---

[505] Michael William Holmes, *The Apostolic Fathers: Greek Texts and English Translations*, Third ed. (Grand Rapids, Mich.: Baker Books, 2007), 33.

households, conduct at meetings, the eating of meat from the marketplace, etc. In his second letter, Paul had to address the so-called "super-apostles," i.e. "false apostles, deceitful workers." He needed to deal with the young congregation's spiritual wellbeing, as well as his authority being undermined.

In fact, First Corinthians is alluded to and quoted some six times in First Clement,[506] which is dated about 95 C.E. Having First Corinthians in mind, Clement of Rome urged the recipients of this letter to "take up the epistle of the blessed Paul the apostle."[507] (I Clem. 47.1) Clement went on to say of the Corinthian congregation,

> (2) What did he first write to you in the beginning of the gospel? (3) Truly he wrote to you in the Spirit about himself and Cephas and Apollos, because even then you had split into factions. (4) Yet that splitting into factions brought less sin upon you, for you were partisans of highly reputed apostles and of a man approved by them. (5) In contrast now think about those who have perverted you and diminished the respect due your renowned love for [the brotherhood].[508] (6) It is disgraceful, dear friends, yes, utterly disgraceful and unworthy of your conduct in Christ, that it should be reported that the well-established and ancient church of the Corinthians, because of one or two persons, is rebelling against its presbyters. (7) And this report has reached not only us, but also those who differ from us, with the result that you heap blasphemies upon the name of the Lord because of your stupidity, and create danger for yourselves as well.[509]

Clement was trying once again to reconcile the Corinthians, to renew their faith. On this, Holmes comments, "The same kind of factiousness that Paul had earlier encountered in Corinth apparently flared up once again in that congregation near the end of the first century. Though (due to restrictions imposed by the genre) details regarding the exact cause or motivation are not clear, it appears that some of the younger men in the congregation had provoked a revolt (this is the Roman point of view; the younger men no doubt defended their action in more positive terms) and succeeded in deposing the established leadership of the church (3.3; 44.6; 47.6). When news of this reached Rome (47.7), the leaders of the

---

[506] Clement draws upon the Septuagint), words of Jesus, the early Christian writings, as well as traditions as sources of authority.

[507] Ibid., 109

[508] Second edition, as it seems the third edition has gone over into the politically correct gender-neutral translation philosophy.

[509] Michael William Holmes, *The Apostolic Fathers: Greek Texts and English Translations*, Third ed. (Grand Rapids, Mich.: Baker Books, 2007), 109.

congregation, there were sufficiently distressed by this breach of proper conduct and order and the damage it inflicted upon the good name of the Corinthian congregation (1.1; cf. 39.1), that they wrote this long letter and even dispatched mediators (63.3; 65.1) in an effort to restore peace and order to the Corinthian congregation."[510]

As an overseer in the congregation at Rome, Clement was the first Apostolic Father of the Church. It is clear that he worked hard for the faith and demonstrated an intense appreciation for the Scriptures.

Ignatius of Antioch: (c. 35 – 108 C.E.) He was a student of the Apostle John and the third bishop [overseer] of Antioch. Ignatius wrote seven letters as he was taken to Rome with a detachment of ten soldiers, where he was to be martyred by being fed to wild animals. Holmes writes, "At a fork in the road at some point along the way through Asia Minor, probably Laodicea, the decision was made to take the northern route through Philadelphia to Smyrna, thus bypassing the churches that lay along the southern route (Tralles, Magnesia, and Ephesus). It is probable that when the northern road was chosen, messengers were sent to these churches informing them of Ignatius's itinerary, and they evidently dispatched delegations to meet him in Smyrna. Ignatius responded to this show of support by sending a letter to each of the three churches, and he also sent one ahead to the church in Rome, alerting them to his impending arrival there. The guards and their prisoners next stopped at Troas, where Ignatius received the news that "peace" had been restored to the church at Antioch (Phld. 10.1; Smyrn 11.2; Pol. 7.1), about which he apparently had been quite worried and sent letters back to the two churches he had visited, Philadelphia and Smyrna, and to his friend Polycarp, bishop of Smyrna. But before he could write any more letters, the group hurried on to Neapolis and then Philippi, where he was warmly received by the church (Pol. Phil. 1.1; 9.1). There he disappears from view. Presumably, he was taken on to Rome and thrown to the lions in the

---

[510] Ibid., 33-34

Coliseum. While it is not absolutely certain that he died a martyr's death, there is no reason to think otherwise."[511]

Seven Authentic Letters:

- The Letter to the Ephesians,

- The Letter to the Magnesians,

- The Letter to the Trallians,

- The Letter to the Romans,

- The Letter to the Philadelphians,

- The Letter to the Smyrnaeans,

- The Letter to Polycarp, Bishop of Smyrna.

Kirsopp Lake notes, "The immediate purpose of each of the letters, except that to the Romans, is to thank the recipients for the kindness which they had shown to Ignatius. The 'Romans' has the object of preventing the Christians at Rome from making any efforts to save Ignatius from the beasts in the arena, and so robbing him of the crown of martyrdom. But besides this immediate purpose, the writer is influenced by three other motives, all or some of which can be traced in each letter.

(1) Ignatius is exceedingly anxious in each community to strengthen respect for the bishop and presbyters. He ascribes the fullest kind of divine authority to their organization, and recognizes as valid no church, institution, or worship without their sanction.

(2) He protests against the form of heresy called docetism (δοκεῖν), which regarded the sufferings, and in some cases the life, of Jesus as merely an appearance. He also protests against any tendency to Judaistic practices, but it is disputed whether he means that this was an evil found in docetic circles, or that it was a danger threatening the church from other directions.

(3) He is also anxious to secure the future of his own church in Antioch by persuading other communities to send helpers."[512]

In regard to Ignatius' use of the New Testament, Holmes adds, "Ignatius may have known a wide range of early Christian literature, but his use of only a few [books] can be demonstrated with any certainty. He

---

[511] Michael William Holmes, *The Apostolic Fathers: Greek Texts and English Translations*, Third ed. (Grand Rapids, Mich.: Baker Books, 2007), 167.

[512] Pope Clement I et al., *The Apostolic Fathers*, ed. Pope Clement I et al., vol. 1, The Loeb Classical Library (London; New York: Heinemann; Macmillan, 1912–1913), 166–167.

probably worked with the Gospel of Matthew (e.g., *Smyrn* 1.1.); there is no evidence of Mark and only minimal (and not conclusive) evidence of Luke (*Smyrn* 3.2). Use of John (cf. *Rom.* 7.3; *Phld.* 7.1) is unlikely. He has read 1 Corinthians, and probably Ephesians. There are numerous echoes of other Pauline documents (his collection may have included 1 Corinthians, Ephesians, Romans, Galatians, Philippians, Colossians, and 1 Thessalonians), but it is difficult to determine whether they reflect the use of traditional elements or literary dependence. The parallel between 1 John and *Eph.* 14.2 is notable, as are parallels between Ignatius and *1 Clement, 2 Clement*, and the *Shepherd of Hermas*, but again these are insufficient to demonstrate knowledge of written documents."[513] In a footnote, Holmes goes on to say, "The limits of this assessment of documents whose use can be demonstrated must be respected (absence of evidence is not evidence of absence). That the use of a particular document cannot be demonstrated does not mean that Ignatius did not know it; it only means that knowledge of it cannot be demonstrated on the basis of a limited number of documents written under very stressful conditions (i.e., traveling as a prisoner)." (p. 175)

Ignatius styled his letters after Paul, Peter, and John, and would quote or paraphrase their books. He quoted the Gospel according to Matthew, e.g. "The tree is known by its fruit" (Matt. 12:33; Eph. 14:2); "The one who accepts this, let him accept it." (Matt. 19:12; Smyr. 6:1); "Be as shrewd as snakes" in all circumstances, yet always "innocent as doves" (Matt. 10:16; Poly. 2:2). He quoted many other New Testament authors as well.

Polycarp of Smyrna: Polycarp was born to Christian parents about 69 C.E. in Asia Minor, in Smyrna. As he grew into manhood, he was known for his kindness, self-discipline, compassionate treatment of others, and thorough study of God's Word. Soon enough he became an elder in the Christian congregation at Smyrna. Polycarp was very fortunate to live in a time when he was able to learn from the apostles themselves. In fact, the apostle John was one of his teachers. Irenaeus[514] says the following about Polycarp:

> Polycarp was not only instructed by apostles and conversant with many who had seen the Lord, but was appointed by apostles to serve in Asia as Bishop of Smyrna. I myself saw him in my early years, for he lived a long time and was very old indeed when he laid down his life by a glorious and most splendid martyrdom. At

---

[513] Michael William Holmes, *The Apostolic Fathers: Greek Texts and English Translations*, Third ed. (Grand Rapids, Mich.: Baker Books, 2007), 174-175.

[514] Irenaeus was born between 120 C.E. and 140 C.E. in or near the city of Smyrna, and died about 200 C.E. He served as an elder in Gaul. He was an early apologist; his principal writing was *The Refutation and Overthrow of the Knowledge Falsely So Called*," which was commonly referred to as "*Against Heresies*."

all times he taught the things which he had learnt from the apostles, which the Church transmits, which alone are true.[515]

Polycarp quoted abundantly from the Scriptures. In his letter to the Philippians, he referred to Matthew, Acts, Romans, 1 Corinthians, 2 Corinthians, Galatians, Ephesians, 2 Thessalonians, 1 Timothy, and 1 Peter, to mention a few. This establishes the use of the Scriptures by an early apologist to defend the truth as he understood it.

We can attribute this spiritual maturity among the Christians in Smyrna to the hard work of the elders, like Polycarp. Throughout the time of Polycarp's serving as an overseer in the congregation, these leaders lived through one difficult religious struggle after another. There was pressure from the Roman government and non-Christian Jews and conflicting creeds and cults. The community they had to enter to spread the gospel was pagan, and the atmosphere was one of godlessness. The martyrdom of Polycarp took place on February 23, 155 C.E., and extremist Jews apparently helped with the gathering of firewood. They did this even though the execution took place on a special Sabbath day.

> After withdrawing from the city, Polycarp is hunted by a police captain named Herod and betrayed by young slaves who belong to his own house (6:2). He is arrested late in the evening in an "upper room" by police armed as if advancing against a robber (7:1; cf. Mt. 26:55). He refuses to flee, but like Jesus in Gethsemane says "the will of God be done." After a long prayer (7:3) he is taken back to the city riding on an ass on a "great Sabbath day" (8:1).[516]

In the arena, Polycarp was standing before the governor and an enormous crowd looking for blood. The governor continued to push him to profess worshipful honor to Caesar:

> But as he continued to insist, saying, "Swear by the Genius of Caesar," he answered: "If you vainly suppose that I will swear by the Genius of Caesar, as you request, and pretend not to know who I am, listen carefully: I am a Christian. Now if you want to learn the doctrine of Christianity, name a day and give me a hearing." (2) The proconsul said, "Persuade the people." But Polycarp said, "You I might have considered worthy of a reply, for we have been taught to pay proper respect to rulers and authorities appointed by

---

[515] Irenaeus Against Heresies 3.3.4; Eusebius, Ecclesiastical History 4.14.3–8. This translation from the edition cited above.

[516] Geoffrey W. Bromiley, vol. 1, *The International Standard Bible Encyclopedia, Revised* (Wm. B. Eerdmans, 1988; 2002), 211.

God, as long as it does us no harm; but as for these, I do not think they are worthy, that I should have to defend myself before them."[517]

Just moments later Polycarp was burned to death because he would not deny Christ.

Hermas, the Shepherd of Hermas, wrote in the first part of the second century. According to the Muratorian Fragment, he was the brother of Pius, bishop of Rome (c. 140 – 154 C.E.), according to the Muratorian Fragment, the oldest existing canon or authoritative list of books of the Christian Greek Scriptures (c. 170 C.E.). Holmes is correct when he writes, "The Hermas, who wrote the Shepherd is certainly not Paul (a suggestion made based on Acts 14:12) or the Hermas mentioned in Romans 16:14 (Origen's suggestion)."[518] In his work the Shepherd, or Pastor, we have a Christian literary work, considered valuable by many Christians as well as canonical Scripture by some of the early Church fathers such as Irenaeus, Clement of Alexandria, and Origen. The manuscript Codex Sinaiticus includes the epistle of Barnabas and the Shepherd of Hermas after the book of Revelation.

The work comprises five visions, twelve mandates, and ten parables. It depends on allegory and pays special attention to the Christian congregation, calling on the faithful to repent of their sins that have harmed it. Unfortunately, the Shepherd of Hermas is of no real help in establishing the original text of the New Testament.

Papias of Hierapolis: Papias (70 – 163 C.E.) was a bishop of the early Church. Eusebius of Caesarea calls him "Bishop of Hierapolis," a city in the region of Asia, which is 6.2 miles (10 km) north of Laodicea and near

---

[517] Michael William Holmes, *The Apostolic Fathers: Greek Texts and English Translations*, Third ed. (Grand Rapids, Mich.: Baker Books, 2007), 315, 317.

[518] Ibid., 446

Colossae (Col. 4:12-13), in the northern edge of the Lycus Valley of Asia Minor; it should not be confused with the Hierapolis of Syria. Christianity came to Hierapolis through the "efforts" of Epaphras. Papias wrote a five-volume work entitled, *An Exposition of the Oracles of the Lord*.

Papias describes his way of gathering information:

I will not hesitate to set down for you, along with my interpretations, everything I carefully learned then from the elders and carefully remembered, guaranteeing their truth. For unlike most people, I did not enjoy those who have a great deal to say, but those who teach the truth. Nor did I enjoy those who recall someone else's commandments, but those who remember the commandments given by the Lord to the faith and proceeding from the truth itself. And if by chance someone who had been a follower of the elders should come my way, I inquired about the words of the elders—what Andrew and Peter said, or Philip or Thomas or James or John or Matthew or any other of the Lord's disciples, were saying. For I did not think that information from books would profit me as much as information from a living and abiding voice.[519]

We know that Papias was a friend and associate of Polycarp (69 – 155 C.E.), who was one year younger than he. As we learned from the above, Polycarp was a student of the apostle John. Papias would have been about 28 years old when John penned First, Second, and Third John in 98 C.E. from Ephesus. When we consider the years in which Papias lived, whom he likely studied under, his associates, his positions as an overseer in the congregation of Hierapolis, his way of taking in knowledge, he was likely very knowledgeable about the Christianity of his era.

According to Irenaeus (130 – 202 C.E.), Papias was an exceptionally learned man held in high esteem and respected as a reliable source for the apostolic teachings. Eusebius (260/265–339/340 C.E.), an early church historian, on the other hand, offers us contradictory information regarding Papias. "Eusebius ('Hist. Eccl.,' iii. 36) says, 'While Polycarp was in Asia, and was Bishop of Smyrna, Papias was well known as Bishop of the Church in Hierapolis, **a man well skilled in all manner of learning**, and well

---

[519] Michael William Holmes, *The Apostolic Fathers: Greek Texts and English Translations*, Third ed. (Grand Rapids, Mich.: Baker Books, 2007), 735.

acquainted with 'the Scriptures.' In 3.39 Eusebius again speaks of him as σφόδρα σμικρὸς ὢν τὸν νοῦν, as being intellectually small or weak. These apparently contradictory passages are not difficult to reconcile."[520] The reason Eusebius took issue with Papias was apparently because Papias believed in a literal millennium, a thousand-year reign of Christ upon the earth. However, this was actually the prevalent view of Christians in the second century, while Eusebius was a determined anti-millenarian.[521]

Papias was writing at a time when Gnosticism was widespread. Gnosticism was an early apostate Christian movement teaching that salvation comes by learning esoteric spiritual truths that free humanity from the material world, intertwining philosophy, speculation, and pagan mysticism. It would seem that Papias' writings of Jesus' sayings were an attempt to slow the rampant growth of Gnosticism. Afterward came Irenaeus, an apologist specifically fighting the Gnostics' false and exaggerated spirituality. The Gnostic literature may have sparked Papias' sarcastic reference to "**those who have so very much to say**, but in those who teach the truth; nor in those who relate foreign commandments, but in those (who record) such as were given from the Lord to the Faith, and are derived from the Truth itself."[522] It appears that Papias' objective was to shine the light of truth on the false teachings. – 1 Timothy 6:4; Philippians 4:5.

About 150 C.E., Papias says of Mark's Gospel, "'Mark, having become the interpreter of Peter, wrote down accurately everything that he remembered.'[523] Irenaeus, writing about A.D. 185, stated: "Now after their decease [Peter and Paul], Mark, the disciple, and interpreter of Peter, also handed down to us in writing what Peter had preached."[524] (Irenaeus, "Against Heresies," 370) Further confirming this Gospel's accuracy, Papias continues, "So then Mark made no mistake when he wrote down thus some things as he remembered them; for he concentrated on this alone—not to omit anything that he had heard, nor to include any false statement among them."[525] Papias also states that Matthew initially penned his Gospel in Hebrew. Papias says, "Matthew put together the oracles [of the Lord] in the

---

[520] H. D. M. Spence-Jones, ed., *St. John*, vol. 1, The Pulpit Commentary (London; New York: Funk & Wagnalls Company, 1909), xxxii.

[521] Philip Schaff and David Schley Schaff, *History of the Christian Church*, vol. 2 (New York: Charles Scribner's Sons, 1910), 696.

[522] Joseph Barber Lightfoot and J. R. Harmer, *The Apostolic Fathers* (London: Macmillan and Co., 1891), 528.

[523] "The Fragments of Papias," p. 265.

[524] Paul P. Enns, *The Moody Handbook of Theology* (Chicago, IL: Moody Press, 1989), 84.

[525] R. A. Cole, "Mark, Gospel Of," ed. D. R. W. Wood et al., *New Bible Dictionary* (Leicester, England; Downers Grove, IL: InterVarsity Press, 1996), 727–728.

Hebrew language, and each one interpreted them as best he could."[526] It is likely that Papias referred to the Gospels of Luke and John and other writings of the Christian Greek New Testament books. If true, he would undoubtedly be one of the earliest witnesses establishing their authority, authenticity, and divine inspiration. Sadly, though, only scant fragments of the writings of Papias have survived. Papias probably suffered martyrdom at Pergamum in 161 or 165 C.E.

Richard Heard observes, "Papias is primarily of interest to us as the last link in a chain of oral tradition going back to the Apostles, and for the information—difficult as it sometimes is to interpret—which he preserved about Peter and Mark, Matthew, Philip, and the Elder John. We are profoundly thankful for his curiosity and for his belief 'that things out of the books did not profit me so much as the utterances of a voice which liveth and abideth', even if some of the oral traditions which he wrote down appear to us legendary, e.g. the report attributed to John, the disciple of the Lord, of the Lord's teaching on the material delights of Paradise, and the account which Papias gives of the death of Judas."[527]

Agnostic Bible scholar Bart D. Ehrman has quite a different opinion about Papias: "There's an even bigger problem with taking Papias at his word when he indicates that Mark's Gospel is based on an eyewitness report of Peter: virtually everything else that Papias says is widely, and rightly, discounted by scholars as pious imagination rather than historical fact."[528] An apologetic Bible scholar, Timothy Paul Jones, offers the following response:

> In fairness to Ehrman's position, some early Christian theologians did engage in pious-as well as, in the descriptions of the heretical Carpocratians in the writings of Clement of Alexandria and Epiphanius of Salamis, quite impious–imaginings.
>
> Still, Ehrman's own declaration at this point is, I think, a bit of an overstatement. The fragments of Papias's writings include stories about a man named justus Barsabas who was poisoned but didn't die and about a dead man who was raised to life. Papias also described traditions, allegedly from john the author of Revelation, about a future epoch of earthly bliss

---

Papias, "Fragments of Papias," in *The Apostolic Fathers with Justin Martyr and Irenaeus*, ed. Alexander Roberts, James Donaldson, and A. Cleveland Coxe, vol. 1, The Ante-Nicene Fathers (Buffalo, NY: Christian Literature Company, 1885), 155.

[527] Richard Heard (1954). (B) Papias' Quotations from the New Testament. New Testament Studies, 1, pp 130-134. doi:10.1017/S0028688500003647.

[528] Bart D. Ehrman, *Peter, Paul and Mary Magdalene: The Followers of Jesus in History and Legend* (Oxford, NY: Oxford University Press, 2006), 95.

and material blessings following the return of Jesus to earth ("the millennium"). Such ideas may strike some persons as odd, but they do not differ significantly from notions that were already present in the New Testament.

Papias did record at least one tradition that could qualify as 'pious imagination.' Recounting the death of Judas Iscariot, Papias recorded a story in which the betrayer–apparently having survived the suicide attempt described in Matthew 27:5–swelled until his eyes could not be seen and his genitals oozed putrid pus. In the end, Judas died on his own land in such a way that the entire property stank; this account seems to expand on the tradition found in Acts 1:18. Although scholars in previous generations were hesitant to ascribe this story to Papias, it appears–based on the report recorded in the writings of Apollinarius of Laodicea–that Papias may actually have preserved this tale about Judas. Responding to the tale of Judas's death, Ehrman comments that 'Papias was obviously given to flights of fancy.'

So what effect do these stories have on the tradition that Papias preserved regarding the Gospels According to Matthew and Mark? Very little, really.

The importance of Papias's testimony is that it verifies that the type of authorial traditions cited by Irenaeus of Lyons–traditions that connected the four New Testament Gospels to Matthew, Mark, Luke and john–existed long before the mid to late second century. Through what remains of Papias's writings, it is clear that these traditions were at least as ancient as the late first or early second century.

Papias faithfully recorded stories that he heard, and it is possible that some of these stories were exaggerated. But the fact that Papias may have recorded some exaggerated stories does not negate the crucial fact that he recorded oral traditions about the Gospels that were in circulation fewer than twenty years after the last of the four New Testament Gospels was written. This fact is already suggested by the consistency with which the various manuscripts connect the four Gospels to the same authors; the testimony of Papias simply confirms this suggestion.[529]

---

[529] Timothy Paul Jones, *Misquoting Truth: A Guide to the Fallacies of Bart Ehrman's "Misquoting Jesus"* (Downer Groves, IL: IVP Books, 2006), 147-8.

Apologists

Apostle John (left) and Marcion of Sinope (right), from Morgan Library MS 748, 11th century

Marcion of Sinope: He was a rich young man who was also a significant leader in early Christianity (c. 85 – c. 160 C.E.). He publicly stated that Christians should reject the Old Testament. The other Church leaders would eventually reject him, and he chose to set himself apart from the orthodox Christianity of the day. According to English historian Robin Lane Fox, "The creator, [Marcion] argued, was an incompetent being: why else had he afflicted women with the agonies of childbirth? 'God' in the Old Testament was a 'committed barbarian' who favored bandits and such terrorists as Israel's King David. Christ, by contrast, was the new and separate revelation of an altogether higher God, a God of love revealed in the New Testament; or, rather, in the parts that Marcion accepted (some of Paul's writings and an edited Luke).

It was not until Marcion that there became a need to create an official canon of Scripture. Marcion built his canon around his doctrinal positions, from a select few of Paul's writings and an abridged form of the Gospel of Luke. This, combined with the ever-growing list of apocryphal literature, moved other church leaders to distinguish between what was Scripture and what was not.

Justin Martyr: The Christian apologetic writer Justin Martyr (c. 100 – 165 C.E.) was a philosopher and theologian who wanted to resolve Christian doctrine and pagan culture. He was born in Flavia Neapolis, a Roman city built on the site of the ancient Shechem in Samaria. His parents were pagans. In his youth, Justin was zealous in his studies of Greek philosophy, particularly the writings of Plato and the Stoic philosophers. It was in Ephesus that he first encountered Christianity. Justin happened upon an old man, an unnamed Christian, who entered into a dialogue about God and spoke of the witness of the prophets as being more trustworthy than the reasoning of philosophers.

"'There existed, long before this time, certain men more ancient than all those who are esteemed philosophers, both righteous and beloved by God, who spoke by the Divine Spirit, and foretold events which would take place, and which are now taking place. They are called prophets. These alone both saw and announced the truth to men, neither reverencing nor fearing any man, not influenced by a desire for glory, but speaking those things alone which they saw and which they heard, being filled with the Holy Spirit. Their writings are still extant, and he who has read them is very much helped in his knowledge of the beginning and end of things, and of those matters which the philosopher ought to know, provided he has believed them. For they did not use demonstration in their treatises, seeing that they were witnesses to the truth above all demonstration, and worthy of belief; and those events which have happened, and those which are happening, compel you to assent to the utterances made by them, although, indeed, they were entitled to credit on account of the miracles which they performed, since they both glorified the Creator, the God and Father of all things, and proclaimed His Son, the Christ [sent] by Him: which, indeed, the false prophets, who are filled with the lying unclean spirit, neither have done nor do, but venture to work certain wonderful deeds for the purpose of astonishing men, and glorify the spirits and demons of error. But pray that, above all things, the gates of light may be opened to you; for these things cannot be perceived or understood by all, but only by the man to whom God and His Christ have imparted wisdom.'"[530]

As the kindhearted man admonished, Justin thoroughly and carefully examined the Scriptures and seemed to have gained a degree of appreciation for them as well as Bible prophecy, as seen in his writings. The books that are credited to Justin are

- The First Apology of Justin addressed to Antoninus Pius, his sons, and the Roman Senate

- The Second Apology of Justin addressed to the Roman Senate

- Dialogue of Justin with Trypho, a Jew

- Justin's Hortatory Address to the Greeks

---

[530] Justin Martyr, "Dialogue of Justin with Trypho, a Jew," in *The Apostolic Fathers with Justin Martyr and Irenaeus*, ed. Alexander Roberts, James Donaldson, and A. Cleveland Coxe, vol. 1, The Ante-Nicene Fathers (Buffalo, NY: Christian Literature Company, 1885), 198.

- Justin on the Sole Government of God

- Fragments of the Lost Work of Justin on the Resurrection

- Other Fragments from the Lost Writings of Justin

- The Martyrdom of the Holy Martyrs

Justin was fascinated and awestruck with the courage and fearlessness of Christians in the face of death. He also valued and respected the teachings of the Hebrew Scriptures. In making his arguments in his *Dialogue with Trypho*, Justin quoted from Genesis, Exodus, Leviticus, Deuteronomy, 2 Samuel, 1 Kings, Psalms, Isaiah, Jeremiah, Ezekiel, Daniel, Hosea, Joel, Amos, Jonah, Micah, Zechariah, and Malachi, as well as the Gospels. His gratefulness for these Bible books is demonstrated in the dialogue with Trypho, as Justin dealt with Messianic Judaism.

Second-century Christians refused to worship pagan gods, so they were labeled atheists. Justin argued, "What sober-minded man, then, will not acknowledge that we are not atheists, worshipping as we do the Maker of this universe .... Our teacher of these things is Jesus Christ ... He is the Son of the true God."[531] In dealing with the folly of idol worship, Justin wrote, "And often out of vessels of dishonor, by merely changing the form, and making an image of the requisite shape, they make what they call a god; which we consider not only senseless, but to be even insulting to God, who, having ineffable glory and form, thus gets His name attached to things that are corruptible, and require constant service .... What infatuation! that dissolute men should be said to fashion and make gods for your worship, and that you should appoint such men the guardians of the temples where they are enshrined; not recognising that it is unlawful even to think or say that men are the guardians of gods."[532]

Justin offers numerous references to the Greek New Testament as he states his belief in the resurrection of Christ, Christian morals, baptism, Bible prophecy (particularly regarding Christ), as well as Jesus' teachings. On the subject of Jesus, Justin quotes Isaiah 9:6, stating, "Unto us a child is born, and unto us, a young man is given, and the government shall be upon His [Christ's] shoulders."[533] Justin also says, "For if we looked for a human kingdom, we should also deny our Christ."[534] He goes on to discuss the trials of Christians as well as their obligations, stating numerous times that true

---

[531] Ibid., 166-7.

[532] Ibid., 165.

[533] Ibid., 174.

[534] Ibid., 166.

worship belongs to those doing the will of God; all others "are sons and angels of the devil, because they do the works of the devil."[535] As for evangelism, Justin writes, "In these books, then, of the prophets we found Jesus our Christ foretold as coming, born of a virgin, growing up to man's estate, and healing every disease and every sickness, and raising the dead, and being hated, and unrecognized, and crucified, and dying, and rising again, and ascending into heaven, and being, and being called, the Son of God. We find it also predicted that certain persons should be sent by Him into every nation to publish these things."[536]

The Second Apology of Justin is directed at the Roman Senate. Justin takes his case before the Romans, sharing how Christians were being persecuted after they had become followers of Christ. Their Christlike moral values set these Christians apart within the Roman Empire, where even acknowledging that one was a Christian could have meant certain death. Urbicus, the prefect, began to persecute Christians severely. Justin quotes Lucius, a former Christian teacher, who upon "seeing the unreasonable judgment that had thus been given, said to Urbicus: 'What is the ground of this judgment? Why have you punished this man, not as an adulterer, nor fornicator, nor murderer, nor thief, nor robber, nor convicted of any crime at all, but who has only confessed that he is called by the name of Christian?'"[537]

The magnitude of hostility against anyone claiming to be a Christian at that time is supported by Justin's statement, "I too, therefore, expect to be plotted against and fixed to the stake, by some of those I have named, or perhaps by Crescens, that lover of bravado and boasting; for the man is not worthy of the name of philosopher who publicly bears witness against us in matters which he does not understand, saying that the Christians are atheists and impious, and doing so to win favor with the deluded mob, and to please them. For if he assails us without having read the teachings of Christ, he is thoroughly depraved and far worse than the illiterate, who often refrain from discussing or bearing false witness about matters they do not understand."[538]

Justin was condemned by the Roman prefecture as one who undermined the Roman government and was sentenced to die. In about 165 C.E. he was beheaded in Rome. His zeal for truth and righteousness was clearly sincere. The writings of Justin are valuable for their historical content, as well as his many references to Scripture. Moreover, they offer the reader insight into the life experiences of Christians of the second century. Justin

---

[535] Ibid., 525.

[536] Ibid., 173

[537] Ibid., 188.

[538] Ibid., 189

rejected pagan religion and any hollow, empty, and deceptive philosophy in favor of God's Word. As an apologist, Justin defended the Christian faith and the Word of God, and as a Christian, he suffered martyrdom. He is known for his love for the truth and his courageous witnessing in the face of persecution.

Tatian the Assyrian: An apologetic writer and theologian who was a native of Syria and traveled extensively. He read prolifically, which made him well-informed in the Greco-Roman culture of the second century (c. 120 – c. 180 C.E.). In the first century, about 56 C.E., the apostle Paul was at the end of his third missionary journey, warning the older men in Ephesus. He cautioned, "I know that after my departure, savage wolves will come in among you, not sparing the flock, and from among your own selves, men will arise, speaking perverse things, to draw away the disciples after them." — Ac 20:29-30.

This dire warning proved true soon after the death of the apostle John in 100 C.E. The second century proved to be a time filled with apostates and apostasy. Gnosticism became a major threat to the church, an early pseudo-Christian religious movement teaching that salvation comes by learning esoteric spiritual truths that free humanity from the material world. This movement caused much spiritual shipwreck among the believers, as it appeared to offer explanations for the suffering of the righteous and the problem of sin.

While Tatian was in Rome, he was introduced to Christianity. He began to associate with Justin Martyr, perhaps becoming his student. In an enlightening account of his conversion to Christianity, Tatian asserts: "I sought how I might be able to discover the truth. And, while I was giving my most earnest attention to the matter, I happened to meet with certain barbaric writings, too old to be compared with the opinions of the Greeks, and too divine to be compared with their errors; and I was led to put faith in these by the unpretending cast of the language, the inartificial character of the writers, the foreknowledge displayed of future events, the excellent quality of the precepts, and the declaration of the government of the universe as centred in one Being."[539] Tatian was eager to invite his contemporaries to investigate Christianity and to witness its simplicity and clearness as opposed to the darkness of heathenism.

The writings of Tatian reveal him as an apologist, one who defended the truth. He had a harsh and aggressive attitude toward pagan philosophy. In his work *Address of Tatian to the Greeks*, he emphasizes the insignificance and irrelevance of paganism and the reasonableness of Christianity. In reference to the philosopher Heraclitus, he states, "Death, however, demonstrated the stupidity of this man; for, being attacked by dropsy, as he had studied the art of medicine as well as philosophy, he plastered himself with cow-dung, which, as it hardened, contracted the flesh of his whole body, so that he was pulled in pieces, and thus died.[540]

Tatian held it in high regard that there was but one God to whom Christians owe their worship, "the builder [Creator] of all things" (Heb. 3:4). In his *Address of Tatian to the Greeks*, he refers to God as "a Spirit" and says, "He alone is without beginning, and He Himself is the beginning of all things. God is a Spirit"[541] (John 4:24). He rejected the use of images in worship, writing, "How can I speak of stocks and stones as gods?"[542] (1 Cor. 10:14). On the resurrection, he writes, "we believe that there will be a resurrection of bodies after the consummation of all things."[543] As to why we grow old and die, he says, "We were not created to die, but we die by our own fault. Our free will has destroyed us; we who were free have become slaves; we have been sold through sin. Nothing evil has been created by God; we

---

[539] Tatian, "Address of Tatian to the Greeks," in *Fathers of the Second Century: Hermas, Tatian, Athenagoras, Theophilus, and Clement of Alexandria (Entire)*, ed. Alexander Roberts, James Donaldson, and A. Cleveland Coxe, trans. J. E. Ryland, vol. 2, The Ante-Nicene Fathers (Buffalo, NY: Christian Literature Company, 1885), 77.

[540] Ibid., 66.

[541] Ibid., 66.

[542] Ibid., 66. [Over again Tatian asserts spirits to be material, though not fleshly; and I think with reference to 1 Cor. 15:44.] – Alexander Roberts, James Donaldson, and A. Cleveland Coxe, eds., Fathers of the Second Century: Hermas, Tatian, Athenagoras, Theophilus, and Clement of Alexandria (Entire), vol. 2, The Ante-Nicene Fathers (Buffalo, NY: Christian Literature Company, 1885).

[543] Ibid., 67.

ourselves have manifested wickedness; but we, who have manifested it, are able again to reject it."[544]

As we examine the writings of Tatian, it becomes clear how familiar he was with the Scriptures, using them in his apologetic work. On the impact they had on him, he writes, "I do not wish to be a king; I am not anxious to be rich; I decline military command; I detest fornication; I am not impelled by an insatiable love of gain to go to sea … I am free from a mad thirst for fame … I see that the same sun is for all, and one death for all, whether they live in pleasure or destitution." Tatian reproves, "Die to the world, repudiating the madness that is in it. Live to God, and by apprehending Him lay aside your old nature"[545] — Matthew 5:45; 1 Corinthians 6:18; 1 Timothy 6:10.

Tatian's other major work was the Diatessaron, a harmony of the four New Testament Gospels in a combined narrative of the life of Jesus. I do not want to leave the reader with the impression that Tatian was biblically correct on every count, however. In a lost writing entitled *On Perfection according to the Doctrine of the Savior*, Tatian attributes matrimony to the Devil. He states that those who marry would be tying the flesh to the perishable world through marriage, which he strongly condemned.

It appears that there are mixed views as to what happened to Tatian after the death of Justin Martyr. Irenaeus says he was expelled from the church for his ascetic views. Eusebius says that Tatian founded or associated with an ascetic sect called the Encratites, who emphasized the importance of strict self-control over one's body. They were required to abstain from wine, marriage, and possessions.

Athenagoras of Athens: He was the most accomplished philosopher and Christian apologist of the second century, having come from Platonism (c. 133 – c. 190 C.E.). Norman L. Geisler writes, "His famous *Apology* (ca. 177), which he called 'Embassy,' petitioned Marcus Aurelius on behalf of

---

[544] Ibid., 69-70.

[545] Ibid., 69.

Christians. He later wrote a strong defense of the physical resurrection … *On the Resurrection of the Dead*. Two later writers mention Athenagoras. Methodius of Olympus (d. 311) was influenced by him in his *On the Resurrection of the Body*. Philip Sidetes (early sixth century) stated that Athenagoras had been won to Christianity while reading the Scriptures 'in order to controvert them' (Pratten, 127). His English translator noted, 'Both his *Apology* and his treatise on the Resurrection display a practiced pen and a richly cultured mind. He is by far the most elegant, and certainly at the same time one of the ablest, of the early Christian Apologists' (ibid.). The silence about Athenagoras by the fourth-century Church historian Eusebius is strange in view of his work."[546]

Gerald Bray comments, "The only way that we can date his works is by internal evidence. The first of his two extant treatises are called *An Embassy on Behalf of the Christians*. It was addressed to the Emperors Marcus Aurelius (161 – 80 C.E.) and his son Commodus (176–92C.E.) so that it has to be placed at some point during the four-year period when they were co-emperors. In this work, Athenagoras presents a calm and elegant refutation of the standard charges made against Christians—that they were atheists, cannibals, and incestuous. Like other Christian writers of his time, Athenagoras asks the pagan rulers to judge Christians on their merits and not

according to the rumors which circulated about them. He was sure that, if they did so, the Christians would be exonerated and allowed to practise their religion freely."[547]

Theophilus of Antioch: He was a late second-century bishop of Antioch and an apologist (d. c. 182 C.E.). As was true of many early Christian writers, he was born a pagan and was led to accept Christianity as the truth by studying the Scriptures, especially the prophetical books. Theophilus writes, "…you

---

[546] Norman L. Geisler, *Baker Encyclopedia of Christian Apologetics*, Baker Reference Library (Grand Rapids, MI: Baker Books, 1999), 59.

[547] Gerald Bray, "Athenagoras of Athens (c. 177–80)," ed. Trevor A. Hart, *The Dictionary of Historical Theology* (Carlisle, Cumbria, U.K.: Paternoster Press, 2000), 42.

call me a Christian, as if this were a damning name to bear, I, for my part, avow that I am a Christian,[548] and bear this name beloved of God, hoping to be serviceable[549] to God."[550] Hans Svebakken tells us that Theophilus

…intends to discredit the myths and philosophical claims of the Greeks and demonstrate the truth of his religion through various 'proofs' from Nature, the consistent, inspired witness of the Hebrew prophets and the antiquity of his tradition. Theophilus seems to have a special affinity for Jewish modes of thought. His most succinct confession is limited to a single, providential Creator, who has revealed his Law for the moral betterment of humanity (3.9). The righteous, through obedience to that Law, will be rewarded with immortality, while the wicked will be punished (2.27). He defines a Christian as one who is anointed with the oil of God (1.12), but he makes no explicit reference to Jesus Christ either in this definition or elsewhere. Such an omission, however, is not unique among second-century apologists. Theophilus is the first Christian to produce an extant commentary on the so-called *Hexaemeron*, or the first 'six days' of the creation account (2.12–19). Here his reliance on the exegetical methods of Hellenistic Judaism is clear; some have suggested that he also makes use of rabbinical interpretations. His continuity, though, with the theological vision of a variety of New Testament texts is indicated by his many clear allusions to them … Perhaps Theophilus's most formative contribution is to the doctrine of creation *ex nihilo*. All things were created out of what did not exist (1.4; 2:10, 13), thus matter itself had a definitive point of origin. For Theophilus, the sovereignty and transcendence of God are here at stake. If matter is uncreated, it is immutable and thus equal to God. God demonstrates his omnipotence and superiority to mortal craftsmen by not being limited merely to the formation of available, pre-existent material (2.4). Irenaeus, writing at roughly the same time, expresses the same thought (Heresies, 2.10.4).[551]

---

[548] [Acts 11:26. Note this as from *an Antiochian*, glorying in the name of Christian.]

[549] Εὔχρηστος, punning on the name *Christian*. [Comp cap xii., *infra*. So Justin, p. 164, vol. i., this series. But he also puns on his own name, "beloved of God," in the text φορῶ τὸ Θεοφιλὲς ὄνομα τοῦτο, κ.τ.λ.]

[550] Theophilus of Antioch, "Theophilus to Autolycus," in *Fathers of the Second Century: Hermas, Tatian, Athenagoras, Theophilus, and Clement of Alexandria (Entire)*, ed. Alexander Roberts, James Donaldson, and A. Cleveland Coxe, trans. Marcus Dods, vol. 2, The Ante-Nicene Fathers (Buffalo, NY: Christian Literature Company, 1885), 89.

[551] Hans Svebakken, "Theophilus of Antioch," ed. Trevor A. Hart, The Dictionary of Historical Theology (Carlisle, Cumbria, U.K.: Paternoster Press, 2000), 542–543.

Clement of Alexandria:[552] Titus Flavius Clemens (c. 150 – 215 C.E.) was born to non-Christian parents. Clement was highly educated and cultured before his conversion to Christianity. Like Just Martyr, he traveled, seeking the truth wherever it might be found. He happened upon a Christian teacher, who was able to defend and share the Christian message from a philosopher's mindset. The teacher was Pantaenus, referred to as "the Sicilian bee" by Clement. After studying under the Christian philosopher Pantaenus, Clement became head of the catechetical school in Alexandria in about 190 C.E., which became famous under his leadership. Thereafter Clement penned three great works: the Protrepticus (Exhortation to the Greeks) – written c. 195, the Paedagogus (Instructor, on ethics) – written c. 198, and the Stromata (Miscellanies) – written c. 198 – c. 203. In 203, Clement left Alexandria during the persecution of the Christians by the Roman Emperor Septimius Severus and went to Caesarea (Mazaca) in Cappadocia. He died about 215 C.E. Origen, who later attained distinction as a prolific writer, teacher, and theologian, was one of Clement's pupils, and it was he who replaced him in Alexandria. Clement wrote, "But those who are ready to toil in the most excellent pursuits, will not desist from the search

after truth, till they get the demonstration from the Scriptures themselves" (Miscellanies 7.16).

Tertullian: Quintus Septimius Florens Tertullianus, known as Tertullian (c. 160 – c. 240 C.E.), was a prolific early Christian author from Carthage in the Roman province of Africa. Tertullian was a notable early Christian apologist and a polemicist against heresy, who produced an extensive amount of Christian literature in Latin. His work is noteworthy for its blunt sarcasm, and concise, witty, and often paradoxical

[552] IMAGE: By André Thévet - Internet Archive scan of Les vrais pourtraits et vies des hommes illustres grecz, latins et payens, Public Domain,

https://commons.wikimedia.org/w/index.php?curid=6885509

statements. Almost no facet of religious life escaped his pen. Tertullian asked, "So, then, where is there any likeness between the Christian and the philosopher? Between the disciple of Greece and of heaven? Between the man whose object is fame, and whose object is life? Between the talker and the doer? Between the man who builds up and the man who pulls down? Between the friend and the foe of error? Between one who corrupts the truth, and one who restores and teaches it? Between its chief and its custodier?"[553]

Tertullian was best known for witty, and often paradoxical statements, such as, "God is then especially great when He is small."[554] "The Son of God died; it is by all means to be believed because it is absurd. And He was buried and rose again; the fact is certain because it is impossible."[555] It would seem that it was the faith of those who suffered horrible martyrdom for Christ, that drew him to Christianity. With reference to Christian martyrdom, he asked, "For who that contemplates it, is not excited to inquire what is at the bottom of it? Who, after inquiry, does not embrace our doctrines?"[556]

Church Fathers

The Church Fathers were prominent theologians and Christian philosophers who lived between the second and fifth centuries C.E. More broadly speaking, Robert M. Grant writes, "In Christian thought since the eighth century, a church father (pater ecclesiae) is a teacher living within the first seven centuries (eight among the Greeks) who's teaching the church has recognized as orthodox. The four basic requirements have been orthodox doctrine, sanctity of life, agreement with the church, and antiquity. (For someone to be named a doctor of the church, outstanding learning is further required.)"[557]

---

[553] Tertullian, "The Apology," in *Latin Christianity: Its Founder, Tertullian*, ed. Alexander Roberts, James Donaldson, and A. Cleveland Coxe, trans. S. Thelwall, vol. 3, The Ante-Nicene Fathers (Buffalo, NY: Christian Literature Company, 1885), 51.

[554] Ibid., Tert., Adv. Marc. 2.2

[555] Ibid., Tert., De carn. *Chr.* 5

[556] Ibid., Tert., Apol. 50

[557] Robert M. Grant, "Church Fathers," *The Encyclopedia of Christianity* (Grand Rapids, MI; Leiden, Netherlands: Wm. B. Eerdmans; Brill, 1999–2003), 521.

Hippolytus of Rome: He is considered the most important third-century theologian in the Christian Church in Rome (170 – 236 C.E.). The Oxford Dictionary of the Christian Church states, "Of his early life, nothing is known. The assertion of Photius that he was a disciple of St Irenaeus is doubtful. During the first decades of the 3rd century, he must have been an important personality among the Roman presbyters; when Origen came to Rome (c. 212), he attended one of his sermons. Soon afterward, Hippolytus took an active part in attacking the doctrines of Sabellius. He refused to accept the teaching of Pope Zephyrinus (198–217), and under his successor, Callistus (217–22), whom he rejected as a heretic, he seems to have allowed himself to be elected as a rival Bp. of Rome. He continued to attack Callistus' successors, Urban (222–30) and Pontianus (230–5). In the persecution of the Emp. Maximin (235–8), however, he and Pontianus were exiled together to Sardinia, and it is very probable that before his death, he was reconciled to the other party at Rome; for under Pope Fabian (236–50) his body with that of Pontianus was brought to Rome (236)."[558]

The Oxford Dictionary continues, "A list of several of Hippolytus' writings as well as his Easter tables were discovered on a statue, long thought to portray him, but now recognized as originally a female figure, perhaps personifying one of the sciences; it was found in Rome and heavily restored in 1551; it is now kept in the Vatican Library. Many other works are listed by Eusebius of Caesarea and St Jerome. Hippolytus' principal work is his 'Refutation of all Heresies' (not listed on the statue). Books 4–10 of this were found in an MS on Mount Athos and published (together with the already known Book 1) under the title 'Philosophumena' in 1851 at Oxford by E. Miller, who attributed it to *Origin; but J. J. I. von Döllinger argued that its author was Hippolytus. Books 2–3 are lost. Its main aim is to show that the philosophical systems and mystery religions described in Books 1–4 are responsible for the heresies dealt with in the later Books."[559]

---

[558] F. L. Cross and Elizabeth A. Livingstone, eds., *The Oxford Dictionary of the Christian Church* (Oxford; New York: Oxford University Press, 2005), 778.

[559] Ibid., 778

Origen of Alexandria and Caesarea: He was a scholar and early Christian theologian who spent the first half of his life and career in Alexandria. Origen was a prolific writer in such areas as theology, apologetics, textual criticism, biblical exegesis and hermeneutics, philosophical theology, preaching, and spirituality (184/185 – 253/254 C.E.). The Oxford Dictionary of the Christian Church states,

He was born in Egypt, prob[ably] at Alexandria, where he received a thoroughly Christian education in his parents' house. During the persecution in Alexandria in 202 when his father, Leonidas, was killed, he was prevented from seeking martyrdom only by a ruse of his mother, who hid his clothes. He taught in Alexandria and, when peace was restored, was recognized by Demetrius as head of the Catechetical School (q.v.), in place of Clement, who had fled the city. He now began to lead a strictly ascetical life of fastings, vigils, and voluntary poverty, and even, acc[ording] to Eusebius, mutilated himself, misinterpreting Mt. 19:12 in a literal sense. He was well versed in the works of the Middle Platonists and studied pagan philosophy and literature under Ammonius Saccas. He undertook several journeys, one to Rome, where he heard a sermon of St Hippolytus, and one to Arabia. When, in 215, troubles broke out in Alexandria in connection with a visit of the Emp. Caracalla, he went to Palestine, where he was asked to preach by the Bps. of Caesarea and Aelia. As he was only a layman, this was regarded as a breach of the Alexandrian ecclesiastical discipline, in consequence of which he was recalled by his bishop, Demetrius. From c. 218 to 230, he devoted himself almost without interruption to literary activities. In 230, he went again to Palestine, where he was ordained priest by the same bishops who had invited him to preach on his previous visit. As a consequence, Bp. Demetrius deprived him of his chair and deposed him from the priesthood, more because of the irregularity of his ordination than, as later opponents asserted, for doctrinal reasons. Origen left Alexandria and found a refuge at Caesarea (231), where he established a school, which soon became famous, and where he continued his literary work and devoted himself to preaching. In 250, in the persecution of Decius, he was imprisoned and subjected to prolonged torture, which he survived only a few years.[560]

---

[560] Ibid., 1200

Eusebius of Caesarea:[561] He was likely born in Palestine about 260 C.E. and died about 340 C.E. When he was quite young, Eusebius befriended Pamphilus, an overseer of the church in Caesarea. He would join the theological school of Pamphilus, becoming an exceptional student. He is regarded as an exceptionally well-learned Christian of his time, making a meticulous use of Pamphilus' magnificent library. He would later refer to himself as "Eusebius of Pamphilus."

Concerning his ambitions, Eusebius stated, "It is my purpose to write an account of the successions of the holy apostles, as well as of the times which have elapsed from the days of our Saviour to our own; and to relate the many important events which are said to have occurred in the history of the Church; and to mention those who have governed and presided over the Church in the most prominent parishes, and those who in each generation have proclaimed the divine word either orally or in writing." (Eusebius, Ecclesiastical History 1.1.1)

Eusebius is known for his highly regarded work entitled *History of the Christian Church*. Ten volumes were published about 324 C.E., and the work has long been considered the most important ecclesiastical history from that era. Because of this achievement, Eusebius is known as the father of church history.

Aside from Church History, Eusebius penned *The Chronicle*, which was divided into two parts. The first volume, the *Chronography*, was an epitome of universal history from the sources, arranged according to nations. In the fourth century, it became the standard text for referencing world chronology. The second volume, the *Canons*, showed dates of historical events. Using parallel columns, Eusebius displayed the successive royalty of different nations.

Eusebius went on to write two other historical works, *Martyrs of Palestine* and *Life of Constantine*. The *Martyrs of Palestine* covers the years 303-310 C.E. and discusses martyrs of that period. Eusebius would have lived through these events. The *Life of Constantine* was published in four books after Emperor Constantine had died in 337 C.E. These volumes contained

---

important historical details. Instead of being a history, it is principally a eulogy.

Eusebius read and referred to an enormous number of books in his eighty years. Without Eusebius' work, we would have little or no knowledge of many prominent persons of the first three centuries after Christ. He has given us accounts that have shed light on important movements. These are from sources to which we have no access. He was hard working, meticulous, and thorough in his gathering of material. Eusebius seems to have cautiously made an effort to distinguish between trustworthy and untrustworthy reports. However, we would be mistaken if we thought his work without error. On occasion, he misjudges and even misunderstands men and their actions. His chronology is sometimes inaccurate. Eusebius let his biases show at times as well. Regardless of obvious imperfections, however, his many works are viewed as a priceless treasure.

Other Church Fathers Honorably Mentioned

Hilary of Poitiers: (c. 310 – c. 367 C.E.) Overseer of Poitiers and a Doctor of the Church. His name comes from the Latin word for happy or cheerful. He was sometimes referred to as the "Hammer of the Arians" and the "Athanasius of the West."

Lucifer of Cagliari: (d. c. 371) Lucifer of Cagliari was a bishop of Cagliari in Sardinia known for his passionate opposition to Arianism. He is venerated as a Saint in Sardinia, though his status remains controversial.

Athanasius of Alexandria: (c. 296–298 – 373) Athanasius I of Alexandria, also called Athanasius the Great, Athanasius the Confessor or, primarily in the Coptic Orthodox Church, Athanasius the Apostolic, was **the 20th bishop of Alexandria** (as Athanasius I).

Ephrem the Syrian: (c. 306 – 373 C.E.) He was born in Nisibis, served as a deacon, and later lived in Edessa. He served as the Syriac Overseer and was a prolific writer. He was also known as Saint Ephrem, Ephrem of Edessa, or Aprem of Nisibis, was a prominent Christian theologian and writer who is revered as one of the most notable hymnographers of Eastern Christianity.

Gregory of Nazianzus: (c. 329 –390 C.E.) Fourth-century Archbishop of Constantinople, and theologian.

Gregory of Nyssa: (c. 335 – c. 395) Overseer of Nyssa. He was also known as Gregory the Theologian or Gregory Nazianzen was a 4th-century Archbishop of Constantinople and theologian. He is widely considered the most accomplished rhetorical stylist of the patristic age.

Ambrose of Milan: (c. 340 – 4 397 C.E.) Overseer of Milan. He was venerated as Saint Ambrose, was the Bishop of Milan, a theologian, and one of the most influential ecclesiastical figures of the 4th century. Ambrose served as the Roman governor of Aemilia-Liguria in Milan when he was unexpectedly made Bishop of Milan in 374 by popular acclamation.

CHAPTER XII

Ancient Versions of the New Testament

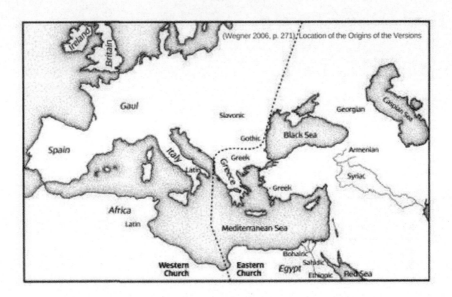

The ancient versions of the New Testament themselves are not what is important to the textual scholar but rather what they provide as they point to the text from which they were translated. Textual scholars must keep some important points in mind as they go about their work in textual criticism with the versions.

(a) Just as it is true that we do not have the originals of the Greek New Testament manuscripts, we do not have the originals of the versions either. Therefore, we are looking at a three-step process. First, we must apply the rules and principles of textual criticism to the version manuscripts, to get back to the original reading of the version. Second, we can then use this original version reading as a means of determining the Greek from which it was translated. Third, the textual scholar will then translate the version back into the original Greek, in an effort to reconstruct the text that was lying behind the version.

(b) It goes almost without saying, when we are dealing with two different languages (the version and the original), that there are some difficulties that will arise. For example, Syriac and Latin, like the Greek of those days, did not have an indefinite article, while Coptic did have an indefinite article. Then again, the Latin had no definite article, which would mean that for a variant issue that involves the definite article, which is very common, especially with proper names, the Latin would not be helpful. Syntax as well, i.e. how words are joined together to make sense, would not be resolved by using the versions that follow a mandatory word order when Greek has no such requirement.

(c) It must be kept in mind that the translators were not always competent in Greek. Metzger notes a significant complaint that Augustine (354-430 C.E.) raised about translations into Latin: "No sooner did anyone gain possession of a Greek manuscript, and imagine himself to have any facility in both languages (however slight that may be) than he made himself bold to translate it." (*De doctrina Christiana* 2.11.16)[562] Augustine went on to write, "As for the books of the New Testament, if the variety of Latin manuscripts leads to any uncertainty, there is no doubt that they should give way to Greek ones, especially those which are found in more learned and responsible churches. As for the translations themselves, the *Itala* [Latin translation] is preferable to the rest; for it keeps more closely to the words and gives the sense with clarity. (*De doctrina Christiana* 2.15.22)

The missionaries produced some of the earliest versions of the New Testament. They sought to make disciples as they proclaimed the Gospel in other languages such as Coptic, Syriac, Latin, and Gothic.[563] Translations into the Syriac and Latin are significant because they came to us two hundred years before the great uncials like Codex Sinaiticus and Codex Vaticanus, dated to the mid-fourth century C.E., the former being slightly later than the latter. Still, other versions include the Armenian, Georgian, Ethiopic, Arabic, Sogdian, Old Church Slavonic, and Nubian.

---

[562] (B. M. Metzger 1964, 1968, 1992, p. 95, n. 76.)

[563] Ibid. 95

The Syriac Versions

Ancient Syria was a region with Mesopotamia to its East, the Lebanon Mountains on the West, the Taurus Mountains to its North, and Palestine and the Arabian Desert to its south. Syria played a very prominent role in the early growth of Christianity. The city of Antioch in Syria was the third-largest city in the Roman Empire. Luke tells us that "those who were scattered because of the persecution that occurred in connection with Stephen [shortly after Pentecost, yet just before the conversion of Paul in 34 or 35 C.E.] made their way to Phoenicia and Cyprus and **Antioch**, speaking the word to no one except to Jews alone. But there were some of them, men of Cyprus and Cyrene, **who came to Antioch** [of Syria] and began speaking to the Greeks also, preaching the Lord Jesus" (Ac 11:19-20, bold mine). Because of the thriving interest in the Gospel manifested in Antioch, where many Greek-speaking people were becoming believers, the apostles in Jerusalem sent Barnabas, who then called Paul in from Tarsus to help (Ac 11:21-26). Both Barnabas and Paul remained there for a year, teaching the people. Antioch became the center for the apostle Paul's missionary journeys. Moreover, "the disciples were first called Christians in Antioch" (Ac 11:26). While the New Testament letters were written in Koine Greek, the common language of the Roman Empire (Latin being the official language) it was thought best to make a translation of the New Testament books into Syriac (a form of Aramaic) in mid-second century C.E. as Christianity spread throughout the rest of Syria.

444

Syriac Sinaiticus, folio 82b, Gospel of Matthew 1:1-17. Superimposed, life of Saint Euphrosyne.

This is why textual scholars so highly prize the Syriac versions.[564] Five different Syriac versions have been differentiated: The Old Syriac, the Peshitta, the Philoxenian Syriac, the Harkleian Syriac, and the Palestinian Syriac.

The Diatessaron (c. 170 C.E.) is the most well-known of the early Gospel harmonies and was produced by the Syrian writer Tatian (c. 120-173 C.E.), an early Christian Assyrian apologist who had also been a pupil of Justin Martyr in Rome. Early in Christianity, critics claimed that the Gospels contradicted each other, and as a result, their accounts could not be trusted. Tatian came to the defense of the Gospels. As an apologist, he concluded that if he could harmonize and blend the four accounts into one narrative, the critics could no longer claim that there were discrepancies. Therefore, Tatian went about preparing what would become known as the Diatessaron (*dia tessarōn*, meaning, "Through [the] four").[565] It is not known whether his original was in Greek or in Syriac. Regardless, he completed his work, and the rest became history. The Diatessaron is the earliest translation of the gospels into Syriac.

In the nineteenth century, some scholars argued that none of the four Gospels was written before the second century but rather between 130 C.E. and 170 C.E., which would mean that they could not be authentic accounts of the life and ministry of Jesus. Of course, if true, this argument would have

---

[564] Bruce M. Metzger, *The Early Versions of the New Testament* (Oxford, England, U.K.: Oxford University Press, 1977), 4-5.

[565] Alex Ramos, "Bible, Ancient Versions of The," ed. John D. Barry et al., *The Lexham Bible Dictionary* (Bellingham, WA: Lexham Press, 2016).

Syriac Sinaiticus, Matthew 15:12–27.

decreased their value to Christianity a thousandfold. The discovery of translations of the Diatessaron into Armenian and Arabic in the twentieth century has given modern Christian apologists decisive evidence that the four Gospels, and the four Gospels alone, were already well known by the mid-second century C.E.; so much so that they were in collections.[566] More evidence of the authenticity of the Gospels came through Ephraem the Syrian (c. 310-373 C.E.), who produced a commentary on the Diatessaron, the Syriac original, which was rediscovered in 1957. This unique fifth/sixth-century commentary contains long excerpts from Tatian's original work. It became clear that Tatian did not make use of any of the so-called apocryphal gospels, as he had done with the four authentic, authoritative Gospels. Therefore, the apocryphal gospels were not viewed as reliable or canonical.

The Old Syriac (180–220 C.E.) came shortly after Titian's Diatessaron in Syriac. The four gospels of the New Testament are contained in two manuscripts in Old Syriac, one discovered in Egypt in 1842 and the other by Agnes Smith Lewis at Mount Sinai in 1892. The former, dates to the fifth century, is known as the Syriac Curetonianus (syr[c]) from being edited and published by William Cureton in 1858. The latter is known as the Syriac Sinaiticus (syr[s]) or Sinaitic Palimpsest, which dates to the late fourth century and contains 358 pages. We recall that a palimpsest is a manuscript written over a partly erased older manuscript in such a way that the old words can be read beneath the new. The Syriac Sinaiticus, four canonical gospels of the New Testament, is beneath a biography of female saints and martyrs, which date to 778 C.E. Metzger writes, "Though these manuscripts were copied in about the fifth and fourth centuries ... the form of the text that they preserve dates from the close of the second or beginning of the third century. When the two manuscripts are compared, it is seen that the Sinaitic Syriac represents a slightly earlier form of text than does the Curetonian, even though in some places it may have corruptions that the Curetonian has escaped."[567]

---

[566] F. L. Cross and Elizabeth A. Livingstone, eds., *The Oxford Dictionary of the Christian Church* (Oxford; New York: Oxford University Press, 2005), 480.

[567567] Bruce M. Metzger, *The Text of the New Testament* (Oxford University Press 2005), p. 96-97.

The Syriac Curetonianus (syr^c) and the Syriac Sinaiticus (syr^s) texts are representatives of the Western text. A few significant variant readings include:

Matthew 12:47: ["And someone said to him, 'Look, your mother and your brothers are standing outside seeking to speak to you.'"] This verse is omitted in early MSS (ℵ* B L it^k **Sy**^c,s cop^sa), and WH, while it is present in the Byz text and the NU Committee enclosed the words within square brackets, suggesting uncertainty. Many believe it is likely the verse was omitted accidentally because of a homoeoteleuton (λαλῆσαι ... λαλῆσαι). They also argue that the following verses seem to suggest the necessity of verse 47. However, the weight of the witnesses supporting the omission is significant, making it highly unlikely that homoeoteleuton could have taken place in so many witnesses.

Mark 10:2: "And **Pharisees** came up, testing him, began questioning him whether it was lawful for a man to divorce a wife." Some witnesses omit "Pharisees" (D it syr^s). This would mean that Matthew failed to name Jesus' critics. Hurtado has commented, "It is highly likely, but not absolutely certain that the original text contained this reference to Pharisees." (Hurtado 1989, 166) The majority of the committee for the Greek New Testament felt that the assimilation to the parallel passage in Matthew 19:3 was weak because it

Syriac Sinaiticus, John 5:46–6:11.

is not absolutely parallel, and the widespread support for the longer reading moved them to retain the longer reading. However, the minority of the committee added, "Inasmuch as the impersonal plural is a feature of Markan style, the words προσελθόντες Φαρισαῖοι are probably an intrusion from Matthew; if retained at all, they should be enclosed within square brackets. B.M.M. and A.W."[568]

Luke 23:34: "[But Jesus was saying, 'Father, forgive them; for they do not know what they are doing.'] And they cast lots, dividing up his garments among themselves." Some important early and diverse manuscripts omit 34a, such as P^75 ℵ^1 B D* W Θ 070 it^a syr^s cop^sa bo, which removes any argument for a scribal error. If Jesus' words were original, he would have been forgiving the Romans who were executing him, as verse 33 says, "And when they [the Romans] came to the place that is called The Skull, there they crucified him."

---

[568] Bruce M. Metzger, *The Text of the New Testament* (Oxford University Press 2005), p. 88.

(UASV) Thus, the argument that the later scribes removed the original reading for anti-Semitic purposes, as Jesus supposedly forgave the Jews, does not hold. WH argued that the words came from an oral tradition. They wrote, "They can only be a fragment from the traditions, written or oral, which were, for a while at least, locally current beside the canonical Gospels, and which doubtless included matter of every degree of authenticity and intrinsic value. These verses and the first sentence of 23:34 may be safely called the most precious among the remains of this evangelic tradition which were rescued from oblivion by the scribes of the second century." (Westcott and Hort 1882, 67) Comfort argues that they were "added to make Jesus the model for Christian martyrs—of offering forgiveness to one's executioners."[569] We know why the words are found in the Byz text, but WH and the NU retain the reading only in double brackets, signifying their strong doubts about its presence in the original. Metzger writes that the fragment, "though probably not a part of the original Gospel of Luke, bears self-evident tokens of its dominical origin, and was retained, within double square brackets, in its traditional place where it had been incorporated by unknown copyists relatively early in the transmission of the Third Gospel."[570] (B. M. Metzger, A Textual Commentary on the Greek New Testament 1994, 154)

The publication of the Syriac Curetonianus (syr^c) and the Syriac Sinaiticus (syr^s) has allowed scholars to examine how the gospel text in Syriac changed over the first few centuries of Christianity, made up of multiple churches of Eastern Christianity.

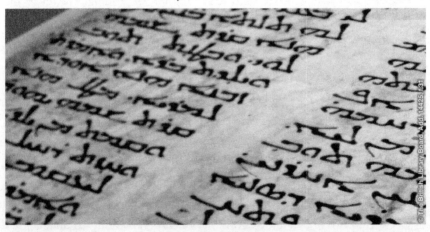

---

[569] Philip W. Comfort, *NEW TESTAMENT TEXT AND TRANSLATION COMMENTARY* (Tyndale House, Carole Stream 2008), p. 240.

[570] Bruce M. Metzger, *The Text of the New Testament* (Oxford University Press 2005), p. 154.

The *Syriac Peshitta* (Syr^p) dates to the late fourth to early fifth century C.E. and is the standard version of the Bible for both Eastern and Western branches of the Syrian Church.

Rabbula was the bishop of Edessa from 411 to 431 C.E. and was long wrongly credited with making the Peshitta translation. However, Metzger suggests, "it is more likely that his revision marked an intermediate between the Old Syriac text and the final form of the Peshitta."[571] Given that the Syrian church split in 431 C.E. and the Peshitta was the standard text for both Western and Eastern Syrian Christianity, the Peshitta had to have time to gain that stature.

Peshitta means "simple" or "common." The Peshitta contained every book of the New Testament except 2 Peter, 2 John, 3 John, Jude, and Revelation. The Syrian church did not recognize these books as canonical at the time. However, these books were later translated and added to the Syrian canon of the New Testament. Still, the early Syrian Church Fathers never referred to these books. More than 250 manuscripts of the Old Testament Peshitta are known.

More than 350 manuscripts of the New Testament Peshitta are known today, a number of them dating to the fifth and sixth centuries C.E. The following manuscripts are found in the British Archives: Rabbula Gospels, Khaboris Codex, Codex Phillipps 1388, British Library, Add. 12140, 14470 (complete text of 22 books), 14479, 14455, 14466, 14467, and 14669.[572] The text of the Peshitta was transmitted with extraordinary faithfulness, resulting in very few significant variants. Metzger tells us that the Gospels of the Peshitta are akin to the Byzantine type of text, while in Acts it agrees more with the Western text. (Metzger and Ehrman, 98)

---

[571] (B. M. Metzger 1964, 1968, 1992, p. 98)

[572] http://www.bl.uk/manuscripts/Default.aspx

The palimpsest called the Sinaitic Syriac. Visible in the margin is the underwriting of the Gospels

The Philoxenian Syriac (Syr[ph]) dates to 508 C.E. when the New Testament was completed by the chorepiscopus (bishop) Polycarp, which Philoxenus of Mabbug had commissioned. This revision also included the books that the Peshitta had omitted. There are only two known manuscripts, one of which contains 2 Peter, 2 John, 3 John, and Jude, while the other contains the book of Revelation. Referring to its character, Sir Frederic Kenyon, the famous archaeologist, and librarian of the British Museum, explained, "the Philoxenian version was written in free and idiomatic Syriac, being the most literary in form of all the translations of the New Testament into this language. The Greek text underlying it was that of the great mass of later MSS., which (as is abundantly clear from other evidence also) was firmly established as the standard type of text in the Greek-speaking Church at the time when Polycarp prepared this version of the Scriptures for Philoxenus."[573]

The *Harkleian Syriac* (Syr[h]) dates to 616 C.E. when Thomas of Harkel completed an Aramaic language translation, which has become known as the Harkleian version. Some argue that Thomas simply added an extensive set of alternate readings in the margins, while others say that Thomas did a complete revision of the Philoxenian Syriac (Syr[ph]), adding readings in the margin that he felt were unworthy of being in the text itself. If we take the first view, there is only the Philoxenian Syriac text with marginal notes, while the second view holds that there are two separate versions. Metzger observes that the Harkleian Syriac (Syr[h]) "apparatus of Acts is the second most important witness to the Western text, being surpassed in this respect only by Codex Bezae." (Metzger and Ehrman, 99)

---

[573] Frederic G. Kenyon, *Handbook to the Textual Criticism of the New Testament* (London; New York: Macmillan and Co., 1901), 142.

The *Palestinian Syriac* (Syr^pal) dates to the eleventh and twelfth centuries C.E. The origin of the Palestinian Syriac Version is likely the fifth century. It is primarily known from three lectionary manuscripts of the Gospels. However, there are fragments of the Gospels in continuous text extant and scraps of the book of Acts and several of Paul's letters. Metzger says that it is based on "the Caesarean type and is quite independent of the other Syriac versions." (Metzger and Ehrman, 100) Agnes Smith Lewis (1843–1926), a Semitic scholar, discovered the manuscript of the Palestinian Syriac, a complete Gospel lectionary, in the library of Saint Catherine's Monastery on Mount Sinai in 1892, which were published by Mrs. Lewis and her sister, Mrs. Gibson, in 1899.[574]

The Latin Versions

Romans 15:24-25 Updated American Standard Version (UASV)

[24] whenever **I journey to Spain**, I hope that I will see you in passing and to be helped on my way there by you after I have first enjoyed your company for a time. [25] But now I am about to travel to Jerusalem to minister to the holy ones. (Bold mine)[575]

The apostle Paul penned those words on his third missionary journey in Rome about 56 C.E. We cannot be certain if Paul ever made his journey to Spain. However, Clement of Rome describes Paul (c. 95 C.E.) as "having taught righteousness to the whole world and having reached the farthest limits of the West."[576] This very well could have included Spain. Regardless, through the efforts of Paul and his more than one hundred traveling companions, as well as other Christian missionaries after him, the Word of God did reach Spain by the second century C.E. As a result, the conditions were right for the Christians in Spain to have the Bible translated into Latin. Latin was the official language of Imperial Rome. However, it was not the common language of the people throughout the Roman Empire the first century C.E. By the last half of the second century C.E., Spain had long been under Roman rule, and Latin had become the common language.

The Latin translations of the Bible were used in the Western part of the Roman Empire to the Reformation. In fact, they are still in use today in

---

[574] *The Palestinian Syriac Lectionary*, re-edited by A. S. Lewis and M. D. Gibson (1899).

[575] Unless otherwise indicated, Scripture quotations are from the forthcoming Updated American Standard Version (UASV) – http://www.uasvbible.org/

[576] Michael William Holmes, *The Apostolic Fathers: Greek Texts and English Translations*, Third ed. (Grand Rapids, MI: Baker Books, 2007), 53.

conjunction with translations from Latin into the common language, in the Roman Catholic Church.

Old Latin Versions (180 C.E.) came into existence prior to the end of the second century C.E. in Carthage, North Africa. Today we have thirty-two Old Latin manuscripts, Codex Vercellenis (it*ᵃ*) being the oldest, dating to the fourth century. None of the Old Latin manuscripts is a complete New Testament, but most of the New Testament is preserved when we consider them all. Scholars typically speak of two basic types of Old Latin text: the African and the European. The sigla that represent the manuscripts of the Itala are italic lower-case letters, such as itᵃ (Vercellenis) Gospels; 4th c., itᵃᵘʳ (Aureus) Gospels; 7th c., itᵇ (Veronensis) Gospels; 5th c., itᵈ (Cantabrigiensis—the Latin text of Bezae) Gospels, Acts, 3 John; 5th c., itᵉ (Palatinus) Gospels; 5th c., itᶠ (Brixianus) Gospels; 6th c., itᶠᶠ² (Corbeiensis II) Gospels; 5th c., itᵍ¹ (Sangermanensis) Matthew; 8th–9th c., and itᵍⁱᵍ (Gigas) Gospels; Acts; 13th c.

Below are the most important Old Latin witnesses of the African and the European type of texts. Old Latin manuscripts are so-called not because they are written in Old Latin, that is, before 75 B.C.E., but rather because they are the oldest versions of the New Testament in Latin.

African Old Latin Manuscripts

itᵉ (Palatinus) Gospels; 5th c.

The Codex Palatinus, designated by itᵉ, is a fifth-century Latin Gospel manuscript that contains portions of the four Gospels. The Gospels follow in the Western order. The text was written on purple-dyed vellum in gold and silver ink. Even though the Latin text of Codex Palatinus is basically an African recension, it was strongly Europeanized.[577]

John 1:34: "And I have seen, and I have borne witness that this one is **the Son** of God."

Byz WH and NU read ὁ υἱὸς τοῦ θεοῦ "the Son of God," which is the reading in the KJV, NKJV, RSV, NIV, NASB, and UASV. It is supported by (P66 P75 P120 ℵ2 A B C W Δ Θ Ψ 083). Variant reading 1 ο εκλεκτος του θεου "the Chosen One of God" is found in the TNIV, NEB, REB, NJB, NLT, and LEB. It is supported by P5vid P106vid ℵ* itᵉ syrᶜ,ˢ. Variant 2 reading "chosen son of God" is found in the NETmg and is supported by itᵃ syrᵖᵃˡ copˢᵃ.

---

[577] (B. M. Metzger 1964, 1968, 1992, p. 102)

Codex Palatinus (it^e) reflects ο εκλεκτος "the Chosen One" along with the other manuscripts (P5vid P106vid ℵ* it^e syr^c,s). These are impressive witnesses, two early papyri, an early uncial, as well as two of the most reliable early Western witnesses. However, the Byz WH NU readings are even a little weightier than Variant 1, with the papyri and early uncials. This means that both readings likely existed in the early third century C.E. "The second corrector of Codex Sinaiticus (sixth or seventh century) deleted εκλεκτος and wrote the nomen sacrum for υιος in the margin."[578] Some scholars have argued that εκλεκτος (Chosen One) is the harder reading; therefore, it is more likely that the reading was changed to υιος (Son) as opposed to εκλεκτος (Chosen One). We also have the fact that "the Son of God" frequently occurs in John's Gospel, while "the chosen one" does not occur in the Gospel of John or his letters (making it the harder reading), and Peter does call Jesus "the Holy One of God" (John 6:69). All of this makes "the Chosen One of God" more appealing as the original reading. However, the external evidence is weightier for "the Son of God," which is also in harmony with the theological terminology of the Gospel of John, as well as his three letters.[579]

it^b (Fleury palimpsest) Matt 3–14; 18–28; Acts; Revelation; Peter's Epistles; 1 John; 5th c.

The Fleury Palimpsest, designated by it^b, is a sixth-century Latin Gospel manuscript which contains portions of Acts, the epistles of Peter, First John, and Revelation. The codex was formerly at Fleury but is now is located in the Bibliothèque nationale de France in Paris. It contains many scribal errors. There are only ten differences in the book of Acts from the text of Acts contained in quotations in the *Testimonia* of Cyprian (c. 200 –258 C.E.),[580] bishop of Carthage, which means that the text is from the third century. The order of books was probably Revelation, Acts, First and Second Peter, then First John.

it^k (Bobbiensis) Matthew, Mark; ca. 400

Codex Bobbiensis, designated by it^k, is one of the oldest and most important African Old Latin manuscripts of the New Testament, and it contains parts of the Gospel of Mark (Mk 8:8-16:9) and Gospel of Matthew (Matt. 1:1-15:36). The Latin of the codex is representative of the Western text-type. It was copied about 400 C.E. Sometime later, it was brought to an

---

[578] Philip W. Comfort, *NEW TESTAMENT TEXT AND TRANSLATION COMMENTARY* (Tyndale House, Carole Stream 2008), p. 259.

[579] (B. M. Metzger, A Textual Commentary on the Greek New Testament 1994, p. 172)

[580] Bruce M. Metzger, *The Early Versions of the New Testament*, Oxford University Press, 1977, pp. 314-315.

Irish monastery in Bobbio in northern Italy. Today it can be viewed in the National Library in Turin. Its text form agrees closely with quotations from Cyprian (c. 200 –258 C.E.), bishop of Carthage. Some scholars feel that it represents a page from the Bible Cyprian used while he was a bishop. After a paleographic study of the text, it has been determined that it was copied from a second-century papyrus. Codex Bobbiensis is the only known example of the intermediate ending of the Gospel of Mark.[581]

Matthew 8:10: "Now when Jesus heard this, He marveled and said to those who were following, 'Truly I say to you, I have not found such great faith **with anyone** in Israel.'" WH and NU have παρ' οὐδενὶ τοσαύτην πίστιν ἐν τῷ Ἰσραὴλ εὗρον "**with no one** in Israel I found such faith." The manuscript support is B W (f¹ 0281) itᵏ copᵇᵒ. This is the preferred reading of the NRSV, ESV, NASB, UASV, HCSB, NET, LEB, and others.

A variant reads ουδε εν τω Ισραηλ τοσαυτην πιστιν ευρον "**not even** in Israel I found such faith." The manuscript support is ℵ C Θ 0233 0250 f¹³ 33 Maj. This is the preferred reading of the KJV, NKJV, ASV, RSV, and NEB. Because the manuscript evidence is so divided and the original reading is only determined with difficulty, the following translations have this variant reading in a footnote: NRSV, ESV, and NASB. Some argue that the variant is the result of adopting the reading from Luke 7:9.

European Old Latin Manuscripts

itᵃ (Vercellensis) Gospels; 4th c.

Codex Vercellensis, designated by itᵃ, is likely the oldest and most important of the European Old Latin manuscripts of the New Testament, which contains Matthew, John, Luke, and Mark respectively, the same order also found in some other very old "Western" manuscripts, such as Codex Bezae. It is housed in the cathedral library of Vercelli, in the Piedmont Region, Italy. It contains the long ending of Mark 16:9-20 on a replacement page, which begins mid-sentence in verse 7 in the Vulgate version. Unfortunately, the final pages of Mark after 15:15 are no longer extant. However, when C. H. Turner analyzed the space in 1928, it seemed unlikely that the original included verses 9-20.

Some would argue that this hypothesis is made on assumptions that only four pages were lost, which cannot be verified, and that the scribe did not accidentally omit anything. It is not likely that some scribe simply made one replacement page. The more likely scenario is that the scribe merely took a

---

[581] K. Aland & B. Aland, *The text of the New Testament: an introduction to the critical editions and to the Theory and Practice of the Modern Textual Criticism*, Wm. Eerdmans, 1995, p. 188.

page from another manuscript instead of making one to place in Codex Vercellensis. The text of the Codex is related to the fifth-century text of it[ff2] (Corbeiensis II), which contains the Gospels and includes the long ending of Mark. According to an old tradition, Codex Vercellensis was penned under the direction of bishop Eusebius of Vercelli, who was martyred in 371, which would date it to the late fourth century. Textual scholar Peter M. Head reports on some important new research from Gregory Heyworth and Roger Easton: "In March 2013, a team from the Lazarus Project[582] traveled to Vercelli to collect spectral images of sample leaves from the codex. In July 2014, they returned to image the entire manuscript (Codex Vercellensis), this time with help from the Early Manuscripts Electronic Library.[583] Spectral imaging involves two distinct phases. First, imagers photograph the manuscript with a 50-megapixel camera fitted with a specially calibrated quartz lens and a dual filter wheel. Specially designed LED light units to illuminate each folio both from above (reflectively) and below (transmissively) in twelve different wavelengths of light between the ultraviolet (365nm) and the infrared (940nm). Fluorescence from the manuscript provoked by ultraviolet and blue light is separated and captured with the help of a dual filter wheel that sits in front of the lens. All told, as many as thirty-three individual images of each page are captured by the computer-driven system, totaling in this case over 20,000 photos in a ten-day period and over 4 terabytes of data." Head goes to say, "Much of the text that is unreadable to the unaided eye reveals itself in the spectral images. Processing of images of the entire manuscript is now ongoing. Additional results are expected by the end of summer 2015, to be followed by a new edition by Heyworth under the auspices of the Vetus Latina Institute."[584]

Matthew 27:9 "Then what was spoken through **Jeremiah** the prophet was fulfilled: 'And they took the thirty silver pieces,[585] the price that was set on the man, the one on whom a price was set by some of the sons of Israel.'" The WH NU Byz have Ἰερεμίου τοῦ προφήτου "Jeremiah the prophet," which is supported by ℵ A B C L W all.

Variant 1 reads Ζαχαριου του προφητου "Zechariah the prophet," which is supported by 22 syr[hmg]. Variant 2 reads Ιησαιου του προφητου "Isaiah the prophet," which is supported by 21 it[l]. Variant 3 reads του προφητου "the

---

[582] (http://www.lazarusprojectimaging.com/)

[583] (http://emel-library.org/)

[584] Seeing the Codex Vercellensis in a New Light .., http://evangelicaltextualcriticism.blogspot.com/2015/03/seeing-codex-vercellensi (accessed April 09, 2017).

[585] I.e. silver shekels; it takes 50 shekels to equal 1 mina, and 60 minas to equal 1 talent.

prophet," which is supported by Φ 33 it[a,b] syr[p,s] cop[boMS] MSS[according to Augustine].

Matthew says that Jeremiah the prophet spoke these words, when the words are actually found in Zechariah the prophet. Therefore, it would seem that Jeremiah was actually quoting Zechariah 11:12–13. Because of this perceived difficulty, some scribes changed "Jeremiah" to "Zechariah" for variant 1, while others changed "Jeremiah" to "Isaiah" for variant 2. Then others simply removed Jeremiah's name, leaving us "the prophet" in the third variant. However, there is no error on the part of Matthew because the prophecy comes from Zech. 11:12–13 and Jer. 19:1–11; 32:6–9.

We should also examine the differences between what Matthew paraphrases and what Jeremiah says. Matthew has the prophet paying out the money for a field rather than giving it personally to the potter as is the case with Zechariah. Also, notice that the entire thrust of Matthew's quotation is on the purchase of the field, while Zechariah does not even mention a field. Now if we look down to Jeremiah 32:6-9, we find the prophet purchasing a field for seventeen shekels of silver. Jeremiah 18:2 informs us that Jeremiah is sent "down to the potter's house," where he was to "hear God's words." Jeremiah 19:2 has Jeremiah being commanded to "go out to the Valley of the Son of Hinnom at the entry of the Potsherd Gate and proclaim there the words that I tell you." Jeremiah 19:11 informs us of Jeremiah's symbolic actions; "and shall say to them, 'Thus says Jehovah of armies: So will I break this people and this city, as one breaks the vessel of the potter so that it can never be repaired; and in Topheth men shall bury because there will be no place else to bury'" (UASV).

We must also keep in mind that Zechariah was fond of using Jeremiah in his prophecy (Zech. 1:4 and Jer. 18:11; Zech. 3:8 and Jer. 23:5; Zech. 1:12 7:5 and Jer. 25:12). Further, if we reread Zechariah's words, we will see that he does not mention the purchase of a field, but Jeremiah does mention such a purchase. Actually, it is Jeremiah who writes, "because they have filled this place with the blood of innocents" (19:4), and says that the name of the potter's field "shall no more be called Topheth, or the Valley of the Son of Hinnom, but the Valley of Slaughter" (19:6), In addition, it must be recalled that it was Jeremiah the prophet who actually purchased a potter's field (Jer. 32:6-9), Thus, it was a common practice for a later prophet to quote or use the information from an earlier prophet. We can see that Zechariah did that, and the apparent mistake is likely just another example of Zechariah's quoting Jeremiah. Zechariah's own words further support this: "were not these the words that Jehovah proclaimed by the former prophets...?" (7:7) It was also a common saying among the Jews that "the spirit of Jeremiah was upon

Zechariah." If we combine this with the fact that Jeremiah was the more prominent prophet, we can see why Matthew credits him.

it[b] (Veronensis) Gospels; 5th c.

Codex Veronensis, designated by it[b], is a fifth-century Latin manuscript written on purple-dyed vellum in silver and occasionally gold ink, which followed the Western order. It contains all four Gospels in almost their entirety: Matthew, John, Luke, Mark.[586] It has several lacunae (Matt. 1:1-11; 15:12-23; 23:18-27; John 7:44-8:12; Lu 19:26-21:29; Mk 13:9-19; 13:24-16:20).[587] The Latin text of Codex Veronensis represents the Western text-type in European recension.[588] Metzger cites Francis Crawford Burkitt (1864–1935) as saying, "It represents the type of text that Jerome used as the basis for the Vulgate."[589]

Several pages are missing from Codex Veronensis, which include the pages that would have contained John 7:44-8:11, and when the spacing is analyzed, it would seem that it would have included John 7:53-8:11, namely, the account of the adulteress. However, the evidence is overwhelming that the account is an interpolation and is not part of John's Gospel.

John 14:14: "If you ask **me** anything in my name, I will do it."

WH NU have ἐάν τι αἰτήσητε **με** ἐν τῷ ὀνόματι μου "whatever you ask **me** in my name," which is supported by P[66] P[75vid] ℵ B W Δ Θ 060 f[13] 33. The variant has εαν τι αιτησητε εν τω ονοματι μου "whatever you ask in my name," which is supported by A D L Q Ψ.

The variant "if you ask **me** anything" has the support of the earliest manuscripts. Scribes likely omitted με ("me") so as to bring 14:14 into harmony with 14:13, as well as 15:16 and 16:23. In Codex Veronensis (it[b]), the entire verse of John 14:14 is omitted along with manuscripts X f[1] 565 1009 ℓ 76 ℓ 253 vg[mss] syr[s, pal] arm geo Diatessaron. Ancient versions were known to omit repetitive material. The omission could have been accidental or intentional.

---

[586] Bruce M. Metzger, *The Early Versions of the New Testament*, Oxford University Press, 1977, p. 296.

[587] Scrivener, Frederick Henry Ambrose; Edward Miller (1894). *A Plain Introduction to the Criticism of the New Testament. Vol. 2* (fourth ed.). London: George Bell & Sons. p. 45.

[588] Gregory, Caspar René (1902). *Textkritik des Neuen Testaments*. Leipzig. p. 601

[589] Bruce M. Metzger, *The Text of the New Testament: Its Transmission, Corruption, and Restoration*, Oxford University Press 2005, p. 102.

it^e (Colbertinus) Gospels; twelfth c.

Codex Colbertinus, designated by it^e and penned in the twelfth century, likely in Southern France, is now housed at the National Library of France at Paris. In the four Gospels and Book of Acts Codex Colbertinus follows the European Old Latin (with traces of African readings), while the rest of the New Testament follows the Vulgate.

Matthew 27:38: "Then two robbers were crucified with him, one on the right and one on the left."

In Codex Colbertinus (it^c), the two robbers, who were crucified on either side of Jesus, are named: Zoatham (right-hand) and Camma (left-hand). In Mark 15:27, virtually the same names are given by the same scribe, as Zoatham and Chammata. Codex Rehdigeranus (it^l) gives the names of the two robbers as Joathas and Maggatras. It was common for scribes to give names to persons whom they felt played a major role in the Scriptures.[590]

it^ff2 (Corbeiensis II) Gospels; 5th c.

Codex Corbeiensis II, designated by it^ff2, is a fifth century Old Latin Gospel, written on vellum, containing 190 parchment folios with the text of the four Gospels, with lacunae (Matt 1:1-11:16; Luke 9:48; 10:20.21; 11:45-12:6.7; John 17:15-18:9; 20:22-21:8).[591] It was penned in a beautiful round uncial hand. The Gospels are as follows: Matthew, Luke, John, Mark. The Latin text of Codex Corbeiensis II is characteristic of the Western text-type.

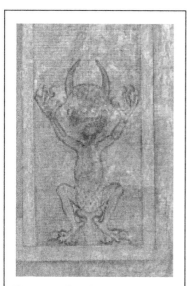

Illustration of the devil, Folio 290 recto.
it^gig (Gigas) Gospels; Acts; 13th c.

It contains a form of text that is akin to that preserved in Codex Vercellensis and Codex Veronensis.[592]

it^gig (Gigas) Gospels; Acts; 13th c.

Codex Gigas is designated by it^gig and is known in English as the Giant Book, as it is the largest extant medieval manuscript in the world (weighing in at 165 pounds). Each page is about 20 by 36 inches. It dates to the thirteenth century. The New Testament is Matthew through Acts, James through Revelation, and Romans through Hebrews.

It is also known as the Devil's Bible because it has a huge illustration of the devil on the inside (Folio 290 recto). The Legend is that a monk who sold his soul to the devil created the codex. The codex was copied by Herman the Recluse in the Benedictine monastery of Podlažice near Chrudim in the Bohemia, to later be acquired by the Imperial Treasury in Prague. At the end of the Thirty Years' War in 1648, the codex was taken by the Swedish army and presented to the Royal Library in Stockholm, where it remained from 1649 to 2007.

---

[590] See Bruce M. Metzger's article, "Names for the Nameless in the New Testament; a Study in the Growth of Christian Tradition," in *Kyriakon: Festschrift Johannes Quasten*, edited by Patrick Granfield and Josef A. Jungmann (Münster/W., 1970), pp. 89 ff., reprinted (with additions) in Metzger, *New Testament Studies*(Leiden, 1980), pp. 33 ff.

[591] Bruce M. Metzger, *The Early Versions of the New Testament*, Oxford University Press, 1977, p. 296.

[592] Bruce M. Metzger, *The Text of the New Testament: Its Transmission, Corruption, and Restoration*, Oxford University Press 2005, p. 102.

The Latin Vulgate (*Vulgata Latina*) is a version of the entire Bible by one of the foremost Biblical scholars of all time, Jerome ([c.346–420 C.E.] Latin: Eusebius Hieronymus). Jerome was a Roman Christian priest, confessor, theologian, and historian who became a Doctor of the Church. He was the son of Eusebius of the city of Stridon, which was on the border of Dalmatia and Pannonia. His parents were prosperous, and he felt the benefits of money at an early age, receiving an education in Rome under the well-known grammarian Donatus. Jerome demonstrated himself to be an exceptional grammar, rhetoric, and philosophy student. Throughout this period, he also studied Greek. He is most famously known for his translation of the Bible from the original languages of Hebrew (OT) and Greek (NT) into Latin (the Vulgate), and his list of works is extensive.

Jerome was born at Stridon about 346 C.E. He was not baptized until about 366 C.E., and shortly after that, he and his friend Bonosus headed for Rome. However, they became wanderers for a time and then finally found themselves in Aquileia, Italy, where Jerome was introduced to the idea of asceticism. He became attracted to this extreme way of life, so he and a group of his friends spent a number of years cultivating it.

In 373 C.E., some unnamed trouble contributed to the group's going their separate ways. Discouraged, Jerome traveled without a purpose and a known destination eastward across Bithynia, Galatia, and Cilicia, and eventually to Antioch, Syria.

Even though he was only in his late 20's at this point, Jerome's health was damaged by fever, and he grew very ill during his journeys. "Oh, if only the Lord Jesus Christ would suddenly transport me to you," he said, writing to a friend, Rufinus. "My poor body, weak even when well, has been shattered by frequent illnesses."

Jerome had already coped with sickness, seclusion, and inner turmoil; he was now thrust into a spiritual crisis. In a dream,

> Suddenly I was caught up in the spirit and dragged before the judgment seat of the Judge; and here the light was so bright, and those who stood around were so radiant, that I cast myself upon the ground and did not dare to look up. Asked who and what I was I replied 'I am a Christian.' But He who presided said: 'Thou liest; thou art a follower of Cicero and not of Christ. For where thy treasure is there will thy heart be also.' Instantly I became dumb, and amid the strokes of the lash—for He had ordered me to be scourged—I was tortured more severely still by the fire of conscience, considering with myself that verse 'In the grave, who

shall give thee thanks?' Yet for all that I began to cry and to bewail myself saying: 'Have mercy upon me, O Lord; have mercy upon me.' Amid the sound of the scourges this cry still made itself heard. At last the bystanders, falling down before the knees of Him who presided, prayed that He would have pity on my youth, and that He would give me space to repent of my error. He might still, they urged, inflict torture upon me, should I ever again read the works of the Gentiles. Under the stress of that awful moment I should have been ready to make even still larger promises than these. Accordingly I made oath and called upon His name, saying 'Lord, if ever again I possess worldly books, or if ever again I read such, I have denied thee.' On taking this oath, I was dismissed, and returned to the upper world.[593]

Sometime later he would sidestep his pledge that he had made in the dream and said that he should not be held answerable for a solemn promise made in a dream. However, Jerome felt somewhat obligated to his vow, so he left Antioch and searched for solitude in Chalcis in the Syrian Desert. Living as a recluse, he submerged himself in the study of the Bible and theological literature. Jerome said, "I read the books of God with zeal greater than I had previously given to the books of men."[594] He likewise learned the local Syriac tongue and started studying Hebrew with the help of a Jew who had become a Christian.

After about five years of living an ascetic life, Jerome returned to Antioch in 378 or 379 C.E. His return to civilization was met with disappointment as the church was profoundly divided. While he had still been in the desert, Jerome had written to the Pope, saying, "The church is rent into three factions, and each of these is eager to seize me for its own."[595]

Jerome eventually decided that he would take the side of Bishop Paulinus, one of three men who claimed the title of Antioch. Jerome unwillingly accepted his being ordained and demanded (1) that he was not to be held back from continuing his ascetic life and (2) that he would remain freed from any priestly duties to minister to a specific church.

---

[593] Rufinus of Aquileia, "The Apology of Rufinus", trans. William Henry Fremantle In , in A Select Library of the Nicene and Post-Nicene Fathers of the Christian Church, Second Series, Volume III: Theodoret, Jerome, Gennadius, Rufinus: Historial Writings, Etc., ed. Philip Schaff and Henry Wace (New York: Christian Literature Company, 1892), 462-63.

[594] Jerome, "The Letters of St. Jerome", Volume VI: St. Jerome: Letters and Select Works, ed. Philip Schaff and Henry Wace (New York: Christian Literature Company, 1893), 36.

[595] Jerome, "The Letters of St. Jerome", Volume VI: St. Jerome: Letters and Select Works, ed. Philip Schaff and Henry Wace (New York: Christian Literature Company, 1893), 20.

Jerome went with Paulinus to the Council of Constantinople and afterward continued with him to Rome in 381 C.E. Pope Damasus soon appreciated Jerome's learning and linguistic expertise. Jerome was raised to the important position of personal secretary to Damasus within a year.

Once in the position of personal secretary, Jerome seemed to attract controversy at every turn. For example, even though he lived in a luxurious papal court, he continued his ascetic lifestyle. This was not only frowned upon, but he even went a step further and spoke out against the excessive lifestyle of the worldly clergy, creating numerous enemies.

Regardless of those who despised him, Jerome had the complete backing of Pope Damasus. Of course, the pope had very good reasons for seeing that Jerome continued in his Bible research. The Latin Bible version was in numerous forms, as many of them had been carelessly translated, filled with errors. Another problem that Damasus faced was the division of his church, the East and the West. Few in the Eastern portion of the church knew Latin, and fewer still in the Western portion knew Greek.

Therefore, Pope Damasus intended to have Jerome create a standard Latin text of the Gospels. Damasus desired a translation that would be a mirror image of the original language Greek texts, yet at the same time be moving, stirring, and powerful, as well as clear in Latin. Jerome and only a handful of other scholars were up to such a task. He was fluent in Greek, Latin, and Syriac and possessed a fundamental knowledge of Hebrew, making him well-suited for the job. Therefore, Jerome was commissioned to a project by Damasus that would not be completed for the next 20 years of his life.

Jerome became a translator with a mission, which was evident from the speed with which he was accomplishing his task. Jerome exhibited a clear technique that would be used by translators and textual scholars over a millennium later. One of the leading textual scholars of the 20th century, the late Bruce M. Metzger, had this to say about Jerome's method:

> Within a year or so Jerome was able to present Damasus with the first-fruits of his work, a revision of the text of the four Gospels, where the variations had been extreme. In a covering letter, he explained the principles which he followed: he used a relatively good Latin text as the basis for his revision and compared it with some old Greek manuscripts. He emphasized that he treated the current Latin text [of his day] as conservatively as possible and changed it only where the meaning was distorted. Though we do not have the Latin manuscripts which Jerome chose as the basis of his work, it appears that they belonged to the European form of the Old Latin (perhaps they were similar to manuscript *b*). The

Greek manuscripts apparently belonged to the Alexandrian type of text.[596]

Initially, Jerome's Latin translation was well received. However, critics came out of the woodwork to complain about the supposed liberties that he took in doing his translation, as he himself testifies:

> After I had written my former letter, containing a few remarks on some Hebrew words, a report suddenly reached me that certain contemptible creatures were deliberately assailing me with the charge that I had endeavored to correct passages in the gospels, against the authority of the ancients and the opinion of the whole world.[597]

These complaints only grew in intensity after the death of Pope Damasus in 384 C.E. The new pope and Jerome did not have a working relationship like the one he had shared with Damasus, so he made the decision to leave Rome. Once again, Jerome was wandering toward the east.

In 386 C.E., Jerome had found his way to Bethlehem, where he would spend the rest of his life. He was traveling with a few of those who had remained loyal to him, as well as Paula, a prosperous woman of nobility from Rome. Paula had grown accustomed to the plain and simple way of life without luxury because of Jerome's influence. However, here in Bethlehem, her wealth was used to establish a monastery under the direction of Jerome. It would be here that he would take his scholarly pursuits to an entirely new level, completing the ultimate work of his life.

Jerome's understanding of Hebrew was only functional, so this new life in Bethlehem would offer him the opportunity to become an extraordinary Hebrew scholar. Paula was able to help him afford several different Jewish tutors, who helped him fully grasp a number of the most difficult characteristics of the language. Concerning one teacher, Jerome said,

> What trouble and expense it cost me to get Baraninas to teach me under cover of night! For by his fear of the Jews he presented to me in his own person a second edition of Nicodemus.[598]

The Jews of Jerome's day were not very receptive to Gentiles due to the latters' failure to pronounce the guttural sounds correctly. This did not

---

[596] Bruce M. Metzger, *The Text of the New Testament: Its Transmission, Corruption, and Restoration*, Oxford University Press 2005, p. 105.

[597] Jerome, "The Letters of St. Jerome", Volume VI: St. Jerome: Letters and Select Works, ed. Philip Schaff and Henry Wace (New York: Christian Literature Company, 1893), 43-44.

[598] John 3:2; Ibid, Volume VI, 176.

dissuade Jerome, though, as he simply put more effort into his studies and was eventually able to master these sounds. In addition, Jerome transliterated numerous Hebrew words into Latin.[599] This method not only assisted him in remembering the words but also preserved the Hebrew pronunciation of that time.

We are not sure how much of the Bible Damasus wanted Jerome to translate. However, we are well aware of how much Jerome intended to accomplish. Jerome was very attentive and resolute and was determined to make available a revised Latin translation of the entire Bible.

> Therefore, I beseech you, Paula and Eustochium, to pour out your supplications for me to the Lord, that so long as I am in this poor body, I may write something pleasing to you, useful to the Church, worthy of posterity. As for my contemporaries, I am indifferent to their opinions, for they pass from side to side as they are moved by love or hatred.[600]

The basis for the Old Testament was the Greek Septuagint (LXX).[601] The Septuagint was viewed by the Christians of the time as though God inspired it.[602] It functioned as Scripture for the Greek-speaking Jews and was used by many Christians down to the time of Jesus and his apostles, as well up to the time of Jerome. In the Greek New Testament, most of the 320 direct quotations and the collective total of perhaps 890 quotations and references to the Hebrew Old Testament are from the Septuagint.

As Jerome delved deeper into the work of translating the Old Testament, he was again met with discrepancies as had been the case with the different Latin manuscripts, and now was evident between the different Greek manuscripts that he was using. One can only imagine the feelings of disappointment, exasperation, and weariness experienced by this man as he realized the work that would be involved in making textual decisions and translating. In the end, Jerome simply decided that it would be more practical

---

[599] Transliteration is the representation of letters and words written in the parent language (Hebrew in this case) using the corresponding letters of another.

[600] Jerome, "Prefaces to the Books of the Vulgate Version of the Old Testament", Second Series, Volume VI: St. Jerome: Letters and Select Works, ed. Philip Schaff and Henry Wace (New York: Christian Literature Company, 1893), 493.

[601] A Greek translation of the Hebrew Bible made between 280 and 150 B.C.E. to meet the needs of Greek-speaking Jews outside Palestine. The Septuagint (Latin for "seventy") contains some books not in the Hebrew canon. According to tradition (the *Letter of Aristeas*) 72 Jewish scholars of Alexandria, Egypt translated the Septuagint in 72 days. It is typically referenced by the Roman numerals for 70, "LXX."

[602] We need to offer a word of caution here, that the Greek Septuagint was not inspired (no translation is). Moreover, there were a number of Greek translations made, and the text was neither carefully guarded nor unified. Thus there are considerable differences between the Greek and the (original) Hebrew Old Testaments.

to scrap his plan of using the Greek manuscripts and even the revered Septuagint and use the Hebrew text as his basis for the translation.

It was here that Jerome found himself being falsely accused as a forger of the text, a man who was disrespectful of God, deserting the church's traditions in favor of the Jews. Even the leading theologian of Jerome's day, Augustine, begged him to abandon the Hebrew text and return to the use of the Septuagint as the basis for his Latin translation, saying: "If your translation begins to be more generally read in many churches, it will be a grievous thing that, in the reading of Scripture, differences must arise between the Latin Churches and the Greek Churches."[603]

Augustine clearly worried that the church would become further divided. He feared that the Western churches would be using Jerome's Latin text based on the Hebrew text, while the Eastern Greek churches would be using the Greek Septuagint. Moreover, Augustine was concerned about setting aside the Greek Septuagint for a translation that only Jerome would be able to defend.

What was Jerome's reaction to all of these critics? He chose to stay true to himself; he simply ignored them. He stayed with the Hebrew text as the basis for his Latin translation of the Old Testament and brought the whole Latin Bible to completion in 405 C.E. It would be labeled the Vulgate (from Latin *vulgatus,* meaning "common") some years later.

The Old Testament portion of Jerome's Latin translation was not just a revision of the current Latin texts. It was the beginning of something far greater, a course change in the way the Bible was studied and translated. "The Vulgate," said historian Will Durant, "remains as the greatest and most influential literary accomplishment of the fourth century." (Durant 1950, 54)

Granted that Jerome possessed a critical manner of speaking and combative temperament, he by himself nevertheless led Bible research back to the inspired Hebrew text. He pored over and compared ancient Hebrew and Greek manuscripts of the Bible that are no longer accessible to us today with a sharp eye. Jerome's monumental work was also accomplished before that of the Jewish Masoretes.[604] Therefore, the Vulgate is a treasured reference tool for comparing alternate renderings of Bible texts. Hence, it would seem that his and his fellow assistant's petitions were heard:

---

[603] Augustine of Hippo, "Letters of St. Augustin", trans. J. G. Cunningham In , in A Select Library of the Nicene and Post-Nicene Fathers of the Christian Church, First Series, Volume I: The Confessions and Letters of St. Augustin With a Sketch of His Life and Work, ed. Philip Schaff (Buffalo, NY: Christian Literature Company, 1886), 327.

[604] The Masoretes were early Jewish scholars. The Masoretic Text was the text revised and annotated by them between the 6th and 10th centuries C.E.

Therefore, I beseech you, Paula and Eustochium, to pour out your supplications for me to the Lord, that so long as I am in this poor body, I may write something pleasing to you, useful to the Church, **worthy of posterity**. As for my contemporaries, I am indifferent to their opinions, for they pass from side to side as they are moved by love or hatred.[605]

Vulgate of Mark 1:1ff in an illuminated manuscript held at Autun

Jerome first embarked on a revision of the Old Latin version of the New Testament in comparison with the Greek text. He started with the Gospels, which were published in 383 C.E. After more than two decades of tremendous labor in translating God's Word and putting out volumes of commentaries, not to mention taking on every theological battle in his time, Jerome, working alone, finally finished his translation in late 404 or 405 C.E.

vg^a or A (Amiatinus), whole Bible; 7th/8th c.

Codex Amiatinus, designated by vg^a or A, is the earliest surviving manuscript of the whole Bible in the Latin Vulgate version. Many scholars view it as the best and most accurate manuscript of the vulgate. Codex Amiatinus is slightly over nineteen inches high, slightly over thirteen inches in breadth, seven inches thick, and it weighs over 75 pounds. "It was written by order of Goelfrid, abbot of Jarrow and Wearmouth and sent by him as a gift to Pope Gregory in 716."[606]

Vg^c or C (Cavensis), whole Bible; 9th c.

Codex Cavensis, designated by vg^c or C, is housed at the abbey of La Trinità della Cava, near Cava de' Tirreni. It contains 330 vellum folios which measure 12.6 by 10.2 inches. Codex Cavensis dates to the ninth century. It contains the whole Bible in the named scribe's (Danila) hand, and textual variations and orthography suggest that the manuscript is representative of the Spanish group of manuscripts. Metzger qualifies it as one of the "chief representatives."

---

[605] Jerome, "Prefaces to the Books of the Vulgate Version of the Old Testament", trans. W. H. Fremantle, G. Lewis and W. G. Martley In , in A Select Library of the Nicene and Post-Nicene Fathers of the Christian Church, Second Series, Volume VI: St. Jerome: Letters and Select Works, ed. Philip Schaff and Henry Wace (New York: Christian Literature Company, 1893), 493.

[606] Bruce M. Metzger, *The Text of the New Testament* (Oxford University Press 2005), p. 106.

Codex Dublinensis Matthew 20:33-34

Vg^d or Z (Dublinensis) Gospel of Matthew; 6th c.

Codex Dublinensis, designated by vg^d Z, is a Greek uncial manuscript of the Gospels which dates to the sixth century. John Barrett discovered it in 1787 under some cursive writing, which he published in 1801, with errors. Codex Dublinensis is now located at the Trinity College Library in Dublin. It contains the bulk of the text of Gospel of Matthew,[607] on 32 parchment leaves with numerous lacunae. It was penned with one column per page. The column is 21 lines, having 27 letters to each line.

Vg^f or F (Fuldensis) NT; 541-546

Codex Fuldensis, designated by vg^f or F, is a New Testament manuscript based on the Latin Vulgate, made in the mid-sixth century. The codex is viewed as the second most important witness of the Vulgate manuscripts. It is also known as the Victor Codex and is currently housed at the Hessian State Library Landesbibliothek at Fulda, in Hesse, Germany. It contains the Diatessaron and 23 of the canonical books of the New Testament, plus the Epistle to the Laodiceans and a copy of Jerome's Prologue to the Canonical Gospels.[608] Codex Fuldensis plays an essential role regarding the authenticity of 1 Corinthians 14:34–35 coming after verse 33, as opposed to after verse 40, which was the case of several Western witnesses (D F G 88* it^d, g Ambrosiaster Sedulius Scotus), as well as one vulgate manuscript (Codex Reginensis), which also places 1 Cor. 14:34-35 after 1 Cor. 14:40. We will look at verse 33 as well below.[609]

1 Corinthians 14:33–35: [33] For God is not a God of confusion but of peace.

---

[607] Matthew 1:17-2:6, 2:13-20, 4:4-13, 5:45-6:15, 7:16-8:6, 10:40-11:18, 12:43-13:11, 13:57-14:19, 15:13-23, 17:9-17, 17:26-18:6, 19:4-12, 21-28, 20:7-21:8, 21:23-30, 22:16-25, 22:37-23:3, 23:15-23, 24:15-25, 25:1-11, 26:21-29, 62-71.

[608] Bruce M. Metzger, *The Early Versions of the New Testament* (Oxford 1977), p. 335.

[609] Philip B. Payne, *Fuldensis, Sigla for Variants in Vaticanus and 1 Cor 14.34-5*, NTS 41 (1995) 251-262.

As in all the congregations of the holy ones, [34] let the women keep silent in the congregations, for it is not permitted for them to speak, but let them be in subjection, as the Law also says. [35] If they want to learn something, let them ask their husbands at home, for it is disgraceful for a woman to speak in the congregation.

WH and NU retain verses 34-35 after 14:33 and are supported by P[46] ℵ A B Ψ 0243 33 81 88[mg] 1739 Maj syr cop Origen Pelagius, which are found in all translations. The alternate variant places verses 34-35 after 14:40 D F G 88* it[b] Ambrosiaster and is found in the footnotes of the NRSV, TNIV, NLT, and NET.

Both Codex Fuldensis and the uncial Vaticanus (B) of the early fourth century possess marginal readings that would lead one to believe their scribes were aware of the textual problem of 14:34-35. On this, Comfort writes, "In Codex Vaticanus, there is a marginal umlaut by the line that contains the end of 14:33, which, in Payne's view, indicates awareness of the textual problem regarding 14:34–35. As for Codex Fuldensis (produced in 546/547), it seems certain that Victor of Capua (the editor and reader of the manuscript) asked the original scribe to rewrite 14:36–40 in the margin. Payne argues that this rewrite was done so as to exclude 14:34–35. However, it must be said that there are no clear sigla in the manuscript which indicate such an omission. Finally, Payne conjectures that manuscript 88 must have originally been copied from an exemplar that did not contain 14:34–35 (see Payne 1998, 152–158). Niccum (1997, 242–255) presents a thorough case against Payne's observations and concludes that there is no textual evidence for the omission of 14:34–35. Miller (2003, 217–236) also sees reasons for the presence of the umlaut in Codex B other than signaling inauthenticity."[610] In addition, verses 14:34-35 are in P[46] (ca. 150 C.E.) after verse 33, not verse 40.

The apostle Paul's instruction to "keep silent" appears three times in 1 Corinthians chapter 14. Each time he is addressing a different group within the congregation. However, all three have the same reason behind the instruction, "let all things be done decently and in an orderly manner"– 1 Corinthians 14:40.

Did this instruction to "be silent" mean that a woman could never speak at a congregational meeting? No. There were occasions when the Holy Spirit moved women to pray or prophesy in the congregation in the first century. They demonstrated their position within God's arrangement by wearing a head covering on these occasions. – 1 Corinthians 11:5.

---

[610] Philip W. Comfort, NEW TESTAMENT TEXT AND TRANSLATION COMMENTARY (Tyndale House, Carole Stream 2008), p. 519.

vg^m or M (Mediolanensis) Gospels; 6th c.

Codex Mediolanensis, designated by vg^m or M: A Gospel vulgate manuscript that is now housed in the Ambrosian library at Milan, dating to the early sixth century. According to Wordsworth and White, Codex Mediolanensis is one of the best witnesses alongside Amiatinus and Fuldensis.[611]

Vg^r or R (Reginensis) Paul; 8th c.

Codex Reginensis, designated by vg^r or R: an eighth-century vulgate manuscript of the Paul's epistles, which is now housed in the Vatican Library in Vatican City State, within the city of Rome.

Vg^s or S (Sangallensis) Gospels; 5th c.

Codex Sangallensis 1395, designated by vg^s or S, is the oldest Vulgate manuscript of the Gospels, dating to the fifth-century and penned on vellum in Verona, Italy. The codex contains the text of the four Gospels (Matthew 6:21 thru John 17:18), with numerous lacunae. It contains 320 parchment leaves which are 9.1 by 7.3 inches. It has some singular readings in the Gospel of Matthew (11:4; 14:2; 16:9.10; 17:26; 18:9; 26:45.47; 27:59; 28:1) and in Mark (4:7; 4:11; 6:33; 14:21).[612] Currently, it is housed at the Abbey library of Saint Gall (1395) in St. Gallen, Switzerland.[613]

Vg^{g1} or G (Sangermanensis) NT; 9th c.

Codex Sangermanensis, designated by vg^{g1} or G: A Vulgate manuscript, dated 822 C.E.[614] The text is written on vellum. The manuscript contains 191 leaves which are 15.5 by 13 inches. In the New Testament, the Gospel of Matthew contains Old Latin readings. It also contains Shepherd of Hermas.[615]

Matthew 3:15-16: [15] But Jesus answering said to him, "Let it be so now, for thus it is fitting for us to fulfill all righteousness." Then he allowed him. [16] After being baptized, Jesus came up immediately from the water; and

---

[611] Bruce M. Metzger, *The Text of the New Testament* (Oxford University Press 2005), p. 108.

[612] C. H. Turner, *The oldest manuscript of the Vulgate Gospels* (Oxford 1931), pp. XXXI–XXXIV.

[613] Metzger, Bruce M. (1977). *The Early Versions of the New Testament.* London: Oxford University Press. p. 335.

[614] Robert L. Bensly, *The Missing Fragment of the Latin Translation of the Fourth Book of Ezra* (1875, Cambridge Univ. Press) page 5.

[615] Ibid., 298.

behold, the heavens were opened up, and he saw the Spirit of God descending as if a dove coming upon him.[616]

In between verses 15 and 16, an Old Latin manuscript and a vulgate manuscript (it[a, g1]) add, *et cum baptizaretur lumen ingens circumfulsit de aqua, ita ut timerent omnes qui advenerant*[617] ("and when he was baptized a great light shone from the water so that all who were gathered were frightened"). F. F. Bruce notes that this interpolation is also present in Tatian's Diatessaron.[618] While these kinds of interpolations are interesting, this was not in the original text of the Gospel of Matthew. There is no place in any of the Gospels that speak of any presence of a light when Jesus was baptized.

The Coptic Versions

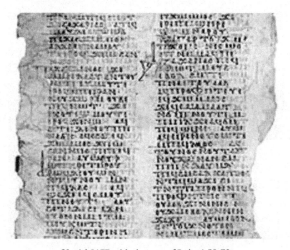

Uncial 0177 with the text of Luke 1:59-73

---

[616] **3:16 BBC: the Spirit of God descending as if a dove coming upon him.** This visible descent upon Jesus was possibly similar to that of the fluttering descent of a dove as it about to land on a branch. (Lu 3:22; Matt. 3:16; Mark 1:10; John 1:32-34) It was the perfect symbol when we consider its characteristics of gentleness, faithfulness to its mate, and its innocence.

[617] Eberhard Nestle and Erwin Nestle, *Nestle-Aland: NTG Apparatus Criticus*, ed. Barbara Aland et al., 28. revidierte Auflage. (Stuttgart: Deutsche Bibelgesellschaft, 2012), 6.

[618] F. F. Bruce, *The Canon of Scripture* (Downers Grove, IL: Inter-Varsity Press, 1988), 127–128.

The earliest translations of the Christian Greek Scriptures were into Syriac, Latin, and Coptic. As Christianity spread, of course, other versions would have been required. Even though Greek was often used in Egypt, in time the need to have a translation in the native language of the growing Egyptian Christian population would come. Coptic was a later form of ancient Egyptian language. In the late first or early second century C.E., a Coptic alphabet was developed using somewhat modified Greek letters (majuscules and seven characters from the demotic,[619] representing Egyptian sounds the Greek language did not have). At least by the end of the second or the beginning of the third century (c. 200 C.E.), the first translation of parts of the New Testament had been produced for the Coptic natives of Egypt. Various Coptic dialects were used in Egypt, and in time, various Coptic versions were made. The most important in the study of the early New Testament is the Sahidic Version of Upper Egypt (i.e., the South) and the Bohairic Version of Lower Egypt (i.e., the North).

The Sahidic cop[sa] (Southern Egypt) All NT; fourth-fifth century

The Sahidic Coptic, designated by cop[sa], is a fourth-fifth century Coptic manuscript of all of the New Testament. The first translation of parts of the New Testament into the Sahidic dialect was made by the end of the second or the beginning of the third century (c. 200 C.E.) in Upper Egypt, where Greek was not understood well. When comparing the different Sahidic texts, the evidence suggests that throughout the third and into the fourth

---

[619] Demotic is a simplified form of Egyptian hieroglyphics. Hieroglyphics is a writing system that uses symbols or pictures to denote objects, concepts, or sounds.

century, different translators worked on different parts of the New Testament. Almost the entire Sahidic New Testament is available in extant manuscripts, made up of completed codices and many fragments from the fourth century and later. Generally speaking, the Sahidic agrees with the Alexandrian text-type, with many Western readings being found in the Gospels and Acts. The books of the NT are in the following order: the Gospels (John, Matthew, Mark, and Luke), the Pauline epistles, with Hebrews between 2 Corinthians and Galatians, the general epistles,[620] Acts, and the book of Revelation.[621]

The Bohairic cop[bo] (Northern Egypt) All NT; ninth century

The Bohairic Coptic, designated by cop[bo], is a fourth-fifth century Coptic manuscript of all New Testament. The Bohairic Coptic dialect of Lower (Northern) Egypt version (near Alexandria and in the delta region) was made a little later than the Sahidic version. The Greek language was more prominent in Lower Egypt, and thus there was no immediate need for a translation into the common language. A very literal translation was made in the beginning of the third century C.E. Most of the more than one hundred Bohairic are from the ninth century and later. This initially led some scholars to conclude that the Bohairic version dated no earlier than the seventh or eighth century. However, some manuscripts go back to the fourth and fifth centuries (Codex Bodmer III).

Middle Egypt falls between Northern and Southern Egypt. The only witnesses that have survived of the Akhmimic and Fayyumic versions are mere fragments. The Schøyen Codex, a papyrus manuscript, contains the Gospel of Matthew and is dated to the early fourth century. It is the earliest copy of Matthew in any Coptic dialect. Codex Glazier contains Acts 1:1-15:3 and is housed at the Pierpont Morgan Library. It is textually very close to Greek Codex Bezae and is dated to the fourth or fifth century. P. Mich. inv. 3521 (Inventory Number) is a Gospel of John in Fayyumic, dating to about 325 C.E.

- cop[fay] (Fayyumic) John; 4th–5th c.

- cop[ach] (Akhmimic) John; James; 4th c.

- cop[ach2] (Subakhmimic) John; 4th c.

---

[620] The epistle of James, the first epistle of Peter, the second epistle of Peter, the first epistle of John, the second epistle of John, the third epistle of John, and the epistle of Jude.

[621] Verses that have been omitted are: Matthew 12:47; Matthew 16:2b-3; 17:21; 18:11; 23:14; Mark 9:44.46; 11:26; 15:28; Luke 17:36; 22:43-44; John 5:4; 7:53-8:11; Acts 8:37; 15:34; 24:7; 28:29; Romans 16:24.

- copG67 (a Middle Egyptian MS) Acts; 5th c.

- copmae (Middle Egyptian) Matthew; 4th–5th c.

The great quality of the Sahidic and Bohairic versions make these very important. Christianity came early to Egypt and we are very fortunate that the Egyptian Christians preserved an early form of the text. The Sahidic and Bohairic versions have the same text type that is found in the Vaticanus and Sinaiticus codices, which have long been the most trustworthy manuscripts.

The Gothic Version

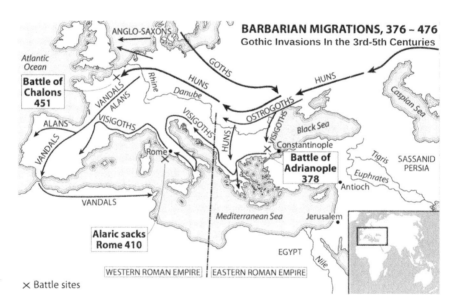

The Goths were a group of loosely allied Germanic tribes, most likely originating in Scandinavia. In the first few centuries after Christ's death and resurrection, they migrated as far south as the Black Sea and the Danube River, to the very outposts of the Roman Empire. The Gothic Bible was the first literary work in any Germanic tongue. Ulfilas (c. 311–383 C.E.) was a missionary translator who was also known as by his Gothic name, Wulfila ("Little Wolf").

Who's Who in Christian History offers us some insights into Ulfilas' life. "Born in Cappadocia (east Asia Minor), Ulfilas may have been captured by Gothic raiders as a youth. Yet his residence by early adulthood was Constantinople, the Roman Empire's eastern capital. He undoubtedly received his education and began his life of service to the church. In 341

Eusebius of Nicomedia, the bishop of Constantinople consecrated Ulfilas as bishop. Soon afterward, the young bishop proceeded to Dacia (north of the Danube River), and for his remaining years, he served as the church's principal missionary to the western Goths in this region. The many converts indicate that Ulfilas's efforts to spread the gospel had extensive results. After several years, persecution forced Ulfilas out of Dacia, and his work thereafter originated from a residence in Moesia (south of the Danube), an area within the empire's borders. Ulfilas's removal to Moesia also saw the project's beginnings for which he is best remembered. This was his translation of the Old and New Testaments into the Goths' vernacular language. Toward this end, Ulfilas first had to reduce Gothic speech to writing, a task involving the invention of an alphabet based on Greek. As copied in the early Middle Ages, surviving remnants of this translation represent the earliest extant examples of Gothic literature. Ulfilas appears to have translated the whole New Testament and also the Old Testament except for the Books of Kings (1 and 2 Samuel, 1 and 2 Kings). It is supposed that the missing Old Testament sections were omitted purposely because of Ulfilas's fear that they would only encourage the aggressive Goths."[622]

Wulfila (Ulfilas) explaining the Gospels to the Goths

Ulfilas finished his translation just two or three years before he died in 383 C.E. The Goths who migrated to Spain and Italy mostly used this translation. Many copies of Gothic Bibles were made. It is probable that several manuscripts were produced in the scriptoria of Ravenna and Verona the areas where the Goths had set up their kingdom. There are surviving fragments of codices of the Wulfila Bible from the 6th to 8th centuries, which contain about half of the Gospels and portions of the apostle Paul's letters.

---

[622] K.J. Bryer, "Ulfilas," ed. J.D. Douglas and Philip W. Comfort, *Who's Who in Christian History* (Wheaton, IL: Tyndale House, 1992), 686.

Eine Seite der Wulfila-Bibel

- goth (Codex Argenteus) part of the four gospels (Matthew, John, Luke, and Mark); 6th c.

- goth (Codex Ambrosianus A-E) Pauline epistles; c. 6th-11th c.

- goth (Codex Carolinus) Romans 11-15; 6th or 7th c.

- goth (Codex Vaticanus Latinus 5750) John; 6th c.

- goth (Codex Gissensis) Luke; 5th c.

Today, the Gothic Bible should be of interest to both the Bible scholar and the serious Bible student. It gives us the history of one translator, Ulfilas, in the sea of many who gave their lives and were filled with a tremendous desire and determination to have the Word of God translated into the common tongue of their days. It was by the work of Ulfilas that the Gothic people were able to have an understanding of the Christian faith. The Gothic Bible gave them a hope that all Christians share, namely, the life that is to come—1 Peter 3:15.

The Armenian Version

Illustrated Armenian Bible from 1256

The Armenian Version of the Bible, designated by *arm*, dates from the early fifth century C.E. It includes all New Testament and was likely prepared from Greek and Syriac texts. It is often called the "queen of the versions," and many regard it as beautiful and accurate. The New Testament is a very literal translation which, of course, is quite helpful to textual criticism.

Isaac or Sahak of Armenia (354–439) was the Patriarch of the Armenian Apostolic Church. Even though Sahak had been abandoned as an orphan at an early age, he still managed to gain an exceptional literary education in Constantinople, especially in the Eastern languages. Around the time that Sahak was elected as the Patriarch of the Armenian Apostolic Church, the Armenians were suffering difficult times. In 387, Armenia had been divided between the Byzantine Empire and Persia. On the Byzantine side, Armenians were not allowed to use the Syriac language, which had to be replaced with the Greek language. This greatly affected their worship and Hellenizing the Armenians in the Byzantine territory. The Armenians were prohibited from using Greek on the Persian side, with Syriac being the chosen language. This could have greatly influenced the culture of the Armenians, removing their national unity. Sahak sponsored Saint Mesrop (c. 362-440), an Armenian linguist who invented the Armenian alphabet (c. 405). After that, Mesrop began to translate the Christian Bible. This was a monumental step in strengthening Armenian national identity.

476

The Armenian version has a record number of copies, at 1,244 cataloged by Rhodes (with hundreds more in the Soviet Union). It is an accurate and literal rendering of the Greek New Testament. Over one hundred of the Armenian manuscripts stop at verse 8 at the end of Mark chapter 16. "One copy of the Armenian Gospels, dated to A.D. 989, says that the last twelve verses of Mark 16 were added by "the presbyter Ariston" (who is mentioned by Papias in the early second century as one of the disciples of the Lord)."[623]

The Georgian Version

The Georgian Version of the Bible is designated by *geo* and dates from the middle of the fifth century C.E. There are no secular records to determine the exact year that Christianity came to Georgia. However, among those who heard Peter's speech at Pentecost 33 C.E. were Jews from Pontus, a district of northern Asia Minor (Ac 2:9). These could have returned home, bringing Christianity there. Clearly, Christian congregations existed in Pontus in about 62-64 C.E., as the apostle begins his first letter "Peter, an apostle of Jesus Christ, to the temporary residents **scattered about** in **Pontus**, Galatia, Cappadocia, Asia, and Bithynia ..." (1 Pet. 1:1). Pontus was on the border of Georgia, which corresponds to the northeastern corner of present-day Turkey. Georgia is the mountainous region between the Black Sea and the Caspian Sea (see Spread of Christianity map below). Note that Peter addressed believers who were "scattered about" in such places as Pontus. The Greek word for "scattered about" is διασπορά (*diaspora*), which literally means "of the Diaspora," i.e., to be spread or scattered throughout a region

[623] Paul D. Wegner, *A Student's Guide to Textual Criticism of the Bible: Its History, Methods & Results* (Downers Grove, IL: InterVarsity Press, 2006), 281.

or avery large area.[624] Peter goes on to say of these people, "In this you greatly rejoice, even though now for a little while, if necessary, **you have been grieved**[625] by various trials" (1 Pet. 1:6). This was probably referring to their being persecuted for their faith.

In about 112 C.E., severe tests were placed on the Christians in Pontus and the surrounding region. "Pliny the Younger was appointed by the emperor Trajan to govern Bithynia-Pontus and reported that he asked suspected Christians three times with threats of punishment, 'Are you a Christian?'[626] The accused proved their innocence by cursing Jesus, which, he says, 'those who are really Christians cannot be made to do.' In the *Martyrdom of Polycarp* 9:3, the proconsul adjures Polycarp, 'Swear and I will release you.' Polycarp replies, 'How can I blaspheme the King who saved me?'"[627] Metzger and others would argue that the gospel message did not reach the Georgian people in the rough mountainous district between the Black Sea and the Caspian Sea until the first half of the fourth century.[628]

The Georgian version was made for the Georgians in the Caucasus, being completed toward the middle of the fifth century C.E. and, although revealing Greek influence, it has an Armenian and Syriac basis. Old Georgian manuscripts of the Gospels, the letters of Paul, and the Psalms have been dated to the mid-fifth century C.E. or even earlier. The alphabet used to translate the New Testament into Georgian was created by the same Mesrop mentioned above, who is credited with the Armenian alphabet. Sidney Jellicoe would argue that the Georgian version was translated from the Armenian version and then revised by comparing it with the Greek text.[629] Georgian was an agglutinative language, meaning that it formed new words by combining simple words without changing their form. The Adysh is the oldest Georgian manuscript (Geo1), dating to 897 C.E., which contains the four Gospels. This is followed by the Opiza manuscript, which dates to 913 C.E., and the Tbet' manuscript that dates to 895 C.E.

---

[624] William Arndt, Frederick W. Danker, and Walter Bauer, *A Greek-English Lexicon of the New Testament and Other Early Christian Literature* (Chicago: University of Chicago Press, 2000), 236.

[625] Or *distressed*

[626] Pliny, *Ep.* 10.96.3.

[627] Clinton E. Arnold, *Zondervan Illustrated Bible Backgrounds Commentary: Matthew, Mark, Luke*, vol. 1 (Grand Rapids, MI: Zondervan, 2002), 293–294.

[628] Bruce M. Metzger, *The Text of the New Testament* (Oxford University Press 2005), p. 108.

[629] Sidney Jellicoe, *The Septuagint and Modern Study* (Oxford: Clarendon, 1968), p. 261.[629]

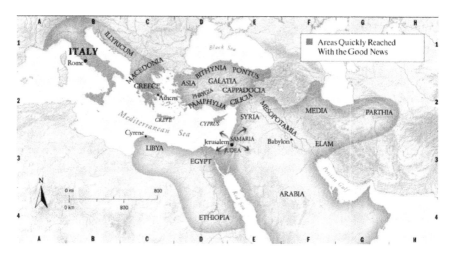

The Ethiopic Version

The Ethiopic Version of the Bible is designated by *eth*, used by the Abyssinians and produced possibly in the fourth or fifth century C.E. Ethiopia was the name given by the ancient Greeks to the region of Africa South of Egypt. Therefore, it corresponded generally with the Hebrew "Cush." The language called Ethiopic was the commonly spoken language during the time of Jesus Christ in the first century until the 14th century and is of Semitic origin. How and when Christianity came to Ethiopia is an unknown. Many point to the Ethiopian eunuch who was "a court official of Candace, queen of the Ethiopians, who was in charge of all her treasure; who had come to worship in Jerusalem," and to whom Philip preached (Ac 8:27-39). Jewish exiles were scattered after their seventy-year exile in Babylon, and this Ethiopian eunuch may have come from an area where many Jews resided. The copy of the scroll of Isaiah that he read was likely a copy of the Greek Septuagint, which was initially produced in Alexandria, Egypt. The Ethiopian kingdom had become partly Hellenized from the time of Ptolemy II (308-246 B.C.E.), and it would be no surprise that he was reading the Greek language.

About 320 C.E. "Frumentius and Aedisius, two Syrian brothers, were rescued from a plundered Roman Ship off the Ethiopian coast. The two lads were escorted to the royal palace in Axum where both served for a number of years in significant administrative and Christianizing roles. Some years later Frumentius traveled to Alexandria to inform Athanasius of the development of Christianity in the Axumite palace, who ordained him bishop." In 327 C.E., newspaper headlines could read, "The Kingdom of Ethiopia adopts Christianity; Ethiopian missionaries sent to convert the Himyarites; the church historian Philostorgios offers first evidence of a Jewish presence in the region."[630]

Over one hundred Ethiopic manuscripts are known but none date earlier than the thirteen-fourteenth centuries. We can say that the Ethiopic version was initially made from Syriac, or possibly Greek, and that it was produced by the fourth or fifth century C.E. A fourteenth-century revision was made in an effort to make the text agree with the Arabic manuscripts of the New Testament. The oldest known extant Ethiopic text is a copy of the four Gospels, which dates to the tenth century C.E. (Abba Garima, MS. 1).[631] According to the Alands, "the translation of Acts seems to have been made from Greek. The Catholic letters were more certainly translated from Greek, and from Revelation, it is possible not only to be certain of the language from which it was translated but to identify the source even more precisely: it represents the text type of A and C, with subsequent influence from the Coptic and the Arabic versions."[632]

The Old Slavonic Version

The Old Slavonic Version of the Bible (designated by *slav*) was created in the ninth century C.E., and has been attributed to two brothers, Cyril (827-869 C.E., originally named Constantine) and Methodius (825-885 C.E.), who were born into a noble family in Thessalonica, Greece. These two brothers are credited with the Glagolitic and the Cyrillic alphabets. "Slavonic" denotes the Slavic dialect that Cyril and Methodius used for their mission and literary work. Some scholars today use the terms "Old Slavonic" or "Old Church Slavonic."

T. O. Kay in Who's Who in Christian History offers us the following insights into these two brothers. "At an early age, Cyril accepted a call to scholarship and was trained at Constantinople by the patriarch Photius. Cyril was ordained, entered a monastery, and was asked to teach philosophy at Constantinople. When he was sent on a mission to Crimea in southern Russia, he took his brother, Methodius, with him. Although that mission resulted in some professions of Christianity, no long-term foundations were laid at that time. Later, Prince Ratislav of Moravia, in reaction to Western

---

[630] Ethiopia | The Center for Early African Christianity, http://www.earlyafricanchristianity.com/research-resources/timelines/ethiopia.html (accessed April 19, 2017).

[631] Metzger, Bruce M. (1977). *The Early Versions of the New Testament*. London: Oxford University Press. p. 224-225.

[632] Kurt and Barbara Aland (1989). *The Text of the New Testament*. Grand Rapids: Wm. B. Eerdmans Publishing. p. 209.

political, cultural, and religious infiltration, requested missionaries from Constantinople. Cyril and Methodius were sent. Cyril created an alphabet, put the Slavonic language into writing for the first time, and then translated the Scriptures. His work thus involved both evangelization and instruction. As a result of conflict with the Western clergy, the missionaries were called to Rome. The pope, however, gave his approval to their work and made Cyril a bishop. Cyril died shortly thereafter and was buried in Rome. The Prince of Pannonia (northern Yugoslavia) then sought the help of Methodius, who left Rome and became archbishop of Sirmium (near modern Belgrade). From there his work spread to other areas, including Bohemia, again with opposition from Western clergy—although his efforts were accepted by the pope and the people. Thus, Cyril and Methodius laid the foundations of the church in Slavic Europe."[633]

The nature of the alphabet Cyril manufactured has triggered much disagreement, as linguists are not certain what alphabet it was. The alphabet called Cyrillic is an old alphabet derived from Greek script, with a little over a dozen additional characters created to denote Slavonic sounds not found in Greek. However, the Slavonic manuscripts use a very different script, known as Glagolitic. It is this script that many scholars think Cyril created. A few of the Glagolitic characters seem to come from cursive Greek or Hebrew. A number of them were likely a result of medieval diacritics. However, most of them are original and complex creations. Glagolitic appears to be a highly distinct and original creation. The late date of the Old Slavonic Version means that it holds little value for the textual scholar as to playing any role in determining original readings. The version belongs to the Byzantine family type of text but also contains a number of Western and Caesarean readings.

᛭	Ⱆ	Ⰲ	℅	Ⰴ	Ə	Ⰶ	Ⰷ	Ⱁ	Ⱂ	Ⱛ
а	б	в	г	д	е	ж	дз	з	и	и

Ⱃ	Ⰿ	Ⰽ	Ⰾ	ℳ	Ⱇ	Ə	Ⱇ	Ⱆ	Ⱀ	Ⱅ
и	г'	к	л	м	н	о	п	р	с	т

Ⱎ	Ⱇ	Ⱈ	Ⱉ	Ⰲ	Ⰲ	Ⱋ	Ⱋ	Ⱚ	Ⱏ	Ⱐ
у	ф	х	о	ш	ц	ч	щ	ъ	ы	ь

Ⰰ	Ⱓ	Ⱑ	Ⱔ	Ⱖ	Ⱗ	Ⱍ	Ⰻ
я	ю	еⁿ	оⁿ	йеⁿ	йоⁿ	ф	и

[633] T.O. Kay, "Cyril (826–869) and Methodius," ed. J.D. Douglas and Philip W. Comfort, *Who's Who in Christian History* (Wheaton, IL: Tyndale House, 1992), 187.

CHAPTER XIII

What Are Textual Variants [Errors] and How Many Are There?

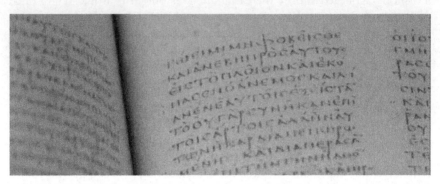

The first part of this chapter will cover the gist of what is most often discussed in New Testament textual criticism today. After that, we will discuss what should be the primary focus of NTTC (New Testament Textual Criticism). It would seem that Bart D. Ehrman and other Bible critics of his persuasion have sent many textual scholars on a quest. These scholars have become obsessed with discussing how many variants there are, how to count the textual variants, and whether they are significant or insignificant. Below, we will cover what is being said about variants and whether some are more significant than others, and then close the chapter with what actually is the most important mission in NTTC.

Some Bible critics seem, to begin with, the belief that if God inspired the originals and they were fully inerrant, the subsequent copies must continue to be inerrant for the inerrancy of the originals to have value. They seem to be asking, "If only the originals were inspired, and the copies were not inspired, and we do not have the originals, how are we to be certain of any passage in Scripture?" In other words, God would never allow the inspired, inerrant Word to suffer copying errors. Why would he perform the miracle of inspiring the message to be fully inerrant and not continue with the miracle of inspiring the copyists throughout the centuries to keep it inerrant? First, we must acknowledge that God has not given us the specifics of every decision he has made in reference to humans. If we begin asking, "Why did God not do this or do that," where would it end? For example, why didn't God just produce the books himself and miraculously deliver them to people as he gave the commandments to Moses? Instead of using humans, why did he not use angelic messengers to pen the message, or produce the message miraculously? God has chosen not to tell us why he did not move the copyists along with the Holy Spirit, so as to have perfect copies, and it remains an unknown. However, it should be noted that if we can restore the text to its original wording through the science of textual criticism, i.e. to an exact representation thereof, we have, in essence, the originals.

We do know that the Jewish copyists and later Christian copyists were not infallible as were the original writers. The Holy Spirit inspired the original writers, while the most that can be said about the copyists is that the Holy Spirit **guided** them. However, do we not have a treasure-load of evidence from centuries of copies, unlike ancient secular literature? Regardless of the recopying, do we not have the Bible in a reliable critical text and trustworthy translations, with both improving all the time? It was only inevitable that imperfect copyists, who were not under inspiration, would cause errors to creep into the text. However, the thousands of copies that we have enable textual scholars to identify and reject these errors. How? For one thing, different copyists made different errors. Therefore, the textual scholar compares the work of different copyists. He is then able to identify their mistakes.

A Simple Example

Suppose 100 people were invited or hired to make a handwritten copy of Matthew's Gospel, with 18,345 words. Further, suppose that these people fit in one of four categories as writers: **(1)** struggle to write and have no experience as a document maker; **(2)** skilled document makers (recorders of events, wills, business, certificates, etc.); **(3)** trained copyists of literature; and **(4)** the professional copyists. There is little doubt that these copyists would make some copying errors, even the professionals. However, it would be impossible that they would all make the same errors. Suppose a trained textual scholar with many years of religious education, including textual studies and decades of experience, was to compare the 100 documents carefully. In that case, he could identify the errors and restore the text to its original form, even if he had never seen that original.

The textual scholars of the last 250 years, especially the last 70 years, have had 5,000+ and now over 5,898 Greek manuscripts at their disposal. A number of the manuscripts are portions dating to the second and third centuries C.E. Moreover, more manuscripts are always becoming known; technology is ever advancing, and improvements are always being made.

Hundreds of scholars throughout the last three centuries have produced what we might call a master text through lifetimes of hard work and careful study. Are there places where we are not certain of the reading? Yes, of course. However, we are considering very infrequent places in the Greek NT text containing about 138,020 words, which would be considered difficult to arrive at what the original reading was. In all these places, the alternative readings are provided in the apparatus. Bible critics who exaggerate the extent of errors are misleading the public on several fronts. First, some copies are almost error-free and negate the critics, who claim, "We have only error-ridden copies."[634] Second, the vast majority of the Greek New Testament has no scribal errors. Third, textual scholarship can easily identify and correct the majority of the scribal errors. In addition, of the remaining errors, we can still say most are solved with satisfaction. Of the small number of scribal errors remaining, we can say that most are solved with some difficulty, and there remain very few errors of which textual scholarship continues to be uncertain about the original reading at this time.

400,000 to 500,000 Supposed Variants in the Manuscripts

With this abundance of evidence, what can we say about the total number of variants known today? Scholars differ significantly in their estimates—some say there are 200,000 variants known, some say 300,000, some say **400,000 or more!** We do not know for sure because, despite impressive developments in computer technology, no one has yet been able to count them all. Perhaps, as I indicated earlier, it is best simply to leave the matter in comparative terms. There are more variations among our manuscripts than there are words in the New Testament.[635]

Bart D. Ehrman has some favorite, unprofessional ways of describing the problems, which he stresses without qualification, in every interview he has for a lay audience or seminary students. Below are several, the first two from the quotation above:

- Scholars differ significantly in their estimates—some say there are 200,000 variants known, some say 300,000, some say **400,000 or more!**

- There are **more variations** among our manuscripts **than there are words** in the New Testament.

---

[634] (Bart D. Ehrman, Misquoting Jesus: The Story Behind Who Changed the Bible and Why 2005, 7)

[635] Ibid., 89-90

- We have only **error-ridden copies**, and the vast majority of these are centuries removed from the originals and different from them, evidently, in thousands of ways. (*Whose Word is It*, 7)

- We don't even have copies of the copies of the originals, or **copies of the copies of the copies of the originals**. (*Misquoting Jesus*, 10)

- **In the early Christian centuries, scribes were amateurs** and as such were more inclined to alter the texts they copied. (*Misquoting Jesus*, 98)

- **We could go on nearly forever** talking about specific places in which the texts of the New Testament came to be changed, either accidentally or intentionally. (*Misquoting Jesus*, 98)

- The Bible began to appear to me as a very **human book**. (*Misquoting Jesus*, 11)

Each of the bullet points above claimed by Ehrman can be categorized as an exaggeration, misinformation, misleading, or just a failure to be truthful. Many laypersons-churchgoers have been spiritually shipwrecked in their faith by such unexplained hype. What the uninformed person hears is that we can never get back to the originals or even close, that there are hundreds of thousands of significant variants that have so scarred the text, we no longer have the Word of God, and it is merely the word of man. How such a knowledgeable man cannot know the impact his words are having is beyond this author.

Miscounting Textual Variants

In 1963, Neil R. Lightfoot penned a book that has served to help over a million readers, *How We Got the Bible*. It has been revised two times since 1963, once in 1988, and again in 2003. There is a "miscalculation" in the book which has contributed to a misunderstanding in how textual variants are counted. In fact, there are several other books repeating it. A leading textual scholar, Daniel B. Wallace, has brought this to our attention in an article entitled, *The Number of Textual Variants an Evangelical Miscalculation*.[636] World-renowned Bible apologist Norman L. Geisler has commented on it as well.

Lightfoot wrote,

From one point of view, it may be said that there are 200,000 scribal errors in the manuscripts. Indeed, the number may well considerably exceed this and obviously will grow, as more and

---

[636] http://bible.org/article/number-textual-variants-evangelical-miscalculation

more manuscripts become known. However, it is wholly misleading and untrue to say that there are 200,000 errors in the text of the New Testament. (Actually, textual critics consciously avoid the word "error;" they prefer to speak of "textual variants.") This large number is gained by counting all the variations in all of the manuscripts (5,898). This means that if, for example, one word is misspelled in 4,000 different manuscripts, and it amounts to 4,000 "errors." Actually, in a case of this kind, only one slight error has been made, and it has been copied 4,000 times. But this is the procedure which is followed in arriving at the large number of 200,000 "errors."[637]

Wallace makes this observation in his article:

In other words, Lightfoot was claiming that textual variants are counted by the number of manuscripts that support such variants, rather than by the wording of the variants. This book has been widely influential in evangelical circles. I believe over a million copies of it have been sold. And this particular definition of textual variants has found its way into countless apologetic works." He goes on to clarify just what a textual variant is, "The problem is, the definition is wrong. Terribly wrong. A textual variant is simply any difference from a standard text (e.g., a printed text, a particular manuscript, etc.) that involves spelling, word order, omission, addition, substitution, or a total rewrite of the text. No textual critic defines a textual variant the way that Lightfoot and those who have followed him have done.

Geisler writes,

Some have estimated there are about 200,000 of them. First of all, these are not "errors" but variant readings, the vast majority of which are strictly grammatical. Second, these readings are spread throughout more than 5300 manuscripts, so that a variant spelling of one letter of one word in one verse in 2000 manuscripts is counted as 2000 "errors."[638]

Lightfoot evidently was thought to have erred by counting manuscripts rather than the variants in the text. In fairness to Lightfoot, it should be pointed out that he deplored the system of counting "errors" by the number of manuscripts, as the quotation above reveals. He was simply saying that critics were doing this, not that it was proper. It is difficult to see why Wallace

---

[637] *How We Got the Bible* (Grand Rapids: Baker, 2003; p). Lightfoot says (53-54)

[638] *Baker Encyclopedia of Christian Apologetics*, by Norm Geisler (Grand Rapids: Baker, 1998; p. 532)

would attribute responsibility for the system to Lightfoot. Also, Wallace cited Lightfoot's 1963 edition that did not include the distinction between "error" and "textual variant."

Let me offer the reader an example for our purposes. First, we should underscore a few important points raised: 1) we have so many variants because we have so many manuscripts. 2) We do *not* count the manuscripts; we count the variants. 3) A variant is any portion of the text that exhibits variations in its reading between two or more different manuscripts. This is more precisely called a **variation unit**. It is important to distinguish variation units from variant readings. Variation units are the places in the text where manuscripts disagree, and each variation unit has at least two variant readings. Setting the limits and range of a variation unit is sometimes difficult or even controversial because some variant readings affect others nearby. Such variations may be considered individually or as elements of a longer single reading.

We should also note that the terms "manuscript" and "witness" may appear to be used interchangeably in this context. Strictly speaking, "witness" (see below) only refers to the content of a given manuscript or fragment, so the witness predates the physical manuscript on which it is written to a greater or lesser extent. However, the only way to reference the "witness" is by referring to the manuscript or fragment that contains it. In this book, we have sometimes used the terminology "witness *of* x or y manuscript" to distinguish the content in this way.

We begin by choosing our "base" or "standard text." We are primarily using the *standard text* (critical or master text), **N**estle-Aland (NA) Greek Text (28th edition), and the **U**nited Bible Society (UBS) Greek Text (5th edition). These two critical texts are the same. However, we also include the 1881 **W**estcott and **H**ort (WH) critical text. Therefore,

Note: When the acronym **NU** is used, **N** stands for **N**estle-Aland, the **U** for **U**nited Bible Societies, since the texts are the same. The apparatuses are different, and the UBS version is designed primarily for translators (more on this below). The acronym **WH** is for Westcott and Hort Greek text. Here is another opportunity to emphasize the documentary approach in making textual decisions, which is shown in the fact that about 155 variant decisions were made by the editors of the NU text when the preferred reading is found in the WH text. When we consider the WH NU texts, we can argue that we have a critical text that is a 99.99% reflection of the original.

In this writer's opinion, the critical WH NU texts are as close as we can get to what the original would have been like.[639] Therefore, we can use the reading in the critical text as the original reading, and anything outside of that in the manuscript history is a variant: spelling, word order, omission, addition, substitution, or a total rewrite of the text. Any difference in two different manuscripts is a variant, technically speaking.

Before going to our example, I want to emphasize that Bible critics, who grumble and repeat over and over again how there are 400,000+ variants in the text of the New Testament, have only one agenda: they want to discredit the Word of God. They use the issue of variants as a misrepresented excuse for their having lost their faith, having shipwrecked their faith, or having had no faith from the start. These Bible critics are no different from the religious leaders Jesus dealt with in the first century. Jesus said of them, "Blind guides! You strain out a gnat yet gulp down a camel!" (Matt. 23:24). They thrust aside 99.99 percent because 0.01 of one percent is not absolutely certain! Now let's turn to our example, which comes from the Apostle Paul's letter to the Colossians.

Example of a Textual Variant

Colossians 2:2 Updated American Standard Version (UASV)

[2] that their hearts may be comforted, having been knit together in love, and into all riches of the full assurance of understanding, and that they may have a complete knowledge[640] of the mystery **of God**, namely **Christ**, [τοῦ θεοῦ Χριστοῦ; tou theou Christou]

See the chart below.

---

[639] It is true that some scholars, such as Philip Comfort, argue that the NU could be improved upon because in many cases it is too dependent on internal evidence, when the documentary evidence should be more of a consideration in choosing readings. It should be pointed out, however, that this is in only a relative handful of places, when one considers 138,020 words in the Greek New Testament, and it is hardly consequential. I would also mention that this writer would agree with Comfort in the matter of giving more weight to documentary evidence.

[640] *Epignosis* is a strengthened or intensified form of *gnosis* (*epi,* meaning "additional"), meaning, "true," "real," "full," "complete" or "accurate," depending upon the context. Paul and Peter alone use *epignosis*.

Variants	Variant	MSS or Versions
NU[641]	of the God of Christ	Standard Text
1	of the God	10 MSS[642]
2	of the Christ	1 MS
3	of the God who is Christ	4 MSS
4	of the God who is concerning Christ	2 MSS
5	Of the God in the Christ	2 MSS
6	of the God in the Christ Jesus	1 MS
7	of the God and Christ	1 MS
8	Of God the father Christ	4 MSS
9	Of God the father of Christ	5 MSS
10	Of God and Father of Christ	2 MSS
11	Of God father and of Christ	4 MSS
12	Of God father and of Christ Jesus	3 MSS
13	Of God father and of Lord of us Christ Jesus	2 MSS
14	Of God and father and of Christ	38 MSS
Total 14	14 Variants in 79 MSS	79 MSS

These variants are found in 79 MSS. Thus, we have 14 variants in 79 manuscripts, not 79 variants. We do not count manuscripts, as most textual scholars know. In trying to paint a picture about the trustworthiness of the text, this author does not think talking about variants is really helpful, and it can confuse the layperson. The churchgoer needs to know what a variant is and the general extent of the variants, but in the long run, it is the places in the text that are affected by variants that most matter and what we have as our text in the end.

The United Bible Society's "A" "B" "C" and "D" ratings are fine, and the definitions by UBS, i.e., [A] **certain**, [B] **almost certain**, [C] **difficulty in deciding**, and [D] **great difficulty in arriving at**, are helpful but should be better qualified, with some numbers of what percentage of the text fall under each area.

---

[641] Recall that NU is an acronym for two critical manuscripts: (1) Nestle-Aland Greek Text (28th ed.) and (2) United Bible Societies Greek Text (5th ed.)

[642] This is only a partial list of the manuscripts, as we are just offering an example, to see how we count the variants.

All Variant Units (Places)

What we need to talk about is how many **places** there are where we find variants. What percentage is this of the entire New Testament text?

We can then discuss:

- What percentage of the text is untouched by variants?

- Of the percentage affected, how much can we say or surmise to be given an "A" rating, a "B" Rating, a "C," or "D" rating?

Variant Reading and Variation Unit

This section is based in large part on the work by Eldon Jay Epp and Gordon D. Fee, *Studies in the Theory and Method of New Testament Textual Criticism* (Grand Rapids, MI: Eerdmans, 1993), wherein Eldon J. Epp expands on the brief 1964 article of Ernest C. Colwell (1901–74) and Ernest W. Tune on "Variant Readings: Classification and Use."

Again, we need to discuss how many variation units (places) there are where we find variations. Before doing so, let us define some terms.

SIGNIFICANT AND INSIGNIFICANT READINGS AND OR VARIANTS: Below, we have what are commonly described as significant and insignificant variants. *Significant* would mean any reading that has an impact on the transmission history of a variant unit. For example, it would apply to how we determine the relationship of the manuscripts to one another, such as where a particular manuscript would fall in the history and transmission of the manuscripts. It would also be impactful if the reading could help the textual scholar establish the original. Therefore, *insignificant* would mean just the opposite, referring to a reading with very little to no impact in *many* aspects of a transmission history. We stop at "many" aspects here because all readings in a manuscript play a role in some aspects of the transmission history, such as the characteristics of the manuscript it is in and the scribal activity within that individual manuscript.

Insignificant—*Nonsense Reading*: As Epp points out, a nonsense reading is "a reading that fails to make sense because it cannot be construed grammatically, either in terms of grammatical/lexical form or in terms of grammatical structure, or because in some other way it lacks a recognizable meaning. Since authors and scribes do not produce nonsense intentionally, it is to be assumed (1) that nonsense readings resulted from errors in transmission, (2) that they, therefore, cannot represent either the original text or the intended text of any MS or alert scribe, and (3) that they do not aid in

490

the process of discerning the relationships among MSS."[643] It should also be stated that the original did not contain any nonsense readings, as the Holy Spirit led the writers. Before publication, the inspired author would have corrected any error by a scribe such as Tertius or Silvanus.

Insignificant—Certainty of Scribal Errors: while these errors "can be construed grammatically and make sense," there is a certainty on the part of textual scholars that these are scribal errors. These are not nonsense readings but rather readings that make sense, which are scribal errors beyond all reasonable doubt. These would "be certain instances of haplography and dittography, cases of harmonization with similar contexts, hearing errors producing a similar-sounding word, and the transposition of letters or words with a resultant change in meaning."[644] The problem that we sometimes encounter here is that what may be listed as a *certainty* of the scribal error to one scholar may instead be an *almost certainty* to another, and even less so to another. The key element here in determining a reading that is understandable as insignificant is that it can be "demonstrated" so by the scholar making such a claim.

Insignificant—Incorrect Orthography (Greek for "correct writing"): this term is used loosely to refer to the spelling of words, which (for Greek) can include breathing and accent marks. Thus, one can refer to variations in the orthography of a word or even to incorrect orthography. When a variation in orthography is due merely to dialectical or historical changes in spelling for variant readings, the variations are often ignored in the decision process because the reading in question is identical to another reading, once the orthographical differences are factored in (*mutatis mutandis*). Epp writes, "Mere orthographic differences, particularly itacisms and nu-movables (as well as abbreviations) are 'insignificant' as here defined; they cannot be utilized in any decisive way for establishing manuscript relationships, and they are not substantive in the search for the original text. Again, the exception might be the work of a slavish scribe, whose scrupulousness might be considered useful in tracing manuscript descent, but the pervasive character of itacism, for example, over wide areas and time-spans precludes the 'significance' of orthographic differences for this important text-critical task."[645]

---

[643] Eldon Jay Epp and Gordon D. Fee, *Studies in the Theory and Method of New Testament Textual Criticism* (Grand Rapids, MI: Eerdmans, 1993), 58.

[644] Ibid. 58.

[645] Ibid. 58.

Insignificant—Singular Readings: a singular reading is technically a variant reading that occurs only once in only one Greek manuscript and is therefore immediately suspect. There is some quibbling over this because critics who reject the Westcott and Hort position on the combination of 01 (Sinaiticus) and 03 (Vaticanus) might call a reading "nearly singular" if it has only the support of these two manuscripts. Moreover, it is understood that not all manuscripts are comparable. Thus, for example, one would comfortably reject a reading found only in a single late manuscript, while many critics would not find it so easy to reject a reading supported uniquely by 03. Some also give more credit to singular readings that have additional support from versions. Singular readings that are insignificant would be nonsense readings, transcriptional errors, meaningless transpositions, and itacisms.

Significant Variants: a *significant* reading/variant is any reading that has an impact on any major facet of the transmission history of a variant unit. One approach to identifying these is to remove the insignificant variants first: nonsense readings, determined (without doubt) scribal errors, incorrect orthography, and singular readings. Those readings that cannot be ruled out in this process are probably significant.

Number of Variants, Significant and Insignificant Variants vs. Level of Certainty

It would seem that some scholars have lost sight of the most important goal of textual criticism, namely, reconstructing the original. There is little doubt that agnostic Bible scholar Dr. Bart D. Ehrman has led the conversation on how many textual variants exist. The author of this publication is focusing their attention on the initial goal of textual criticism, returning to the original. We believe that even now, the Greek New Testament is entirely reliable. However, some 2,000 textual places within the New Testament need to be dealt with because the witnesses and internal evidence require consideration and deliberation.

Level of Certainty

The level of certainty charts below is generated from A TEXTUAL COMMENTARY ON THE GREEK NEW TESTAMENT (Second Edition), A Companion Volume to the UNITED BIBLE SOCIETIES' GREEK NEW TESTAMENT (Fourth Revised Edition) by Bruce M. Metzger.

The letter {A} signifies that the text is certain.

The letter {B} indicates that the text is almost certain.

The letter **{C}** indicates that the Committee had difficulty in deciding which variant to place in the text.

The letter **{D}**, which occurs only rarely, indicates that the Committee had great difficulty in arriving at a decision. In fact, among the **{D}** decisions sometimes none of the variant readings commended itself as original, and therefore the only recourse was to print the least unsatisfactory reading.

The Greek-English New Testament Interlinear (GENTI), Produced by Christian Publishing House, Cambridge, Ohio seeks to make a notable addition to the Greek-English Interlinear family by providing a text of the Greek New Testament that is based on the most recent research and is grounded in the earliest manuscript witnesses, to ascertain the original wording of the original texts.

TERMS AS TO HOW WE SHOULD OBJECTIVELY VIEW THE DEGREE OF CERTAINTY FOR THE READING ACCEPTED AS THE ORIGINAL by GENTI[646]

The modal verbs are ***might*** *have been* (30%), **may** *have been (40%),* **could** *have been* (55%), **would** *have been (80%)*, **must** *have been (95%)*, which are used to show that we believe the originality of a reading is certain, probable or possible.

The letter **[WP]** stands for **Weak Possibility (30%)**, which indicates that this is low-level proof that the reading *might have been* original in that it is enough evidence to accept that the variant *might have been possible*, but it is improbable. We can say the reading **might** have been original, as there is *some evidence* that is derived from manuscripts that carry very little weight, early versions, or patristic quotations.

The letter **[P]** stands for **Plausible (40%)**, which indicates that this is low-level proof that the reading *may have been* original in that it is enough to accept a variant to be original, and we have enough evidence for our belief. The reading **may have** been original but is probably not so.

The letter **[PE]** stands for **Preponderance of Evidence (55%)**, which indicates that this is a higher-level proof that the reading *could have been* original in that it is enough to accept as such *unless another reading emerges as more probable.*

The letter **[CE]** stands for **Convincing Evidence (80%)**, which indicates that the evidence is an even higher-level proof that the

---

[646] https://christianpublishinghouse.co/greek-english-interlinear/

reading *surely* was the original in that the evidence is enough to accept it as substantially *certain* unless proven otherwise.

The letter **[BRD]** stands for **Beyond Reasonable Doubt (95%)**, which indicates that this is the highest level of proof: the reading **must have been** original in that *there is no reason to doubt it*. It must be understood that feeling as though we *have no reason to doubt* is not the same as one hundred percent absolute certainty.

NOTE: This system is borrowed from the criminal just legal terms of the United States of America, the level of certainty involved in the use of modal verbs, and Bruce Metzger in his A Textual Commentary on the Greek New Testament (London; New York: United Bible Societies, 1994), who borrowed his system from Johann Albrecht Bengel in his edition of the Greek New Testament (Tübingen, 1734). **In addition**, the percentages are in no way attempting to be explicit, but instead, they are nothing more than a tool to give the non-textual scholar a sense of the degree of certainty. However, this does not mean the percentages are not reflective of the certainty.

The word count below is taken from the Nestle-Aland Novum Testamentum Graece using Logos Bible Software.[647] While this author has compiled the numbers regarding the level of certainty of readings from Metzger's Textual Commentary, he has not gone to the point of counting the letters or words at each variant place. We will just offer the reader the general statement that almost all textual variants in the commentary were based on a letter or a few letters in a Greek word, to two-three words. Seldom was it an entire sentence or verse, very rarely several verses like the long ending of Mark. Therefore, we have chosen three words as the average to multiply the total number of variants so that the reader can see the truly small number of variants that are even worthy of consideration instead of the total number of words in the New Testament. For example, Matthew has 18,346 words with a mere 153 places where we find variants selected for the GNT, affecting about 459 words.

We need to add and emphasize that the GNT editors selected all of the variants counted as relevant for translation, and the total does not include other variant units that were not considered relevant for that purpose. A good number of these additional variants can be found in the NA apparatus, but only with considerable difficulty in many cases because the same variants are frequently handled differently in the GNT and NA apparatuses. The author of this book does consider all variant units relevant even if a good number

---

[647] Word Counts for Every Book of the Bible ..., http://overviewbible.com/word-counts-books-of-bible/ (accessed April 20, 2017).

of them are difficult or virtually impossible to represent in translation (depending on the target language). We recommend that the reader adjust the figures offered below by multiplying the numbers of variants by a factor of two, which should compensate for any variants that are not reported in the GNT text. We see no reason to assume a significantly different outcome in the ratings that might have been assigned to these variants if they had been included in the GNT, except possibly where no decisions might be possible in the cases of competing readings that were fully acceptable (rather than difficult).

For readers who have a working knowledge of NT Greek, it may be informative simply to select a few random pages of corresponding text from the GNT and NA and compare the apparatuses to see what is missing from the GNT relative to the NA apparatus. We believe that our suggestion of multiplying the variant figures below by a factor of two will appear more than reasonable; however, even using a factor of three or four will still leave a relatively minute percentage of "C" and "D" readings, as revealed below.

So then, if we look at Matthew and first multiply the GNT variant units by three for an average of three words a variant, we have 459 words. Of the 153 variant units found in Matthew, we are certain of about 32 of them, almost certain about 70, have a little difficulty deciding on 50, and great difficulty deciding on only one variant unit. When we say that we have difficulty deciding, this does not mean that we cannot decide as we can. Moreover, a good translation will list the alternative reading in a footnote. So, in the entirety of the Gospel of Matthew, there is only one variant place (Matt 23:26) which we would count as about three out of 18,346 words, where there was great difficulty in deciding the original. As it turns out, in this case, the GNT apparatus handles it as a variant of eight words, while NA breaks it into two variants, thus illustrating our point about the difficulty of comparing the two apparatuses. Some translations have incorporated the variant (ESV, NASB, NIV, TNIV, NJB, and the NLT), viewing it as the original, while other translations (NRSV, NEB, REB, NAB, CSB, and the UASV) see the variant as an addition taken from the previous verse.

Matthew 23:26 Blind Pharisee, cleanse first the inside of the cup,[648] so that the outside of it may also become clean. (UASV)

NU has καθάρισον πρῶτον τὸ ἐντὸς τοῦ ποτηρίου, ἵνα γένηται καὶ τὸ ἐκτὸς αὐτοῦ καθαρόν "first cleanse the **inside of the cup, that the outside**

---

[648] The NU (D Θ f¹ itᵃˑᶜ syrˢ) has the above reading. A variant, WH and Byz (א (B²) C L W 0102 0281 Maj) add "and of the dish." The variant is an addition taken from the previous verse.

495

of it may also become clean," which is supported by D Θ f¹ it^{a,c} <u>syr^s</u> (bold mine).

Variant/Byz WH καθαρισον πρωτον το εντος του ποτηριου και της παροψιδος ινα γενηται και το εκτος αυτων καθαρον have "first cleanse the **inside of the cup [and the dish], that the outside** of them may also become clean," which is supported by ℵ (B²) C L W 0102 0281 Maj.

Looking at the above support alone, it would seem that the witnesses for the longer reading ("and the dish") are weightier, making the longer reading the likely original. Then, when we consider the presence of a few manuscripts (B* f¹³ 28 *al*) that are not listed for the shorter reading because they have the longer reading ("and the dish"), the weight shifts over to the shorter reading's being the original. Why? Because these few manuscripts have the singular αυτου instead of αὐτῶν, even though they have the longer reading. This tells us that the archetype text was the shorter reading. Clearly, the copyist added ("and the dish") from the previous verse, Matthew 23:25, which reads, "Woe to you, scribes and Pharisees, hypocrites! because you cleanse **the outside of the cup and of the dish**, but inside they are full of greediness and self-indulgence."

Below, we will look at all of the numbers, the total words in the Greek New Testament, the number of A, B, C, and D variants in each book as they were selected by the GNT committee, followed by the total number of variants listed in Metzger's textual commentary.

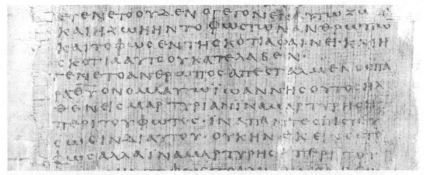

The Entire New Testament (138,020 Words)

{A-D}	New Testament
{A}	505
{B}	523

{C}	354
{D}	10
Total Var.	1,392
Words	138,020

The Gospels (64,767 Words)

{A-D}	Matt	Mark	Luke	John
{A}	32	45	44	44
{B}	70	49	73	62
{C}	50	45	44	41
{D}	1	1	0	2
Total Var.	153	140	161	149
Words	18,346	11,304	19,482	15,635

The Acts of the Apostles (18,450 Words)

{A-D}	Acts
{A}	74
{B}	82
{C}	40
{D}	1
Total Var.	197
Words	18,450

Paul's Fourteen Epistles (37,361 Words)

{A-D}	Rom	1 Cor	2 Cor	Gal.	Eph.	Php	Col.
{A}	39	21	12	16	16	10	8
{B}	19	22	17	3	11	7	12
{C}	20	15	10	8	7	3	8

{D}	1	1	0	0	0	0	0
Total Var.	79	59	39	27	34	20	28
WORDS	7,111	6,830	4,477	2,230	2,422	1,629	1,582

{A-D}	1 Th	2 Th	1 Tim	2 Tim	Tit	Phm.	Heb.
{A}	9	3	15	2	2	2	20
{B}	2	3	2	6	1	3	11
{C}	3	2	2	1	1	0	12
{D}	0	0	0	0	0	0	0
Total Var.	14	8	19	9	4	5	43
WORDS	1,481	823	1,591	1,238	659	335	4,953

The General Epistles (7,591 Words)

{A-D}	Jam	1 Pet	2 Pet	1 Jn	2 Jn	3 Jn	Jude
{A}	7	21	8	18	4	1	9
{B}	12	9	7	7	1	1	0
{C}	4	7	6	4	0	0	3
{D}	0	0	1	0	0	0	1
Total Var.	23	37	22	29	5	2	13
WORDS	1,742	1,684	1,099	2,141	245	219	461

The Book of Revelation (9,851 Words)

{A-D}	Revelation
{A}	23
{B}	31
{C}	18
{D}	1
Total Var.	73
Words	9,851

As noted above, the author of this publication maintains that all variation units or places where variations occur are significant because we are dealing with the Word of God, and reconstructing the original wording is of the utmost importance. Recall Lightfoot once more. "What about the significance of these variations? Are these variations immaterial, or are they important? What bearing do they have on the New Testament message and on faith? To respond to these questions, it will be helpful to introduce three types of textual variations, classified in relation to their significance for our present New Testament text. 1. Trivial variations which are of no consequence to the text. 2. Substantial variations which are of no consequence to the text. 3. Substantial variations that have a bearing on the text."[649]

Whether we are talking about the addition or omission of such words as "for," "and," and "the," or different forms of similar Greek words, differences in spelling, or the addition of a whole verse or even several verses, the importance lies **not with the significance of the impact** on the meaning of the text but rather **the certainty** of the wording in the original. What we want to focus on is the certainty level of reconstructing every single word that Matthew, Mark, Luke, John, Paul, Peter, James, and Jude penned.

We will use Lightfoot's example of Matthew 11:10-23, that is, fourteen verses of 231 words; we have eleven variants in verses 10, 15, 16, 17, 18, 19(2), 20, 21, and 23(2). This may seem worrisome to the churchgoer or someone new to textual criticism. However, while all variants are found in the NA28 critical apparatus (2012), pp. 31–32,[650] the following sources below only covered seven of them because four are not even an issue. Why are they not an issue? We know what the original reading is with absolute certainty. The seven that have some uncertainty are mentioned in the textual commentaries below.

- Comfort *New Testament Text and Translation* covers verses 15 and 19

- Comfort *Commentary on the Manuscripts and Text of the New Testament* covers verses 12 and 19

- Metzger's *Textual Commentary on the Greek New Testament* covers 15, 17, 19, and 23.

Immediately we need to note that verse 12 is absolutely certain as to the original words as well. Verse 19a is mentioned in Comfort's textual commentary because he is drawing attention to the "Son of Man" being written as a nomen sacrum ("sacred name" that is abbreviated) in two early manuscripts (א W), as well as in L. Therefore, verse 19a is absolutely certain as well. We are now down to five variants. The original readings of verses 15, 17, 19a and the two in verse 23 where variants occur are almost certain. The committee's textual scholars for four leading semi-literal and literal

---

[649] *How We Got the Bibles*, by Neil R. Lightfoot (Grand Rapids: Baker, 1998; p. 95-103)

[650] Eberhard Nestle and Erwin Nestle, *Nestle-Aland: NTG Apparatus Criticus*, ed. Barbara Aland et al., 28. revidierte Auflage. (Stuttgart: Deutsche Bibelgesellschaft, 2012), 31–32.

translations (ESV, LEB, CSB, and the NASB) agree on ten of the eleven variants. There is disagreement on **Matthew 11:15**. Even so, the reader has access to the original and alternatives in the footnote.

"He who has ears to hear, let him hear." (ESV, NASB, UASV)

The variant is ο εχων ωτα ακουειν ακουετω "the one having ears to hear let him hear," which is supported by ℵ C L W Z Θ f[1,13] 33 Maj syr[c,h,p] cop

"The one who has ears to hear, let him hear!" (LEB, cf. CSB)

WH and NU have ὁ ἔχων ὦτα ἀκουέτω "the one having ears let him hear," which is supported by B D 700 it[k] syr[s]

As is usually the case in more difficult decisions, the variant readings are divided in their support between the leading Alexandrian manuscripts. One reading has 01 (Sinaiticus) on its side, the other has 03 (Vaticanus). This tends to cancel out the weight of documentary evidence.

Now, we return to the charts above. There are 138,020 words in the New Testament. Just 1,392 textual variants deemed relevant for translation have enough of an issue to even be considered in the textual commentary. Again, if we average three words per variant, this amounts only to about 3.026 percent of the 138,020 words, or about 6 percent when we compensate for variant units ignored by the GNT editors. We can also remove the 505 {A} ratings because they are certain. Then, we really have no concerns about the {B} ratings because they are almost certain as well. This means that out of 138,020 words in the Greek New Testament, we only have 364 variants (1,092 words by our average) with which we have difficulty, a mere 10 of which involve great difficulty in deciding which reading to put in the text. Our average would make these variants 0.791 percent of the text without accounting for any difficult variants not included because they were considered irrelevant for translation.

We need not be disturbed or distracted by worries of how many variants there are, or whether they are significant or insignificant. We need only to deal with the certainty of each variation unit, endeavoring to determine the original reading. We should also be concerned with the role textual criticism plays in apologetics. There is no possibility of apologetics if we do not have an authoritative and true Word of God. J. Harold Greenlee was correct when he wrote, "Textual criticism is the basic study for the accurate knowledge of any text. New Testament textual criticism, therefore, is the basic biblical study, a prerequisite to all other biblical and theological work. Interpretation, systemization, and application of the teachings of the NT cannot be done until textual criticism has done at least some of its work."[651] We would add apologetics to that list for which textual criticism is a prerequisite. How are we to defend the Word of God as inspired, inerrant, true, and authoritative if we do not know whether we even have the Word of God? Therefore, when Bible critics try to muddy the waters of truth with misinformation, it is up to the textual scholar to correct the Bible critic's misinformation.

Again, it is true that Lightfoot erred if he was counting the manuscripts instead of the variants. However, we need not count variants either but rather variation units, namely, the places where there are variations. The above Colossians 2:2 example of variations that are found in 79 manuscripts was seen to have 14 variants in 79 manuscripts, not 79 variants. While this is true, it is also true that this is simply one variation unit, i.e., one place, where a variation occurs. This may sound as though we are trying to rationalize a major problem of hundreds of thousands of variants. However, it is actually the other way around. The Bible critic is misrepresenting the facts, trying to talk about an issue without giving the reader or listener all of the facts. We need to consider Benjamin Disraeli's words on statistics: "There are three types of lies: lies, damn lies, and statistics."

The certainty of the Original Words of the Original Authors

Virgil (70-19 B.C.E.) wrote the *Aeneid* between 29 and 19 B.C.E. for which only five manuscripts are dating to the fourth and fifth centuries C.E.[652] Jewish historian Josephus (37-100 C.E.) wrote *The Jewish Wars* about 75 C.E., for which we have nine complete manuscripts, seven of major importance dating from the tenth to the twelfth centuries C.E.[653] Tacitus (59-129 C.E.) wrote *Annals of Imperial Rome* sometime before 116 C.E., a work considered vital to understanding the history of the Roman Empire during the first century, and we have only thirty-three manuscripts, two of the earliest that date 850 and 1050 C.E. Julius Caesar (100-44 B.C.E.) wrote his Gallic Wars between 51-46 B.C.E.,[654] which is a firsthand account in a third-

---

[651] *Introduction to New Testament Textual Criticism*, by J. Harold Greenlee (Peabody: Hendrickson Publishers, 1995; p. 7)

[652] Preface | Dickinson College Commentaries. (April 25, 2017) http://dcc.dickinson.edu/vergil-aeneid/manuscripts

[653] Honora Howell Chapman (Editor), Zuleika Rodgers (Editor), 2016, A *Companion to Josephus* (Blackwell Companions to the Ancient World), Wiley-Blackwell: p. 307.

[654] Carolyn Hammond, 1996, Introduction to *The Gallic War*, Oxford University Press: p. xxxii.

Max Radin, 1918, The date of composition of Caesar's Gallic War, *Classical Philology* XIII: 283–300.

person narrative of the war, of which we have 251 manuscripts dating between the ninth and fifteenth centuries.[655]

On the other hand, New Testament textual scholars have over 5,898 Greek manuscripts, not to mention ancient versions such as Latin, Coptic, Syriac, Armenian, Georgian, and Gothic, which number into the tens of thousands. We have many early and reliable manuscripts in Greek and the versions, a good number that cover almost the entire New Testament dating within 100 years of the originals. Therefore, reconstructing the original Greek New Testament is a realistic goal for Bible scholars. This belief and goal that we could anticipate a time when we would recover the original wording of the Greek New Testament had its greatest advocates in the nineteenth century, in Samuel Tregelles (1813-75), B. F. Westcott (1825-1901), and F. J. A. Hort (1828-92). While they acknowledged that we would never recover every word with absolute certainty, they knew that it was always the primary goal to come extremely close to the original. When we entered the twentieth century, there were two textual scholars who have since stood above all others, Kurt Aland and Bruce Metzger. These two men carried the same purpose with them, as they were instrumental in bringing us the Nestle-Aland and the United Bible Societies' critical editions, which are at the foundation of almost all modern translations.

From the days of Johann Jacob Griesbach (1745-1812) to Constantin Von Tischendorf (1815-1874), to Samuel Prideaux Tregelles (1813-1875), to Fenton John Anthony Hort (1828-1892), to Kurt Aland (1915-1994), to Bruce M. Metzger (1914-2007),[656] we have been blessed with extraordinary textual scholars. These scholars have devoted their entire lives to providing us with the transmission of the New Testament text and the methodologies by which we can recover the original words of the New Testament authors. They did not construct these histories and methodologies from textbooks or in university classrooms. No, they spent decades upon decades working with

---

[655] O. Seel, 1961, *Bellum Gallicum.* (Bibl. Teubneriana.) Teubner, Leipzig.

W. Hering, 1987, *C. Iulii Caesaris commentarii rerum gestarum, Vol. I: Bellum Gallicum.*(Bibl. Teubneriana.) Teubner, Leipzig.

Virginia Brown, 1972, *The Textual Transmission of Caesar's Civil War*, Brill.

Caesar's Gallic war - Tim Mitchell. (April 25, 2017)
http://www.timmitchell.fr/blog/2012/04/12/gallic-war/

[656] These textual scholars provided us with histories of the transmission of the New Testament text and methodologies. However, we have had dozens of textual scholars who have given their lives to the text of the New Testament. To mention just a few, we have Brian Walton (1600-1661), John Fell (1625-1686), John Mill (1645-1707), Edward Wells (1667-1727), Richard Bentley (1662-1742), Johann Albert Bengel (1687-1752), Johann Jacob Wettstein (1693-1754), Johann Salomo Semler (1725-1791), Johann Leonard Hug (1765-1846), Johann Martin Augustinus Scholz (1794-1852), Karl Lachmann (1793-1851), Erwin Nestle (1883-1972), Allen Wikgren (1906-1998), Matthew Black, (1908-1994), Barbara Aland (1937-present), and Carlo Maria Martini (1927-2012).

manuscripts and putting their methods of textual criticism into practice, as they provided us with one improved critical edition after another. As their knowledge grew, the number of manuscripts they had to work with fortunately grew.

Samuel Tregelles stated that his purpose was to restore the Greek New Testament text "as nearly as can be done on existing evidence."[657] B. F. Westcott and F. J. A. Hort declared that their goal was "to present exactly the original words of the New Testament, so far as they can now be determined from surviving documents."[658] Metzger said that the goal of textual criticism is "to ascertain from the divergent copies which form of the text should be regarded as most nearly conforming to the original."[659] Sadly, after centuries, textual criticism is losing its way, as new textual scholars have begun to set aside the goal of recovering and establishing the original wording of the Greek New Testament. They have little concern for the certainty of a reading as to whether it is the original.

In speaking of the positions of agnostic Bart D. Ehrman (author of *The Orthodox Corruption of Scripture*) and David Parker (author of *The Living Text of the Gospels*), Elliott overserved, "Both emphasize the living and therefore changing text of the New Testament and the needlessness and inappropriateness of trying to establish one immutable original text. The changeable text in all its variety is what we textual critics should be displaying."[660] Elliott then reflects further on his goals within textual criticism: "Despite my own published work in trying to prove the originality of the text in selected areas of textual variation ... I agree that the task of trying to establish the original words of the original authors with 100% certainty is impossible. More dominant in text critics' thinking now is the need to plot the changes in the history of the text. That certainly seemed to be the consensus at one of the sessions of the 1998 SBL conference in Orlando, where the question of whether the original text was an achievable goal received generally negative responses."[661]

We strongly disagree. The goal of textual criticism had been and still should be **to restore** the New Testament Greek text **in every word that the New Testament authors originally penned** in a critical edition. Suppose we are aiming only "to plot the changes in the history of the text," as Elliott put it. In that case, we are unable to do so precisely at the time when we have

---

[657] Tregelles, *An Account of the Printed Text of the Greek New Testament*, 174.

[658] Westcott and Hort, *Introduction to the New Testament in the Original Greek*, 1.

[659] Metzger, *The Text of the New Testament*, v.

[660] J. K. Elliott, *New Testament Textual Criticism: The Application of Thoroughgoing Principles: Essays on Manuscripts and Textual Variation*, 592.

[661] Ibid. 592.

the greatest need to see what happened, i.e., soon after the NT books were first published, if we actually deny and rob ourselves of any chance to recover the original. Then we must admit either that we can never have the complete word of God (the new position), or that any and potentially every quality Greek witness must be considered the word of God. The latter might even be said of a quality version, or at least of readings clearly inferred from such a version. In reality, however, any manuscript that departs from the original in its witness is more or less damaged goods.

We obviously do not think such pessimism is the necessary or inevitable response. In looking at the numbers above as to the certainty level of the restoration of the original Greek New Testament, we have come a long way since John Fell (1625-1686). A spot comparison of changes in ratings between GNT5 and previous GNT editions indicates that the level of certainty is increasing in most cases, and when it does not, the preference tends toward the earliest and most reliable manuscripts.[662] To set aside the primary goal of textual criticism now would be an insult to the lives of many textual scholars who preceded us, not to mention to the authors who penned the New Testament books and the Almighty God who inspired them.

---

[662] Sample comparisons of the General Epistles in GNT5 with previous GNT editions led to this conclusion. When the level of certainty decreased–which was infrequent compared to the reverse–the trend seemed to be that more weight was being given to 03 and/or 01 in opposition to internal factors. It is also expected that certainty levels will increase with the use of the CBGM.

CHAPTER XIV

The Printed Text of the Greek New Testament

By 1450 Johannes Gutenberg began printing with movable type in Germany.

Separated into Families

We have textual traditions or families of texts, which grew up in specific regions. For example, we have the **Alexandrian text-type**, which Westcott and Hort called the Neutral text that came from Egypt. Then, there is the **Western text-type**, which came from Italy and Gaul as well as North Africa and elsewhere. There was also the **Caesarean text-type**, which came from Caesarea and is characterized by a mixture of Western and Alexandrian readings.[663] The **Byzantine text-type**, also called **Majority Text**, came from Constantinople (i.e., Byzantium).

In short, early Christianity gave rise to what is known as "local texts." Christian congregations in and near cities, such as Alexandria, Antioch, Constantinople, Carthage, or Rome, were making copies of the Scriptures in

---

[663] B. M. Metzger, *A Textual Commentary on the Greek New Testament* 1994, Page xxi

a form that would become known as their text-type. In other words, manuscripts grew up in certain areas, just like a human family, becoming known as that text-type, having their own characteristics. In reality, it is not as simple as this because there are mixtures of text-types within each text-type. However, generally, each text-type resembles itself more than it does the others. It should also be remembered that most of our extant manuscripts are identical in more than seventy-five percent of their texts. Thus, it is the twenty-five percent of variation that identifies a manuscript as a certain text-type, i.e., what one could call "agreement in error."

Therefore, the process of classifying manuscripts for centuries was to label them a certain text-type, such as Alexandrian, Western, Caesarean, or Byzantine. However, this practice is fading because technology has allowed the textual scholar to carry out a more comprehensive comparison of all readings in all manuscripts, supposedly blurring the traditional classifications. The new method primarily responsible is the Coherence-Based Genealogical Method (CBGM). In this method, an "initial text" is reconstructed that is considered "relatively close to the form of the text from which the textual tradition of a New Testament book has originated." (Stephen C. Carlson)

The original New Testament authors were inspired by God and error-free. The copyists were not inspired, and errors did show up in the texts as a result. These errors help us to place these texts into specific families. Very early in the transmission process, copies of the originals worked their way to these four major religious centers. The copying traditions that distinguish these text-types began to occur. The Alexandrian text-type is the earliest and reflects the work of professional and semi-professional scribes who treated the copying process with respect. The text is simple, without added material, and lacking the grammatical, stylistic polish sometimes imposed by Byzantine scribes. The Western text-type is early to the mid-second century. These manuscripts reflect the work of scribes who were given to paraphrasing. Scribes freely changed words, phrases, clauses, and whole sentences as they felt it necessary. At times, they were simply trying to harmonize the text or even add apocryphal material to spice it up. The Caesarean text-type is a mixture of Western and Alexandrian readings. The Byzantine text-type had its beginning in late fourth century C. E. It shows the hand of scribes who, as noted, attempted to smooth out both grammar and style, often with a view to making the text easier to understand. These scribes also combined differing readings from other manuscripts that contained variants. The period of 50 to 350 C.E. certainly saw its share of errors (variants) entering into the text, but the era of corruption is the period when the Byzantine text would become the standard text.

The Corruption Period

To round out our understanding of this early history, we need at least a short overview of what happened after 350 C.E. After Constantine legalized Christianity, giving it equal status with the pagan religions, it was much easier to have biblical manuscripts copied. In fact, Constantine ordered 50 copies of the whole of the Bible for the church in Constantinople. Over the next four centuries or so, the Byzantine Empire and the Greek-speaking church were the dominant factors in making the Byzantine text the standard. It was not a matter of its being the better, i.e., more accurate text. From the eighth century forward, the Byzantine text had displaced all others.

After the invention of the Guttenberg printing press in 1455, it would be this Byzantine text that would become the first printed edition by way of Desiderius Erasmus in 1516. Thanks to an advertisement by the publishers, it was referred to as the Textus Receptus or the "Received Text."[664] Over the next four centuries, many textual scholars attempted to make minor changes to this text based on the development of the science of textual criticism, but to no real effect on its status as the Greek text of the church. Worse still, this inferior text would lay at the foundation of all English translations until the *Revised English Version* of 1881 and the *American Standard Version* of 1901. Not until 1881, two Cambridge scholars, B. F. Westcott and F. J. A. Hort replace the Textus Receptus with their critical text. This critical edition of the Westcott and Hort text is the foundation for most modern translations and all critical editions of the Greek New Testament, UBS[5], and the NA[28].

---

[664] Dr. Wilkins writes, "The nuance between 'receive' and 'accept' is often overlooked in discussing the TR, and the Latin "receptus" could just as well mean "accepted" (i.e. 'the text accepted by all'), which I suspect was the intent of the advertisement."

Desiderius Erasmus and the Greek Text

I WOULD have these words translated into all languages, so that not only Scots and Irish, but Turks and Saracens too might read them . . . I long for the ploughboy to sing them to himself as he follows his plough, the weaver to hum them to the tune of his shuttle, the traveler to beguile with them the dullness of his journey. (Clayton 2006, 230)

Dutch scholar Desiderius Erasmus penned those words in the early part of the 16th century. Like his English counterpart, William Tyndale, his greatest desire was that God's Word is widely translated and that even the plowboy would have access to it.

Much time has passed since the Reformation, and 98 percent of the world we live in today has access to the Bible. There is little wonder that the Bible has become the bestseller of all time. It has influenced people from all walks of life to fight for freedom and truth. This was especially true during the Reformation of Europe throughout the 16th century. These leaders were of great faith, courage, and strength, such as Martin Luther, William Tyndale, while others, like Erasmus, were more subtle in the changes that they brought. Thus, it has been said of the Reformation that Martin Luther only opened the door to it after Erasmus picked the lock.

Not a single historian of the period would deny that Erasmus was a great scholar. Remarking on his character, the *Catholic Encyclopedia* says: "He had an unequalled talent for form, great journalistic gifts, a surpassing power of expression; for strong and moving discourse, keen irony, and covert sarcasm, he was unsurpassed." (Vol. 5, p. 514) Consequently, when Erasmus went to see Sir Thomas More, the Lord Chancellor of England, just before Erasmus revealed himself, More was so impressed with his exchange that he shortly said: "You are either Erasmus or the Devil."

Erasmus's wit was evidenced in a response that he gave to Frederick, elector of Saxony, who asked him what he thought about Martin Luther. Erasmus retorted, "Luther has committed two blunders; he has ventured to touch the crown of the pope and the bellies of the monks." (*Cyclopedia of Biblical, Theological, and Ecclesiastical Literature*: Vol. 3 – p, 279) However, we must ask what type of influence did the Bible have on Erasmus and, in turn, what did he do to affect its future? First, we will look at the early years of Erasmus' life.

Erasmus' Early Life

He was born in Rotterdam, the Netherlands, in 1466. He was not a happy boy, living in a home as the illegitimate son of a Dutch priest. He was faced with the double tragedy of his mother's death at seventeen, and his father shortly thereafter. His guardians ignored his desire to enter the university; instead, they sent him to the Augustinian monastery of Steyn. Erasmus gained a vast knowledge of the Latin language, the classics, and the Church Fathers. In time, this life was so detestable that he jumped at the opportunity to become secretary to the bishop of Cambrai, Henry of Bergen, in France at the age of twenty-six. This afforded him his chance to enter university studies in Paris. However, he was a sickly man, suffering from poor health throughout his entire life.

It was in 1499 that Erasmus was invited to visit England. He met Thomas More, John Colet, and other theologians in London, which fortified his resolution to apply himself to Biblical studies. In order to understand the Bible's message better, he applied himself more fully in his study of Greek, soon being able to teach it to others. It was around this time that Erasmus penned a treatise entitled *Handbook of the Christian Soldier*, in which he advised the young Christian to study the Bible, saying: "There is nothing that you can believe with greater certitude than what you read in these writings." (Erasmus and Dolan 1983, 37)

While trying to escape the plague and make a living in an economy that had bottomed worse than our 20th-century Great Depression, Erasmus found himself at Louvain, Belgium, in 1504. It was there that he fell in love with the study of textual criticism while visiting the Praemonstratensian Abbey of Parc near Louvain. Erasmus discovered a manuscript of Italian scholar Lorenzo Valla within the library: *Annotations on the New Testament*. Thereupon Erasmus commissioned to himself to restore the original text of the Greek New Testament.

Erasmus moved on to Italy and subsequently pushed on to England once again. It is this trip that brought to mind his original meeting with Thomas More, meditating on the origin of More's name (moros, Greek for "a fool"); he penned a satire which he called "Praise of Folly." In this work, Erasmus treats the abstract quality "folly" as a person and pictures it as encroaching in all aspects of life, but nowhere is folly more obvious than amid the theologians and clergy. This is his subtle way of exposing the abuses of the clergy. These abuses had brought on the Reformation, which was now festering. "As to the popes," he wrote, "if they claim to be the successors of the Apostles, they should consider that the same things are required of them as were practiced by their predecessors." Instead of doing this, he perceived, they believe that "to teach the people is too laborious; to interpret the scripture is to invade the prerogative of the schoolmen; to pray is too idle." There is little wonder that it was said of Erasmus that he had "a surpassing power of expression"! (Nichols 2006, Vol. 2, 6)

The First Greek Text

While teaching Greek at Cambridge University in England, Erasmus continued with his work of revising the Greek New Testament text. One of his friends, Martin Dorpius, attempted to persuade him that the Latin did not need to be corrected from the Greek. Dorpius made the same error in reasoning that the "King James Only" people make, arguing: "For is it likely that the whole Catholic Church would have erred for so many centuries, seeing that she has always used and sanctioned this translation? Is it probable that so many holy fathers, so many consummate scholars would have longed to convey a warning to a friend?" (Campbell 1949, 71) Thomas More joined Erasmus in replying to these arguments, making the point that what matters is having an accurate text in the original languages.

In Basel, Switzerland, Erasmus was about to be harassed by the printer Johannes Froben. Froben was alerted that Cardinal Ximenes of Toledo, Spain, had been putting together a Greek and Latin Testament in 1514. However, he was delaying publication until he had the whole Bible completed. The first printed Greek critical text would have set the standard, with any other being all but ignored. Erasmus published his first edition in 1516, while the Complutensian Polyglot (Greek for "many languages") was not issued until 1522.

The fact that Erasmus was terribly rushed resulted in a Greek text that contained hundreds of typographical errors alone.[665] Textual scholar Scrivener once stated: '[It] is in that respect the most faulty book I know' (Scrivener 1894, 185). This comment did not even take into consideration the blatant interpolations into the text that were not part of the original. Erasmus was not oblivious to the typographical errors, which were corrected in a good many later editions. This did not include the textual errors. Martin Luther used his second edition of 1519 in his German translation and William Tyndale's English translation. This is exactly what Erasmus wanted, writing the following in that edition's preface: "I would have these words translated into all languages. . . . I long for the ploughboy to sing them to himself as he follows his plough."

Unfortunately, this debased Greek New Testament's continuous reproduction gave rise to its becoming the standard, called the Textus Receptus ("Received Text"), reigning 400 years before it was dethroned by the critical text of B. F. Westcott and F. J. A. Hort in 1881. Regardless of its imperfections, the Erasmus critical edition began the all-important work of

---

[665] In fact, his copy of Revelation being incomplete, Erasmus simply retranslated the missing verses from the Latin Vulgate back into Greek.

textual criticism, which has only brought about a better critical text and more accurate Bible translations.

Erasmus was not only concerned with ascertaining the original words; he was just as concerned with achieving an accurate understanding of those words. In 1519, he penned *Principles of True Theology* (shortened to *The Ratio*). Herein he introduces his principles for Bible study, his interpretation rules. Among them is the thought of never taking a quotation out of its context nor out of the line of thought of its author. Erasmus saw the Bible as a whole work by one ultimate author, and as such, it should interpret itself.

Erasmus Contrasted with Luther

Erasmus penned a treatise called *Familiar Colloquies* in 1518, in which again he was exposing corruption in the Church and the monasteries. Just one year earlier, in 1517, Martin Luther had nailed his 95 theses on the church door at Wittenberg, denouncing the indulgences, the scandal that had rocked numerous countries. Many people likely thought that these two could bring about change and reform. This was not going to be a team effort, though, as the two were at opposite ends of the spectrum on how to bring reform about. Luther would come to condemn Erasmus because he was viewed as being too moderate, seeking to make change peacefully within the Church.

The seemingly small bond they may have shared (by way of their writings against the Church establishment) was torn apart in 1524 when Erasmus wrote his essay *On the Freedom of the Will*. Luther believed that salvation results from "justification by faith alone" (Latin, *sola fide*) and not from priestly absolution or works of penance. In fact, Luther was so adamant in his belief of "justification by faith alone" that in his Bible translation, he added the word "alone" to Romans 3:28. Luther failed to understand that Paul was writing about the works of the Mosaic Law. (Romans 3:19, 20, 28) Thus, Luther denied the principle that man possesses free will. However, Erasmus would not accept such faulty reasoning in that it would make God unjust because this would suggest that man would be unable to act in such a way as to affect his salvation.

As the Reformation was spreading throughout Europe, Erasmus saw complaints from both sides. Many religious leaders who supported the reform movement chose to leave the Catholic Church. While they could not predict the result of their decision, they moved forward, many meeting their deaths. This would not be true of Erasmus, though, for he withdrew from the debate, yet he did refuse to be made cardinal. His approach was to try to appease both sides. Thus, Rome saw his writings as heretical, prohibiting them, while the reformers denounced him for refusing to risk his life for the cause. Here was a man emotionally broken over criticism but in fear of burning bridges with Rome, so he cautiously sat on the sideline.

The affairs of Erasmus in relation to the Reformation can be summarized as follows: "He was a reformer until the Reformation became a fearful reality; a jester at the bulwarks of the papacy until they began to give way; a propagator of the Scriptures until men betook themselves to the study and the application of them; depreciating the mere outward forms of religion until they had come to be estimated at their real value; in short, a learned, ingenious, benevolent, amiable, timid, indecisive man, who, bearing the responsibility, resigned to others the glory of rescuing the human mind from the bondage of a thousand years. The distance between his career and that of Luther was therefore continually enlarging, until they at length moved in opposite directions and met each other with mutual animosity."—(McClintock and Strong 1894, 278).

The Reformation's greatest gain is that the common person can now hold God's Word in his hand. In fact, the English-language person has over 100 different translations from which to choose. From these 16th-century life and death struggles, Erasmus shared that there has materialized dependable and accurate Bible translations. Consequently, the "plowboy" of 98 percent of the world can pick up his Bible, or at least part of it.

"The text we have, now received by all" is the words from the Elzevier 1633 edition, in Latin, from which the term "Textus Receptus" was derived.

The Textus Receptus

The Dark Ages (5th to 15th centuries C.E.) was a time when the Church had the Bible locked up in the Latin language, and scholarship and learning were nearly nonexistent. However, with the birth of the Morning Star of the Reformation, John Wycliffe (1328-1384), and the invention of the printing press in 1455, the restraints were loosened, and there was a rebirth of interest in the Greek language. Moreover, with the fall of Constantinople to the Turks in 1453 C. E., many Greek scholars and their manuscripts were scattered abroad, resulting in a revival of Greek in the Western citadels of learning.

About fifty years later, or at the beginning of the sixteenth century, Ximenes, archbishop of Toledo, Spain, a man of rare capability and honor, invited foremost scholars of his land to his university at Alcala to produce a multiple-language Bible—not for the common people, but for the educated. The outcome would be the Polyglot, named Complutensian, corresponding to the Latin of Alcala. This would be a Bible of six large volumes, beautifully bound, containing the Old Testament in four languages (Hebrew, Aramaic, Greek, and Latin) and the New Testament in two (Greek and Latin). These scholars had only a few manuscripts available to them for the Greek New Testament, and those of late origin. One may wonder why this was the case when they were supposed to have access to the Vatican library. This Bible was completed in 1514, providing the first printed Greek New Testament, but it did not receive approval by the pope to be published until 1520 and was not released to the public until 1522.

Froben, a printer in Basel, Switzerland, became aware of completing the Complutensian Polyglot Bible and its pending consent by the pope to be published. Immediately, he saw a prospect of making profits. He at once sent word to Erasmus, who was the foremost European scholar of the day and whose works he had published in Latin, pleading with him to hurry through a Greek New Testament text. In an attempt to bring the first published Greek text to completion, Erasmus was only able to locate, in July of 1515, a few late cursive manuscripts for collating and preparing his text. It would go to press in October of 1515 and would be completed by March of 1516. In fact, Erasmus was in such a hurried mode that he rushed the manuscript containing the Gospels to the printer without first editing it, making such changes as he felt were necessary on the proof sheets. Because of this terrible rush job, the work contained hundreds of typographical errors, as we noted earlier. Erasmus himself admitted this in his preface, remarking that it was "rushed through rather than edited." Bruce Metzger referred to the Erasmian text as a "debased form of the Greek testament." (Metzger and D 1964, 1968, 1992. 2006, 103)

As one would expect, Erasmus was moved to produce an improved text in four succeeding editions of 1519, 1522, 1527, and 1535. We are informed that Erasmus' editions of the Greek text ultimately proved an excellent achievement, even a literary sensation. They were inexpensive, and the first two editions totaled 3,300 copies compared to the 600 copies of the large and expensive six-volume Polyglot Bible. In the preface to his first edition, Erasmus stated, "I vehemently dissent from those who would not have private persons read the Holy Scriptures, nor have them translated into the vulgar tongues." (Baer 2007, 268)

Except for everyday practical consideration, the editions of Erasmus had little to vouch for them, for he had access only to five (some say eight) Greek manuscripts of relatively late origin, and none of these contained the entire Greek New Testament. Instead, these comprised one or more sections into which the Greek texts were normally divided: (1) the Gospels; (2) Acts and the general epistles (James through Jude); (3) the letters of Paul; and (4) Revelation. In fact, of the some 5,750 Greek New Testament manuscripts that we now have, only about fifty are complete.

Consequently, Erasmus had but one copy of Revelation (twelfth-century). Since it was incomplete, he merely retranslated the missing last six verses of the book from the Latin Vulgate back into Greek. He even frequently brought his Greek text in line with the Latin Vulgate; this is why some twenty readings in his Greek text were not found in any other Greek manuscript.

Martin Luther would use Erasmus' 1519 edition for his German translation, and William Tyndale would use the 1522 edition for his English translation. Erasmus' editions were also the foundation for others' later Greek editions of the New Testament. Among them were the four published by Robert Estienne (Stephanus, 1503-59). The third of these, published by Stephanus in 1550, became the Textus Receptus or Received Text of Britain and the basis for the King James Version. This took place through Theodore de Beza (1519-1605), whose work was based on the Erasmian text's corrupted third and fourth editions. Beza would produce nine editions of the Greek text, four being independent (1565, 1589, 1588-9, 1598), and the other five smaller reprints. It would be two of Beza's editions, that of 1589 and 1598, which would become the English Received Text.

Beza's Greek edition of the New Testament did not even differ as much as might be expected from those of Erasmus. Why do I say, as might be expected? Beza was a friend of the Protestant reformer, John Calvin, succeeding him at Geneva, and was also a well-known classical and biblical scholar. In addition, Beza possessed two important Greek manuscripts of the fourth and fifth century, the D and D^P (also known as D^2), the former of which contains most of the Gospels and Acts as well as a fragment of 3 John, and the latter containing the Pauline epistles. The Dutch Elzevir editions followed next, which were virtually identical to those of the Erasmian-influenced Beza text. It was in the second of seven of these, published in 1633 that there appeared the statement in the preface (in Latin): "You therefore now have the text accepted by everybody, in which we give nothing changed or corrupted." This edition became the Textus Receptus or the

Received Text on the continent. It seems that this success was in no small way due to the beauty and useful size of the Elzevir editions.

The Restoration Period

For the next 250 years, until 1881, textual scholarship was enslaved to the Erasmian-oriented Received Text. As these textual scholars[666] became familiar with older and more accurate manuscripts and observed the flaws in the Received Text, they would publish their findings in introductions, margins, and footnotes of their editions instead of changing the text. In 1734, J. A. Bengel of Tübingen, Germany, made an apology for again printing the Received Text, doing so only "because he could not publish a text of his own. Neither the publisher nor the public would have stood for it," he complained. (Robertson 1925, 25)

The first one to break free from this enslavement to the Textus Receptus, in the text itself, was Bible scholar J. J. Griesbach (1745-1812). His principal edition comes to us in three volumes, the first in Halle in 1775-7, the second in Halle and London in 1796-1806, and the third at Leipzig in 1803-7. However, Griesbach did not fully break from the Textus Receptus. Nevertheless, Griesbach is the real starting point in the development of classifying the manuscripts into families, setting down principles and rules for establishing the original reading, and using symbols to indicate the degree of certainty as to its being the original reading. We will examine his contributions in more detail below.

Karl Lachmann (1793-1851) was the first scholar fully to get out from under the influence of the Textus Receptus. He was a professor of ancient classical languages at Berlin University. In 1831, he published his edition of the Greek New Testament without any regard to the Textus Receptus. As Samuel MacAuley Jackson expressed it: Lachmann "was the first to found a text wholly on ancient evidence; and his editions, to which his eminent reputation as a critic gave wide currency, especially in Germany, did much toward breaking down the superstitious reverence for the textus receptus." Bruce Metzger had harsh words for the era of the Textus Receptus as well:

> So superstitious has been the reverence accorded the Textus Receptus that in some cases attempts to criticize it or emend it have been regarded as akin to sacrilege. Yet its textual basis is essentially a handful of late and haphazardly collected minuscule manuscripts,

---

[666] Brian Walton (1600-61), Dr. John Fell (1625-86), John Mill 1645-1707), Dr. Edward Wells (1667-1727, Richard Bentley (1662-1742), John Albert Bengel (1687-1752), Johann Jacob Wettstein (1693-1754), Johann Salomo Semler (1725-91), William Bowyer Jr. (1699-1777), Edward Harwood (1729-94), and Isaiah Thomas Jr. (1749-1831)

and in a dozen passages, its reading is supported by no known Greek witnesses. (Metzger and D 1964, 1968, 1992. 2006, 106)

After Lachmann came Friedrich Constantine von Tischendorf (1815-74), was best known for discovering the famed fourth-century Codex Sinaiticus manuscript, the only Greek uncial manuscript containing the complete Greek Greek New Testament. Tischendorf went further than any other textual scholar to edit and made accessible the evidence in leading and less important uncial manuscripts. Throughout the time that Tischendorf was making his valuable contributions to the field of textual criticism in Germany, another great scholar, Samuel Prideaux Tregelles (1813-75) in England made other valued contributions. Among them, he was able to establish his concept of "Comparative Criticism." That is, the age of a text, such as Vaticanus 1209, may not necessarily be that of its manuscript (i.e. the material upon which the text was written), which was copied in 350 C.E., since the text may be a faithful copy of an earlier text, like the second-century P[75]. Both Tischendorf and Tregelles were determined defenders of divine inspiration of the Scriptures, which likely had much to do with the productivity of their labors. If you take an opportunity to read about the lengths to which Tischendorf went in his discovery of Codex Sinaiticus, you will be moved by his steadfastness and love for God's Word.

The Climax of the Restored Text

Leading textual scholars have commended the critical text of Westcott and Hort of 1881 over the last one hundred and forty years, and still stands as the standard. Numerous additional critical editions of the Greek text came after Westcott and Hort: Richard F. Weymouth (1886), Bernhard Weiss (1894–1900); the British and Foreign Bible Society (1904, 1958), Alexander Souter (1910), Hermann von Soden (1911–1913); and Eberhard Nestle's Greek text, *Novum Testamentum Graece*, published in 1898 by the Württemberg Bible Society, Stuttgart, Germany. The Nestle in twelve editions (1898–1923) to subsequently be taken over by his son, Erwin Nestle (13th–20th editions, 1927–1950), followed by Kurt Aland (21st–25th editions, 1952–1963), and lastly, it was coedited by Kurt Aland and Barbara Aland (26th–28th editions, 1979, 1993, 2012).

Many of the above scholars gave their entire lives to God and the Greek text. Each of these could have an entire book devoted to them and their work alone. The amount of work they accomplished before the era of computers is nothing short of astonishing. Rightly, the preceding history should serve to strengthen our faith in the authenticity and general integrity of the Greek New Testament. Unlike Bart D. Ehrman, men like Sir Frederic Kenyon have been moved to say that the books of the Greek New Testament have "come down to us substantially as they were written." And all this is especially true of the critical scholarship of the almost two hundred years since the days of Karl Lachmann, due to which all today can feel certain that what they hold in their hands is a mirror reflection of the Word of God that was penned in twenty-seven books, some two thousand years ago.

CHAPTER XV

The Arrival of the Critical Text

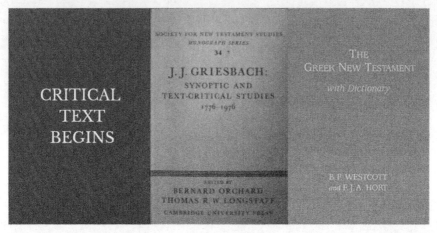

In the third century of our common era, New Testament textual criticism goes back to Origen (185-254). The historical roots of textual scholarship actually reach back to the 3rd-century B.C.E. in the Library of Alexandria. We are going to the 18th-19th centuries for the purposes of this chapter.

From 1550, the New Testament Greek text was in bondage to the popularity of the Textus Receptus as though the latter were inspired itself, and no textual scholar would dare make changes regardless of the evidence found in older, more accurate manuscripts that later became known. The best textual scholars would offer to publish these new findings in their editions' introductions, margins, and footnotes. Bengel, as we noted above, apologized for repeating the printing of the Textus Receptus "because he could not publish a text of his own. Neither the publisher nor the public would have stood for it." (Robertson 1925, 25)

Karl Lachmann (1793-1851), Professor of Classical and German Philology at Berlin, was the first to make a clean break with the influential Textus Receptus. In 1831, he published his edition of the Greek text overthrowing the Textus Receptus at Berlin. Ezra Abbot says of Lachmann, "He was the first to found a text wholly on ancient evidence; and his editions, to which his eminent reputation as a critic gave wide currency, especially in Germany, did much toward breaking down the superstitious reverence for the textus receptus." (Schaff, Companion to the Greek Testament, 1883, 256-7)

Johann Jakob Griesbach [1745-1812]

Griesbach obtained his master's degree at the age of 23. He was educated at Frankfurt and the universities of Tubingen, Leipzig, and Halle. Griesbach became one of Johann Salomo Semler's most dedicated and passionate students. Semler (1725 – 1791) persuaded him to focus his attention on New Testament textual criticism. Even though it was Semler who introduced Griesbach to the theory of text-types, Griesbach is principally responsible for the text-types that we have today. Griesbach made the Alexandrian, Byzantine, and Western text-types appreciated by a wide range of textual scholars over two centuries.

After his master's degree, Griesbach traveled throughout Europe examining Greek manuscripts: Germany, the Netherlands, France, and England. Griesbach would excel far beyond any textual scholar who had preceded him, publishing his Greek text first at Halle in 1775-77, followed by London in 1795-1806, and finally in Leipzig in 1803-07. It would be his latter editions that would be used by a number of Bible translators, such as Archbishop Newcome, Abner Kneeland, Samuel Sharpe, Edgar Taylor, and Benjamin Wilson.

Griesbach was the first to include manuscript readings that were earlier than what Erasmus had used in his Greek text of 1516 C.E. The Society for New Testament Studies comments on the importance of his research: "Griesbach spent long hours in the attempt to find the best readings among the many variants in the New Testament. His work laid the foundations of modern text criticism, and he is, in no small measure, responsible for the secure New Testament text which we enjoy today. Many of his methodological principles continue to be useful in the process of determining the best readings from among the many variants which remain." (B. Orchard 1776-1976, 2005, xi)

The Fifteen Rules of Griesbach

In the Introduction to his Second edition of the **Greek New Testament** (Halle, 1796) **Griesbach** set forth the following list of critical rules for weighing the internal evidence for variant readings within the manuscripts.

1. **The shorter reading is to be preferred over the more verbose**, if not wholly lacking the support of old and weighty witnesses,

for scribes were much more prone to add than to omit. They hardly ever leave out anything on purpose, but they added much. It is true indeed that some things fell out by accident; but likewise not a few things, allowed in by the scribes through errors of the eye, ear, memory, imagination, and judgment, have been added to the text.

The shorter reading is especially preferable (even if by the support of the witnesses it may be second best),

(a) if at the same time it is harder, more obscure, ambiguous, involves an ellipsis, reflects Hebrew idiom or is ungrammatical.

(b) if the same thing is read expressed with different phrases in different manuscripts.

(c) if the order of words is inconsistent and unstable;

(d) at the beginning of a section;

(e) if the fuller reading gives the impression of incorporating a definition or interpretation, or verbally conforms to parallel passages, or seems to have come in from lectionaries.

But on the contrary, we should set the fuller reading before the shorter (unless the latter is seen in many notable witnesses),

(a) if a "similarity of ending" might have provided an opportunity for an omission;

(b) if that which was omitted could to the scribe have seemed obscure, harsh, superfluous, unusual, paradoxical, offensive to pious ears, erroneous, or opposed to parallel passages;

(c) if that which is absent could be absent without harm to the sense or structure of the words, for example, prepositions which may be called incidental, especially brief ones, and so forth, the lack of which would not easily be noticed by a scribe in reading again what he had written;

(d) if the shorter reading is by nature less characteristic of the style or outlook of the author;

(e) if it wholly lacks sense;

(f) if it is probable that it has crept in from parallel passages or from the lectionaries.

On Griesbach's principle of preferring the shorter reading, James Royse offers a word about appreciating the complexity and exceptions to the rule: "I would certainly accept Silva's reminder that Griesbach's formulation of the *lectio brevior potior* principle is far from a simple preference for the shorter reading, and that its correct application requires a sensitivity to the many exceptions and conditions that Griesbach notes." (J. R. Royse 2007, 735) Kurt and Barbara Aland qualify the principle as well: "The venerable maxim lectio brevior lectio potior ("the shorter reading is the more probable reading") is certainly right in many instances. But here again the principle cannot be applied mechanically. It is not valid for witnesses whose texts otherwise vary significantly from the characteristic patterns of the textual tradition, with frequent omissions or expansions reflecting editorial tendencies (e.g. D)." (Aland and Aland, The Text of the New Testament 1995, 281) Harold Greenlee offers a simple (or perhaps simplistic), balanced view of the principle:

(b) The *shorter* reading is generally preferable if an *intentional change* has been made. The reason is that scribes at times made intentional additions to clarify a passage, but rarely made an intentional omission. Of course, this principle applies only to a difference in the number of words in the reading, not to the difference between a longer and a shorter word.

(c) The *longer* reading is often preferable if an *unintentional change* has been made. The reason is that scribes were more likely to omit a word or a phrase accidentally than to add accidentally. (Greenlee, Introduction to New Testament Textual Criticism 1995, 112)

Of Griesbach, Paul D. Wegner writes, "While Griesbach sometimes would rely too heavily on a mechanical adherence to his system of recensions, by and large he was a careful and cautious scholar. He was also the first German scholar to abandon the Textus Receptus in favor of what he believed to be, by means of his principles, superior readings." (Wegner, A Student's Guide to Textual Criticism of the Bible: Its History Methods & Results 2006, 214)

His choosing the shorter reading of the Lord's Prayer at Luke 11:3-4 evidenced Griesbach's ability as a textual scholar. He made this decision based on only a handful of minuscule and uncials, patristic, and versional evidence. A few short years later, the Vaticanus manuscript would confirm that Griesbach's choice was correct. Today we have one of the oldest and most valued manuscripts, P75, and it has the shorter reading as well. Many scribes from the fourth century onward harmonized Luke's form of the prayer with Matthew's Gospel.

Luke 11:3-4 New American Standard Bible (NASB / NU)	Luke 11:3-4 New King James Version (NKJV / TR)
³ Give us each day our daily bread, ⁴ and forgive us our sins, for we ourselves forgive everyone who is indebted to us. And lead us not into temptation."	³ Give us day by day our daily bread. ⁴ And forgive us our sins, For we also forgive everyone who is indebted to us. And do not lead us into temptation, **But deliver us from the evil one.**"

Karl Lachmann [1793-1851]

After two and a half centuries, in 1831, a German classical philologist and critic, Karl Lachmann, had the courage to publish an edition of the New Testament text he prepared from his examination of the manuscripts and variants, determining on a case-by-case basis what he believed the original reading was, never beholding to the Textus Receptus. However, he did not include his textual rules and principles in his critical text. He simple stated that these principles could be found in a theological journal. "Karl Lachmann, a classical philologist, produced a fresh text (in 1831) that presented the Greek New Testament of the fourth century."[667]

The *Interpreter's Dictionary of the Bible* sums up Lachmann's six textual criteria as follows:

- Nothing is better attested than that in which all authorities agree.

- The agreement has less weight if part of the authorities is silent or in any way defective.

---

[667] (P. Comfort, Encountering the Manuscripts: An Introduction to New Testament Paleography and Textual Criticism 2005, 294)

- The evidence for a reading, when it is that of witnesses of different regions, is greater than that of witnesses of some particular place, differing either from negligence or from set purpose.

- The testimonies are to be regarded as doubtfully balanced when witnesses from widely separated regions stand opposed to others equally wide apart.

- Readings are uncertain which occur habitually in different forms in different regions.

- Readings are of weak authority which are not universally attested in the same region.[668]

It was not Lachmann's intention to restore the text of the New Testament back to the original, as he believed this to be impossible. Rather, his intention was to offer a text based solely on documentary evidence, setting aside any text that had been published prior to his, producing a text from the fourth century. Lachmann used no minuscule manuscripts, but instead, he based his text on the Alexandrian text-type and the agreement of the Western authorities, namely, the Old Latin and Greek Western Uncials if the oldest Alexandrian authorities differed. He also used the testimonies of Irenaeus, Origen, Cyprian, Hilary, and Lucifer. As A. T. Robertson put it, Lachman wanted "to get away from the tyranny of the Textus Receptus." Lachmann was correct in that he could not get back to the original, at least for the whole of the NT text, as he simply did not have the textual evidence that we have today, or even what Westcott and Hort had in 1881. Codex Sinaiticus had yet to be discovered, and Codex Vaticanus had yet to be photographed and edited. Moreover, he did not have the papyri that we have today.

Samuel Prideaux Tregelles [1813-1875]

Tregelles was an English Bible scholar, textual critic, and theologian. He was born to Quaker parents at Wodehouse Place, Falmouth, on January 30, 1813. He was the son of Samuel Tregelles (1789–1828) and his wife Dorothy (1790–1873). His education began at Falmouth Grammar School. He lost his father at the

[668] Biographies of Textual Critics - SkyPoint,
http://www.skypoint.com/members/waltzmn/Bios.html (accessed June 10, 2016).

young age of fifteen, compelling him to take a job at the Neath Abbey ironworks. However, he had a gift and a love of language, which led him to study Hebrew, Greek, Aramaic, Latin, and Welsh in his free time. He began the study of the New Testament at the age of twenty-five, which would become his life's work.

Tregelles discovered that the Textus Receptus was not based on any ancient witnesses. He determined that he would publish the Greek text of the New Testament grounded in ancient manuscripts and the citations of the early church fathers exactly as Karl Lachmann was doing in Germany. In 1845, he spent five months in Rome, hoping to collate Codex Vaticanus in the Vatican Library. Philip W. Comfort writes, "Samuel Tregelles (self-taught in Latin, Hebrew, and Greek) devoted his entire life's work to publishing one Greek text (which came out in six parts, from 1857 to 1872).[669] As is stated in the introduction to this work, Tregelles's goal was 'to exhibit the text of the New Testament in the very words in which it has been transmitted on the evidence of ancient authority.'[670] During this same era, Tischendorf was devoting a lifetime of labor to discovering manuscripts and producing accurate editions of the Greek New Testament."[671]

Friedrich Constantin von Tischendorf [1815-1874]

Tischendorf was a world-leading biblical scholar who rejected higher criticism, which led to his noteworthy success in defending the authenticity of the Bible text. He was born in Lengenfeld, Saxony, in northern Europe, the son of a physician, in the year 1815. Tischendorf was educated in Greek at the University of Leipzig. During his university studies, he was troubled by higher criticism of the Bible, as taught by famous German theologians, who sought to prove that the Greek New Testament was not authentic. Tischendorf became convinced, however, that thorough research of the early manuscripts would prove the trustworthiness of the Bible text.

---

[669] Because he was very poor, Tregelles had to ask sponsors to help him with the cost of publishing. The text came out in six volumes over a fifteen-year period—the last being completed just prior to his death. I consider myself fortunate to own a copy of Tregelles's *Greek New Testament* with his signature.

[670] See Prolegomena to Tregelles's *Greek New Testament*.

[671] (P. Comfort, Encountering the Manuscripts: An Introduction to New Testament Paleography and Textual Criticism 2005, 100)

We are indebted to Tischendorf for dedicating his life and abilities to searching through Europe's finest libraries and the monasteries of the Middle East for ancient Bible manuscripts, and especially for rescuing the great Codex Sinaiticus from destruction. However, our highest thanks go to our heavenly Father, who has used hundreds of men since the days of Desiderius Erasmus, who published the first printed Greek New Testament in 1516, so that the Word of God has been accurately preserved for us today. We can be grateful for the women of the twentieth and now the twenty-first century who have given their lives to this great work as well, such as Barbara Aland.

In the second principal recension of Tischendorf (as enumerated in Reuss 1872), the Introduction sets forth the following canons of criticism with examples of their application (see Tregelles 1854, pp. 119-21):

Basic Rule: "The text is only to be sought from ancient evidence, and especially from Greek manuscripts, but without neglecting the testimonies of versions and fathers."

1. "A reading altogether peculiar to one or another ancient document is suspicious; as also is any, even if supported by a class of documents, which seems to evince that it has originated in the revision of a learned man."

2. "Readings, however well supported by evidence, are to be rejected, when it is manifest (or very probable) that they have proceeded from the errors of copyists."

3. "In parallel passages, whether of the New or Old Testament, especially in the Synoptic Gospels, which ancient copyists continually brought into increased accordance, those testimonies are preferable, in which precise accordance of such parallel passages is not found; unless, indeed, there are important reasons to the contrary."

4. "In discrepant readings, that should be preferred which may have given occasion to the rest, or which appears to comprise the elements of the others."

5. "Those readings must be maintained which accord with New Testament Greek, or with the particular style of each individual writer."[672]

---

[672] Bibliography of Textual Criticism "T", http://www.bible-researcher.com/bib-t.html (accessed June 12, 2016).

Westcott's and Hort's 1881 Master Text

B. F. Westcott
1825-1901

F. J. A. Hort
1828-1892

The climax of this restoration era goes to the immediate successors of these men, the two English Bible scholars B. F. Westcott and F. J. A. Hort, upon whose text the United Bible Society is based, which is the foundation for all modern-day translations of the Bible. Westcott and Hort began their work in 1853 and finished it in 1881, working for twenty-eight years independently of each other, yet frequently comparing notes. As the Scottish biblical scholar Alexander Souter expressed it, they "gathered up in themselves all that was most valuable in the work of their predecessors. The maxims which they enunciated on questions of the text are of such importance." (Souter 1913, 118) They considered all imaginable factors in laboring to resolve the difficulties that conflicting texts presented, and when two readings had equal weight, they indicated that in their text. They emphasized, "Knowledge of documents should precede final judgment upon readings" and "all trustworthy restoration of corrupted texts is founded on the study of their history." They followed Griesbach in dividing manuscripts into families, stressing the significance of manuscript genealogy. In addition, they gave due weight to internal evidence, "intrinsic probability" and "transcriptional probability," that is, what the original author most likely wrote and wherein a copyist may most likely have made a mistake.

Westcott and Hort relied heavily on what they called the "neutral" family of texts, which involved the renowned fourth-century vellum Vaticanus and Sinaiticus manuscripts. They considered it quite decisive whenever these two manuscripts agreed, particularly when reinforced by other ancient uncial manuscripts. However, they were not thoughtlessly bound to the Vaticanus manuscript as some scholars have claimed, for by assessing all the elements, they frequently concluded that certain minor interpolations had crept into the neutral text that was not found in the group more given to interpolations and paraphrasing, i.e. the Western manuscript family. E. J. Goodspeed has shown that Westcott and Hort departed from Vaticanus seven hundred times in the Gospels alone.

According to Bruce M. Metzger, "the general validity of their critical principles and procedures is widely acknowledged by scholars today." In 1981 Metzger said,

> The international committee that produced the United Bible Societies Greek New Testament, not only adopted the Westcott and Hort edition as its basic text, but followed their methodology in giving attention to both external and internal consideration.

Philip Comfort offered this opinion:

> The text produced by Westcott and Hort is still to this day, even with so many more manuscript discoveries, a very close reproduction of the primitive text of the New Testament. Of course, I think they gave too much weight to Codex Vaticanus alone, and this needs to be tempered. This criticism aside, the Westcott and Hort text is extremely reliable. (...) In many instances where I would disagree with the wording in the Nestle / UBS text in favor of a particular variant reading, I would later check with the Westcott and Hort text and realize that they had often come to the same decision. (...) Of course, the manuscript discoveries of the past one hundred years have changed things, but it is remarkable how often they have affirmed the decisions of Westcott and Hort.[673]

Critical Rules of Westcott & Hort

The following summary of principles is taken from the compilation in Epp and Fee, *Studies in the Theory and Method of New Testament Textual Criticism* (1993, pages 157-8). References in parentheses are to sections of Hort's *Introduction*, from which the principles have been extracted.

1. Older readings, manuscripts, or groups are to be preferred. ("The shorter the interval between the time of the autograph and the end of the period of transmission in question, the stronger the presumption that earlier date implies greater purity of text.") (2.59; cf. 2.5-6, 31)

2. Readings are approved or rejected by reason of the quality, and not the number, of their supporting witnesses. ("No available presumptions

---

[673] Philip Comfort, *Encountering the Manuscripts: An Introduction to New Testament Paleography & Textual Criticism*, (Nashville, 2005), p. 100.

whatever as to text can be obtained from number alone, that is, from number not as yet interpreted by descent.") (2.44)

3. A reading combining two simple, alternative readings is later than the two readings comprising the conflation, and manuscripts rarely or never supporting conflate reading are text antecedent to mixture and are of special value. (2.49-50).

4. The reading is to be preferred that makes the best sense, that is, that best conforms to the grammar and is most congruous with the purport of the rest of the sentence and of the larger context. (2.20)

5. The reading is to be preferred that best conforms to the usual style of the author and to that author's material in other passages. (2.20)

6. The reading is to be preferred that most fitly explains the existence of the others. (2.22-23)

7. The reading is less likely to be original that combines the appearance of an improvement in the sense with the absence of its reality; the scribal alteration will have an apparent excellence, while the original will have the highest real excellence. (2.27, 29)

8. The reading is less likely to be original that shows a disposition to smooth away difficulties (another way of stating that the harder reading is preferable). (2.28)

9. Readings are to be preferred that are found in a manuscript that habitually contains superior readings as determined by intrinsic and transcriptional probability. Certainty is increased if such a better manuscript is found also to be an older manuscript (2.32-33) and if such a manuscript habitually contains reading that prove themselves antecedent to mixture and independent of external contamination by other, inferior texts (2.150-51). The same principles apply to groups of manuscripts (2.260-61).[674]

J. W. Burgon

Setting Straight the Indefensible Defenders of the Textus Receptus

While Karl Lachmann was the one to overthrow the Textus Receptus, it would be B. F. Westcott and F. J. A. Hort in 1881 who would put the nails in the coffin of the Textus Receptus. The

---

[674] Studies in the Theory and Method of New Testament Textual .., https://www.logos.com/product/46572/studies-in-the-theory-and-method-of-new-test (accessed June 12, 2016).

1881 British Revised Version (RV), also known as the English Revised Version (ERV) of the King James Version, and the 1881 New Testament Greek text of Westcott and Hort did not set well with the King-James-Version-Only[675] advocate John William Burgon (1813–1888), E. H. A. Scrivener (1813–1891), and Edward Miller (1825–1901), the latter authoring *A Guide to the Textual Criticism of the New Testament* (1886). We do not have the space nor the time to offer a full-scale argument against the King James Version Only and the Textus Receptus Only groups. However, we will address what amounts to their main arguments. This should help the reader to see how desperate and weak their arguments are.

Bible scholar David Fuller brings us **the first argument** in his book, *Which Bible*, where he writes, "Burgon regarded the good state of preservation of B (Codex Vaticanus) and ALEPH (Codex Sinaiticus) in spite of their exceptional age as proof not of their goodness but of their badness. If they had been good manuscripts, they would have been read to pieces long ago. We suspect that these two manuscripts are indebted for their preservation, solely to their ascertained evil character …. Had B (Vaticanus) and ALEPH (Sinaiticus) been copies of average purity, they must long since have shared the inevitable fate of books which are freely used and highly prized; namely, they would have fallen into decadence and disappeared from sight. Thus, the fact that B and ALEPH are so old is a point against them, not something in their favour. It shows that the Church rejected them and did not read them. Otherwise, they would have worn out and disappeared through much reading."

Thus, Vaticanus and Sinaiticus, leading representatives of the Alexandrian family of manuscripts, are in such great condition because they are full of errors, alterations, additions, and deletions, so they would have had little chance of wear and tear, never having been used by true believers. This argument is simply the weakest and most desperate that this author has ever heard. **First**, many of the papyrus Alexandrian manuscripts are in terrible shape. Some are 200 years older than codices Vaticanus and Sinaiticus, which would mean that they must have been read very often by true believers. **Second**, a number of old Byzantine and Western manuscripts are in good condition as well, which by this argument would indicate that they are also guilty of never having been read because they were full of errors, alterations, additions and deletions, so they would have had little chance of wear and tear. **Third**, the size of Sinaiticus with the Old Testament, the New Testament,

---

[675] A connected group of Christians promotes the King James Only movement. It is their position that the King James Version of the Bible is superior to all other English translations, and that all English translations based on the Westcott and Hort text of 1881 (foundation text of UBS5 and NA28) are corrupt due to the influence of the Alexandrian Greek manuscripts.

and apocryphal books, among other books would have weighed about 50+ lbs. This book was not read in the same manner that Christians would read their Bibles today. The same would be true of Codex Vaticanus as well. **Fourth**, both were written on extremely expensive and durable calfskin. **Fifth**, the period of copying the Byzantine text type was c. 330 – 1453 C.E., and it progressed into the most corrupt period for the Church (priests to the popes: stealing, sexual sins, torture, and murder); so much so, it ends with the Reformation. Thus, the idea of **true believers** wearing out manuscripts is ludicrous. **Sixth**, the Bible was locked up in Latin. Jerome's Latin Vulgate, produced in the 5th century to make the Bible accessible to all, became a means of keeping God's Word hidden. Almost all Catholic priests were biblically illiterate, so one wonders who these so-called true believers were and how were they reading God's Word to the point of wearing it out. For centuries, manuscripts were preserved, even when the Catholic priests could no longer understand them.

In their second argument, Burgon, Miller, and Scrivener maintained that the Byzantine text was used by the church for far more centuries, which proved its integrity, as God would never allow the church to use a corrupt text. B. F. Westcott wrote, "A corrupted Bible is a sign of a corrupt church, a Bible mutilated or imperfect, a sign of a church not yet raised to complete perfection of the truth." (*The Bible in the Church*, 1864, 1875) The reader can determine for themselves if it is a mere coincidence that as the church grew corrupt, the most corrupt manuscript of all grew right along with it for a thousand years.

As was stated earlier, Lucian produced the Syrian text, renamed the Byzantine text. About 290 C.E., some of his associates made various subsequent alterations, which deliberately combined elements from earlier types of text, and this text was adopted about 380 C.E. At Constantinople, it became the predominant form of the New Testament throughout the Greek-speaking world. The text was also edited, with harmonized parallel accounts, grammar corrections, and abrupt transitions modified to produce a smooth text. This was not a faithfully accurate copy. As we had just learned earlier under the corruption period, after Constantine legalized Christianity, giving it equal status with the pagan religions, it was much easier for those possessing manuscripts to have them copied. In fact, Constantine had ordered 50 copies of the whole of the Bible for the church in Constantinople. Over the next four centuries or so, the Byzantine Empire and the Greek-speaking church **were the dominant factors** as to why this area saw their text becoming the standard. It had nothing to do with it being the better text, i.e., the text that more accurately reflected the original. From the eighth century forward, the corrupt Byzantine text was the standard text and had displaced all others; it makes up about 95 percent of all manuscripts that we have of the Christian Greek Scriptures.

In their third argument, Burgon, Miller, and Scrivener continued with the belief that it would be foolish to set aside thousands of manuscript witnesses (the Byzantine text-type) for a few *supposedly* early manuscript witnesses (the Alexandrian text-type). But in truth, the majority of anything does not automatically mean that it is the best or even correct. Today we can easily produce thousands of copies of a faulty manuscript with a machine, and every copy displays the same errors. If we were to hand-copy the same manuscript a thousand times, obvious errors probably would be corrected in many copies, but new errors would be introduced, many of them probably the result of a well-intended "correction." A textual criticism principle that has been derived from this observation is that manuscripts should be weighed (i.e. for value), not counted.

In their **fourth argument,** Burgon, Miller, and Scrivener maintained that the Byzantine text-type was actually older and superior to the Alexandrian text-type. To refute this, we can go back to our patristic quotations, which reveal the Alexandrian text-type as earlier than the Byzantine text-type. Greenlee writes, "The fallacy in this argument was that the antiquity of a 'Syrian' (i.e., Byzantine) reading could be shown only when the Byzantine text was supported by one of the pre-Byzantine texts, which proved nothing in favor of the Byzantine, since WH maintained that Syrian readings were largely derived from the pre-Syrian texts. That the traditional text was intrinsically superior was more nearly a matter of subjective opinion; but extensive comparison of text-types has left most scholars convinced that the late text [Byzantine] is in general inferior, not superior."[676]

Metzger (whom I cite at length) writes,

The Alexandrian text, which Westcott and Hort called the Neutral text (a question-begging title), is usually considered to be the best text and the most faithful in preserving the original. Characteristics of the Alexandrian text are brevity and austerity. That is, it is generally shorter than the text of other forms, and it does not exhibit the degree of grammatical and stylistic polishing that is characteristic of the Byzantine type of text. Until recently the two chief witnesses to the Alexandrian text were codex Vaticanus (B) and codex Sinaiticus (ℵ), parchment manuscripts dating from about the middle of the fourth century. With the acquisition, however, of the Bodmer Papyri, particularly P[66] and P[75], both copied about the end of the second or the beginning of the third century, evidence is now available that the Alexandrian type of text goes

---

[676] (Greenlee, Introduction to New Testament Textual Criticism 1995, 76-7)

back to an archetype that must be dated early in the second century. The Sahidic and Bohairic versions frequently contain typically Alexandrian readings …. It was the corrupt Byzantine form of text that provided the basis for almost all translations of the New Testament into modern languages down to the nineteenth century. During the eighteenth-century scholars assembled a great amount of information from many Greek manuscripts, as well as from versional and patristic witnesses. But, except for three or four editors who timidly corrected some of the more blatant errors of the Textus Receptus, this debased form of the New Testament text was reprinted in edition after edition. It was only in the first part of the nineteenth century (1831) that a German classical scholar, Karl Lachmann, ventured to apply to the New Testament the criteria that he had used in editing texts of the classics. Subsequently other critical editions appeared, including those prepared by Constantin von Tischendorf, whose eighth edition (1869–72) remains a monumental thesaurus of variant readings, and the influential edition prepared by two Cambridge scholars, B. F. Westcott and F. J. A. Hort (1881). It is the latter edition that was taken as the basis for the present United Bible Societies' edition. During the twentieth century, with the discovery of several New Testament manuscripts much older than any that had hitherto been available, it has become possible to produce editions of the New Testament that approximate ever more closely to what is regarded as the wording of the original documents.[677]

History of the Nestle-Aland Edition

It seems best to allow the German Bible Society and the Institute for New Testament Textual Research to tell their own history:

In 1898, Eberhard Nestle published the first edition of his Novum Testamentum Graece. Based on a simple yet ingenious idea it disseminated the insights of the textual criticism of that time through a hand edition designed for university and school studies and for church purposes. Nestle took the three leading scholarly editions of the Greek New Testament at that time by Tischendorf, Westcott/Hort and Weymouth as a basis. (After 1901 he replaced the latter with Bernhard Weiss 1894/1900 edition.) Where their textual decisions

[677] Bruce Manning Metzger, United Bible Societies, *A Textual Commentary on the Greek New Testament, Second Edition a Companion Volume to the United Bible Societies' Greek New Testament (4th Rev. Ed.)* (London; New York: United Bible Societies, 1994), xx, xxv.

differed from each other Nestle chose for his own text the variant, which was preferred by two of the editions included, while the variant of the third was put into the apparatus.

The text-critical apparatus remained rudimentary in all the editions published by Eberhard Nestle. It was Eberhard Nestle's son Erwin who provided the 13th edition of 1927 with a consistent critical apparatus showing evidence from manuscripts, early translations and patristic citations. However, these notes did not derive from the primary sources, but only from editions.

This changed in the nineteen-fifties, when Kurt Aland started working for the edition by checking the apparatus entries against Greek manuscripts and editions of the Church Fathers. This phase came to a close in 1963 when the 25th edition of the Novum Testamentum Graece appeared; later printings of this edition already carried the brand name "Nestle-Aland" on their covers.

The 26th edition, which appeared in 1979, featured a fundamentally new approach. Until then the guiding principle had been to adopt the text supported by a majority of the critical editions referred to. Now the text was established on the basis of source material that had been assembled and evaluated in the intervening period. It included early papyri and other manuscript discoveries, so that the 26th edition represented the situation of textual criticism in the 20th century. Its text was identical with that of the 3rd edition of the UBS Greek New Testament (GNT) published in 1975, as a consequence of the parallel work done on both editions. Already in 1955 Kurt Aland was invited to participate in an editorial committee with Matthew Black, Bruce M. Metzger, Alan Wikgren, and at first Arthur Vööbus, later Carlo Martini (and, from 1982, Barbara Aland and Johannes Karavidopoulos) to produce a reliable hand edition of the Greek New Testament.

The first edition of the GNT appeared in 1966. Its text was established along the lines of Westcott and Hort and differed considerably from Nestle's 25th edition. This holds true for the second edition of the GNT as well. When the third edition was prepared Kurt Aland was able to contribute the textual proposals coming from his preliminary work on the 26th edition of the Nestle-Aland. Hence the process of establishing the text for both editions continued to converge, so that eventually they could share an identical text. However, their external appearance and the design of their apparatus remains different, because they serve different purposes. The GNT is primarily intended for translators, providing a reliable Greek initial text and a text-critical apparatus showing variants that are relevant for translation. In the case of the passages selected for this purpose the evidence is displayed as completely as possible. The Novum Testamentum Graece is produced primarily for research, academic education and pastoral practice. It seeks to provide an apparatus that enables the reader to make a critical assessment of the reconstruction of the Greek initial text.

The text of the 26th edition of the Nestle-Aland was adopted for the 27th edition also, while the apparatus underwent an extensive revision. The text remained the same, because the 27th edition was not "deemed an appropriate occasion for introducing textual changes". Since then the situation has changed, because the Editio Critica Maior (ECM) of the Catholic Letters is now available. Its text was established on the basis of all the relevant material from manuscripts and other sources. The ECM text was adopted for the present edition following approval by the editorial committee of the Nestle-Aland and the GNT.[678]

This makes more certain for us the Apostle Peter's words: "But the word of the Lord endures forever." (1 Peter 1:25, NASB) We can have the same confidence that the One who inspired the Holy Scriptures, giving us His inerrant Word, has also used his servants to preserve them throughout the last two thousand years, "who desires all men to be saved and to come to an accurate knowledge[679] of truth." (1 Tim. 2:4) The beloved Bruce Manning Metzger was right; the text of the New Testament was transmitted; then, it entered a 1,400-year period of corruption and has been enjoying a 500-year period of restoration. If one has a restored text, then, in essence, they have the originals.

---

[678] Nestle Aland Novum Testamentum Graece: History, http://www.nestle-aland.com/en/history/ (accessed June 12, 2016).

[679] *Epignosis* is a strengthened or intensified form of *gnosis* (*epi*, meaning "additional"), meaning, "true," "real," "full," "complete" or "accurate," depending upon the context. Paul and Peter alone use *epignosis*.

CHAPTER XVI

The Practice of Textual Criticism to Determine the Original Reading

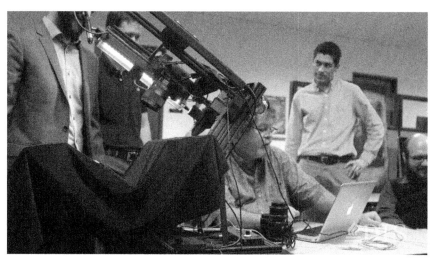

Dr. Daniel Wallace and his team digitizing Ancient manuscripts for The Center for the Study of New Testament Manuscripts

Major Critical Texts of the New Testament

- **Byz RP**: 2005 Byzantine Greek New Testament, Robinson & Pierpont

- **TR1550**: 1550 Stephanus New Testament

- **Maj**: The Majority Text (thousands of minuscules which display a similar text)

- **Gries**: 1774-1775 Johann Jakob Griesbach Greek New Testament

- **Treg**: 1857-1879 Samuel Prideaux Tregelles Greek New Testament

- **Tisch**: 1872 Tischendorf's Greek New Testament

- **WH**: 1881 Westcott-Hort Greek New Testament

- **NA28**: 2012 Nestle-Aland Greek New Testament

- **UBS5**: 2014 Greek New Testament

- **NU**: Both Nestle-Aland and the United Bible Society

- **TGNT**: 2017 The Greek New Testament by Tyndale House
- **GENTI**: 2021 Greek-English New Testament Interlinear[680]

Collecting the manuscript evidence is a laborious process, but it is a little more straightforward than the evaluation process. In the collection process, the goal is to gather as much evidence as possible concerning various readings of a specific text. In the evaluation process, the aim is to determine which reading has the best evidence for being the original reading. The evaluation process is complicated by the fact that not all scholars agree on which evaluation principles are to be used or the relative importance of each of them.[681]

Evaluation Principles

- There can only be one reading, which is the original reading.
- Manuscripts are to be weighed not counted. Certain families of manuscripts are more trustworthy (e.g., Alexandrian over Byzantine, Western, or Caesarean). In addition, certain manuscripts within a family are more faithful than others (e.g., P66 P75 01 03)
- Generally, the reading that is weighty from both internal and external evidence is preferred.[682]
- The external evidence of the manuscript witnesses is to be evaluated first; thereafter, will the internal evidence be considered.
- The primary weight of external evidence goes to the original language manuscripts. If the weight is so evenly distributed, it is difficult to make a decision; the versions and Church Fathers may serve to tip the scales.
- Probability is determined based on paleographical details and the habits of scribes.

The Internal Textual Criticism Process

- The reading that the other reading(s) most likely came from is likely the original. This is the fundamental principle of textual criticism.
- The *more difficult* or *awkward* reading is often preferable. The reading at first will seem to be more difficult or awkward to understand, but

---

[680] https://christianpublishinghouse.co/greek-english-interlinear/

[681] Paul D. Wegner, A Student's Guide to Textual Criticism of the Bible : Its History, Methods & Results (Downers Grove, Ill.: InterVarsity Press, 2006), 239.

[682] However, the Documentary Approach gives great weight to the external evidence of the documents.

after further investigation, it will be discovered that a scribe deliberately or mistakenly changed the text to an easier reading.

- The *shorter* reading is generally preferred if the change is *intended*. This is a reflection of scribal tendency, as a scribe is far more likely in his efforts at clarification, willfully to make an addition to a text. Very rarely will a scribe intentionally add to his text by mistake.

- The *longer* reading is generally preferred if the change is *unintended*. This again is a reflection of scribal activity, in that a scribe is far more likely to omit a word or phrase mistakenly, as to intentionally adding.

- The *longer* reading is preferred if there is clear reason(s) internally as to why the scribe omitted a word or phrase, like difficulties (perceived contradictions) or awkwardness. For example, a scribe may willfully remove or alter a verse that is repeating one of the previous verses.

- Within the synoptic gospels especially, a *less identical* reading is preferred as scribes had a tendency to harmonize readings.

- An *author-style* reading is preferred. If a reading matches the style of the author, it is preferred, and the variants that are foreign to that style are questionable.

- An *author-vocabulary* reading is preferred. If a reading matches the vocabulary of the author, it is preferred, and the variants that are foreign to that vocabulary are questionable.

- An *author-doctrine* reading is preferred. If a reading matches the doctrine of the author, it is preferred, and the variants that are foreign to that doctrine are questionable, especially if they are of a later period in Christian history, anachronistic.

- The reading that is deemed *immediately at odds with the context* is preferred if deemed intentional because a scribe is more likely to have smoothed the reading out.

The External Textual Criticism Process

- The *Alexandrian text*-type is generally preferred (especially P[66] P[75] 01 03), unless it appears to be a "learned" correction.

- A *represented* reading from more than one geographical area may be preferred to even an Alexandrian text-type reading. The reason is that the odds are increased greatly against a reading being changed from the original in such a wide geographical and family spectrum.

- An *overwhelming* Alexandrian representation (P^{66} P^{75} 01 03), numerous Alexandrian manuscripts of great quality and trustworthiness can overrule a widely *represented* reading from all geographical areas and families.

- The *Byzantine reading* is always questionable until proven otherwise.

- The *most faithful* to a text-type is preferred if they are divided in support.

New Testament textual criticism is the study of the existing manuscripts of the New Testament to establish the most accurate and original text. The field seeks to identify and resolve any discrepancies, variations, or errors that may have occurred during the copying and transmission process throughout history. Scholars employ various approaches to achieve this goal. Two of the main approaches are the Thoroughgoing Eclecticism and the Reasoned Eclecticism.

Different Approaches to New Testament Textual Criticism

1. **Thoroughgoing Eclecticism**: This approach, also known as radical eclecticism, is characterized by evaluating every individual variant reading in the New Testament manuscripts without giving priority to any particular text type, group, or family. This means that each variant is assessed on its own merits, rather than favoring certain manuscripts based on their age, geographical distribution, or other factors. Thoroughgoing eclectics believe that the best way to establish the most original reading is through an in-depth examination of each variant.

This method relies on several key principles:

a. **Internal evidence**: This includes evaluating the reading based on the linguistic style, grammar, and vocabulary of the author, as well as the context within the passage.

b. **Transcriptional probability**: This principle seeks to determine which reading is more likely to have led to the other(s) by examining the potential scribal errors or intentional changes that may have occurred during copying.

c. **Intrinsic probability**: This considers the author's intention, theological views, and the overall coherence of the passage.

538

Thoroughgoing Eclecticism has its strengths and weaknesses. Its main strength lies in its objective and impartial evaluation of the text, which can help uncover the most accurate reading. However, its weakness is that it can sometimes lead to an overly individualistic and subjective assessment of variants, making it difficult to arrive at a consensus.

2. **Reasoned Eclecticism**: This approach is a more moderate form of eclecticism that combines both internal and external evidence to establish the original text. Reasoned eclectics give more weight to certain text types, families, or groups based on their age, geographical distribution, and overall quality.

In addition to considering the principles of internal evidence, transcriptional probability, and intrinsic probability, Reasoned Eclecticism also takes into account the following factors:

a. **Manuscript evidence**: The age, quality, and geographical distribution of the manuscripts that contain a particular variant are taken into consideration.

b. **Textual relationships**: The affiliations between manuscripts, text types, or families are examined, with preference often given to the Alexandrian text type or the earliest attested readings.

Reasoned Eclecticism aims to strike a balance between relying solely on internal evidence and giving undue preference to certain text types. Its strength lies in its balanced and systematic approach, which can lead to a more reliable reconstruction of the original text. However, critics argue that this method can still be influenced by the subjective preferences of scholars and may overlook significant individual readings in favor of established text types.

3. **Reasoned Conservatism**: Reasoned Conservatism, as advocated by H. A. Sturz in his work "The Byzantine Text-Type & New Testament Textual Criticism," is another approach to New Testament textual criticism. This method is characterized by giving more weight to the Byzantine text-type, also known as the Majority Text, which is the textual family found in the majority of extant Greek New Testament manuscripts.

Sturz's Reasoned Conservatism is based on the following principles:

a. **Byzantine priority**: While Sturz does not argue that the Byzantine text-type should be followed blindly, he contends that it should not be dismissed outright, as is the case with some critics. Sturz believes that the Byzantine text-type has preserved many early readings and that these readings should be considered carefully.

b. **Manuscript evidence**: Sturz emphasizes the importance of evaluating all available manuscript evidence, including those from the Byzantine text-type, before making a decision on the most likely original reading. This approach requires scholars to consider the full range of manuscript evidence without automatically dismissing readings found in the Byzantine text-type.

c. **Internal and external evidence**: Like Reasoned Eclecticism, Reasoned Conservatism also takes into account both internal and external evidence when evaluating variant readings. However, the key difference lies in the weight assigned to the Byzantine text-type.

The strengths of Reasoned Conservatism include its openness to considering the Byzantine text-type as a valuable source of early readings and its comprehensive evaluation of manuscript evidence. This approach can lead to the identification of genuine early readings that might otherwise be overlooked.

However, the main criticism of Reasoned Conservatism is that it might assign too much importance to the Byzantine text-type, which is generally considered to be a later, more secondary text-type. This could potentially result in the selection of later readings instead of the original ones. Despite this, H. A. Sturz's work has contributed to a more balanced and inclusive approach to New Testament textual criticism by advocating for the careful consideration of the Byzantine text-type.

4. **Byzantine Priority**: The Byzantine Priority approach to New Testament textual criticism, as championed by scholars like Maurice A. Robinson, Zane C. Hodges, and Arthur L. Farstad, gives primary importance to the Byzantine text-type, also known as the Majority Text. This textual family is found in the majority of extant Greek New Testament manuscripts and is characterized by a more standardized and harmonized text.

The main principles of Byzantine Priority are:

a. **Majority support**: Advocates of Byzantine Priority argue that the sheer number of manuscripts supporting the Byzantine text-type should not be ignored, as it indicates a strong and consistent transmission history. They contend that the majority of the manuscripts must have been based on an earlier, reliable text.

b. **Byzantine antiquity**: While the majority of Byzantine manuscripts are from the later period, proponents of Byzantine Priority maintain that the text-type itself can be traced back to a much earlier stage in the textual transmission history, potentially even to the autographs (original writings) themselves. Daniel Wallace has shown this to be false, which we have known for many decades.

c. **Consistency and accuracy**: Scholars who support Byzantine Priority emphasize the consistency and accuracy of the Byzantine text-type compared to other text-types. They believe that the process of transmission and copying was more controlled and stable in the Byzantine tradition, leading to a more accurate representation of the original text.

The strengths of Byzantine Priority include the acknowledgment of the significance of the majority of manuscripts and the attention given to the possibility of early and accurate readings within the Byzantine text-type. By focusing on the majority of the manuscripts, this approach can reveal readings that may have been overlooked by other methods.

However, the main criticism of Byzantine Priority is that it often neglects or downplays the importance of other text-types, such as the Alexandrian, which is generally considered to be earlier and closer to the original text. Critics argue that the sheer number of manuscripts does not necessarily imply greater accuracy or reliability and that the Byzantine text-type can sometimes reflect a later, more harmonized version of the text.

Despite these criticisms, the work of Robinson, Hodges, and Farstad has contributed to the ongoing debate in New Testament textual criticism and has encouraged scholars to reevaluate the role of the Byzantine text-type in reconstructing the original text.[683]

5. **Documentary Approach**: The Documentary Approach to New Testament textual criticism, as advocated by scholars like F. J. A. Hort, Ernest C. Colwell, and Philip W. Comfort, focuses on the study of individual manuscripts, text-types, and families, with the goal of reconstructing the original text by examining the genealogical relationships between these documents.

The main principles of the Documentary Approach are:

a. **Textual genealogy**: This approach emphasizes the importance of understanding the relationships between manuscripts, text-types, and families in order to trace the development and transmission of the text. Scholars examine the shared readings, omissions, and variations in the manuscripts to establish the most likely genealogical lineage.

b. **Text-types and families**: The Documentary Approach gives significant weight to the identification and analysis of distinct text-types, such

---

[683] David Alan Black, New Testament Textual Criticism: A Concise Guide (Grand Rapids, MI.: Baker Books, 1994), 39.

as Alexandrian, Western, and Byzantine, as well as smaller manuscript families. Each text-type or family is evaluated based on its age, geographical distribution, and textual characteristics.

c. **External evidence**: The Documentary Approach relies heavily on external evidence, including the age and quality of the manuscripts, their geographical distribution, and the patristic citations (quotations from early church fathers). This approach tends to prioritize older manuscripts and text-types that are considered to be closer to the original text, such as the Alexandrian text-type.

d. **Critical editing**: Scholars using the Documentary Approach often engage in critical editing, a process in which they compare and analyze the variant readings in the manuscripts and then produce a critical edition of the text that represents their best reconstruction of the original.

The strengths of the Documentary Approach lie in its systematic and comprehensive examination of the manuscript evidence and its emphasis on the genealogical relationships between the manuscripts. By focusing on text-types and families, this approach can provide valuable insights into the transmission history of the New Testament text.

However, the main criticism of the Documentary Approach is that some fell that it can sometimes prioritize certain text-types or families at the expense of others, potentially overlooking valuable readings in less favored text-types, such as the Byzantine. This just is not the case, as the Documentary Approach does consider all manuscript families. Additionally, the reconstruction of the original text based on genealogical relationships can be complex and subjective, as it often involves making difficult decisions about which readings are more likely to be original.

Despite these challenges, the Documentary Approach has been influential in the field of New Testament textual criticism and has contributed to a better understanding of the textual transmission history and the relationships between the manuscripts.

This author's approach to New Testament Textual Studies is almost identical to Philip W. Comfort. I started my research and studies in NTTC in 1996. Metzger's TEXT OF THE NEW TESTAMENT was the book to read. I respect the textual scholars from the 1700s to the 21st century, some being J. J. Griesbach (1745–1812), Karl Lachmann (1793-1851), to Samuel Tregelles (1813–1875), to Constantin von Tischendorf (1815–1874), to Westcott (1825 – 1901) and Hort (1828 – 1892), to the Nestles and Alands of the Nestle Aland Text.

The Coherence-Based Genealogical Method (CBGM)

The Coherence-Based Genealogical Method (CBGM) is a computational approach to textual criticism, developed by the Institute for New Testament Textual Research (INTF) in Münster, Germany. The goal of this method is to reconstruct the genealogical relationships among the thousands of existing manuscripts of the New Testament, in order to determine the most likely original text.

The CBGM operates on the principle of "coherence," which refers to the consistency of readings found within a group of related manuscripts. The method involves a series of steps:

1. **Collecting and analyzing manuscript data**: The CBGM starts with the collection and analysis of data from thousands of Greek New Testament manuscripts, including information about their text, date, and geographical origin.

2. **Comparing textual variants**: The CBGM analyzes the differences between the manuscripts, known as textual variants. It then quantifies the relationships between these variants, calculating the degree of agreement between them.

3. **Constructing a local stemma**: For each textual variant, the CBGM constructs a "local stemma," which is a hypothetical family tree that shows the relationships between the manuscripts containing that variant. This process involves comparing the coherence of various possible stemmata and selecting the one that best explains the available data.

4. **Merging local stemmata into a global stemma**: The CBGM then combines the local stemmata into a "global stemma," which is a comprehensive family tree representing the relationships between all the manuscripts under consideration.

5. **Assessing the initial text**: Based on the global stemma, the CBGM identifies the most likely original text of the New Testament, also known as the "initial text." This text is the one that best explains the relationships among the existing manuscripts and the development of the textual tradition.

Critics of the CBGM argue that the method is too complex and relies too heavily on computer algorithms, making it difficult for scholars to understand and evaluate its results. However, proponents of the CBGM argue that it represents a significant advancement in the field of textual criticism, offering a more objective and reliable approach to reconstructing the original text of the New Testament.

Aland's Local-Genealogical Method

Aland's Local-Genealogical Method is a textual criticism approach developed by Kurt Aland, who argued that it is impossible to determine the original New Testament text by using a single manuscript family tree. Instead, he suggested that decisions must be made on a case-by-case basis, considering both external and internal criteria. This method has been criticized for leading to extensive eclecticism, where editors make decisions about the original text on a variant-unit basis, resulting in potential inconsistencies.

The Local-Genealogical Method assumes that any manuscript may have preserved the original text for a specific variant unit. However, this leads to a problem when editors must decide what the authors most likely wrote for each variant unit. This can result in atomistic eclecticism, where editors accept or reject manuscript readings based on internal evidence, leading to potential inconsistencies within single verses.

Several examples of such inconsistencies can be found in the New Testament, such as Mark 6:51, Matthew 8:21, John 9:4, and Romans 8:11. In each case, the selection of variant readings seems to be influenced by eclecticism, often prioritizing internal evidence over strong documentary attestation. This can result in accepting one manuscript's reading in one part of a verse and rejecting the same manuscript's reading in another part of the same verse.

To address this issue, it is suggested that textual critics should first determine the best manuscripts or groups of manuscripts for each specific book or section of the New Testament. Once these are identified, the burden of proof for any textual variation is to show that these manuscripts do not have the original wording. Transcriptional errors should be considered first, followed by internal evidence criteria. However, strong arguments on internal grounds are required to overthrow strong documentary attestation.

In conclusion, Aland's Local-Genealogical Method is an approach to New Testament textual criticism that focuses on making decisions on a variant-unit basis, considering both external and internal criteria. Despite its potential for leading to inconsistencies due to atomistic eclecticism, it remains an important contribution to the field of textual criticism. Critics should be well-versed in each manuscript and scribe's tendencies to make informed decisions about the original text.

Metzger's Evaluation of Variant Readings Based on Text-Types

Given the vast number of individual manuscripts, textual critics face the challenge of understanding the unique characteristics of each manuscript. To address this, many critics, including renowned textual critic Bruce Metzger, classify the manuscripts into text-types, which are then used to evaluate textual variants. Metzger identified four primary text-types: Alexandrian, Western, Caesarean, and Byzantine, each of which warrants further explanation.

1. Alexandrian Manuscripts

Alexandrian manuscripts were produced by scribes trained in the Alexandrian scriptoral tradition, considered the best in Greco-Roman times. These scribes were skilled in creating accurate and well-crafted copies. New Testament manuscripts include early (or proto-Alexandrian) and later Alexandrian manuscripts. Generally, earlier manuscripts are purer, as they are closer to the original writings and exhibit minimal creative interaction with the text.

A notable example of a faithful transmission is the high percentage of textual agreement between 𝔓75 and Codex Vaticanus (B), supporting Hort's theory that Codex Vaticanus traces back to an early, pure text. Metzger (1992) lists numerous Alexandrian witnesses, categorized as "Proto-Alexandrian" and "Later Alexandrian."

2. Western Manuscripts

The "Western" text is a loosely defined category, characterized by scribal expansion, harmonization, and amelioration. Proponents of this text-type argue that it likely developed in the mid-to-late second century in Western Christendom. This version of the Gospels, Acts, and Paul's Epistles circulated in North Africa, Italy, and Gaul, as well as Egypt and other Eastern locations. The Western text is represented in Old Latin manuscripts, Syriac manuscripts, and the D-text, and is prevalent in the writings of Marcion, Tatian, Irenaeus, and Tertullian. Metzger (1992) lists several "Western" witnesses.

3. Caesarean Manuscripts

A small group of manuscripts, known as the Caesarean text, emerged when scholars such as Streeter and Lake demonstrated that Origen brought a text from Egypt to Caesarea, which was then transported to Jerusalem. This text, exhibiting a mix of Alexandrian and Western readings, is apparent in several Gospel manuscripts, including 𝔓45, W, family 1 (f1), family 13 (f13), Θ, 565, and 700.

4. Byzantine Manuscripts

The Byzantine manuscripts constitute the largest group and are typically the furthest removed from the original text in most New Testament sections, with the notable exception of the book of Revelation. Several Byzantine manuscripts preserve a purer form of the text in Revelation. Metzger lists numerous Byzantine manuscripts.

According to Metzger (1992), a variant reading supported by a combination of Alexandrian and Western witnesses is generally superior to other readings. However, he also emphasizes the importance of evaluating all variant readings in light of both transcriptional and intrinsic probabilities, and the possibility that the original reading may be preserved in any group of manuscripts, even in rare instances within the Koine or Byzantine text.

It is crucial to consider that diverse testimony among later manuscripts signals the reading's widespread copying in various church sectors, but does not necessarily validate its originality. Early and diverse documentary support is essential in determining the originality of a reading.

In summary, Metzger's approach to evaluating variant readings based on text-types offers valuable insights for textual critics. By categorizing manuscripts into Alexandrian, Western, Caesarean, and Byzantine text-types, critics can better understand the origins, characteristics, and transmission histories of these texts.

However, it is essential to remember that diverse testimony among later manuscripts might not necessarily indicate the originality of a reading. Instead, critics should prioritize early and diverse documentary support when assessing the originality of a reading. This approach allows for a more nuanced and comprehensive understanding of the New Testament manuscripts and their variant readings, contributing to the ongoing quest for the original text of the New Testament.

The Importance of the Documentary Approach

Reasoned eclecticism, or the local-genealogical method, often prioritizes internal evidence over external evidence, which can lead to atomistic eclecticism. In order to recover the original text, it is crucial to prioritize external evidence. Westcott and Hort, in their work on The New Testament in the Original Greek, stressed the importance of documentary evidence over internal evidence.

Colwell similarly emphasized the importance of considering documentary evidence and urged scholars to reconstruct the history of the manuscript tradition. However, many scholars were skeptical about reconstructing a stemma, or a manuscript family tree, for the Greek New Testament. A stemma can help scholars understand the relationships between manuscripts, their origins, and their associations, and it may reveal that some of the earliest manuscripts are the closest to the original text.

One key piece of evidence for the importance of documentary considerations is the second-century papyrus 𝔓75. This manuscript, containing the Gospels of Luke and John, has been recognized as a highly accurate copy. Its close textual relationship with Codex Vaticanus demonstrates that it was not the result of a fourth-century recension but a direct copy of an early, accurate manuscript.

Prior to the discovery of 𝔓75, scholars believed that second- and third-century papyri displayed a text in flux, characterized by individual independence. They thought that scribes in Alexandria must have used several such manuscripts to produce a good recension, as seen in Codex Vaticanus. However, 𝔓75's close affinity with Vaticanus disproved this theory, revealing that Vaticanus was a copy of a manuscript much like 𝔓75.

The discovery of 𝔓75 also changed Kurt Aland's thinking about the textual history of the New Testament. Aland used to describe second- and third-century manuscripts as exhibiting a text in flux or a mixed text, but after the discovery of 𝔓75, he stated that a recension of the text at Alexandria in the fourth century was no longer a valid supposition.

Gordon Fee argued that there was no Alexandrian recension before the time of 𝔓75 and that both 𝔓75 and Vaticanus represented a relatively pure form of preservation from the original text. This suggested that the original text of Luke and John was virtually preserved in 𝔓75.

Despite these findings, some scholars remain unconvinced that the 𝔓75/B type of text is superior to another early text called the Western text. This form of text circulated primarily in western regions and was used by early Christian figures such as Marcion, Irenaeus, Tertullian, and Cyprian. However, many scholars recognize that the Western text is not a true text-type, but rather a loose categorization of early non-Alexandrian texts.

Critics argue that the preference for 𝔓75 and B is based on subjective appreciation rather than theoretical reconstruction. However, many textual critics who have worked extensively with actual manuscripts maintain that manuscripts like 𝔓75 and B represent the best textual purity, as they contain fewer errors, expansions, harmonizations, and interpolations than Western manuscripts.

In conclusion, it is essential to prioritize documentary considerations in textual criticism to better understand the relationships between manuscripts and their origins. 𝔓75's discovery has significantly impacted the field, demonstrating the importance of documentary evidence and providing insights into the transmission history of the New Testament. This evidence supports the notion that some of the earliest manuscripts, such as 𝔓75 and Codex Vaticanus, may be the closest replications of the original text.

Determining the Original Text

As we've discussed, there are numerous instances in the New Testament where ancient manuscripts, translations, and quotations from early church figures differ. With so many variations, how can we determine the original text of the New Testament? How can we know what the inspired authors actually wrote?

Firstly, it's essential to remember that despite the significant number of variations, most of the manuscript texts agree with each other. Secondly, most of these variations do not impact the overall meaning of the text. Only a few variants present meanings that may be considered false, usually due to scribal errors found in a single manuscript or a small number of them.

Therefore, the purpose of studying these manuscripts is not to determine if the New Testament teaches specific fundamental truths, but rather to decide on minor details and subtle nuances. Some might question the necessity of such studies if no significant truths are at stake. However, the New Testament holds such immense importance that any effort to bring our understanding closer to the original text or to confirm that our current text is as close to the original as possible is undoubtedly worthwhile.

Most individuals, of course, lack the expertise to study the Greek manuscripts and must rely on translations or versions in their native languages. This is entirely appropriate. These readers trust the decisions made by the translators of the versions they are reading. Even so, these readers may sometimes wonder about differences between various translations. So, how do we decide between the differences in the manuscripts to determine which version is most likely the original text?

Textual scholars employ various methods and principles to assess the numerous variations and determine the most probable original reading. These methods involve analyzing both internal and external evidence, as well as considering the history and context of the manuscripts. Internal evidence looks at factors such as the writing style of the author, the context of the passage, and the likelihood of scribal errors or intentional changes. External evidence examines the manuscripts themselves, their dates, and the geographical distribution of the readings.

By carefully considering both internal and external evidence, textual critics can make informed decisions about which reading is most likely to be the original. This process is not infallible, and some variations may remain unresolved. However, the extensive study of these manuscripts has led to a high degree of confidence in our current understanding of the New Testament text, ensuring that it remains a reliable source of spiritual guidance and historical insight.

Determining the Original Reading

The formatting below is similar to and borrowed from Philip W. Comfort, New Testament Text and Translation Commentary: Commentary on the Variant Readings of the Ancient New Testament Manuscripts and How They Relate to the Major English Translations (Carol Stream, IL: Tyndale House Publishers, Inc., 2008)

Matthew 5:44 - Analyzing Textual Variants

In Matthew 5:44, there are two primary readings:

1. **WH NU**: "pray for those persecuting you" Supported by: ℵ B f1 itk syrc, cop Origen

2. **Variant/TR**: "bless those who curse you, do good to those who hate you, pray for those who despitefully use you and persecute you" Supported by: D L W Θ f13 33 Maj

The textual evidence favors the shorter reading (WH NU) for three reasons: (1) the Greek manuscripts supporting the shorter reading are from the 4th century, which is one century earlier than those supporting the longer reading (5th century and later); (2) the quotations from early church fathers supporting the shorter reading come from earlier sources; and (3) the additional words in the longer reading (variant/TR) appear to have been borrowed from Luke's account of the Sermon on the Mount (Luke 6:27-28). If the longer reading had originally been in Matthew's gospel, there would be no reasonable explanation for its removal.

Although Jesus did teach that we should bless those who curse us and do good to those who hate us, these specific words were not recorded by Matthew but by Luke. It seems that Jesus gave several similar sermons, using varying language as He saw fit. Consequently, Matthew's "Sermon on the Mount" is not an exact replica of Luke's "Sermon on the Plain." However, some scribes felt compelled to harmonize the two gospels in passages they believed were describing the same event. The Textus Receptus (TR) includes most of these harmonizations, which were then translated into the King James Version (KJV) and the New King James Version (NKJV). Most modern translations do not include this harmonization in Matthew 5:44.

Matthew 6:13 - Analyzing Textual Variants

In Matthew 6:13, there are six primary variants related to the doxology at the end of the Lord's Prayer:

1. **WH NU**: Omit doxology at end of prayer Supported by: ℵ B D Z 0170 f1

2. **Variant 1**: Add αμην ("amen") Supported by: 17 vgcl

3. **Variant 2**: Add "because yours is the power forever." Supported by: itk syrp

4. **Variant 3**: Add "because yours is the power and the glory forever. Amen." Supported by: copsa (Didache omits αμην)

5. **Variant 4**: Add "because yours is the kingdom and the glory forever. Amen." Supported by: syrc

6. **Variant 5/TR**: Add οτι σου εστιν η βασιλεια και η δυναμις και η δοξα εις τους αιωνας. αμην. "because yours is the kingdom and the power and the glory forever. Amen." Supported by: L W Δ Θ 0233 f13 33 Maj syr

7. **Variant 6**: Add οτι σου εστιν η βασιλεια του πατρος και του υιου και του αγιου πνευματος εις τους αιωνας. αμην. "because yours is the kingdom of the Father and the Son and the Holy Spirit forever. Amen." Supported by: 157 (1253) None

The textual evidence suggests that the original version of the Lord's Prayer concluded with a petition for deliverance from evil. The diversity of variants and their gradual expansion indicate that the doxology was added later. Early scribes adapted terms like "power" and "glory" from verses such as 1 Chr 29:11, Ps 62:3 LXX, Dan 2:37, 1 Pet 4:11, and Jude 25. The Didache, a compilation of early church traditions, contains a longer form of the Lord's Prayer, which may have been in use as early as the end of the 1st century. This form gained popularity due to its inclusion in the Textus Receptus (TR) and the King James Version (KJV).

Modern translations generally exclude the doxology, but it remains ingrained in Christian tradition and is still recited in private and public worship. The doxology is likely included because it offers a glorious and uplifting conclusion to the prayer, which would have motivated early scribes to add it.

Matthew 8:28 - Analyzing Textual Variants

Main Text (WH NU): τὴν χώραν τῶν Γαδαρηνῶν "the country of the Gadarenes" Supported by: (Γαζαρηνων ℵ*) B C Θ syr,p,

Variant 1 (TR): την χωραν των Γεργεσηνων "the country of the Gergesenes" Supported by: 2ℵ L W f1, Maj

Variant 2: την χωραν των Γερασηνων "the country of the Gerasenes" Supported by: 892c syrhmg copsa

In each Synoptic Gospel that records Jesus' visit to the region on the eastern side of the Sea of Galilee (where he healed the demoniac), there is textual variation concerning the region's name. In Matthew 8:28, Mark 5:1, and Luke 8:26, all three readings occur: "Gerasenes," "Gergesenes," and "Gadarenes." The textual variations in the three synoptic gospels reflect the scribes' confusion (Bruce 1979, 144).

Origen (Comm. Jo. 5.41.24), while commenting on John 1:28, discussed this confusion. He objected to Gadara (a reading he saw in a few manuscripts), located about five miles southeast of the Sea of Galilee. He also rejected Gerasa, situated thirty miles southeast of the Sea of Galilee. Origen suggested the name Gergesa based on some local tradition and because its name supposedly meant "dwelling of those that have driven away." Fond of finding etymological significance in names, Origen said the name suited the place because the citizens asked Jesus to leave their territory.

"Gadarenes" has the best testimony in Matthew and adequately suits the context for the story. Josephus (Life 42.9) stated that Gadara had territory and villages on the border of the lake; one of these villages must have been called "Gerasa," the name found in the best manuscripts in Mark 5:1 and Luke 8:26. The first variant, "Gergesenes," likely demonstrates the influence Origen had on later traditions, while the second variant, "Gerasenes," represents scribal harmonization to Mark 5:1 and Luke 8:26.

Mark 9:44, 46 - Analyzing Textual Variants

Main Text (WH NU): omit verses 44 and 46 Supported by: ℵ B C L W Δ Ψ 0274 f1 28 565 itk syrs cop

Variant (TR): add verses 44 and 46 (which are identical to 9:48 in NU) οπου ο σκωληξ αυτων ου τελευτα και το πυρ ου σβεννυται. "where the worm does not die and the fire is not extinguished" Supported by: A D Θ f Maj

Although one could argue that scribes omitted these verses, considering the repetition unnecessary, such deletion is unlikely to occur in manuscripts with as much diversity as those supporting the absence of these verses. On the other hand, verses 44 and 46 were likely added as a sort of prophetic refrain that enhances oral reading. Many textual variants entered the textual stream due to scribes improving the text for oral reading in the church, and this case serves as a classic example. Several modern English versions omit these verses, but they include notes for readers familiar with their place in the KJV tradition. By retaining the verses in the text, the HCSB maintains the KJV tradition.

Luke 22:43-44 - Analyzing Textual Variants

Main Text (TR WH NU): include verses 43-44 "43 And an angel from heaven appeared to him, strengthening him. 44 And being in agony, he prayed more earnestly, and his sweat became like great drops of blood falling down on the ground." Supported by: ℵ*, D L Θ Ψ 0171 0233 f Maj (with asterisks or obeli: Δc Πc 892c 1079 1195 1216 copMSS) most Greek MSS according to Anastasius MSS according to Jerome MSS according to Epiphanius, Hilary Justin Irenaeus Hippolytus Eusebius

Variant 1: place verses after Matt 26:39 Supported by: f13 (13*) and some lectionaries with additions

Variant 2: omit verses Supported by: 𝔓69 𝔓 ℵ A B N T W itf syrs copsa some Greek MSS according to Anastasius MSS according to Jerome some Greek and Old Latin MSS according to Hilary Marcion Clement Origen

These verses are absent from ancient witnesses across diverse text-types. Other factors suggesting their non-originality include (a) some manuscripts marking them with asterisks or obeli, indicating doubt about their originality, and (b) their placement after Matt 26:39 in family 13 manuscripts and several lectionaries. Despite this, their presence in many manuscripts (some ancient) and their citation by various early Christian writers indicate the account's antiquity.

It is more likely that these verses were added from an early source of extra-canonical traditions concerning Jesus' life and passion, rather than being original but omitted by those who found Jesus' display of human weakness inconsistent with his divine omnipotence. Nevertheless, the passage is retained in double square brackets in some texts due to its antiquity and importance in the textual tradition. Modern translations are divided: some omit the verses (RSV), some include them (NIV, NJB, REB, TEV, TOB, Seg), and others place them within square brackets (FC) or double brackets (NRSV).

The absence of Luke 22:43-44 from the manuscript P.Oxy. 2383 (designated as 𝔓69) was not acknowledged in the third edition of the United Bible Societies (UBS3), but it is now indicated in the fourth edition (UBS4) in parentheses. The editors of 𝔓69 were convinced that the only explanation for the large gap in the manuscript (from Luke 22:41 to Luke 22:45) is that the copyist's source did not include Luke 22:43-44 and the scribe's eye moved from προσηυχετο in 22:41 to προσευχης in 22:45. This was because they calculated that these two words would have been located at the end of lines, four lines apart. The manuscript 0171 should be listed as "vid" (as in UBS4), as it only shows a part of 22:44, but there are no obeli or asterisks, as indicated in UBS4.

The manuscript evidence for this textual variation strongly supports the exclusion of Luke 22:43-44. This is evident from the impressive list of Greek manuscripts (dating from the 2nd to 5th century) that favor its exclusion, including 𝔓69, 𝔓, ℵ, B, T, and W. Additionally, manuscripts that mark the passage with obeli or cross it out, such as the first corrector of ℵ, further support its dubious nature. Its transposition to Matt 26 in some manuscripts and lectionaries indicates that it was a free-floating passage that could be inserted into any passion narrative.

On the other hand, the manuscripts that support the inclusion of the verses are fewer and date from the 5th century or later. The earliest witness is 0171vid, which dates to around 300. However, several early church fathers, such as Justin, Irenaeus, Hippolytus, Dionysius, and Eusebius, recognized this portion as part of Luke's gospel.

Examinations of the writings of early church fathers reveal that many of them noted both the presence and absence of the "bloody sweat" passage in the manuscripts they were familiar with. For instance, Epiphanius indicated that the verses were found in some "uncorrected copies" of Luke, suggesting that the Gospel of Luke was being copied in two forms, one with and one without the "bloody sweat" passage, in the early stages of textual transmission.

Metzger, as well as Westcott and Hort, believed that it was more likely that the verses were added from an early source (oral or written) of extra-canonical traditions concerning the life and passion of Jesus, rather than deleted by those who felt the account of Jesus being overcome by human weakness was incompatible with his sharing the divine omnipotence of the Father. Despite considering the passage to be a later addition to the text, a majority of the Committee decided to retain the words in the text but enclose them within double square brackets due to its antiquity and importance in the textual tradition.

As a result, Luke 22:43-44 shares a similar position with the pericope of the adulterous woman (John 7:53-8:11) in the NU text, as both are kept in the text due to their place in tradition, even though they are not part of the original writings. Most Bible translations keep these passages in the text, providing notes about their absence in ancient witnesses, perpetuating their authenticity in the minds of Christians who rely solely on translations. The only exception was the Revised Standard Version (RSV), which excluded both passages. However, due to outside pressure, John 7:53-8:11 was restored to the text after its initial printing, but Luke 22:43-44 was not.

Most Christians believe that the detail about Jesus' passion in Luke 22:43-44, which is often referred to as the "bloody sweat" passage, is authentic and came from Luke as he received it from the eyewitnesses of Jesus (Luke 1:1-4). However, it is often misinterpreted to mean that Jesus was sweating blood, when in fact, the text says that he was sweating so profusely that it appeared like blood dripping from a wound.

John 7:53-8:11 - A More Constructive Comprehensive Explanation

The Pericope Adulterae, found in John 7:53-8:11, is a passage that has been widely debated among scholars due to its presence in some New Testament manuscripts and absence from others. Its origins, placement, and authorship have been questioned, as there is substantial external evidence against its inclusion as part of the original Gospel of John.

1. **Manuscripts that omit the passage**: The passage is absent from many early and diverse manuscripts, including the oldest forms of the Syriac, Sahadic, sub-Achmimic, and older Bohairic versions. It is also missing from some Armenian manuscripts, Old Georgian versions, the Gothic version, and several Old Latin manuscripts.

2. **Manuscripts that include the passage**: Despite the strong evidence against its inclusion, the passage is present in other manuscripts, such as D, F, G, H, K, M, U, and Γ. It is also found in various positions in different manuscripts, indicating uncertainty about its original placement.

3. **Stylistic and contextual differences**: The style and vocabulary of the passage differ noticeably from the rest of the Fourth Gospel, and its presence interrupts the narrative flow between John 7:52 and 8:12.

4. **Indications of historical truth**: The account has signs of historical truth and seems to be a piece of oral tradition that circulated in parts of the Western church. This oral tradition was eventually incorporated into various manuscripts at different locations.

5. **Copyists' uncertainty**: In many of the manuscripts that contain the passage, it is marked with asterisks or obeli, indicating that the copyists were aware that it was not part of the original text.

6. **Inclusion in double square brackets**: Although the passage is not considered part of the original Fourth Gospel, it is enclosed in double square brackets in certain editions (NA27 and UBS4) due to its antiquity and significance in the Christian tradition.

The pericope of the adulteress (7:53–8:11) is not found in any of the earliest manuscripts of the New Testament, including 𝔓66 and 𝔓75, which date back to the second to fourth centuries. The other witnesses, such as the fourth-century codices (ℵ A B C T), Diatessaron, the early versions, and most of the early church fathers, also exclude this passage. Its first appearance in a Greek manuscript is in Codex D from around 400, but it was not included in other Greek manuscripts until the ninth century. Although the story may have been circulating in the oral tradition as early as the second century, the pericope's appearance in the written text is an example of how oral tradition can eventually be incorporated into the written text.

Many scholars have pointed out that the vocabulary used in the pericope is not consistent with the rest of John and that its insertion in the text greatly disrupts the narrative flow. The pericope also interrupts the connection between 7:40–52 and 8:12–20. The internal evidence, therefore, suggests that the pericope was not written by John.

Despite the strong evidence against its Johannine authorship, the Pericope Adulterae remains an important passage in the biblical tradition and continues to be studied and commented on by scholars. Its historical and spiritual value makes it a significant part of the Christian faith, even though its origins and placement in the Gospel of John are certain. It must be emphatically stated that 7:53–8:11 was not part of the Gospel of John.

Romans 11:6 - Analyzing Textual Variants

Main Text (WH NU): οὐκέτι γίνεται χάρις "it [grace] would no longer be grace" Supported by: 𝔓46 ℵ* A C D F G 1739 cop

Variant 1 (TR): ουκετι γινεται χαρις. ει δε εξ εργων ουκετι εστι χαρις, επει το εργον ουκετι εστιν εργον "it [grace] would no longer be grace. But if it is of works, then it is no longer grace; otherwise work is no longer work." Supported by: (B omits εστι and replaces final εργον with χαρις) 2ℵ Ψ 33 Maj (syr)

The textual variants in Romans 11:6 revolve around whether the passage should include the additional sentence found in the variant/TR. In analyzing the textual evidence, the main text (WH NU) has significant support, including 𝔓46, ℵ*, A, C, D, F, G, and 1739.

The variant reading, on the other hand, has a smaller but still considerable group of witnesses, including 2ℵ, Ψ, 33, and the Majority text. Notably, this variant includes an additional sentence: "But if it is of works, then it is no longer grace; otherwise work is no longer work."

There is no compelling reason to account for the omission of the second sentence in the main text if it were originally part of the epistle. Consequently, the variant is likely an interpolation that may have been created as early as the fourth century. Furthermore, this gloss does not help clarify the passage's message. The main text clearly conveys the nature of grace as being a free gift, not a reward for doing work. The variant's additional sentence, rather than enhancing this meaning, detracts from it with the ambiguous statement, "otherwise work is no longer work."

Considering the strong textual evidence supporting the main text and the lack of clarity added by the variant's additional sentence, the main text's shorter reading is more likely to be the original version of Romans 11:6.

Romans 16:24 - Analyzing Textual Variants

Main Text (WH NU): omit verse Supported by: 𝔓46 𝔓61 ℵ (A) B C 1739 it cop

Variant 1 (TR): include verse (same as in 16:20—see note) Supported by: D (F G omit Ιησου Χριστου [Jesus Christ]) Ψ Maj syrh

The textual issue in Romans 16:24 revolves around whether the verse should be included or omitted. The main text (WH NU) omits the verse, and this reading is strongly supported by the earliest manuscripts, including 𝔓46, 𝔓61, ℵ, A, B, C, and 1739.

On the other hand, the variant (TR) includes the verse, which is the same as in 16:20. This reading is supported by a smaller group of witnesses, including D, Ψ, and the Majority text. The Western manuscripts (D, F, G) add the benediction at 16:24 because they do not include 16:25–27. The verse's inclusion in the TR and Majority Text leads to its presence in the KJV and NKJV translations.

The omission of this verse is more plausible, as it is likely that a scribe (or scribes) copied the verse from 16:20, thinking it was appropriate to follow the postscript (see note on 16:20). All modern translations, following superior testimony, do not include the verse. However, these translations provide a textual note concerning this verse due to its presence in traditional English translations.

In summary, considering the strong textual evidence supporting the omission of Romans 16:24 and the fact that it duplicates the content found in 16:20, it is more likely that the original text of Romans did not include this verse.

1 Timothy 3:16 - Analyzing Textual Variants

Main Text (WH NU): ὃς ἐφανερώθη "who was manifested" Supported by: ℵ* A* C* F G 33 Didymus

Variant 1: ὃ εφανερωθη "which was manifested" Supported by: D*

Variant 2/TR: θεος εφανερωθη "God was manifested" Supported by: אc Ac C2 D2 Ψ 1739 Maj

The textual problem in 1 Timothy 3:16 generated significant debate in the nineteenth century, as it deals with the doctrine of the incarnation. The issue revolves around whether the original text read "who was manifested," "which was manifested," or "God was manifested."

The main text (WH NU) reads "who was manifested," supported by the earliest manuscripts, including א*, A*, C*, F, G, and 33. The first variant reads "which was manifested," found in manuscript D*. The second variant, "God was manifested," is the reading in the TR and is supported by later corrected manuscripts and the Majority text. This reading is also found in the KJV translation.

It has been suggested that a scribe mistook OC (equivalent to ος) for Θ͞C (the nomen sacrum for θεος) and made the change. However, it is unlikely that multiple scribes would make this error. The more plausible explanation is that scribes intentionally altered the text to emphasize that it was "God" who was manifested in the flesh.

Although some scholars feared that the doctrine of the incarnation would be undermined by the reading "he who was manifest in the flesh," the subject of the verse is still Christ. Most commentators identify "who" (or "he") with Christ, the God-man who revealed his deity through his humanity. Modern English translations, beginning with the ASV and ERV, reflect the superior text, and most provide the variant readings in marginal notes. The debate surrounding this textual issue does not undermine the doctrine of the incarnation but merely highlights the importance of accurately preserving the original text.

1 Peter 5:8 - Analyzing Textual Variants

Main Text (NU): ζητῶν [τινα] καταπιεῖν "seeking someone to devour" Supported by: Maj

Variant 1/TR: ζητων τίνα καταπιειν "seeking whom he may devour" Supported by: L P 1739

Variant 2/WH: ζητων καταπιειν "seeking to devour" Supported by: B Ψ 0206

The textual issue in 1 Peter 5:8 involves the precise wording of the description of the devil's actions, whether he is "seeking someone to devour," "seeking whom he may devour," or simply "seeking to devour." The manuscripts 𝔓72, א, and A are not listed above, as the word τινα is unaccented in these manuscripts and could have been interpreted as either a definite or indefinite pronoun by ancient readers. In the majority of later manuscripts, the word was accented to indicate a specific interpretation.

The second variant, "seeking to devour," has the support of two fourth-century manuscripts (B and 0206) and is likely the original reading. This variant probably gave rise to the other variants, each of which adds a substantive after ζητων ("seeking"). With this reading, the focus is on the activity of the devil, who is described as a lion-like figure seeking to devour, rather than the object of his action, which can be assumed. This interpretation emphasizes the relentless and dangerous nature of the devil's pursuits, urging believers to remain vigilant and resist his advances.

Jude 5 - Analyzing Textual Variants

Main Text (WH) NU: πάντα ὅτι [ὁ] κύριος ἅπαξ "[knowing that] the Lord having once for all" Supported by: C* (ℵ Ψ omit ο) syrh Examples of English translations: RSVmg, NRSV, ESVmg, NASB, NIV, TNIV, NEB, REB, NJB, NAB, NLTmg, HCSB

Variant 1: απαξ παντα, οτι Ιησους "[knowing] once for all, that Jesus" Supported by: A, B, 33, Cyril, Jerome, Bede

Variant 2: παντα, οτι Ιησους απαξ "[knowing] everything, that Jesus once" Supported by: 1739, 1881, Origen (according to mg), cop

Variant 3: απαξ παντα, οτι θεος Χριστος "[knowing] once for all, that God [the] Messiah (or, Messiah God)" Supported by: 𝔓72 (𝔓* παντας)

Variant 4: απαξ παντα, οτι ο θεος "[knowing] once for all, that God" Supported by: C2, vgMS

Variant 5/TR: απαξ τουτο, οτι ο κυριος "once [you knew] this, that the Lord" Supported by: (K L) Maj

The primary textual issue in Jude 5 concerns the identity of the one who delivered the people out of Egypt. The first two variants present "Jesus" as the deliverer, while the other variants use "Lord," "God," or "God the Messiah." The reading with "Jesus" is found in several important early manuscripts, including A, B, 33, 1739, 1881, and the writings of Origen, Cyril, Jerome, and Bede. 𝔓72 may also indirectly support this reading, as it contains a messianic title, "Christ."

From a textual perspective, it is easier to argue that the reading with "Jesus" is the original one, as scribes were not known for inventing difficult readings. Some scholars have suggested that Jude might have intended "Joshua" instead of "Jesus," but this is unlikely, as Joshua led the Israelites into Canaan, not out of Egypt. Instead, Jude likely viewed Jesus as Yahweh the Savior, present with the Israelites and operative in their deliverance from Egypt. Paul shared a similar view in 1 Corinthians 10:4 and 10:9.

The first English translation to adopt the reading with "Jesus" was NLT, with other recent versions such as TNIV and NET also adopting this reading. Most other English translations have included it in the margin. While the United Bible Societies' Greek New Testament initially contained the reading with "Jesus," a slim majority of editors later voted to change it to "Lord." Despite this change, the reading with "Jesus" should be considered the original and more accurate reading.

Revelation 11:8 - Analyzing Textual Variants

Main Text (WH) NU: ὁ κύριος αὐτῶν ἐσταυρώθη "their Lord was crucified" Supported by: ℵc, A, C, P, syr

Variant 1/TR: ο κυριος ημων εσταυρωθη "our Lord was crucified" Supported by: 1

Variant 2: ο κυριος εσταυρωθη "the Lord was crucified" Supported by: 𝔓47, ℵ*

The textual issue in Revelation 11:8 involves the identity of the Lord in relation to the witnesses or those in Jerusalem. The three textual variants show three different scribal perspectives on this issue.

The WH NU reading indicates that "the Lord" (referring to Jesus) is either the Lord of the two witnesses or the Lord of those in Jerusalem, symbolized by the names "Sodom and Egypt." This reading could be interpreted as Jesus being the Lord of the witnesses or the Lord of Jerusalem.

In contrast, variant 1, found in minuscule 1 and incorporated by Erasmus in the Textus Receptus, changes the text to "our Lord," reflecting a personalization of the text or an attempt to resolve a perceived theological issue. The question raised here is how Jesus could be the Lord of the city that crucified him.

The third variant, supported by the two earliest manuscripts (𝔓47 and ℵ*), is neutral because it lacks a pronoun and simply states that "the Lord was crucified." This reading could either be the original wording or a scribal alteration to remove the ambiguity of the expression "their Lord."

It is worth noting that the scribe of 𝔓47 wrote the verb "crucified" as a nomen sacrum with an unusual form: εστρω. While other early scribes (𝔓46, 𝔓66, 𝔓75) also used the nomen sacrum form for "cross" and "crucify," this is the only instance of its use in Revelation among extant papyri predating 300 C.E.

The preferred method of getting at the original words of the original text is the **documentary method**, which considers internal and external evidence, as well as all manuscripts, yet giving the greater weight to the trusted documents (dates of the manuscripts supporting a reading, the geographical distribution of the manuscripts, and the overall quality both of the individual manuscripts and textual "families."), and so, it is Codex Vaticanus and Codex Sinaiticus that are the deciding factor in going against the NU text.

Worksheet for New Testament Textual Criticism[684]

PASSAGE: _____

Various Readings		
Variant 1	Variant 2	Variant 3
Internal Evidence:	Internal Evidence:	Internal Evidence:
External Evidence:	External Evidence:	External Evidence:
What is the weight of the external evidence?		
What textual principles apply?		
Conclusion:		

---

[684] Paul D. Wegner, *A Student's Guide to Textual Criticism of the Bible: Its History, Methods & Results* (Downers Grove, IL: InterVarsity Press, 2006), 228.

CHAPTER XVII

The Collation and Classification of Manuscripts

Variant Reading(s): differing versions of a word or phrase found in two or more manuscripts within a variation unit. Variant readings are also called alternate readings. **Variation Unit**: any portion of text that exhibits variations in its reading between two or more different manuscripts. It is important to distinguish variation units from variant readings. Variation units are the places in the text where manuscripts disagree, and each variation unit has at least two variant readings. For example, in **COLOSSIANS 1:2**, we have "God our Father" in the following manuscripts (B D K L Ψ 33 1739 it syr cop) and "God our Father and the Lord Jesus Christ" in (א A C F G I Maj it (syrh**) cop Jerome). **COLOSSIANS 2:2** is a great example of a number of variants in a variation unit. We have the reading found in the critical texts WH NA and UBS "the mystery of God, Christ" in (P46 B), **variant 1** "the mystery of God, which is Christ" (D*), **variant 2** "the mystery of God" (D1 H P 1881), **variant 3** "the mystery of Christ" (81 (1739) itb) **variant 4** "the mystery of God, Father of Christ" (א* A C 048vid) **variant 5** "the mystery of God, even the Father of Christ" (2א Ψ 0208) **variant 6/TR** "the mystery of God and of the Father and of Christ" (D2 Maj syr**). Having so many variants is an indication that the scribes struggled with this text. Comparing the manuscripts with another is called collating.

Simple Textual Variant

Simple Textual Variant

John 3:13 The Greek-English New Testament Interlinear (GENTI) [WH NU]

<small>And no one has ascended into the heaven if not the (one) out of the heaven having descended, the Son</small>
13 καὶ οὐδεὶς ἀναβέβηκεν εἰς τὸν οὐρανὸν εἰ μὴ   ὁ   ἐκ τοῦ οὐρανοῦ καταβάς, ὁ υἱὸς
<small>of the   man.</small>
τοῦ ἀνθρώπου.

P66 P75 א B L T Ws 083 086 cop Diatessaron

John 3:13 Updated American Standard Version (UASV)

13 And no one has ascended into heaven except the one who descended from heaven, the Son of man.

John 3:13 variant/ Stephanus New Testament (TR1550)

<small>And no one has ascended into the heaven if not the (one) out of the heaven having descended, the Son</small>
13 καὶ οὐδεὶς ἀναβέβηκεν εἰς τὸν οὐρανὸν εἰ μὴ   ὁ   ἐκ τοῦ οὐρανοῦ καταβάς, ὁ υἱὸς
<small>of the   man.   who is in the   heaven</small>
τοῦ ἀνθρώπου **ο ωνεντωουρανω**

(A* omit ων) Θ Ψ 050 f1, Maj

John 3:13 New King James Version (NKJV)

13 No one has ascended to heaven but He who came down from heaven, *that is*, the Son of Man **who is in heaven**.

Collation: a base text of the Greek New Testament together with an apparatus of variant readings for any place in the text where the manuscripts selected for the collation disagree. Disagreements can range from a single letter to a phrase, and the latter sometimes includes the order of the words. Diacritical marks are noted as well, but of course, these marks are late additions and are subject to change at the will of the critic. The formal term for places of disagreement is "variation unit" (q.v.). - Don Wilkins

Collating in New Testament Textual Studies is comparing and analyzing one NT manuscript with another. One can only imagine the daunting task of comparing and analyzing every NT manuscript. This is especially true when we consider that the New Testament has 5,898 Greek New Testament manuscripts, 10,000 Latin manuscripts, and an additional 9,300 other manuscripts in such languages as Syriac, Slavic, Gothic, Ethiopic, Coptic, and Armenian. Then, we must consider the Scriptural quotations from the Apostolic Fathers of the late first and early second centuries C.E., as well as the churchmen who were called Apologists and other early Church Fathers near the middle of the second century C.E. through its end, and the Church Fathers of the third to the sixth centuries C.E. If it was not for the scholars who poured through these manuscripts, comparing and analyzing (collating) them, we would have no practical way of putting them to use.

Collating, comparing, and analyzing every manuscript is how we know what variants there are in a given variation unit. **Variant Reading(s)**: differing versions of a word or phrase found in two or more manuscripts within a variation unit. Variant readings are also called alternate readings. **Variation Unit**: any portion of text that exhibits variations in its reading between two or more different manuscripts. It is important to distinguish variation units from variant readings. Variation units are the places in the text where manuscripts disagree, and each variation unit has at least two variant readings. For example, in **Colossians 1:2**, we have [θεοῦ πατρὸς ἡμῶν] "God our Father" in the following manuscripts (B D K L Ψ 33 1739 it syr cop) and [θεου πατρος ημων και κυριου Ιησου Χριστου] "God our Father and the Lord Jesus Christ" in (ℵ A C F G I Maj it (syrh**) cop Jerome). **Matthew 22:30** is a great example of a number of variants in a variation unit. We have the reading found in WH NA and UBS [ὡς ἄγγελοι ἐν τῷ οὐρανῷ εἰσιν] "they are like angels in heaven" in (B D 700), **variant 1** [ως οι αγγελοι εν τω ουρανω εισιν] "they are like angels in heaven" (Θ f), variant 2 [ως αγγελοι θεου εν τω ουρανω εισιν] "the mystery of God" (D1 H P 1881), **variant 2**/TR "they are like angels of God in heaven" (ℵ L f¹³ 33; W Maj add οι before αγγελοι = the angels). Having so many variants is an indication that the scribes struggled with this text. Comparing the manuscripts with another is called collating.

In addition, in textual studies, collation is also comparing the manuscripts with a critical text like 1881 WH, 2012 NA (28th ed.), 2015 UBS (5th ed.), or 2017 THGNT. As you can see from Colossians 2:2, we refer to the first reading within the critical texts WH NU and the others are listed as variants, even the TR. By doing this, we have access to the entire Greek NT and its differences without having to look through all of the manuscripts. In this, the critical text (WH WH NU THGNT) is the standard upon which all of the other manuscripts are compared. Then, the differences are listed in the apparatus of the critical text. If more evidence were to come to light; then. a variant reading in the apparatus could very well be placed in the main text and the reading in the main text becomes a variant reading in the apparatus. Then again, more evidence could be discovered that adds more testimony to the reading in the critical text, reinforcing the decision that has already been made.

The textual scholar of a translation committee, for example, in certain circumstances should be willing to verify the decisions that have been made by the textual scholars of the critical text. For instance, there may be a reading that has long been disputed as to what the manuscript contains because of damage to that manuscript. Aside from this rare occasion, the textual scholars over the centuries and recent decades have compiled a storehouse of information on as they have collated the manuscripts for us. Nevertheless, the textual scholar working on a translation or another critical text could differ in the decision made by the manuscript evidence as well. As we have learned early on the NA text is supposed to be a reasoned eclectic text where the scholars consider internal and external evidence equally. However, the textual scholars of the NA text tend to lean toward internal evidence often. In other words, the textual scholars might refer to the excellent weighty evidence (P66, P75 ℵ B) in the first half of a verse and then ignore that same evidence in the second half of a verse, favoring internal evidence, which shows an inconsistency. This author favors the documentary approach in making textual decisions, which means that I look at both internal and external, giving a little extra weight to the external, which is less subjective. I have thus decided against a number of decisions made by the editors of the NU text. Below is one example.

Matthew 9:26 2019 *Greek-English New Testament Interlinear* (GENTI WH)

And went out the report of [about] her into whole the land that.

26 Καὶ ἐξῆλθεν ἡ φήμη **αὐτῆς** εἰς ὅλην τὴν γῆν ἐκείνην.

ΚΑΤΑ ΜΑΤΘΑΙΟΝ 9:26 2012 Nestle-Aland / Stephanus New Testament (TR NU TGNT SBLGNT)

And went out the report this into whole the land that.

26 Καὶ ἐξῆλθεν ἡ φήμη **αὕτη** εἰς ὅλην τὴν γῆν ἐκείνην.

Matthew 9:26 Updated American Standard Version (UASV)	Matthew 9:26 English Standard Version (ESV)	Matthew 9:26 New American Standard Bible (NASB)
26 And the **report about her** spread into that whole region.	26 And the **report of this** went through all that district.	26 This news spread throughout all that land.

GENTI εξηλθεν η φημη αυτης "the report of [about] her went out" ℵ C* Θ f¹ 33	Variant 1/TR WH NU TGNT SBLGNT εξηλθεν η φημη αυτη "this report went out" B W f¹³ Maj	Variant 2 εξηλθεν η φημη αυτου "his fame went out" D cop

The likely original wording in Matthew 9:14 is "the report of [about] her went out" (εξηλθεν η φημη αυτης) in good documentary witnesses ℵ C* Θ f¹ 33 and GENTI. We have **a variant**, "this report went out" (εξηλθεν η φημη αυτη) in B W f¹³ Maj and TR WH NU TGNT SBLGNT. There is a second variant, "his fame went out" (εξηλθεν η φημη αυτου) in D cop.

Some Sopherim (scribes) of the Hebrew Old Testament altered the text if they felt it showed irreverence for God or the attention was focused on something else instead of God Himself. In the marginal notes of the Masoretic text, there are notes that read: "This is one of the eighteen emendations of the Sopherim," or comparable words. "The report of [about] her went out" (εξηλθεν η φημη αυτης) was likely altered by the scribes who felt the attention was being given to the girl as opposed to the fact that it was Jesus who raised her from the dead. Therefore, the words "the **report about her**" was likely changed with one letter from αυτης [of her] to αυτη [this] making it "the **report of this**." Others made the change from αυτης [of her] to αυτου [of him], which would be similar to Luke 4:14 (καὶ φήμη ἐξῆλθεν καθ᾽ ὅλης τῆς περιχώρου περὶ αὐτοῦ) "and a report about him went out through all the surrounding country."

Example of a Collation

John 1:16	John 1:16	John 1:16	John 1:16
GENTI WH NU	p[66] p[75] א B C* D L 33	TR MAJ BYZ	A C[3] W[s] Θ Ψ f[1,]
[16] **ὅτι** ἐκ τοῦ πληρώματος αὐτοῦ ἡμεῖς πάντες ἐλάβομεν, καὶ χάριν ἀντὶ χάριτος·	[16] **ὅτι** ἐκ τοῦ πληρώματος αὐτοῦ ἡμεῖς πάντες ἐλάβομεν, καὶ χάριν ἀντὶ χάριτος·	[16] **Καὶ** ἐκ τοῦ πληρώματος αὐτοῦ ἡμεῖς πάντες ἐλάβομεν, καὶ χάριν ἀντὶ χάριτος.	[16] **Καὶ** ἐκ τοῦ πληρώματος αὐτοῦ ἡμεῖς πάντες ἐλάβομεν, καὶ χάριν ἀντὶ χάριτος.
[16] **For from** his fullness we have all received, and grace upon grace.	[16] **For from** his fullness we have all received, and grace upon grace.	[16] **And of** his fullness have we all received, and grace upon grace.	[16] **And of** his fullness have we all received, and grace upon grace.

On this Philip Comfort writes, "The replacement of **καὶ** for **ὅτι** is a scribal adjustment intended to make a more logical connection between 1:15 and 1:16. However, **ὅτι** in 1:16 connects with 1:14 inasmuch as 1:15 is a parenthetical statement (usually set off by parentheses in English translations). Connecting the end of 1:14 with **ὅτι** at the beginning of 1:16 gives this reading: "we saw his glory, glory as of the only Son of the Father, full of grace and truth … because (**ὅτι**) from his fullness we have all received, even grace added to grace." John was saying that he (and the other apostles) knew by experience that the Son of God was full of grace and truth because they had continually been recipients of that full supply."[685]

---

[685] Philip W. Comfort, *New Testament Text and Translation Commentary: Commentary on the Variant Readings of the Ancient New Testament Manuscripts and How They Relate to the Major English Translations* (Carol Stream, IL: Tyndale House Publishers, Inc., 2008), 254.

The originals were perfect in every sense because the authors were moved along by the Holy Spirit. The copyist was not inspired and, in some cases,, they were not even Christian but worked at scriptoriums. We had 1,400 years of mostly accidental errors and some intentional errors, and now we have 500 years of restoration. In these latter parts of the last day, it falls on textual scholars to give a restored text that is a mirror-like reflection of the original. We must remember that Westcott and Hort brought us so very close in 1881 as their text is 99.5% the same as the 2012 Nestle-Aland Greek New Testament. I believe that between WH and NA, we have a restored text of 99.99 percent. The literal translations today are based on these restored texts of WH and NA. This would not have been possible without collations. Modern technology has made it so much easier to collate. We can see from the Logos Bible Software below just how easy it is to compare the differences.

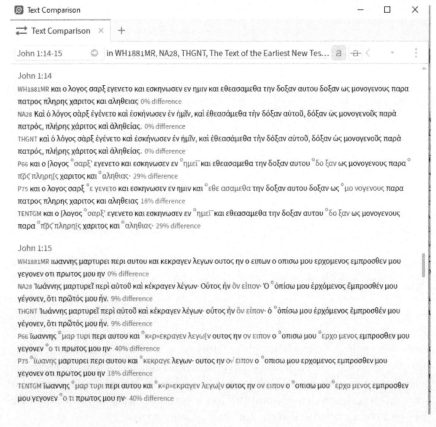

A Brief History of Collation

John Mill (1645-1707) was a fellow at Queen's College, Oxford, who spent some 30 years in textual studies, which ended with his majorly important Greek text that ended up being published a mere two weeks before he died at the age of 62. Mill had a critical introduction to his Greek text, wherein his work recorded over 30,000 discrepancies between some 100 extant New Testament manuscripts. He decided against changing Stephanus's 1550 Textus Receptus Greek text or adding an apparatus in the critical text. So, he left the time-honored corrupt Textus Receptus undamaged. Nevertheless, here is where we find the first real Textus Receptus Only arguments. Mill's Greek New Testament and especially his critical introduction to his Greek text came under attack by Daniel Whitby and Anthony Collins. Whitby's *Examen* claimed that Mill had basically, in essence, began the destruction of the Word of God. Whitby argued that Mill had damaged the authority of God's Word and that his tampering with the text was tampering with the Word of God. These same arguments are still used today by what we call the Textus Receptus Only and the King James Version Only. Bentley came to Mill's defense remarking that actually, Mill was not accountable for the differences between the various manuscript, they were already there, Mill simply pointed them out. John Mill, *Novum Testamentum Graecum, cum lectionibus variantibus MSS* (Oxford 1707). In 1710 Ludolf Küster reprinted Mill's *Testament* at Amsterdam with the readings of twelve additional manuscripts.

Edward Wells (1667-1727) was an English mathematician, geographer, and controversial theologian, who published a ten-part Greek New Testament text with helps for his readers. From 1709 to 1719, Wells produced a critical Greek edition of the New Testament, which was published in Oxford. Some 210 times, Wells would abandon the Textus Receptus, with the vast majority of his decisions agreeing with the critical texts that would come about 150+ years later when far more textual evidence was available. Even though his work got little press, he goes down in history as the first to abandon the Textus Receptus in a complete Greek New Testament text. Wells had used the variant readings that had been collated in the edition of John Mill in the construction of his Greek New Testament text. As was stated above Mill's edition had involved the most thoroughgoing critical apparatus up to its time and would only be outmatched by Tischendorf some 140+ years later. However, as was stated, the actual text was simply a reprint of that of 1550 Stephanus. So, it bears repeating that it was Wells' edition to be the first to give scholars the complete Greek New Testament as he moved away from the Textus Receptus and to what we now consider the standard critical text, such as the Nestle-Aland.

Richard Bentley (1662-1742), master of Trinity College, Cambridge was an English classical scholar, critic, and theologian. In 1716, Bentley sent in a letter to William Wake, Archbishop of Canterbury, announcing his plan to prepare a critical edition of the Greek New Testament. Throughout the next four years, he was assisted by J. J. Wetstein, a prominent biblical critic, he gathered materials for the work that lie ahead. In 1720 Bentley published *Proposals for a New Edition of the Greek Testament*, wherein he gave examples of how he intended to proceed. In the example of the last chapter of Revelation, he abandoned the Textus Receptus in 40+ places. He was determined to compare the text of the Vulgate with that of the oldest Greek manuscripts. Bentley intended to restore the Greek text as the church has received it at the time of the Council of Nicaea in 325 C.E. Bentley's primary foundational manuscript was *Codex Alexandrinus*, which he described as "the oldest and best in the world." Bentley's intention was to supplant the Textus Receptus. However, the Textus Receptus was so revered it would not be so easily displaced.

Johann Albert Bengel (1687-1752) was a Lutheran pietist clergyman and a Greek-language scholar. Bengel's belief in the plenary inspiration of the Bible coupled with John Mill's 30,000 textual variants is what motivated him to investigate the transmission of the text. In 1734, Bengel's edition of the Greek New Testament without the critical apparatus was published at Tübingen and Stuttgart. As early as 1725, in an addition to his edition of *Chrysostoms De Sacerdotio*, he had given an account in his *Prodromus Novi Testamenti Graeci recte cauteque adornandi* (An essay of the New Testament correctly and cautiously adorned) of the principles on which his intended edition was to be based. as he was preparing to get his work underway, Bengel was able to acquire the collations of upwards of twenty manuscripts. However, none of them were of great importance, not having much influence on his decisions. Twelve of them he had collated himself. Then, he imposed on himself the rule of not inserting any variant reading which had not already been used in an earlier printed edition of the Greek text. However, in the case of Revelation, he deviated from his rule because of the text being so corrupt, he chose to insert certain readings based on manuscript authority. Using the first five letters of the Greek alphabet to establish the level of importance, he inserted a selection of various readings in the lower margin of the page: α was used to indicate the reading Bengel felt to be the original reading, even though he failed to put it in the main text; β indicated a reading that was more likely than that in the main text; γ indicated that it was equal to the reading in the main text, and δ indicated readings that were inferior to those in the text.

Bengel's text was followed by his critical apparatus. The beginning of which was an introduction to his analysis of the New Testament. He explained his famous well-known textual principle in the thirty-fourth section *Proclivi scriptioni praestat ardua* (The difficult reading is to be preferred to that which is easy). This sound principle has held on with textual scholars ever since. The next part of his critical apparatus was his observations of the various readings, wherein he gives the reader the evidence for or against the different readings. Bengel was the first to develop textual families. As he had invested these manuscripts, he began to see a certain resemblance of some Greek NT manuscripts, versions, and church fathers, while others had certain characteristics that grouped them together. For example, particular readings might be found in one particular grouping of manuscripts but not the others. While later the manuscripts would be gathered into four different families: Alexandrian, Caesarean, Western, and Byzantine. Bengel broke it down into two families: The African family and the Asiatic family, the former he considered older and the latter he considered of less value or less weighty as we would say. The next to accept families of manuscripts, which they tweaked, were J. S. Semler and J. J. Griesbach. Modern scholars are now trying to move away from the manuscript family theory. Like those who came before him, like Brian Walton and John Mill, he was criticized for exposing the variant readings and point out the differences in the manuscripts. Again, many felt that his exposing these scribal errors was tantamount to undermining the Word of God. On the other hand, J.J. Wetstein accused Bengel of holding back and that Bengel should have leaned into his critical materials even more. Bengel decided to address all these accusations from both sides in his *Defence of the Greek Text of His New Testament*, which he published in 1736. It contained answers to complaints of both sides, but he focused more attention on Wetstein. The text of Bengel may have hit a few speed bumps in his day but scholars since have recognized its value long after his death, even being frequently reprinted.

Johann Jacob Wettstein (1693-1754) was a Swiss Protestant theologian, best known as a New Testament critic and he was one who collated manuscripts for Bentley. Wettstein gave his lifework to the study of the New Testament manuscripts and other sources and his collection of various readings. He put much labor and love into his study of Codex Alexandrinus. Strangely, he was stumbled in his faith in the Divinity of Christ when he discovered in the Codex Alexandrinus with no corrected reading, the original itself the reading (Ὃς ἐφανερώθη ἐν σαρκί) "who was manifested in the flesh" in 1 Timothy 3:16, as opposed to (θεος ἐφανερώθη ἐν σαρκί) "God was manifested in the flesh." In the Alexandrinus Codex, the contraction for "God," formed by two Greek letters "ΘС," appears originally to have read "OC," which is the Greek word for "who." Bruce M. Metzger in his *Textual Commentary on the Greek New Testament* concludes: "No uncial (in the first hand) earlier than the eighth or ninth century (Ψ) supports θεὸς [theos]; all ancient versions presuppose ὅς or ὅ; and no patristic writer prior to the last third of the fourth century testifies to the reading θεὸς [theos]. The reading θεὸς [theos] arose either (a) accidentally, through the misreading of ος as ΘΣ, or (b) deliberately, either to supply a substantive for the following six verbs, or, with less probability, to provide greater dogmatic precision."[686]

After forty-years of laborious research, in 1751-2, Wettstein published ar Amsterdam, the Greek New Testament in two volumes. He too published the Textus Receptus text but within the margins, he placed readings that he thought were original. In the appendix, Wettstein offers his reader the advice "manuscripts must be evaluated by their weight, not by their number." This is our 'manuscripts must be weighed not counted.' Being weighed means assessing the importance of one manuscript over another, especially with a view to a decision of what the original reading is. The thing is, Wettstein had good rules or principles but he did not apply them consistently. Ironically, considering the line of textual evidence that was coming to light up unto his life's work, he seemed to go against Bengel in his belief that the early Greek manuscripts had been contaminated by the Latin versions and that textual scholars should instead rely on the later witnesses for establishing the original readings. Some of his opponents valued his work less because he did not value the Latin versions, as well as group manuscripts into families of manuscripts, which had also been done by Richard Bentley and J. A. Bengel.

Johann Salomo Semler (1725-1791) was a German church historian, biblical commentator, and textual critic who was also known as "the father of German rationalism." Semler adopted Wettstein's manuscript classification into families but took it a little further. He renamed Bengel's Asiatic group "eastern," assigning the origin to the recension of the early fourth century by Lucian of Antioch. He renamed Bengel's "African" group "Western" or "Egypto-Palestinian" and assigned the source to Origen. He had three classifications for the manuscripts: **(1)** Alexandrians from Origen that was found in Syriac, Bohairic, and Ethiopic; **(2)** Eastern that was prevailing in the Antiochian and Constantinopolitan churches; **(3)** Western that was found in the Latin version and church fathers. Semler thought that the later manuscripts were distinguished by combining all of the recensions.

Johann Jakob Griesbach (1745-1812) was a was a German textual scholar. Griesbach's notoriety comes from his work in New Testament textual studies, in which he introduced a new milestone. He laid the groundwork for all the work in NT textual studies that would follow. He had

---

[686] Bruce Manning Metzger, *United Bible Societies, A Textual Commentary on the Greek New Testament*, Second Edition a Companion Volume to the United Bible Societies' Greek New Testament (4th Rev. Ed.) (London; New York: United Bible Societies, 1994), 574.

been a student of Semler at Halle. Griesbach's critical edition of the Greek New Testament first emerged at Halle, in three volumes, in 1774-1775. He used the *Elzevir* edition of the Textus Receptus in his critical text. When he disagreed with the TR, he would place the TR reading on the inner margin along with other readings that concerned him that he printed in smaller type. The readings found in the margins received special markings as to what he felt their probability was. As he weighed these probabilities and investigated the transmission history of the NT manuscripts, he continued categorizing the manuscripts as J. A. Bengel, and J. S. Semler had. Griesbach placed all then known manuscripts into three categories: **(1)** the Alexandrian, **(2)** the Western, and **(3)** the Byzantine recensions. Griesbach was the beginning of the modern era of New Testament Textual studies, which was followed by such scholars as Karl Lachmann (1793-1851), F. J. A. Hort (1828-1892) and B. F. Westcott (1825-1901) AKA Westcott and Hort (WH), Erwin Nestle (1883-1972), Allen Wikgren (1906-1998), Matthew Black, (1908-1994), Barbara Aland (1937-present), and Carlo Maria Martini (1927-2012). Collation in those early days was no easy task because they were working with the manuscripts themselves, not some digitally enhanced copy. Those collating the manuscripts would have to often travel the globe on ships, trains, even by horse. Now, we can turn on our computers and get an enhanced image like the one below within seconds.

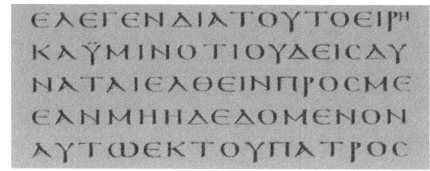

Codex Vaticanus (300-330 C.E.) Gospel of John

The Apparatus

Eberhard Nestle and Erwin Nestle, Nestle-Aland: NTG Apparatus Criticus, ed. Barbara Aland et al., 28. revidierte Auflage. (Stuttgart: Deutsche Bibelgesellschaft, 2012) Some of the symbols in the critical apparatus are as follows. The words enclosed between □ and ⌐ in the text are omitted. ¦ Separates different variants referring to the same variation unit. The symbol ⌐ represents the next word in the text is transmitted with variants. The words enclosed between ⌐ and ⌐ in the text are transmitted with variants. The symbol ° represents the next word in the text is omitted. The symbol * identifies the original reading when a correction has been made. The symbol ⊤ stands for the place marked in the text where an addition is transmitted.

Future Work in Collation

On this, Dr. Don Wilkins writes,

One thing that is immediately apparent for collation from the present onward is that we can say goodbye to much of the tedious work because computers are very good at doing these jobs. We, humans, were created for better things—not that I do not honor and admire the dedication of those who did such work in the past! We cannot eliminate all of the tedium, unfortunately. For example, humans still have to input or at a minimum verify the accuracy of inputting ancient handwritten text into machine-readable form. But once the text is accurately recorded for all time, we can have computers check the texts of different manuscripts against each other for agreements and disagreements and perform most other tasks of collation that previously had to be done by humans.

Now then, if you have purchased NA28 or GNT5 recently and have discovered that only James through Jude has been reedited, you may feel a little short-changed. You probably should not. If nothing else, you at least have a window into the future of collation. What you find in these short books is the result of the ECM2 committee's work applying the massive collation of the Institute for New Testament Textual Research and using the tools of the Coherence-Based Genealogical Method. In the NA28 and GNT5 apparatuses, you have additional citations of papyri, but also the loss of citations of various variant readings, so *do not* throw away your previous editions of these texts unless you also plan to purchase the ECM2 itself.

Permit me to do some forecasting and advisement beyond this. If you want to know as much as possible about the Greek text, and if NA28 and GNT5 are representative of what the final NA and GNT texts and apparatuses will be (as I suspect they are), then NA28 and GNT5 will be inadequate for you. For a full reporting of the text and accompanying collation in printed form, you will need the ECM2. On the other hand, if you are content with the methods of traditional TC, then NA26/27 and GNT4 will continue to serve you well, and if you wish, you can consult the online CBGM tools or purchase NA28 or GNT5 to see where the editors have changed their previous decisions in the General Epistles. GNT5, of course, will supply the additional information of ratings and have a clearer apparatus, but at the expense of omitting numerous variant readings.

Whether you purchase the ECM2 or not, I *strongly* encourage you to consult the online CBGM tools, which I will discuss in chapter xii. They provide invaluable information and are free to all users, at least for now. These tools are actually much better as a source of information than the NA28 and GNT5 apparatuses, and even extend the usefulness of the ECM2 considerably.

As to other collations, I can hardly think of any organizations more resourceful than Zondervan and the SBL, and so far neither has made any discernable attempt to add collations to their published Greek texts (*A Reader's Greek New Testament* and the SBLGNT respectively). Indeed, as we have seen, they have not even clarified for their readers what individual manuscripts their texts are based upon when they differ from the NA.

The closest thing we have seen to a rival collation, at least in my experience, is Swanson's work. No one has stepped in to complete that project after his death, and for good reason, I think. Swanson had complained about unidentified mixture in base texts, but now what we have with all of our resources and computing power is common material among all the Greek manuscripts in existence. When we had only print resources, using Swanson's interlinear layout was a pleasure compared to the relative eyesore encountered in the NA apparatus, and Swanson had the extant sources accounted for just as well. Now, however, the Institute for New Testament Textual Research (INTTR) has virtually all the Greek NT manuscripts in existence[687] online, and one can easily see clean representations of all the variants and can even choose any variant temporarily as the base text for comparison.

I think it would be impossible to compete with such a resource and organization, at least so long as the organization provides convenient, free access to its sources. It has flaws, certainly, some of which I will point out in the chapter on the CBGM, and we can only hope that these will be addressed. The intention has also been expressed to make the ECM available online, and that has yet to be implemented. So long as the database is properly managed and good access provided, however, I expect that it will be the one everyone uses in place of everything else that may still be available.

Ultimately, then, I foresee everyone who edits a Greek text of the New Testament linking it to the ECM in some way. Today, probably the only way to do this, at least off-site, would be to set up one's preferred readings as the chosen text and copy and record the results from the CBGM tools, variant by variant. It would undoubtedly be better for someone planning a new edition of the Greek NT to do it by consulting the CBGM, taking full advantage of the information available nowhere else.

In the publication of a new Greek text, we should then expect to see some accounting of the sources behind the editor's (or editors') choices relative to the ECM. I do not know what, if any, copyright issues might be involved at present in listing the actual manuscripts, but I would think that at least it would be possible for editors to note that a particular choice was the 'b' or 'c' etc. reading in the ECM.

---

[687] This includes only a selected group of representative Byzantine manuscripts.

In closing out this chapter we can again say that the purpose of collation is to acquire all of the information about the manuscripts without ever having the texts of the manuscripts in full. We can compare a family of manuscripts with a standard critical text (TR WH NA THGNT) and then noting all of the significant differences. Or we can compare one manuscript against another. The amount of space that we save is enormous.

Before you begin collating the manuscript maybe take some time and collate a couple of the chapters first to get your feet wet and familiarize yourself with the manuscript: handwriting style, odd or unusual feature or habit of the scribe, how the document is laid out. Every textual student or scholar should try their hand at collating. The collation should be done two times at minimum and then compared and even shared with others. Collating is no easy task, so one should not overwhelm themselves by spending hours collating to then get burned out, take a few days off, which has no rhythm to it. Regular and consistent is best, maybe one hour a day in the beginning. Then, gradually increase your time until you reach two hours a day. The work area for the collation should be comfortable but not too comfortable. There should be no distractions like playing music and you should turn off your cellphone. Nothing should distract you from the task at hand. When you are two hours a day, take a 15-minute break in between the hours. As you work do quick reviews along the way to make certain that you have made no mistakes. As you are working your way through the collation take note of how many correctors worked on the copy and how their habits differ from one another and if the copyist himself was involved in any of the corrections.

CHAPTER XVIII

Modern Translations and the New Testament Text

There indeed has been a renewed interest in the field of textual criticism, which had lain relatively dormant for several decades. What has contributed to this renewed interest? Several factors have contributed to the rehabilitated awareness: **the internet** has provided such tools as Yahoo and Google discussion boards and Twitter, where scholars and laypersons alike can discuss the science and art of textual criticism. The internet has given the layperson many free websites that offer comprehensive information about textual criticism.[688] **Evangelism** is another reason for the resurgence of textual criticism. Evangelism is defined as "planting the seeds of the Gospel," while Preevangelism is defined as *"tilling the soil of people's minds and hearts to help them be more willing to listen to the truth"* (Geisler and Geisler 2009, p. 22). This leads us to the third leading reason for the renewed interest: The **New Atheist, Agnostic, and Skeptic**, who seek to cast doubt on the existence of

---

[688] https://christianpublishinghouse.co/ot-and-nt-textual-studies/

God and his Word. These new critics of God and the Bible are different from those of 60 years ago or so, as they are far more evangelistic than even Christians are. These new critics pen many books, magazine articles, advertising on billboards, news, and radio shows, and publicly debate Bible scholars. They seem to be everywhere and are significant contributors to the spiritual shipwreck of hundreds of thousands of Christians if not more.

The fourth contributing factor to this renewed interest is **scholarly books written for the layperson**, which have enabled the churchgoer to enter the conversation. We now have a plethora of books dealing with numerous biblical fields, which allow Christians to avoid falling into the trap of doubting that what they have is, in fact, the Word of God, inspired and fully inerrant. There is absolutely no one to be blamed if we end up in repeated conversations that cast doubt on our beliefs and the Word of God, except ourselves. Suppose the average Christian is going to be effective in his Preevangelism (apologetics) of helping those with receptive hearts to overcome the assault on God's Word. In that case, they need proper Bible study tools.

In addition, the renewed interest in textual criticism brings up why it is important to all churchgoers who may simply own a few good English translations. What is the benefit of all Churchgoers knowing about textual criticism? First, we might all agree on two essential points as it relates to translation differences. Most churchgoers would agree that what they want in their Bible is what God had the original authors write translated into English (ASV, RSV, NASB, ESV, CSB, UASV), not some interpretive translation, not what a translator thinks God meant in its place. (CEV, NLT, NIV, NRSV,) The same holds true with textual criticism. Most churchgoers would agree that what they want in their Bible is what God had the original authors, who were moved along by Holy Spirit to write. Namely, they want the inspired, inerrant Word of God (ASV, RSV, ESV, CSB, UASV), not the thousands of intentional and unintentional textual errors of copyists that crept into the text over 1,400 years of copying. (KJV, NKJV, NASB) The same holds true with textual criticism. So, our understanding of the foundations of the basics of Bible translation philosophy and textual criticism can enable us to make the best choice when selecting a Bible translation.

As Bible readers seeking what God had penned under inspiration, do we want the King James Version or the New King James Version based on the text of the 16th century (TR), the corrupt Byzantine text-type represented in the great majority of Greek Manuscripts? Or, rather, do we want the up-to-date Bible translations that rely upon the modern critical text of Westcott and Hort, the Nestle-Aland and the United Bible Society, which departs from the Byzantine tradition (WH NU). The following are critical texts:

the **TR** stands for **T**extus **R**eceptus text (1550), **WH** stands for **W**estcott and **H**ort text (1881), and **NU** stands for the **N**estle-Aland text (2011) and the **U**nited Bible Societies text (2015). If we want to make such choices, eyes wide open, we must fully understand how the Greek text came down to us.

Why are Jehovah's Witnesses so easily able to convert Christians over into their religion by the millions? It is because the Christians, sadly, are unaware, they have not taken in enough knowledge of God's Word; in short, they lack knowledge and understanding. Therefore, what the Jehovah's Witnesses teach sounds perfect, reasonable, and even very biblical to a person who requires Bible knowledge. The same is true with this King James Version Onlyist cult, which can hold millions of Christians under their influence because the Christian lacks an accurate knowledge (Gr. *epignosis*, used by Paul 21 times) of exactly how the Greek New Testament came down to us. Yes, there are some KJVOist out there who have a good measure of knowledge about the text of the New Testament. Still, it is through the prism of the mind control of the KJVOist, who has impacted their thinking and their way of thinking, so any real evidence is dismissed out of hand or seen as mere trickery by those who have the accurate knowledge of the Greek text of the New Testament. This is how the Jehovah's Witnesses operate, sowing doubt about all others. Witnesses say that true Christianity is the whore of Babylon and the tool of Satan and that we should only trust the Jehovah's Witnesses, as trusting "Christendom" is tantamount to trusting Satan and denying the truth. The KJVOist does the same in saying that all translations other than the KJV are the product of Satan.

In addition, understanding textual criticism is the same as understanding Bible translation philosophy in another way. Those choosing literal translation do so because they do not want a translator making interpretive choices for them. The churchgoer can use textual criticism for the very same reason, removing the textual scholar from the driver's seat so they can determine for themselves if a particular reading is original or not. As they read the Bible, the churchgoer encounters textual footnotes, and they are left out of the discussion if they have no knowledge of textual studies.

There is both good news and bad news. The good news is that all of the significant English translations give the reader footnotes where major textual issues will affect the translation. However, the bad news is, this footnote means very little in the grand scheme of things. Let's consider Matthew 6:13.

Matthew 6:13 (ESV)	Matthew 6:13 (CSB)	Matthew 6:13 (NASB)	Matthew 6:13 (NIV)
13 And lead us not into temptation, but deliver us from evil.[a] [a] some manuscripts add *For yours is the kingdom and the power and the glory, forever. Amen*	13 And do not bring us into temptation, but deliver us from the evil one.[b] [b] Or from evil; some later mss add For yours is the kingdom and the power and the glory forever. Amen.	13 'And do not lead us into temptation, but deliver us from [a]evil. [b][For Yours is the kingdom and the power and the glory forever. Amen.'] [b] This clause not found in early mss	13 And lead us not into temptation,[a] but deliver us from the evil one.[b]' [b] some late manuscripts one, / for yours is the kingdom and the power and the glory forever. Amen.

Matthew 6:13 Updated American Standard Version (UASV)

13 And do not lead us into temptation, but deliver us from the wicked one.[1]

[1] Matthew 6:13 ends with "but deliver us from the wicked one." This is supported by the earliest and best manuscripts (א B D Z 0170 f1). Within the other extant manuscripts, there are six different additions to the end of Matthew 6:13, which is evidence against any addition at all. Within this footnote, we will deal with just one, which is found in the Textus Receptus and the King James Version, "for yours is the kingdom and the power and the glory forever, amen." (L W Δ Θ 0233 f13 33 Maj syr) These later manuscripts do not outweigh the earlier Alexandrian manuscripts (א B), the Western (D), and most Old Latin, as well as other (f1) text types, and the early commentaries on the Lord's prayer (Tertullian, Origen, Cyprian). It seems that the scribes were looking to conclude the Lord's Prayer with an uplifting message, or in the case of a couple of additional support for the Trinity doctrine. "because yours is the kingdom of the Father and the Son and the Holy Spirit forever. Amen." (157 1253)

What do these textual footnotes in the ESV, CSB, NASB, and the NIV tell you about this interpolation? Basically, 'some late manuscripts added this doxology at the end of the Lord's Prayer.' The NKJV is just the opposite by saying, "NU omits the rest of v. 13." The NASB is basically with the NKJV in that it has the textual interpolations in the main text of the Bible itself and a footnote that reads, "This clause not found in early MSS." The reader has no way of knowing if it is true. They have no way of defending it when they talk with the KJVOist on social media. All they can say in response is, 'it is what my Bible says in a footnote.' The Updated American Standard Version footnote offers the reader far more.

King James Onlyist (KJVO): Of course, the New Testament of the King James Version and the New King James Version is based on the Textus Receptus. Both the King James Onlyist (KJVO) and the Textus Receptus Onlyist (TRO) agree. The King James Onlyist believes that the King James Version is the only English Bible that should be viewed as God's Word.

Textus Receptus Onlyist (TRO): These scholars and their followers believe that the critical Text of Erasmus of 1516, the 1550 Stephanus New Testament, and all the critical New Testament Texts up until 1633 better preserve the original. While the Textus Receptus is based on the Byzantine text, it is only based on about seven manuscripts out of thousands. Daniel B. Wallace has counted 1,838 differences between the Textus Receptus and the Majority Text of Hodges and Farstad. – "Some Second Thoughts on the Majority Text," Bibliotheca Sacra 146 (July–September 1989): 276.)

Majority Text Onlyist (MTO): These scholars and their followers believe that the words penned by the original authors are better preserved in the thousands of Byzantine texts.

Significant Editions of the Greek New Testament

[There are] four [major] editions of the Greek New Testament: (1) the Textus Receptus, (2) Westcott and Hort's *The New Testament in the Original Greek*, (3) the United Bible Societies' *Greek New Testament* (third and fourth editions), and (4) the Nestle-Aland *Novum Testamentum Graece* (twenty-sixth and twenty-seventh editions).

The Textus Receptus (TR)

The Textus Receptus (abbreviated TR in the commentary) has its roots in the early fourth century, when Lucian of Antioch produced a major recension of the New Testament (see Jerome's introduction to his Latin translation of the Gospels, PL 29:527c). This text is sometimes called "Syrian," because of its association with Antioch in Syria. Lucian's work was a definite recension (i.e., a purposely created edition), in contrast to the Alexandrian text-type (see appendix D). The Alexandrian scribes did some minimal editing, such as we would call copy editing. By contrast, the Syrian text is the result of a much larger endeavor; it is characterized by smoothness of language, which is achieved by the removal of obscurities

---

and awkward grammatical constructions, and by the conflation of variant readings.

Lucian's text was produced prior to the Diocletian persecution (ca. 303), during which many copies of the New Testament were confiscated and destroyed. Not long after this period of devastation, Constantine came to power and recognized Christianity as a legal religion. There was, of course, a great need for copies of the New Testament to be made and distributed to churches throughout the Mediterranean world. It was at this time that Lucian's text began to be propagated by bishops going out from Antioch to churches throughout the East. Lucian's text soon became standard in the Eastern Church. For century after century—from the sixth to the fourteenth—the great majority of Greek New Testament manuscripts were produced in Byzantium, the capital of the Eastern Empire. All of these copies bore the same kind of text, one directly descended from Lucian's Syrian recension. When the first Greek New Testament was printed (ca. 1525), it was based on a Greek text that Erasmus had compiled using a few late Byzantine manuscripts (notably, minuscules 1 and 2 of the twelfth century). This text went through a few more revisions by Robert Stephanus and then by Theodore Beza. Beza's text was published by the Elzevir brothers in 1624, with a second edition in 1633. In this printing they announced that their edition contained "the text which is now received by all, in which we give nothing changed or corrupted." In this way, "textus receptus" (the "received text") became the name of this form of the Greek New Testament.

The edition of the Textus Receptus cited throughout [Christian Publishing House blog] is that of Stephanus (1550). The Elzevirs' text (1624) is virtually the same. Both can be called the Textus Receptus (TR).

In recent years, a few scholars have attempted to defend the validity of the Textus Receptus or what they would call the Majority Text. The Majority Text is nearly the same as the Textus Receptus, since TR was derived from manuscripts produced in Byzantium, where the majority of other Greek New Testaments were produced. The two terms are not completely synonymous, however, because TR did not attempt to reproduce the reading found in a statistical majority of witnesses. Thus, it does not consistently reflect the Majority Text throughout. Majority Text is more nearly synonymous with the Byzantine text-type because it was in Byzantium (and surrounding regions) that Lucian's recension was copied again and again in thousands of manuscripts.

Modern advocates of the superiority of the Majority Text over other text-types are Hodges and Farstad, who produced *The Greek New Testament according to the Majority Text*. Their arguments are more theological than textual. They reason that God would not have allowed a corrupt or inferior text to be found in the majority of manuscripts, while permitting a superior text to be hidden away in a few early manuscripts somewhere in the sands of Egypt. Further, they argue that the church's adoption of the Majority Text was a vindication of its correctness, while the obscurity of the Egyptian text was a sign of its rejection.

Most contemporary scholars contend that a minority of manuscripts—primarily the earliest ones—preserve the most authentic wording of the text. Those who defend the Majority Text (and its well-known incarnations, TR and KJV) would have to prove that these earlier manuscripts, usually having a slimmer text than what appears in later manuscripts, were purposefully trimmed at an early stage in the textual transmission. In other words, they would have to present good arguments as to why early scribes would have purposely excised the following passages: Matthew 5:44b; 6:13b; 16:2b–3; 17:21; 18:11; 20:16b, 22–23; 23:14; 27:35b; Mark 7:16; 9:44, 46; 11:26; 15:28; 16:8–20; Luke 4:4b; 9:54c–56; 11:2; 17:36; 22:43–44; 23:17, 34; John 5:3b–4; 7:53–8:11; Acts 8:37; 15:34; 24:6b–8a; 28:16b, 29; Romans 16:24; 1 John 5:6b–8a. Had these portions originally been in the text, there are no good explanations why they would have been eliminated. On the other hand, there are several good explanations why they were added, such as gospel harmonization, the insertion of oral traditions, and theological enhancements (see commentary on the above passages). It is true that some of the earliest scribes were prone to shorten their texts in the interest of readability, but these deletions usually involved only a few words. Thus, most scholars see TR as being the culmination of textual accretions.

Westcott and Hort, The New Testament in the Original Greek (WH)

Aided by the work of scholars such as Tregelles and Tischendorf, two British scholars, Brooke Westcott and Fenton Hort, worked together for twenty-eight years to produce an edition entitled *The New Testament in the Original Greek* (2 volumes, 1881–1882; abbreviated WH in the commentary). In this publication, they made known their theory (which was chiefly Hort's) that Codex Vaticanus and Codex Sinaiticus (along with a few other early manuscripts) represented a text that most closely replicated the original writing. This is the text, which they called the Neutral Text, that Westcott and Hort attempted to reproduce in their edition. Their work was historically significant in that it dethroned reliance on the Textus Receptus.

In my opinion, Westcott and Hort's edition is still to this day, even with so many more manuscript discoveries, a very close reproduction of the primitive text of the New Testament. Of course, like many others, I think they gave too much weight to Codex Vaticanus alone. This criticism aside, the Westcott and Hort text is extremely reliable. In my own studies of textual variants, in many instances where I would disagree with the wording in the NU edition in favor of a particular variant reading, I would later check with WH and realize that they had come to the same decision. This revealed to me that I was working on a similar methodological basis as they. Since the era of Westcott and Hort, hundreds of other manuscripts have been discovered, notably the early papyri. Were Westcott and Hort alive today, they would be pleased to see that several of these papyri affirm their view that Codex Vaticanus and Codex Sinaiticus are reliable witnesses of a very primitive form of the Greek New Testament. They would have undoubtedly altered some of their textual choices based on the evidence of the papyri. For example, the testimony of $\mathfrak{P}^{75}$ (with א and B) in several Lukan passages clearly indicates that Westcott and Hort were wrong to have excluded several passages in Luke 22–24 based on their theory of "Western noninterpolations."

The Nestle-Aland Novum Testamentum Graece (26th and 27th editions) and The United Bible Societies' Greek New Testament (3rd and 4th corrected editions) (NU)

In the [Christian Publishing House Blog] these two editions, which have the same text, are referred to jointly as NU; when it is necessary to refer to the volumes individually, the sigla NA[26], NA[27], NA[28], UBS[3], and UBS[4] UBS[5] are used.

The United Bible Societies prepared an edition of the *Greek New Testament* as a tool for their Bible translators, in which a full citation of witnesses was given in the critical apparatus for significant variants. After the United Bible Societies had published two editions of the *Greek New Testament*, they decided to unite with the work being done on the twenty-sixth edition of the Nestle-Aland text, a scholarly reference tool.

Thus, the United Bible Societies' third edition of the *Greek New Testament* and the Nestle-Aland twenty-sixth edition of *Novum Testament Graece* have the same text. Each, however, has different punctuation and a different critical apparatus. The United Bible Societies' text has a plenary listing of witnesses for select variation units; the Nestle-Aland text has a condensed listing of the manuscript evidence for almost all the variant-units. Both works have since gone into another edition (the fourth and twenty-seventh, respectively), manifesting a multitude of corrections to the critical apparatus but not to the wording of the text itself.

In *The Text of the New Testament*, Kurt and Barbara Aland argue that the Nestle-Aland text "comes closer to the original text of the New Testament than did Tischendorf or Westcott and Hort, not to mention von Soden" (1991, 32). And in several other passages they intimate that this text may very well be the original text. This is evident in Kurt Aland's defense (1979, 14) of NA[26] as the new "standard text":

The new "standard text" has passed the test of the early papyri and uncials. It corresponds, in fact, to the text of the early time.... At no place and at no time do we find readings here [in the earliest manuscripts] that require a change in the "standard text." If the investigation conducted here in all its brevity and compactness could be presented fully, the detailed apparatus accompanying each variant would convince the last doubter. A hundred years after Westcott-Hort, the goal of an edition of the New Testament "in the original Greek" seems to have been reached.... The desired goal appears now to have been attained, to offer the writings of the New Testament in the form of the text that comes nearest to that which, from the hand of their authors or redactors, they set out on their journey in the church of the first and second centuries.

Though the Alands should be commended for their work, it remains to be seen whether or not the Nestle-Aland text is the best replication of the original text. As noted before, I have my doubts. ... Nonetheless, the Nestle-Aland Greek text is now truly recognized as the standard text, accepted by most of the academic community as representing the best attempt at reconstructing the original text of the Greek New Testament.

Since the scholarly community worldwide is most familiar with NU, this is the edition given first in each listing of textual variants. The NU reading is printed as it stands in the UBS[4] edition, including accents. All the variants are unaccented, as in the critical apparatus of NA[27]. This presentation should not be interpreted as implying, however, that this text is "inspired" or infallible—as many scholars will readily attest. The NU editors were able to take into consideration the newly discovered documents as they sought to produce a more accurate text. In many places they no doubt have achieved their goal to produce a more accurate text than did Westcott and Hort. However, their strong reliance on the eclectic method has produced an uneven documentary text. In some, but not all, instances, the Nestle-Aland text presents an advance beyond Westcott and Hort.

Nonetheless, the reader will see that the NU and WH editions often agree on matters of major textual significance. Where the WH and NU diverge, however, NU far more frequently concurs with TR than does

> WH. Furthermore, where WH and NU differ, I am inclined quite frequently to agree with WH on the basis of documentary evidence.[689]

The ESV, CSB, NASB, and the NIV, as well as most other major translations, including the dynamic equivalent, do not provide the readers with what they need to be able to make an informed decision about these significant textual variants. These footnotes do not allow the reader a non-textual scholar to truly evaluate the different variants (textual errors) of a variant unit (place in the manuscript where there are multiple differences) because they do not know what internal and external evidence supports each variant, or how to evaluate the weight of these manuscripts behind the variants. If the reading in the main text has (א B P75 and P66) and the variant has (L W Δ Θ 0233 f13 33 Maj syr), most churchgoers are going to think, wait, the variant has far more manuscript support than the reading in the main text, not knowing manuscripts are weighed not counted.

All the reader knows in the ESV, CSB, NASB, and the NIV, as well as most other major translations, is that the Bible translation has made the decision for them, for they (1) do not have enough information in the footnote for them to evaluate the variants, and (2) if they were given external manuscript evidence, this would still prove to be unhelpful without knowing how to weigh the manuscript support. Moreover, how many churchgoers out of 2 billion can evaluate the variant readings for themselves by considering the internal evidence, such as context, style, and theological inferences. Thus, the reader is at the mercy of the translation's textual committee choosing for them. Think this through for a moment. The reader who has chosen a literal translation has done so because he did not want translators making interpretive choices for him. Now, we have the translation doing just that with the textual decision if the reader had enough information by way of appendices Basics of Old Testament Textual Criticism and Basics of New Testament Textual Criticism and a footnote that gave them the external manuscripts.

Romans 16:24 Updated American Standard Version

24 _____ [1]

[1] P46 P61 א A B C 1739 It[b] cop omit; DItVg[c], [The grace of our Lord Jesus Christ be with you all. Amen.], which is the same as the end of vs 20.

---

[689] Philip W. Comfort, *New Testament Text and Translation Commentary: Commentary on the Variant Readings of the Ancient New Testament Manuscripts and How They Relate to the Major English Translations* (Carol Stream, IL: Tyndale House Publishers, Inc., 2008), xxiii–xxvi.

The earliest MSS support the omission of this verse. All modern translation does not include this verse because of superior testimony.

Thus, what is the benefit of knowing 'later manuscripts add this ...' or 'early manuscripts do not contain this ...'? Or, what is the benefit if the translation even listed the manuscript support if the reader cannot weigh the evidence himself for or against to determine for himself, which is the original reading?

The answer to our problem is quite simple for both internal and external evidence. There needs to be an appendix that makes the reader aware of how to weigh the manuscript evidence (Basics of Old Testament Textual Criticism and Basics of New Testament Textual Criticism) and a chart at the outset of the translation that lists the major Manuscripts and Ancient Versions.

Utilizing the Families in Translation

In quest of the genuine (i.e., inspired) text of the New Testament, scholars have differed as to which is the best family. All agree that no family is perfect, but most accept the Alexandrian family as the most reliable of the four. A few view the Western to be superior. An even smaller number endorses the Byzantine as retaining the correct reading most often.

Available English translations represent each of these three families (no English translation uses the Caesarean). The King James Version (also call the Authorized Version) is an example of a New Testament which shows closest kinship to the Byzantine family (Textus Receptus, i.e., 'received text', is another title that in general designates this same family). The Douai Version is an example of a version which shows greatest affinity for the Western family. Examples of English translations made from the Alexandrian family are the English Revised Version (1881, 1885) and the American Standard Version (1901).

A pertinent question about the Byzantine family is, how did it come to dominate English translations of the New Testament for so long if it is a secondary or later-in-origin text-type? The answer lies in its dominance of Greek manuscripts of the New Testament from the fifth or sixth century onward. This dominance is explainable perhaps by the relocation of the capital of the Roman Empire from Rome to Asia Minor in the fourth century, and perhaps by growing disuse of the Greek languages in areas outside the Byzantine area (Turkey and Greece in modern times) in these early centuries of the Christian era. In other words, the only Greek manuscripts being produced were in the territory where the Byzantine family was influential.

The dominance of the Byzantine Greek manuscripts through the Middle Ages led to the dominance of the Byzantine family in English translations for so long. When Erasmus edited the first printed Greek New Testament in the early sixteenth century, the only manuscripts available to him were late ones of a Byzantine type. Tyndale depended on this Greek New Testament when he translated his New Testament, the first to be translated from Greek to English. Hence, it was inevitable that Tyndale's work carried this family resemblance.

From then on, practically all new English translations were simply revisions of works done earlier. The Tyndale tradition of dependence on the Byzantine text-type continued through the King James Version of 1611. The King James Version continued its exclusive reign in the English-speaking Protestant church for approximately three and a half centuries.

In the late nineteenth century, however, revisers of the King James Version launched a serious challenge to that textual basis. The challenge came at a time when manuscripts of a more ancient vintage than those available to Erasmus had surfaced. An awareness dawned that the Byzantine family was not the most accurate source for the New Testament text.

The influence of two British scholars, Brook Foss Westcott and Fenton John Anthony Hort, caused that change in appraisal of text-types. The English Revised Version, New Testament, of 1881 translated primarily a Greek text prepared by these two scholars. Their Greek Testament used Alexandrian-type readings rather than Byzantine. Their case for the superior reliability of this family was convincing, so much so that from the turn of the century to the present, most English translations made have been from predominantly Alexandrian sources.

Despite the twentieth-century trend toward the Alexandrian-type translations, some still prefer a Byzantine-based translation. They do so for a variety of reasons. One is the theoretical presumption that the numerical dominance of Greek manuscripts indicates that the Byzantine family is the oldest and therefore the best representative of the original Greek New Testament. This theory, an impressive one on the surface, falters, however, when taking into account the impact of international political and linguistic changes in the early centuries of the Christian era.

Another reason advanced to support the *Textus Receptus* is God's providential care. His providence provided for the preservation of this family in English in the form of the King James Version. The other families were not translated into English early because they were not inspired, says this theory. This line of reasoning is one-sided. It fails to notice that God's providence provided for the preservation of the Alexandrian and Western families too, text-types preserved in languages other than English. People in other parts of the world have preserved and used those two continuously since the second century. We must accept that God in His providence has seen fit to preserve several families of readings, not just one.

To explain the absence of second-century evidence for the existence of the Byzantine, the pro-Byzantine viewpoint sometimes theorizes that Greek manuscripts of this family were worn out through repeated use because of a recognition of their inspiration, whereas early manuscripts of the other families survived because they experienced only limited use. This explanation is at best highly speculative. Furthermore, it does not explain why the ancient versions and early church writers have no Byzantine readings.

Differences Between the Alexandrian and Byzantine Families

The question often arises: how much difference is there between translations based on different families of manuscripts, particularly the Byzantine and the Alexandrian? Table I provides a partial answer to the question. It lists 165 passages where variations between the two families are noticeable to English readers. The list is by no means an exhaustive list of differences, but presents typical passages where manuscript sources have differing readings of the same passages.

Table I usually does not cite complete verses, only the portions of verses that show the contrasting renderings. The translation is not that of one particular version, but is a literal translation to which any translation can be compared. In the Table contemporary English has been chosen in lieu of Elizabethan English except when Deity is addressed in the text. The Table uses American spellings (e.g., Savior) whenever they differ from English spellings (e.g., Saviour). Readings found in the Textus Receptus sometimes differ from the Byzantine family; the Table does not include these (e.g., Acts 9:6a; 1 John 5:7b–8a). Also excluded from consideration are variants where the Byzantine or the Alexandrian family is evenly divided in support of one reading or the other. An English version often indicates that a passage is in doubt by use of brackets or other special markings; in such cases the Table of comparisons assumes the translators' preference for the omission.[690]

---

[690] Robert L. Thomas, *How to Choose a Bible Version: An Introductory Guide to English Translations* (Fearn, Great Britain: Christian Focus Publications, 2000), 60–63.

In summary, almost all modern translations of the New Testament use the Nestle-Aland-United Bible Society critical text that is reflective of the early Alexandrian family of texts. Nevertheless, these translations do offer the reader the briefest of footnotes that address the significant variants. At present, these footnotes do very little to offer the uninformed reader any means of weighing the evidence for or against a particular reading. Until this is made available in modern translations, readers are going to have to invest in a critical commentary that will enable them to hear reasoned arguments on most of the significant variants of the Greek New Testament as to why one reading was chosen over another. The score below is based on whether the translation has textual footnotes, the detail of those notes, and is there any information provided so the reader can comprehend and make an informed decision about the footnotes.

Comparison Results by Score of to What Degree the Reader Is Informed about Textual Issues

Bible Version	Score	NT Textual Base
New King James Version (NKJV)	20%	Textus Receptus
New American Standard Bible (NASB)	30%	UBS5 & Nestle-Aland 28
English Standard Version (ESV)	30%	UBS5 & Nestle-Aland 28
Christian Standard Bible (CSB)	30%	UBS5 & Nestle-Aland 28
New Revised Standard Version (NRSV)	30%	UBS5 & Nestle-Aland 28
New International Version (NIV)	30%	UBS5 & Nestle-Aland 28
Updated American Standard Version (UASV)	100%	Wescott and Hort UBS5 & Nestle-Aland 28

LIST OF TRANSLATION

KJV   King James Version, 1611
NKJV   New King James Version, 1982
ASV   American Standard Version, 1901
UASV   Updated American Standard Version, 2020
RSV   Revised Standard Version, 1952
NRSV   New Revised Standard Version, 1990
ESV   English Standard Version, 2001
LEB   Lexham English Bible, 2012
NASB   New American Standard Bible, 1964, 1995
NIV   New International Version, 1978
TNIV   Today's New International Version, 2005
NEB   New English Bible, 1961
REB   Revised English Bible, 1989
CEV   Contemporary English Version, 1995
TEV   Today's English Version, 1976
NJB   New Jerusalem Bible, 1986
NAB   New American Bible, 1984 (revised NT)
NLT   New Living Translation (second edition), 2004
HCSB   Holman Christian Standard Bible, 2004
CSB   Christian Standard Bible, 2017
NET   The NET Bible (New English Translation), 1996
TNIV   Today's New International Version, 2005

What lies below is from Wikipedia, Bible Gateway, Philip Comfort, and Edward D. Andrews.

LITERAL TRANSLATIONS (Word-for-Word)

The terms Dynamic equivalence (interpretive meaning for meaning) and formal equivalence (literal word-for word), coined by Eugene Nida, are associated with two dissimilar translation approaches that are employed to achieve different levels of literalness between the source text and the target text, as evidenced in biblical translation.

KJV King James Version, 1611

In 1604, King James I of England authorized a new translation of the Bible into English. It was finished in 1611, just 85 years after the first translation of the New Testament into English appeared (Tyndale, 1526). The Authorized Version, or King James Version, quickly became the standard for English-speaking Protestants. Its flowing language and prose rhythm have had a profound influence on the literature of the past 400 years. Textual basis for the OT: Masoretic Text, some LXX and Vulgate influence. NT: Textus Receptus, similar to the Byzantine text-type; some readings derived from the Vulgate. The translators of the King James Version used the corrupt Textus Receptus for the New Testament. The translators did as well as expected, but their tools were flawed. Many thousands of manuscripts have been discovered since 1611, enabling publishers to produce translations that are far more reflective of what the original had said.

NKJV New King James Version, 1982

Commissioned in 1975 by Thomas Nelson Publishers, 130 respected Bible scholars, church leaders, and lay Christians worked for seven years to create a completely new, modern translation of Scripture, yet one that would retain the purity and stylistic beauty of the original King James. With unyielding faithfulness to the original Greek, Hebrew, and Aramaic texts, the translation applies the most recent research in archaeology, linguistics, and textual studies. Textual basis   NT: Textus Receptus, derived from the Byzantine text-type. OT: Masoretic Text with Septuagint influence. Even though they knew better, the New King James Version translators used the corrupt Textus Receptus for the New Testament.

ASV American Standard Version, 1901

From Wikipedia: The American Standard Version (ASV) is rooted in the work that was done with the Revised Version (RV) (a late 19th-century British revision of the King James Version of 1611). In 1870, an invitation was extended to American religious leaders for scholars to work on the RV project. A year later, Protestant theologian Philip Schaff chose 30 scholars representing the denominations of Baptist, Congregationalist, Dutch Reformed, Friends, Methodist, Episcopal, Presbyterian, Protestant Episcopal, and Unitarian. These scholars began work in 1872.

The RV New Testament was released In 1881; the Old Testament was published in 1885. The ASV was published in 1901 by Thomas Nelson & Sons. In 1928, the International Council of Religious Education (the body that later merged with the Federal Council of Churches to form the National Council of Churches) acquired the copyright from Nelson and renewed it the following year.

The divine name of the Almighty (the Tetragrammaton) is consistently rendered Jehovah in the ASV Old Testament, rather than LORD as it appears in the King James Bible.

The ASV was the basis of four revisions. They were the Revised Standard Version, 1971, the Amplified Bible, 1965, the New American Standard Bible, 1995, and the Recovery Version, 1999. A fifth revision, known as the World English Bible, was published in 2000 and was placed in the public domain. The ASV was also the basis for Kenneth N. Taylor's Bible paraphrase, The Living Bible, 1971. Comfort writes, "These men were greatly influenced by Codex Sinaiticus and Codex Vaticanus, but not by the papyri, since only a few had been discovered and published by then."[691]

Textual basis NT: Westcott and Hort 1881 and Tregelles 1857, (Reproduced in a single, continuous, form in Palmer 1881). **OT**: Masoretic Text with some Septuagint influence).

Translation type: Formal equivalence, that is, it is one of the most literal translation in English.

RSV Revised Standard Version, 1952

The Revised Standard Version of the Bible (RSV) is an authorized revision of the American Standard Version, published in 1901, which was a revision of the King James Version, published in 1611.

The King James Version has with good reason been termed "the noblest monument of English prose." Its revisers in 1881 expressed admiration for "its simplicity, its dignity, its power, its happy turns of expression ... the music of it cadences, and the felicities of its rhythm." It entered, as no other book has, into the making of the personal character and the public institutions of the English-speaking peoples.

The Revised Standard Version of the Bible, containing the Old and New Testaments, was published on September 30, 1952, and has met with wide acceptance.

The Revised Standard Version Bible seeks to preserve all that is best in the English Bible as it has been known and used through the years. It is intended for use in public and private worship, not merely for reading and instruction. We have resisted the temptation to use phrases that are merely current usage and have sought to put the message of the Bible in simple, enduring words that are worthy to stand in the great Tyndale-King James tradition. We are glad to say, with the King James translators: "Truly (good Christian Reader) we never thought from the beginning, that we should need

---

[691] Philip W. Comfort, *New Testament Text and Translation Commentary: Commentary on the Variant Readings of the Ancient New Testament Manuscripts and How They Relate to the Major English Translations* (Carol Stream, IL: Tyndale House Publishers, Inc., 2008), xxvii.

to make a new Translation, nor yet to make of a bad one a good one … but to make a good one better."

Textual basis NT: Novum Testamentum Graece. **OT**: Biblia Hebraica Stuttgartensia with limited Dead Sea Scrolls and Septuagint influence. Apocrypha: Septuagint with Vulgate influence.

Translation type: Borderline of formal equivalence (literal) and dynamic equivalence (interpretive).

NASB New American Standard Bible, 1964, 1995, 2020

While preserving the literal accuracy of the 1901 ASV, the NASB has sought to render grammar and terminology in contemporary English. Special attention has been given to the rendering of verb tenses to give the English reader a rendering as close as possible to the sense of the original Greek and Hebrew texts. In 1995, the text of the NASB was updated for greater understanding and smoother reading. The New American Standard Bible present on the Bible Gateway matches the 1995 printing.

The New American Standard Bible Update - 1995

Easier to read:

- Passages with Old English "thee's" and "thou's" etc. have been updated to modern English.

- Words and Phrases that could be misunderstood due to changes in their meaning during the past 20 years have been updated to current English.

- Verses with difficult word order or vocabulary have been retranslated into smoother English.

- Sentences beginning with "And" have often been retranslated for better English, in recognition of differences in style between the ancient languages and modern English. The original Greek and Hebrew did not have punctuation as is found in English, and in many cases modern English punctuation serves as a substitute for "And" in the original. In some other cases, "and" is translated by a different word such as "then" or "but" as called for by the context, when the word in the original language allows such translation.

More accurate than ever:

- Recent research on the oldest and best Greek manuscripts of the New Testament has been reviewed, and some passages have been updated for even greater fidelity to the original manuscripts.

- Parallel passages have been compared and reviewed.

- Verbs that have a wide range of meaning have been retranslated in some passages to better account for their use in the context.

And still the NASB:

- The NASB update is not a change-for-the-sake-of-change translation. The original NASB stands the test of time, and change has been kept to a minimum in recognition of the standard that has been set by the New American Standard Bible.

- The NASB update continues the NASB's tradition of literal translation of the original Greek and Hebrew without compromise. Changes in the text have been kept within the strict parameters set forth by the Lockman Foundation's Fourfold Aim.

- The translators and consultants who have contributed to the NASB update are conservative Bible scholars who have doctorates in Biblical languages, theology, or other advanced degrees. They represent a variety of denominational backgrounds.

Continuing a tradition:

The original NASB has earned the reputation of being the most accurate English Bible translation. The NASB update carries on the NASB tradition of being a true Bible translation, revealing what the original manuscripts actually say--not merely what the translator believes they mean.

Philip Comfort writes, "this translation is clearly lacking in terms of textual fidelity: though it was originally supposed to follow the twenty-third edition of the Nestle text, it tends to follow the Textus Receptus. This commentary cites the 1964 edition, as this is the version that most readers have in hand. An updated version appeared in 1995, but this update has only a few textual changes in the translation, with a few more changes in the marginal notes."[692]

Textual basis OT: Biblia Hebraica Stuttgartensia with Septuagint influence. **NT**: Novum Testamentum Graece

---

[692] IBID, xxviii.

Translation type is Formal Equivalence, meaning a literal translation. It is one of the most literal modern translations.

Has the New American Standard Bible (NASB) 2020 Revision Stepped Away from Its Literal Translation Philosophy?

Lockman goes on to say that the NASB 2020 is a Bible that is accessible to all readers and is presented in a way that clearly and accurately communicates the content, so it is understood in the same way it would have been to the original audience. Most importantly, the NASB 2020 provides a literal translation of the Bible that clearly communicates God's message to the modern English reader so that everyone can continue to grow in their knowledge and love of our Lord, God, and Savior, Jesus Christ. Again, with the delving into the interpretive translation philosophy and having corrupt readings in the main text, this is not entirely true.

Starting in 2018, the Lockman Foundation posted some passages from "NASB 2020", an update of the 1995 revision.[39] Key differences from the 1995 revision include an effort to improve "gender accuracy" (for example, adding "or sisters" in italics to passages that reference "brothers", to help convey the mixed-gender meaning of a passage that might otherwise be misunderstood as only speaking of men), a shift (where applicable) from the common construct "let us" when proposing action to the more-contemporary construct "let's" (to disambiguate a sort of "imperative" encouragement rather than a seeking of permission that could otherwise be misunderstood from a given passage), and a repositioning of some "bracketed text" (that is, verses or portions of verses that are not present in earliest Biblical manuscripts, and thus printed in brackets in previous NASB editions) out from inline-and-in-brackets down instead to footnotes.[693]

The reader of the CPH blog has continuously read interpretive and translation principles that are not only sound but also aid the Christian in understanding the Bible more fully. One such interpretive principle is about the meaning that we are after, what the author meant by the words that he used as should have been understood by his initial intended audience.

When we look at the controversy over gender-inclusive language and the use of plurals, the above principles come into play, as does the historical-grammatical approach, which means that God personally chose the time, the place, the language, and the culture into which his Word was inspirationally penned. Who are we to disrespect that because we wish to appease the modern man or woman, who may be offended? Their offense is nothing more than self-centeredness, refusing to wrap their mind around the idea that

---

[693] "More Information About NASB 2020". lockman.org. Retrieved February 17, 2021.

the Creator of all things chose the setting, the language, and time in which his Word was to be introduced to man. One of the last bastions of literal translation philosophy, the New American Standard Bible, has given into the gender-inclusive translation philosophy. How are we to translate the Greek word ἀδελφοί (brothers)?

NEW AMERICAN STANDARD BIBLE (NASB 1995/2020): The 1995 edition **was*** very literal. The NASB Translates "brothers" or "brethren," to "brothers and sisters." The NASB has gender-inclusive changes to the word "man" in Romans 2:1-11 and Micah 6:8.

*The NASB 2020 revision has taken the first steps at abandoning their literal translation philosophy. One of the updates is what the NASB (the Lockman Foundation) calls the use of the "**Gender Accurate**" language. This is actually good marketing skills to call an abandonment of your core translation values "accurate" when it is anything but accurate.

1 Thessalonians 5:14: *We urge you, **brethren**, admonish the unruly, encourage the fainthearted, help the weak, be patient with everyone.* NASB 1995

1 Thessalonians 5:14: *We urge you, **brothers and sisters,** admonish the unruly, encourage the fainthearted, help the weak, be patient with everyone.* NASB 2020

Romans 2:1: *Therefore you have no excuse, **you foolish person**, everyone of you who passes judgment, for in that which you judge **someone else** [another], you condemn yourself; for you who judge practice the same things…*

Romans 2:3: *But do you suppose this, **you foolish person** [O man] **who passes** [when you pass] judgment on those who practice such things and **yet does them as well** [do the same yourself], that you will escape the judgment of God?*

Micah 6:8: *He has told you, **O man**, what is good…* NASB 1995

Micah 6:8: *He has told you, **a human**, what is good; and what does the LORD require of you but to do justice, to love kindness, and to walk humbly with your God?* NASB 2020

From what the Lockman Foundation has released about the 2020NASB, the 2020 update seems like it is a more significant release than their 1995 update was. Taking everything into account, there are gender-neutral language changes. There is an attempt to remove archaic language which has also led to removing literal renderings, and that is not a good thing. We can say, some of the changes are good, some are irrelevant, some are wordy, and some are poor. Looking at all the pluses and minuses. There seem to be more minuses than pluses. We have not even delved into the Lockman's Foundation obsession with retaining the corrupt readings from the King

James Version NT (Textus Receptus) in the main text instead of relegating them to footnotes.

Translators

The translation work was done by a group sponsored by the Lockman Foundation.[694] According to the Lockman Foundation, the committee consisted of people from Christian institutions of higher learning and from evangelical Protestant, predominantly conservative, denominations (Presbyterian, Methodist, Southern Baptist, Church of Christ, Nazarene, American Baptist, Fundamentalist, Conservative Baptist, Free Methodist, Congregational, Disciples of Christ, Evangelical Free, Independent Baptist, Independent Mennonite, Assembly of God, North American Baptist, and "other religious groups").[695]

The foundation's Web site indicates that among the translators and consultants who contributed are Bible scholars with doctorates in biblical languages, theology, "or other advanced degrees", and come from a variety of denominational backgrounds. More than 20 individuals worked on modernizing the NASB in accord with the most recent research.[696]

The Bible that Will Replace the NASB

The Updated American Standard Version (UASV) will be released by the end of 2021 for a 120-year anniversary of the American Standard Version (ASV). Unlike the NASB2020, the UASV has **no intention** of ever abandoning the literal translation philosophy or even stepping away from it even in minor ways. It will not be our desire to bend toward the dynamic equivalent translations (NIV, CEV, TEV, NLT, etc.) and the quasi literal translations (ESV CSB) but rather to educate the readers of those translations of the importance of the literal translation philosophy and bring them into our camp.

Our primary purpose is to give the Bible readers what God said by way of his human authors, not what a translator thinks God meant in its place.—Truth Matters! Our primary goal is to be accurate and faithful to the original text. The meaning of a word is the responsibility of the interpreter (i.e., reader), not the translator.—Translating Truth!

---

[694] Metzger, Bruce (2003). The New Testament: Its Background, Growth, and Content (3rd ed.). Nashville: Abingdon Press. p. 336.

[695] BeDuhn, Jason David (2003). *Truth in Translation — Accuracy and Bias in English Translations of the New Testament*. University Press of America. p. 35,39.

[696] "The Lockman Foundation – NASB, Amplified Bible, LBLA, and NBLH Bibles". The Lockman Foundation.

The translation of God's Word from the original languages of Hebrew, Aramaic, and Greek is a task unlike any other and should never be taken lightly. It carries with it the heaviest responsibility: the translator renders God's thoughts into a modern language. The **Updated American Standard Version (UASV)** is a literal translation. What does that mean?

LEB Lexham English Bible, 2012

With approximately one hundred different English translations of the Bible already published, the reader may well wonder why yet another English version has been produced. Those actually engaged in the work of translating the Bible might answer that the quest for increased accuracy, the incorporation of new scholarly discoveries in the fields of semantics, lexicography, linguistics, new archaeological discoveries, and the continuing evolution of the English language all contribute to the need for producing new translations. But in the case of the *Lexham English Bible* (LEB), the answer to this question is much simpler; in fact, it is merely twofold.

First, the LEB achieves an unparalleled level of transparency with the original language text because the LEB had as its starting point the *Lexham Hebrew-English Interlinear Bible* and the *Lexham Greek-English Interlinear New Testament*. It was produced with the specific purpose of being used alongside the original language text of the Bible. Existing translations, however excellent they may be in terms of English style and idiom, are frequently so far removed from the original language texts of Scripture that straightforward comparison is difficult for the average user. Of course, distance between the original language text and the English translation is not a criticism of any modern English translation. To a large extent this distance is the result of the philosophy of translation chosen for a particular English version, and it is almost always the result of an attempt to convey the meaning of the original in a clearer and more easily understandable way to the contemporary reader. However, there are many readers, particularly those who have studied some biblical Hebrew, Aramaic, or Greek, who desire a translation that facilitates straightforward and easy comparisons between the translation and the original language text. The ability to make such comparisons easily in software formats like Logos Bible Software makes the need for an English translation specifically designed for such comparison even more acute.

Second, the LEB is designed from the beginning to make extensive use of the most up-to-date lexical reference works available. For the Old Testament this is primarily *The Hebrew and Aramaic Lexicon of the Old Testament (HALOT)*, and for the New Testament this is primarily the third edition of Walter Bauer's *A Greek-English Lexicon of the New Testament and Other Early Christian Literature* (BDAG). Users can be assured that the LEB as a translation is based on the best scholarly research available. The Hebrew text on which the LEB Old Testament is based is that of *Biblia Hebraica Stuttgartensia*. The Greek text on which the LEB New Testament is based is that of *The Greek New Testament: SBL Edition* (SBLGNT), a new edition produced by Michael W. Holmes in conjunction with the Society of Biblical Literature and Logos Bible Software. In its evaluation of textual variation, the SBLGNT uses modern text-critical methodology along with guidance from the most recently available articles, monographs, and technical commentaries to establish the text of the Greek New Testament.

Naturally, when these two factors are taken into consideration, it should not be surprising that the character of the LEB as a translation is fairly literal. This is a necessary by-product of the desire to have the English translation correspond transparently to the original language text. Nevertheless, a serious attempt has been made within these constraints to produce a clear and readable English translation instead of a woodenly literal one.

There are three areas in particular that need to be addressed to make a translation like the LEB more accessible to readers today, while at the same time maintaining easy comparison with the original language text. First, differences in word order have to be addressed. In this regard, the LEB follows standard English word order, not the word order of biblical Hebrew, Aramaic, or Koiné Greek. Anyone who needs to see the word order of the original languages can readily consult the *Lexham Hebrew-English Interlinear Bible* or the *Lexham Greek-English Interlinear New Testament*, which contain a sequence line which gives this information. Second, some expressions in biblical languages are idiomatic, so that a literal translation would be meaningless or would miscommunicate the true meaning. The LEB uses ⌊lower corner⌋ brackets to indicate such expressions, with a literal rendering given in a note. Third, words which have no equivalent in the original language text must sometimes be supplied in the English translation. Because the LEB is designed to be used alongside the original language texts of Scripture, these supplied words are indicated with italics. In some cases, the need for such supplied words is obvious, but in other cases where it is less clear a note has been included.

Finally, the reader should remember that any Bible translation, to be useful to the person using it, must actually be read. We encourage every user of the LEB, whether reading it alongside the original languages text or not, to remember that once we understand the meaning of a biblical text we are responsible to apply it first in our own lives, and then to share it with those around us.

Textual basis NT: SBL Greek New Testament. The Society of Biblical Literature is not really to be too trust as they are filled with higher critics and has an Agnostic Bart D. Ehrman on staff who has spent much of his life undermining the New Testament for churchgoers through his books, wherein he intentionally misrepresents the information.

Translation type is Formal Equivalence, namely a literal translation.

Updated American Standard Version (UASV)

GREEK TEXT: The primary Greek texts used to prepare the English text of the Greek Scripture portion of the Updated American Standard Version were the WH NA. The Wescott and Hort Greek New Testament and the Kurt Aland et al., Novum Testamentum Graece, 27th/28th Edition. (Stuttgart: Deutsche Bibelgesellschaft, 1993/2012).[697]

The Updated American Standard Version (UASV) holds to the classic literal translation philosophy of English Bible translations over the past five hundred years. The source of this philosophy was William Tyndale's New Testament of 1526; the King James Version of 1611 (KJV), the English Revised Version of 1885 (RV), and the foundation text for the UASV, the American Standard Version of 1901 (ASV).

The Updated American Standard Version endeavors to give its readers a deeper, more accurate translation that remains faithful to the original words. By translating Scripture into the closest possible corresponding modern English, the UASV allows readers to encounter God's Word at it was originally intended.

Developed by one Bible scholar, in the translation legacy of William Tyndale, the Updated American Standard Version remains faithful to the Bible's original text; therefore, the original author's meaning is never endangered for the sake of readability, for it is the reader's task to determine what the Bible author meant by the words that he used. In this literal translation that remains faithful to its translation philosophy, the reader can be secure in knowing that they are always getting the Word of God in English not what a translator has interpreted it to be. In order to achieve this, by way of the good judgment of the translator, every word and phrase in the UASV has been considered against the original Hebrew, Aramaic, and Greek, to give its readers the fullest accuracy.

The UASV was produced using lexical or linguistic translation philosophy that focuses on the accuracy of translating from the original languages into modern English, painstakingly deciding what English word or

---

[697] *Updated American Standard Version* (Cambridge, Ohio: Christian Publishing House, 2020). https://www.uasvbible.org/

phrase most closely corresponds to a given word of the original text never sacrificing accuracy for the sake of readability. The translator has given the reader a literal word-for-word translation in almost every case. It is understandable. However, in the rarest of exceptions, if it has been determined that the rendering will be misunderstood or misinterpreted, there is no going to extremes in the literal translation of the text just for the sake of being literal. At times, the translator has retained the literal rendering, such as "slept," for example, and added the phrase "in death," which completes the sense in the English text. (1 Kings 2:10) This process assures that the words of the original text chosen under inspiration by its authors are translated as accurately as possible for our readers.

ESSENTIAL-OPTIMALLY LITERAL

ESV English Standard Version, 2001

The English Standard Version (ESV) stands in the classic mainstream of English Bible translations over the past half-millennium. The fountainhead of that stream was William Tyndale's New Testament of 1526; marking its course were the King James Version of 1611 (KJV), the English Revised Version of 1885 (RV), the American Standard Version of 1901 (ASV), and the Revised Standard Version of 1952 and 1971 (RSV). In that stream, faithfulness to the text and vigorous pursuit of accuracy were combined with simplicity, beauty, and dignity of expression. Our goal has been to carry forward this legacy for a new century.

To this end each word and phrase in the ESV has been carefully weighed against the original Hebrew, Aramaic, and Greek, to ensure the fullest accuracy and clarity and to avoid under-translating or overlooking any nuance of the original text. The words and phrases themselves grow out of the Tyndale-King James legacy, and most recently out of the RSV, with the 1971 RSV text providing the starting point for our work. Archaic language has been brought to current usage and significant corrections have been made in the translation of key texts. But throughout, our goal has been to retain the depth of meaning and enduring language that have made their indelible mark on the English-speaking world and have defined the life and doctrine of the church over the last four centuries.

The ESV is an "essentially literal" translation that seeks as far as possible to capture the precise wording of the original text and the personal style of each Bible writer. It seeks to be transparent to the original text, letting the reader see as directly as possible the structure and meaning of the original.

Derived from the RSV—1971 Revision.

Textual basis for the OT: Biblia Hebraica Stuttgartensia with Septuagint influence **Deuterocanonical/Apocrypha:** Göttingen Septuagint, Rahlf's Septuagint and Stuttgart Vulgate. **NT**: 83% correspondence to Nestle-Aland Novum Testamentum Graece 27th edition.

Translation type is Formal Equivalence, meaning that it is a literal translation. However, it is not as literal as it could be, meaning that having Bill Mounce as the Chief translator when he favors interpretive translations cause the ESV to be dynamic equivalent in many places when it did not have to be. The stated intent of the translators was to follow an "essentially literal" translation philosophy while taking into account differences of grammar, syntax, and idiom between current literary English and the original languages. The ESV uses some gender-neutral language.

HCSB Holman Christian Standard Bible, 2004

The Holman Christian Standard Bible (HCSB) is a trusted, original translation of God's Word. A team of more than 100 scholars from 17 denominations pursued two ideals with every translation decision: each word must reflect clear, contemporary English and each word must be faithful to the original languages of the Bible.

Holman Bible Publishers assembled an international, interdenominational team of 100 scholars and proofreaders, all of whom were committed to biblical inerrancy. The translation committee sought to strike a balance between the two prevailing philosophies of Bible translation: formal equivalence (literal or word-for-word) and dynamic or functional equivalence (thought-for-thought). The translators called this balance "optimal equivalence."

According to the translators, the goal of an optimal-equivalence translation is "to convey a sense of the original text with as much clarity as possible." To that end, the ancient source texts were exhaustively scrutinized at multiple levels (word, phrase, clause, sentence, discourse) to determine their original meaning and intent. Afterwards, using the best language tools available, the semantic and linguistic equivalents were translated into as readable a text as possible.

Textual basis NT: Novum Testamentum Graece 27th edition. **OT**: Biblia Hebraica Stuttgartensia with some Septuagint influence.

Translation type is Mediating, meaning that it is halfway between literal translation philosophy and dynamic equivalent, i.e., interpretive.

CSB Christian Standard Bible, 2017

The Christian Standard Bible aims to draw readers into a deeper, more meaningful relationship with God. By translating Scripture into the clearest possible modern English, the CSB allows readers to experience God's Word at its fullest.

Developed by 100 scholars from 17 denominations, the Christian Standard Bible faithfully and accurately captures the Bible's original meaning without compromising readability.

The CSB was created using Optimal Equivalence, a translation philosophy that balances linguistic precision to the original languages and readability in contemporary English. In the many places throughout Scripture where a word-for-word rendering is clearly understandable, a literal translation is used. When a word-for-word rendering might obscure the meaning for a modern audience, a more dynamic translation is used. This process assures that both the words and thoughts contained in the original text are conveyed as accurately as possible for today's readers.

The CSB provides a highly accurate text for sermon preparation and serious study, translated from the biblical languages by scholars who love God's Word. Yet it doesn't compromise readability and clarity for those who may be less familiar with the traditional (and sometimes difficult) vocabulary retained in some translations. Research shows the CSB is both highly literal to the original languages and highly readable, achieving an optimal balance of the two.

Pastors and laypeople can read and share the Christian Standard Bible with confidence, knowing truth of God's Word will be communicated effectively.

Derived from the Holman Christian Standard Bible

Textual basis of the **NT**: Novum Testamentum Graece 28th edition. **OT**: Biblia Hebraica Stuttgartensia 5th Edition with some Septuagint influence.

Translation type Optimal Equivalence, meaning that it is not a true literal translation any will be an interpretive translation where the translators take liberties with the text at times giving you what they believe the Bible authors meant not what the Bible authors said.

Reading level 7.0

NET The NET Bible (New English Translation), 1996

The NET Bible is a completely new translation of the Bible, not a revision or an update of a previous English version. It was completed by more than 25 biblical scholars—experts in the original biblical languages—who worked directly from the best currently available Hebrew, Aramaic, and Greek texts. Most of these scholars teach Old or New Testament exegesis in seminaries and graduate schools. Furthermore, the translator assigned to prepare the first draft of the translation and notes for each book of the Bible was chosen in every instance because of his or her extensive work in that particular book—not only involving teaching but writing and research as well, often extending over several decades. Many of the translators and editors have also participated in other translation projects. They have been assisted by doctoral students and advised by style consultants and Wycliffe field translators. Hence, the notes alone are the cumulative result of hundreds of thousands of hours of biblical and linguistic research applied to the particular problems of accurately translating and interpreting the text. The translators' notes, most of which were created at the same time as the initial drafts of the translation itself, enable the reader of the NET Bible to "look over the shoulders" of the translators as they worked and gain insight into their decisions and choices to an extent never before possible in an English translation.

One of the goals of the NET Bible with the complete set of translators' notes is to allow the general public—as well as Bible students, pastors, missionaries, and Bible translators in the field—to be able to know what the translators of the NET Bible were thinking when a phrase or verse was rendered in a particular way. Many times, the translator will have made informed decisions based on facts about grammatical, lexical, historical, and textual data not readily available to English-speaking students of the Bible. This information is now easily accessible through the translators' notes.

tn: Translator's Note

Explains the rationale for the translation and gives alternative translations, interpretive options, and other technical information.

sn: Study Note

Incudes comments about historical or cultural background, explanation of obscure phrases or brief discussions of context, discussions of the theological point made by the biblical author, cross references and references to Old Testament quotations or allusions in the New Testament, or other miscellaneous information helpful to the modern reader.

tc: Text-critical Note

Discusses alternate (variant) readings found in the various manuscripts and groups of manuscripts of the Hebrew Old Testament and Greek New Testament.

Textual basis Self-described "transparent": Inter-dependent textual basis as evidenced in extensive text-notes. **NT**: Novum Testamentum Graece 27th edition. **OT**: Biblia Hebraica Stuttgartensia with Septuagint influence.

Translation type Mid-range functional or dynamic equivalence prevalent in the text, with formal equivalent renderings very often given in the footnotes. The primary purpose of an effective translator or translation committee is to give the Bible readers what God said by way of his human authors, not what a translator thinks God meant in its place. That is not what we have here. The primary goal of an effective translator or translation committee is to be accurate and faithful to the original text. The meaning of a word is the responsibility of the interpreter (i.e., reader), not the translator. Again, that is not what we have here.

Reading level Middle School

RNJB Revised New Jerusalem Bible, 2018, 2019

The Revised New Jerusalem Bible (RNJB) is an English translation of the Bible published by Darton, Longman & Todd. The New Testament and the Psalms were released in February 2018, with the full Bible released in July 2019. It is a revision of the Jerusalem Bible and the New Jerusalem Bible undertaken by the British biblical scholar and Ampleforth Abbey monk Henry Wansbrough. Whereas the New Jerusalem Bible and its predecessor The Jerusalem Bible featured the use of Yahweh some 6800+ times for the Divine Name, YHWH, the RNJB reverts to the use of LORD. Substantially revising the JB and NJB texts, the new translation "applies formal equivalence translation for a more accurate rendering of the original scriptures, sensitivity to readable speech patterns and more inclusive language." It contains new study notes and book introductions, written by Henry Wansbrough.

Textual basis Old Testament: Biblia Hebraica Stuttgartensia with Septuagint influence. **New Testament**: Novum Testamentum Graece 27th edition, i.e., "NA27."

Translation type is claimed to be Formal equivalence, i.e., literal translation. However, it is a gender inclusive Bible even more so than the NJB. For instance, Matthew 4:4 reads, "A human lives not on bread alone." Therefore, regardless of its claim about itself, it is not a true literal translation.

605

MIDDLE-GROUND

NRSV New Revised Standard Version, 1990

The *New Revised Standard Version of the Bible* (*NRSV*) was published in 1989 and has received the widest acclaim and broadest support from academics and church leaders of any modern English translation.

It is the only Bible translation that is as widely ecumenical:

- The ecumenical *NRSV* Bible Translation Committee consists of thirty men and women who are among the top scholars in America today. They come from Protestant denominations, the Roman Catholic church, and the Greek Orthodox Church. The committee also includes a Jewish scholar.

- The *RSV* was the only major translation in English that included both the standard Protestant canon and the books that are traditionally used by Roman Catholic and Orthodox Christians (the so-called "Apocryphal" or "Deuterocanonical" books). Standing in this tradition, the *NRSV* is available in three ecumenical formats: a standard edition with or without the Apocrypha, a *Roman Catholic Edition*, which has the so-called "Apocryphal" or "Deuterocanonical" books in the Roman Catholic canonical order, and *The Common Bible*, which includes all books that belong to the Protestant, Roman Catholic, and Orthodox canons.

- The *NRSV* stands out among the many translations available today as the Bible translation that is the most widely "authorized" by the churches. It received the endorsement of thirty-three Protestant churches. It received the imprimatur of the American and Canadian Conferences of Catholic bishops. And it received the blessing of a leader of the Greek Orthodox Church.

The *NRSV* differs from the *RSV* in four primary ways:

- updating the language of the *RSV*, by replacing archaic forms of speech addressed to God (Thee, Thou, wast, dost, etc.), and by replacing words whose meaning has changed significantly since the *RSV* translation (for example, Paul's statement in 2 Corinthians 11.25 that he was "stoned" once)

- making the translation more accurate,

- helping it to be more easily understood, especially when it is read out loud, and

- making it clear where the original texts intend to include all humans, male and female, and where they intend to refer only to the male or female gender.

Textual basis OT: Biblia Hebraica Stuttgartensia with Dead Sea Scrolls and Septuagint influence. **Apocrypha**: Septuagint (Rahlfs) with Vulgate influence. **NT**: United Bible Societies' The Greek New Testament (3rd ed. corrected). 81% correspondence to Nestle-Aland Novum Testamentum Graece 27th edition.

Translation type Formal equivalence, with minimal gender-neutral paraphrasing. It is not a true literal translation and will be an interpretive translation where the translators take liberties with the text at times giving you what they believe the Bible authors meant not what the Bible authors said. The primary purpose of an effective translator or translation committee is to give the Bible readers what God said by way of his human authors, not what a translator thinks God meant in its place. That is not what we have here. The primary goal of an effective translator or translation committee is to be accurate and faithful to the original text. The meaning of a word is the responsibility of the interpreter (i.e., reader), not the translator. Again, that is not what we have here.

Reading level High School

NIV New International Version, 1978, 1984, 2011

The New International Version (NIV) is a completely original translation of the Bible developed by more than one hundred scholars working from the best available Hebrew, Aramaic, and Greek texts.

The initial vision for the project was provided by a single individual – an engineer working with General Electric in Seattle by the name of Howard Long. Long was a lifelong devotee of the King James Version, but when he shared it with his friends he was distressed to find that it just didn't connect. Long saw the need for a translation that captured the truths he loved in the language that his contemporaries spoke.

For 10 years, Long and a growing group of like-minded supporters drove this idea. The passion of one man became the passion of a church, and ultimately the passion of a whole group of denominations. And finally, in 1965, after several years of preparatory study, a trans-denominational and international group of scholars met in Palos Heights, Illinois, and agreed to begin work on the project – determining to not simply adapt an existing English version of the Bible but to start from scratch with the best available manuscripts in the original languages. Their conclusion was endorsed by a large number of church leaders who met in Chicago in 1966.

A self-governing body of fifteen biblical scholars, the Committee on Bible Translation (CBT) was formed and charged with responsibility for the version, and in 1968 the New York Bible Society (which subsequently became the International Bible Society and then Biblica) generously undertook the financial sponsorship of the project. The translation of each book was assigned to translation teams, each made up of two lead translators, two translation consultants, and a stylistic consultant where necessary. The initial translations produced by these teams were carefully scrutinized and revised by intermediate editorial committees of five biblical scholars to check them against the source texts and assess them for comprehensibility. Each edited text was then submitted to a general committee of eight to twelve members before being distributed to selected outside critics and to all members of the CBT in preparation for a final review. Samples of the translation were tested for clarity and ease of reading with pastors, students, scholars, and lay people across the full breadth of the intended audience. Perhaps no other translation has undergone a more thorough process of review and revision. From the very start, the NIV sought to bring modern Bible readers as close as possible to the experience of the very first Bible readers: providing the best possible blend of transparency to the original documents and comprehension of the original meaning in every verse. With this clarity of focus, however, came the realization that the work of translating the NIV would never be truly complete. As new discoveries were made about the biblical world and its languages, and as the norms of English usage developed and changed over time, the NIV would also need to change to hold true to its original vision.

And so, in the original NIV charter, provision was made not just to issue periodic updates to the text but also to create a mechanism for constant monitoring of changes in biblical scholarship and English usage. The CBT was charged to meet every year to review, maintain, and strengthen the NIV's ability to accurately and faithfully render God's unchanging Word in modern English.

The 2011 update to the NIV is the latest fruit of this process. By working with input from pastors and Bible scholars, by grappling with the latest discoveries about biblical languages and the biblical world, and by using cutting-edge research on English usage, the Committee on Bible Translation has updated the text to ensure that the New International Version of the Bible remains faithful to Howard Long's original inspiration.

Textual basis NT: Nestle-Aland Greek New Testament. **OT**: Biblia Hebraica Masoretic Hebrew Text, Dead Sea Scrolls, Samaritan Pentateuch,

Aquila, Symmachus and Theodotion, Latin Vulgate, Syriac Peshitta, Aramaic Targums, for Psalms Juxta Hebraica of Jerome.

Translation type Mixed formal & dynamic equivalence. It is not a true literal translation and will be an interpretive translation where the translators take liberties with the text at times giving you what they believe the Bible authors meant not what the Bible authors said. The primary purpose of an effective translator or translation committee is to give the Bible readers what God said by way of his human authors, not what a translator thinks God meant in its place. That is not what we have here. The primary goal of an effective translator or translation committee is to be accurate and faithful to the original text. The meaning of a word is the responsibility of the interpreter (i.e., reader), not the translator. Again, that is not what we have here.

Reading level 7.80

NJB New Jerusalem Bible, 1986

The New Jerusalem Bible (NJB) is an English-language translation of the Bible published in 1985 by Darton, Longman and Todd and Les Editions du Cerf, edited by Henry Wansbrough and approved for use in study and personal devotion by Roman Catholics. The New Jerusalem Bible includes the deuterocanonical books and sections. The text of these is included where they occur in the context of the complete Septuagint, rather than being grouped together in an appendix. Deuterocanonical sections of books in the Hebrew canon are identified by the use of italics. This version of scripture is translated directly from the Hebrew, Greek or Aramaic. The 1973 French translation, the Bible de Jérusalem, is followed only where the text admits to more than one interpretation. The introductions and notes, with some modifications, are taken from the Bible de Jérusalem.[1] The NJB's New Testament is translated from the Novum Testamentum Graece 25th ed., with occasional parallels to Codex Bezae. Its Old Testament is drawn from the Biblia Hebraica Stuttgartensia with Septuagint, and the Deuterocanon from the Septuagint with Vulgate influence.

It is not a true literal translation and will be an interpretive translation where the translators take liberties with the text at times giving you what they believe the Bible authors meant not what the Bible authors said. The primary purpose of an effective translator or translation committee is to give the Bible readers what God said by way of his human authors, not what a translator thinks God meant in its place. That is not what we have here. The primary goal of an effective translator or translation committee is to be accurate and faithful to the original text. The meaning of a word is the responsibility of the interpreter (i.e., reader), not the translator. Again, that is not what we have here. The translation uses some inclusive language, as in Exodus 20:17: "You shall not set your heart on your neighbor's spouse", rather than "neighbor's wife" or "neighbor's woman". For the most part, however, the inclusive language is limited to avoiding a "preference" for the masculine, as the translators write in the foreword. The New Jerusalem Bible uses more gender inclusive language than the Jerusalem Bible

NABRE New American Bible Revised Edition, 1984 (revised NT)

The New American Bible Revised Edition (NABRE) is an English-language Catholic Bible translation, the first major update in 20 years to the New American Bible (NAB), originally published in 1970 by the Confraternity of Christian Doctrine. Released on March 9, 2011, it consists of the 1986 revision of the NAB New Testament with a fully revised Old Testament approved by the United States Conference of Catholic Bishops in 2010.

Approved for private use and study by Catholics, the NABRE has not received approval for Catholic liturgical use. Although the revised Lectionary based on the original New American Bible is still the sole translation approved for use at Mass in the dioceses of the United States, the NABRE New Testament is currently being revised so that American Catholics can read the same Bible translation in personal study and devotion that they hear in Mass.

Derived from the Confraternity Bible, New American Bible

Textual basis OT (2011 revision): Biblia Hebraica Stuttgartensia with Dead Sea Scrolls and minor Septuagint influence. Deuterocanonicals: Septuagint, Dead Sea Scrolls, and some Vulgate influence. **NT**: (1986 revision): "UBS3," the third edition of United Bible Societies' Third Edition Greek New Testament, and consultations of Novum Testamentum Graece 26th edition, i.e., "NA26."

Translation type Formal equivalence (from the Preface), moderate use of dynamic equivalence.

Reading level High School

It is not a true literal translation and will be an interpretive translation where the translators take liberties with the text at times giving you what they believe the Bible authors meant not what the Bible authors said. The primary purpose of an effective translator or translation committee is to give the Bible readers what God said by way of his human authors, not what a translator thinks God meant in its place. That is not what we have here. The primary goal of an effective translator or translation committee is to be accurate and faithful to the original text. The meaning of a word is the responsibility of the interpreter (i.e., reader), not the translator. Again, that is not what we have here.

DYNAMIC EQUIVALENT (Interpretive Meaning for Meaning)

NEB New English Bible, 1961

The New English Bible (NEB) is an English translation of the Bible. The New Testament was published in 1961 and the Old Testament (with the Apocrypha) was published on 16 March 1970.[1] In 1989, it was significantly revised and republished as the Revised English Bible.

Near the time when the copyright to the English Revised Version was due to expire (1935), the Oxford University Press (OUP), and the Cambridge University Press (CUP), who were the current English Revised Version copyright holders, began investigations to determine whether a modern revision of the English Revised Version text was necessary. In May 1946 G.S. Hendry, along with the Presbytery of Stirling and Dunblane produced a notice, which was presented to the General Assembly of the Church of Scotland, indicating that the work of translating should be undertaken in order to produce a Bible with thoroughly "modern English." After the work of delegation was finished, a general conference was held in October 1946 where it was determined that a completely fresh translation should be undertaken rather than a revision as originally suggested by the University Presses of Oxford and Cambridge.

In due time, three committees of translators and one committee of literary advisers were enlisted and charged with the task of producing the New English Bible. Each of the three translation committees was responsible for a different section of the Bible. These three sections consisted of the Old Testament, the Apocrypha, and the New Testament.

The work of translating was typically undertaken in this fashion: A member, or members, of one of the committees, would produce a draft of a book, or books, of the Bible (typically from the section in which they were assigned) and submit the draft to the section committee. Occasionally a scholar outside the committee would be invited to participate in this phase of the translation process and was asked to submit a draft of the book or books with which he or she had renowned experience. This draft was then distributed among the members of the appropriate committee. Members of the committee would then meet and discuss the translation choices made in the draft. The draft that resulted from this meeting of the concerned committee was then sent to the committee of literary advisers, who would revise the draft in co-operation with the translators. When a consensus on the draft was reached, the final draft would be sent on to the Joint Committee, which was head over the four sub-committees.

For the Old Testament the translators primarily made use of the Masoretic Text as presented by Rudolf Kittel in his 3rd Edition of the Biblia Hebraica (1937). In addition to the Masoretic Text, the translators also made use of the Dead Sea Scrolls, the Samaritan Pentateuch, the Greek Septuagint, the Aramaic Targums, and the Syriac Peshitta.

For the Apocrypha the translators made the decision to follow The Old Testament in Greek according to the Septuagint, edited by H.B. Swete. Also, the translators made use of the Codex Sinaiticus (for the Book of Tobit), Theodotion's translation of the Apocrypha (for The Song of the Three, Daniel and Susanna, and Daniel, Bel and the Snake (sometimes referred to as the Dragon)), Codex Vaticanus Graecus 1209 (for Sirach), Codex 248 (also for Sirach), and R.L. Bensly's Latin text The Fourth Book of Ezra for 2 Esdras.

For the New Testament the New English Bible Translators relied on a large body of texts including early Greek New Testament manuscripts, early translations rendered in other languages (those aside from Greek), and the quotations of early Christian writers and speakers. The text adhered to by the translators of the New English Bible can be found in The Greek New Testament, edited by R.V.G. Tasker and published by the University Presses of Oxford and Cambridge (1964).

The translators of the New English Bible chose to render their translation using a principle of translation called dynamic equivalence (also referred to as functional equivalence or thought-for-thought translation). C.H. Dodd, Vice-Chairman and Director of the Joint Committee, commented that the translators "...conceived our task to be that of understanding the original as precisely as we could... and then saying again in our own native idiom what we believed the author to be saying in his."

This method of translation is in contrast to the traditional translations of the Authorized Version (King James Version), English Revised Version, American Standard Version, Revised Standard Version, and others, which place an emphasis on word-for-word correspondence between the source and target language. C.H. Dodd goes on to summarize the translation of the New English Bible as "...free, it may be, rather than literal, but a faithful translation nevertheless, so far as we could compass it."

As a result, the New English Bible is necessarily more paraphrastic at times in order to render the thoughts of the original author into modern English.

Because of its scholarly translators, the New English Bible has been considered one of the more important translations of the Bible to be produced following the Second World War. Biblical scholar F.F. Bruce declared that "To the sponsors and translators of the New English Bible the English-speaking world owes an immense debt. They have given us a version which is contemporary in idiom, up-to-date in scholarship, attractive, and at times exciting in content..." T.S. Eliot, however, commented that the New English Bible "astonishes in its combination of the vulgar, the trivial and the pedantic."[698] Henry Gifford argued that "the new translators ... kill the wonder."

Textual basis NT: R.V.G. Tasker Greek New Testament. **OT**: Biblia Hebraica (Kittel) 3rd Edition.

Translation type Dynamic equivalence

It is not a literal translation at all and translators are giving their readers an interpretive translation where the translators will quite often take liberties with the text at times giving the reader what they believe the Bible authors meant not what the Bible authors said. The primary purpose of an effective translator or translation committee is to give the Bible readers what God said by way of his human authors, not what a translator thinks God meant in its place. By far that is not what we have here. The primary goal of an effective translator or translation committee is to be accurate and faithful to the original text. The meaning of a word is the responsibility of the interpreter (i.e., reader), not the translator. Again, that is not what we have here. This is not a Bible translation regardless of what it claims, rather it is a mini-commentary and if viewed as such, it can be used as a study tool.

REB Revised English Bible, 1989

The Revised English Bible (REB) is a 1989 English-language translation of the Bible that updates the New English Bible (NEB) of 1970. As with its predecessor, it is published by the publishing houses of both the universities of Oxford and Cambridge. It is not to be confused with the Revised English

---

[698] Nicolson, Adam (31 May 2004). Power and Glory: Jacobean England and the Making of the King James Bible. HarperCollins Pub Ltd.

Eliot, T.S. (16 December 1962). "Letter of T.S. Eliot on the style of the New English Bible". Sunday Telegraph: 7. Retrieved Friday, February 21, 2020.

Bible of 1877, which was an annotated and slightly corrected version of the King James Bible.

The REB is the result of both advances in scholarship and translation made since the 1960s and also a desire to correct what have been seen as some of the NEB's more egregious errors (for examples of changes, see the references). The changes remove many of the most idiosyncratic renderings of the NEB, moving the REB more in the direction of standard translations such as the New Revised Standard Version (NRSV) or the New International Version (NIV).

The translation is intended to be somewhat gender-inclusive, though not to the same extent as translations such as the NRSV. Psalm 1 offers an illustration of the REB's middle-ground approach to gender-inclusive language. On one side are more traditional translations, such as the King James Version (KJV) and the English Standard Version (ESV), that use the word "man" and the masculine singular pronoun in Psalm 1. The ESV, for example, has "Blessed is the man who walks not in the counsel of the wicked...; but his delight is in the law of the Lord." On the other side are more gender-inclusive translations such as the NRSV that avoid any masculine nouns and pronouns in Psalm 1. The NRSV uses plurals: "Happy are those who do not follow the advice of the wicked...; but their delight is in the law of the Lord." In between these two approaches is the translation of Psalm 1 in the REB, which avoids using a male noun ("man") but retains the masculine singular pronouns ("his"): "Happy is the one who does not take the counsel of the wicked for a guide... His delight is in the law of the Lord."

The style of the REB has been described as more "literary" than that of the NRSV or NIV. It tends slightly further in the direction of "dynamic equivalence" than those translations, but still translates Hebrew poetry as poetry and reflects at least some of the characteristics of that poetry. The REB's general accuracy and literary flavour has led Stephen Mitchell and others to compliment it as one of the best English renderings. The translators of the REB gave particular attention to its suitability for public reading, especially in the Book of Psalms.

The NEB "had a considerable British flavor" but the REB "removed much of this distinctiveness and aimed to be more accessible to an American audience."

Derived from the New English Bible

Textual basis NT: Medium correspondence to Nestle-Aland Novum Testamentum Graece 27th edition, with occasional parallels to Codex Bezae. OT: Biblia Hebraica Stuttgartensia (1967/77) with Dead Sea Scrolls and Septuagint influence. Apocrypha: Septuagint with Vulgate influence.

Translation type Dynamic equivalence

Reading level High school

It is not a literal translation at all, and translators are giving their readers an interpretive translation where the translators will quite often take liberties with the text at times, giving the reader what they believe the Bible authors meant, not what the Bible authors said. The primary purpose of an effective translator or translation committee is to give the Bible readers what God said by way of his human authors, not what a translator thinks God meant in its place. By far, that is not what we have here. The primary goal of an effective translator or translation committee is to be accurate and faithful to the original text. The meaning of a word is the responsibility of the interpreter (i.e., reader), not the translator. Again, that is not what we have here. This is not a Bible translation regardless of what it claims, rather it is a mini-commentary and if viewed as such, it can be used as a study tool.

Philip Comfort writes, "The REB is a revision of The New English Bible (neb). The revisers of the New Testament used NA[26]. This choice resulted in several textual changes from neb, which had followed a very eclectic text. The translators of neb had adopted readings never before put into print by English translators, but the scholars working on REB adjusted many of these readings back toward the norm. At the same time, they also made some significant textual changes, the most outstanding of which was their treatment of the story of the woman caught in adultery (John 7:53–8:11). Reflecting the overwhelming evidence of the Greek manuscripts, this story is not included in the main body of John's Gospel. Rather, it is printed as an appendix after the Gospel of John."[699]

CEV Contemporary English Version, 1995

Uncompromising simplicity marked the American Bible Society's (ABS) translation of the Contemporary English Version (CEV) that was first published in 1995. The text is easily read by grade schoolers, second language readers, and those who prefer the more contemporized form. The CEV is not a paraphrase. It is an accurate and faithful translation of the original manuscripts.

The CEV began as a result of studies conducted by biblical scholar Dr. Barclay M. Newman in 1984 into speech patterns used in books, magazines, newspapers, and television. These studies focused on how English was read

---

[699] Philip W. Comfort, *New Testament Text and Translation Commentary: Commentary on the Variant Readings of the Ancient New Testament Manuscripts and How They Relate to the Major English Translations* (Carol Stream, IL: Tyndale House Publishers, Inc., 2008), xxviii.

and heard, especially by children. This led to a series of test volumes being published in the late 1980s and early 1990s.

The CEV New Testament was released in 1991, the 175th anniversary of ABS. The CEV Old Testament was released in 1995 and the Apocryphal/Deuterocanonical Books were published in 1999.

The translators of the CEV followed three principles: that the CEV:

- must be understood by people without stumbling in speech

- must be understood by those with little or no comprehension of "Bible" language

- must be understood by all.

"The drafting, reviewing, editing, revising, and refining the text of the Contemporary English Version has been a worldwide process extending over a period of slightly more than ten years. It has involved a wide variety of persons beyond the core team of ABS translators and the consultant experts who have worked closely with the team. The creative process has also involved scholar consultants and reviewers representing a wide range of church traditions and with expertise in such areas as Old Testament, New Testament, Hebrew language, Greek language, English language, linguistics, and poetry. In all, this process involved more than a hundred people in the various stages of the text creation and review process. And it is this process, carried out in constant prayer for the guidance of the Spirit of God, that guarantees the accuracy, integrity and trustworthiness of the CEV Bible" (from *Creating and Crafting the Contemporary English Version: A New Approach to Bible Translation*—New York: American Bible Society, 1996).

Translation type Dynamic equivalence

It is not a literal translation at all and translators are giving their readers an interpretive translation where the translators will quite often take liberties with the text at times giving the reader what they believe the Bible authors meant not what the Bible authors said. The primary purpose of an effective translator or translation committee is to give the Bible readers what God said by way of his human authors, not what a translator thinks God meant in its place. By far that is not what we have here. The primary goal of an effective translator or translation committee is to be accurate and faithful to the original text. The meaning of a word is the responsibility of the interpreter (i.e., reader), not the translator. Again, that is not what we have here. This is not a Bible translation regardless of what it claims, rather it is a mini-commentary and if viewed as such, it can be used as a study tool.

TEV Todays English Version [Also known as the Good News Translation], 1976

The Good News Translation (GNT), formerly called the Good News Bible or Today's English Version, was first published as a full Bible in 1976 by the American Bible Society as a "common language" Bible. It is a clear and simple modern translation that is faithful to the original Hebrew, Koine Greek, and Aramaic texts. The GNT is a highly trusted version.

It first appeared in New Testament form in 1966 as *Good News for Modern Man: The New Testament in Today's English Version*, translated by Dr. Robert G. Bratcher in consultation with a committee appointed by the American Bible Society.

Textual basis Medium Correspondence to Nestle-Aland Novum Testamentum Graece 27th edition

Translation type   Dynamic equivalence

It is not a literal translation at all and translators are giving their readers an interpretive translation where the translators will quite often take liberties with the text at times giving the reader what they believe the Bible authors meant not what the Bible authors said. The primary purpose of an effective translator or translation committee is to give the Bible readers what God said by way of his human authors, not what a translator thinks God meant in its place. By far that is not what we have here. The primary goal of an effective translator or translation committee is to be accurate and faithful to the original text. The meaning of a word is the responsibility of the interpreter (i.e., reader), not the translator. Again, that is not what we have here. This is not a Bible translation regardless of what it claims, rather it is a mini-commentary and if viewed as such, it can be used as a study tool.

NLT New Living Translation (second edition), 2004

The goal of any Bible translation is to convey the meaning of the ancient Hebrew and Greek texts as accurately as possible to the modern reader. The New Living Translation is based on the most recent scholarship in the theory of translation. The challenge for the translators was to create a text that would make the same impact in the life of modern readers that the original text had for the original readers. In the New Living Translation, this is accomplished by translating entire thoughts (rather than just words) into natural, everyday English. The end result is a translation that is easy to read and understand and that accurately communicates the meaning of the original text.

The New Living Translation used translators from a variety of Christian denominations. The method combined an attempt to translate the original texts simply and literally with a dynamic equivalence synergy approach used to convey the thoughts behind the text where a literal translation may have been difficult to understand or even misleading to modern readers. A part of the reasoning behind adapting the language for accessibility is the premise that more people will hear the Bible read aloud in a church service than are likely to read it or study it on their own.

It has been suggested that this "thought-for-thought" methodology, while making the translation easier to understand, is less accurate than a literal (formal equivalence) method, and thus the New Living Translation may not be suitable for those wishing to undertake detailed study of the Bible.[700]

Textual basis Revision to the Living Bible paraphrase. **NT**: Greek New Testament (UBS 4th revised edition) and Nestle-Aland Novum Testamentum Graece 27th edition. **OT**: Biblia Hebraica Stuttgartensia, with some Septuagint influence.

Translation type Formal and Dynamic equivalence

It is not a literal translation at all and translators are giving their readers an interpretive translation where the translators will quite often take liberties with the text at times giving the reader what they believe the Bible authors meant not what the Bible authors said. The primary purpose of an effective translator or translation committee is to give the Bible readers what God said by way of his human authors, not what a translator thinks God meant in its place. By far that is not what we have here. The primary goal of an effective translator or translation committee is to be accurate and faithful to the original text. The meaning of a word is the responsibility of the interpreter (i.e., reader), not the translator. Again, that is not what we have here. This is not a Bible translation regardless of what it claims, rather it is a mini-commentary and if viewed as such, it can be used as a study tool.

TNIV Today's New International Version, 2005

Today's New International Version (TNIV) was an English translation of the Bible which was developed by the Committee on Bible Translation (CBT). The CBT also developed the New International Version (NIV) in the 1970s. The TNIV is based on the NIV. It is explicitly Protestant like its predecessor; the deuterocanonical books are not part of this translation. The TNIV New Testament was published March 2002. The complete Bible was

---

[700] Rhodes, Ron (2009). The Complete Guide to Bible Translations: How They Were Developed. Harvest House Publishers. p. 152.

published February 2005. The rights to the text are owned by Biblica (formerly International Bible Society). Zondervan published the TNIV in North America. Hodder & Stoughton published the TNIV in the UK and European Union.

A team of 13 translators worked on the translation, with forty other scholars reviewing the translation work. The team was designed to be cross denominational.

In 2011 both the 1984 NIV and the TNIV were discontinued following release of a revised and updated version of the NIV.

The translation took more than a decade to complete; 13 evangelical scholars worked on the translation: Ronald F. Youngblood, Kenneth L. Barker, John H. Stek, Donald H. Madvig, R. T. France, Gordon Fee, Karen H. Jobes, Walter Liefeld, Douglas J. Moo, Bruce K. Waltke, Larry L. Walker, Herbert M. Wolf and Martin Selman. Forty other scholars, many of them experts on specific books of the Bible, reviewed the translation teams' work. They came from a range of Evangelical denominational backgrounds.

The intent of the TNIV translators was to produce an accurate and readable translation in contemporary English. The Committee on Bible Translation wanted to build a new version on the heritage of the NIV and, like its predecessor, create a balanced mediating version—one that would fall in-between the most literal translation and the most free; between word-for-word (Formal Equivalence) and thought-for-thought (Dynamic Equivalence).

For translation a wide range of manuscripts were reviewed. The Masoretic text, the Dead Sea Scrolls, the Samaritan Pentateuch, the Greek Septuagint or (LXX), the Aquila, Symmachus and Theodotion, the Latin Vulgate, the Syriac Peshitta, the Aramaic Targums, and for the Psalms the Juxta Hebraica of Jerome were all consulted for the Old Testament. The Dead Sea Scrolls were occasionally followed where the Masoretic Text seemed inconsistent. The United Bible Societies Nestle-Aland Greek New Testament text was used for the New Testament.

Translation type Dynamic and Formal Equivalence

It is not a literal translation at all and translators are giving their readers an interpretive translation where the translators will quite often take liberties with the text at times giving the reader what they believe the Bible authors meant not what the Bible authors said. The primary purpose of an effective translator or translation committee is to give the Bible readers what God said by way of his human authors, not what a translator thinks God meant in its place. By far that is not what we have here. The primary goal of an effective translator or translation committee is to be accurate and faithful to the original text. The meaning of a word is the responsibility of the interpreter (i.e., reader), not the translator. Again, that is not what we have here. This is not a Bible translation regardless of what it claims, rather it is a mini-commentary and if viewed as such, it can be used as a study tool.

Glossary of Technical Terms[701]

Alexandrian Text: the Greek text was produced in Alexandria, Egypt, where there was a high degree of scholarship due to the famous library and museum. This was undoubtedly responsible in large part for the more meticulous care taken in the copying of manuscripts. The chief manuscripts representing the Alexandrian text are Codex Vaticanus, also designated as B and 03; Codex Sinaiticus, designated by the first letter of the Hebrew alphabet, א (aleph), and 01, and the papyri p75 and p66. Codex Alexandrinus designated 02, is characteristic of the Byzantine text in the Gospels, but Alexandrian elsewhere. Vaticanus and Sinaiticus are both dated fourth-century. One of the more notable characteristics of the Alexandrian text is the tendency to display the harder variant readings, which usually are the best candidates for the original reading or autograph. Vaticanus seems to be slightly superior to Sinaiticus in its readings. It also rates as closest to the initial text (q.v.) of the ECM (q.v.).

Amanuensis: Latin term for a scribe or clerk (plural "amanuenses"). When used in the context of textual criticism, it refers specifically to a person who served as a secretary to record first-hand the words of a New Testament book, if the author chose to use a secretary rather than write down the words himself. Tertius (Rom. 16:22) is an example. The degree to which an amanuensis may have contributed to the content of any particular book is a matter of speculation and controversy. At one end of the spectrum is the amanuensis who merely took dictation (the position preferred here); at the other is the possibility that a New Testament author may have told his amanuensis what he wished to communicate in general terms, leaving it to the amanuensis to actually compose the book.

Apparatus: information about variant readings to the text chosen for a critical edition of the Greek New Testament. Such information is also called a textual or critical apparatus. The standard layout is footnotes covering all the variants identified on the page, listing the manuscripts supporting the variants. With the exception of the ECM (see below), it is not the intent of the editors to note every known variant to the text, because doing so would expand the edition to a large, multi-volume work. Thus, only a selection of all the variants is actually provided, usually focusing on variants deemed to be of some significance. The extent of the selection varies from one apparatus to another. The two that are best known are included respectively with the Nestle-Aland text and the United Bible Societies' text (GNT). The

---

[701] Glossary is by Dr. Don Wilkins, a Senior Translator for the New American Standard Bible. Used with permission.

former, designed principally for scholarly research, notes more variants than the latter, while the latter is easier to read and provides ratings of confidence levels for many variants. Bruce Metzger also provided *A Textual Commentary on the Greek New Testament* as a companion volume to the GNT, sharing valuable notes about committee decisions for the readings that have ratings. Since the NA and GNT have had the same texts for many years under the same leadership, Metzger's *Textual Commentary* is relevant and helpful for both. It should be noted, negatively, that translator's notes or notes about alternate translations in modern versions are not the same as a textual apparatus, though the information may also be helpful. The apparatus must list variant readings and the ancient manuscripts that support them.

Archetype: the original text, or ancestor (in genealogical terms), from which a group of manuscripts ultimately derive. Using "ultimately" in the fullest sense, all biblical manuscripts ultimately derive from the autograph as their archetype, but in textual criticism "archetype" is distinguished from the autograph. Since it is by definition the original text behind a group (larger or smaller) of copies, it is not possible to identify a particular manuscript as an archetype, and typically archetypes are assumed to be lost.

Assimilation: a deliberate alteration of the text by a scribe when he encountered a parallel passage elsewhere that exhibits some differences with the one he was copying. The resulting manuscript has the passages in agreement, while another extant manuscript–possibly exhibiting the text of the scribe's exemplar–reveals differences between the passages; there may, of course, be others with differing texts as well. Assimilation is assumed as a variation of the harder reading (*lectio difficilior*) principle. That is, a scribe would have found differences in the parallel passages, e.g. OT quotations, troubling, and therefore would have "corrected" them in his copy. This may sometimes be indicated more or less by interlinear or marginal notations in a manuscript used as an exemplar. If so, the textual critic can select the text with the differing parallel as the most likely original with considerable confidence. Otherwise, unless the differences are accountable as errors, the same text is still preferable because there is no good reason why the scribe of that text would change it to make it differ from its parallel.

Asterisk (*): a common notation in the apparatus of a critical text. Often a reading in a manuscript has been altered by a scribe as a correction from the scribe's perspective. Scribes were careful not to blot out the original lettering etc., but to make an interlinear or marginal notation of the correction instead. Sometimes readings have been "corrected" in this way more than once, and by different scribes. To show the distinction, a superscript number is added to the notation for the manuscript in question, such as "B[1]." By this format the reader is informed that a particular variant is supported by the first corrector of manuscript B; other correctors, if there are others, are indicated by successive superscript numbers. When one or more corrections are listed as support for variants, an asterisk (e.g. "B*") is usually added to a manuscript notation to indicate that the variant reading is the one originally found in that manuscript, as opposed to a correction. When this happens, then, the same manuscript will be listed with at least two different variant readings. Therefore, it is very important to be aware of these superscript characters attached to manuscript notations, especially the asterisk.

Atticism: a stylistic, grammatical, or lexical feature in New Testament Greek that is thought by many to be secondary, added by a later scribe who was trying to "improve" the Greek. Attic Greek, the Greek of golden-age Athens that was so often imitated for so many centuries later, is taken to be the standard. The position assumed here is that Attic Greek really did become the standard for Greek, including that of the New Testament, and so-called Atticisms are not necessarily foreign to the language of the New Testament. One could say that the New Testament basically is Attic Greek, so long as one allows that for the most part it is not literary Greek, and eyewitness accounts of events seem to have been kept in the style of the original language.

Authorities: often used as a general term for manuscripts but can have a wider application to other sources (e.g. ancient translations and patristic citations) that have some value as support for variant readings.

Autograph: The autograph (self-written) was the text actually written by a New Testament author, or the author and scribe as the author dictated to him. If the scribe was taking it down in dictation (Rom: 16:22; 1 Pet: 5:12), he might have done so in shorthand.[702] Whether by shorthand or longhand, we can assume that both the scribe and the author would check the scribe's work. The author would have authority over all corrections since Holy Spirit did not move the scribe. If the inspired author wrote everything down himself as the Spirit moved him, the finished product would be the autograph. This text is also often referred to as the original. Hence, the terms *autograph* and *original* are often used interchangeably. Sometimes textual critics prefer to make a distinction, using "original" as a reference to the text

---

[702] Andrews says, again, there is the **slight possibility** of Tertius or other Bible author's scribes taking it down in shorthand and after that making out a full draft, which would have been reviewed by both Paul and Tertius. This is only the case if it is comparable to what a modern-day court reporter does. In some sense, they are taking down whoever is speaking down in shorthand. Imagine a courtroom where you have a witness talking fast, the prosecution interrupts, the defense jumps in with his rebuttal and the judge snaps his ruling, and the witness resumes his or her account of things. All of that is taken down explicitly word for word in shorthand, and if ever turned into longhand, it would be exactly what was said, down to the uh and um common in speech. So, if the shorthand of the day had that kind of capability; then, it is conceivable. We must remember these are the Bible author's dictated words to the scribe based on their inspiration, not the word choice or writing style of the scribe.

that is correctly attributed to a biblical author. This is a looser distinction, one that does not focus on the process of how a book or letter was written.

Base Text: in a collation, the text chosen to display to the reader. The readings of any other texts are listed as variant readings to this text and included in an apparatus, usually as footnotes. The first Greek text used as a base text was the Textus Receptus. In modern times the common practice has been for the editors of the Greek text to display a base text which they have determined themselves by following principles of textual criticism. The principles vary from one circle of critics to another and undergo some refinement as research in textual criticism continues. The leading base texts today are the text shared by Nestle-Aland and the United Bible Societies, and the Majority Text (edited by the late Zane Hodges and Arthur Farstad). A third text may gain traction at some point, that of the Greek New Testament published by the Society of Biblical Literature and edited by Michael Holmes.

Biblical Uncial: a traditional term for manuscripts written in the large Greek letters loosely described as "capitals." This term has fallen into disfavor, and "majuscule" (see below) is preferred.

Byzantine Family: the second of the three principal families recognized today, along with the Alexandrian and Western. For a traditional account of the Byzantine family or text, see above p. 51. Most modern scholars doubt the traditional explanation of the rise of the text or view it as unhelpful in understanding it. It seems clear that the text existed in some form as early as the fourth century, but that it continued to be developed after that. The ECM editors have confirmed that the Byzantine text took a consistent form after the ninth century. They have also defined it for their own purposes of collation: Byzantine readings are those which agree with the majority of witnesses but differ from the initial text of the ECM. In contrast, Majority Text readings are those supported by the majority of witnesses and *may* also agree with the ECM initial text.

Caesarean Family: a group of manuscripts once identified as a fourth family of manuscripts. The family is discussed above on pp. 174 f. It is no longer considered viable by most scholars, in view of the high degree of mixture among NT witnesses and the difficulty of establishing consistency in such families.

Canon: used in two senses: 1) the 27 New Testament books accepted as inspired and uniquely comprising the New Testament; and 2) a term for the principles or rules of textual criticism accepted by most critics (see above p. 159). Most textual critics today would use less absolute language for these principles, in some cases even calling them "guidelines." Most of the principles are subject to qualification, with exceptions, and even to debate in some cases.

CBGM: The Coherence-Based Genealogical Method, a computer-assisted system for determining genealogical relationships between manuscripts. For details see the chapter on the same. The system relies on internal evidence and is designed to cope with the high level of contamination or mixture of texts found in NT manuscripts.

Cluster: a replacement term for the geographical nomenclature traditionally associated with families of texts. As applied by Eldon Epp (see above, pp. 234 f.), the Western text becomes, for example, the "D-text cluster," referring to the manuscripts exhibiting common traits associated with the text represented by manuscript D (05). Positively, one can say that new terminology is desirable given that we are now aware of the high degree of mixture or contamination among NT witnesses that makes geographical identifiers largely obsolete. Negatively, "cluster" is a vague concept and does not account for the genealogical connections between witnesses. Retaining "family" without a geographical reference might be better.

Codex: a physical book of scripture in contrast to the ancient scroll. The church began to produce codices early in the second century or perhaps at the end of the first. Aside from whatever monetary savings may have resulted, the codex provided a great advantage in locating passages: quite literally what we can call random access as opposed to the serial access necessitated by unwinding a scroll.

Collation: a base text of the Greek New Testament together with an apparatus of variant readings for any place in the text where the manuscripts selected for the collation disagree. Disagreements can range from a single letter to a phrase, and the latter sometimes includes the order of the words. Diacritical marks are noted as well, but of course, these marks are late additions and are subject to change at the will of the critic. The formal term for places of disagreement is "variation unit" (q.v.).

Colophon: from a Greek word for "finishing." In the context of copying manuscripts, "a finishing touch," referring to comments that scribes sometimes added at the end of a copy. The comment could be anything but might provide valuable information as to when and where the manuscript was written.

Commentaries: these exist in two forms: 1) a more or less complete set of marginal or interlinear notes added by instructors to the text of a manuscript, and 2) conventional commentaries written by church fathers. The latter can be valuable to the extent that they usually include scripture quotations, often of substantial length, which may provide insight into the text used by the father. If that can be established, then the dates associated with the father also stand as evidence for dating the text.

Conflation or Conflated Readings: when a variation unit (q.v.) includes a reading that in effect combines the other variant readings for the unit, that reading is considered a conflation (or conflated reading) according to the principles of textual criticism. The assumption behind this conclusion is that when faced with two (or possibly more) choices that seemed to have equal merit as original, the scribe's primary concern was that the original reading is not lost. The other possibility is that the conflation is the original reading, and the other readings are shorter due to erroneous omission. However, conflation is usually the more likely explanation (see above p. 241).

Conjectural Emendation: this is a controversial practice, highly so in some circles. It is based on the corollary to the "harder reading" principle that the harder variant reading is to be rejected if it is so difficult as to be impossible. Usually, the alternative is to choose an easier reading, but in rare instances, some textual critics may conclude that there is no acceptable alternate reading. In that case, they may propose, based on conjecture (a highly educated "guess"), another reading that does not exist in any extant manuscript. In defense of this practice, it can be argued that in fact many early manuscripts have been lost to us, and the practice has been routinely used to repair other ancient Greek manuscripts. I (Wilkins) can attest to the latter, having seen at least one instance where a conjectural emendation on a classical text later proved to be correct. However, there are major differences between classical and biblical manuscripts, one of which is that we have many more of the latter, arguably eliminating the need for this practice. There is also the theological issue of divine preservation (a case in which defenders of the Textus Receptus and textual critics at large ironically find some common ground). Most textual critics of faith take a *de facto* position that God has preserved the NT text in extant Greek manuscripts. Defenders of conjectural emendation can argue, along with advocates of the MT or TR, that the resultant text of any of these critics does not exist in any extant manuscript (and never will). The response is the fact of mixture (or contamination) in all extant manuscripts: we are trying to reconstruct the original; if the result agreed with any extant manuscript, then it would either be a failure, or we would have the incredible outcome that the resultant Greek text would both be the original, and the extant manuscript with which it agreed would be a copy of the original.

Copyist: generally, a synonym for an ancient scribe, in the context of textual criticism. The quality of the manuscript is a good indicator of the professionalism of the copyist, and a colophon (q.v.), if included, may provide information about the copyist's credentials. If the quality seems more like that of an amateur, it is quite possible that the copyist was not a scribe, but just someone with the ability to write who made a copy for his own purposes or for the benefit of friends or others. Thus "copyist" can have a wider reference than "scribe."

Corpus: a Latin term meaning "body," this refers to a complete collection of some kind. One typical use is the reference to all of Paul's letters as the "Pauline corpus." Any group of writings with a common trait can be collected together under that trait as a category.

Corrector and Corrections: the term "correction(s)" can have its ordinary meaning, but in the context of TC often refers to a change in the text of a manuscript made by a scribe or copyist, sometimes the same person who made the copy of the manuscript, and sometimes by one or more others. The one who has made the change is often called the "corrector," and if the handwriting indicates that writers other than the original copyist have added corrections, they may be designated as separate correctors (see on "Asterisk" above; see also "Assimilation"). From the viewpoint of the critic, these corrections are always intrusions on the text, unless it is clear that they have been made by the same person who produced the manuscript, in which case they indicate what exemplars (q.v.) he had before him. Corrections result in mixed (contaminated) texts, and they can be very difficult to sort out. When made by the copyist of the manuscript, they are simply a choice of wording that is only recognized by comparison with other texts that have different wording.

Corruption: a reading in the text that is judged by textual critics to be a mistake grammatically or lexically and virtually unreadable or senseless. If it is readable but does not seem to make good sense in the context, reasonable scholars may disagree, depending on their tolerance of the NT author's flexibility in the Greek and the range of possibility for the context. It is probably safe to say that more corruptions are observed or declared in the Hebrew OT than in the NT.

Critical Edition or Critical Text: any biblical text in the original language that includes a legitimate apparatus of variant readings linked to the text. To be legitimate, the readings must consistent mainly of alternatives found in ancient manuscripts, which usually include ancient versions (translations) and citations in the church fathers. This format, which is a collation (q.v.), is the most practical way to provide the user a convenient source providing a great deal of textual information for making textual decisions. The text itself represents all the choices of its editors for every variation unit (q.v.) in the text.

Cursive Manuscripts: from a Latin word meaning "running," cursive refers to a handwriting style in smaller (minuscule, "rather small") Greek letters developed for the purpose of easier, quicker writing. Cursive manuscripts seem to have come into existent about the beginning of the ninth century. One can therefore easily identify these copies as late.

Dittography: a scribal error, the copying of a letter, word, or combination of words twice. It is easy for any writer to commit from a momentary lapse of concentration, particularly if the doubled wording has the same ending as that of the text to which it was added. See above p. 142 for an example.

Documentary Evidence: extant manuscripts of significance supporting a variant reading. The date of the manuscript and the quality of the text it contains according to text-critical principles are the chief determinants of significance. Documentary evidence is usually contrasted with internal evidence and often posed in opposition to it, though in fact the quality of the text is decided by internal evidence. Earlier manuscripts usually have better readings by this standard. However, textual mixture or contamination is always assumed, so in the minds of many or most textual critics, internal evidence should prevail over documentary when the two are in opposition. Others maintain that superior documentary evidence should prevail over internal. This amounts to deciding whether a manuscript is consistently presenting superior readings elsewhere should be preferred when its reading in a passage seems in some way inferior to that of lesser manuscripts.

Eclecticism: within the discipline of textual criticism, eclecticism can be viewed as a preference for internal criteria in deciding variant readings in opposition to external criteria. The degree to which this is done has led to two recognized types of eclecticism, most often called "thoroughgoing" and "reasoned" (see pp. 248 ff.). The former ignores external criteria while the latter accords value to it. In practice, internal and external criteria usually point to the same readings. When they conflict, however, thoroughgoing eclecticism prefers the choice of internal criteria, while reasoned eclecticism may allow external evidence priority over internal.

Eclectic Edition: an edition of the Greek New Testament created by using some form of eclectic method (see above). It is assumed that the readings chosen for the editions have to some extent been chosen by favoring internal criteria over external. The text of NA28/GNT5 is an example. Unless one were to assume, however, that a particular manuscript actually was a copy of the original text (as described hypothetically under Conjectural Emendation), every extant manuscript ultimately is a result of some degree of eclecticism on the part of ancient scribes. Thus, distinguishing any Greek

NT text as "eclectic" is a matter of degree depending to some extent on the perspective of the critic. In most circles, an edition called "eclectic" is substantially based on internal criteria.

ECM (*Edition Critica Maior*): the critical text and apparatus published by the Institute for New Testament Textual Research in Munich. Now in its second edition, the ECM2 is based on a nearly exhaustive collection of Greek manuscripts, ancient versions that attest to readings in the Greek text, and readings attested by the Greek fathers. The text, which appears in NA28 and GNT5 is, as noted elsewhere, eclectic, relying on genealogical relationships between witnesses that are determined by statistical agreements of variant readings. For details about the text, see chapter 13 on the CBGM, the computer-based methodology used to produce the ECM. At the time of this writing, only the General (Catholic) Epistles have been published.

Ellipsis: for our purposes, this term has two contexts. The first is a piece of missing text in an ancient manuscript or fragment due to wear and tear or other misfortunes. When ellipses occur, the task of the textual critic is to use the spacing of other letters in the text to estimate one or more letters that were lost. The context as found in corresponding manuscripts may make the task easy, or it may be difficult or impossible to arrive at certainty if more than one option is plausible. The second context is that of a negative apparatus in ECM2, indicated by an ellipsis in the a-reading; see note 423 on p. 295 above. This is simply a space-saving device, and the bulk of information included in ECM2 needs to be streamlined whenever possible.

Emendation: see Conjectural Emendation above.

Exemplar: from a Latin word for "pattern" or "archetype," a manuscript that a scribe was tasked to copy. It seems probable that in many instances a scribe used more than one exemplar, though probably not more than two or three for any one copy. In these cases, one exemplar probably served as the primary source to be copied, while another was used for comparison, and "correction," so to speak. That is, the scribe could "correct" the primary exemplar by sometimes choosing a reading for his copy found in another exemplar he was using. Whenever a reading is found in at least one other extant source, we can assume for practical purposes that the scribe of the manuscript copied the reading and did not invent it.

Extant: i.e. actually existing, as opposed to a hypothetical reading or manuscript. Many textual critics take the position that only readings found in extant texts are acceptable for consideration in a variation unit. The argument against this position is that many manuscripts–particularly the earlier ones–have been lost, so there is always the possibility that a conjectured reading could have existed. Conjectural emendations are the logical opposite to extant readings. Since they are typically invented to solve a problem in the text, one argument against them is that they are easier readings which should have survived. Yet one or more harder readings survived, while the (easier) conjecture did not.

External Evidence: nearly synonymous with Documentary Evidence (q.v.), which focuses on particular manuscripts. External evidence focuses on external criteria for evaluating manuscripts. Originally the chief criteria were the dates of the manuscripts supporting a reading, the geographical distribution of the manuscripts, and the overall quality both of the individual manuscripts and textual "families." For textual critics who favor traditional methods, all three criteria continue to carry weight, and external evidence, as a rule, prevails over internal when the two sets of criteria point to opposing readings. Among other critics, research on NT manuscripts such as that pursued with the CBGM has eliminated geographical distribution as a criterion due to textual contamination/mixture. The same research has also cast doubt on the value of dating and has largely homogenized text families (the Byzantine text continues to be recognized as its own family). The superiority of some manuscripts continues to be acknowledged both by traditionalists and other critics, but this factor only plays a role in the decision practice of the former. Non-traditionalists rely on internal evidence.

Facsimile: in the context of textual criticism, a photographic reproduction in accurate color of a manuscript. A facsimile copy is essential for the expert who must evaluate a reading, because even slight differences in color may help to determine the outline of a character or other mark in a text. Facsimiles can be very expensive; today, fortunately, photographs on the internet may suffice.

Folio: a single leaf, or page, of a book. The "front" of the page is called the *recto*, while the back that is read after turning it is called the *verso*. This is the system for describing an ancient codex.

Fragment: as the name indicates, a portion of a text, the remainder of which has been lost. The term may be used to refer to a fairly significant amount of text or as little as a mutilated piece containing only a few letters. The value of very small fragments is that if they can be dated and identified, they may establish an early date for a particular reading. Identification is often very difficult or impossible, however.

Generation: in the language of genealogy-based textual criticism, a text that is basically a copy of an earlier text and/or the exemplar for a later text. The reality is more complex, however. The distinction between "text" and "manuscript" can easily be blurred, the text being the manuscript's content, and it is possible for the text of one manuscript to actually be earlier than that of an earlier manuscript to which it is compared. Ultimately it is the date of the text that matters. Furthermore, research has established the reality of mixture or contamination among texts, to such an extent that any two related texts will exhibit readings that appear to be both earlier and later in each text. That is, when readings differ, one text will not exhibit all earlier readings relative to the other, but both earlier and later readings, and vice-versa. So, when two texts are judged sufficiently alike to be related, a system must be used to assign a genealogical priority to the one text or the other.

Genealogy: the metaphor that has gained the most acceptance among textual critics for describing the relationship between New Testament manuscripts. It has been said that all manuscripts, or more precisely, texts, are related since they all derive more or less from an autograph. In the Coherence-Based Genealogical Method, which is poised to be the leading system, the texts of individual manuscripts are for example categorized as potential ancestors or descendants of each other. This system and the metaphor itself are not without its shortcomings, including assumptions that are difficult or impossible to prove.

Gloss: a very short commentary on a detail in the text, written by the scribe or a teacher. Most often it is a brief definition or explanation of an uncommon word in the text and will be written in the margin. Glosses often pose a problem for the textual critic because they may have appeared to be alternative readings to previous scribes, and in some cases, those scribes may have misunderstood a gloss in question as a preferred reading. The result, in these cases, is that a scribe replaces the word in the text with the gloss as he makes his own copy. The textual critic is left to reverse-engineer the situation and identify the original reading. It may not be difficult if one of the readings is clearly harder, but that is not always the case.

Haplography: the scribal error of copying two identical letters, words, or phrases in close proximity only once by accident. For an example see above, pp. 141 f. This is one of several "errors of the eye."

Harmonization: an intentional scribal error, viewed by the scribe as a necessary correction. It essentially takes two forms: 1) revising a quotation of scripture to match the original, or 2) changing the reporting of any details to match the original account of the details. One sees the former mainly as NT quotations of OT passages, routinely following the LXX. It is possible that scribes sometimes made these changes unconsciously due to the intrusion of their own memories. When done intentionally, the changes can be viewed as another case of rejecting harder readings, since the scribe was uncomfortable with the quotation's differing from the original as he knew it. The same can be said of the harmonization of details found elsewhere, such as differing reports of events in the Synoptics. It is important to distinguish harmonization in textual criticism from exegetical harmonization. Scribal harmonizations are to be rejected in the search for the original text, but interpretations of seemingly conflicting reports, etc. that harmonize them to remove contradictions can be legitimate. This approach always accepts the best text-critical readings.

Homoeoarcton: the phenomenon of two lines of text having the same or similar beginnings, leading a scribe to skip part or all of the first line as he mistakenly copies the second line without finishing the first.

Homoeoteleuton: the phenomenon of two lines of text having the same or similar endings, the counterpart to homoeoarcton ("similar beginning"). Homoeoteleuton often is loosely used in reference to both phenomena, even though it only refers by definition to endings. See also parablepsis.

Homophony: the phenomenon of words that sound alike but are spelled differently. This undoubtedly has always been a problem for copyists, and it became an even greater problem in late Greek as certain vowels tended to be pronounced alike. For scribes, it was inevitable that mistakes would be made due to homophony when copies were being made by dictation. However, it is natural for anyone making a copy of a text to make homophonic mistakes even when working alone, as the mind unconsciously produces mistaken homophones. The confusion of "there" with "their" is one of many in English. Fortunately, homophonic errors usually result in nonsense and for the most part, can easily be identified by textual critics, but this is not always the case. The situation is complicated in Greek, where homophony results in mistakes in grammatical endings.

Initial Text: this is defined variously, but for conservatives, it can be equated with the autograph. For others, it is the text that became the origin of all copies of the NT, but it was not the autograph itself. This conclusion is based in part on the assumption that the text of the autograph cannot be reconstructed with complete confidence, due to uncertainties about variant readings. It is also assumed that we cannot know what happened to the text between the time that it was first penned by the author (the autograph) and first copies were produced that became the exemplars for all subsequent copies.

Inscription: See Superscription:

Interlinear: writing between lines of text. Scribes sometimes did this to supply translation and notes or other helps.

Internal Evidence: evidence supporting or opposing a reading based on scribal habits or the original author's style, in contrast to external or documentary evidence. Since the goal of textual criticism is to determine the reading most likely to be the original, the leading criterion of internal evidence is that the harder reading is to be preferred. The determination of difficulty can relate to a number of different factors, essentially anything that would make a reading uncomfortable to a scribe. Compare "Documentary Evidence," "Eclecticism," and "External Evidence" above.

Interpolation: the addition of spurious material to the text by a scribe, often for harmonization (q.v.). Other additions probably were glosses (q.v.) that were moved to the text, or paraphrases such as are found in the Western text.

Intrinsic Probability: internal evidence related to the original author, primarily stylistic matters. The goal is to make the best estimation of what the author is likely to have written. This can be very difficult to determine with any real confidence and should be done cautiously. For details see above, pp. 244 ff.

Itacism: scribal errors based on confusion of certain vowel sounds in Greek. The term is based on the letter iota, which tended to be the sound (a long "ee" in English) of three vowels and additional two-vowel combinations. Long and short "o" sounds were also confused, however. The substitution of mistaken vowels when copying was done at dictation could result in a confusion of Greek pronouns and verb constructions among other things. Doubtless the same mistakes might also be made as a result of homophony (q.v.) even when copying was done without dictation. The textual critic must be alert to the possibility, which can provide a simple explanation to variant readings whose vowels could be confused.

Lacuna (pl: Lacunae): an unfortunate loss of text within a manuscript due to accident or wear and tear. Even more unfortunate, lacunae usually are more frequent and more damaging in early manuscripts, especially the papyri. The essential elements of the missing text can be supplied from other manuscripts, of course, but not sufficiently to reconstruct a variant reading. To attempt any kind of reconstruction, one must have access to an accurate facsimile of the damaged manuscript.

Leather, Vellum: See Parchment.

Leaves: the same as folios (see "Folio" above).

Lectio Brevior: Latin for "shorter reading." In traditional TC, when there is a difference in the length of variant readings, it has been a criterion that the shorter reading is preferred as the original, other factors being equal.

The reasoning is that a scribe is more likely to add material (e.g. an interpolation) than to delete it. This criterion has fallen on hard times, however, as critics have produced evidence that scribes were more likely to omit material by accident than to add it (see above, pp. 240 ff.). We take the position that the criterion still has merit but must be applied with certain conditions in mind (pp. 241 f.).

Lectio Difficilior: Latin for "more difficult reading," also called simply "the harder reading." Often mentioned in this book, the criterion is the leading rule of TC, but also problematic because of the associated provision that the reading must not be so difficult as to be impossible. The criterion is based on the assumption that a conscientious scribe would not change an easy or clear reading in the text to a more difficult one, but only the reverse. Other internal criteria often relate to this criterion as subcategories of it. The provision ruling out impossibilities is easy to apply when the difficulty can be explained as an error. When that is not the case, however, critics may disagree as to whether the harder reading in question really is impossible, or extremely difficult but possible.

Lectionaries: books of NT passages chosen by the Christian church for reading at services. For the most part, they represent the Byzantine text and are of use in reconstructing the history of that text.

Lector: Latin for "reader," referring to the person whose task it was in a Scriptorium to read the text of a manuscript for a group of copyists or scribes (see p. 10 above).

Liturgical Influence: a factor, like theology, that may have led a scribe to choose one reading over another. The tendency would be to prefer a reading that was customarily followed in a text read for services.

Majority Text: a text of the NT in which variant readings are chosen that are found in the majority of all Greek NT manuscripts (cf. "Byzantine Family" above). One could consider this external (objective) evidence and maintain that it is the leading criterion for establishing the text. Credit for this text is due primarily to Zane Hodges and Arthur Farstad, though the latter once humbly told me (Wilkins) that the text was mainly Hodges' work. Hodges maintained that mathematical probabilities pointed to the text with the greatest number of surviving manuscripts as the one closest to the original. Thus, the name is an accurate description, though Hodges' theory about the text's relation to the original is arguable at best. Of greater value and importance, the Majority Text has essentially purged the Byzantine text of its negative association with the Textus Receptus. Nevertheless, most textual critics maintain that those favoring the MT rely heavily on theological arguments and thin objective evidence in their defense of the text. In particular, easier readings tend to prevail over harder in the MT and BT.

Majuscule: Latin for "somewhat larger," referring to the large Greek letter set that is commonly considered the capitals. All of the earlier manuscripts were written in this style. Other features of the style in its pristine form are the lack of punctuation, spaces between words, and accents (in some majuscules punctuation and accents have been added). The lack of spacing, one would think, was perhaps due in part to writing down words as they were spoken, without pauses or other space markers between the words. It is assumed that spacing was omitted beginning with papyrus, which was expensive, and it may be true that some expense was saved thereby. However, margins were wide, which certainly was not a cost-saving measure.

Manuscript (MS), Manuscripts (MSS): essentially any physical container of text, but usually a reference to a codex of some length in contrast to a papyrus of short length, and typically excluding fragments. In the context of the CBGM (q.v.), a manuscript is carefully distinguished from the text it contains.

Metathesis: the scribal error of switching the order of one or more letters in a word, such as "hte" for "the" in English. For a Greek example see pp. 142 f. above.

Minuscule: from a Latin word meaning "somewhat smaller," a set of small, cursive Greek letters as opposed to majuscules (q.v.). In a loose sense, minuscles are often thought of as lowercase Greek letters. They seem to have been invented in the ninth century to speed and lower the cost of book production.

Nomen Sacrum, Nomina Sacra: standard abbreviations developed by Christian scribes for sacred names or nouns such as "God," "Jesus," "savior," etc. Usually, the formula was the first and last letters of the word, with a horizontal line drawn over the top of them. There is no definitive explanation for their invention, but one can guess that the nomina sacra made a small contribution to the saving of space and time in the copying process. It has been observed that they provide the benefit today of indicating at first sight that the manuscript in which they occur is a Christian work. For the textual critic, however, the nomina sacra mostly are another source of scribal errors and complications in reconstructing the original text. For an example, see above, pp. 153 f.

Oral reading: reading aloud. This was the typical way that anything was read, even when the reader was alone. It was of course done when an NT letter was read to a church, and when a lector (q.v.) dictated a text to be copied by scribes. The prevalence of oral reading must be borne in mind by the textual critic because of the potential for confusion between vowels due to itacism (q.v.), and between any words that happen to be homophonic (see "Homophony").

Original Text: see "Autograph."

Oral tradition: in the context of textual criticism, biblical texts as preserved in the memory of early Christians, including the church fathers. Considerable accuracy often is attributed to these versions of the NT text on the ground that oral tradition was highly valued and great care was taken to preserve it. In TC, however, authority cannot be accorded to oral tradition (at least in most conservative circles), and it mainly provides an explanation for deviations from bona fide texts.

Orthography: Greek for "correct writing," this term is used loosely to refer simply to the spelling of words, which (for Greek) can include breathing and accent marks. Thus, one can refer to variations in the orthography of a word, or even to incorrect orthography. When a variation in orthography is due merely to dialectical or historical changes in spelling for variant readings, the variations are often ignored in the decision process because the reading in question is identical to another reading, once the orthographical differences are factored in (*mutatis mutandis*).

Paleography: from Greek for "old writing," the study of ancient writing, primarily the form of the letters, e.g. majuscule vs. minuscule (q.v.). There are distinct differences that Greek letter sets have in common from various historical periods, and paleographers and textual critics can usually make an immediate guess as to the relative and general dating of texts from different periods, based on these common differences.

Palimpsest: a Greek word meaning "scraped again," referring to a manuscript that has been written on used parchment as a cost-saving measure. In these cases, the parchments originally contained biblical texts, and the ink was scraped off so that a new text of some kind could be written on the erased parchment. Almost needless to say, the new text is usually worthless compared to the old, whose loss can bring tears to the eye of any Bible student. Fortunately, modern technology can be used to recover most of the original text.

Papyrus, Papyri: named for the Egyptian plant from which it is made, in the proper climate this is a very durable writing material that was made by bonding vertical strips of the papyrus pith to horizontal strips. Writing could easily be done on the side with the horizontal strips, and with some difficulty on the other side (called an "opisthograph" when written on both sides). The oldest manuscripts of the NT were written on papyrus; some of them are as early as the second century.

Parablepsis: ("looking to the side") another scribal error of the eye, resulting in the omission of material when the scribe skips a line due to homoeoteleuton (see above). Parablepsis describes the visual process (looking at the right side and missing the left), while haplography describes the result.

Paraphrase: this term usually is understood as a relatively loose translation, conveying the meaning of the text as the translator understands it rather than a translation meant to exhibit a direct correspondence between the words in the original and those in the translation. In textual criticism, it is an appraisal of a reading that is typically longer than corresponding readings and appears to explain or "correct" difficult terminology in another reading. It seems to be a trait of the Western text, as exhibited in particular by D (05). It is also typical of citations by the church fathers.

Parchment: thin leather, the best material for the ancient production of books. It was naturally more durable than papyrus, and since both sides of a parchment page could be smoothed out for writing, it was much better for writing on both sides and producing books. It seems to have begun to replace papyrus in the early fourth century. Like papyrus, however, it was expensive, as one can imagine, and as the existence of palimpsests (see above) confirm.

Passage: most often a general term referring to a single verse, but not limited to that. The term may refer to a larger or smaller selection of text, and sometimes variant readings cross traditional verse boundaries. One must keep in mind, of course, that verse divisions are simply a modern convenience and can be changed at will. They do not play a role in textual criticism.

Pericope: a particular passage of several verses or longer on a single event or story. One of the more famous is the story of the woman caught in adultery (John 7:53-8:11), known (in Latin) as the *periscope de adultera*. To have this designation, a passage usually needs to have special significance. It is well-known, often cherished, and in textual criticism a periscope is usually suspect for being of doubtful authenticity. Critics frequently conclude that such an account is not scriptural but has marks of historical authenticity. It lacks scriptural authenticity if it does not have credible manuscript support.

Quire: in book production, a sheet of writing material folded into a number of rectangles that are to become pages. Once folded, the edges of the rectangles are cut to form pages (see page 12 above).

Reasoned Eclecticism: the method of textual criticism that aims to give about equal weight to external and internal evidence (cf. "Eclecticism"). It is also called the local-genealogical method as developed by Kurt and Barbara Aland. Variant readings are evaluated on a case-by-case basis. The extent to which external evidence, e.g. the age of important manuscripts, is taken into account can be difficult to judge.

Recension: a revision of the Greek NT combining various sources. The term has particular relevance to Lucian, a presbyter of Antioch, who was martyred in 312. In the traditional criticism of Westcott and Hort, Lucian produced the recension that came to be called the Byzantine Text (among other names) and was adopted by the church. There is no absolute proof of the recension, the theory of which rests largely on references to it by Jerome. Even assuming the veracity of the theory; however, the value of it has been called into question in modern research. The Byzantine Text does not appear to have reached a consistent form until after the ninth century.

Recto: Latin for "directly" or "rightly," but a technical term for papyri and codices. For papyri, it is the side of the page with the fiber strips running horizontally, preferred for writing. For codices, the meaning "rightly" applies because the term refers to the right-hand page when the codex (book) is open.

Redaction: editorial work on a manuscript that involves deletions and additions of material. The product of the work is also called a redaction.

Rigorous Eclecticism: see Thoroughgoing Eclecticism.

Scholium, Scholia: interpretive or explanatory notes added (normally in the margin) to a Greek manuscript by a teacher or scribe.

Scribe(s): in Jewish culture scribes were meticulous copyists of scripture who also were recognized as experts on the scripture as a result of their work. Scribes of the NT, on the other hand, could have been either professional copyists or amateurs, and the quality of their work varied. Research shows, however, that NT scribes recognized the value of works they were producing and for the most part were careful to preserve what had been entrusted to them.

Scriptio Continua: a written form of text without spaces between words, punctuation, or other marks (see "Majuscle" above). This was the oldest form of New Testament Greek. For the most part it does not pose a problem for the textual critic. Sometimes, however, options in word divisions and diacriticals (e.g. breathing marks) create ambiguity in the deciphering of individual words. This becomes serious when more than one option is plausible in the context. We assume that what is unclear to the modern reader was clear to the original reader.

Scriptorium: a professional business that was a crude version of a modern printer. Books were mass-produced by scribes who hand-copied pages dictated to them by a *lector* reading aloud. When the copies were completed, they were usually reviewed by correctors. Scriptoria (plural) became mainstream sources for New Testament copies in the fourth century.

Scroll: the original form of a copy of scripture. A roll of papyrus sheets would be glued together, or parchment sewed together.

Sigla: from Latin for "stamped figures," a list of special signs used in a critical text of the Greek NT to indicate variant readings by types, such as omissions and replacements. If NA28 and UBSGNT are compared, one can see that the signs are harder to follow in the former. The NA28 sigla are designed to save space, and more variant readings are noted there than in UBSGNT.

Significant Reading: one can interpret "significant" in two ways: 1) readings with adequate textual support, and 2) readings that are significantly different, as opposed to having differences (like a movable Greek nu or final sigma) that do not distinguish them in meaning from another reading. Adequate textual support can be a matter of opinion, however (compare "Singular Reading" below). For example, a reading with only Byzantine Text support would be rejected by those who favor the position taken by Westcott and Hort. It would be chosen by those who prefer the Majority Text.

Singular Reading: technically, a variant reading that occurs in only one Greek manuscript and is therefore immediately suspect. There is some quibbling over this because critics who reject the Westcott and Hort position on the combination of 01 (Sinaiticus) and 03 (Vaticanus) might call a reading "nearly singular" if it has only the support of these two manuscripts. Moreover, it is understood that not all manuscripts are comparable. Thus, for example, one would comfortably reject a reading found only in a single late manuscript, while many critics would not find it so easy to reject a reading supported uniquely by 03. Some also give more credit to singular readings that have additional support from versions.

Solecism: any reading that is a conspicuous error of some kind in the original language, at least by conventional standards. One such example is found in Rev. 1:4, where the preposition APO is followed by an object in the nominative (subject) case. The case is "corrected" in a number of inferior texts. If the error can be accounted for, then the reading displaying it is to be preferred as the harder reading (*lectio difficilior*).

Text: this term has several meanings, the simplest of which is the content of a manuscript as opposed to its materials. This is a non-technical meaning, the same as the content of any book, or a portion of the content. The term also has two technical meanings, one of which is roughly synonymous with "text-type." This use of the term is accompanied by a geographical or qualitative adjective, usually proper, such as "Alexandrian" or

"Byzantine." There is a significant difference between it and "text-type": "text" by itself takes into account modern considerations regarding textual contamination and redefinitions of traditional text-types. The other technical meaning is roughly synonymous with "witness" (q.v.). It focuses, as one would expect, on content, while "witness" focuses on the text as content entirely separate from the manuscript and predating it, possibly by many centuries.

Text-Type: a technical term in textual criticism referring to a unique combination of characteristics that a specific group of manuscripts is thought to have in common. These characteristics, such as longer variant readings and harmonizations, are determined by comparison of the variant readings found in different manuscript groups. Often the term "text-type" is used not only of the characteristics but of the variant readings themselves. In modern textual criticism, the term is generally considered no longer viable, due mainly to textual contamination (q.v.). The term "text" by itself (see above) is, however, sometimes used to refer to much the same thing, taking into account contamination and other issues.

Textual Mixture: a positive term for textual contamination (q.v.).

Textual Contamination: or often simply "contamination." Previously mentioned under several topics above, this is the inclusion of material from other manuscripts into a text being copied from an exemplar. We cannot know the circumstances under which a case of contamination took place, but it seems likely that the scribe who incorporated the text was attempting to correct or improve upon the exemplar. Some scholars prefer a neutral or positive term for the phenomenon–granting that the incorporated text is scripture–but the result of contamination is a complication that makes it more difficult to construct a genealogy of manuscripts or the texts they contain.

Textual Critic: a scholar whose goal is reconstruct from extant manuscripts either the autograph or the initial text of the NT from which all existing copies originated. The methodology is the same in either case. The critic uses mental, and computer-based tool sets to decide between variant readings among the manuscripts. There are different schools of thought, which tend to prefer either the early manuscripts with more difficult readings or the later manuscripts exhibiting what has been called the Majority Text.

Textual Criticism: the art and science (some would say only art) of determining the original text from variant readings exhibited by extant manuscripts. At present, a good deal of scientific methodology seems to be used as statistics, and computer processing are heavily employed. At the same time, however, TC is also faith-based (at least among conservative theologians), and the results are arguably impossible to verify. Faith plays a role in the belief by many that God has preserved His word somewhere among extant Greek manuscripts, which makes conjectural emendation unnecessary and unacceptable. As to verification, logic and the genealogical relationships between texts than can be constructed are often very convincing, but sometimes a decision is somewhat tenuous. Some critics would claim that no decision can really be verified, but many theories are accepted today without physical verification, on the strength of reasonable probability.

Textual Family: a group of manuscripts that are observed to share common traits. The groups have been distinguished by geography, but textual contamination has cast major doubt on the relevance of that factor (see "Cluster" above). The concept of a family (or sub-family) of manuscripts is certainly relevant, however, and it appears that the old geographic identifiers continue to be used for convenience at least.

Textus Receptus: for the history of the Textus Receptus (TR), see pp.. The name is Latin and usually translated as "received text," based on a comment in Latin in the publisher's preface to the 1633 edition, referring to the text and (again) usually translated "...now received by all..." (*nunc ab omnibus receptum*). We doubt, however, that "received" as it is normally understood is what the Elziver brothers had in mind. Much more likely is the possibility that *receptum* was to be understood as "accepted" in the fullest sense of that term. For some time now a very loyal audience of readers has preferred the TR, which should be distinguished from the MT/Byz text. The TR contains passages such as the Johannine Comma (the Trinitarian version of 1 John 5:7-8) that are foreign to the majority of NT Greek manuscripts.

Thoroughgoing Eclecticism: as briefly described above (see "Eclecticism"), this form of eclecticism, also known as "radical" or "rigorous" (among other designations), uses internal criteria to evaluate variant readings without giving significant attention to external criteria. It does not matter what manuscripts support a reading, and in the mind of a thoroughgoing eclectic, the support of a particular manuscript or group of manuscripts should not be allowed to prevail when internal evidence points to a different reading. We have noted before that internal evidence usually is consistent with external, in that the manuscripts or texts with better external credentials tend to display readings with strong internal support, so the interplay between internal and external evidence usually is significant only when the two are in opposition. In these circumstances reasoned eclectics may choose a reading with better external support over another with better internal support. This would draw the disapproval (and even the ire) of a thoroughgoing eclectic.

641

Transcription: this term is commonly used in two contexts: 1) an ancient scribe's process of copying a text, and 2) the modern reproduction of an ancient text in printed form, as opposed to a facsimile. See more on (1) below under "Transcriptional Error." As to (2), this is what we encounter for any edition of the NT, including the readings found in the apparatus of a critical edition. While the great majority of the time the printed reproductions are trustworthy, they cannot be trusted by the textual scholar when there is any question about the identification of characters or other marks. Full-color facsimiles are best consulted under these circumstances.

Transcriptional Error: this is any error in the text that is a result of the copying process by a scribe. Many are mentioned in this book, such as haplography and metathesis. Variant readings that can be attributed to transcriptional errors can be dismissed, provided that it is reasonable for an otherwise competent scribe to have committed the error in question.

Translation: see Version.

Transposition: the scribal error of accidentally inverting words or phrases (sometimes letters are included, but see "Metathesis"). Usually, the words themselves are correct; only their order is mistaken. The error is common enough that it has its own markers in an apparatus.

Uncial: a term commonly used to refer to majuscule (q.v.) letters. It is agreed, however, that the term, taken from Latin and meaning "one-twelfth," should be applied only to a particular type of Latin script or document.

Variant Reading(s): differing versions of a word or phrase found in two or more manuscripts within a variation unit (see below). Variant readings are also called alternate readings.

Variation Unit: any portion of text that exhibits variations in its reading between two or more different manuscripts. It is important to distinguish variation units from variant readings. Variation units are the places in the text where manuscripts disagree, and each variation unit has at least two variant readings. Setting the limits and range of a variation unit is sometimes difficult or even controversial because some variant readings affect others nearby. Such variations may be considered individually, or as elements of a single reading. One should also note that the terms "manuscript" and "witness" may appear to be used interchangeably in this context. Strictly speaking "witness" (see below) will only refer to the content of a given manuscript or fragment, which it predates to a greater or lesser extent. However, the only way to reference the "witness" is by referring to the manuscript or fragment that contains it. In this book, we have sometimes used the terminology "witness *of* x or y manuscript" to distinguish the content in this way.

Vellum: See Parchment.

Version: in textual criticism and some other fields, this term refers exclusively to ancient Bible translations, such as the Septuagint, Vulgate, and Syriac. An abbreviation of the term is often found in an apparatus or other textual notes.

Verso: from Latin for "turn," the opposite (left) page to the right (recto, q.v.) page in an open codex. For papyri, the back side of the page, where the fiber strips run vertically. Usually, this side is left blank because it is hard to write across the vertical strips.

Vorlage: the German equivalent of "Exemplar," q.v.

Western Text: another textual family or "type" in traditional TC with a geographical identifier that continues to be used more for convenience than for accuracy. Compared to the Alexandrian text, the so-called Western text appears to feature paraphrased readings and other significant departures from the original. There are significant exceptions, however, such as places where Western and Alexandrian readings agree, and some places where the Western seems preferable. Most scholars are on the whole skeptical of Western readings, but some defend them.

Witness: the content of a manuscript, viewed as existing separately from it and predating it. Since all biblical manuscripts are copies of other manuscripts, the content of any manuscript predates it by at least one generation in the form of its exemplar(s), which is (are) probably lost. No two manuscripts agree completely, and the unknown exemplar or exemplars may predate the manuscript in question to an insignificant degree, or perhaps by many centuries. It is theoretically possible that the witness of a late manuscript predates the witness of an earlier manuscript. This calls into question the significance of the dates of the manuscripts themselves. The dates do at least establish terminal points for the creation of the exemplars; that is, the later the date of the manuscript, the later the date that its exemplar(s) could have been produced.

Bibliography

Abbot, Nabia. 1938. *STUDIES IN ANCIENT ORIENTAL CIVILIZATIONS*. Chicago: The University of Chicago Press.

Aland, Barbara. 2004. *The Significance of the Chester Beatty in Early Church History, in: THE EARLIEST GOSPEL ed. Charles Horton*. London: Bloomsbury T & T Clark.

Aland, Kurt, and Barbara Aland. 1995. *The Text of the New Testament*. Grand Rapids: Eerdmans.

—. 1987. *The Text of the New Testament*. Grand Rapids: Eerdmans.

Aland, Kurt, Matthew Black, and Carlo M. Martini. 1993; 2006. *The Greek New Testament, Fourth Revised Edition (Interlinear With Morphology)*. Deutsche Bibelgesellschaft: United Bible Society.

Arndt, William, Frederick W. Danker, and Walter Bauer. 2000. *A Greek-English Lexicon of the New Testament and Other Early Christian Literature. 3rd ed.*. Chicago: University of Chicago Press.

Baer, Daniel. 2007. *The Unquenchable Fire*. Maitland, FL: Xulon Press.

Bagnall, Roger S. 2009. *The Oxford Handbook of Papyrology (Oxford Handbooks)*. Oxford, NY: Oxford University Press.

Balz, Horst, and Gerhard Schneider. 1978. *Exegetical Dictionary of the New Testament*. Edinburgh: T & T Clark Ltd.

Barnett, Paul. 2005. *The Birth of Christianity: The First Twenty Years (After Jesus, Vol. 1)*. Grand Rapids, MI: Wm. B. Eerdmans .

Bauckham, Richard. 1993. *The Theology of the Book of Revelation (NTT)*. Cambridge, UK: Cambridge University Press.

Bercot, David W. 1998. *A Dictionary of Early Christian Beliefs*. Peabody: Hendrickson.

Black, David Alan. 1994. *New Testament Textual Criticism: A Concise Guide*. Grand Rapids, MI: Baker Books.

—. 2002. *Rethinking New Testament Textual Criticism*. Grand Rapids: Baker Books.

Bock, Darrell L, and Daniel B Wallace. 2007. *Dethroning Jesus: Exposing Popular Culture's Quest to Unseat the Biblical Christ*. Nashville: Thomas Nelson.

Borgen, Peder. 1997. *Philo of Alexandria: An Exegete for His Time.* Leiden, Boston: Brill.

Brand, Chad, Charles Draper, and England Archie. 2003. *Holman Illustrated Bible Dictionary: Revised, Updated and Expanded.* Nashville, TN: Holman.

Brown, Virginia. 1972. *The Textual Transmission of Caesar's Civil War.* Leiden: Brill.

Capes, David B, Rodney Reeves, and E. Randolph Richards. 2007. *Rediscovering Paul: An Introduction to His World, Letters and Theology .* Downers Grove: IVP Academic.

Carson, D. A, and Douglas J Moo. 2005. *An Introduction to the New Testament.* Grand Rapids, MI: Zondervan.

Carson, D. A. 1994. *New Bible Commentary: 21st Century Edition. 4th ed.* Downers Grove: Inter-Varisity Press.

Clayton, Joseph. 2006. *Luther and His Work.* Whitefish: Kessinger Publishing.

Cmfort, Philip Wesley. 2015. *A Commentary On the Manuscripts and Text of the New Testament.* Grand Rapids: Kregel Publications.

Colwell, E. C. 1969. *Methods in Evaluating Scribal Habits: A Study of P45, P66, P75, in Studies in Methodology in Textual Criticism of the New Testament.* Leiden and Boston: Brill.

Colwell, Ernest C. 1965. *Scribal Habits in Early Papyri: A Study in the Corruption of the Text.* Grand Rapids: Eerdmans.

Comfort, Philip. 2005. *Encountering the Manuscripts: An Introduction to New Testament Paleography and Textual Criticism.* Nashville: Broadman & Holman.

Comfort, Philip W. 2008. *New Testament Text and Translation Commentary.* Carol Stream: Tyndale House Publishers.

Comfort, Philip Wesley. 1992. *The Quest for the Original Text of the New Testament.* Eugene: Wipf and Stock.

Comfort, Philip, and David Barret. 2001. *The Text of the Earliest New Testament Greek Manuscripts.* Wheaton: Tyndale House Publishers.

Cruse, C. F. 1998. *Eusebius' Eccliatical History.* Peabody, MA: Hendrickson.

Deissmann, Adolf. 1910. *LIGHT FROM THE ANCIENT EAST: The New Testament Illustrated by Recently Discovered Texts of the Graeco-Roman World.* New York and London: Hodder and Stoughton.

Dell 'Orto, Luisa Franchi. 1990. *Riscoprire Pompei (Rediscovering Pompeii)*. Italy: L'Erma di Bretschneider.

Durant, Will & Ariel. 1950. *The Story of Civilization: Part IV—The Age of Faith*. New York, NY: Simon & Schuster.

Ehrman, Bart D. 2005. *Misquoting Jesus: The Story Behind Who Changed the Bible and Why*. New York: Harper One.

—. 2006. *Peter, Paul and Mary Magdalene: The Followers of Jesus in History and Legend*. Oxford: Oxford University Press.

Ehrman, Bart D, and Michael W. Holmes. 2012. *The Text of the New Testament in Contemporary Research: Essays on the Status Quaestionis. Second Edition*. Leiden and Boston: Brill.

Ehrman, Bart D. Holmes, Michael W. 1995. *The Text of the New Testament in Contemporary Research: Essays on the Status Quaestionis* . Grand Rapids, MI: Eerdmans.

Ehrman, Bart D. 2003. *Lost Christianities: The Battles for Scripture and the Faiths We Never Knew* . New York: Oxford University Press.

Elliott, J. K. 2010. *New Testament Textual Criticism: The Application of Thoroughgoing Principles: Essays on Manuscripts and Textual Variation (Novum Testamentum, Supplements)*. Leiden: Brill.

Epp, Eldon J. 1993. *Studies in the Theory and Method of New Testament Textual Criticism*. Grand Rapids: Wm. B. Eerdmans Publishing Co.

—. 1989. *Textual Criticism*. Atlanta: Scholars Press.

Evans, Craig A. 2002. *Fabricating Jesus: How Modern Scholars Distort the Gospels*. Downers Grove, IL: InterVaristy Press.

—. 2012. *Jesus and His World: The Archaeological Evidence*. Louisville: Westminster John Knox Press.

Fahlbusch, Erwin (Editor), Jan Milic (Editor) Lochman, John (Editor) Mbiti, Jaroslav (Editor) Pelikan, and Lukas (Editor) Vischer. German 1986, 1989, 1992, 1996, 1997; English 1999, 2001, 2003, 2005. *The Encyclopedia of Christianity (Vol. 1-3)*. Grand Rapids: Eerdmans Publishing Company and Koninklijke Brill NV.

Fee, Gordon D. 1993. *P75, P66, and Origen: The Myth of Early Textual Recension in Alexandria, in: E. J. Epp & G. D. Fee, Studies in the Theory & Method of NT Textual Criticism*. Grand Rapids: Wm. Eerdmans.

Fee, Gordon D. 1974. *P75, P66, and Origen: The Myth of the Early Textual Recension in Alexandria*. Grand Rapids: Zondervan.

—. 1979. *The Textual Criticism of the New Testament*. Grand Rapids: Zondervan.

Ferguson, Everett. 2003. *Backgrounds of Early Christianity*. Grand Rapids, MI: Wm. B. Eerdmans.

Ferguson, Everett. 2005. *Church History ,Volume One: From Christ to Pre-Reformation: The Rise and Growth of the Church in Its Cultural, Intellectual, and Political Context*. Grand Rapids, MI: Zondervan.

Freeman, James M. 1998. *THE NEW MANNERS & CUSTOMS OF THE BIBLE*. Gainesville: Bridge-Logos.

Gamble, Henry Y. 1995. *Books and Readers in the Early Church: A History of Early Christian Texts*. New Haven, CT: New Haven University Press.

Geisler, Norman L, and William E Nix. 1996. *A General Introduction to the Bible*. Chicago: Moody Press.

Geisler, Norman, and David Geisler. 2009. *CONVERSATION EVANGELISM: How to Listen and Speak So You Can Be Heard*. Eugene: Harvest House Publishers.

Greenlee, J Harold. 1995. *Introduction to New Testament Textual Criticism*. Peabody: Hendrickson.

—. 2008. *The Text of the New Testament*. Peabody: Henrickson.

Guthrie, Donald. 1990. *Introduction to the New Testament (Revised and Expanded)*. Downers Grove, IL: InterVarsity Press.

Hammond, Carolyn. 1996. *Introduction to The Gallic War*. Oxford: Oxford University Press.

Hatch, William Henry Paine. 45. "A Recently Discovered Fragmrnt of the Epistle to the Romans." *Harvard Theological Review* 81-85.

Head, Peter M. 2004. "The Habits of New Testament Copyists Singular Readings in the Early Fragmentary Papyri of John." *Biblica, Vol. 85, No. 3* 399-408.

Hill, Charles E., and Michael J. Kruger. 2012. *The Early Text of the New Testament*. Oxford: Oxford University Press.

Hixon, Elijah, Gurry, Peter J. 2019. *MYTHS AND MISTAKES iN NEW TESTAMENT TEXTUAL CRITICISM*. Downer Groves: InterVarsity Press.

Holmes, Michael W. 1989. *New Testament Textual Criticism*. Grand Rapids: Baker.

——. 2007. *The Apostolic Fathers: Greek Texts and English Translations.* Grand Rapids: Baker Academics.

Hurtado, Larry. 1989. *New International Bible Commentary: Mark. .: .* Peabody, Mass: Hendrickson.

Hurtado, Larry. 1998. "The Origin of the Nominal Sacra." *Journal of Biblical Literature* 655-673.

Johnson, William A. 2012 (Reprint). *Readers and Reading Culture in the High Roman Empire: A Study of Elite Communities (Classical Culture and Society).* Oxford, New York: Oxford University Press.

Johnson, William A, and Holt N Parker. 2011. *Ancient Literacies: The Culture of Reading in Greece and Rome.* Oxford, United Kingdom: Oxford University Press.

Jones, Timothy Paul. 2007. *Misquoting Truth: A Guide to the Fallacies of Bart Ehrman's Misquoting Jesus.* Downer Groves: InterVarsity Press.

Komoszewski, J. Ed, James M. Sawyer, and Daniel Wallace. 2006. *Reinventing Jesus .* Grand Rapids, MI: Kregel Publications.

Lane Fox, Robin. 2006. *Pagans and Christians: In the Mediterranean World from the Second Century AD to the Conversion of Constantine.* City of Westminster, London: Penguin.

Lea, Thomas D., and Hayne P. Griffin. 1992. *The New American Commentary, vol. 34, 1, 2 Timothy, Titus.* Nashville: Broadman & Holman Publishers.

Lightfoot, Joseph Barber, and J. R Harmer. 1891. *The Apostolic Fathers.* London: Macmillan and Co.

Lightfoot, Neil R. 1963, 1988, 2003. *How We Got the Bible.* Grand Rapids, MI: Baker Books.

McCarthy, Dan, and Charles Clayton. 1994. *Let the Reader Understand: A guide to Interpreting and Applying the Bible.* Wheaton, Illinois: BridgePoint.

McKenzie, John L. 1975. *Light on the Epistles: A Reader's Guide.* Chicago, IL: Thomas More Press.

McRay, John. 2003. *Paul: His Life and Teaching.* Grand Rapids, MI: Baker Academics.

Metzger, Bruce M. 1964, 1968, 1992. *The Text of the New Testament: Its Transmission, Corruption, and Transmission.* New York: Oxford University Press.

Metzger, Bruce M. 1994. *A Textual Commentary on the Greek New Testament.* New York: United Bible Society.

Metzger, Bruce M., and Bart D. Ehrman. 2005. *The Text of the New Testament: Its Transmission, Corruption, and Restoration (4th Edition).* New York: Oxford University Press.

Metzger, Bruce. 1981. *Manuscripts of the Greek Bible: An Introduction to Palaeography* . New York, NY: Oxford University Press.

Millard, Alan. 2000. *READING AND WRITING IN THE TIME IF JESUS.* New York, NY: NYU Press.

Mounce, Robert H. 2001. *The New American Commentary.* Nashville, TN: Broadman & Holman Publishers.

Mounce, William D. 2006. *Mounce's Complete Expository Dictionary of Old & New Testament Words.* Grand Rapids, MI: Zondervan.

Myers, Allen C. 1987. *The Eerdmans Bible Dictionary* . Grand Rapids, Mich: Eerdmans.

Nestle, Eberhard, and Erwin Nestle. 2012. *Nestle-Aland: NTG Apparatus Criticus, ed. Barbara Aland et al., 28. revidierte Auflage (Revised Edition).* Stuttgart: Deutsche Bibelgesellschaft.

Orchard, Bernard (Editor), Longstaff, Thomas R. W. (Editor). 2005. "J. J. Griesbach: Synoptic and Text - Critical Studies 1776-1976." *Society for New Testament Studies Monograph Series (Book 34)* xi.

Orchard, Bernard. 1776-1976, 2005. *J. J. Griesbach: Synoptic and Text - Critical Studies* . Cambridge: Cambridge University Press.

Parker, David C. 1992. *Codex Bezae: An Early Christian Manuscript and its Text.* Cambridge: Cambridge University Press.

Parker, David C. 1997. *The living Text of the Gospels.* Cambridge: Cambridge University Press.

Porter, Stanley E. 2013. *How We Got the New Testament (Acadia Studies in Bible and Theology).* Grand Rapids, MI: Baker Publishing Group.

Price, Randall. 2007. *Searching for the Original Bible.* Eugene: Harvest House.

Richards, E. Randolph. 2004. *PAUL AND FIRST-CENTURY LETTER WRITING: Secretaries, Composition and Collection.* Downers Grove: InterVarsity Press.

—. 1991. *The Secretary in the Letters of Paul* . Heidelberg, Germany: Mohr Siebeck.

—. 1990. *The Secretary in the Letters of Paul.* Tübingen: J.C.B. Mohr.

Roberts, C. H. 1970. *Books in the Graeco-Roman World and in the New Testament in the Cambridge History of the Bible, Vol. 1, From the Beginnings to Jerome .* Cambridge: Cambridge University Press.

Roberts, Colin H. 1979. *Manuscript, Society, and Belief in Early Christian Egypt.* London: Oxford University Press.

Roberts, Colin H., and Theodore C. Skeat. 1987. *The Birth of the Codex.* London: Oxford University Press.

Robertson, A. T. 1925. *An Introduction to the Textual Criticism of the New Testament.* London: Hodder & Stoughton.

Royse, James R. 2008. *Scribal Habits in Early Greek New Testament Papyri (New Testament Tools and Studies) (New Testament Tools, Studies and Documents).* Leiden & Boston: Brill Academic Pub.

Schaff, Philip, and David Schley Schaff. 1910. *History of the Christian Church, vol. 2.* New York: Charles Scribner's Sons.

Schurer, Emil. 1890. *A HISTORY OF THE JEWISH PEOPLE IN THE TIME OF JESUS CHRIST (Volume II).* Edinburgh: T. & T. Clark.

Scott, Julius J. Jr. 1995. *Jewish Backgrounds of the New Testament.* Grand Rapids, MI: Baker Academic.

Souter, Alexander. 1913. *The Text and Canon of the New Testament.* New York: Charles Scribner's Sons.

Stark, Rodney. 1996). *The Rise of Christianity: A Socialist Reconsiders History.* Princeton, NJ: Princeton University Press.

Starr, Raymond J. 1987. "The Circulation of Literary Texts in the Roman World." *The Classical Quarterly* 213-223.

Towns, Elmer L. 2006. *Concise Bible Dictrines: Clear, Simple, and Easy-to-Understand Explanations of Bible Doctrines.* Chattanooga: AMG Publishers.

Tregelles, Samuel Prideaux. 1854. *An Account of the Printed Text of the Greek New Testament: With Remarks on Its Revision Upon Critical Principles.* London: S. Bagster and Sons.

Tuckett, Christopher M. 2001. "P52 and Nomina Sacra." *New Testament Study* 544-48.

Wachtel, Klaus, and Michael W Holmes. 2011. *The Textual History of the Greek New Testament: Changing Views in Contemporary Research, Text-Critical Studies*. Atlanta: Society of Biblical Literature.

Wallace, Daniel B. 2011. *Revisiting the Corruption of the New Testament: Manuscript, Patristic, and Apocryphal Evidence*. Grand Rapids, MI: Kregel Publications.

Wallace, Daniel. 2011. *The Reliability of the New Testament: Bart Ehrman and Daniel Wallace in Dialogue*. Minneapolis, MN: Fortress Press.

Warfield, B. B. 1948. *The Inspiration and Authority of the Bible*. Philadelphia, PA: Presbyterian and Reformed Pub. Co.

Wegner, Paul D. 2006. *A Student's Guide to Textual Criticism of the Bible: Its History Methods & Results*. Downers Grove: InterVarsity Press.

—. 1999. *The Journey from Text to Translation*. Grand Rapids: Baker Academic.

Westcott, B. F., and F. J. A. Hort. 1882. *Introduction to the New Testament in the Original Greek*. New York: Harper & Brothers.

—. 1882. *The New Testament in the Original Greek, Vol. 2: Introduction, Appendix*. London: Macmillan and Co.

Whiston, William. 1987. *The Works of Josephus*. Peabody, MA: Hendrickson.

Wright, Brian J. 2017. *COMMUNAL READING IN THE TIME OF JESUS: A Window Into Christian Reading Practices*. Minneapolis, MN: Fortress Press. Accessed March 22, 2017. https://www.academia.edu/18281056/_Ancient_Romes_Daily_N ews_Publication_With_Some_Likely_Implications_For_Early_Chr istian_Studies_TynBull_67.1_2016_145-160.

Wright, G. Ernest. 1962. *Biblical Archaeology*. London, United Kingdom: Gerald Duckworth & Co.

Zuntz, Gunther. 1953. *The Text of the Epistles: A Disquisition upon the Corpus Paulinum*. London: Oxford University Press.

INDEX OF SUBJECTS